Cultural
Anthropology

The McGraw-Hill Companies

Higher Education

CULTURAL ANTHROPOLOGY: TRIBES, STATES, AND THE GLOBAL SYSTEM,
Fourth Edition
Published by McGraw-Hill Higher Education, a business unit of The McGraw-Hill
Companies, Inc., 1221 Avenue of the Americas, New York, NY, 10020. Copyright ©
2005, 2000, 1997, 1994 by The McGraw-Hill Companies, Inc. All rights reserved.
No part of this publication may be reproduced or distributed in any form or by any
means, or stored in a database or retrieval system, without the prior written consent of
The McGraw-Hill Companies, Inc., including, but not limited to, in any network
or other electronic storage or transmission, or for broadcast or distance learning.

Some ancillaries, including electronic and print components, may not be available to
customers outside the United States.

This book is printed on acid-free paper.

4 5 6 7 8 9 FGR/FGR 0 9 8 7

ISBN   978-0-07-287049-7
MHID 0-07-287049-4

Publisher: Phil Butcher
Sponsoring Editor: Kevin Witt
Development Editor: Gabrielle Goodman White
Permissions Coordinator: Marty Granahan
Marketing Manager: Dan Loch
Media Producer: Shannon Gattens
Project Manager: Roger Geissler
Interior Designer: Susan Breitbard
Cover Designer: Violeta Diaz
Art Editor: Robin Mouat
Photo Research Coordinator: Natalia Pescheira
Production Supervisor: Tandra Jorgensen
Media Supplement Producer: Marc Mattson
Compositor: Thompson Type

Library of Congress Cataloging-in-Publication Data

Bodley, John H.
    Cultural Anthropolgy: tribes, states, and the global system /
John H. Bodley. — 4th ed.
    p. cm.
Includes bibliographical references and index.
ISBN 0-07-287049-4
1. Ethnology.   I. Title
GN316.B63 2005   200412137
306—dc21

www.mhhe.com

Cultural Anthropology

TRIBES, STATES, and the GLOBAL SYSTEM

Fourth Edition

JOHN H. BODLEY
Washington State University

Boston   Burr Ridge, IL   Dubuque, IA   Madison, WI   New York
San Francisco   St. Louis   Bangkok   Bogotá   Caracas   Kuala Lumpur
Lisbon   London   Madrid   Mexico City   Milan   Montreal   New Delhi
Santiago   Seoul   Singapore   Sydney   Taipei   Toronto

Brief Contents

Contents

3 Native Amazonians: Villagers of the Rain Forest   63

4 African Cattle Peoples: Tribal Pastoralists   99

5 Body, Mind, and Soul: The Quality of Tribal Life   133

PART TWO

The Imperial World: The End of Equality

6 Pacific Islanders: The Ranked Chiefdoms   166

Preface

Given the interconnections among cultural groups on the current world stage (and the rapidity with which those dynamics change), it is imperative that we learn as much as we can about world culture, history, and geography in order to lead informed, productive lives in our global village. What better way to start than by applying the traditional methods of anthropology to a modern view of the world? With this as my underlying goal, I've presented the basic concepts of cultural anthropology in this introductory text by comparing cultures of increasing scale and focusing on universal human concerns. The end result, I hope, is a stimulating, culturally integrated approach to the discipline.

Throughout the text, I've challenged students to consider the big questions about the nature of cultural systems: How are cultures structured to satisfy basic human needs? What is it like to be human under different cultural conditions? Are race, language, and environment determinants of culture? Are materialist explanations more useful than ideological ones? What are the major turning points in human history?

The culture-scale perspective highlights the unique problems of the present world system. Roughly one-third of the text is devoted to issues of current concern, especially the problem of inequality and how to make our world sustainable. A wide range of global humanitarian issues such as ethnocide, genocide, and ecocide also are con-sidered, along with a variety of more narrow theoretical and methodological issues. My hope is that understanding how tribes, states, and global systems work and how they differ might help citizens design a more secure and equitable world.

PERSONAL PROLOGUE: A CHALLENGE TO THE READER

I intend this book to be a provocative alternative to bland, topically arranged, encyclopedic texts. Anthropology is a subversive science. This book provides students with anthropological tools to question the status quo and its representation of the world. Readers are invited to ask what's going on, and who's in charge in the world and in their own culture. This book has a viewpoint. It offers a radical anthropological critique of firmly-held cultural beliefs and practices that threaten the well-being and continued survival of humanity in the twenty-first century. I invite students to explore the relationship between growth, scale, and power throughout human history and prehistory. I suggest that our most serious human problems are caused by a collective social failure to restrain the natural individual drive to increase personal social power at the expense of others. Given the opportunity, unrestrained aggrandizing individuals will use culture to transform society to benefit themselves and their direct descendants. Elites will alter people's perceptions of reality. They will manipulate cosmologies and technologies to create the belief that elite-directed growth is natural and inevitable, even though it disproportionately concentrates social power and makes everyone else pay the costs.

Throughout history, growth has intensified human problems. These are problems of growth in scale, power, and complexity. Growth first became a problem 7,000 years ago when a few aggrandizing individuals took advantage of local crises created by global climate change at the end of the Ice Age, and were able to centralize social power in the first chiefdoms. Power elites then promoted growth to increase their power, setting off cycles of growth, cultural transformation, and crises, culminating in the creation of a global commercial world dominated by U.S. elites. It is possible that further growth beyond the present threshold may prove unsustainable. The global evidence of cultural crisis is overwhelming: billions of people are impoverished, malnourished and unhealthy, economic and political systems are in turmoil, nature is under siege, and human activities are changing global climate in ways that could be catastrophic. Millions of people are immigrants and refugees fleeing intolerable conditions. Even the richest and most powerful nation is unable to guarantee employment, education, basic health care, and keep the lights on. We all need to question how this state of human affairs came to be, and to concentrate our efforts on creating a better future.

ORGANIZATION OF THE BOOK

To demonstrate the vitality of fieldwork and to generate enthusiasm for the discipline, Chapter 1 begins with a personal account of my fieldwork with the Ashâninka of Amazonia. Not only does it explain why I was inspired to approach anthropology from a humanistic, culture-scale perspective, but it also introduces the field methods employed by cultural anthropologists. Ensuing chapters examine a representative sample of cultures in sufficient depth to maintain cultural context and to provide students with a sound understanding of the world's major cultural areas and dominant civilizations.

The book is designed to provide balanced coverage of three dramatically different cultural worlds. After its introduction to doing fieldwork, Part One examines domestic-scale, autonomous cultures in the tribal world. Part Two presents politically organized, class-based civilizations and ancient empires in the imperial world, and Part Three surveys global, industrial, market-based civilizations in the commercial world. Scale is used as an organizing principle in order to provide a basis for comparison; however, I've avoided the implicit value judgments that are part of popular ideas about evolutionary progress. The following universal issues about the human conditions are explored from a comparative, anthropological perspective: What is "natural" about humans? What is "cultural" about humans? Which human *inequalities* are natural? Which are cultural? Is *population growth* natural or cultural? Is *economic growth* natural or cultural? What are the human costs and benefits of socioeconomic growth? The ethnographic material will focus on the influence of culture scale and the distribution of social power on such basic matters as quality of life, domestic organization, intergroup relations, and relationship to the environment. The causes and consequences of changes in culture scale and the role of elite decision-makers are central themes.

Ethnographic case studies are used to describe the functional interconnections between the material bases and the social and ideological systems of representative cultures in each of the three cultural worlds. The cultures selected as case studies are those that are best described in ethnographic films and monographs, and they are the subject of abundant analytical materials. Australian aborigines, Amazonian villagers, and East African pastoralists represent tribal cultures and are treated in separate chapters. Politically centralized cultures are represented by Pacific Island chiefdoms and the ancient and modern great civilizations of Mesopotamia, the Inca, China, Islam, and Hindu India. The commercial cultures of the United States, the British empire, contemporary indigenous peoples, and the rural peasantry are examined as part of the global commercial system. The text shows cultures in depth—as adapting, integrated systems—and as part of regional, continental, and global systems, as appropriate.

FEATURES FOR STUDENTS

An important objective for this edition was to make the text more appealing and accessible to students by removing much of the academic debate and jargon that were not central to the discipline, or that had less utility for helping students understand the contemporary world. This makes it possible to focus on culture, social power, and scale as analytical tools, and on how individuals solve universal human problems. The core concepts that remain are explained more fully, without assuming previous knowledge on the part of the reader. Diagrams, graphs, and tables have been carefully selected and reformatted to highlight key concepts and for ease of interpretation. The book includes the following features:

NEW! ◆ **Master Timeline Table**—A full-page table, "Major Events in the Development of World Cultures," in the front of the book shows major culture areas from 100,000 BP to the present. This helps students see time and space relationships at a glance, and to understand the successive development of distinct cultural worlds.

NEW! ◆ **Part Openers**—Each of the three parts of the book, covering the tribal, imperial, and commercial worlds, now have brief introductions highlighting the central features of each cultural world, and showing students how each group of chapters fits together.

NEW! ◆ **Learning Objectives**—At the beginning of every chapter a list of clear, specific objectives tells students what they should be able to do after studying the chapter material.

NEW! ◆ **Pronunciation Guides**—Opening Chapters 1–9, these guides set the stage for improved readability and reading comprehension, providing students with handy pronunciation suggestions for many of the foreign words they'll encounter in the text.

◆ **Concept Tables**—Show how different concepts relate to each other, to help remember key terms and quickly see how they relate to each other.

◆ **Timeline Tables**—To help students visualize and understand the historical sequence of major cultural and environmental events in specific culture areas.

NEW! ◆ **Power Rank Tables**—The distribution of households by super-elite, elite, maintenance and poor social power rank is shown for representative societies in the imperial and commercial worlds.

◆ **Kinship Diagrams**—Standard kinship terminology diagrams are presented using native terms for Iroquois, Omaha, Hawaiian, and Chinese systems to help students understand and compare these systems.

◆ **Boxed Material**—Brief case studies illustrate selected concepts in greater detail than provided in the main text, and may be assigned as enrichment.

◆ **Key Terms**—Important terms and concepts are in boldface when they first appear, and are defined in a running glossary at the bottom of the page.

NEW! ◆ **Glossary**—All key terms are defined in an alphabetical Glossary at the end of the book.

◆ **Chapter Summaries**—Review and synthesize the main points of each chapter.

◆ **Study Questions**—At the end of each chapter, a set of essay or discussion questions builds on the chapter's learning objectives, and helps students review chapter material.

◆ **Suggested Readings**—At the end of each chapter a short, annotated list of books offers students resources to explore issues in greater depth.

◆ **Bibliography**—Key authorities and published sources are cited throughout the text, and appear in an extensive Bibliography at the end of the book.

NEW IN THIS EDITION

Those familiar with the third edition will find several significant changes. Throughout, the concept of "cultural world" replaces cultural scale as an organizing device. Domestic-scale, political-scale, and commercial-scale cultures are now the tribal, imperial, and commercial worlds. Labeling these cultures "worlds" calls attention to their distinctive features, and the functional connections among cultural elements. New tables summarize the characteristics of each world referring to both cultural processes and ethnographic details within the infrastructure, structure, and superstructure framework. Scale continues to be important throughout, but it now refers explicitly to the size of societies and economies, rather than cultures. Culture is treated as a tool created by self-interested individuals.

Throughout, the timeline tables giving prehistory and historic background have been abbreviated to highlight the broadest trends. This will make it easier for students to situate each culture in the new master timeline table "Major Events in the Development of World Cultures," located in the front of the book. There are also many more specific cross-cultural comparisons between societies used as case studies. For example, East African cosmologies are compared with Amazonian cosmologies in Chapter 4. In Chapter 6,

the symbolic structures describing the relations between men and women in Hawaiian society are compared with similar symbolic structures in Amazonian cosmologies described in Chapter 3. Also in Chapter 6, the Hawaiian gods, as transcendent, non-empirical concepts, are compared to Australian Dreaming beings, and Amazon spirits. In Chapter 7, there are specific comparisons of the way the Ubaid chiefs of Mesopotamia, Hawaiian kings, and the Inca emperor maintained and exercised social power.

Chapter 1 contains a new section on biocultural evolution to examine the problem of individuals seeking their own biological self-interest in genetic fitness, and the human need to maintain and reproduce society and culture. The concept of cultural relativism now takes into account the fact that culture provides people with a theory of how the world works, but it may not always provide an *accurate* image of the real world. The discussion of social power is applied more consistently throughout the text, and is revised to include a fuller treatment of the ideological, economic, military, and political power aspects of the personal power networks that individuals construct.

Chapter 2 includes a new discussion of the Dreaming and the supernatural as a non-empirical way of knowing the world that can be as "true" or useful as a scientific epistemology. The discussion of band and tribe is abbreviated. A new section, "Affluence as Mode of Thought," shows that how Australian aborigines think about sharing and generosity in relation to nature and other people may be the most important feature of their culture, perhaps even more important than the technology of foraging. To provide students with a graphic illustration of "tribal affluence," a new box describes the daily life of a foraging band. The discussion of kinship now includes the moral dimension of proper kinship behavior.

In Chapter 3, the treatment of war is completely revised to show that violent conflict in Amazonian societies is an aspect of tribal culture in the absence of formal government. The Yanomami case study is thoroughly revised with new sections to show both the limitations and complementarity of materialist and evolutionary explanations, and to take into account the ethical issues raised by the "Darkness in El Dorado" controversy.

Chapter 4 gives special attention to feminist perspectives with a new section, "The Status of Women in East African Pastoral Society: Ideology vs. Reality." There is also a new box, "Turkana Household Symbolism and Cosmology," that adds rich details showing the pervasiveness of female symbols in daily life. A new section, "Bigman Wealth and Power in Herding Societies," highlights the social power differences that cattle make possible when they are treated as moveable wealth. This helps students see important differences between East African bigmen, Amazon bigmen, and Polynesian chiefs.

The discussion in Chapter 5 on health in the tribal world includes a new report by the World Health Organization on non-communicable diseases attributed to lifestyles that are unique problems in the commercial world.

New sections in Chapter 6, "Elite-Directed Cultural Transformation in Polynesia," "Chiefdoms and the Politicization Process," and a new box, "A Matter of Scale: The Political Transformation of Tribes into Chiefdom," explore the human implications of chiefdoms. They discuss the origin of chiefdoms in general, and use Polynesian examples to show why even a small chiefdom of 5,000 people is a significant scale difference from tribal societies. The general ethnographic account of Polynesian chiefdoms and the Hawaiian kingdom is completely revised and updated. There are four new sections: "Hawaii: From Kinship to Kingship," "High Chiefs, Gods, and Sacrifice," "Hawaiian Daily Life: Commoner Men and Women," and "Two Headed Children and Hawaiian Kinship." There is also a new diagram to illustrate the simplicity of Hawaiian kinship. This addition means that each tribal area now includes a representative kinship system.

The introductory section on empires in Chapter 7 is completely rewritten to focus on scale and power dimensions with three new figures to show the relationship between social scale, cultural complexity, and the concentration of social power. Sections on state origins are completely rewritten to incorporate new perspectives. New boxed materials includes "Before Civilization: Abu Hureyra, 4,000 Years of Tribal Village Autonomy," and "The Mesopotamian Elite and the Rewards of Leadership." The ethnographic account of the Ur III Empire is extensively revised to incorporate much new material focused on social power. A new table sorts households into four ranks by social power: super-elite, elite, maintenance, and poor. These ranks are used for comparative purposes in later chapters covering other Great Tradition civilizations as well as societies in the commercial world. The description of the Inca is extensively revised to incorporate new material. A new box "Before the Inca: Moche and Chimú Lords" describes the royal compounds in the city of Chan Chan and finds from the Moche royal tombs of Sipán.

A new section, "Power and Scale in the Thai Kingdom and Mughal Empire," in Chapter 9 adds new ethnohistorical material on social ranking. The treatment of Hindu caste, pollution, and cosmology is extensively revised with new material and new figures, including a new section "Food, Eating, and Caste in Hindu Culture," and descriptions of temple ritual.

A new section, "Growth Thresholds and Scale Limits in Ancient Empires" in Chapter 10 examines growth trends and the physical limits to the size of armies, cities, and empires in the imperial world.

Chapter 11 on the commercial world, includes a new section, "Energy and Population Growth in the Commercial World," showing per capita and aggregate global levels of energy use for different cultures over time, in relation to energy consumption by the contemporary U.S. The discussion of the "Nature of Capitalism" is extensively revised, making the treatment of wealth and capital more understandable. There is new material on the elites who created the institutional foundations of capitalism and invested in colonialism.

In Chapter 12, the description of the United States now includes a discussion of the contrasts between progressivist and neo-conservative political ideology, and a new section "The Construction of Corporate America, 1790–1920." The discussion of the food system and social class in the U.S. is extensively updated, and includes a new section, "Social Power, Personal Imperia, and Family in the U.S., 1980–2003, and a new table on the distribution of wealth and income. The statistics on global poverty and population are updated, and a new table is included to show the distribution of global wealth and income by household rank.

Chapter 13 uses Paul Farmer's concept of "structural violence" to help students better understand the human significance of poverty. There is also new material on global income distributions and the issue of evaluating global living standards.

The discussion of global warming, habitat loss, and species extinctions in Chapter 15 is updated. A new table on "Global Crises and Cultural Response, 12,000 BP–2050 AD" puts the present sustainability crisis in a larger perspective and looks ahead to the near future. The final sections offer an optimistic view of how scale and power solutions can help resolve global problems.

SUPPLEMENTAL RESOURCES

The Online Learning Center at www.mhhe.com/bodley4 provides interactive resources to address the needs of a variety of teaching and learning styles. For every chapter, students and instructors can access chapter outlines, sample quizzes with feedback, crossword puzzles using key terms, and more. For instructors specifically, the Online Learning Center offers a downloadable Instructor's Resource Manual with topical outlines and test questions, and downloadable PowerPoint Lecture outlines.

In addition, instructors also receive an Instructor's Resource CD-ROM (IRCD) containing the Instructor's Resource Manual, Testbank, and PowerPoint lecture outlines.

ACKNOWLEDGMENTS

This book began as a one-page outline in the spring of 1981, and over the years it has benefited greatly from discussions with my colleagues and suggestions from numerous readers. I'm very grateful to all who offered me advice and support.

I'd like to thank especially Jan Beatty, Gerald Berreman, Geoffrey Gamble, and Thomas Headland, who wrote in support of my sabbatical leave from Washington State University in 1990, which enabled me to complete much of the primary research and writing in one concentrated effort. In July 1991, I made the first public presentation of the culture-scale approach in a paper entitled "Indigenous Peoples vs. the State: A Culture Scale Approach," which I gave at a conference called "Indigenous People in Remote Regions: A Global Perspective," organized by historian Ken Coates at the University of Victoria, British Columbia.

My students and colleagues at Washington State University who listened to my ideas and offered suggestions and materials were particularly helpful; I'd like to thank Robert Ackerman, Diana Ames-Marshall, Michael Blair, Brenda Bowser, Mark Collard, Ben Colombi, Mark Fleisher, Lee Freese, Chris Harris, Fekri Hassan, Christa Herrygers, Barry Hewlett, Barry Hicks, Michael Kemery, Tim Kohler, Grover Krantz, William Lipe, Robert Littlewood, William Lyons, Jeannette Mageo, Nancy McKee, Peter J. Mehringer, Jr., Frank Myka, John Patton, Mark Pubols, Margaret Reed, Vanessa Ross, Allan Smith, Linda Stone, Matt Wanamaker, Brad Wazaney, and Troy Wilson. Special thanks also to Shila Baksi for help with Sanskrit pronunciation, and Xianghong Feng for help with Chinese pronunciation.

At the risk of omitting someone, I also want to thank those who provided me with materials that found their way into the book: Mary Abascal-Hildebrand, Clifford Behrens, Diane Bell, Gerald D. Berreman, Jean-Pierre Bocquet-Appel, Cecil H. Brown, Stephen B. Brush, John W. Burton, Gudren Dahl, Shelton H. Davis, Paul L. Doughty, Nancy M. Flowers, Richard A. Gould, Brian Hayden, Thomas Headland, Howard M. Hecker, L. R. Hiatt, Arthur Hippler, Betty Meehan,

Peter G. Roe, Nicholas Thomas, Norman B. Tindale, and Gerald Weiss.

For the second edition, I owe special thanks to Bill Lipe and Linda Stone in my department for directing me to new material on the global culture. Also thanks to Barry Hicks of the Health Research and Education Center, Washington State University, Spokane, for assistance with my state- and county-level research. Kevin Norris in the Information Systems Department of Spokane County, Washington, provided me with data on Spokane County land ownership. Zoltan Porga, system analyst, and Gilbert A. Pierson, Information Technology, at Washington State University, guided me through the intricacies of SAS. The staff in my department, especially LeAnn Couch and Joan Pubols, provided important support as I served as department chair while preparing this revision.

Special thanks to Kevin Witt, Sponsoring Editor for Anthropology at McGraw Hill Higher Education, for directing this project, and to my development editor, Gabrielle Goodman White, for her painstaking help in making the text more useful for students. Thanks also to the rest of the book team at McGraw Hill who contributed to this edition: Marketing Manager Dan Loch, Editorial Coordinator Kathleen Cowan, Project Manager Roger Geissler, Designer Susan Breitbard, Cover Designer Violeta Diaz, Media Producer Shannon Gattens, and Supplements Producer Marc Mattson.

I am grateful to the reviewers of the all editions of this book whose thoughtful comments contributed much:

Fourth Edition Reviewers
Scott E. Antes, Northern Arizona University; Jeffrey Cohen, Pennsylvania State Univesity; Rebecca Cramer, Johnson County Community College; Jerry Hanson, College of Lake County; Sandra L. Orellana, California State University.

Third Edition Reviewers
Jeffrey H. Cohen, Texas A&M University; Robert Dirks, Illinois State University; Michael P. Freedman, Syracuse University; Susan A. Johnston, University of Rhode Island; Adrian S. Novotny, Long Beach City College; and Lars Rodseth, University of Utah.

Second Edition Reviewers
James Armstrong, State University of New York, Plattsburgh; Diane Baxter, George Washington University; Michael P. Freedman, Syracuse University; Josiah McC. Heyman, Michigan Technological University; David T. Hughes, Wichita State University; Ronald R. McIrvin, University of North Carolina, Greensboro; David McMahon, Saint Francis College; Richard K. Reed, Trinity University; and William Stuart, University of Maryland, College Park.

First Edition Reviewers
Gerald D. Berreman (University of California, Berkeley), Peter J. Bertocci (Oakland University), Daniel L. Boxberger (Western Washington University), Jill Brody (Louisiana State University), Thomas E. Durbin (California State University, Stanislaus), James F. Eder (Arizona State University), James F. Garber (Southwest Texas State University), James W. Hamilton (University of Missouri, Columbia), Patricia Lyons Johnson (Pennsylvania State University), Arthur C. Lehmann (California State University, Chico), Fran Markowitz (DePaul University), David McCurdy (Macalester College), Michael D. Olien (University of Georgia), Mary Kay Gilliland Olsen (Pima Community College and University of Arizona), Aaron Podolefsky (University of Northern Iowa), Scott Rushforth (New Mexico State University), and Daniel J. Yakes (Muskegon Community College).

Finally, I'd especially like to thank Kathi, Brett, and Antonie for their encouragement and patience. Kathi helped create the index and offered her support throughout the entire project. We walked together through every edition.

About the Author

John H. Bodley is Edward R. Meyer Distinguished Professor in Anthropology, Washington State University, where he has taught since 1970. He chaired the Department of Anthropology from 1992–96, and has held visiting teaching positions at University of Vermont, the University of Alaska–Fairbanks, and the University of Uppsala, Sweden. In 1980 he was a visiting researcher at the International Work Group for Indigenous Affairs (IWGIA) in Copenhagen. In 1986 he served on the Tasaday Commission, sponsored by the Department of Anthropology, University of the Philippines. He was a member of the American Association for the Advancement of Science Committee on Scientific Freedom and Responsibility, 1991–94. His other books include *Tribal Peoples and Development Issues* (1988), *Victims of Progress* (4th edition 1999), *Anthropology and Contemporary Human Problems* (4th edition 2001), and *The Power of Scale* (2003).

Bodley is a third generation Oregonian, and has an M.A. and Ph.D in anthropology from the University of Oregon. Before turning to anthropology, his earliest fieldwork was in mammalogy and ornithology in the Pacific Northwest. In 1960 he collected mammal and bird museum specimens in Mexico and Guatemala, and in 1961–62 he was an assistant field naturalist in Mexico for the Museum of Natural History of the University of Kansas. In 1964 he collected zoological specimens in Ecuador and Peru. These field experiences convinced him that misguided economic development was threatening ecosystems and indigenous peoples worldwide, and led him to become an anthropologist focused on global problems.

With support from the National Science Foundation, Bodley carried out anthropological field research in the Peruvian Amazon with the Asháninka and Conibo in 1966, with the Asháninka in 1968–69, and with the Shipibo in 1976–77. This research examined the effects on indigenous peoples of their integration into national and global economies. Throughout the 1970s and 1980s he published and lectured widely as an advocate for the rights of indigenous peoples. Between 1986 and 1988 he visited indigenous groups in Alaska, the Philippines, and Australia. Since 1990 his attention has shifted to an examination of social power in the commercial world, the significance of growth and scale, and the role of most powerful individuals and institutions in transforming the world.

PART ONE

THE TRIBAL WORLD
The World Before the State

Most of human existence has been in the tribal world. With small societies living in an uncrowded world, and a minimum of social inequality except for natural differences of age and gender, tribal people could enjoy a maximum of human freedom. People living in the tribal world were able to make their first priority the satisfaction of their individual self-interest in maintaining and reproducing successful households. Self-interest was easily compatible with the interests of society. Because tribal societies typically contained fewer than 2000 persons, there was no need for government. At birth all tribal people received a personal estate that guaranteed them access to all the natural, social, and cultural wealth needed to make a successful living. Everyone shared natural resources and the goods that they produced, while at the same time maintaining clear property rights. Global population remained below 100 million, and because there was little incentive to increase production, tribal societies could generally maintain a sustainable relationship with their natural resources and ecosystems. Tribal lifestyles promoted good health, and generally low population densities minimized the occurrence of communicable disease. Conflict certainly occurred, both within and between groups, and feuds were sometimes difficult to contain, but on balance life in the tribal world was probably good.

The following three chapters describe three culture areas that are representative of the tribal world: aboriginal Australia, Amazonia, and the East African pastoral zone. Each area includes a brief description of the natural ecosystem, how people came to be living there, and some of the details of making a living. There are descriptions of daily life in tribal households, kinship relations, relations between men and women, and beliefs and practices related to the supernatural. Chapter 5 examines how outsiders have evaluated the quality of life in the tribal world, and offers an objective assessment of its human benefits.

1

Understanding Culture

Kathleen Bodley showing an Asháninka woman how to use a fingernail file.

Learning Objectives

After studying this chapter you should be able to do the following.

1. Describe what cultural anthropologists do, what their goals are, and what their principal methods of field research are. Explain why anthropology is useful.

2. Describe the different aspects, features, and functions of culture.

3. Differentiate between the biological and cultural aspects of human beings, explaining how individual self-interest shapes culture.

4. Compare and contrast inside and outside views of culture, and explain how each relates to the problem of observer bias. Explain why ethnocentrism is a problem.

5. Distinguish among the three functionally interconnected aspects of all cultural systems: *superstructure, structure,* and *infrastructure,* in relation to the mental, behavioral, and material aspects of culture. Explain why these distinctions are useful.

6. Distinguish among the three cultural worlds: *tribal, imperial,* and *commercial,* identifying the most important cultural processes at work in each.

7. Discuss the relationship between scale of society and organization of social power.

8. Explain how the concept of the "good life" can be used to evaluate cultures.

PRONUNCIATION GUIDE

Peruvian place names and Asháninka words are written using Spanish orthography. Their approximate pronunciation for English speakers are as follows:

Key
a = a in father
o = o in go
ay = ay in day
ee = ee in beet
oo = oo in food
h = h in hat
• = Syllable division
/ = Stress

Asháninka = [a • sha / neen • ka]
Chonkiri = [Chon / kee • ree]
cushma = [coosh / ma]
Gran Pajonal = [Gran Pa / ho • nal]
Obenteni = [O • bayn • tay / nee]

2

Cultural anthropology will help you understand culture's contribution to the security and well-being of individual humans and of humanity as a whole. This book examines many representative cultures in depth in order to understand the diverse ways people in different cultures relate to one another—both as individuals and as groups—and to the natural environment. This is useful because the cultural world is now so complex and people are so interconnected and interdependent that cultural understanding has become an essential survival skill. Understanding culture matters because culture is the tool kit that people use to solve human problems. Anthropological description and analysis can reveal the internal meaning and practical utility of cultural beliefs and practices that might seem irrational to an outsider. An anthropological view of culture can also help people understand their own culture in new ways that can reveal new possibilities for improvement. Cultural systems that successfully foster human well-being certainly deserve our respect and tolerance. Anthropological analysis can also identify cultural practices that people might choose to modify because they cause war, poverty, disease, and environmental degradation.

Anthropology is the most holistic academic discipline. Cultural anthropologists need to be both scientists and humanists, because they examine any and all aspects of what people think, do, and make everywhere in the world, from the beginning of time into the future. Anthropologists must consider both the material and the symbolic meanings that people use to maintain and reproduce themselves and their culture. At the same time anthropologists need the insights about nature that come from the physical and biological sciences.

The first part of the chapter draws on my field experiences in South America to show what it is like to actually do anthropology and to explain why I use culture scale as an organizing principle. The chapter then introduces the key concepts of culture and ethnocentrism, and discusses

how culture scale, growth, and process will be used throughout the book. Here, we review some major turning points in human history and demonstrate that anthropology has enormous practical significance and is directly concerned with the great public issues of our time.

DOING ANTHROPOLOGY

Adventures in the Field

Doing cultural anthropology is a continuous adventure. It means exploring the unknown to gain a better understanding of other peoples and cultures. Such understanding can be obtained indirectly from books and class work, but it is most exciting and vivid when it comes directly from real-life experiences—sometimes in unexpected ways. For example, my richest understanding of native Amazonian political leadership was gained during a two-day encounter with Chonkiri, a proud and independent Asháninka **bigman,*** who lived with his small band in the rugged foothills of the Andes along the headwaters of the Peruvian Amazon (Figure 1.1). Bigman leadership is based entirely on force of personality, and Chonkiri displayed this quality admirably (Figure 1.2).

In 1969, my wife, Kathleen, and I were exploring the remote interior of the Asháninka homeland to assess the living conditions of those Asháninka still maintaining a self-sufficient way of life. A bush pilot flew us to Obenteni, a tiny frontier outpost in the Gran Pajonal, five days by mule trail from the nearest truck road and fifty air miles from the nearest town. At that time the

---

bigman A self-made leader in a tribal culture. His position is temporary, depending on personal ability and the consent of his followers.

---

*Key terms are set in bold type and are defined on the outside column of the page spread where they first appear.

FIGURE 1.1   Map of the territory of the Asháninka in the Peruvian Amazon.

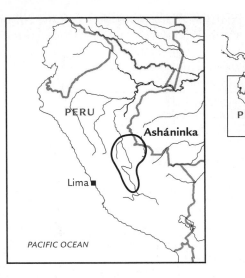

Gran Pajonal was an unmapped maze of savanna-covered ridges and deep forested canyons. It was a vast wilderness, inhabited by the isolated, still fiercely independent Asháninka.

After a hard day's walk from Obenteni, we spotted a column of four Asháninka men on the skyline of an intersecting ridge. Carrying bows and arrows and shotguns, they were an awe-inspiring sight in their long brown cotton robes *(cushmas)* and bright red face paint. They approached briskly and then halted astride the trail a few paces in front of us. With potentially hostile strangers meeting, there was fear and uncertainty on both sides. But the Asháninka were armed and on their home ground, so they controlled the situation. Their leader Chonkiri, obviously a traditional bigman, stepped forward, struck a defiant pose, and shouted a tirade of angry questions at me. The same scene might have greeted the first European explorers to enter Asháninka territory in 1673.

Chonkiri demanded to know where we were going, why we had come, and whether we were bringing sickness. These were legitimate questions, and, although I knew his hostile manner was a formal ritual, I was still uneasy because the Pajonal Asháninka had every reason to resent outsiders. Recent measles epidemics had killed many Asháninka, and colonists and missionaries were appearing in ever greater numbers. In isolated areas such as this, Asháninka often fled at the approach of strangers. However, Chonkiri betrayed no fear. He was playing the role of a powerful and supremely self-confident bigman.

Satisfied with my answers, Chonkiri became a generous host (Figure 1.3). He led us to his house and offered his hospitality—cooked manioc and taro tubers along with handfuls of live ants, which he and his sons had just collected. (I knew that insects were an important food throughout the Pajonal, because game was scarce, but I was amazed to see children sorting through heaps of corn husks to extract fat, inch-long white grubs and pop them, still wiggling, into their mouths.)

After dinner, Chonkiri and his well-armed men followed us back to our camp. They were eager to see what we had brought, and Chonkiri insisted that we unload our backpacks for his inspection (Figure 1.4). Smiling broadly, he immediately took possession of the box of shotgun shells that I had tucked into my pack for trading purposes. "These are mine!" he announced, handing the shells out one at a time to his men. I nodded my approval, hoping that he would be satisfied with such a lavish gift but feeling more and more uneasy at his brashness.

FIGURE 1.2 Chonkiri, the Asháninka bigman, at home—on the left, sitting on the beer trough.

The next morning, Chonkiri returned with a gift basket of corn and bananas. This was simple sharing, giving and receiving, with no monetary scorekeeping. Intellectually, I recognized his gesture as a textbook example of **generalized reciprocity** in a **nonmarket economy.** His generosity reminded me that yesterday Chonkiri had behaved like a tribal bigman by giving away things, even if they were my things.

My instinctive distrust of Chonkiri's real motives was immediately justified. With no further preliminaries, he began to root through our possessions, snatching up whatever he wanted—clothing, trade goods, medical supplies, food, and utensils. In my culture, this was armed robbery, and we were outnumbered, unarmed, and virtually defenseless. An earlier warning that some

Pajonal bigmen were killers suddenly flashed to mind, and I graciously allowed Chonkiri's followers, including his sons, to share my entire assortment of little mirrors and all the rest of my trade goods, even though this would leave me in an awkward position (Figure 1.5).

Chonkiri betrayed his own nervousness when he ripped open a box of unexposed film and started to unreel it, but dropped it with a start

generalized reciprocity The distribution of goods and services by direct sharing. It is assumed that in the long run giving and receiving balances out, but no accounts are maintained.

nonmarket economy Goods and services distributed by direct exchange or reciprocity in the absence of markets and money.

FIGURE 1.3   Women and children in Chonkiri's group.

FIGURE 1.4   Chonkiri, the Asháninka bigman, seated, investigating the contents of my backpack. The ears of corn in the left foreground are his reciprocal gift. The boy in shirt and pants is the son of one of my Asháninka field assistants.

when my wife, Kathleen, blurted, "Stop!" He quickly regained his composure, and his boisterous demands soon became so outrageous that we were forced to call his bluff. He was turning our encounter into a test of will. First, he demanded the hunting knife that Kathleen wore in a sheath on her belt. She refused, insisting that it belonged to her father. Becoming frustrated, Chonkiri picked up my *cushma*, which I used as my only blanket, announcing loudly that it was newer than his and that he intended to take it. When I said "No!," he flung it to the ground, angrily stomping his feet in a display of temper befitting a true bigman. I cautiously assumed that this outburst was for show and would not escalate to violence.

I had a general understanding of the rules. Normally, one was expected to show generosity by giving away anything that was asked for, but now, clearly, Chonkiri was asking for too much. He was showing his bigman status by pushing the limits. I was obliged to refuse his request with no show of fear, although I had no idea how the game would end. The final test came when Chonkiri appropriated the fat roll of cash (50 Sole bills worth approximately $2 each) hidden in my pack. He triumphantly peeled off the bills and handed them out to his men. Using unmistakable gestures, I responded with my most emphatic "No!" If I had not shown personal strength at

FIGURE 1.5 Chonkiri's sons eagerly snatching up all of my trade goods.

that moment, it would have been a humiliating, perhaps even dangerous, defeat. To my considerable relief, he promptly collected the money and restored it to my pack. Chonkiri and I had reached an understanding based on mutual respect. In this situation, familiarity with the culture was as important as courage. I realized that Chonkiri's bravado and bluster betrayed his personal vulnerability as a bigman. If he failed to command the respect of his followers, they could simply walk away. A bigman had no means of coercing loyalty in a culture in which every household could be economically self-sufficient.

After our standoff, Chonkiri became the generous host again. He gave us a grand tour of his house and garden, and provided one of his sons to serve as a trail guide. However, he continued to emphasize his dominance by firmly kicking aside Kathleen when she sat on the overturned beer trough that he wanted to occupy. I chose not to consider that gesture a personal affront, but it helped me decide that we would cut short our visit. We parted on friendly terms.

This episode gives a brief glimpse into the daily politics in an autonomous *tribal culture* be-

yond the reach of government control. However, the apparent isolation was illusory, for Chonkiri and his band were part of the global market economy, even though its direct influence was slight. Several of Chonkiri's men were wearing factory-made pants under their *cushmas*. There were steel axes and metal pots lying about. Obenteni had been a Franciscan mission since the 1930s, and the entire region had been briefly missionized in the eighteenth century. Chonkiri's house was located near an abandoned cattle ranch that three years earlier had served as a temporary base for Marxist guerrillas. Nevertheless, we were inspired to witness the vitality and autonomy of Ash culture after three centuries of European pressure.

Anthropological Research in Amazonia

During my first visit to the Peruvian Amazon in 1964, my experience with the Ash led me to question many fundamental assumptions about the place of tribal cultures in the contemporary world. I developed a profound respect for the Ash and their ability to live so well and so self-sufficiently in their rain forest environment. I also recognized that even though the Ash were one of the largest indigenous groups in the entire Amazon basin, outsiders seeking to exploit Ash resources were threatening their independence and their culture. I learned that although some Ash were avoiding all contacts with the colonists who were invading their territory, others were attempting to adjust to their changing circumstances by establishing economic relationships with the intruders.

According to conventional anthropological theory, the Ash were undergoing rapid **acculturation,** and their culture would soon disappear as Ash society was absorbed into the

---

acculturation Culture change brought about by contact between peoples with different cultures. Usually refers to the loss of traditional culture when the members of tribal cultures adopt elements of commercial-scale cultures.

dominant Peruvian national society. I was disturbed by the obvious negative aspects of this process and wanted to learn how their increasing involvement with the global system was affecting the Asháninka and Asháninka culture. My knowledge of the long history of Asháninka resistance to foreign intrusion convinced me that, contrary to popular wisdom, there was nothing inevitable about acculturation. Furthermore, the neutral term *acculturation* seemed to disguise the harsh fact that the Asháninka were being forcibly conquered and dispossessed. This did not seem to be a natural process and was perhaps neither fair nor beneficial. But no one had gone to the trouble of asking the questions that would illuminate the process. I hoped that my research findings would contribute to new government policies that would allow the Asháninka and similar peoples to maintain their independent lifestyle.

Altogether I spent some fifteen months working on this problem on three separate visits to Peru over a five-year period. I wanted to understand how specific changes in Asháninka economic adaptation were reflected in changes in their society. I collected most of my data by directly observing and participating in the daily life of Asháninka settlements. This basic anthropological field method, called **participant observation,** involves total immersion in the alien culture and a suspension of one's own cultural judgments about appropriate behavior. However, the participant observer never loses his or her own cultural identity, and can never become a full member of the other culture. I never pretended to be an Asháninka, although I lived in their houses, studied their language, shared their food and drink, accompanied them to their gardens and on foraging expeditions, and listened to their nightly stories and songs. This allowed me to *see* Asháninka economy and society in ways that would never have been possible if I had remained a complete outsider. Participant observation also generates empathy and respect for the other culture, especially when it is used as a method of learning, rather than as a means to induce others to change their way of life.

Effective participant observation is combined with the **ethnographic method.** That is, the anthropologist observes everyday activities and asks informal questions, often working closely with a few **key informants,** rather than relying entirely on formal interviews or impersonal survey questionnaires. The key informant may be one's host in the community or a hired guide, translator, or teacher. Because cultures are integrated in complex, often unexpected ways, at first I could not be sure which Asháninka activities had economic or social implications. Thus, it was critical that I observe with an open mind and record as much as possible. I kept a daily journal in which I recorded all my observations and interviews with informants. Even the most obscure observations might have eventually proved useful. For example, it turned out that knowing the native names of the palm trees used for roof thatch became a clue to the intensity with which forest resources were being used in a given area.

Anthropologists often work intensively in a single village, with one or two key informants, but my research required a broader approach. Relying on photos taken from aircraft to locate isolated settlements, I worked in four different regions, collecting detailed census data on more than four hundred Asháninka households living in some forty local groups and speaking four dialects. Altogether, six men, one twelve-year-old boy, and one woman were my primary Asháninka assistants.

The key to much of my work was the **genealogical method.** This involved sitting down with the senior man in a group or household and asking him to name his wife or wives and all his children by relative age. I would ask where everyone was born and determine where they were living or where and how they had died. If possible, I would compile similar information on more distant kin. Then I would draw a sketch map of the village, numbering each house and identifying the occupants by name (Figure 1.6). I also worked intensively with many individuals to outline their life histories in greater detail. All this material allowed me to begin recognizing culturally meaningful social patterns. Without

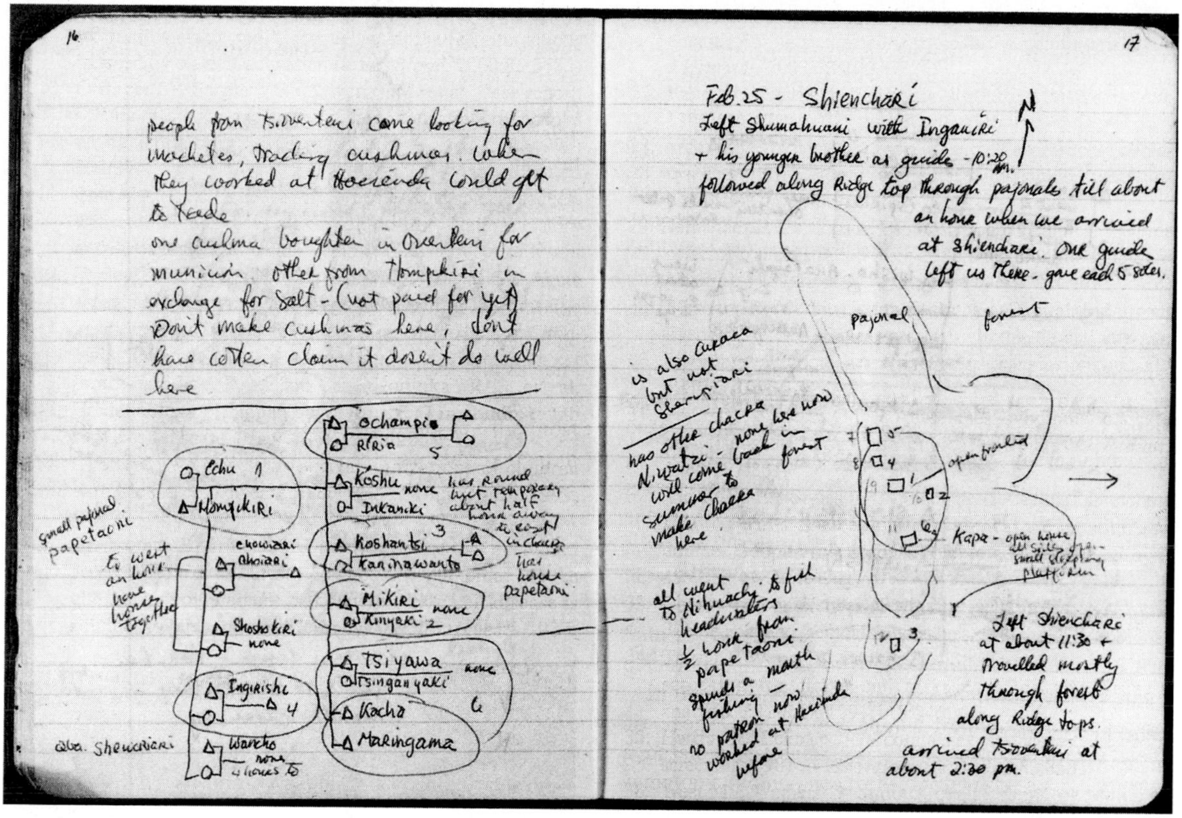

FIGURE 1.6 A page from my field notebook showing an Asháninka local group and genealogical relationships. Kinship diagrams such as these will be discussed in Chapter 2.

knowing who people were by name, where they lived, and who their relatives were, I would have remained an outsider. This information allowed me to analyze settlement and household structures, migration patterns, marriage and kinship terms, and fertility and mortality rates, and it proved indispensable for understanding the impact of changing economic patterns.

What emerged from these data was a shocking pattern of Asháninka depopulation and exploitation. For example, I found that diseases spread by uncontrolled contact with colonists had dramatically elevated Asháninka mortality. In some areas, the Asháninka were indeed disappearing. Many had died violently or been taken captive to work for colonists. Local groups and families were fragmented and scattered, and subsistence activities suffered as people were drawn into virtual debt slavery. Opportunities for individual Asháninka

participant observation Field method in which the observer shares in community activities.

ethnographic method Reliance on direct participant observation, key informants, and informal interviews as a data-collecting technique.

key informant A member of the host culture who helps the anthropologist learn about the culture.

genealogical method Method used to trace the marriage and family relationships among people as a basis for identifying cultural patterns in a community.

to participate successfully in the market economy were extremely limited. Many joined mission communities in hopes of escaping exploitation, but living conditions at the missions often were poor because the concentrated population quickly depleted local resources. Furthermore, the missionaries disapproved of many Asháninka cultural practices. It was a discouraging picture; however, Asháninka culture was extremely resilient, and vast areas of their traditional lands remained undisturbed. I was certain that both people and culture could survive if given the chance.

Eventually, I presented my findings in a doctoral dissertation (Bodley 1970) and in a series of published papers (Bodley 1972a, 1972b, 1973, 1981a, 1992, 1993). Some of my Asháninka ethnographic material illustrates important aspects of independent, tribal cultures as they existed in the **ethnographic present** before they were seriously disrupted by intruders from politically centralized, politically organized cultures (see Chapters 3 and 5). Of course, anthropology involves much more than ethnographic description. It can also provide insights on critical issues of national and international policy. For example, my research has led me to recommend that the Peruvian government legally recognize and respect the political and economic autonomy of the Asháninka on the lands that they traditionally occupied (see Chapter 14).

My research on the Asháninka also has forced me to ask questions about my own culture. I was impressed by the contrast between the precariousness and inequality of our market-based, industrial way of life and the ability of the Asháninka to provide for all of their material needs—food, clothing, and shelter—while maintaining a high-quality environment and high levels of social equality. In this respect, their culture seems to be more effective than our own, and its integrity deserves to be safeguarded from uninvited intrusion. This realization has launched me into a much larger research project to systematically compare tribal cultures, like the Asháninka, with larger-scale cultures in politically organized states and

modern, industrial cultures whose influences span the globe. Understanding how tribes, states, and global systems work and how they differ might help us design a more secure and equitable world. This book is a product of this ongoing investigation.

CULTURE AND ETHNOCENTRISM: THE KEY ANTHROPOLOGICAL CONCEPTS

Culture: The Human Way of Life

Culture is the most basic concept in anthropology, yet there is remarkable variation in how anthropologists define culture and what aspects of culture they think are important. The most widely cited technical definition of culture, as socially patterned human thought and behavior, was originally proposed by pioneering British anthropologist Edward Tylor:

> Culture . . . is that complex whole which includes knowledge, belief, art, law, morals, custom, and any other capabilities and habits acquired by man as a member of society. (Tylor 1871)

Virtually all anthropologists take Tylor's definition as a starting point. Tylor assumed that culture was a uniquely human trait, but he distinguished between biologically inherited and socially transmitted human traits. It is useful to consider humans as the product of this dual inheritance (biological and cultural) because, as a learned inheritance, culture can be unlearned and modified to help solve human problems. If all aspects of culture were biologically inherited, we would need to resort to genetic engineering to solve certain human problems.

Although early anthropologists acknowledged the close biological kinship between humans and the great apes—especially gorillas and chimpanzees—they maintained that it was *culture* that produced a uniquely human way of life. They also assumed that culture requires superior, bio-

TABLE 1.1   KEY ASPECTS, FEATURES, AND FUNCTIONS OF CULTURE

Aspects	Features	Functions
Mental	Patterned	Regulation
Behavioral	Symbolic	Maintenance
Material	Shared	Survival and reproduction
	Socially transmitted	Fitness-enhancement
	Ethnocentric	
	Conservative	
	Normative	
	Dynamic	
	Historical	

logically based mental abilities, which for Tylor were best demonstrated by the powerful symbolism of human speech:

> To use words in themselves unmeaning, as symbols by which to conduct and convey the complex intellectual processes in which mental conceptions are suggested, compared, combined, and even analyzed, and new ones created—this is a faculty which is scarcely to be traced in any lower animal. (Tylor 1875)

This emphasis on words and symbols certainly identifies one of the most important features of culture, but Tylor left unanswered many questions concerning how to make sense of the rest of culture. Anthropologists since Tylor have debated the most useful attributes that a technical conception of culture should stress. How particular anthropologists define culture is important because the definition influences their choice of research problems, their methods and interpretations, and their positions on public policy issues. At one extreme, culture may be considered a thing in itself that simply evolves as an abstract system. This view may be helpful for understanding the impact of cultures on the physical environment, but it fails to consider the decision making of individual human actors. Some contemporary anthropologists emphasize that culture itself, as

well as every ethnographic description of culture, is constructed and interpreted by individuals. In this sense, there is no absolute cultural reality. Rather, culture consists of the narratives and symbolic dialogues that individuals construct—a view that emphasizes the fluidity and dynamism of culture. This view is a humbling reminder of the difficulties involved in sorting out cultural meanings. It is also a valuable anthropological tool for learning how people construct and manipulate culture to gain power over others.

Throughout this text, different dimensions of the various aspects, features, and functions of culture will be examined (Table 1.1). The multiple aspects of culture include (1) *mental,* or what people think, (2) *behavioral,* or what people do, and (3) *material,* or what people produce. Thus, just as Tylor originally proposed, mental processes, beliefs, knowledge, and values all can be considered

---

ethnographic present An arbitrary time period when the process of culture change is ignored in order to describe a given culture as if it were a stable system.

culture Socially transmitted, often symbolic, information that shapes human behavior and that regulates human society so that people can successfully maintain themselves and reproduce. Culture has mental, behavioral, and material aspects; it is patterned and provides a model for proper behavior.

part of culture, but human actors and actions also are important. In this respect, culture is the socially transmitted information that shapes human action. Some anthropologists would define culture entirely as mental rules guiding behavior, although they would recognize as well the often wide gap between the acknowledged rules for correct behavior and people's actual conduct. Consequently, some researchers focus on human behavior and its material products, rather than on the underlying mental information producing them.

In addition to these aspects, culture has several important *features*. As already noted, culture is socially transmitted and shared, symbolic and patterned. Culture is conservative, yet it changes, it has a history, and it tells people what is best and proper. The shared aspect of culture means that it is a social phenomenon; idiosyncratic behavior is not cultural. Culture is learned, not biologically inherited, and as Tylor noted, it involves arbitrarily assigned, symbolic meanings. For example, Americans are not born knowing that the color white means purity, and indeed this is not a universal **symbol** for purity. (In East Asia, white often symbolizes death.) The human ability to assign arbitrary meaning to any object, behavior, or condition makes culture enormously creative and helps distinguish culture from animal behavior. This also means that people can change cultures in positive ways.

Culture also has primary *functions*. Culture exists to guarantee human survival and reproduction. Culture is the unique means by which people in a given **society** satisfy their human needs, regulate the size of their society and the distribution of social power, and manage natural resources. Culture gives people power to produce and distribute resources in ways that can make entire groups prosper or decline. How culture is used as a means of power over the natural environment is clearly one of the keys to human survival and well-being. Effective adaptation to the natural environment means more than mere survival; it involves establishing a sustainable balance between resources and consumption while maintaining a satisfying and secure society.

Because environments change constantly, adaptation is an ongoing process.

Tylor's basic definition of culture has served anthropology well, but in his day little was known about the behavior of chimpanzees, our closest nonhuman relatives. Recent research with chimpanzees suggests that many aspects of culture may not be unique to humans.

Chimpanzee Culture?

Unquestionably, speech is the key human feature that greatly facilitates the human ability to symbol, or assign to symbolic meaning (White 1949). Speech also greatly accelerates the overall production and transmission of culture. It is possible that a single genetic mutation occurring perhaps 100,000 years ago gave our ancestors finer control over movement of the mouth and larynx, making human speech possible (Enard, et al. 2002). However, more recent research with "cross-fostered" chimpanzees—raised by humans and enculturated like children—demonstrates that chimpanzees can learn to communicate symbolically. Although their vocal anatomy prevents chimpanzees from speaking effectively, they can be taught to use ASL (American Sign Language), a gesture language created for those with hearing impairments. The most famous experimental work with cross-fostered chimpanzees was begun in 1966 by R. Allen Gardner and Beatrix Gardner (Gardner and Gardner 1994a, 1994b) and continued by Roger Fouts (1994). This research began as Project Washoe, named for Washoe, a ten-month-old wild chimpanzee who was cross-fostered and intensively taught ASL over a four-year period. Washoe and the other chimpanzees in these experiments proved able to learn up to 150 ASL signs over five years of training. They signed to themselves, to one another, and to humans, producing novel phrases such as "ICECREAM HURRY GIMME." They also taught signs to one another, thereby reproducing symbolic, shared, learned behavior (which certainly could be called culture), but they did not construct new signs. Although the limits of chimpanzee language ability under human fosterage have not been established, such symbolic constructions clearly are not prominent in free-ranging chimpanzees.

During the first half of the twentieth century, conventional anthropological views of human evolution identified toolmaking as the earliest evidence for human culture. Anthropologists argued that toolmaking is a uniquely human trait, functionally connected to increased brain size and upright posture, or bipedalism, which freed the hands. Field research with free-ranging chimpanzees—especially primatologist Jane Goodall's work in Tanzania—demonstrated that chimpanzees make and use simple tools fairly extensively, which suggests the presence of shared, learned cultural behavior. As many as nineteen different tool uses have been identified for wild chimpanzees, including stones used as hammers and missiles, and sticks and branches used as clubs, flails, probes, extractors, and carrying devices. Chimpanzees also use leaves for sponges, napkins, grooming implements, and even medicine (McGrew 1992).

Many anthropologists and primatologists do not hesitate to speak of chimpanzee "culture," "cultural traditions," and "chimpanzee politics" (de Wall 1982, Goodall 1986, McGrew 1992). Humans and chimpanzees appear to differ only in the quantity of culture that they produce. Humans do make many more types of tools. In addition, human speech permits vast increases in the scale of human culture and in the ways that it can be produced, reproduced, and accumulated. Human culture is more complex, with more parts and subparts, and with many culturally defined roles that support much larger societies. Indeed, humans have elaborated culture to such a degree that they are unique in the animal world in their total dependence on culture (Slurink 1994).

Given that most human behavior is socially, rather than biologically, motivated, we still cannot neatly separate human behavior from animal behavior. Learned and shared "cultural traditions" have even been attributed to mountain

sheep, as when all the animals in particular herds shared distinctive behaviors (Geist 1994). However, important distinctions between human and animal culture can be made. Michael Tomasello (1994) observes that human cultural behavior is highly uniform, whereas chimp learned behavior often is idiosyncratic and individually produced. A particular chimp may learn a very efficient way to crack open a nut, but it might never be copied by any other chimp. Human culture always involves numerous behaviors that are uniform and universally shared by all members of a given cultural tradition. For example, all adult Asháninka share the learned behaviors of wearing the *cushma*, applying red face paint, and believing that the forest is populated by dangerous spirit demons. In contrast, only a few of the thirty-six known groups of African chimpanzees display any specific, universally shared, learned behaviors such as using sticks to dig for termites.

Tomasello suggests that chimpanzees may be limited in their ability to produce and transmit culture because they tend to *emulate* rather than *imitate* the behavior of their fellows. That is, they may be inspired to achieve the results that others produce, but they do not precisely copy their behavior. Learning by imitation requires the ability to understand the intentions of others and to make careful observations. Both observation and imitation are greatly enhanced by the rich conceptualization and symbolism encouraged by human speech.

Self-Interest, Selfish Genes, and the Biology of Culture

In understanding how people use culture, it is useful to assume that individual humans generally behave in self-interested ways. Biological evolution operating through natural selection programs us to propagate our individual genetic

symbol Anything with a culturally defined meaning.
society An interacting, intermarrying human population sharing a common culture.

material through our descendants and closest relatives. Like our genes (Dawkins 1976), we are naturally selfish individuals, but we cooperate and form groups when it is beneficial to us. Altruism, or self-sacrifice (helping others at one's own expense), is probably extremely rare, because we are naturally driven to do things that favor the well-being of ourselves and our children above everyone else. Culture is the primary tool that individuals use to pursue actions that they perceive to be in their self-interest.

Human culture includes all the social things that people think, do, and make that are *not* in themselves biologically inherited. Human biology provides us with the physical abilities and psychological propensities that make culture possible, such as the ability to speak, and to manipulate symbols with our minds and objects with our hands. Biology also gives us a bundle of very general behavioral predispositions, or inborn drives, such as a propensity to selfishly do things that will increase our own reproductive success, to accumulate information, to see cause-and-effect relationships, and to competitively emulate and imitate individuals who we think are more successful. Emulation is a more efficient way to learn than trial and error, and is an important means of cultural transmission. We humans have highly developed abilities to monitor what others do, to persuade others to believe they will benefit by doing what we want, even when they don't, and to detect similar deceits on the part of others. This means that in many respects our relationship to other people, and our use of culture, is more important than our relationship to nature.

In realizing our individual self-interest, we use culture to secure energy and materials to meet our biological needs for maintenance and reproduction and to deal with other people. Learning how to successfully relate to other individuals and other human groups is perhaps the most critical human problem, because human conflict can be so costly, and because getting others to do our work can be so beneficial. Groups of people form human societies to maximize their self-interest and resolve their "natural" conflicts of interest

by agreeing on cultural, or "moral," rules. However, culture is an imperfect tool. We know that people do not always follow the rules. People are also sometimes wrong about what they perceive to be in their self-interest. Furthermore, it is not always easy to correctly identify the short-term actions that will best meet our long-term objectives, because the world is so full of uncertainties. Also, people are not always consciously aware of, or knowledgeable about, their long-term interests.

Culture and nature are so closely intertwined that it would be misleading to speak of an essential, unchanging human nature, given the dynamics of change. Our biology allows us to respond in novel ways to novel situations, such that the outcome of cultural development is neither preordained nor inevitable. Culture is a humanly directed response to historical events. We use culture to change our behavior and the behavior of others for personal benefit, but the conscious choices that we make are aimed at immediate outcomes, which may be poorly related to the long-term goal of the survival of human beings as a species. Personal survival, high social status, and access to resources are short-term goals of self-interested individuals that hopefully will also benefit humanity.

Viewing Other Cultures: The Problem of Observer Bias

It is impossible to really know any culture except from the inside, as a native member. Even the most skilled anthropologist will always be an outsider when viewing a different culture. The problem for anthropologists is how to overcome, or at least become aware of, their own cultural biases, while attempting to understand other cultures from the inside. Translation of symbols from a given culture into categories that will be meaningful to outsiders will often be imprecise. The problem is compounded by the fact that cultural insiders may be quite unconscious of the underlying meanings of their own cultural categories.

One of anthropology's most important contributions toward the understanding of other cultures is its recognition of the problem of **ethnocentrism**—the tendency to evaluate other cultures in reference to one's own (presumably superior) culture (see the box entitled "An Ethnocentric Look at Australian Aborigines"). Ethnocentrism contributes to internal social solidarity, but it can seriously distort one's perception of others and hinders cross-cultural understanding. For example, some Christian missionaries disapproved of Asháninka shamans, disregarding their valuable skills as curers and herbalists. In addition, outside developers mistakenly regarded indigenous shifting cultivation in the tropical rain forest as backward and wasteful "slash and burn." But when anthropologists actually examined the internal logic of these practices, they found that native Amazonian cultivation patterns were sustainable, productive, and energy efficient.

Anthropologists must constantly strive to recognize their own ethnocentrism and consciously suspend it when attempting to understand other cultures. As an alternative to ethnocentrism, anthropologists often advocate **cultural relativism**—the position that other cultures have intrinsic worth and can only be usefully evaluated or understood in their own terms. The ideal of cultural relativism can be applied to anthropological research using functionalist methods. **Functionalism** is the belief that particular cultural traits may play a role in maintaining the culture. It is a powerful analytic tool to help anthropologists view each culture as an interconnected system of parts and subparts, and to look for the function of each part. Even practices such as infanticide may in some way contribute to the survival of the total culture. However, identifying the *functions* of particular customs does not explain why they exist or whether they should exist. Anthropologists are interested in evaluating the impact of specific cultural practices on individuals, households, communities, nations, and ecosystems. Making such evaluations in a systematic and unbiased way is one of anthropology's great strengths.

Cultural relativism does not mean that all aspects of every culture are somehow ultimately "true." One of the paradoxes of culture is that it provides its members with a particular way

of knowing the world. A culture is an epistemology—a theory of knowledge—and a cosmology—a theory of how the world is ordered as a system—but because culture is created by self-interested individuals, cultural knowledge and cosmologies may provide distorted views of the world. Cultural meanings may be "true" in that they are internally logical and consistent, and they may function to maintain the culture, but they may not always give people an accurate image of the physical world or the actual operation of society. How people imagine both their own societies and the physical world may be wrong in a cosmic sense as well as in a practical sense. One of anthropology's great advantages is that it offers us tools for asking the big questions about human beings and their place in the universe, and for questioning the significance and utility of our own culture.

Acknowledging one's own ethnocentrism and applying cultural relativism does not mean abandoning judgments and values. For example, when I compiled my first life history of an Asháninka man, I learned that when he was orphaned as a child, a shaman had called him a witch. He would have been burned to death if he had not escaped to a mission. Many Asháninka themselves condemn witch burning, but killing witches was understandable within the Asháninka belief system, just as it was in Salem, Massachusetts, in 1692. I, however, consider killing witches, children or not, to be repulsive. Such practices are also a gross violation of internationally recognized human rights standards. Asháninka bigmen organized intergroup raids—killing men and kidnapping women and children. I found abundant evidence of these practices in my genealogies and life histories, and I understood them to be part of a complex of cultural practices

---

ethnocentrism Evaluation of other cultures from the perspective of one's own—presumably superior—culture.
cultural relativism Understanding of other cultures by their own categories, which are assumed to be valid and worthy of respect.
functionalism Assumption that particular cultural traits may have a role in maintaining the culture.

An Ethnocentric Look at Australian Aborigines

Ethnocentric distortion is well illustrated by an outrageous paper on Australian aborigines read before the Anthropological Institute in London in 1871 by the institute's director, Charles Staniland Wake (1872). (Chapter 2, which is entirely devoted to Australian aboriginal culture, will demonstrate how misleading Wake's views were.) The language of Wake's paper is so offensive that it is difficult to imagine that it was presented as objective science. Wake's ethnocentrism is readily betrayed by his derogatory references to "moral defects" and the "barbarity" and "absurdity" of aboriginal customs, which he claimed were founded on "unmitigated selfishness." Such ethnocentrism had its origins in the assumptions of racial and cultural superiority that supported European colonialism.

In Wake's view, aborigines, with their simple material culture, were living examples of the earliest stage of human evolution. He sought to describe their mental characteristics but felt that it was inaccurate to speak of their "intellectual" abilities, because aborigines operated almost by instinct, barely above the animal level. They had "no aim in life but the continuance of their existence and the gratifications of their passions, with the least possible trouble to themselves."

Their technological achievements, such as the boomerang, were derided as accidental discoveries, while their art was likened to "the productions of children." Even aboriginal languages and complex marriage systems were treated as mere unconscious developments, reflecting no particular intellectual ability.

Morally, aborigines were described as children, who enjoyed song and dance and became "extremely indolent" when food was abundant. The aboriginal mind was "saturated with superstition," but the aborigines had no religion. In Wake's view, they also had no abstract concept of morality, could not form any idea of death, and routinely mistreated women, the young, and the weak. They cannibalized their children and beat, speared, and enslaved their wives. Wake even had doubts about whether aboriginal mothers had "natural affection" for their children, although he also accused them of being overindulgent parents.

In regard to their relations with Europeans, Wake found the aborigines to be haughty, insolent, cunning, and treacherous thieves and liars who unpredictably

centered on the bigman in the absence of centralized political authority. Both witchcraft and raiding no doubt were intensified by the intrusion of outsiders.

From a functionalist, nonethnocentric perspective, cultures can be seen to form logical wholes, but they need not be viewed as discrete, static, perfectly balanced systems. Cultures are open-ended networks of ideas, objects, and people that constantly change as their circumstances change.

A major part of understanding culture is evaluating how successfully different cultures meet basic human needs.

Ethnocentrism can influence both what an observer sees and how observations are interpreted. Ethnocentrism also can influence a researcher's choice of research problem and the mode of explanation adopted. The problem of ethnocentrism is now a standard part of modern anthropological training, but at the height of colonial expan-

killed strangers. He made no connection between these negative personality traits and the obvious facts of colonial invasion, yet he did attribute their treachery to suspicion. Wake's interpretation of aboriginal culture did not go beyond his original assumption that aborigines represented the very "childhood of humanity." They were moral and intellectual children, not degenerates from a higher state. Given Wake's assumptions that European culture was the most highly evolved and that Europeans would inevitably dominate the world, his ethnocentrism is hardly surprising. Wake never actually saw an aborigine, and his knowledge of the culture apparently did not go beyond the superficial stereotypes of unsympathetic European explorers and settlers.

Not even modern anthropologists have been immune from this kind of ethnocentrism. In 1978, American anthropologist Arthur Hippler published a remarkably similar characterization of Australian aboriginal personality. Hippler deprecated the aboriginal personality and worldview as "infantile." Aborigines were "superstitious" and had difficulty separating reality from fantasy. They routinely mistreated women. Aboriginal parents were thoughtless, selfish, inconsistent, harsh, and lacking in empathy toward their children.

Hippler's work was not typical of contemporary anthropology and was promptly condemned by outraged aboriginal specialists. Nevertheless, it illustrated how easily the ethnocentrism of an earlier century can be repeated. Hippler only briefly visited the aboriginal community he described and relied heavily on other sources. His research was based on his prior theory that the child-rearing practices of tribal cultures are inferior and thus produce inferior adults. Hippler deliberately rejected the anthropological standard of cultural relativism—that one at least attempt to view other cultures in their own terms. Furthermore, he began with the openly ethnocentric assumption that "there is no question that Euro-American culture is vastly superior in its flexibility, tolerance for variety, scientific thought, and interest in emergent possibilities to any primitive society extant" (Hippler 1981:395).

---

sion in the nineteenth century, European anthropologists were convinced of their own cultural superiority and were blissfully unaware of the concept of ethnocentrism.

Beyond Ethnocentrism: Emic and Etic Views

One way to move beyond ethnocentric bias is to self-consciously try to view another culture through the eyes of a cultural insider. This requires the use of insider cultural categories. Anthropologists use the terms **emic** and **etic** to refer to the inside and outside perspective on a culture

emic Relating to cultural meanings derived from inside a given culture and presumed to be unique to that culture.
etic Relating to cultural meanings as translated for cross-cultural comparison.

(Headland, Pike, and Harris 1990). For example, an insider emic understanding of Asháninka leadership would start with the Asháninka term *pinkatsari,* literally, "big man." I learned that a *pinkatsari* was a prominent person with a forceful personality. If I had applied the outsider etic category "chief" to Chonkiri, I would have completely misunderstood his cultural role. As a *pinkatsari,* Chonkiri could harangue and persuade, but he held no coercive authority over his followers. He did not inherit his position and could not automatically pass it on to his sons. In fact, the Asháninka reject the kind of central political authority implied by the outsider word *chief.*

This distinction between *emic* and *etic* is based on the use of these terms in linguistics to refer to phon*emic* and phon*etic* transcription, following Kenneth Pike (1954). **Phonemes** are the unique sounds recognized as significant by speakers of a given language. For example, the words *pray* and *play* are distinguished by speakers of English because *r* and *l* are different phonemes and are thus heard as different sounds. Speakers of another language might not hear any difference between *pray* and *play*. A phonetic transcription records the sounds as heard by a nonspeaker of the language who does not know which sound distinctions are meaningful. Phonetic transcriptions may be clumsy approximations of the "real" sounds of a language. Similarly, the meanings of unique words, symbols, rituals, and institutions may be difficult to translate cross-culturally. Even a trained observer can only watch what people do and record native explanations. Observations must be selectively screened through the observer's own cultural categories; then, in effect, an interpretation of the culture must be created.

CULTURE SCALE, GROWTH, AND PROCESS

The past century of astounding material and technological progress has produced a global middle class of some 1.5 billion well-off people—one-fourth of humanity whose private cars, comfortable homes, and abundant consumer goods reflect a standard of prosperity absolutely unprecedented in human experience. These figures, and how they were derived, will be discussed in more detail in Chapter 13. Paradoxically, the bottom 70 percent of the global population, more than 4 billion people, are now poor, if not totally destitute. When uneven development leaves this many people disempowered, the potential for social upheaval is large. Furthermore, human activities are disturbing natural processes on a scale that may threaten everyone's future well-being through undesirable ecosystem modification, species extinctions, and global climate change. How could cultural development have become such a mixed blessing? Does gross inequity and massive social and environmental stress inevitably flow from human nature? Is growth in human population and cultural complexity a natural process, or can individuals and societies shape culture for their own benefit? A knowledge of cultural anthropology can help today's global citizens understand the cultural processes that produce growth and distribute social power.

This book explores what is "natural" and what is "cultural" about human behavior by using the basic concepts of cultural anthropology to examine the full range of cultural diversity, worldwide and throughout history and prehistory. The nature-culture question is crucial because if extreme poverty and environmental degradation are indeed natural, we can only seek to mitigate their most severe consequences. But if poverty and environmental deterioration are under cultural, and therefore human, control, they could be significantly reduced, or even eliminated, by intentional cultural design and change. Culture growth and the distribution of social power in different cultural settings are important variables, because growth in the scale of human activities has the potential to produce both wealth and poverty. If growth is a purely natural process, we remain spectators; but if growth is a human-directed process, then as em-

TABLE 1.2 DOMESTICALLY DIRECTED HUMANIZATION SUBPROCESSES

Conceptualization	Producing abstract concepts and symbols that shape behavior
Materialization	Giving physical form to concepts
Verbalization	Producing human speech
Socialization	Producing human societies
Cultural transmission	Reproducing culture

powered global citizens, we can consciously shape growth to meet our human needs.

The Humanization Process: Reproducing and Maintaining People

Culture, conceived of as the socially transmitted information that shapes human behavior, is part of a biocultural evolutionary process that produced and sustained *Homo sapiens*, the human species. Biocultural theorists Robert Boyd and Peter Richerson (1985) and William Durham (1991) point out that our genes and our culture are interdependent, and have coevolved as a dual inheritance. Genes and culture must be reproduced and transmitted to the next generation. However, there is a crucial difference between natural selection operating on genes and cultural selection operating on culture: People often quite deliberately guide cultural selection. Genes and culture are connected because people are likely to adopt and transmit cultural patterns that they think will improve their *genetic fitness*, or the degree to which their genes are reproduced.

Cultural ideas constitute the templates for a series of human actions that produce outcomes chosen by individual human actors. These actions can be called *cultural processes*. The most important cultural process is **humanization**—the production and maintenance of people, societies, and cultures. Humanization involves a tightly integrated series of subprocesses that collectively define a uniquely human way of life centered on marriage, the family, and the household (Table 1.2). The most crucial humanization subprocess is the human ability to conceptualize and thereby pro-

duce the abstract concepts and symbols, such as father, mother, son, and daughter, that define the family as a social unit and the foundation of human society. Speech, or the ability to verbalize concepts, makes it possible for people to store and efficiently transmit vast quantities of cultural information. Cultural concepts also are frequently given physical form, or materialized, when people build shelters and make tools and ornaments or art objects, or when they act out their beliefs in rituals or stories. For culture to exist, it must be stored and transmitted, or reproduced in the next generation. Cultural transmission can occur in many ways, including by observation and borrowing, but transmission from parents to children within the household is the most basic transmission process.

Social Power in Three Cultural Worlds

This book emphasizes one of the most important and interesting functions of culture: *the way people use culture to produce **social power** to achieve their goals in relation to other people and the natural environment.* Social power is not easily defined or measured, but it is a familiar feature of daily life. Broadly, it is a measure of a person's

---

phoneme The minimal unit of sound that carries meaning and is recognized as distinctive by the speakers of a given language.

humanization The production and maintenance of human beings, human societies, and human cultures, based on social power organized at the household, or domestic, level.

social power An individual's ability to get what he or she wants, even when others might object.

ability to get what he or she wants, even when others might object. From a biocultural perspective, individuals are naturally predisposed to seek social power in order to improve their genetic fitness. However, individuals need social support. Therefore, social power must be culturally regulated, because if individuals gain too much power or misuse their power, they can weaken the social cohesion necessary for successful biological and cultural reproduction. Social power also must be regulated when it is applied to other societies and to the natural environment, because cultural and biological interchange between societies is too important to be permanently disrupted by all-out conflict, and natural resources are too vulnerable to overexploitation.

Culture is all about social power. Thus, much of human mental ability deals with improving our ability to monitor the perceptions, beliefs, and desires of other people to better interpret and direct their behavior (Boyer 2000). This situation evolved as people came to depend on reciprocity from other people. Perceptions are crucial in the struggle for self-interest. What people know and do influences what other people know and do. Human society became more complex when people began to realize that they could use culture to manipulate other people's perceptions of the world in order to gain personal benefits.

Theories about human nature can help us understand why people seek social power and the general methods they employ. However, the particular distributions of social power, such as between men and women, between the young and the old, between social classes in a given culture, or between nations cannot be easily attributed to genetic differences in human populations. We must examine the details of culture, history, and the natural environment, and the actions of individuals to understand how cultures are created and transformed.

Following the lead of historical sociologist Michael Mann (1986), in this book we will distinguish among four types of social power: ideological, economic, military, and political (Table 1.3).

TABLE 1.3 SOCIAL POWER: HOW PEOPLE ACHIEVE THEIR GOALS IN RELATION TO OTHERS

Types of Social Power	
Ideological	Military
Economic	Political
Cultural Organization of Social Power	
By kin in the tribal world	
By rulers in the imperial world	
By business owners, managers, and financiers in the commercial world	

Ideological power refers to control over what people know. Some anthropologists consider ideological power to be the least important form of social power, but it is arguably the most important, because it may be the most effective and efficient way to secure one's self-interest. The common expression "knowledge is power" reflects the importance of ideology. Assuming that people act purposefully according to their knowledge, control over knowledge is also control over human behavior. Ideological power includes control over *how* people know, the methods of knowing, or *epistemology;* control over *what* people know by sight and sound, or phenomena known through the senses; and pure ideas, or **noumenal** things that we know only as conceptions in the mind. Rulers demonstrate the power of ideas when they materialize them, or make them physical objects. For example, they may transform noumenal deities into stone monuments to make them phenomena that their followers can see. It may be less costly to build monuments to persuade people to accept the legitimacy of the social establishment, rather than to threaten them with physical violence.

Economic power is the ability to direct the labor of other people to one's own advantage and to control and accumulate wealth, income, and material resources. *Political power* is personal power over the institutions of government, and is typically linked to military power, which is the use of, or threats to use, organized physical violence.

Individuals construct self-centered networks of power, or **imperia,** incorporating all the people and institutions they can personally command or call on to do things for them in times of need. The *imperium* describes how individuals organize their personal power to realize their self-interest. Personal power networks are based on kinship, marriage, friendship, and patronage, and they can crosscut otherwise functionally separate ideological, economic, military, and political institutional sources of social power. This means that a single person, or a small oligarchy, can command an entire society. The larger and more diverse the personal imperium, the more people one can command, the larger and more successful one's household can be, and the more numerous and successful one's children and grandchildren might become.

Over the past 50,000 years of cultural development people have successively created three distinctive cultural worlds based on the organization of social power: tribal, imperial, and commercial. Each world can be defined by the size of the largest independent societies they contained, or still contain in the case of the commercial world, and the size of global population they sustained. A cultural world is composed of interacting societies in which people use culture to organize social power in broadly similar ways. In the tribal world people have direct access to all forms of social power by means of personal imperia based on kinship and marriage relations. Virtually everyone in the social universe is treated as family, and the household is the central social institution. In the imperial world political rulers monopolize military, economic, and ideological sources of institutionalized social power. In the commercial world business elites use unequal exchanges to amass tangible and intangible wealth, and income, even as they use their economic power to gain political and ideological power. People in the same cultural world may be members of different autonomous societies, may speak different languages, and may make their living in different ways, but they have the same expectations about the grand purpose of their cultures and what cultural tools can be employed for human ends.

Functioning cultural systems in each cultural world emphasize different cultural processes (Table 1.4). The tribal world is remarkable in comparison with other worlds in that the humanization process, the maintenance and reproduction of people and households, is the only major cultural process. However, humanization is not a simple task. In addition to maintaining their families, people must always pay extra costs to create, maintain, and reproduce the culture and society that their survival ultimately depends on. The advantage of the tribal world is that the functional aspects of tribal culture are directly related to human needs, and the costs and benefits are widely and equitably shared.

The tribal world was the only world until about 7,000 years ago, and total global population probably remained below a critical threshold of 100 million people. The largest independent social units were bands and villages that seldom exceeded 500 people, and, because densities were very low, communication technology was so limited, and the household was the dominant social institution, personal imperia necessarily remained small. From the perspective of individual self-interest, the downside of the tribal world was that no one was able to concentrate very much social power, and it was difficult for anyone to create a dynasty. However, the combination of a very small global population and very small societies made it possible for average people in the tribal world to be richer in natural wealth and to enjoy

---

noumenal Relating to mental constructs, concepts, things that people know through the mind, rather than phenomena observed or perceived through the senses.

imperia imperium (*singular*) An individual's personal power network, including everyone that one might command or call on for assistance, as well as the institutional structures that one might direct.

TABLE 1.4 CULTURAL PROCESSES AND SUBPROCESSES BY CULTURAL WORLD

Tribal World
Humanization: the production, maintenance, and reproduction of human beings and culture. • Conceptualization: producing abstract concepts and symbols that shape behavior • Materialization: giving physical form to concepts • Verbalization: producing speech • Socialization: producing human societies by exogamy • Cultural Transmission: reproducing culture
Imperial World
Politicization: the production and maintenance of centralized political power by co-opting the humanization process. • Taxation: extracting surplus production to support government • Conquest: extracting booty, slaves, and tribute • Specialization: government employment • Militarization: development of professional military • Bureaucratization: hierarchical command structures • Urbanization: development of cities
Commercial World
Commercialization: the production and maintenance of private profit-making business enterprise as a means of accumulating capital, by co-opting the humanization and politicization processes. • Commodification: market for land, labor, money, basic goods and services • Industrialization: mass production, distribution, and consumption of goods and services • Capitalization: ownership of means of production separated from labor • Corporatization: business enterprise becomes suprahuman • Externalization: costs of commercial growth are socialized • Supralocalization: business enterprise is detached from community • Financialization: finance institutionalized, separated from production

greater personal autonomy and freedom than at any time since. Because everyone's basic needs were generally satisfied and there were few possibilities for power accumulation, cultural systems tended toward stability. As long as they worked well, there was no need to change them.

The rulers of the imperial world extracted taxes and tribute from the majority in order to improve the well-being of their own households, and in the process they subordinated the interests and life chances of most of the rest of society. In effect, rulers made maintaining and reproducing the institutions of government the dominant purpose of society, even though only a few elite households received the primary benefits. A small network of a few hundred people invariably occupied the top of the imperial social hierarchy and were in a position to direct their own growth projects to enlarge society and increase production in ways that would make them more powerful. As societies grew larger they necessarily required specialization and bureaucratic institutions, and they required a larger and larger subsidy from ordinary people and natural resources.

The largest ancient agrarian civilizations often included tens of millions of subjects, and by AD 1200 global population peaked at about 360 million people. This was probably a threshold for how many people could be persuaded of the legitimacy of rulers who took far more than they returned to their followers. Not surprisingly, giant cultural systems in the imperial world attracted enemies, underwent frequent transformations, and often quickly collapsed.

The commercial world was constructed by economic elites who sought to escape the growth and power limits of the politically organized imperial world. They did so by reducing government controls over business activities, while simultaneously drawing on political and military power to protect their accumulations of private property and expand the size of business enterprises and markets, until business corporations and their markets ultimately encompassed the entire globe. The power imbalances this commercially directed development process initiated caused individual societies to rapidly expand into hundreds of millions of people. Global population exceeded one billion shortly after 1800, doubled to two billion by 1927, and doubled again by 1974. Most people found it increasingly difficult to make a living, because even as population expanded at an unprecedented rate, merchants, manufacturers, and landlords gained greater control over life necessities and turned them into commercial commodities. The effect of this expansion and cultural transformation process was to subordinate the interests of both governments and ordinary households to the interests of economic elites and the institutions they dominated. The commercialization process has produced truly amazing levels of material progress for millions of very fortunate people, but these benefits have not been evenly distributed.

The diverse ways that people in a given society organize social power are perhaps the most important cultural variables for anthropological analysis, because the organization of power limits the scale of society and shapes all aspects of culture. Every successful society is a system of social power based on shared cultural understandings. People must agree to organize and distribute power in particular ways. They must believe that the power structure will work to their advantage or that they are making the best available choices under existing circumstances. The tremendous diversity of world cultures is a result of creative people designing and transmitting cultural understandings acceptable to others. Cultures change when people are persuaded to accept new ideas about power or when they withdraw their consent from existing power systems.

The Functional Organization of Societies and Cultures

In addition to the ideological, economic, military, and political sources of social power, personal imperia, and the three cultural worlds discussed above, it will be helpful to distinguish three functionally interconnected aspects of all cultural systems: *superstructure, structure,* and *infrastructure* (Table 1.5), following an analytic framework introduced by anthropologist Marvin Harris (1980). These categories crosscut in illuminating ways the mental, behavioral, and material aspects of culture that individual human beings experience. They help us understand how the different parts of societies and cultures work together to produce distinctive cultural worlds. *Superstructure, structure,* and *infrastructure* are functional categories describing components of the sociocultural system viewed as a whole. They connect empirical knowledge, and noumenal beliefs and practice in the *superstructure,* with the institutional forms that direct human behavior and interaction in the *structure.* The superstructure is what people collectively know about their society, culture, and natural environment, both the things that they can verify empirically by observation and experiment and the things that they only imagine and believe to be true. Superstructure is information encoded in language and other symbols. *Structure* is primarily behavior. It is how people organize their activities within visible social groups and institutions such as households, families, villages, political

TABLE 1.5 INFRASTRUCTURE, STRUCTURE, AND SUPERSTRUCTURE IN THREE CULTURAL WORLDS

	Tribal World	Imperial World	Commercial World
Infrastructure: Material Basis of Society & Culture			
Human Population	6–84 million	100s of millions	billions
Nature, Energy, and Materials	natural resources & services	natural resources & services	natural resources & services, fossil fuels
Technology	tools of foraging, gardening, herding	tools of intensive agriculture, irrigation, plows, metal, writing	industrial tools, factory farming, mechanized transport, electronic information systems
Structure: Organization of Society			
Economy	domestic sub-sistence, feasting, reciprocal exchange	tribute, tax, plunder, conquest, slavery, specialization, coins, unequal exchange, limited markets, long-distance luxury trade	global markets, commodities, money, factories, financial institutions, public debt, corporations, capital accumu-lation, unequal exchange
Society	low density rural, bands of 50, tribes and villages of 500, family, kin, affines, young, old, male, female, language	high density rural, cities of 100,000, social class: royalty, nobles, com-moners, slaves, castes, ethnicity	high density rural, cities of millions, capitalists, laborers, consumers, race, ethnicity, nationality, social classes, community, commonwealth
Polity/Government	autonomous bands and villages of 500, descent groups	chiefdoms of 5,000, city-states of 50,000, kingdoms of 5 million, empires of 50 million, armies, tyranny, bureaucracy	constitutional nation states of 100s of millions, courts, police, professional military, democracy, universities
Superstructure: Empirical Knowledge, Noumenal Beliefs & Practice			
Ideology	animism, shaman-ism, ancestor cults, spirits, myth, ritual, taboo, magic, divi-nation, animal sacrifice	mana, high gods, polytheism, divine kings, priests, sacred texts, human sacrifice	nationalism, patriotism, monotheism, knowledge, advertising, economic growth, progress, free market

units, and economic structures and practices. Contained within the structure is the organization of social power, whether by domestic households in the tribal world, by political rulers in the imperial world, or by economic elites and their political allies in the commercial world. The *infrastructure* is the physical basis of society. It includes flows of energy and raw materials, all the natural resources and services that support human life and culture, and physical tools, animals, plants, and machines that people employ. Human beings themselves are included in the infrastructure as biological organisms. Without this physical infrastructure there could be no human society and no culture. Particular details of infrastructure are functionally connected with but do not cause structure, and superstructure.

Sociocultural Growth and the Scale of Culture

The enormous differences in the distribution of social power in each of the three cultural worlds suggest that the great transformations of the tribal world into the imperial world, and the imperial world into the commercial world were elite-directed growth processes that intentionally changed the scale of society, wealth, and power. These transformations appear to be elite-directed because the outcome was so inequitable. Growth in scale concentrated social power in a few hands, whereas the majority paid the costs, effectively subsidizing the growth process. The significance of this interpretation is that these great cultural transformations were neither natural, nor inevitable. They were humanly directed. Elites apparently took advantage of crisis events to persuade people that it would be in their best interests to give them more power. It is possible that if the majority had a clearer understanding of the cultural and physical realities of their world, they could take democratic control over cultural development and create a world that distributed costs and benefits more equitably, more humanely, and more sustainably, especially in times of crisis. The crucial problem is thus what people know, and that is why control over the cultural superstructure is so important.

Each cultural system of social power produces a different growth trajectory and scale of culture, and a distinctive distribution of social power and household living standards. When any sociocultural system grows larger, it can be expected to undergo organizational and technological changes simply because it is larger. The quality of everyday life and human relationships will necessarily change. Most people will have less control over their daily affairs; new, more powerful leaders will emerge; and the familiarity characteristic of village life will disappear. Direct participatory democracy is impossible in a large nation. Likewise, when every household cannot be self-sufficient, production systems must become larger, more energy intensive, and more centralized. When households lose control over production, they may have more difficulty meeting their basic material needs, and poverty may emerge.

Ethnographic analysis reveals that as societies adopt larger-scale power systems, order-of-magnitude differences appear in the quantity and concentration of social power as measured on various socioeconomic dimensions. As the case studies in the following chapters will demonstrate, when social power is organized exclusively at the domestic level, the largest politically autonomous social unit seldom exceeds five hundred people. But when power is centralized and politically organized power becomes dominant, millions of people can be politically integrated. Likewise, maximum household wealth, measured by the number of people the richest household could support in a year, can be millions of times greater in commercially organized societies than in domestically organized societies, where wealth is not accumulated. Differences of this magnitude, and the cultural changes that make them possible, are so striking that cultures that organize power differently have come to constitute distinctive scales of culture.

Scale differences have such an important effect on the distribution of social power that it is helpful to refer to cultures in the tribal world as **domestic-scale**, in the imperial world as **political-scale**, and in the commercial world as **commercial-scale**. Recognizing the scale distinctions highlights the reality that growth concentrates power.

---

domestic-scale Characterized by small, kinship-based societies, often with only 500 people, in which households organize production and distribution.

political-scale Characterized by centrally organized societies with thousands or millions of members and energy-intensive production directed by political rulers.

commercial-scale Organized by impersonal market exchanges, commercial enterprises, contracts, and money, and potentially encompassing the entire world.

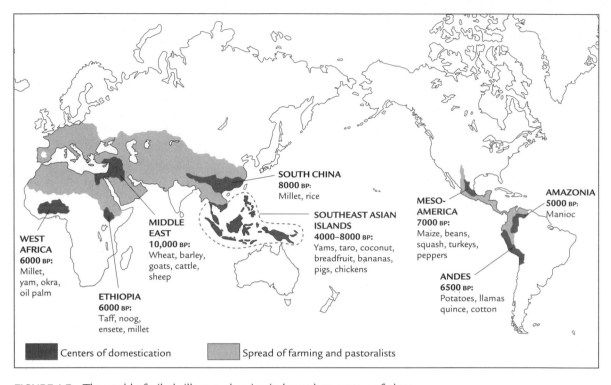

FIGURE 1.7   The world of tribal villagers, showing independent centers of plant and animal domestication and the areas where farming or pastoralism had spread by approximately 5000 BP.

Sociocultural growth, and accompanying changes in the scale of culture, has been neither a steady nor a totally predictable process. The anthropological record shows a very long, relatively stable era, from approximately 50,000 to 8000 years ago, when all societies were organized as domestic-scale, tribal cultures. During this phase of cultural development, humanity spread in great migrations around the globe and diversified into thousands of ethnolinguistic groups adapted to innumerable local ecosystems. They lived exclusively in small-scale, self-sufficient local and regional societies based initially on mobile foraging and later on sedentary village life (Figure 1.7). All the major domestic technologies, including ceramics, textiles, farming, and herding, were invented and disseminated during this time. These technologies uniformly improved

the quality of daily life, because they were equally available to every household. Regional populations remained small, and densities were low. Limits were established by the optimum size of households and kinship groups and by the population density that local ecosystems and domestic technologies could sustain, as will be discussed in the following chapters.

Under the influence of the politicization process, which began perhaps 8000 years ago, chiefdoms, small agrarian kingdoms, and then larger political empires emerged wherever more energy-intensive production systems could be developed and populations enlarged (Figure 1.8). Global population peaked and then receded as various empires proved unsustainable.

Cultural changes associated with the **commercialization** process, beginning about AD 1400,

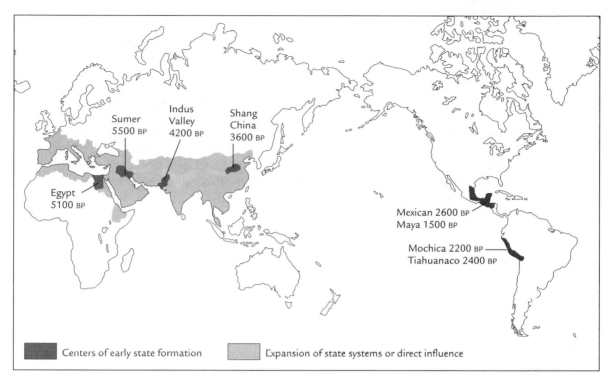

FIGURE 1.8 Six early centers of state formation from 5500 to 1500 BP and the regions that they influenced.

led to increased economic activity culminating in a new wave of technological development that permitted faster and larger-scale production and distribution systems. World population rapidly soared, but along with growth and change came enormous social upheaval and widespread impoverishment. Resource consumption rates grew rapidly, but dramatic improvements in living standards did not become widespread in the industrialized nations until the 1950s. Influenced by the bustling money economy and the use of cheap fossil fuels, growth accelerated exponentially, unfettered by cultural limits.

The emergence of commercial-scale cultures is a challenging anthropological problem. Socioeconomic growth is difficult to explain because at national and global levels it produces few immediate benefits for most people and creates obvious new burdens such as taxes, wars, insecurity, and dependency. Throughout this book, we will examine the possibility that cultural developments, as measured by population growth and increased economic indicators, are caused not by popular demand, but by individual power seekers striving to increase their immediate personal power. Elites can attain more power only by having more people to control and more economic resources to exploit, and this necessarily requires growth. Elites may gain the power to direct culture change in their own short-term interests. However, they cannot predict the long-term consequences of their actions, nor can they necessarily control the

commercialization The production and maintenance of private profit-making business enterprises.

events that they set in motion, including the counterforces of popular social movements led by disaffected people.

The diverse selection of world cultures presented in the following chapters will allow us to test the hypothesis that socioeconomic growth is an elite-directed process that concentrates social power in direct proportion to increases in culture scale. This hypothesis runs counter to the conventional understanding of how economic growth works in the contemporary world: Everyone supposedly benefits from growth, and growth supposedly is natural and inevitable. If the power-elite hypothesis proves correct, then larger-scale cultural systems should have more concentrated social power, and people may be disproportionately impoverished and disempowered by certain growth processes. This analysis raises important questions about the relative benefits of different cultural systems, and it can provide an informed basis for the argument that growth itself may be the biggest human problem and that development without growth may be a solution.

Culture Scale and the Quality of Life: Evaluating Cultures and Cultural Worlds

Recent technological innovations and economic growth undoubtedly have improved the lives of many people, especially since the 1870s. Electric power, antibiotics, water and sewage systems, telephones, personal computers, home appliances, mechanized transportation, printing—all certainly have enhanced our lives in many ways. These technologies were produced by commercial-scale cultures in which commercial elites also came to dominate the sources of social power, but they now are part of the cultural heritage of all of humanity. However, it is an open question what cultural arrangements can best produce, maintain, regulate, and distribute these technologies and their byproducts to ensure that their benefits are most widely shared and that they remain available to future generations.

Many anthropologists theorize that technology determines social organization and that social organization determines ideology. According to this misleading simplification, technology is the supreme cultural determinant. But technologies are *human* creations. They are tools that are directed and controlled by human agents motivated by cultural information and by innate drives. Technology need not dictate the distribution of social power and thereby determine the form of our societies and the quality of our daily lives. Quite possibly, advanced technologies and their benefits can be best sustained by smaller-scale cultural systems based on an equitable balance between domestic, political, and commercial power structures. To discover the best balance, we must first understand how power, growth, and scale are culturally regulated in different societies, and then carefully evaluate the human impact of these differences. Cultural evaluation of this sort is perhaps anthropology's most important function, but it must be done objectively to avoid the pitfalls of ethnocentrism.

In assessing how well different cultures function to meet human needs, it will be helpful to use a working definition of the universal good life, the *summum bonum*, or supreme good. Following political scientist Leopold Kohr, it can be assumed that in addition to household well-being, individuals also need sociability, material prosperity, security, and the opportunity to enjoy expressive culture (Kohr 1977). In practice, this means that the "best" culture would maximize human freedom, happiness, and the general welfare, and would sustain a just and moral society. Individual freedom can be defined positively as the realization of self-interest and negatively as freedom from interference.

The inherent tension between individual freedom and the necessity for social cooperation is the basis of morality. Moral philosophers debate over whether the "right" is a transcendent value, or simply a culturally relative social construction. The problem is that morality defined as a shared understanding of what is "right" might conflict with individual freedom. Social norms might also violate universal *summum bonum* values, sometimes making cultural relativity difficult to either defend or challenge.

This book assumes that a just society would promote the universal good life, but this might not be the "good life" recognized by the culture of a particular community. It is inadequate to either remain neutral on community cultural conventions or to simply accept them as "good" by definition. Rather, we can judge cultural definitions of the "right" in reference to what Sandel (1998:xi) calls "the moral importance of the ends they serve." Aristotle (*The Politics* 1323a14) made the same point when he said, "If we wish to investigate the best constitution appropriately, we must first decide what is the most desirable life." We can't avoid talking about "moral worth," but at the same time what is moral can't be culturally relative.

Any culture's moral worth could be its effectiveness in providing the universal good life measured by individual human health and well-being, human freedom, social stability, and the sustainability of its natural resource base. To the extent that all members of any culture are able to secure these benefits, that culture could be considered successful and morally worthy, even though individuals and communities may vary in how the "goods" of the "good life" are defined in detail. All cultures produce both "bads" and "goods," or costs and benefits. What matters is how these are distributed in society, and that the goods truly outweigh the bads. The accounting is not always easy, because culture itself often obscures reality. However the ethnographic material presented in the following chapters suggests that most people were best able to enjoy the good life in the tribal world, where individual freedom was the highest, and everyone was assured an irreducible minimum of material benefits and opportunities. The imperial world gave a few people a very good life, while exploiting, and pushing down the majority. The commercial world accepts extreme levels of inequality, poverty, sickness, conflict, and environmental degradation,

even as large numbers of people enjoy high levels of material prosperity.

Social cohesion is closely related to equitable distribution of social power: Societies that are more equitable are likely to be more cohesive, and they may generate fewer incentives for destabilizing growth. Conspicuous concentrations of wealth can create a maladaptive, runaway growth process when people support and emulate elite cultural patterns, because they believe that by copying the elite, they will improve their own life chances. Significantly, health and well-being in industrialized societies, as measured by life expectancy, have now been found to be improved more by social equality and social cohesion than by absolute increases in wealth. The distribution of wealth and power thus may be the most important cultural pattern determining the success of the humanization process. The following chapters will explore these issues in depth.

SUMMARY

Culture, the most important concept of cultural anthropology, refers to the socially transmitted, often symbolic, information that shapes human behavior. Culture has mental, behavioral, and material aspects. It is patterned and provides a model for proper behavior, and it regulates human society so that people can successfully maintain themselves and reproduce. The goal of cultural anthropology is to increase cultural understanding. Cultural anthropology's most important research technique, the ethnographic method, relies on participant observation and key informants, and strives to achieve a sympathetic, nonethnocentric view of other cultures from an inside, or emic, perspective.

A major objective of cultural analysis is to sort out the different ways people use culture as a source of social power to achieve their goals in relation to other people and the natural environment. Although not all aspects of culture are unique to humans, humans are unique in their emphasis on linguistically patterned symbolic meanings. All people have the same potential to create culture, and all cultures share many universal features. The most important cultural differences concern the three distinctive ways that people can organize social power: (1) domestically by households, (2) politically by rulers, or (3) commercially by business enterprises. Each method of organization involves its own dominant culture process, whether humanization, politicization, or commercialization, and each requires distinctive ideologies and progressively larger-scale societies, more complex polities, and more intensive technologies. Humanization is the most crucial cultural process, because it is centered on the household and involves the maintenance and reproduction of individual humans, human society, and human culture. Cultures can be grouped according to their dominant mode of organizing social power: (1) domestic-scale cultures (tribes), (2) political-scale cultures (nation-states), and (3) commercial-scale cultures (the global system).

SUGGESTED READING

DeVita, Philip R. 1990. *The Humbled Anthropologist: Tales from the Pacific.* Belmont, Calif.: Wadsworth. A collection of personal accounts of fieldwork experiences in the Pacific written by twenty anthropologists.

Fagan, Brian. 1992. *People of the Earth.* New York: HarperCollins. An overview of world prehistory.

Gamst, Frederick C., and Edward Norbeck. 1976. *Ideas of Culture: Sources and Uses.* New York: Holt, Rinehart & Winston. An extensive examination of the culture concept.

Dreaming beings portrayed at Nourlangie Rock, Kakadu National Park. The primary figure is Namondjok.

PRONUNCIATION GUIDE

There are many variant spellings of aboriginal words. For example, *Kakadu* of Kakadu National Park has also been written Gagadu, and Gagudju, and is also the name of a resident aboriginal language. Nourlangie Rock, a major rock art site within the park, is known to the aborigines as Burrungguy, or Nawulandja. The following pronunciations are recommended by the Australian Nature Conservation Agency as English equivalents for aboriginal terms:*

Key
a = a in father   oo = oo in food
o = o in go   rr = rr in carry, with trill
ay = ay in day   ng = ng in sing
e = e in bed   • = Syllable division
i = i in bit   / = Stress
ee = ee in beet

Anbarra = [an • ba / rra]
borrmunga = [borr • moo / nga]
Gidjingarli = [gij • ing • ar / li]
gurrurta = [goorr • oor / ta]
Kakadu = [ka / ka • doo]
Manggalili = [mang • ga • lee / lee]
molamola = [mo / la • mo / la]
Murrumbur = [moorr • oom / boor]
Nourlangie = [nor • layng / ee]
Oenpelli = [o • en • pel / lee]

*Adapted from Morris, Ian. 1996. Kakadu National Park Australia. Steve Parish Natural History Guide. Fortitude Valley, Queensland: Steve Parish Publishing.

2

Australian Aborigines: Mobile Foragers for 50,000 Years

Learning Objectives

After studying this chapter you should be able to do the following.

1. Describe the physical challenges that faced the first aboriginal peoples who settled Australia.

2. Explain how both empirical and nonempirical knowledge operate in aboriginal culture, discussing the role of each.

3. Explain the central contribution of the Dreaming and totemism to the long-term success of the aboriginal way of life.

4. Describe the basic structure of aboriginal society, distinguishing band, clan, and tribe by composition and function.

5. Explain why size of social units was such an important feature of aboriginal society, and how size contributed to the long-term success of the aboriginal way of life.

6. Explain how aborigines made a living and why they may be considered "the original affluent society," drawing specific comparisons with contemporary commercial societies.

7. Explain why aboriginal society can be considered egalitarian, even though aboriginal social status differs significantly by age and gender, with old men apparently having the most social power.

8. Describe aboriginal marriage practices, including rules of marriageability, who arranges marriages, and the function of polygyny.

The Australians have been the historical, evolutionary and sociological prototype for the study of hunter-gatherers and for the relations between man and nature. From the onset of modern anthropology they have inspired, challenged or provided the limiting case for nearly every view of man's behavior. . . . (Peterson 1986:v)

Australia, the only continent in the modern world to have been occupied exclusively by tribal foragers, has always been central to anthropological theories about tribal cultures. The 50,000-year prehistory of aboriginal culture raises major questions about cultural stability and change, carrying capacity and population regulation, quality of life, and the inevitability of cultural evolution. Furthermore, Australian aborigines are justly famous for their elegant kinship systems and elaborate ritual life, supported by one of the world's simplest known material technologies. The Australian aboriginal culture also raises important questions about the function of initiation rituals and the meaning of equality in a tribal society in which the old men appear to control much of the ideological system. The extent to which such cultures can be considered affluent, egalitarian, and "in balance with nature" is also an issue for debate. All of these issues are discussed in this chapter.

The discovery and successful colonization of the Australian continent by foraging peoples and its continuous occupation for 50,000 years is surely one of the most remarkable events in human history. It clearly demonstrates the tremendous potential of mobile foraging technology and egalitarian social systems, which adapted to diverse, and often unpredictable, environments and to long-term climatic change. The foraging way of life is certainly one of the most successful human adaptations ever developed and persists in scattered locations throughout the world.

Aboriginal culture persisted for millennia because it allowed people to enjoy the good life. The culture was sustainable because it worked for people. It helped people meet their needs fairly, reliably, and easily, and therefore they willingly reproduced the system with only minimal, fine-tuning changes. Aborigines designed and reproduced a cultural system that rewarded people

for keeping their families small and their material requirements low. They correctly imagined that nature would generously provide all of their material needs in return for minimal human effort. They also believed that everyone was family. As members of the same family everyone was entitled at birth to an estate that gave them access to the natural, cultural, and human resources needed to make a living and form a successful household. There was no conflict between individual self-interest and the needs of society, or between the needs of nature and the needs of culture. The genius of the system was that it treated individual and society, nature and culture, male and female, young and old as complementary oppositions that worked together for mutual benefit. Mobile foraging set a low threshold for total population and density and made nature itself the primary form of material wealth. Under these conditions it was difficult for anyone to concentrate enough social power to promote destabilizing growth in society or economy.

It is estimated that at the time of European contact in 1788, Australia was occupied by at least 300,000 people and perhaps a million or more, representing some 600 culturally distinct groups and speaking some 200 languages (Tindale 1974). Throughout the millennia, the aborigines intensified their subsistence techniques and managed and shaped their natural resources, but they never resorted to farming or sedentary village life. Australia was, in fact, the largest world area to avoid domestication and social stratification and the associated burdens of agriculture. The aboriginal "mode of thought" represented by the "Dreaming" seems to be the central integrative key to the entire culture. The Dreaming was an integrated set of ideas, stories, rituals, objects, and practices that explained the origin and meaning of nature and culture, and told people how to live harmoniously.

CONSTRUCTING A SUSTAINABLE DESERT CULTURE

Imagine yourself with 500 other people of all ages—men, women, and children—naked and empty-

TABLE 2.1 AUSTRALIAN PREHISTORY, 60,000 BP–AD 1788

AD 1500–1788	1788	European colonization
	1500	Indonesian fishermen visit
5000–6000 BP	5000	Small Tool Tradition; spear points, backed-blade microliths, spear-thrower; dingo; subsistence intensification
8000–15,000 BP	8000	Cape York separated from New Guinea
	10,000	Earliest dated wooden implements: spear, digging stick, firestick, boomerang
	12,000	Tasmania cut off from mainland
	15,000	Sea levels begin to rise
20,000–60,000 BP	20,000	Widespread occupation
	12,000–50,000	Pleistocene extinctions of megafauna
	40,000–60,000	Initial settlement

SOURCES: Flood (1983), Lourandos (1987), and White and O'Connell (1982).

handed on the shore of an uninhabited desert continent. You are all participants in a great human experiment. Your collective challenge is more than mere survival. The experiment requires you to design a fully self-sufficient culture that will satisfy everyone's human needs while guaranteeing the same security for all future generations. Without machines, metal tools, or libraries, you need to find food and shelter in your strange surroundings. This task requires extensive, highly specialized knowledge and skills, which need to be acquired, stored, and reproduced. Perhaps even more difficult, you need to establish rules to regulate marriage, prevent conflict, and reproduce the culture. Whatever culture you create will need to provide enough human satisfaction that the majority supports it. There will be no chance to start over. This *was* the challenge that faced the first Australians, and they solved it brilliantly.

The great achievement and continuity of aboriginal culture took on a personal meaning for me in 1988 when I visited Nourlangie Rock and the rock shelter of Ubirr in Kakadu National Park on the edge of the great Arnhem Land escarpment. Both of these sites contain richly painted galleries with pictures of people, mythological figures, fish, and animals, many in the unique x-ray style of contemporary Arnhem Land bark painting. Some of the most recent paintings date to the 1960s, but there are multiple layers of increasingly faded red ochre and white line drawings that shade into the remote past. There are also stenciled hand prints, hauntingly reminiscent of those seen in Ice Age cave paintings in France. Archaeological excavations show that people lived in the Kakadu more than 20,000 years ago. Aborigines living in the Kakadu today assert their traditional ownership over these sites and are extremely protective of these direct links to their land and culture. Later, I went on a foraging expedition on the floodplain of the South Alligator River escorted by members of the Murrumbur clan. I saw wallabies, saltwater crocodiles, goannas (lizards), and cockatoos in this game-rich country, and watched my guides gather wild tomatoes and edible waterlilies. They made fire by twirling a stick, and we dined on roast magpie geese and long-necked turtles that the women extracted from the muddy bottom of a shallow lake.

The Earliest Australians

The first major event in Australian prehistory was the original settlement of the continent (Table 2.1). Archaeologists have obtained absolute dates—ages of objects given in years rather than less precisely—of 50,000–60,000 BP for human occupation

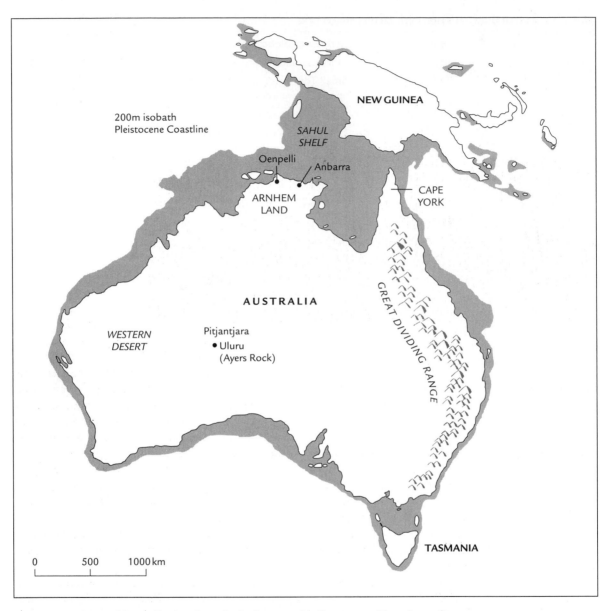

FIGURE 2.1   Map of Australia showing principal geographic features and locations of groups and sites. (SOURCE: Adapted from Lourandos 1987, Figure 2.)

in northern Australia using thermoluminescence—a technique for directly calculating the age of certain minerals (Roberts, Jones, and Smith 1990). Genetic evidence suggests that the ancestors of Australian aborigines must have come from Southeast Asia, but it will never be known precisely how they crossed the 70-kilometer (44-mile) stretch of open water that separated the closest Asian islands from Australia. Because this must have occurred during the Ice Age when Australia and New Guinea were connected by the Sahul Shelf, any evidence of these earliest pioneers would have been obliterated by rising sea levels (Figure 2.1).

FIGURE 2.2 Desert landscape in the Olga National Park, Australian Northern Territory. The luxuriant vegetation followed an unusually wet year.

The suitability of Australia for occupation by foraging peoples, those who use no domesticated plants or herd animals, is determined by the availability of wild plants and animals, which in turn is shaped by the complex interaction of geological history and geography. Remarkably, the Australian continent, which has the same land area as the lower forty-eight United States, is almost totally lacking in major rivers and mountains, and has been called the driest continent in the world. This is because Australia is situated in the southern hemisphere astride the Tropic of Capricorn so that much of the rain that comes from the east across the south Pacific is stopped by the Great Dividing Range that fringes the east coast. This mountain barrier creates a vast rain shadow and makes the interior a desert. Aridity is the principal factor limiting the density and diversity of organisms, including foraging humans, throughout the continent (Figure 2.2).

Biologically, Australia is famous for its unique flora and fauna, especially the numerous gum trees (eucalyptus), the marsupials (the pouch-bearing kangaroos and opossums), and the world's only egg-laying mammals (the platypus and echidna).

Because the aborigines did not raise domestic crops or animals, they were totally dependent on the natural productivity of the environment, as measured by the biomass available for human consumption. Human population density was thus largely determined by rainfall, and was highest in the biologally rich coastal regions, especially in the tropical north and east. Population densities remained extremely low in the dry interior.

In the arid center of Australia, water is certainly the most critical factor shaping the availability of both plant and animal foods, and determining human population movements and density. Conditions are most extreme in the Western Desert, where there is no real seasonality or predictability in rainfall, and drought conditions may continue for years. In the open country, distant rainstorms can be observed for up to 50 miles (80 km), and people watch the clouds and rely on their detailed knowledge of the locations of specific rock holes and soaks to plan their nomadism. Population densities there were among the lowest for foragers in the world, averaging less than 0.01 person per square kilometer (Gould 1980).

Population Stability and Balance with Nature?

Given the vast time period that people have lived in Australia and the relatively low total population when Europeans arrived, many anthropologists have wondered whether aborigines achieved a balance between population and resources. Joseph Birdsell (1957) believed that aborigines rapidly reached the maximum potential population that could be supported by their foraging technology throughout Australia and then maintained a constant balance between population and resources. Others suggest that aborigines very gradually expanded their population and elaborated their technology over many thousands of years (Bowdler 1977, Lourandos 1985, 1987). In either case, the aboriginal achievement is impressive.

During the Pleistocene geological epoch, which ended some 10,000 years ago, glaciation caused global sea levels to drop to 328–492 feet (100–150 m) below present levels. As the ice retreated at the end of the Pleistocene, sea levels began to rise, inundating the Sahul Shelf and cutting New Guinea and Tasmania off from the mainland. It is estimated that the sea advanced across the Sahul by as much as 3 miles (5 km) in a single year and 62 miles (100 km) in a generation (Flood 1983). These events have been enshrined in aboriginal myths. It is a tribute to the success of the forager mode of thought as enshrined in the Dreaming that aborigines were able to resist environmental pressures to intensify their forager subsistence production system. We can only assume that aboriginal culture was so well integrated that it could adjust to major environmental perturbations with minimal change. This also suggests that social power was so evenly distributed that no one was able to take advantage of circumstances to promote their self-interest over the interests of society in stability.

Australian aboriginal society offers an interesting test case for the proposition that foraging peoples were more "in balance" with the environment than village farmers or large-scale societies. The archaeological record shows that the foraging way of life has existed vastly longer than any other, and there is no evidence that foraging peoples experienced periodic population crashes or depleted their resources (except in the most extreme cases, as in the Arctic). The implication is that stationary populations, in which births exactly replace deaths, must have been the norm. Some culturally regulated population controls must have operated because even the smallest deviation from balanced fertility and mortality rates operating over thousands of years would have led either to extinction, overpopulation, and hardship or to drastic cultural change. Aboriginal societies had optimum sizes, but it is not certain how population actually was regulated.

Carrying capacity is the term anthropologists use to describe the number of people who could, in theory, be supported indefinitely in a given environment with a given technology and culture. Birdsell (1973) estimated that tribal territories were optimally populated at 60 percent of their carrying capacity to allow for random fluctuation in resources. He assumed that intentional infanticide involving up to 50 percent of births was the primary mechanism limiting population. It is known that babies were sometimes killed at birth, but there is little direct evidence for the actual rate. Infanticide was most likely carried out by women who were motivated by their desire either to eliminate deformed children or to space out their families in order to have only one child at a time under 3 or 4 years of age to carry and nurse. This kind of family planning increased the likelihood that a given child could be raised to maturity. Given the presumed relatively high "natural" infant mortality rates and overall low life expectancy that apparently characterized tribal demography, spacing births every 4 years could produce a stationary population.

Infanticide was related to foraging conditions because both mobility and the burden of carrying children increase when resources are scarce. Similarly, given existing food sources and preparation techniques, there was no baby food other than mothers' milk; thus, nursing would be prolonged, often for 4 years or more. The balance between population and resources was also under unconscious biological control because extended lactation and nutritional deficiencies can lower fertility by causing hormonal changes in a woman's reproductive cycle.

Infanticide reflected the autonomy that women maintained in reproductive decision making, and it also gave them some covert political leverage in a society that was publicly dominated by men. Gillian Cowlishaw (1978) has argued that some women expressed their resentment over arranged marriages by killing their firstborn, although this type of infanticide would not be a response to resource depletion.

It has sometimes been suggested, on the basis of census data showing sex ratios skewed in favor of boys, that girls were more likely to be killed than boys, thereby making infanticide a more powerful means of population control. However, these data are suspect because girls may have been hidden from census takers, and a careful review of completed families in Australia shows no evidence that girls were selectively killed (Yengoyan 1981). Computer simulation studies also suggest that, if systematically applied, even very low rates of selective female infanticide would have led to population extinction. The concept of selective female infanticide, which is related to theories about a widespread male supremacy cult in tribal societies, will be discussed further in Chapter 3.

The Dreaming and the Structure of Aboriginal Society

It is impossible to discuss Australian culture without confronting the metaphysical aspects of aboriginal understandings about the invisible world of the Dreaming and associated totems, souls, and spirits, and their representation in nature, myth, ritual, and society.

The key element of aboriginal culture is the complex, multidimensional concept aborigines call the Dreaming, which recognizes the interdependence and vitality of all parts of the cosmos. Humans are actors along with other species in a balanced living system whose goal is the continuity of life and the maintenance of the cosmos itself. Regardless of what anthropologists decide about the balance and stability of aboriginal culture, aborigines themselves believe their culture to be fundamentally changeless and in balance with nature.

The emic term *Dreaming* refers variously to creation, the moral order, an ancestral being, people, a spirit, the origin point of a spirit, a specific topographic feature, and a **totem** species, object, or phenomenon. Furthermore, all of these can be thought of as the same, whereas in Western thought they would be sharply distinguished. Outsiders have treated the Dreaming as aboriginal religion, but it is a profound concept that permeates all aspects of the culture and defies easy categorization. Aborigines identify themselves completely with their culture and their land through the Dreaming in a way that nonaborigines have difficulty comprehending. For an aborigine to say, "I am a kangaroo," might sound like nonsense, but within the Dreaming context such a statement carries special significance.

Generations of anthropologists have called these aboriginal beliefs "totemism," or "animism," and often deprecated them as childish, unscientific, and basically false, even though they served obvious individual and social functions. However, it is more helpful to view totemism and the Dreaming as a particular way of knowing the world, an aboriginal epistemology. What qualifies these beliefs as "supernatural" is that they are based on the *noumenal,* a nonempirical way of knowing. They are ideas, or concepts in the mind, of beings whose physical existence may not be verified by observation and experiment.

---

carrying capacity The number of people who could, in theory, be supported indefinitely in a given environment with a given technology and culture.

totem In Australia, specific animals, plants, natural phenomena, or other objects that originate in the Dreaming and are the spiritual progenitors of aboriginal descent groups. Elsewhere, it refers to any cultural association between specific natural objects and human social groups.

Spirits are normally not directly visible to the senses, although they may be embodied in physical objects. Some anthropologists might not consider the noumenal world of spirits to be part of "reality," or things that exist. In this strictly scientific view totems are culture rather than nature, but they are part of aboriginal cultural reality, and knowing about their existence has profound human consequences. Totemism is a way of understanding the world that can be as useful and therefore is as "true" as a scientific empirical epistemology. Beliefs about the supernatural can also be considered religious when they connect with morality, and this is certainly the case with Australian totemism.

In aboriginal culture the nonempirical way of knowing exists alongside of, and does not conflict with, a scientific epistemology that aboriginal people use to create, store, and reproduce detailed information about the *phenomenal* world that appears to their senses. This empirical knowledge tells people what plants and animals are good to eat, where they live, when to collect them, and how to prepare them. Aborigines know that it is both logical and useful to view things in different ways. They recognize that things can, in effect, be two things at once.

Totemism is based on beliefs in the supernatural that are virtually universal in all societies. Souls and spirits fit normal expectations about natural beings, but what makes them *super*natural beings is that they may behave in ways that violate the intuitive understandings that people have about how persons, animals, plants, and objects behave in the natural world (Boyer 2000). For example, spirits are named, and they may have human-like personalities, with beliefs and intentions, and they may assume physical form, but when they become invisible or pass through other objects they are supernatural, and they may have supernatural effects on people. These supernatural qualities make spirit beings memorable, and this makes them useful vehicles for storing and transmitting information, for building moral systems, and for manipulating other

people. Supernatural beliefs and practices are tools that people use in their daily lives.

The early British anthropologist A. R. Radcliffe-Brown (1929) thought that aborigines first ritualized species because they were good to eat, and then adopted them as totemic emblems for their social groups. In this view totems functioned to support group identity and maintain social integration, but this was not a fully satisfactory explanation of their origin. Later, French structuralist Levi-Strauss (1963, 1968) added a new dimension to the functionalist interpretation when he suggested that totemism resulted from a universal tendency of people to create mental sets of paired opposites, such as day and night, male and female, nature and culture. Such complementary oppositions were "good to think" because they were intellectually satisfying and because they created memorable chains of meaning, analogies, and metaphor from which social solidarity could be constructed. Totems helped make aboriginal society seem natural and permanent. It was useful to imagine that the members of clan A and clan B were culturally different, just as their respective ritual namesakes, the emu and the kangaroo, were naturally different. Each member of the pair existed only in relation to the other, and this mutual interdependence created an alliance. Recognizing such complementarity was the basis of exogamy, or marriage exchanges between social groups, which in turn was the very basis of human society.

As a philosophy of life, the Dreaming provides both a **cosmogony** to account for the origin of everything and a **cosmology** to explain the fundamental order of the universe. The Dreaming thus answers the basic meaning-of-life questions; offers a detailed charter for day-to-day living, including basic social categories and ritual activities; and ascribes cultural meanings to the natural environment (Figure 2.3).

When regarded as a mythic cosmogony, the Dreaming is sometimes imprecisely called the Dreamtime, referring to the creation time when a series of heroic ancestor beings crisscrossed the landscape and transformed specific topographic

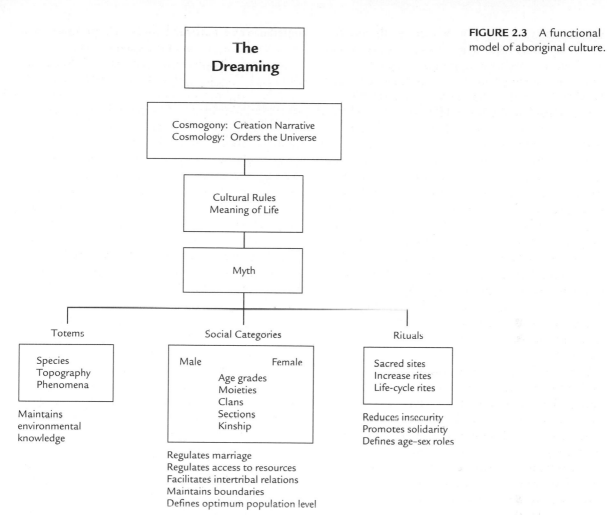

FIGURE 2.3 A functional model of aboriginal culture.

features as a permanent record of their activities. The problem with referring to creation as the Dreamtime is that aborigines are not really concerned with origins as historical events; instead, origin myths are timeless explanations. Time, culture, and nature are viewed as cyclical and changeless. The Dreamtime ancestors followed the same cultural rules that are practiced today, and their influence is still so vital that it is more reasonable to refer to the Dreaming as the Everywhen, or the Eternal Dreamtime, than to place it in the Dreamtime past (see the box entitled "An Aboriginal Woman Talks About the Dreaming").

When the Dreaming is referred to as the moral authority for behavior, it may be called simply the *Law,* or the *Dreaming Law,* and in this respect it is beyond question. Stability is thus a fundamental feature of the culture.

The aboriginal cosmos differs in striking ways from the religions of larger-scale cultures. There

cosmogony An ideological system that seeks to explain the origin of everything: people, nature, and the universe.
cosmology An ideological system that explains the order and meaning of the universe and people's places within it.

An Aboriginal Woman Talks About the Dreaming

During an Australia-wide conference of aboriginal women held in Adelaide in 1980, Nganyintja Ilyatjari, a Pitjantjatjara woman from central Australia, interpreted the Dreaming and related it to the land. Ilyatjari drew a series of small circles on a map of Australia and explained in Pitjantjatjara:

> I am drawing the places all over Australia where our Dreamtime started a long long time ago—Listen! . . . This is Dreaming, Dreaming of the kangaroo, the goanna, the wild fig and lot of other different ones—a long time ago the Dreaming was there, a very long time ago.
>
> This is what all people have always listened to, this Dreaming is ours. . . In all these different places all over Australia lots of aboriginal people have always lived since the beginning. If I could speak English well I would tell you in English.
>
> Our country, the country out there near Mt. Davies, is full of sacred places. The kangaroo Dreaming has been there since the beginning, the wild fig Dreaming has been there since the beginning, many other women's Dreamings are also there. In other places men and women's Dreaming were together from a long time ago. . . .
>
> These places have been part of the sacred Dreamtime since the beginning of time. They were made then by our Dreamtime ancestors—like the kangaroo. Our country is sacred, this country is sacred. (Ilyatjari 1983:55–57)

is no all-powerful god and no rank order in the Dreaming. Similarly, there is no heaven or hell, and the distinctions between sacred and profane, natural and supernatural, are blurred. Aborigines experience the mystical as a perpetual unity with the cosmos as they follow the Dreaming Law in their daily life. For example, a seemingly mundane activity, such as seasonally burning grass, can be considered a religious act because it perpetuates life and the cosmic balance between sun and rain, people, plants, and animals.

Sacred Sites and Dreamtime Pathways at Uluru

Misunderstanding of aboriginal culture began with the British colonization of Australia in 1788. Because they saw no aboriginal farms or permanent houses, British authorities mistakenly concluded that the aborigines had no fixed relationship to the land. Australia was declared *terra nullius,* an empty wasteland, free for the taking, and so aboriginal land was appropriated. Nineteenth-century evolutionary anthropologists did little to help the situation. Lewis Henry Morgan (1877),

one of the founding fathers of cultural anthropology, considered aborigines to be living representatives of his evolutionary stage of "middle savagery." This would make aborigines roughly equivalent to Neanderthals, who had little if any symbolic culture or ritual, and may have even lacked speech. Only over the past hundred years have anthropologists begun to appreciate the subtle complexities of the aborigines' enduring ties to their land. The anthropological debate over government policies toward aborigines is explored in Chapter 14, as part of the broader discussion of the place of tribal cultures within the global system.

The Dreamtime ancestors, or totemic beings, make a direct link between people and their land by means of the sacred sites, which are the physical remains of ancestral beings or their activities. The role of these beings is dramatically illustrated at Uluru, or Ayers Rock, a giant monolith in central Australia (Figure 2.4). Uluru is a weathered dome, some 5 miles (8 km) around and rising more than 1100 feet (335 m) above the desert floor. As the largest such monolith in the world, it was designated as a national park and bio-

FIGURE 2.4 Uluru, or Ayers Rock. Rising from the desert center of Australia, this giant monolith contains many important Dreaming sacred sites.

sphere reserve in 1985, and is administered jointly by the aboriginal owners and the Australian National Park and Wildlife Service. More importantly for aborigines, Uluru is a perpetual Dreamtime monument crammed with cultural meaning.

The north side of the rock belongs to the clan of hare wallabies, rabbit-sized kangaroos, while the south side belongs to the carpet boa clan. A series of stories recounts the activities of ten totemic beings and their relatives, including various snakes, reptiles, birds, and mammals, who created the existing landscape and established the clan boundaries. Charles Mountford (1965), who recorded some of these myths from the Pitjantjatjara people between 1935 and 1960, published some 200 photographs detailing specific rock outcrops, stains, caves, and pockmarks that represent the bodies, camps, and physical signs of these totemic beings.

The same totemic beings who created sites at Uluru traveled widely across the country, leaving permanent Dreaming paths. During their travels, they interacted with other beings and created similar sites elsewhere. Specific Dreaming pathways can stretch for hundreds of miles, crossing the territory of different clans and tribes.

Dreaming locations, or sacred sites, such as those at Uluru, are centers for ritual activity and help define territorial boundaries and regulate use of resources. Some sites contain the spirit essence of their creators and are the places where special "increase ceremonies" are performed to perpetuate particular species. For example, control of a kangaroo increase site means ritual control over the supply of kangaroos. Entry to or even knowledge of such sites often is restricted, and unauthorized intrusion may be severely punished. Other sites are believed to contain especially dangerous supernatural substances that can kill, or make people violently ill, and must be avoided by everyone. To avoid the risks of trespassing, people must seek permission before entering unfamiliar areas. Since 1976, many of these sacred sites

FIGURE 2.5 A Dreaming kangaroo in a rock painting from the Northern Territory.

have been officially protected by federal legislation, and fines can be levied for trespass.

The spirit essence localized at certain sites also completes the direct link between people and their individual Dreamings, because this animating power is believed to be an essential but not an exclusive element in human conception and reproduction. Pregnancy is identified with the totemic "soul stuff" emanating from a specific Dreaming site, and this soul stuff returns to the site at death. Thus, in a real sense, an individual is a physical part of the Dreaming, and this spiritual connection is a more important cultural fact than biological paternity. Some early anthropologists misinterpreted aboriginal beliefs in totemic conception and assumed that they did not understand the "facts of life," but this was clearly not the case.

An added value of the Dreaming tracks is that they serve as mnemonic devices to help fix in memory the location of permanent waterholes, which are critically important. The Dreaming myths and related rituals are dramatic reminders of specific geographic details and preserve them in people's minds as accurately as would any large-scale printed map. The Dreaming also takes on visible form in body paint, sand drawings, rock art, and paintings or carvings on ritual objects, all of which may incorporate an elaborate iconography (Munn 1973) (Figure 2.5).

Aboriginal Band, Clan, and Tribe: Equality and Flexibility

Australian society is based on highly flexible, multifamily foraging groups or **bands,** and a ritual **estate,** or religious property, which is tied to the land. Band and estate are functionally interconnected in the territory defined by Dreaming sacred sites and occupied by the band. This band–estate system serves a resource management function and helps space out and define the optimum limits for local populations, thus contributing directly to long-term stability.

Because aborigines tend to form their bands around a core of male members and their in-marrying wives, anthropologists often speak of **patrilocal bands,** and call the estate-owning groups

FIGURE 2.6 An aboriginal camp—an Aranda family in Alice Springs, 1896. The man is smoothing a spear shaft and a woman is grinding grain. Families that camp and forage together make up the band.

patriclans. The underlying cultural rules are clan **exogamy,** the requirement to marry outside of the clan, and **patrilocality,** the expectation that a woman will join her husband's band. However, for aborigines the band is a group of households that live on and use the resources of the estate (Figure 2.6). They may speak of the camp, the residents of the camp, and the country they occupy, but for aborigines these terms may have multiple meanings. For example, depending on the context, country may refer to land as a religious estate or as a foraging territory. Band members may be referred to as "people of" a particular place, but they may claim affiliation with several countries. In practice, the band is not exclusively patrilocal and may change composition frequently as individual families visit relatives in other areas. Nevertheless, the band is an important social group, and individual bands retain their unity during temporary multiband encampments.

Likewise, the clan is not a sharply defined unit in a fixed hierarchical structure. This gives people numerous possibilities for making claims on other people and resources, and makes the entire system more flexible. Flexibility seems not to generate conflict, because in a small face-to-face society where everyone is family and resources

are not really scarce, the human problem is how best to allocate people to resources.

Clan members control a diverse bundle of supernatural property, as well as social connections with other people and places. The same ancestral beings may belong to multiple clans, and they may even extend to different tribes speaking different languages. The important point is that there are cultural rules and structures, but they may sometimes be intentionally vague to give people more advantages in daily life. It should not be surprising that aboriginal clans do not constitute sharply distinguished groups, because they are shaped by dynamic historic processes in which clans die out and new ones are created, and their

band A group of twenty-five to fifty people who camp and forage together.

estate Property held in common by a descent group, perhaps including territory, sacred sites, and ceremonies.

patrilocal band A theoretical form of band organization based on exogamy and patrilocal residence.

clan A named group claiming descent from a common but often remote ancestor and sharing a joint estate.

exogamy Marriage outside a culturally defined group.

patrilocality A cultural preference for a newly married couple to live near the husband's parents or patrilineal relatives.

constitutive elements get resorted. Different people belonging to the same clan do not always agree on either its components or membership. The Yolngu in Arnhem Land conceive of their social groups as yam plants, or trees with branches, where the ancestors are roots. They use the phrase "same but a little bit different" in describing their social identities, which they also characterize as "bundled together, just like a bundle of sticks" (Keen 2000:429).

The band forages over a discrete territory containing the critical resources that sustain the band during normal years. Band territorial boundaries are recognized but not directly defended. Visitors must observe special entry rites upon arrival at a camp. They also must ask permission before they can forage within band territory. Under this system, the "owners" of the country operate as resource managers. Permission to forage would rarely be denied, but knowing who is foraging where makes resource exploitation much more efficient and minimizes potential conflicts.

It is important to distinguish between use rights to band territory and ownership rights to the land as a religious estate. All band members and those asking permission can use range resources, but only those qualified to be estate owners can give permission and act as managers. The legal nature of the aboriginal land-holding system was formally recognized by an Australian judge who presided over a court hearing in 1970 in which the Yolngu people tried to prove their traditional ownership of their land. The three weeks of direct testimony about clans, spirit beings, and the land included the following exchange between the court and a man from the Manggalili clan about permission to use clan land:

Q: Before you went hunting kangaroos, did you talk to anyone?

A: Yes, we would talk together.

Q: Who would you talk to?

A: If I was living with the Rirratjingu [clan], I would talk to those Rirratjingu people.

Q: And what did you say to them?

A: I am going to get animals—kangaroos.
(Williams 1986:171)

The judge found that the Yolngu land tenure system was "highly adapted to the country" and "remarkably free from the vagaries of personal whim or influence" (Justice Blackburn, cited in Williams 1986:158).

Many sorts of overlapping claims are recognized, both to the right to ask to use a territory and to the right to estate ownership. Patrilineal descent from an owner invariably provides the strongest claim, but a person also has special claims on a mother's estate and use rights in a spouse's country. Extended residence also can provide a claim, as can one's place of conception and birth and the burial place of kin. Under this system, ownership and use are distributed in a way that discourages any concentration of social power. Households always have many places to go during droughts or famines. An owner can also be sure that visitors will return to their own countries where their Dreaming connections are strongest. The ease with which people can move among bands helps reduce conflict because people who are not getting along can simply move apart.

The size and density of the band is in part determined by environmental, demographic, and cultural factors. Worldwide, band populations average twenty-five to fifty people. Because food, especially game, is pooled among families within the band, the minimum average of twenty-five is probably determined by the number required to maintain foraging security by ensuring that enough adult food producers are available. There are strong reasons for people to hold down the upper limits of band size. Given fixed territories, increased numbers above minimum levels would soon result in a reduction in leisure and more frequent moves as resources became depleted.

The minimum size of bands also may be shaped by the need to maintain marriage alliances that would reduce the likelihood of interband conflict. Bands tend to space themselves uniformly across the landscape in roughly hexagonal territories, such that each band is surrounded by five or six neighboring bands. The cultural requirement of band exogamy is a good excuse for marrying otherwise potentially hostile neighbors.

Like all domestic-scale, tribal societies, Australian aborigines recognize no political leaders beyond their local residential communities. Band leaders are coordinators with little coercive power. Decision-making is by consensus. Aboriginal bands are politically autonomous, but the requirements of exogamy mean that they are not totally self-sufficient. Aboriginal people are members of a broader social network linking people in neighboring bands through common language and culture, marriage alliances, joint ceremonies, feasting, and frequent visits. This larger decentralized society can be called a **tribe.** Its members typically consider themselves to be kin, and self-identify with a group designation that often means "the people." The tribe must be large enough to support a demographically viable population through intermarriage (**endogamy**), and to reproduce a distinct language and culture. Australian tribes apparently averaged about 500 people, men, women, and children (Birdsell 1973). If tribes dropped below 200 people, tribal members would have difficulty finding mates, whereas tribes of more than 1,000 people would split up because of internal conflicts and the infrequency of social interaction. The demographics of aboriginal society were so predictable that the optimum sizes of 50 for Australian bands and 500 for tribes have been called "magic numbers." Thus, estimating the aboriginal population in 1788 at 300,000, there may have been some 600 tribes. Approximately 200 aboriginal languages have been identified.

Australian tribes were normally fully self-sufficient, although they maintained sporadic social interaction with the members of neighboring tribes. As with band territories, tribal territories varied in size according to the richness of natural resources. In areas where rainfall was sufficient to increase natural biological productivity, food supplies improved and tribal territories became smaller than in drier zones. In the driest interior deserts territories were vast and population densities very low. People were forced to move frequently to find food and water.

Aborigines are multilingual, and intermarriage and joint ceremonies between people speaking different languages and dialects are common. Language groups often are associated with territories, but such territories are probably de facto artifacts of the aggregated territorial estates when viewed from the outside. There are few, if any, occasions when the members of a tribe would act as a unit, and joint defense of tribal territory must have been a rare event. However, there is often a strong sense of "tribal" identity reflecting shared language, territory, and culture.

Aboriginal Australia comprises overlapping networks of social interaction that span the entire continent. Aboriginal material culture is the simplest of any ethnographically known people. In the next section, we examine how they remain well fed and comfortable in the desert, with nothing more than fire and a few implements of wood and stone.

MAKING A LIVING WITH FORAGING TECHNOLOGY

Foraging technology is a brilliant human achievement based on mobility and the productivity of natural ecosystems. Foraging allows an appropriately organized and culturally outfitted regional population of a mere 500 people to maintain itself indefinitely in virtually any environment with no outside assistance. Human survival under

tribe A politically autonomous, economically self-sufficient, territorially based society that can reproduce a distinct culture and language and form an in-marrying (endogamous) society.

endogamy Marriage within a specified group.

such conditions is an impressive achievement. It is unlikely that a contemporary urban population of 500 people, including families with dependent children and elderly, could survive if placed empty-handed in a wilderness. Foraging requires a vast store of knowledge about plants and animals, specialized manufacturing and food-processing techniques, and hunting-and-gathering skills, as well as assorted material implements and facilities.

Foragers ultimately are constrained by the level of food resources produced by the natural ecosystems they occupy, but many options exist for adjusting subsistence output to meet basic human needs, including the tools used, the species eaten, and the organization of labor. Most important is the ability to move as local resources are consumed.

For optimum efficiency and sociability, foragers in temperate and tropical areas typically organize themselves into camps of twenty-five to fifty people, based on a flexible division of labor by gender: Women collect plant food and small animals within a 3-mile (5-km) radius of camp, and men hunt within a 6-mile (10-km) range. These distances allow people to return easily to camp each day. Except as compensation for severe seasonal shortages, food storage was rare, and camps were moved as soon as food yields declined. The degree of mobility was directly related to the size of camps and resource availability. As long as the human population density remained low, there was little danger of serious resource depletion.

Lizards and Grass Seeds: Aboriginal Food Resources

Virtually every edible plant and animal has been part of the aboriginal diet somewhere in Australia. The list would include insects, lizards, whales, birds, mammals, turtles, fish and shellfish, and nuts, fruits, greens, and grass seeds. Aborigines commonly distinguish between plant and animal foods, with the latter usually ranked

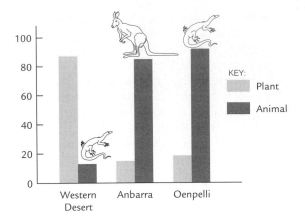

FIGURE 2.7 Food consumption patterns, in percentage by weight, of plants and animals by three aboriginal groups: Western Desert (Gould 1980), Anbarra (Meehan 1982), and Oenpelli (McArthur 1960).

higher. Animal fat, rather than meat as such, is often the food most desired by foragers.

Although animal food might be preferred, there is great variation throughout Australia in actual consumption patterns (Figure 2.7). The Anbarra and Oenpelli aborigines, who live in the tropical monsoon north, have enjoyed the greatest abundance of animals, especially when they have had access to marine ecosystems (Figure 2.8). Foragers have considerable difficulty maintaining a high intake of meat in the desert, where species diversity and abundance are low, and they rely heavily on lizards as a staple, supplemented with insects.

The importance of lizard meat in the Western Desert is striking (Figure 2.9). Lizards made up nearly half, by weight, of the total meat animals brought in by a group of ten aborigines observed in the 1960s (Gould 1980). Lizards represent one of the most efficient desert resources considering the time and energy needed to collect and process them in relation to their food value (O'Connell and Hawkes 1981). It takes only 15 minutes to capture and cook 2.2 pounds (1 kilogram [kg]) of lizard, which yields more than 1000 kilocalories (kcal) of food energy. Kangaroos, though

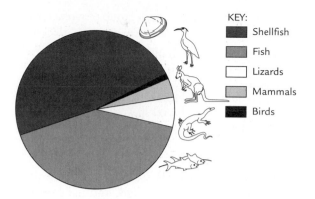

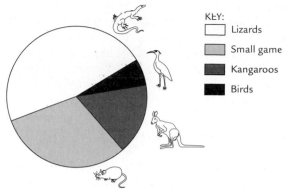

FIGURE 2.8   Meat consumption pattern, in percentage by weight, of shellfish, fish, reptiles, mammals, and birds by Anbarra (coastal) aborigines. (SOURCE: Meehan 1982.)

FIGURE 2.9   Meat consumption pattern, in percentage by weight, of lizards, small game, kangaroos, and birds by desert aborigines. (SOURCE: Gould 1980.)

highly desired, are not so easy to secure and contributed only 16 percent to the total meat supply. The famous Witchetty grub, actually a wood-boring moth larva extracted from the roots of certain desert trees, is also quite energy-efficient. The grubs, which weigh a little over 1 ounce (30 g) each, are almost pure fat and protein. Aborigines can extract 1 kilogram of grubs in 30 minutes (O'Connell and Hawkes 1981, Tindale 1981).

Desert aborigines have relatively few plant foods available to them, but they use them intensively. In the Central Desert, more than one hundred plant species are consumed, especially grasses and seeds, which are among the most costly food resources. Seed collecting and grinding requires up to 6 hours of work per kilogram produced (O'Connell and Hawkes 1981:123). The use of seeds is a testimony to the skill and resourcefulness of the desert foragers.

Throughout Australia, the primary concern traditionally was to maintain long-term food security, because unpredictable fluctuations and shortages of key staples could occur even in the richest areas. Techniques of food storage were known, but they were used only to address short-term emergencies or to sustain temporary aggregations of people. Rather than stockpiling food, the basic strategy was to maintain access to

resources over a wide area through kinship ties and social networks. In the desert, a combination of rain and an unusual abundance of kangaroos might provide the occasion for a joint encampment of a hundred or more people for feasting, performing rituals, and arranging marriages. The most remarkable food bonuses were the great masses of moths that congregated in the summer on the rock walls of the Great Dividing Range (Flood 1980, 1983, Gould 1980). A rich source of fat, the moths could be eaten immediately or ground to a paste and shaped into cakes. The moth feast supported temporary aggregations of up to 700 aborigines at specific campgrounds.

Aboriginal Tools: Digging Stick, Firestick, and Spear

The diverse foraging activities of the aborigines have been supported for 50,000 years by a remarkably sparse tool kit of simple stone, bone, and wood implements, which expanded only about 4000–5000 years ago. The oldest and most universal food-getting tools in Australia are the digging sticks used by women to collect roots and small animals, the men's wooden hunting spear, and the firestick.

FIGURE 2.10   The spear-thrower, or *woomera,* a tool that has been in use in Australia for at least 5000 years. (a) Side and top views—note the gum-mounted, chipped-stone blade and wooden hook on the ends; (b) an aboriginal man launching a spear using a spear-thrower.

This division of tools by gender is symbolically valid, but in practice the aborigines are much more pragmatic than anthropological stereo-

types suggest. For example, a group of women from Borroloola, on the Gulf of Carpentaria, declared:

> We are Aboriginal women. We talk for our hunting business, ceremony business. We used to go hunting. We can't wait for the men. We are ladies, we go hunting and feed the men too. . . . Sometimes we use that shovel spear—kangaroo, emu and fish, all that with the spears. . . . Sometimes camping out, leave husbands, just the women go hunting. (Gale 1983:70–71)

The tools themselves are simple, but they can be manufactured, maintained, and used only in combination with a vast store of specialized environmental knowledge. Aborigines on the move always carry glowing firesticks and in the dry season intentionally set fire to large areas of brush and grassland. This is a resource management tool that aborigines use to drive game, facilitate growth of wild food plants, and keep the country open for easier travel. Many plants will not reproduce without periodic burning, and frequent burning prevents the accumulation of plant litter that might fuel destructive fires. Signal fires also help widely scattered groups keep track of one another.

About 5000 years ago, a technological change known as the Small Tool Tradition spread throughout Australia. It was distinguished by the mounting of small stone flakes on spear shafts, the use of the spear-thrower, and the appearance of the dingo, a semidomesticated dog. These new developments may have increased hunting efficiency and made possible increased ritual activities and the expansion of social networks.

The *woomera,* or spear-thrower, increases the power and accuracy of the spear. It is a long, thin, curved piece of wood with a hook on one end and a chipped-stone blade, or adze, mounted on the other end (Figure 2.10). This multipurpose tool also can be used as a shovel, fire starter, or percussion musical instrument (Gould 1970).

In much of Australia, very simple stone-flaked tools satisfied all aboriginal cutting needs. However, where boomerangs and throwing clubs were frequently used, as Brian Hayden (1977) notes, it made sense to use edge-ground rather than chipped-stone tools. Grinding an edge is more work than chipping, but a ground tool can be re-sharpened many times. Furthermore, because they are so durable, edge-ground tools can be mounted on handles to make a stone ax with twice the striking force of a hand-held tool (Dickson 1981). The edge must be carefully aligned and painstakingly ground on sandstone with water. Crafting the head shape is not easy, and the hafting technique requires much skill. The haft must be rigid enough to keep the head in place while maintaining enough handle flexibility to cushion the shock of chopping blows. The head usually is grooved to receive a wraparound, heat-treated, wooden handle, which is glued with vegetable gum and tied in place. Stone axes can be very sharp and efficient tools, but they take longer for a given cutting task than steel axes because the stone blade is thicker and more wood must be removed to cut to a given depth (Dickson 1981).

The Forager Way of Life: Aboriginal Affluence As Mode of Thought

For centuries social theorists have had difficulty imagining what life was like before the creation of politically organized societies, and before agriculture. English philosopher Thomas Hobbes (1588–1679) in a famous passage in his classic book on the state, *Leviathan* (1651), imagined that life for all pre-state peoples was "poor, nasty, brutish, and short" (Chapter 13, Paragraph 9). This resembles archaeologist Robert Braidwood's description of pre-Neolithic life as: ". . . a savage's existence, and a very tough one. A man who spends his whole life following animals just to kill them to eat, or moving from one berry patch to another, is really living just like an animal himself" (Braidwood 1964:122, cited Winterhalder 1993). Europeans readily applied this negative view of the tribal world to Australian aborigines because they raised no crops and had no permanent villages and no government to protect private property. These were important points of contrast, but in reality tribal life was rich, satisfying, and sustainable. The ob-

vious simplicity of aboriginal material culture created an illusion of poverty that misled generations of superficial European observers.

The illusion of aboriginal poverty was intensified by the material impoverishment, sickness, and death that followed the disruption of aboriginal social networks, the displacement of aboriginal food sources by sheep and cattle, and the deliberate destruction of aboriginal culture following the European conquest of aboriginal territory after 1788. The descriptions of aboriginal life offered in this chapter refer primarily to pre-European conditions, or contemporary aborigines living independently in rural communities. The official Australian census counted 386,000 "people of aboriginal descent" in 1996, most of whom were living in towns and cities. However, the Dreaming still shaped the lives of many of the 105,000 who were living in rural areas of the country. Many living on designated aboriginal land continued to forage for "bush foods."

Modern anthropologists have variously identified details of subsistence, society, or ideology as the most remarkable features of foragers in comparison with other types of society. These dimensions of culture are so interconnected that they are all equally important. However, in the analysis offered in this book, the small size of forager bands and tribes is treated as perhaps their most important physical feature shaping the forager way of life. The scale or small size of aboriginal society is such a significant factor that it can help explain other details of forager subsistence, society, and beliefs.

Surprisingly, when twentieth-century anthropologists began to scientifically examine the material aspects of foraging systems, they soon discovered that aborigines were actually quite healthy, and were comfortably meeting their material needs. Marshall Sahlins (1968) concluded that foragers in fact represented "the original affluent society," citing Arnhem Land aborigines who were able to keep themselves well nourished by only four to five hours a day of foraging and processing food (Figure 2.11). Significantly, this was a weekly average (see box "A Day in the Life

FIGURE 2.11 Aboriginal men spearfishing in the coastal waters of the tropical north. They have speared a stingray.

of the Fish Creek Band"). Actual time expenditures were quite variable, and there was plenty of time for daytime relaxing. Likewise, in the harsh Western Desert the Pitjantjatjara aborigines spent five to seven hours a day on subsistence, even under drought conditions, and still managed to thrive (Gould 1969, 1980). Sahlins noted that outsiders thought that tribal people refused to accumulate wealth because they were lazy and improvident, but tribal nonaccumulation was actually a measure of tribal affluence. The key point of misunderstanding was that aboriginal wealth did not consist of stored food, structures, or other familiar forms of tangible wealth in the commercial world. Paradoxically, even though aborigines had the absolute minimum of material culture, they were very wealthy. Their wealth was in nature and the land, people, and intangible culture. Nature provided most of the goods and services that

they required, and this made it reasonable to credit nature's services as forager income, and to count nature as wealth, even though aborigines did not buy and sell anything. Aboriginal income, or tribal product, was primarily food production, and it was consumed daily, but their primary investment effort was in raising children, maintaining social relations, and reproducing the ideas and information stored in their culture. Aborigines worked at subsistence only until their material needs were satisfied, and they did not store food because they could gather what they needed every day. As long as foraging bands remained small and moved frequently, there was no scarcity of food. Forager subsistence workloads varied considerably under different conditions, but the logic of their system, which emphasized sharing and abundance, always remained the same. Sahlins suggested that the key to aboriginal affluence was

A Day in the Life of the Fish Creek Band

It is impossible to know in exact detail what daily life was like for prehistoric aboriginal peoples, but modern ethnographies can give a reasonable picture of the ease of making a living by foraging. From October 7 to 20, 1948, anthropologists Frederick McCarthy and Margaret McArthur (1948:147–180) kept a careful diary of the daily activities of a small group of aborigines foraging in the monsoon forest in Arnhem land a few miles from Oenpelli Mission. This research was part of a larger study of the health, nutrition, and food consumption of aborigines who relied heavily on bush foods. The Fish Creek band included three older men with three of their wives, and three younger, unmarried initiated adolescents, all led by Wilira, a 35-to-40-year-old man. The group used wooden digging sticks, dip-nets, spears, and spear-throwers, as well as a metal ax, metal spear points, a hunting dog, and iron rods for digging. This was late in the dry season, and wild plants were in short supply, but even so, during 11 days the group consumed 390 pounds of kangaroo and wallaby, 116 pounds of fish, 7 pounds of honey, and 35 pounds of plant food, including 28 pounds of wild yams. This exceeded their per capita caloric requirements and provided 300 grams of protein per person per day, which was more than 5 times their recommended daily requirements. October 7 unfolded as follows:

8:00 AM	Breakfast of yams.
8:00–9:30	Men work on their hunting equipment.
9:30–2:00	Five men stalk kangaroo and wallaby, killing one kangaroo.
8:30 AM–12:45 PM	The women walk through the forest, dig out a bandicoot, extract a honey hive from an anthill, catch a few fish by hand from a pool, dig roots, and catch a goanna lizard.
12:45–2:00	Women rest, then prepare and cook food.
2:00–3:45	Men rest, women gather firewood, men eat kangaroo innards, roast the carcass in earth oven, divide and eat it.
3:45–6:30	Everyone rests.
6:30–10:00	Everyone sings and dances.

their cultural ability to limit their material needs to levels that could be easily satisfied. This means that the aboriginal definition of what constituted the good life determined their choice of technology and mode of production. Perhaps most importantly, the tribal good life depended on social units maintaining a small-scale optimum size, but this was easy because when bands grew too large, workloads increased, quarrels might occur, and the group would split.

Aboriginal foragers represent what Sahlins (1974) called a **"domestic mode of production,"** where production decisions are made at the household level with minimal outside pressure. Aborigines did not use labor, technology, and resources to their maximum productive potential, choosing instead to maximize their leisure, sharing, and ceremonial activities above purely material concerns. The relative uniformity and durability

domestic mode of production Material production organized at the household level, with distribution between households based on reciprocal sharing.

of their forager system suggests that aborigines had designed a sustainable no-growth culture, whether intentionally or not. Aborigines did not "invest" surplus production in either supporting larger populations or expanding economic production, instead they directed it into activities that helped individuals build their social and cultural capital in ways that also benefited society as a whole and contributed to the reproduction of the culture. Food sharing, ceremonial feasting, and leisure provided growth-dampening effects and helped aborigines avoid the Malthusian dilemma of endless cycles of population growth and subsistence intensification (Sahlins 1974, Peterson 1997). When people shared food, there was little incentive to produce beyond their immediate needs. The absence of wealth accumulation also left little basis for individuals to build large personal command structures, and this made it easier for everyone's needs to be met.

Limited material production by aborigines can be partially understood as the outcome of cost benefit decisions given forager technology. The more hours per day foragers work, the less efficient their efforts become, because their prey becomes scarcer relative to the number of people to be fed. Bruce Winterhalder (1993) used computer simulations to show that relatively low work effort actually produces the largest sustainable human population and the best return for forager effort. It may seem counterintuitive, but increased effort in the form of longer hours spent foraging appears to only reduce efficiency because of resource depletion. Of course, aborigines could have intensified their food production by becoming farmers, but they chose not to, even though their New Guinea neighbors did.

It is not always obvious what constitutes production (Allen 2002). What some observers consider leisure may be social investment, or may indirectly support food production. Discussing the day's events over the evening fire may be an exchange of economic information rather than leisure (Smith 1988), and applying body paint to a kinsman or preparing a dance ground is providing a service (Altman 1987:221–22, 228–30).

Sharing among kin can also be considered the extraction of social surplus. The continuous pressure of **demand sharing** may push people to produce more than they would need for their own consumption, especially when they can gain benefits from sharing viewed as social investment. Demand sharing is when people ask for things based on kinship obligations (Peterson 1997). In Australia giving away meat helped men build support networks to gain access to social capital such as wives, hunting territory, and sacred property. The important point is that in small-scale societies there were severe limits on how much social capital anyone could accumulate, because there were very few people to command and the ideology was emphatically anti-growth and anti-accumulation.

In comparison with people in the imperial and commercial worlds, Australian aborigines and other foraging peoples exemplify a distinctive mode of thought that is shared by tribal peoples generally and that persists even when modes of production change (Barnard 2002). The forager mode of thought is part of forager self-identity, and includes beliefs related to many social power issues involving production, consumption, politics, and society. Foragers expect people to readily share things for immediate consumption by everyone. Accumulation is antisocial. In contrast, the "accumulation mode of thought" characteristic of people in the commercial world generally treats sharing and consumption only within one's own household as proper, and considers not saving and not accumulating to be antisocial. In political affairs, foragers are suspicious of anyone who takes a leadership position, and they prefer to follow the group consensus. Tribal leaders are deferred to out of respect for their special skills that come with age and experience. In contrast, in the commercial world, leadership is seen as a positive trait, and to be a follower suggests weakness.

Under the forager mode of thought, society is based on what has been called "universal kinship" (Barnard 2002). This means that all members of a forager society are placed in a kinship category and treated as "family." Nurit Bird-

David (1992) calls this the "cosmic economy of sharing." Foragers recognize a direct kinship with spirit beings who socialize and share food with people as part of the natural order of existence. This is the essence of Dreamtime symbolism. Thus, Australian aborigines call everyone kin, and they do not consider themselves to be members of any centrally controlled, territorially based political unit, although they do recognize common language and culture. Foragers treat their territory as an inviolable possession, a common property that is too sacred to be sold or alienated, although individuals do own their scant moveable possessions. Foragers consider individuals to be free and autonomous, and reject the constraints imposed by government. In contrast, in commercial societies land is bought and sold by individuals, and private property must be protected by government authority.

The foraging technological subsystem provides the energy, nutrients, and raw materials needed by the population, but the technology depends on a much more complex social and ideological system. Tribal cultures generate social status and power only through marriage and the family. In this section, we look at how these social networks are organized and how power is obtained.

DAILY LIFE IN FORAGER SOCIETY: KINSHIP, AGE, AND GENDER

Australian aboriginal society, although rooted in antiquity and sustained by simple technology, is a fully developed and dynamic system. It is not a fragile relic of the Paleolithic or a step on the way to political centralization. The basic challenge for aborigines is the circular problem of maintaining a tribal system that will perpetuate their population and, in turn, reproduce the culture. Understanding how aborigines solve this problem has preoccupied anthropologists for more than a century.

Anthropological interpretations of aboriginal culture have shifted dramatically over time as theoretical perspectives have changed and new data have become available. This debate has helped establish many of the most basic concepts of cultural anthropology while gradually revealing the genius of aboriginal culture. The broadest theoretical issues concern how the culture actually works: the role of the belief system and the way the culture relates to environmental and demographic factors. Important humanistic issues concern how much social equality there is and whether women and young men are being exploited by old men.

A Kinship-Based Society

Aboriginal society is highly decentralized and egalitarian, with people in overlapping and interdependent roles that minimize the possibility that divisive interest groups will come into serious conflict. Under this social system, an individual might encounter as many as 500 or so people and be able to sort them into a workable number of social categories that specify appropriate interpersonal behavior, especially in the critical areas of marriage and access to spiritual property. The totemic estate groups are among the most important social categories. In a given aboriginal society, there might be dozens of totemic estate groups, or clans, that regulate rights in spiritual property and indirectly provide access to natural resources. Who one marries is partly determined in reference to the totemic groups of one's parents, and marriage establishes access to territory associated with one's spouse's totemic estates.

All social interaction takes place between people who can place themselves in specific kinship categories. Kinship terms simplify social relations by categorizing people. Terms such as mother, father, uncle, and sister define an individual's personal network of culturally significant categories that are conceptually based on the relationships arising from the **nuclear family** of mother, father,

demand sharing Requesting food or other things from kin who are obligated to give.

nuclear family The primary family unit of mother, father, and dependent children.

and children. Aboriginal **kinship terminology** systems typically distinguish some fifteen to twenty relationship pairs such as father/daughter, brother/sister, and so on. Kin terms may distinguish gender and relative age or generation, and whether one is a **consanguine** (related by a common ancestor) or an **affine** (related by marriage). Aboriginal kin terms also indicate marriageability and relative totemic estate group affiliation. Because everyone must be fitted into a "kinship" category, most people are not necessarily what nonaboriginals would consider "real kin," but aborigines *do* treat them as kin. The terms reflect shared understandings of social status, and they become basic guides for expected behavior.

Kinship terms represent cultural categories, and their specific application varies considerably cross-culturally. For example, in a given system, someone might refer to several women using the same term applied to *mother*. The term *mother* might then mean "woman of mother's generation who belongs to mother's totemic estate group (clan)." The biological facts of motherhood might be irrelevant in this context. When the biological relationship needs to be designated, a modifier such as *true* or *real* might be attached to the term. Similarly, a man might refer to several women as "wife's mother," yet not be married to any of their daughters. From an aboriginal viewpoint, what is most important is potential marriageability and relationship to totemic estate groups.

The kinship terminologies and estate groups are further simplified by another system of categories in aboriginal society known as moieties and sections. **Moieties** sort people in each tribe into two sides by estate groups, or from the viewpoint of a specific individual, they may divide the entire society into "own group" and "other group." In some aboriginal societies, all people, totems, and natural phenomena are assigned to a specific moiety. For example, one-half of a society might be associated with the color black, kangaroos, acacia trees, and goanna lizard Dreaming sites, whereas the other half is white, emus, gum trees, and rainbow serpent Dreaming sites.

Membership may be assigned through mother (matrimoiety) or father (patrimoiety) or by generation level.

Moiety groupings help organize ritual activities and can be used to specify roles in initiation ceremonies, marriages, and funerals. For example, one moiety may "own" a particular ritual, while the other moiety actually carries out the ritual. This is a form of **complementary opposition**, because the ceremony could not be performed without the cooperation of both groups.

The **section system** simply extends the number of summary social categories from two moieties to four sections and sometimes eight subsections. Because a given society may be crosscut by overlapping moiety systems, sections can significantly simplify social status and help determine whom people can marry (see the boxes entitled "Cross-Cousins and Marriage Sections" and "Kinship and Mother-in-Law Avoidance"). People belong to the same section category in relation to everyone, unlike the case of kinship terms that depend on each person's unique network of kin. Thus, sections serve as convenient identifying labels, especially because aborigines often consider it rude to use personal names in public. Knowing someone's section would allow one to make reasonable inferences about more specific social categories. Furthermore, because sections are recognized intertribally, strangers can quickly fit into a local social network.

Moieties, sections, totems, and kinship terms all work together in a neatly integrated system to guide people in their daily interaction with one another and in their relationships to their countries and spiritual properties. It is a remarkably successful system that significantly reduces the potential for conflict and makes authoritarian rule unnecessary.

The emphasis that aborigines place on following social rules makes it clear that the early anthropologists who thought that aborigines epitomized selfish immorality were mistaken. Hiatt (2002) shows that the Gidjingarli people of Arnhem Land in northern Australia make altruism a central value, and this is strongly reflected in their language. The Gidjingarli have terms for "good" (*molamola*) and "bad" (*werra*). These terms may be used for moral judgments about individuals, such that a *molamola* person cares for others and shares, whereas a *werra* person is unkind and perhaps harmful. The value of benevolence and mutual support are expressed in terms for kin or countrymen (*borrmunga*), for kin responsibilities (*gurrurta*), and kin reciprocity (*gurrurta-gurrurta*). Marriage and trading partnerships are important reciprocal obligations that are contractual agreements involving trust. Such contracts are moral concerns and may be expressed in kinship terms, but the partners may not be "real" kin. Thus, a good person is someone who behaves like close kin, who are assumed to be good. Hiatt suggests that extending the sentiments of kinship to society at large converts potential enemies into friends. There are many Gidjingarli customs based on the Dreaming that specify polite speech and overall proper behavior covering all aspects of interaction with kin, especially with universal life-cycle events such as initiation, betrothal, marriage, childbearing, and death. People who repeatedly threaten the well-being of the community may be killed by mutual agreement.

In contrast to the simplicity and functionality of aboriginal society, in commercial societies it is impossible for any individual to be acquainted with more than a tiny sample of the many individuals, social statuses, and corporate groups that exist. For example, in the United States there were 272 million people, some 20,000 occupational titles, and nearly 5 million for-profit business corporations in 1999.

Polygyny, Gerontocracy, and Social Equality

Many aspects of aboriginal society are related to the widespread practice of **polygyny** (plural wives). Polygyny automatically creates a scarcity of potential wives, which is partially alleviated by the large age difference between men and women at marriage. Girls may be promised in marriage long before they are born, and men might be well beyond 30 years of age before their first marriage, perhaps to a much older widow, while a 12-year-old girl might marry a 50-year-old man. If one assumes an even sex ratio, then the only way in which some men could have more than one wife would be for women to marry at a younger age than men. The wider the age differential at marriage, the more polygynous marriages can take place. A recent study in Arnhem Land found that nearly one-half of the men over 40 years of age had more than one wife, and one-third had three or more (Shapiro 1981). More than one-third of the men ages 20–40 were still unmarried.

In some respects aboriginal society is a polygynous **gerontocracy** in which the old men use polygyny and Dreamtime ideology to control women and the labor supply. The young men are deprived of wives and kept subservient by the male initiation system (see the box entitled "Male Initiation: The Terrible Rite"). This interpretation may reflect the perceptions of some of the old men, particularly when they are describing the system to male anthropologists, but it is a misleading generalization. Emphasis on male gerontocracy ignores the important role of women both in the ritual system and in domestic life, and it obscures the essentially egalitarian nature of aboriginal society.

---

kinship terminology An ego-centered system of terms that specifies genealogical relationships of consanguinity and affinity in reference to a given individual.

consanguine A relative by culturally recognized descent from a common ancestor; sometimes called a "blood" relative.

affine A relative by marriage.

moiety One part of a two-part social division.

complementary opposition A structural principle in which pairs of opposites, such as males and females, form a logical larger whole.

section system A social division into four (sections) or eight (subsections) intermarrying, named groups, which summarize social relationships. Members of each group must marry only members of one other specific group.

polygyny A form of marriage in which a man may have more than one wife.

gerontocracy An age hierarchy that is controlled or dominated by the oldest age groups.

Cross-Cousins and Marriage Sections

Aboriginal marriage practices provide an important key to understanding many aspects of the social system. Marriages, normally arranged by the elders, fit within precisely defined cultural categories, which vary in detail from group to group. Frequently, the ideal mate for a man (Ego in Figure 2.A) would be the daughter of someone he would refer to as "wife's mother" (WM). WM might also be a woman of the father's totemic clan and in the "father's sister" (FZ) category. WM might be married to a man whom ego would place in the "mother's brother" (MB) category. MB could be any man who was a member of the same totemic clan to which ego's actual mother belonged. Of course, several men could be in this category, and they would not need to be the actual brother of ego's actual mother. Also, an appropriate spouse often will be someone in the kinship category of *cross-cousin* (the daughter of mother's brother or father's sister—MBD or FZD) because these women could not belong to ego's descent group.

A person would be expected to marry within a certain range of ego-based kin and in reference to specific clan, moiety, and section categories. One would always

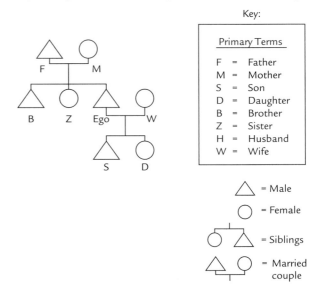

FIGURE 2.A Conventions of kinship diagramming. Anthropologists describe all kinship relationships using a set of eight primary terms with standard abbreviations (shown in key). These terms are then combined to describe additional relationships. Thus, FB = father's brother, MB = mother's brother, FF = father's father, FBD = father's brother's daughter, MBD = mother's brother's daughter, and so on. Ego, always the reference point in any kinship diagram, is the person who applies the terms shown. These designations are culturally specific social categories; they need not represent actual biological relationships. Even primary terms such as *mother* can be applied to several people who are not one's biological mother.

marry outside of one's own clan and might even refer to one's own-generation fellow clan members as brother and sister, emphasizing the incestuous nature of clan *endogamy*—marriage within a culturally defined group. Where society-wide moieties exist, spouses would be drawn from opposite moieties, and the moiety groups could be called exogamous.

Appropriate marriages also can be described in relation to the section system. With a four-section system, there are four named sections, and an individual can marry into only one specific section (Figures 2.B–D). Siblings always belong to the same section but belong to different sections from their parents, reflecting the fact that marriage within parent–child and sibling categories would be incestuous. Sections only indirectly regulate marriage because not all women in the appropriate section will be in the marriageable MBD category. Knowing someone's section identity simply narrows the search.

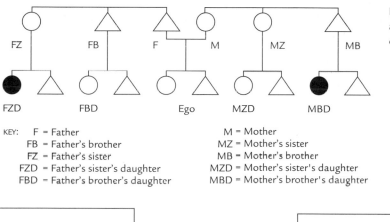
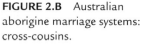

FIGURE 2.B Australian aborigine marriage systems: cross-cousins.

KEY: F = Father   M = Mother
         FB = Father's brother   MZ = Mother's sister
         FZ = Father's sister   MB = Mother's brother
         FZD = Father's sister's daughter   MZD = Mother's sister's daughter
         FBD = Father's brother's daughter MBD = Mother's brother's daughter

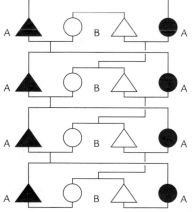

FIGURE 2.C A simple two-section moiety system.

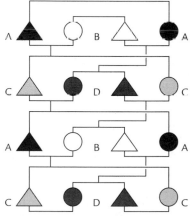

FIGURE 2.D A four-section system, in which there are four-named sections (A, B, C, D distinguished by shade). Each person marries into only one section, and section membership alternates by generation (each person is in the same section as a grandparent).

Kinship and Mother-in-Law Avoidance

One striking form of aboriginal kinship behavior is the extreme avoidance operating between a man and any woman whom he calls wife's mother (WM). In some aboriginal groups, a man cannot look at, remain near, or speak directly to his WM. She is considered to be a source of "shame," and he must avoid any sexual references in her presence and may even use a special form of avoidance speech full of circumlocutions to avoid embarrassment. Early observers thought such customs were absurd, but in cultural context, they make a great deal of sense.

L. R. Hiatt (1984b) points out that in Australia, a man often may live in close proximity to his WM and may provide her with meat as a form of bride-service, even before marrying his WMD. Given the often great age differential at marriage, a man may be nearly the same age as his WM and could find her attractive, while the WM might find a young daughter's husband more attractive than the old man who would be her husband. Meat-giving also has sexual implications and takes place between husband and wife. Under these circumstances, extreme avoidance would certainly reduce the possibility of conflict between a man and his wife's father (WF). Avoidance also would prevent the possibility of father–daughter incest because if a man did have an affair with his WM, he could be his own WF.

Although the marriage age differential facilitates polygyny, the existence of polygyny itself remains to be explained. It may appear to be the direct result of manipulation by self-interested and influential older men, but this is a narrow view. Polygyny also offers important benefits for the entire society. Polygynous households may provide childbearing women with greater security. An older man is more likely than a young man to have a thorough knowledge of the territory and a wider network of kinship connections, which will benefit his entire household, especially in times of resource shortage. Similarly, delaying marriage provides the young men with an opportunity to learn the intricacies of the totemic landscape and the locations of critical waterholes while they remain free of domestic responsibilities.

The way in which aboriginal marriage customs are discussed by anthropologists, as with the terms *wife-givers* and *wife-receivers,* often implies male domination where it is not present. The terms *wife bestowal* and even *mother-in-law bestowal* are sometimes applied to the spouse selection process.

Mother-in-law bestowal refers to a ceremony in which a young girl is publicly designated as wife's mother to a young man. The term *bestowal,* rather than the more neutral term *betrothal,* may suggest that a father is "giving away" a daughter, when, in fact, the girl's mother or mother's brother is more likely to make the arrangements. Furthermore, the term suggests that the marriage might never take place. Given a man's age at marriage, he might not even be around when his daughter actually marries, although he might have had some involvement in her prenatal betrothal.

The place of women in aboriginal culture has been interpreted in many different ways. Ethnocentric European travelers mistakenly described these women as degraded and passive servants of the men. The seemingly sharp gender divisions in the activity spheres of aboriginal culture made it difficult for anthropologists to obtain a balanced picture. Early anthropologists were mostly men who necessarily observed male culture and talked to male informants. These male anthropologists were also quite comfortable with the male superiority view because it corresponded closely to their own Victorian biases. Victorian anthropologists considered women in general to be spiritually inferior and even described them as "profane," whereas men were seen as "sacred." More recent fieldwork by female anthropologists working with aboriginal women has broadened the picture by showing that these women have a very active secret ritual life and exercise considerable autonomy in domestic affairs.

Australian anthropologist Diane Bell (1983, 1987) spent many months living in aboriginal communities in northern Australia. As a divorced woman with children, she was treated as an adult widow, given a kinship status, and included in public ceremonies. When her female hosts were satisfied that she would respect their secrecy, she was allowed to participate in women's secret rituals. From this perspective, she discovered that aboriginal women share joint and complementary responsibility with men for maintaining their spiritual heritage. Whereas men's rituals emphasize creative power, women's rituals focus on the nurturing role of women, health, social harmony, and connections with the land.

Women also play a major role in subsistence, may arrange marriages, control family size by means of infanticide, and can influence the choice of conception totems. Some anthropologists still consider aboriginal men "superior" but would grant women the status of "junior partners." However, the notion of rank by sex is probably not a culturally significant issue for aborigines. Throughout the world, foraging peoples that are characterized by high mobility and low population density are the most egalitarian societies known. Equality is reflected in the conspicuous absence of differences in material wealth among individuals, in the availability to each household of the resources needed to secure its existence, and in the absence of permanent political leaders with coercive power over others. However, social equality does not mean that everyone is alike. Obvious differences exist between men and women, between young and old, and between individuals with different personalities and physical characteristics.

Foragers, like the aborigines, who operate with immediate-return systems, provide little basis for people or corporate groups to maintain coercive power over others (Lee 1981, Woodburn 1982). With immediate-return systems, there is no investment of labor in fixed structures, gardens, or herds that will produce a delayed-return system and that might require long-term storage. Thus, there is no particular advantage in long-term control of a labor force. When basic production is left to nature and food is harvested and consumed on a daily basis, population densities must remain low, and social groups must be highly flexible and mobile to respond to natural fluctuations in supply. Reciprocity, especially pooling and sharing of food, levels out individual variation in production, reduces individual risk, and operates among all households in a camp. In immediate-return production systems, every household has freely available the productive tools and natural resources that it requires. Mobility reduces the potential for social domination and exploitation by discouraging wealth accumulation and making it easy for people to walk away from adverse interpersonal situations.

Social equality also is closely related to the "openness" of aboriginal society. Open societies derive their special characteristics from their mobility and the absence of permanent houses, tombs, temples, and institutionalized leadership. Domestic life takes place in the open, where people can pay close attention to one another (Wilson 1988). Under these conditions, there are few secrets and few sources of conflict. Furthermore, with weapons always at hand, the use of force is available to everyone and is less likely to become a means for domination.

Outsiders may be struck by the apparent frequency of conflict in aboriginal society, the violence of domestic quarrels, and the charges of infidelity or failure to share. Conflicts of this sort apparently are more common under the crowded conditions of modern settlements. Furthermore, any conflict is a public event in an open society and cannot be hidden behind walls as may be the

Male Initiation: The Terrible Rite

The physical ordeals of scarification, nose piercing, bloodletting, tooth evulsion, genital mutilation, and fingernail extraction associated with aboriginal male initiation rituals have been a continuing source of amazement for outsiders and have generated endless speculation about their origins and persistence. These rites occur throughout Australia, but not all groups share the same specific forms. For males, the rituals mark different age grades in social maturity and acquisition of ritual knowledge. Women and girls pass through similar maturation grades but with few physical ordeals.

The obvious functionalist interpretation of these rituals is that they are **rites of passage** publicly marking an individual's change of status. For example, a boy must be circumcised before he can marry. The pain makes the new status more valuable and increases one's pride of membership, thus contributing to social solidarity. The value of body mutilation, especially where little clothing is worn, is that the change in status is permanently visible and unlikely to be faked; genital mutilation is performed only on males. These rituals are part of the formal instruction in ritual lore and make the ritual more valuable and more memorable. The initiates must accept the discipline of the older men, and they owe respect and gifts of meat to their tutors.

The most dramatic male ordeal is subincision, which follows circumcision and involves slitting the underside of the penis lengthwise to open the urethra. The operation is performed by the initiate's MB or WF, who uses a very sharp stone knife. The initiate must remain passive and show no signs of experiencing pain. After healing, the incision remains open, but infection or reproductive impairment does not normally occur.

case in other societies. Victoria Burbank (1994) recorded hundreds of incidents of verbal and physical aggression between individuals during 18 months of research in an aboriginal community in Arnhem Land. Contrary to the way Americans view domestic conflict in their own culture, she found that aboriginal women were not passive victims of male aggression. Women initiated fights nearly as often as men, sometimes physically assaulting men. Burbank emphasizes that for aborigines, aggression is culturally constructed as an often-legitimate expression of anger. Its openness means that kin may intervene to prevent serious injuries. The cultural support for aboriginal women taking an aggressive stance toward men is a way of balancing the otherwise unequal physical differences between men and women that could be expressed as unequal social power.

The religious life in open societies is primarily concerned with healing, love magic, and natural fertility rather than with witchcraft. Individual souls are recycled and may exist briefly as ghosts, but they are not permanently commemorated in ancestor cults. Groups, even those based on kinship, are not rigidly bounded corporate entities. Both individual friendships and kinship categories define social relationships; they are not exclusively determined by genealogical criteria.

Paradoxically, aboriginal society is at the same time intensely egalitarian and religiously authoritarian (Hiatt 1987). Although aboriginal society is sometimes described as a society without poli-

Subincision appears to have been a recent invention and was actively spreading from tribe to tribe when Europeans arrived. Young men willingly submit to the ordeal because it admits them to the privileges of manhood in a society in which other tests of strength and courage such as warfare are of little importance. As psychologist S. D. Porteus (1931) explained, "It is the price that must be paid for tribal membership, and all must pay. . . . that the price is high puts an enhanced value on these bonds of tribal union" (280–281).

From the aboriginal viewpoint, subincision requires no special explanation beyond the fact that it originated in the Dreaming. Aborigines may point to the physical resemblance between the subincised penis and the genitals of kangaroos and emus as confirmation of the Dreaming connection (Cawte 1974).

Psychoanalysts have suggested that subincision is a subconscious way for aboriginal men to deal with oedipal fears, castration anxiety, or their supposed envy of female reproductive powers. In opposition to the aboriginal interpretation, the subincision would represent a woman's vagina, not a totemic kangaroo penis. The best support for the psychoanalytic view is that the initiates are symbolically killed in the ritual and reborn as men. However, because men already have a culturally acknowledged role in fertility through totemic increase ceremonies, vagina envy seems unnecessary. A conflicting psychological argument is that boys who grow up too closely associated with their mothers need a painful initiation to affirm their identity as males.

We may never know how rituals such as subincision originated in the first place. But they play an important role in the culture and are best understood as expressions of the overwhelming importance of the Dreaming.

tics because of the absence of formal chiefs, elders do have moral authority, based on the Dreaming, over their juniors, both men and women. Relationships among individuals at different generation levels are hierarchical and may be expressed as a kinship responsibility to "hold" or "look after" or "raise" the junior (Myers 1980). This is considered nurturing and guiding behavior, not domination or exploitation. In aboriginal English, one's elder may be referred to as a "boss" who has control over one's marriage and ritual advancement. Such an elder–junior system extends throughout the society so that everyone but the youngest child would be responsible for a junior, but the context is always specific. No one has generalized power over all others.

An age hierarchy is different from a government bureaucracy because, in the age system, status is always relative, everyone at a given level is equivalent, and everyone moves up. No one is permanently excluded from access to basic resources or political power by membership in a lower social class. As they mature, everyone—men and women alike—move to positions of greater decision-making ability in society. People in commercial societies often imagine their societies as ladders that people ascend. This is certainly

rite of passage A ritual marking culturally significant changes in an individual's life cycle, such as birth, puberty, marriage, old age, and death.

the hope, but in class-based societies there is never room at the top for everyone who aspires to "rise." However, everyone does move up the ladder of aboriginal society.

For aborigines, the ideological foundation of their society is the Dreaming, which defines and is perpetuated by the generational hierarchy. Knowledge of the Dreaming is concentrated in the elders, who are obligated to transmit it to the juniors. Holding and transmitting such knowledge can be considered an exercise of political power, but it is a very special kind of power that cannot be directly compared with the political power in large-scale, nonegalitarian societies.

There often are aboriginal "bigmen" or "men of high renown" who stand out because of their vast ritual knowledge or oratorical skills, but their range of action is limited. They may have considerable influence in the ceremonial life and may be able to manipulate certain social relationships to their advantage with threats of supernatural punishment. However, in the larger society, even such powerful individuals can take little political action without broad popular consensus.

SUMMARY

Australian aborigines demonstrate that a domestic-scale culture can remain egalitarian and in balance with its resource base indefinitely as long as it is not invaded by larger-scale neighbors. For over 50,000 years, gradual adjustments in aboriginal technology occurred as environmental conditions changed, and the ritual system and social organization underwent continuous elaboration; aboriginal culture, however, retains its fundamental character as a domestic-scale system. This is clearly a dynamic, responsive, and highly creative system, but it appears to have changed in such a way that the most fundamental cultural elements remain in place. The Dreaming itself, and all its associated features, seems to

be the key element in understanding this remarkable cultural stability.

STUDY QUESTIONS

1. In what sense could the aboriginal subsistence system be considered an affluent economy?
2. Discuss the role of women in aboriginal society. Are they really oppressed and exploited by the old men as some suggest?
3. Demonstrate the connections between religion and society *or* between religion and adaptation to the natural environment in aboriginal Australia.
4. Discuss explanations for the remarkable initiation practices of the aboriginals, distinguishing between how aborigines view these practices and how anthropologists and other outsiders see them.
5. Describe the significance of cross-cousin marriage in aboriginal society.
6. In what sense can aboriginal society be considered egalitarian? What cultural mechanisms contribute to equality?
7. Evaluate the relative importance of mode of thought and mode of production as the most crucial cultural elements in aboriginal culture.
8. What factors helped regulate the size of aboriginal social units?

SUGGESTED READING

FLOOD, JOSEPHINE. 1983. *Archaeology of the Dreamtime.* Honolulu: University of Hawaii Press. A comprehensive overview of the prehistory of Australia.

GOULD, RICHARD A. 1980. *Living Archaeology.* Cambridge, Eng.: Cambridge University Press. An engaging work by an archaeologist who studied contemporary aborigines in the Western Desert to help understand the prehistoric remains.

SAHLINS, MARSHALL. 1968. "Notes on the Original Affluent Society." In *Man the Hunter,* edited by Richard B. Lee and Irven DeVore, pp. 85–89. Chicago: Aldine. A short section that compares foraging and market economies.

TONKINSON, ROBERT. 1991. *The Mardudjara Aborigines: Living the Dream in Australia's Desert,* 2nd ed. New York: Holt, Rinehart & Winston. A well-rounded ethnography of aboriginal culture in the Western Desert.

3

Native Amazonians: Villagers of the Rain Forest

Achuar boy with blowgun, Conambo River, Ecuadorean Amazon, 1998.

PRONUNCIATION GUIDE

Amazonian place names and terms are variously derived from Spanish, Portuguese, Quechua, and numerous tribal languages. Their most common pronunciation can be approximated by English speakers using the following orthography and sounds:

Key
a = a in father
o = o in go
ay = ay in day
ee = ee in beet
oo = oo in food
ng = ng in sing
• = Syllable division
/ = Stress

Aguaruna = [ag • wa • roo / na]
Asháninka = [a • sha / neen • ka]
Ge = [shay]
Huambisa = [wam • bee / sa]
Kuikuru = [koo • ee • koo / roo]
Matsigenka = [ma • tsi • gen / ka]
Mundurucú [moon • doo • roo • koo/]
Waiwai = [wai / wai]
Xingu = [shing • goo/]
Yanomami [ya • no • ma / mee]

Learning Objectives

After studying this chapter you should be able to do the following.

1. Describe the main climatological and biological features of the Amazon environment that distinguish this region from temperate environments.
2. Define tropical forest village culture and explain how the process of subsistence intensification is related to cultural development in Amazonia.
3. Describe shifting cultivation in Amazonia and explain why manioc is so important.
4. Describe the environmental and cultural factors that shape settlement patterns and population density in Amazonia, and evaluate the relative importance of each factor.
5. Evaluate the evidence for affluence in tribal Amazonia, and explain the cultural conditions that make affluence possible.
6. Compare the social organization and belief systems of Amazon villagers with Australian aborigines, identifying and explaining the most important similarities and differences.
7. Distinguish between raiding and feuding in the tribal world, and war in the imperial and commercial worlds.
8. Discuss different explanations for raiding and feuding in Amazonia, and explain the ethical problems for anthropologists in dealing with these issues.

Since early in the sixteenth century, European accounts of the native inhabitants of Amazonia have fueled the myth of the "noble savage." The earliest European explorers correctly described the relative social and political equality and the communalism of the rain forest villagers, but they mistakenly equated the prevailing nudity of the natives with the innocence and perfection of the biblical Eden. Native Amazonians were not perfect peoples, but their cultures still fascinate outsiders because they continue to offer a dramatic contrast to life in the imperial and commercial worlds.

Amazonia was one of the last large areas of the world where many tribal societies existed with minimal direct influences from the commercial world. By the beginning of the twenty-first century, only a handful of very small tribal societies remained isolated enough to retain their autonomy. Many Amazonian peoples continue to make a living in the rain forest, but they may also engage in various commercial activities and are citizens of modern nation states. Amazonia is still home to the world's largest tropical rain forest, which is now receiving international attention from environmentalists and humanitarians because of the global implications of deforestation and the related issue of the destruction of traditional cultures.

Like Australian aborigines, Amazonians live in small-scale tribal societies, but they have gardens and villages, and their populations may sometimes be larger and denser. A small Amazonian village may have only twenty-five to fifty people and resemble an Australian band, but many larger Amazonian villages may contain a few hundred people and be nearly as large as an Australian tribe. Larger, more sedentary settlements intensify interpersonal stress, and this is reflected in more concern with dangerous spirit beings and violent feuding. However, both Amazonian and Australian societies are highly egalitarian. Men and women have separate, but complementary roles. Amazonian villages have nominal leaders who may be warriors, and they may have large, polygynous households, but they must be especially generous. Cross-cousin marriage, local group exogamy, and polygyny are common features of Australian and Amazonian societies, but age grades and severe male initiations are largely absent in Amazonia. The requirements of shifting cultivation mean that villages are moved frequently, and this limits material wealth accumulation. With rain forest subsistence based on hunting and gardening, the availability of natural resources sets an upper limit on population density and the amount of social power that even the most aggrandizing individual can acquire, just as in Australia.

This chapter focuses on an ethnographic present that assumes political and economic independence of tribal Amazonia. (Chapter 14 examines the problems created by the intrusion of the commercial world.)

LIVING IN THE TROPICAL RAIN FOREST

The Fragile Abundance of the Rain Forest

Amazonia contains one of the world's great ecosystems, combining the largest continuous stand of tropical rain forest with the greatest river system in the world (Figure 3.1). The Amazon River drains an area of 2.2 million square miles (mi^2) (5.8 million square kilometers [km^2]) and discharges four times the volume of water carried by the Congo, the next largest river in the world. The rain forest stretches for some 2000 miles (3218 km) east to west across the center of South America. This warm, wet region is an ideal climate for plant growth and serves as a veritable treasury of biological diversity (Figure 3.2).

Amazonia is a land without winter. In the coolest month, the temperature does not drop below 64°F (18°C), and no month receives less than 2.4 inches (6 centimeters [cm]) of rain. Amazonia is entirely in the tropics, mostly within 10 degrees of the equator, so there are 12 hours of daylight every day and the sun's rays strike the region with maximum intensity. Rainfall is abundant throughout the region, usually averaging over 80 inches (203 cm) a year. Daytime high temperatures reach 90°F (32°C), and nighttime lows

FIGURE 3.1 Map of the Amazonian culture area showing the culture groups discussed. Note that the Amazon basin proper covers only part of the culture area.

about 70°F (21°C). This daily range is greater than the seasonal variation in temperature.

The basic biological productivity of tropical rain forest is three to five times that of most temperate forests, and the total biomass (weight of plants and animals) is among the highest of any terrestrial ecosystem. The forest is composed predominantly of woody plants, and familiar temperate plants such as violets and grasses are represented here as trees. Rain forest trees are usually straight and tall, their interlocking limbs forming a closed canopy laced with woody vines.

FIGURE 3.2   Achuar hunter with blowgun, Ecuadorean Amazon.

The number of plant and animal species in Amazonia is remarkable. Worldwide tropical forests cover only six percent of the earth's surface, yet they contain half of all species. The upper Amazon is known to contain some 50,000 plant species, or about 20 percent of the world's plant species (Wilson 2002). It is not unusual to find twenty to eighty or more species of trees per acre, whereas temperate forests might have only four tree species per acre (Richards 1973). A study from central Amazonia reported some 500 plant species over 4 feet (1.2 m) high in a plot of less than half an acre (Fittkau and Klinge 1973). Amazonian rivers may contain as many as 3000 fish species (Goulding 1980), whereas only 60 species occur in the rivers of western Europe, and only 250 species occur in the Mississippi system. There are probably more species of birds in Amazonia than in any other area of similar size

in the world. More than 500 species were found in one 2-mile^2 (5-km^2) area in the Peruvian Amazon, whereas only 440 species are known in the entire eastern half of North America.

The biological wealth of the rain forest hides some curious paradoxes. High productivity does not mean high human carrying capacity because much energy goes to the production of inedible forest litter. Soil fertility often is very low and quickly depleted. There are few easily harvested carbohydrates in the woody vegetation, and 90 percent of the animal biomass is composed of ants, termites, and other small invertebrates that can eat leaves and wood. Large vertebrates are relatively scarce, and animal protein is difficult for hunters to secure because game often is nocturnal or hidden in the forest canopy. Natural food resources for people are so scarce that some authorities argue that no full-time foraging peoples have been able to live in the rain forest unless they have had access to aquatic resources or been able to obtain garden produce from village farmers (Bailey et al. 1989).

The infertility of Amazonian soils is due to the combination of heavy humidity and warm temperature, which fosters both luxuriant growth and the rapid breakdown of forest litter. The top humus layer of the soil is actually very shallow, and most tree roots are near the surface where they can quickly take in the nutrients liberated by decomposition. Trees recycle litter so efficiently that more nutrients are held in the forest itself than in the soil. The forest also regulates the water cycle, contributing directly to the daily thundershowers through water given off daily by plants, and moderating the potential for erosion by cushioning and dispersing the heavy downpours. The forest also sustains the Amazon's wealth of fish, because many species are specialized to feed on fruit on the floor of seasonally flooded forests (Goulding 1980). The scientific community still has a poor understanding of the extreme complexity of the Amazonian ecosystem, but it is apparent that successful long-term human utilization of this region requires maintaining the forest.

The Origins of Tropical Forest Village Culture

The physical evidence of teeth, bones, and blood indicates that people reached the New World from Asia by at least 12,000 BP (see Table 3.1). Periods of lowered sea levels during the Ice Age created a land bridge between Asia and America that facilitated the first settlement of the New World. There is no archaeological record of the occupation of the Amazonian rain forest by mobile foragers, but people may have lived in that region for many thousands of years, without leaving a trace, especially during drier climate phases that turned rain forest into scrub forest and savanna environments more favorable for foragers.

Beginning about 10,000 BP, a steady intensification of subsistence activities must have occurred in Amazonia, paralleling similar events that occurred throughout the world, including Australia, at the end of the Ice Age in response to global changes in climate, vegetation, and fauna. Rising sea levels reduced productive coastal zones, and many big game animals disappeared. People had to work harder to make a living and expanded their food base to include not only the smaller, more numerous species, such as fish and shellfish, but also a broad range of plant species. These changes meant more careful scheduling of seasonal activities and more work in food acquisition and processing, but they resulted in greater food production per unit of territory and more permanent settlement at greater densities. This process has been called **subsistence intensification.**

In Amazonia, and worldwide, subsistence intensification marked the transition from mobile foraging to settled village life and plant domestication. However, it is important to recall, as noted in Chapter 2, that Australian aborigines apparently managed to remain in balance with their resources during this time without turning to domestication. Anthropologists at first considered domestication to be a remarkable invention or discovery that occurred in very few places. But, in fact, there were many centers of domesti-

TABLE 3.1 PREHISTORY OF AMAZONIA, 12,000 BP–AD 1542

AD 1542	European invasion begins
2000 BP	Chiefdoms on central Amazon floodplain
5000–2000 BP	Spread of tropical forest tribal villagers
7000–5000 BP	Domestication of manioc and maiz, forest expands
12,000–7000 BP	First settlers, hunters and foragers
	Post-glacial climate changes, forest retreats

cation, and domestication was a gradual process, not an instant discovery (see Figure 1.7). It must have been compelled by intractable imbalances between population and resources. Paradoxically, domestication represented a technological response to the need to produce more food from a given area of land. People did not intend to increase their total food supply. The unintended consequence was that intensification promoted further population growth by reducing the incentives for family planning encouraged by mobile foraging and by making further increases in food production readily achievable. Thus, village farmers were more likely to experience gradual population growth and had to work harder to maintain a balance with natural resources than did mobile foragers. They also were prone to migrate into territories formerly occupied exclusively by foragers.

The crucial condition that made it easier for Amazonian peoples to maintain small-scale societies and prevent the concentration of social power was their reliance on shifting cultivation and hunting that required vast tracts of forest. Consequently, their settlements were small and impermanent, and there was no incentive to accumulate

---

subsistence intensification Technological innovations that produce more food from the same land area but often require increased effort.

material wealth. In contrast, more intensive, more permanent farming systems, such as those in Hawaii and Mesopotamia, supported larger-scale populations that offered greater scope for aggrandizing individuals to concentrate social power, even as it became more difficult for people to resist. When people intensified their subsistence efforts, they sacrificed freedom of mobility, but they gained the selective advantage of greater short-term control over their energy sources. The problem was that villagers, living in large sedentary settlements sustained by permanent agriculture, had difficulty restraining the growth of political power. By contrast, mobile foragers and shifting cultivators could readily abandon oppressive leaders. Subsistence intensification was a necessary condition for scale increases, but whenever ordinary people remained mobile or self-sufficient, elites were not able to turn growth into concentrated social power.

Domestication requires drastic changes in human activities because, even as plants become dependent on people for their care and reproduction, people become increasingly specialized and dependent on the plants. People made major sacrifices in personal freedom to till their new gardens. In its earliest stages, domestication is not distinguishable from the careful management of wild resources or the simple transplanting of wild plants to more convenient locations. The transition from dependence on wild to genetically altered, domestic plants, and from mobile foraging to relatively permanent villages, took a thousand years or more. This transition did not occur everywhere, and some village farmers, such as those in Amazonia, never became dependent on domesticated animals.

Archaeologist Donald Lathrap (1977) speculated that early plant domestication in Amazonia resulted from efforts to intensify fishing production, in response to the decline in the amount of game as the forest expanded. Increased use of nets and fish poisons would have encouraged people to selectively cultivate cotton (for nets and lines), bottle gourds (for floats), and poisonous plants in easily tended house gardens near their settlements. Cultivation would have been an advantage because in the tropical forest, most plant species are widely dispersed and might be naturally unavailable in the quantity needed.

The domestication of manioc (genus *Manihot*), the most important food plant in Amazonia, probably took place more than 5000 years ago. Manioc is a woody shrub that grows readily from cuttings, and the tuber can be stored in the ground until needed. Although deficient in protein, manioc is very rich in carbohydrates, is highly productive even in poor soils, and is an ideal complement to the fish and game of Amazonia. It can also be fermented to produce a nutritious, mildly alcoholic drink, which may have been an important incentive for its domestication. As a *root crop,* it represents a distinctive cultivation system from maize, the major New World *seed crop* that originated in Mesoamerica and spread to Amazonia.

By at least 2000 BP, the tropical forest cultural pattern of small, autonomous tribal villages—based on shifting cultivation, hunting, and fishing—was established throughout Amazonia. With average population densities of perhaps 0.4 persons per square mile, the total population may have exceeded 1 million people. At least five major language groups—Tupi, Carib, Arawak, Panoan, and Ge—diversified into some 200 languages (Migliazza 1982). People lived in small, widely separated villages of up to 500 people, sometimes in large communal houses *(malocas).* The bow and arrow was the most common weapon. Dugout canoes provided river transport, while an impressive array of implements of wood, stone, basketry, and pottery were used in food processing. Cotton was used to make hammocks and clothing, while colorful plumes were made into elaborate headdresses and other ornaments. Diverse regional culture patterns, or culture areas, can be distinguished based on variations in material culture and details of social organization and religion, but the broad pattern is the same.

Rain Forest Gardening and Manioc Processing

Manioc production, the key to successful human occupation of Amazonia, depends on a specialized

(b)

(a)

FIGURE 3.3 Shifting cultivation in Amazonia: (a) an Ashá-ninka mother and child rest in the shade in a newly cleared swidden; (b) an Asháninka man plants manioc cuttings.

system of shifting cultivation that minimally disrupts the forest ecosystem. It is the forest that ultimately maintains soil quality, regulates the local climate, recycles nutrients and water, and sustains fish and game resources. With shifting cultivation, as still practiced by native peoples throughout Amazonia, food is harvested from small, temporary forest clearings containing mixed gardens.

In comparison with the large monocrop farms and plantations that have recently been introduced in Amazonia for commercial purposes, native gardens, or *swiddens,* rely on a diverse mix of crops. The overlapping layers of different plant species minimize erosion and losses to insects and disease while making efficient use of the space. Sweet potato vines and beans quickly cover the ground, then are shaded by maize and manioc, which in turn are shaded by bananas and various fruit trees.

This gardening system is sometimes called **slash and burn** because it is based on an apparently simple technology of cutting the forest, and then burning the dry slash (Figure 3.3). The burn is usually incomplete, and many trees survive and quickly regrow. Some wild plants may even be deliberately protected. The burning concentrates nutrients in the ash, thus eliminating the need for additional fertilizer. Unburned logs provide an easy source of wood for cooking fires.

Shifting cultivation requires a great deal of specialized knowledge, which has an elaborate vocabulary. Native Amazonians distinguish several different types of soil and forest, and they take

slash and burn A farming technique in which forest is cleared and burned to enrich the soil for planting; a forest fallow system depending on forest regrowth. Also called *swidden cultivation.*

TABLE 3.2 MATSIGENKA SUBSISTENCE PER HOUSEHOLD PER YEAR

	Production		Energy Cost	Subsistence
	(kg)	(%)	(kcal/kg)	Effort (%)
Gardening*	6755	93	80	55
Fishing	298	4	740	22
Hunting/ gathering	194	3	1151	22
Total	7247	100	1971	99

SOURCE: Johnson and Behrens (1982).
*Manioc alone = 4887 kg, or 67 percent of total production weight.

into account the special characteristics of each when selecting a garden site. Because many varieties of manioc require more than six months to produce large tubers, manioc must be grown on land that is not seasonally flooded; thus, manioc gardens cannot take advantage of the annually renewed alluvial soils along the major rivers. Gardens typically are about an acre in size. Although they are seldom carefully tended for more than one year, they may yield manioc for up to three years. New gardens might be made each year, so that at a given time every household has gardens at different stages of production. In this **forest fallow system,** a plot usually would not be replanted for at least twenty-five years to allow ample time for forest regrowth. Actually, full forest regrowth might require fifty to one hundred years or more, but as long as gardens remain small and widely scattered, a twenty-five-year cycle can adequately protect the forest. Shifting cultivation works well under tribal conditions, but when commercial agriculture invades tribal areas, large-scale corporate owners may displace subsistence cultivators, pushing them into marginal areas where they are forced to shorten the fallow cycle. Under these conditions shifting cultivation cannot be sustained, and people and lands are impoverished.

Native peoples prefer the forest fallow system to more intensive cultivation for several reasons. Gardens are abandoned in part because rapid forest regrowth makes weeding a burdensome task. In most forest soils, continuous replanting would soon lead to a decline in fertility and yield. Reclearing of old garden sites is avoided because, during the early stages of forest succession, the vegetation is very dense and difficult to clear with hand tools. Village sites themselves may be shifted every few years to reduce conflict or to find better hunting ground.

The productivity of manioc is truly impressive and readily explains its importance in the subsistence system. A single garden belonging to an Asháninka household in the Peruvian Amazon potentially could produce some 30,000 pounds of manioc in a year. This is more than double the household's consumption requirements and disregards replanting. Such apparent overproduction provides an important security margin. Other researchers found that the nearby Matsigenka people obtained more than two-thirds of their food by weight from manioc, which was produced at roughly 10 percent of the labor cost by weight of food produced by hunting, foraging, and fishing (Table 3.2). The recent use of metal axes has no doubt increased the relative advantage of manioc by making tree felling easier, but even with stone tools, manioc cultivation would have been very attractive. The Matsigenka allocated just over half of their total subsistence effort to gardening, which produced over 90 percent of their total food by weight (Johnson and Behrens 1982). But manioc alone does not provide an adequate diet, so the Matsigenka raise a dozen other important crops and cultivate some eighty named plant varieties for various purposes (Johnson 1983).

Most Amazonians grow a dozen or more varieties of manioc, carefully distinguishing them based on characteristics of tuber and leaf. The Kuikuru

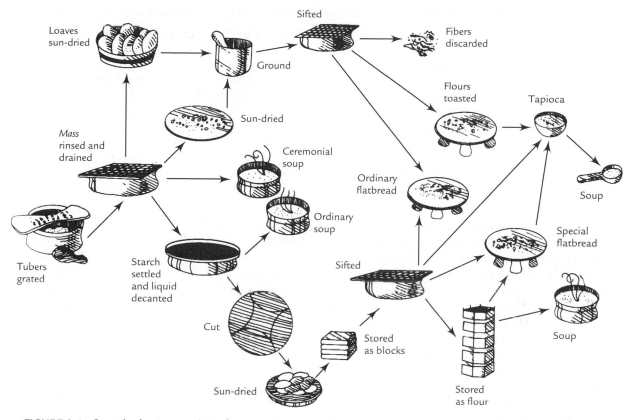

FIGURE 3.4 Steps in the preparation of manioc among the Kuikuru.
(SOURCE: Adapted from Dole 1978.)

on the upper Xingu River in Brazil can name 46 manioc varieties, while the Aguaruna and Huambisa of Peru recognize more than 100 (Boster 1983, Carneiro 1983). Such diversity suggests that long-term selective breeding is taking place.

All manioc tubers contain potentially toxic substances. In "sweet" varieties, they can be eliminated merely by peeling and cooking, but the "bitter" varieties require more elaborate processing. The quality of the starch in bitter manioc is especially suitable for flour, which is made by an elaborate, labor-intensive process of squeezing, sifting, and roasting the grated pulp. The Waiwai of Guyana have developed at least fourteen types of bread and fourteen beverages based on bitter manioc and its by-products (Yde 1965). The flour may be sifted in various ways, baked

in bread, toasted, or used in soups and stews. The juice is used directly in soups, and there are several uses for the tapioca starch extracted from the juice (Figure 3.4).

Manioc may be stored in the ground until it is used, or it may be stored as processed flour or bread as long as it is kept dry. Potentially, it could provide an important **surplus** that could help support a political-scale society, but as will be shown, a variety of other factors—both cultural and ecological—keep this surplus only potential.

forest fallow system A system of cultivation in which soil nutrients are restored by allowing the forest to regrow.
surplus Subsistence production that exceeds the needs of the producer households and that is extracted by political leaders to support nonfood-producing specialists.

Village Size Limits: Gardens, Protein, or Autonomy?

It is a striking fact that rain forest villages usually remain small, averaging less than 100 people and seldom exceeding 300 people. These villages are relatively impermanent, as villagers relocate every few years. Anthropologists often have assumed that environmental factors in Amazonia must set upper limits on village size.

Although environmental factors do have a limiting effect, they cannot fully account for the small size of Amazonian villages. The most obvious natural environmental factors limiting the size and density of human populations in Amazonia are the productivity of soils and gardens and the availability of animal protein. There are two broad ecosystems in the Amazon that offer very different biological potentials: the main Amazon River, with its floodplains and oxbow lakes, and the interior forests. Before Europeans arrived in 1542, the banks of the Amazon River were annually enriched by deposits of waterborne (alluvial) soil, and there were abundant fish, manatees, caimans, and turtles. Prehistorically, the main Amazon flood plain supported dense permanent villages that often exceeded 500 people and were organized into politically centralized chiefdoms. These societies were quickly destroyed by European colonists, whereas the tribal villagers hidden in the interior upland forests survived.

The forests, and smaller or less productive river systems supported fewer people, at lower densities, and less permanent villages, but these smaller-scale tribal societies were not smaller simply because the environment limited growth. Robert Carneiro (1960) demonstrated that manioc gardening produced such abundant carbohydrate that it could easily support villages of 500 people, even with shifting cultivation, as long as people could get the 50 grams of protein they needed per capita daily from fish and game (see the box entitled "Carrying-Capacity Calculations"). In fact, the protein intake of tribal Amazonians typically exceeded this minimum (Gross 1975). Furthermore, it appears that wild game might theoretically support human densities as high as one person per square kilometer, and even more if fish and edible insects are included. However, actual tribal densities were much lower than this. The Asháninka averaged only 0.4 persons/km^2, suggesting that the size, density, and permanence of human settlements in the Amazon were also determined by cultural factors such as beliefs about what constituted the good life.

Apparently, villages could be larger throughout Amazonia if people were willing to either hunt and fish more intensively, rely more on plant protein, maintain domestic animals, or accept a nutritionally lower standard of living and/or the higher levels of political authority that such changes might require. Cultural factors connected with the advantages of domestic-scale society encourage people to halt gardening, hunting, and fishing production at levels well below what would be theoretically sustainable. Cultural preferences for large game animals, maximum leisure, and household-level autonomy seem to be more important objectives than supporting the largest possible villages. It seems that the tropical forest village way of life offers Amazonian peoples sufficient personal satisfactions that they choose to maintain and reproduce it as long as they have enough personal freedom to make that choice. This suggests that the transformation of the tribal world first into the imperial and then into the commercial world involved a loss of human freedom in the sense that the range of lifestyle choices became much narrower.

Biodiversity and Ethnoecological Knowledge

One evening, I loaned my portable tape recorder to a small group of Asháninka who were visiting my camp. They immediately created a word game in which they excitedly passed the microphone back and forth until the tape was filled with a steady stream of Asháninka words. They were spontaneously reciting a seemingly endless list of animal names, playing with their working knowledge of rain forest biological diversity. The Asháninka not only knew the names of the animals but understood many details of their natural history and imbued many species with rich cultural significance. Biological diversity is the foundation on which the Asháninka way of life depends. They are, in effect, treating biodiversity as natural capital; it is their investment in the future. In contrast, in our commercial-scale culture, we relegate biological diversity to the concern of a handful of specialized ecologists, biologists, and industrial technicians. We also make biodiversity a commercial product to be bought and sold for private gain, and in policy debates we wonder if we can "afford" to maintain natural diversity in parks and nature preserves as a public good where it does not produce direct monetary profits.

I later found that the Asháninka's knowledge of rain forest animals was matched by their knowledge of useful cultivated plants. I found dozens of named varieties of manioc and bananas in Asháninka gardens. This genetic diversity was produced without the incentive of commercial markets or tax-supported research grants. People experimented with new varieties and were eager to discuss their different qualities. Most adults in these domestic-scale cultures can readily name 500–1000 plants, whereas few urban Americans are likely to know more than 50–100.

The breadth of indigenous knowledge of Amazonian biodiversity also is indicated by the detailed work of Berkeley anthropologists Brent and Elois Berlin (1983), who collected 875 animal names from the Jivaroan-speaking peoples near the Ecuadorean border. Carneiro (1978a) elicited 187 tree identifications from the Kuikuru in Brazil and obtained 45 named trees in a 0.17-acre (0.07-hectare) tract and 43 plants from a 10-foot^2 (0.9-m^2) tract. He even found that the Kuikuru could identify 45 plant varieties based on the decomposing leaves collected from 1 foot^2 (0.09 m^2) of forest floor. They also had an intimate understanding of the relationships between specific animals and specific plants.

It is hardly surprising that rain forest peoples are interested in biological diversity, because it is the very source of their existence. In 1976–1977, I documented some thirty-five species of forest palm trees that the Shipibo in Peru used to produce roofs, floors, and walls for houses, as well as basketry, bows and arrows, foodstuffs, and cosmetics (Bodley and Benson 1979). In the 1960s, I visited isolated Asháninka household groups that, with the exception of a few metal pots, knives, and axes, were entirely self-sufficient, drawing all that they needed from the forest and their gardens. They made their own houses, food, medicine, and clothing directly from the raw materials that they personally extracted from their local environment. The important point about Asháninka self-sufficiency is that they live well. They are well fed, comfortably housed and clothed, healthy, and self-confident. They are not impoverished and do not need to be "developed." Like many indigenous peoples, they secure most of their livelihood directly from the biological diversity that they produce and maintain.

Rain Forest Affluence

Amazonian villages clearly demonstrate some striking advantages of life in tribal societies. The villagers have developed an equitably balanced subsistence system. Men do the heavy work of garden clearing in seasonally concentrated bursts of effort, and women carry out the bulk of routine cultivation, harvesting, and food processing. Men, women, and children forage for wild plant food, insects, and small animals. Everyone may join large-scale fishing expeditions, but men provide most of the daily animal protein by hunting and fishing. Meat and fish are pooled and distributed to each household in the village to smooth out the variation in productivity between households. All of these activities are individually directed, and everyone controls the necessary tools. There are no inequalities here.

This production system guarantees that each household can meet its nutritional needs with relatively moderate work loads while maintaining a reasonable labor balance between the sexes. It also provides strong incentives for maintaining low population densities because, as densities

Carrying-Capacity Calculations: Manioc Starch Versus Animal Protein

Robert Carneiro devised a formula to specify the critical variables that determine the maximum size of a village as limited by the productivity of manioc under shifting cultivation (Figure 3.A). The amount of arable land is set by the maximum distance women choose to carry produce from the garden—usually about 3 miles (5 km), yielding 18,000 acres (7290 hectares). Assuming Carneiro's modest figure of 13,350 acres (5468 hectares) of arable land, gardens cultivated for 3 years, and a 25-year fallow, a village of 2043 people could meet its manioc needs without ever moving. This is more than six times the observed upper limit for Amazonian villages. Extending the fallow to 100 years would reduce the potential size of the village to 561 people, still well above average for Amazonia. These figures demonstrate that manioc shortages do not limit village size.

Village size limits based on the productivity of rain forest hunting are more difficult to estimate because we do not have accurate figures for game populations. Figure 3.B lists some of the variables that must be taken into account, along with a formula for calculating the number of people who theoretically could obtain

FIGURE 3.A A formula for environmental limits on gardening on Amazonian villagers. (SOURCE: Carneiro 1960.)

Basic Formula:

$$P = \frac{[T/(R + Y)]Y}{A}$$

Where P = village population, T = arable land, R = years in forest fallow, Y = years garden cultivated, and A = garden area per person.

If T = 13,350 acres, R = 25 yr, Y = 3 yr, and A = .7 acres, then P = 2043 people.

If R = 100 yr, then P = 561 people.

increase, work loads quickly accelerate due to game depletion and the increasing distances that women must walk to their gardens. Work loads also would be increased dramatically if people needed to produce food to support the nonfood-producing specialists, who inevitably accompany increases in societal scale. Thus, an incentive to maintain social equality is also the foundation of domestic-scale societies.

Subsistence work loads in Amazonia are not significantly different from those reported earlier for Australian aborigines. In both cases, there is abundant leisure time. On average, all food pro-

duction needs can be met with just two to three hours of work a day (Bergman 1974, Flowers 1983, Johnson 1975, Lizot 1977, Werner 1983). Men average about three hours and women about two hours. Total work loads, including everything that must be done around the house, require only five to seven hours daily and would be unlikely to exceed eight hours. This means that if the workday begins at six AM, with the equatorial sunrise, one can possibly spend the whole afternoon lounging in a hammock.

These figures must be interpreted with caution because they were collected by different research-

2 ounces (50 g) of protein from game per year per 0.4 mile² (1 km²) on a sustained basis. The most critical value is the *biomass* (the total weight of biological organisms living in a given area) of the game, but this can be estimated based on zoological surveys of rain forest mammals (Eisenburg and Thorington 1973, Walsh and Gannon 1967), allowing for cultural definitions of edibility, technology, and sustainability. These calculations predict a potential village size remarkably close to that seen ethnographically. The high estimate for biomass suggests that up to 300 people could supply their protein needs within a 6 mile (10 km) hunting radius of a permanent village.

Basic Formula: $P = \dfrac{BHSCN}{R}$

P = Persons per square kilometer. B = Biomass of mammals per square kilometer of forest. H = Hunted mammals (proportion of mammal biomass hunted annually). S – Sustainable Harvest (proportion of hunted biomass sustainably harvested, allowing for the low reproductive rate of rain forest mammals). C – Carcass (proportion of sustainable harvest in dressed carcass). N = Protein (proportion of protein in kilograms of dressed carcass). R = Protein required per person per year.

If B – 5300 kg/km², H – .43, S – .10, C – .50, N = .16, and R = 50 g × 365 days = 18 kg, then P – 1 person/km².

Therefore, a 10-km hunting radius covering an area of 314 km² supports 314 people.

FIGURE 3.B A formula for estimating the number of people who could be supported by hunting within a 6-mile (10-km) radius of a rain forest village.

ers who did not always classify activities in the same way. Some researchers did not regard child care as work. There is also the basic problem of the cross-cultural validity of the concept of "work." For example, should hunting, which is often an exciting and enjoyable activity, be considered work? Researchers also used different techniques for recording time expenditures.

Johnson (1985) made a useful comparison of the work load of the Matsigenka, which is heavy by Amazonian standards, with the way modern urban French people spend their time (considering women working both in and outside the

home). He showed that although both the Matsigenka and the French get about eight hours of sleep a night, the Matsigenka work about two hours less a day than the French to satisfy their basic needs. The Matsigenka have fewer other demands on their time than the French and enjoy five hours more of free time a day, which they spend resting and visiting. Data such as these tend to confirm the idea of affluence in tribal societies, lending credibility to the early reports from frustrated colonial plantation owners that Native Amazonians were "lazy" and hated to work. In fact, they do work, but only until their needs are satisfied, and their society is structured so that no one works for an overlord.

It would be a mistake to view these systems as underdeveloped technological stages that will inevitably evolve into something better. These are already highly developed systems that elegantly solve the problems posed for them. They would be difficult to improve upon, given their culturally defined objective of equitably meeting the physical needs of small communities.

Workloads are kept low in village Amazonia both by the limited demand on food production in a system where each household is basically self-sufficient in food, but also by the limited range of material culture that people produce, own, and maintain. The Asháninka make only about 120 separately named material items apart from food products (Weiss 1975). This list includes a full range of domestic articles such as the house (Figure 3.5), and tools for hunting, gardening, fishing, and trapping; food processing implements such as grinders, ceramic pots, baskets, strainers, trays, gourd containers, pounders, stirrers, grills; looms and spindles; clothing and adornments such as robes, headdresses, necklaces, bandoliers, pendants, face paint, combs, and depilators; and toys and musical instruments such as drums, flutes, and panpipes. Only about a dozen additional industrially manufactured items are imported, most importantly metal knives, axes, needles, and pots, but these things can usually be obtained by trade. This is all the material culture needed to maintain the Asháninka good life on the fringes of the commercial world. This is a substantially richer list of things than possessed by Australian aborigines, and reflects the more sedentary lifestyle of the Amazon villagers, but it is far less than the thousands of material items possessed by households fully dependent on the commercial world and its products.

Every Asháninka adult owns all the basic tools needed for daily life and has free access to all necessary natural resources. Because they pay no taxes and do not need money to buy anything, the Asháninka are free to devote 70 percent of their productive time to hunting, foraging, gardening,

cleaning, bathing, food preparation, childcare, and eating to satisfy all their direct household and personal requirements. Their remaining productive time is evenly divided, 15 percent to making domestic material goods and 15 percent to maintaining their social connections and reproducing their culture through visiting, feasting, singing and dancing, and storytelling.

Affluence depends on wealth. Given the richness of the tropical forest ecosystem, it would be reasonable to estimate that most of Asháninka wealth is in nature, because as with Australian aborigines, nature's services provide most of their material needs. The rest of their wealth is in the value of the human effort invested in their households, their individually owned stock of material culture, and the shared value of their society and culture. Considering their time expenditures, and allowing for depreciation and maintenance, an average Asháninka household has perhaps 80 percent of its social and cultural wealth in people, 15 percent in society and intangible culture, and only 5 percent in material culture.

VILLAGE LIFE IN AMAZONIA: DOMESTIC SOCIAL POWER

Village life in tribal Amazonia is characterized by great diversity in social organizational details, but the overall pattern is for households to be highly self-reliant, and for individuals to enjoy high degrees of personal autonomy. The crucial importance of kinship relationships in everyday village life would be no surprise to a visiting Australian aborigine, who would even find the Asháninka using the same system of kinship categories as their own, and practicing cross-cousin marriage just as in Australia. An aborigine would readily understand Amazonian beliefs and practices concerning the supernatural world of spirit beings. Gardening and sedentary village life would show the most striking differences, but these cultural practices would not alter the fundamental freedoms and independence that define life in the

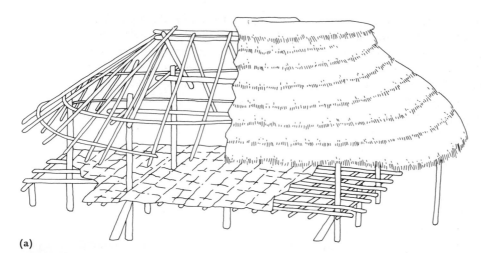

FIGURE 3.5 An Asháninka house. Each household usually occupies a single palm leaf–thatched house constructed of posts and beams, with slats peeled from palm trunks as flooring: (a) construction details; (b) a photograph of the house in the diagram.

(a)

(b)

tribal world for both Australian foragers and Amazonian villagers.

Among villagers, interpersonal conflict and tension are always just beneath the surface in the struggle between self-interest and the demands of society, but daily life seems harmonious, and, overall, people appear to be content. Many Amazonian peoples like the Asháninka and their

Matsigenka neighbors maximize individual freedom by living in very small settlements of twenty-five to fifty or fewer people, sometimes in only a single isolated family. These small groups resemble Australian bands, but they can be more sedentary because high garden productivity makes individual households more self-sufficient than if they relied entirely on foraging. In comparison with those living in very small villages, those like the Mundurucú, who live in larger villages of up to a hundred people, can enjoy a more intense social life. They can defend themselves more easily against hostile neighbors, but the daily presence of more people makes internal conflict more likely.

In comparison with politically organized chiefdoms, where 500 to 1,000 people or more may live in a single settlement, all Amazon tribal peoples conduct their daily affairs in a small scale, face-to-face society, where inherited rank and social classes are conspicuously absent. Small-scale residential units are favored by relatively peaceful conditions and by the cultural fact that wealth in tribal Amazonia, as in Australia, is primarily held as natural capital in publically owned nature, rather than as individual moveable property, or permanent structures. Control over material wealth does not give anyone greater social power. Under these conditions adults do not need rulers and government to protect their property, and they can focus their energies on the everyday practical problems of managing and enlarging their households. Given low population densities, there are only a few dozen other men that even the most powerful big men could possibly command, and except for orphans, or especially lazy or very unfortunate men, other men are all too self-reliant to be forced to comply with the demands of any bigman.

The most frequent and intense expressions of social power in Asháninka and Matsigenka households occur in interactions between husband and wife, between co-wives, between parents and children, and among siblings (Allen Johnson 2003: 152–159). The daily substance of family life involves people using their authority or respect to get others to do things for them, or they respond to others by being either supportive or unsupportive. In this context, social power is largely expressed through entitlements defined by age, gender, and relative kinship status. Infants are entitled to nurture from their mothers. Husbands are entitled to cooked food, beer, and clothing from their wives, and wives are entitled to a house, a cleared garden site, and meat from their husbands. As in Australia, there are power asymmetries between

men and women, and young and old, but when individuals behave properly the household can prosper. This kind of social power is neither exploitation nor oppression. Infants generally get what they want, but when they grow older and throw tantrums to gain inappropriate support they are ignored (Allen Johnson 2003:96–113). Noncompliance between adults, as in adulterous affairs, can be countered with threats, blows, or withdrawal of support. Unrestrained self-seeking in food and sex or lack of support are always potential sources of anger and conflict within the household.

Beyond the household, there are no permanent leaders with the authority to command other people against their will. Leaders are coordinators, distinguished by their generosity and public service. All adults are expected to share food and possessions, help others perform common tasks, socialize by feasting and partying, arrange marriages, and confront enemies, but more public service is expected from the most respected individuals heading the largest households. Inequalities can be measured by the number of wives, children, and other dependents in different households. Larger households are likely to receive more visitors, exchange food and labor with more households, and host more feasts, and of course their male heads are likely to be "big men" who father more children than less successful men (Allen Johnson 2003:177–184). However, such opportunities for personal success are technically available to every man, subject only to the vagaries of individual fortune and personal ability. The social power of successful big men peaks and quickly declines as they age, and is not automatically transmitted to any of their children. Women build networks of personal power through their husbands, junior co-wives, and kin. Both men and women may have supernatural spirit helpers.

Domestic Residence, Kinship, and Descent in Amazonia

Local settlements in Amazonia also resemble the bands of Australian aborigines in that both are usually exogamous groups. Because rain forest villages are frequently moved, individual houses and landholdings are not inherited. Ordinarily, gardens are only owned by those who clear and cultivate them until they are abandoned to the forest. In addition, sacred sites are not typically owned, Australian style, by **descent groups.** Typically, there are no named kinship-based **unilineal descent groups** in Amazonia such as clans, based on remote ancestors, or lineages with membership assigned by descent from mother or father and known ancestors (see the box entitled "Domestic Residence and Descent Groups in Amazonia"). Descent groups are corporate groups whose existence continues beyond the life of any individual member, but they are very uncommon in Amazonian societies, which are often highly individualistic. The Mundurucú, who have clans and moieties, are a notable exception and are discussed below. Societies that do not have descent groups are said to have *bilateral* descent and ego-based **kindreds.** The kindred is the network of family members and relatives that individuals in all human societies recognize. Kindreds form overlapping networks and are unique to each individual and their full siblings. Nearly three quarters of Amazonian societies are organized bilaterally by kindreds (Table 3.3). Genealogical reckoning is shallow and even discouraged in such societies by frequent taboos on speaking the names of dead ancestors. This prevents the emergence of ancestor cults and invidious ranking of descent lines that are the ideological foundations of the inherited status of chiefs, kings, and emperors in the imperial world. The result is a highly egalitarian social system that encourages easy access to natural resources. Larger social groups often are named after rivers, but territories frequently overlap and generally seem much more flexible than in Australia.

Life in houses has the potential to change the relationships among people and between people and place. Mobile foragers are likely to be socially more open than sedentary villagers, because the privacy of houses creates a potentially closed society in which suspicion can thrive and a social hierarchy can arise. The house itself can be treated metaphorically in the cosmology as the foundation for ancestor cults, tombs, and hierarchical descent groups. However, except for the chiefdoms along the Amazon itself, most native Amazonians have not taken this route. The communal *maloca* (large common household) certainly minimizes household privacy, and the requirements of rain forest hunting and shifting horticulture make hierarchical organization distinctly unattractive. Native Amazonians clearly prefer low-density, domestic-scale societies and minimize the disadvantages of domesticated society.

Men and Women in the Mundurucú Village

Gender roles are critical for understanding how rain forest cultures work because age and sex, not wealth and class, are the primary differences between people in these tribal cultures. The Mundurucú illustrate how the antagonisms between men and women are played out in the daily life of village cultures in Brazilian Amazonia. In 1953, anthropologists Yolanda and Robert Murphy spent a year with 350 Mundurucú, who lived in small villages of 50–100 people in the savannas and forests of the upper tributaries of the Tapajos River (Murphy and Murphy 1974). As a husband and wife team, the Murphys could observe Mundurucú culture from both sexes' viewpoint.

The world of Mundurucú men and women is sharply divided. Men are primarily hunters, although they also do the heavy work of garden clearing. Women cultivate, harvest, and process bitter manioc. Mundurucú men assume public roles, which is symbolically reflected in the physical structure of the village. Adult males and older boys sleep communally and spend much of their time in the *eksa*, an open-walled men's house, whereas all females and young boys sleep in individual, close-walled domestic houses.

descent group A social group based on genealogical connections to a common ancestor.

unilineal descent group Membership based on descent traced through a line of ancestors of one sex to a common ancestor.

kindred Ego-based, overlapping network that includes all of an individual's relatives.

Domestic Residence and Descent Groups in Amazonia

When descent groups in the form of clans or lineages are advantageous, people can construct them out of the spatial alignments produced when a newly married couple chooses to live near the husband's or wife's parents, either patrilocal, or matrilocal, respectively (Murdock 1949). Figure 3.C illustrates the domestic groupings that are created by patrilocality and matrilocality. Patrilocality and matrilocality create de facto patrilineages and matrilineages, respectively. There are also interesting cases, such as the Mundurucú, in which residence matrilocality occurs with patrilineal descent groups.

In Amazonia, the emphasis on manioc gardening seems to encourage matrilocal residence patterns, in which a husband lives with or near his wife's family. This may be because mothers, daughters, and sisters often form cooperative work groups when gardening, processing manioc, or making ceramics. More than 80 percent (31) of a sample of 37 Amazonian societies either are listed as matrilocal (17) or show matrilocality as a temporary or alternative pattern (14) (Table 3.3). With temporary matrilocality, a newly married couple will remain near the wife's mother until after their first child is born so that the new mother has help from her mother and the new husband can perform bride-service. The high frequency of patrilocality may be related to the occurrence of revenge raiding in Amazonia, which makes it advantageous for closely related men to remain close together.

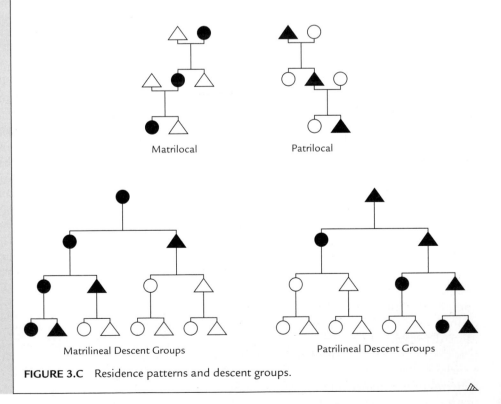

FIGURE 3.C   Residence patterns and descent groups.

TABLE 3.3   RESIDENCE AND DESCENT IN AMAZONIA

| Residence | Descent | | | |
	Patrilineal	Matrilineal	Bilateral	Total
Patrilocality	6	0	10	16
Matrilocality	2	2	13	17
Other	0	0	4	4
Total	8	2	27	37

SOURCE: Murdock (1981).

As is common in Australian aboriginal society, the Mundurucú are divided into exogamous moieties. Mundurucú moieties are color-coded "red" and "white," and membership in them is allocated through males. People marry their **cross-cousins,** who belong to opposite moieties. The moieties are subdivided into 38 patrilineal clans (16 red, 22 white), each with an animal founder, like the Australian Dreaming ancestors. Clan loyalties are strong, and ancestral spirits are symbolically present in sacred flutes, which are hidden in the men's house. The potential for intervillage conflict is reduced by the Mundurucú practice of **matrilocality,** which contrasts significantly with the patrilocality of Australian aborigines. Matrilocality requires that a young man, who must marry outside of his clan and moiety, leave his own village and move into the men's house in his new wife's village. The result is that village residence crosscuts clan loyalties such that the men of a given village, who cooperate daily, are unlikely to fight their fellow clansmen in another village.

According to the Murphys, men consider themselves to be the superior sex, and they frequently draw on symbolic support for this position, but the women reject this male understanding. The entire mythic charter for the male view is enshrined in the central myth of the phallic sacred flutes. The myth tells how women originally possessed mysterious flutes that reversed normal gender roles. As long as women had the flutes, they occupied the men's house, relegating the men to the domestic houses to cook, carry water and

firewood, and be seduced by aggressive women. The downfall for the women was that the flutes demanded meat, but only men could hunt. Eventually, the men grew impatient with this arrangement and threatened to stop hunting, thereby forcing the women to surrender the flutes and restoring normal gender roles. The myth explains why men are both sexually and publicly dominant. Men are superior to women—not because they are inherently superior, but because gender roles differ and male hunting is culturally the most important gender role. Hunting and meat are thus crucially important for understanding Amazonian cultures.

The sacred flute myth highlights a central human problem: Men are sexually attracted to women and physically dependent on them, but they fear their power. Patrilineality gives men rights over the status of children, but only women can produce children. The myth suggests that men know their vulnerability and must constantly assert themselves, or women will overcome them. The mythic flutes are symbolically embodied in four-foot-long hollow wooden tubes, which are stored and regularly played in the men's house. Sometimes the flutes are paraded about the village, but the women are never supposed to view them; women who do see them can expect to be

cross-cousin The son or daughter of one's mother's brother or father's sister, and often considered to be in a marriageable category.

matrilocality Residence near the wife's kin, normally near her parents.

gang raped. The flutes reinforce the male role in patrilineality and hunting because they contain the spirits of the *patriclan* (a named descent group with membership assigned through male lines), and they must be offered meat. The phallic symbolism of the flutes is explicitly recognized by the Mundurucú, and men openly joke about penis power and vaginas with teeth.

Mundurucú male dominance is a male ideology of gender roles. Publicly, women remain in the background, actively maintaining their separation from men, but in practical terms, they have real power in their daily lives. Regardless of male ideology, Mundurucú women are in charge of their **households.** Each house contains a single cooking hearth to serve an **extended family,** with twenty to twenty-five people in four to five **nuclear families.** Senior women direct household activities and control food distribution, handing out both manioc and meat. Given matrilocality, households are centered predominantly on sisters, mothers, and daughters. Kin ties between women are very strong and are expressed in the question, "How would a girl manage without her mother to help her?" (Murphy and Murphy 1974:122). Thus, women are likely to be supported by close kin in any domestic struggle. Women also gain solidarity by routinely working together in the manioc processing shed. Women carry out all their daily activities in groups, because a woman alone is assumed to be sexually available. Thus, women are effectively united in their resistance to male ideological domination.

The Mundurucú women questioned Yolanda Murphy about her daily home life (Murphy and Murphy 1974:219). Recognizing the apparent social isolation of American women, they asked, "But if you don't go with the other women to get water and to bathe, aren't you lonely?" Yolanda responded, "Yes, we are."

Although in Mundurucú society the nuclear family is not the primary domestic unit, marriage and nuclear families perpetuate moieties, clans, and the kinship roles that structure everything. The Asháninka of the Peruvian Amazon provide an example of the specific kinship categories that are functionally connected to simple moiety systems and cross-cousin marriage, which are so common in domestic-scale cultures (see the box entitled "The Basics of Asháninka Society and Kinship").

The Headman and Village Politics: Society Against the State

One of the most distinctive features of tribal cultures is the way they preclude any concentration of political power that might threaten the autonomy of households and communities. Village leaders serve the people and are granted no undue power. Christopher Boehm (1993) calls this distinctive political arrangement in tribal cultures a **reverse dominance hierarchy.**

The largest local settlement in Amazonia is a politically autonomous unit, even if it contains only twenty-five people. Political autonomy in this context means that villagers can move the village whenever they choose, can kill intruders, and can control their natural resources. Given exogamy, there cannot be complete village autonomy, because spouses must be drawn from other settlements. A leader, or **headman,** often is recognized and may even be called a "chief" by outsiders, but his authority is extremely limited. A headman's responsibilities increase with the size of the village, but normally he is a powerless coordinator who formally announces what everyone had already decided to do, such as clean the village plaza or begin a group fishing expedition. Such a headman cannot force anyone to do anything against his or her will.

As the French ethnologist Pierre Clastres (1977) observed, an Amazon village is essentially a "society against the state" in that it is designed to prevent the concentration of political power that would allow anyone to gain control of the economy for his own benefit. In some respects, the headman is held hostage by the community. He is granted a certain degree of privileged status, often indicated by polygyny, which is more likely to be practiced by a headman. But he also frequently works harder than everyone else and is denied real power. Polygyny is not an exclusive prerogative of headmen and should not be construed as payment for the headman's leadership services. Rather, it is a requirement of the job because more wives are needed to help brew the extra manioc beer expected from a generous headman. Society is not paying for his services, but he can hold his position only as long as he serves the community. As Claude Lévi-Strauss (1944) described it, leadership in this system is its own reward, and only a few would take on the responsibility.

A good headman must be a good public speaker and be especially generous, giving things away on request, but he is not distinguished by special dress or insignias of office. The importance of the headman's oratorial skills further shows that he cannot use coercive violence. He must be verbally persuasive at settling intravillage conflicts; but if he fails as a peacemaker, the village simply breaks apart. Society's refusal to grant political power to the headman may be the most critical limit on the size of villages in Amazonia. Amazonian political organization relates to game resources because disputes over meat distribution increase as villages become larger. When a headman's powers are limited to verbal persuasion, he may be unable to keep the peace in a community larger than 200–300 people.

Janet Siskind (1973) argued that the underlying source of village conflict is the shortage of game and the related competition between village men for access to women, which in the absence of a powerful headman can lead to village fragmentation. Sexual competition is intensified by the relative scarcity of women created by exogamy and by even a limited practice of polygyny. Throughout Amazonia, hunting success is equated with virility, and the successful hunter can support wives and lovers through gifts of meat. Successful hunters also have free time to engage in infidelities while less skilled hunters are still in the forest. This leads to conflict, and villages break apart before potentially irreversible game depletion sets in (Figure 3.6). When game is really abundant, Siskind argued, individual differences in hunting abilities are less prominent, and men may turn to raiding other villages

to capture women. Successful raiding would increase village size, raise the pressure on hunters, and result in village fragmentation.

The Spirit World: Sexual Symbols, Shamans, and Forest Demons

The Amazonian equivalent of the Australian Dreaming is found in a rich body of myth, beliefs, and ritual practices that, like the Dreaming, help people answer basic questions about the meaning of life and death, the origin of things, how people should behave, and the relationship between nature and culture. Amazonian cosmology also helps people deal with their reasonable fears that uncontrolled self-seeking, lust, anger, and jealousy will destroy society. Their myths are conveyed in the colorful and entertaining stories that people share in the evening. These stories describe exciting encounters between people and supernatural beings, spirits, and demons in which thoughtless or greedy individuals do bad things, and as a consequence, are killed and eaten, transformed into monsters, or meet some other equally unpleasant fate. Amazon myths are not acted out in dramatic rituals as frequently as in Australia, but nevertheless they help sustain the moral order by demonstrating the horrible consequences of bad behavior. The cosmology also explains why people get sick, offers therapy, and provides routine procedures that help hunters, gardeners, and warriors feel more confident and be more successful

---

household A social unit that shares domestic activities such as food production, cooking, eating, and sleeping, often under one roof, and is usually based on the nuclear or extended family.

extended family A joint household based on a parent family and one or more families of its married children.

nuclear family The primary family unit of mother, father, and dependent children.

reverse dominance hierarchy System whereby the members of a village or community intentionally limit the power of leaders, keeping them subservient to the group will.

headman A political leader who coordinates group activities and is a village spokesman but who serves only with the consent of the community and has no coercive power.

The Basics of Asháninka Society and Kinship

Asháninka villages consist of a few individual houses—often only two and usually located in the same ridgetop clearing—occupied by closely related individual nuclear families (husband, wife, and dependent children). A village, or household group, is either an extended family or households connected by sibling ties (see Figure 3.D). Extended families are formed when married children reside near their parents, either matrilocally or patrilocally. Each married couple constitutes an independent domestic unit with its own kitchen hearth and garden, but there is daily economic cooperation between households, and fish and game are pooled. Household groups might be an hour's walk from any neighboring groups, but such groups might periodically socialize over manioc beer and sing and dance. They also might combine to form raiding parties.

The Asháninka recognize three categories of people: kin, formal trading partners, and strangers who are potential enemies. If friendly interaction is to take place, strangers are immediately placed in a kinship category and treated appropriately. For example, men who want to request a favor from me would address me as "brother." When they want to show deference, they call me "father-in-law."

The distinctive feature of the Asháninka kinship terminological system is that one's immediate kin are sorted into just two groups: (1) parents and siblings, and stepparents and stepsiblings, who are close family and thus not marriageable, and (2) those who are potential in-laws and spouses (Figure 3.E). As is common in Australian aboriginal society, one marries someone in the category of cross-cousin, and the parents of cross-cousins are called in-laws. Parallel cousins, the children of one's father's brother and mother's sister, are often treated as siblings, and their parents are treated like one's own parents.

Figure 3.F illustrates some of the actual terms that are used in one Asháninka language. Father is called *Pawa,* and one's father's brother is called *Pawachori,* which might be translated as "step" or "potential" father. *Pawachori* might, in fact, marry one's mother if one's father died (a practice known as the *levirate*), and his spouse would be called *Nanayni,* or mother's sister.

When an Asháninka man seeks a spouse, he must find someone whom he can call *Ingyayni,* or cross-cousin. The terms need not refer to actual biological relationships. Any unrelated woman might be placed in that category if everyone agrees, but this is an important decision because it has obvious sexual implications. A man's lover will almost certainly be called *Ingyayni.* The parents of someone called *Ingyayni* would be called *Kongki* and *Iyoeni* (in-laws). A husband would show respect for his in-laws and would be expected to work for them during the initial, often matrilocal, phase of his marriage.

Although the Asháninka kin system reflects cross-cousin marriage, it can also be characterized as a sibling-exchange system in which a brother and sister marry a brother and sister. Figure 3.G illustrates how the Asháninka terms accommodate both forms of marriage. Cross-cousin marriage could be conceptualized as the continuation of sibling exchanges in consecutive generations, and with the Asháninka, sibling-exchange marriages are more common than marriages of "biological" cross-cousins.

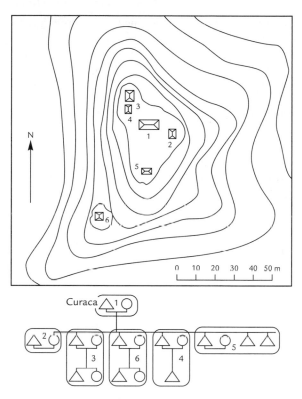

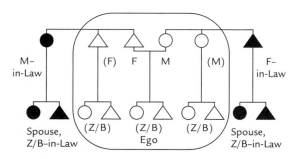

FIGURE 3.D Ground plan of an Asháninka extended-family household group situated on a ridgetop clearing. *Curaca* is the Quechua (Inca) term for headman. House numbers correspond to the circled household members in the genealogical diagram.

FIGURE 3.E Asháninka kinship system.

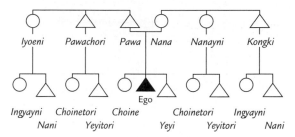

FIGURE 3.F Asháninka kinship terminology.

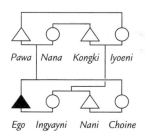

FIGURE 3.G Sibling-exchange marriages and cross-cousin marriages as reflected in Asháninka kinship terminology.

FIGURE 3.6 Zaparo hunter with White-lipped Peccary, Ecuadorean Amazon, 2002.

in relating to others in society. Supernatural beliefs do function to integrate society, as Radcliffe-Brown suggested, but they also serve important psychological functions that benefit individuals (Malinowski 1948).

In domestic-scale societies, there are no priests, no full-time professionals to formalize the belief system, and nothing codified in writing. And despite considerable fluidity in individual beliefs, there are underlying uniformities. E. B. Tylor (1871) called the unifying ideological theme **animism,** a belief in spirits. The spirit world is animated with human, animal, and plant souls and a wide variety of anthropomorphic beings with superhuman characteristics. These beings can intrude directly in the affairs of humans and control natural resources. Individuals may have personal spirit helpers, but **shamans** are the religious spe-

cialists who by training and self-selection, are particularly adept at communicating with the spirit world. Shamans may have especially powerful spirit helpers that allow them to perform remarkable supernatural feats, diagnose and cure illness, and harm enemies through sorcery. In the absence of centralized political authority, shamans often play a key role in the politics of village life by using their spirit power to enforce social control. Shamans can also use their supernatural powers to counterbalance the political power of village headmen.

Gertrude Dole (1964) provided a dramatic example of the political role of a Kuikuru shaman on the upper Xingu in central Brazil. When a house unexpectedly burned down, the villagers asked Metse, their most skilled shaman, to use spirit divination to determine the cause. Metse went into a tobacco-smoke-induced trance and announced that three mysterious strangers had started the fire with a flaming arrow, as the villagers suspected. He added that they were attempting to plant a magical lightning rod in his house in order to kill him. Remarkably, within three weeks Metse's house was struck by lightning. His house burned, and Metse was injured. Metse went into a trance again and accused another village's shaman of being the sorcerer responsible for the fires and the lightning attack. Shortly thereafter, a spontaneous avenging party ambushed and killed the accused shaman. It turned out that Metse's kinsmen had good reason to fear their victim, because the rival shaman had created resentment among the villagers after breaking an agreement to marry a local woman. People suspected him because the fire broke out in the woman's house as soon as Metse's younger brother had arranged to marry her. Given their belief in Metse's spirit powers, the villagers had little difficulty in accepting his interpretation of events, and they felt fully justified in killing a potentially dangerous sorcerer. The lightning strike enormously enhanced Metse's prestige as a powerful shaman.

The fear of being accused of sorcery is a powerful means of enforcing social control and strengthening kin ties in a small community. Behaving aggressively or doing anything that deviates from social norms can bring one under suspicion of sorcery. The shaman whom Metse accused not only had behaved inappropriately but also had little support in the village. His only brother was considered weak, and he had also left the village. Kin ties are critical because individuals who are surrounded by supportive kin rarely are accused of sorcery.

Amazonian ideology is part of a highly elaborate, logical, and consistent philosophy of life. Spirit beings normally are invisible, but they can assume visible form and freely transform from human to animal form and back again. In Asháninka thought, any unusual animal or otherwise unexplained event may be attributed to a spirit (Weiss 1975). The Asháninka recognize and name scores of specific spiritual entities; some include the souls of their own ancestors, which are ordinarily considered harmless. Malevolent spirit beings may appear as blue butterflies, tapirs, jaguars, hairy red humanoid dwarfs, or hoof-footed human impersonators. They are found in the deep forest, and they frequent whirlpools and rocky cliffs. Human contact with or even sight of malevolent spirit beings may cause illness or death.

A central feature in Amazonian cosmology is the theme that women in animal form were originally the possessors of culture, which was wrested from them by men who humanized them and took control of culture in the form of fire and cultivated plants. This theme is present in the Mundurucú myth of the sacred flutes and in related rituals. The entire cosmology is permeated by sexual antagonism; it is primarily a male construction, relegating women to a negative role, as in their symbolic association with sickness and death. The principal actors in the **myths** and their spirit representatives in the forest and rivers invariably are oversexed demons seeking to seduce people, especially vulnerable women. In their sexual natures people are also most like animals, so it is not surprising that sexual themes are projected onto animal-like supernatural beings. The sexual content of myths and symbols of course also makes them memorable, entertaining, and

readily reproduced, but uncontrolled sex, incest, and adultery are perpetual threats to the integrity of any society, and they both attract and repel people. Adultery is a common source of conflict in village life, but fear of supernatural sexual encounters must act as a powerful deterrent to such misbehavior (Allen Johnson 2003:98). For example, the Asháninka told me about a prominent local man who was seduced by a strange beautiful woman who entered his hunting blind in the forest. As he described it, she then turned into a tapir and ran away, and he realized that she was a demonic spirit and the encounter would almost certainly kill him. He came home, immediately fell ill, vomited green, and died. This tragic event was still so fresh in people's memories that several recalled it in precisely the same detail. Eventually the story would become an object lesson to be retold as myth.

Amazonian myths consistently focus on the cosmic issues of reproduction and fertility, the relationship between the sexes, the origin of culture, and illness and death. The dominant characters are drawn from especially powerful **natural symbols** found in the rain forest, such as the anaconda, jaguar, tapir, caiman, and harpy eagle (see the box entitled "An Anaconda Myth"). To introduce novelty, Amazonian storytellers might explore the classic themes using a complex series of character transformations based on logical chains of association that may depend on specific knowledge of the animal in question. For example,

animism A belief in spirits that occupy plants, animals, and people. Spirits are supernatural and normally invisible but may transform into different forms. Animism is considered by cultural evolutionists to be the simplest and earliest form of religion.

shaman A part-time religious specialist with special skills for dealing with the spirit world; may help his community by healing, by divination, and by directing supernatural powers against enemies.

myth A narrative that recounts the activities of supernatural beings. Often acted out in ritual, myths encapsulate a culture's cosmology and cosmogony and provide justification for culturally prescribed behavior.

natural symbols Inherent qualities of specific plants and animals used as signs or metaphors for issues that concern people.

An
Anaconda
Myth

The following myth was recounted to archaeologist Peter Roe by my Shipibo assistant Manuel Rengifo in 1971. It portrays the anaconda as a source of noxious pests and illustrates how spirit beings take on human form and can influence hunter success.

One day a man who was a very bad hunter set out once more to pursue the game of the forest with his blowgun. He had had no luck, as usual, until he approached the shores of a lake. There he noticed a man wearing a decorated *cushma* [woven cotton robe]. The man greeted him and asked him if he would like to accompany him so that the strange man could show the hunter his "real *cushma*." The hunter agreed, and they set off, only to finally encounter a huge coil "Mother of All Boas," the anaconda. This, the man informed the hunter, was his real *cushma*. The hunter was very frightened, but the man reassured him and said that he would show him how to be a good hunter. The anaconda man first blew through his blowgun but out came only a horde of stinging, poisonous animals like mosquitos, black biting flies, stingrays, scorpions, and spiders. When the stranger blew again, hosts of deadly vipers as well as all the other evil snakes of the jungle poured forth from the tip of his blowgun. He then handed his blowgun to the hunter, whom he instructed to do as he had done. The hunter blew through the instrument and immediately killed a monkey. From that day on the hunter, thanks to his friendship with the anaconda man, always enjoyed success as a great hunter. (Roe 1982:52)

the anaconda, caiman, tapir, king vulture, and frog may all be associated as feminine symbols. The anaconda has multiple associations, and may be seen as both masculine and feminine. Hollow bee hives may replace gourds as a feminine symbol, while the giant anteater may replace the anaconda as a masculine symbol because he introduces a long, phallic tongue into the hive (see the box entitled "Mythic Jaguars and Anaconda Rainbows").

Roe relates this sexual antagonism in the cosmology to the striking gender division in Amazonian society, which often physically separates men and women, as demonstrated by the Mundurucú. The vivid sexual imagery also can be attributed to the fact that sex is one of the only activities that men and women engage in together and thus is a major preoccupation. Furthermore, men seem to be jealous of women's role in reproduction, and in the myths masculine characters sometimes assume important creative roles. This jealousy is reflected in the special vulnerability of women to assaults by demons when their biological role is especially evident at puberty, menstruation, and

pregnancy. During these times, women may be secluded and may observe specific food taboos.

Gerardo Reichel-Dolmatoff (1971, 1976), who analyzed the cosmology of the Tukano of the Colombian Amazon, has called attention to the similarity between Tukano cosmology and basic ecological principles. He notes that the Tukano believe in a circuit of solar sexual energy that fertilizes the earth and flows through both people and animals. They assume that a balance must be maintained between a finite supply of fish and game and the human population that depends on them. People threaten that balance through overhunting and through uncontrolled sexual behavior, which leads to overpopulation. Sexual repression through observation of the rules of exogamy and basic restraint helps maintain the energy cycle. The game animals are protected by a spirit being, the Keeper of the Game, who is identified with the jaguar in Roe's model but who can exist in many forms. The Keeper of the Game regulates the supply of animals and may release them to be hunted at the request of the shaman who communicates with him while in a hallucinogenic, drug-induced trance or with the aid of tobacco smoke. This explains the obsessive concern of the Keeper of the Game with the sex life of humans. He may withhold game or send sickness if he feels that people are being irresponsible. Hunting itself is replete with sexual imagery: It is literally seen as making love to the animals and, in preparation for hunting, people must practice sexual abstinence and observe other specific requirements.

There is no doubt a connection between the belief systems of native Amazonians, as seen in their cosmologies, and sexual behavior, food taboos, and hunting patterns—all of which can have important adaptive significance. Hornborg (2002) emphasizes that a significant part of the culture of Amazonian peoples involves subtle feelings and observations about the environment such as subtle signs and sounds associated with particular animals that might be transmitted mimetically, rather than linguistically, for example, by hunters watching and copying each other. From a semiotic or symbolic perspective, particular animals may be eaten or avoided because of metaphorical, idiosyncractic associations that people draw, contingent on specific circumstances. For example, a particular fish prone to rot quickly might be avoided at planting time, on the theory that the fish and the garden might affect each other.

RAIDING AND FEUDING IN THE TRIBAL WORLD

The downside of the apparent harmony and tranquility of Amazon village life is that personal conflicts between individual men can sometimes escalate to violence and homicide. This is of course true in any society, but in the tribal world there are no central political authorities or institutions with police, courts, and judges that could curb offenders, settle disputes, and prevent endless cycles of revenge and killing. People fear internal conflict and might simply move out of a village if violence threatens, although sometimes angry people are allowed to come to blows with fists or clubs and inflict minor injuries in a public setting. Tribal people often clearly distinguish the use of episodes of dueling to dissipate anger from intergroup violence with lethal weapons, or "war," intended to kill. When a man participates in a successful attack on another community he may be rewarded with increased status and perhaps an additional wife. This means that the world outside of one's immediate circle of kin and family is a dangerous place where one must constantly be on guard. I experienced this directly when my Asháninka guide reacted with immediate alarm at our discovery of strange footprints on a faint trail deep in the forest. In this case, the possibility of an unexpected encounter with an enemy produced an exhilarating sense of danger rather than immobilizing fear, because the Asháninka are generally confident in their capability for self-defense.

Violence in the tribal world is best called raiding and **feuding** rather than war, because the objective is not conquest, and actions are small-scale and brief. Tribal fighting typically involves at most a few dozen warriors, fighting sporadic raids in hit-and-run fashion. Although any conflict directed at another group can technically be considered war, there are enormous qualitative differences between tribal intergroup conflict and wars fought between governments. Typically, tribal raids are neither sustained nor coordinated, and their objective is to kill someone in revenge for previous killings or to capture women and children, but not ordinarily to kill everyone or to take territory or property. In contrast, political rulers in the imperial and commercial worlds use organized violence as instruments of state policy to conquer other societies, take property, territory, and resources, and collect tribute. Conflicts between states may properly be called war, and the scale and scope of destruction

feuding Chronic intergroup conflict that exists between communities in the absence of centralized political authority. It may involve a cycle of revenge raids and killing that is difficult to break.

Mythic Jaguars and Anaconda Rainbows: The Symbolic Structure of Amazonian Cosmology

French anthropologist Claude Lévi-Strauss (1969, 1973, 1978), demonstrated that Amazonian people construct their myths logically from very simple binary oppositions that metaphorically restate the central contrast between nature and culture. He believed that myths help people cope with life's basic contradictions by allowing them to manipulate them symbolically and intellectually. For example, in the myths the everyday conflicts and contradictions between nature and culture and male and female are explained metaphorically and symbolically in the formula: Male is to Female as Culture is to Nature. This makes the claim that men have culture and women are like animals, and may help men deal with their inferior role in reproductive biology.

Following Lévi-Strauss's lead, Peter Roe (1982) sifted through hundreds of myths in order to understand the internal logic linking the symbols. He selected the relationships between the most prominent symbols and constructed a simplified model of Amazonian cosmology that would be generally recognizable by most tribal Amazonian people (Figure 3.H). Roe's basic model depicts a three-tiered cosmos of earth, celestial world, and underworld, centered on the communal house and joined together by a world tree rooted in the underworld. Three cosmic layers account for the daily cycle of sun and moon. The house is surrounded by a cleared Plaza that represents culture in opposition to the surrounding forest, which is savage nature inhabited by demons. The underworld is a source of death and disease and has many feminine associations, whereas the celestial world is dominated by male symbols. The underworld is represented in the night sky as the Milky Way, which is also associated with the rainbow and the multicolored anaconda.

The dominant symbol in the cosmology is the world tree represented by the kapok or silk cotton tree (Ceiba) and its relatives. This tree has predominantly feminine associations because it is soft, hollow, and filled with water. It is considered to be a source of life and culture and may appear in myths in varied form, sometimes as a dragon tree, a fish woman, a tree with fish and frogs inside, and so on.

Two primary opposing associations center on the dragon and the jaguar. The dragon, usually represented by the caiman, is a sinister underworld being. The jaguar has both male and female associations and is an ambiguous figure, mediating between oppositions. The most striking natural features of real jaguars are that they are active day and night, they are at home in the water and on land—in trees and on the ground—and they are dangerous to humans. It is not surprising, then, that powerful shamans may transform themselves into jaguars.

in such war is vastly greater than the raids and feuds in the tribal world.

Many tribal groups are relatively peaceful, but when violence does occur it is too horrible to forget, and is likely to generate outrage and desire for revenge. Although the total casualties from tribal conflict are tiny compared with the hundreds of millions killed in the politically directed wars that were fought by governments in the twentieth century (Rummel 1997), mortality rates in the tribal world can sometimes be extremely high in particular villages (Keeley 1996). Further-

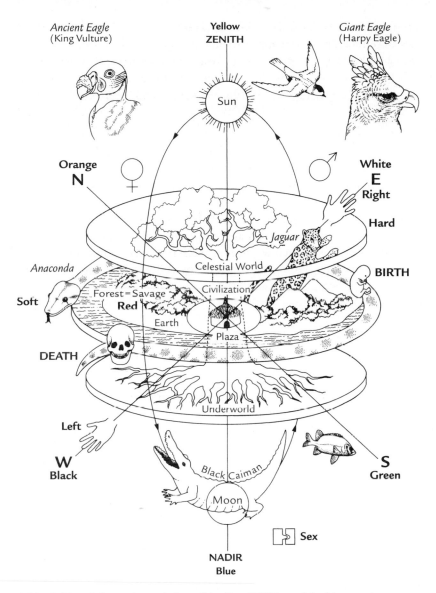

Ancient Eagle
(King Vulture)

Yellow
ZENITH

Sun

Giant Eagle
(Harpy Eagle)

♀

♂

Orange
N

White
E
Right

Hard

Jaguar

Celestial World

BIRTH

Anaconda

Forest = Savage

Civilization

Soft

Red

Earth

Plaza

DEATH

Underworld

Left

W
Black

Black Caiman

Moon

S
Green

□ **Sex**

NADIR
Blue

FIGURE 3.H   Schematic rendering of the Roe (1982) model of Amazonian metacosmology.

more, the possibility of low level, sometimes devastating violence of this sort encourages people to maintain a hostile stance toward outsiders.

In the absence of any legal authority such as a police force, people must resort to self-help in the event of serious trouble. A single homicide can set off a chain of revenge killings, which can go on for years because there are few mechanisms for making peace. This is a situation of political anarchy in the sense of an absence of formal government, but it does not mean that total chaos reigns. There is great variability in the frequency and intensity of such conflict, but normally the loss of life is not great. Exogamy works to reduce the potential for conflict by creating in-law/kinship relationships between people in different villages. Formal trading partnerships and feasting can prepare the way for marriage ties. Everyday objects such as arrows may be traded on the basis of **deferred exchanges** in which the initial gift giving will not be reciprocated for several months or even years. In this way, a continuing relationship is maintained, and there is always an excuse for further visits.

Whatever its extent, even the possibility that such conflict might occur has consequences for the pattern of life in Amazonia. For example, villages may be located on easily defended ridgetops, or they may be encircled by stout log palisades. There may also be pressures to maintain larger villages for defense. Where raiding is especially common, extensive "no-man's lands" may develop between hostile groups and can serve as de facto game reserves to replenish adjacent hunting territories.

Anthropologists have variously explained Amazonian raiding and feuding as examples of individual men striving consciously or unconsciously for reproductive success, measured as **inclusive fitness** (Chagnon 1968, 1979, 1983, 1988), as a cultural adaptation centered on a **male supremacy complex** (Divale and Harris 1976, Harris 1971b, 1974), or more broadly in reference to the perceived benefits that warriors and their families apparently derive from combat (Durham 1991). Clearly, in the tribal world warfare is a complex, multidetermined activity. Men presumably have a biologically driven propensity, and the physical ability, to use violence to advance their self-interest, but culture and society regulate this propensity to promote domestic tranquility even in tribal societies that maximize individual freedom and autonomy.

Amazonia is an especially fertile area for theorists interested in understanding armed conflict in the tribal world, because many groups have remained beyond the effective reach of government control until very recent times. Nevertheless, it must be understood that using ethnographic data to describe war in the "tribal world" necessarily refers to an imaginary ethnographic present for academic purposes. All of the peoples referred to in this chapter are encompassed by the commercial world and have been influenced by it in varying degrees for centuries. Anthropologists have sometimes conducted fieldwork with people where raids and feuds were either ongoing or had occurred within recent memory. For example, I interviewed several Asháninka who remembered being kidnapped and seeing their family members killed by raiders a few years earlier. I assumed that raiding continued in the most remote Asháninka areas, and on one occasion I saw an armed group attempt to barter a captive woman in exchange for a shotgun. Today, outsiders and many Asháninka might consider such activities to be either expressions of political autonomy, or examples of criminality.

Certainly armed conflict in any society merits scientific explanation, but it is impossible for an anthropologist to be totally objective and dispassionate about tribal warfare, because, except in self-defense, armed conflict in any society is a violation of basic human rights, and assaults on women and children and noncombatants are a violation of the civilized rules of war and offend our sense of humanity. Furthermore, it would be difficult for a field researcher to remain neutral or have no influence in a tribal combat zone if their material wealth and power as an outsider were conspicuous. Even more problematic, any published descriptions or analysis of tribal warfare could have a negative impact on the people described if it made them appear excessively savage, nasty, or animal-like. These are serious ethical issues that cannot be ignored. The following sections examine both the scientific and ethical dimensions of these issues using examples drawn from the Yanomami and Mundurucú.

Yanomami Armed Conflict: Scientific Issues

The Yanomami people of the Orinoco headwaters in southern Venezuela and adjacent areas of Brazil are very well known to the educated public as prototypical Amazon Indians thanks to the many generations of anthropology students who have read the various editions of Napoleon Chagnon's *Yanomamö: The Fierce People* (1968, 1983, 1992, 1997), those who may have followed the very contentious and public scientific debates between Chagnon and Marvin Harris over the explanation of Yanomami warfare, and more recently those who may have read Patrick Tierney's popular book, *Darkness in El Dorado* (2000), attacking Chagnon's professional ethics.

The Yanomami resemble the Asháninka in many ways. Although they live at opposite sides of the Amazon basin, both groups are gardeners who rely heavily on hunting and foraging in the forest, move their settlements frequently, and have similar kinship and marriage systems, cosmologies, and bigman leadership. Both groups numbered more than 20,000 people in the 1960s, and were among the largest, most independent indigenous groups in Amazonia. The most conspicuous difference between them is that Yanomami villages are larger, averaging a hundred people living in a single circular maloca opening on a central plaza. Feuding and raiding occur in both groups, but Chagnon's research has made Yanomami violence more thoroughly documented.

Chagnon began his research among the Yanomami in 1964 specifically to study on-going warfare, treating raiding and feuding as the centerpiece of Yanomami culture. Initially, Chagnon (1968b) explained Yanomami warfare as a political expression of village autonomy, recognizing that wife stealing was the proximate cause of their conflicts. The Yanomami, by their own admission, were fighting over women, and this was aggravated by an apparent scarcity of women, which Chagnon attributed to the effects of polygyny, and **selective female infanticide**. Later, Chagnon (1979, 1983, 1988) turned to evolutionary biology for explanations and stressed the genetic value of violent, and even homicidal, behavior for individual Yanomami men. From this view, he explained Yanomami fighting as the self-interested result of the "reproductive strivings" of individual Yanomami men. Chagnon argued that gaining a reputation for fierceness by swift

retaliation against aggressors would make a Yanomami man a more attractive mate and make it easier for him to prevent others from stealing his wives. This would increase his individual inclusive fitness, or the proportion of his genetic material that would be contributed to succeeding generations (Figure 3.7a).

Marvin Harris (1971b) offered cultural materialist, functionalist explanations that stressed the presumed adaptive advantages of warfare for Yanomami society and culture, rather than its benefits to individuals. His theory was that warfare was an example of the "male supremacy complex" and functioned to balance population and resources (Divale and Harris 1976). This culture complex was presumably characteristic of tribal societies and interconnected warfare, female infanticide, patrilocality, polygyny, a male-dominated division of labor, male headmanship, male shamanism, and the ritual subordination of women. Divale and Harris offered cross-cultural statistical evidence to demonstrate connections among these patterns. The driving force behind this cultural complex was population growth causing resource shortages (Figure 3.7b). Harris believed that in Amazonia game shortages would be crucial, and they would be expressed as protein deficiencies or as **diminishing returns** to the

---

deferred exchange A form of trade in which gift giving is reciprocated with a return gift at a later time, thus providing an excuse for maintaining contacts and establishing alliances between potentially hostile groups.

inclusive fitness A biological concept referring to the degree to which individuals are successful in passing on a higher proportion of their genes to succeeding generations.

male supremacy complex A functionally interrelated series of presumably male-centered traits, including patrilocality, polygyny, inequitable sexual division of labor, male domination of headmanship and shamanism, and ritual subordination of women.

selective female infanticide According to cultural materialist theory, a cultural pattern in which infant girls are selectively killed or neglected in favor of boys who will become hunters and warriors.

diminishing returns A decline in output for each increase in effort that accompanies an attempt to increase total production beyond a certain point. Overhunting often produces diminishing returns.

FIGURE 3.7 Interpre-
tations of Yanomami
feuding: **(a)** as an improved inclusive fitness
(Chagnon 1979, 1988).
(b) As an example of
cultural materialism
theory and male
supremacy complex
(Divale and Harris
1976, Harris 1984).

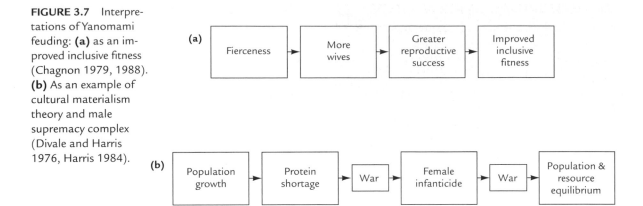

hunting effort. Warfare was a crucial causal variable that encouraged people to selectively raise
boys to become warriors while systematically ne-
glecting and even killing girls. This practice, in
turn, would in theory increase hostilities by un-
balancing the sex ratio and making wives scarce,
but it would limit population more severely than
killing males.

Chagnon's and Harris's interpretations of Yanomami violence are complementary, with Chagnon
focused on its possible genetic benefits for individuals. Harris saw group benefits, and emphasized
etic, cross-cultural comparisons. Both explanations offer plausible functionalist connections
among a series of cultural practices, and both are
reasonable ways of understanding tribal warfare.
However, neither set of explanations is fully satisfactory, and there are many reasons to challenge their applicability to the Yanomami case
(Ferguson 1995, Gross 1975). This is an example of logical scientific hypotheses that cannot be
readily verified or satisfactorily tested. Explanations of cultural variation that draw on evolutionary biology are often problematic because
culture can vary independently of human genetics.
Genes can determine only the broadest parame-
ters of human behavior. Likewise, functionalist
explanations can never fully explain the existence of any particular cultural patterns because
some other trait might always function equally
well. For example, peaceful cooperation could

always be more beneficial than war for both individuals and groups. There are also many possible ways to relieve population pressure and
protein shortages. How people imagine the world
to be, and how they want it to be, may ultimately
be more crucial than purely material limits. Culture is not beyond direct human control, and
people are not helpless automatons driven solely
by their genes and the forces of nature. The cultural traditions established in particular areas of
the world also shape the levels of violence in particular cultures quite independently of material
conditions. For example, Australian aborigines
created a continent-wide cultural system that reduced the likelihood that men would fight over
women. Equally important, historical circumstances, such as the presence of trade goods, missionaries, anthropologists, invading miners, and
exotic diseases, can change the dynamics of tribal
cultures in ways that disturb even the best scientific theories.

In addition to the difficulty of verifying the validity of any scientific interpretation of violence,
there are serious doubts about the legitimacy of
characterizing the Yanomami as violent people
(Sponsel 1998). Other anthropologists with extensive field experience describe peaceful Yanomami
(Figure 3.8). For example, anthropologist Kenneth
Good (1991), who was commissioned by Chagnon
and Harris to investigate the protein deficiency
issue, was more impressed by the peace and harmony

FIGURE 3.8 Daily life in Amazonia is primarily peaceful. Here a Quichua woman in the Ecuadorean Amazon is finishing a ceramic pot by coating it with resin.

of Yanomami life, than by violence and conflict. Going far beyond the expectations of participant observation, he married a Yanomami woman, and lived virtually as a "native" from 1975 to 1986. Not surprisingly, he reported that the Yanomami "didn't seem at all menacing" and declared, "They're happy, much happier, I think, than anybody in our society—rich or poor. Despite everything, despite the diseases, the raids, the anger and fights, at bottom they are a happy people living in a harmonious society" (Good 1991:81). Other researchers have presented ethnographic portrayals of the Yanomami that are so strikingly different that they are powerful reminders that anthropological writing is not pure observation or pure science (Ramos 1987). For example, Jacques Lizot

(1985) focuses on the romantic adventures that fill the daily life of the Yanomami, and Bruce Albert (1985) explores their intellectual life, symbolic systems, and related beliefs about illness.

The Yanomami and the Ethics of Anthropology

The most important human problem with any anthropological portrayal of the Yanomami as "fierce people" is that it suggested to the public that the Yanomami were violent remnants of the stone age and unfit for survival in the contemporary world. This was an unfortunate image because by the late 1980s the very existence of the Yanomami was in doubt, not because of their own violence but because they were being invaded. The Venezuelan Yanomami were dying in epidemics introduced by miners and other outsiders, and in Brazil they also faced settlers, highway construction, and the Brazilian government's policies to reduce their land rights. These events overshadowed any scientific debate about the causes of Yanomami tribal violence and spurred many anthropologists to re-examine the issue of the ethics of anthropology, and to campaign actively for indigenous rights.

The possibility that Chagnon's image of the Yanomami as "the fierce people" may have actually harmed them is serious enough, but journalist Patrick Tierney (2000) also accused Chagnon of intentionally promoting Yanomami warfare and violence to make his books and related films more profitable, and suggested that he and his associate James Neel deliberately spread measles that killed many Yanomami in order to test their inclusive fitness theories. Such sensational charges prompted the American Anthropological Association to convene a wide-ranging formal inquiry in 2001. The inquiry task force concluded that the most sensational charges against both men were unfounded, but ethical mistakes were made (American Anthropological Association 2002). The researchers had not always worked with full, informed consent from the Yanomami, and some of their activities may have inadvertently caused harm. The panel defended Chagnon's right to conduct field research on Yanomami violence, but acknowledged that his research may have had unintended negative consequences that he should have anticipated. They also stressed that Chagnon was too slow to moderate his negative image of the Yanomami. The panel admonished anthropologists not to deny the "coevalness" of the people they study. To the extent that Chagnon's work represented the Yanomami as "stone age" peoples, he obscured the reality that they exist in the contemporary world and are of the same age as other peoples. All of these matters are crucial issues for anthropologists because they call attention to the complexities, dangers, and responsibilities of conducting any kind of research on people. The overriding ethical standard spelled out in the American Anthropological Association 1971 Principles of Professional Responsibility is that "Anthropologists must do everything in their power to protect the physical, social, and psychological welfare and to honor the dignity and privacy of those studied."

Mundurucú Headhunting and Resource Competition

William Durham's (1991) analysis of the persistence of Mundurucú warfare provides a biocultural evolutionary perspective on Yanomami violence, demonstrating the utility of diverse approaches. From the time they were first encountered by Europeans in the 1760s until well into the twentieth century, the Mundurucú were feared throughout the central Brazilian Amazon because they conducted long-distance raids against neighboring tribes to take heads and capture children. Robert Murphy (1957, 1960) originally considered Mundurucú headhunting to be a "safety valve" that diffused potential aggression among unrelated men living in the same village. However, such a functionalist explanation is hard to defend, because many other cultural patterns might serve equally well to reduce internal tensions. More recently, Durham has pro-

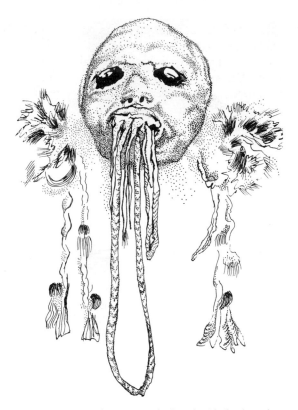

FIGURE 3.9   Mundurucú trophy head with feathered ear ornaments.

posed that the cultural ideas behind Mundurucú headhunting, and the practice itself, persisted because the Mundurucú themselves believed that it effectively reduced intertribal competition for game animals.

The Mundurucú told Murphy that they fought because they thought it was fun and exciting. They also liked to barter captives for European trade goods, and they enjoyed the increased social status that warriors received because of the ritual value of the trophy head (Figure 3.9). Durham accepts that these personal motives certainly helped perpetuate headhunting. But he argues that historically the practice probably preceded the arrival of European manufactured goods and is best explained as part of a complex of cultural beliefs related to hunting. Like many other Amazonian peoples, the Mundurucú always faced the possibility of game shortages, and they explicitly linked head-taking with improved game supplies. Successful Mundurucú headhunters were given the honorific title of *Dajeboishi*, or "mother of the peccary," and the trophy head was thought to magically guarantee general hunting success by promoting animal fertility. More directly, the head also effectively demonstrated that they had eliminated a competing hunter who might have invaded Mundurucú hunting territory. The Mundurucú explicitly compared warfare to hunting, and it seems likely that at one time they ate their victims, like game animals; after all, their close relatives, the Tupinamba, and many other Tupi speakers, were enthusiastic cannibals. Durham argues that the Mundurucú remained headhunters because the practice worked well for them. All the men shared in the risks, the entire society enjoyed the perceived benefits that it produced, and better hunting improved everyone's genetic fitness. Thus, Durham's all-inclusive biocultural explanation takes into account history, food resources, cultural meanings, personal motivations, and reproductive success.

SUMMARY

Amazonia provides a background for discussing a variety of theories on the causes and consequences of sedentary village life based on domesticated plants. Sedentary living is certainly a great divide, and it undermines many of the mechanisms that promote social equality and stability among mobile foragers. Major issues for villagers include resolving conflict, limiting individual acquisition of political power, and maintaining access to resources as density increases. Ecological factors, in combination with cultural preferences for wild game and a desire to maintain light work loads, help keep villages small and population densities low. The Asháninka kinship system shows how kin terms are used to

define social relationships and are related to marriage and family patterns.

Structuralist interpretations of Amazonian life use examples of Amazonian myth and symbolism and related ritual practices, which express an underlying pan-Amazonian cosmology. This cosmology illustrates symbolic patterns that are virtually universal, but it also distinctly reflects tribal culture in the rain forest environment and provides an important point of comparison and contrast with the cosmology underlying the Inca empire to be described in Chapter 7. In functional terms, Amazonian cosmology works to resolve important logical contradictions while contributing to the basic adaptation of the culture.

Important cultural ecological issues in Amazonia include the contrasts between the river and the forest environments, the success of shifting cultivation, and the controversy over the cultural importance of animal protein. Conflicting sociobiology and cultural materialist interpretations of infanticide and raiding in Amazonia have been advanced. A biocultural interpretation of Mundurucú headhunting helps synthesize many diverse interpretations of these issues.

Revenge killing, homicide in general, and raiding for women can be a chronic problem of tribal life in the Amazon, but the small scale of Amazonian societies, their low population density, and the ease with which households change residence minimize the frequency of violence. Under some conditions violence can advance both individual and group interests, however, such benefits are an inadequate explanation for the occurrence of violence in tribal societies, because peace and cooperation are also beneficial. Any explanation of tribal warfare needs to take into account the overall cultural context and history of particular cultures, as well as the impact of influences from the imperial and commercial worlds. At the present time anthropologists dealing with tribal violence also need to consider the ethical aspects of their research, especially when the existence of many tribal groups is at risk due to the intrusion of outsiders.

STUDY QUESTIONS

1. Why might protein be considered a population control factor in Amazonia? What other factors also influence village size?
2. How is shifting cultivation adapted to the special conditions of the tropical rain forest environment?
3. Describe the kinship terminology system of the Asháninka, and show how it is related to marriage practices.
4. In what ways do the religious beliefs and practices of Native Amazonians relate to social and ecological conditions?
5. How did Chagnon and Harris each attempt to explain Yanomami warfare and how have their explanations been criticized?
6. What are the ethical problems with the image of "fierceness" that Chagnon used to portray the Yanomami in the early editions of his ethnography?

SUGGESTED READING

CHAGNON, NAPOLEON. 1997. *Yanomamö*. 5th ed. Fort Worth, Texas: Harcourt Brace College Publishers. Well-rounded ethnography, but focused on the issue of conflict.

JOHNSON, ALLEN W. 2003. *Families of the Forest: The Matsigenka Indians of the Peruvian Amazon*. Berkeley: University of California Press. Full ethnography of people who are closely related, and whose culture is very similar to the Asháninka. Family life, kinship, and ideology are highlighted.

REICHEL-DOLMATOFF, GERARDO. 1971. *Amazonian Cosmos: The Sexual and Religious Symbolism of the Tukano Indians*. Chicago: University of Chicago Press. Very detailed analysis of an Amazonian belief system covering ritual and myth and relating it to rain forest adaptation.

SPONSEL, LESLIE E. 1995. *Indigenous Peoples and the Future of Amazonia: An Ecological Anthropology of an Endangered World*. Tucson & London: The University of Arizona Press. A collection of articles examining key issues focused on native peoples and environment in Amazonia, emphasizing changing rather static elements in Amazonian human ecology.

Maasai young men.

4

African Cattle Peoples: Tribal Pastoralists

Learning Objectives

After studying this chapter you should be able to do the following:

1. Describe the physical features of the East African environment that make pastoralism an attractive form of subsistence.

2. Explain the strategies that cattle people use to maximize their return from cattle and minimize the risk of material shortages in an unpredictable environment.

3. Define "cattle complex," and explain the central importance of cattle in the material, social, and ideological aspects of African pastoral life.

4. Describe how cattle peoples structure their intergroup relations in the absence of centralized political authority.

5. Evaluate the status of women in herding societies in comparison with that of men, judging the extent of gender equality or inequality.

6. Explain how men use cattle to extend their personal imperia beyond their immediate kin in ways that prevent the creation of permanent concentrations of social power and hierarchy.

7. Compare the ideological systems and cosmologies of African herders, Australian foragers, and Amazonian villagers.

8. Describe how the Maasai age class system organizes the life cycle of Maasai, and explain how it contributes to social stability.

PRONUNCIATION GUIDE

Tribal names and vocabulary in Nilotic languages are usually pronounced by English speakers according to the following orthography and sounds:

Key
a = a in father
o = o in go
ay = ay in day
ai = i in ice
e = e in bed
oo = oo in food
• = Syllable division
/ = Stress

Nuer = [noo • ayr/]
Maasai = [ma / sai]
eunoto = [ay • oo • no / to]
moran = [mo • rän/]

The Nuer, Karimojong, Maasai, and other Nilotic-speaking peoples in East Africa have fascinated casual European observers and anthropologists for more than a century. The pride and arrogant self-confidence of these peoples were so striking, and their warriors were so brave and numerous, that they commanded the immediate respect of the first European colonialists. The Maasai were viewed with special awe, because their warriors made a contest out of killing lions with spears and wore their manes as a badge of courage. It was even more impressive that these peoples could support themselves almost entirely from their cattle in an environment that Europeans considered a wilderness paradise for big game. In fact, cattle dominated all aspects of their culture, to a degree that outsiders thought irrational and obsessive. However, these East Africans, who may be respectfully called "cattle peoples," have survived droughts and epidemics, and some have retained much of their autonomy despite many government-imposed changes.

After the Ice Age ended, animals were domesticated in many parts of the world. This opened up new possibilities for people while creating many new problems. In the absence of animal domesticates, the population density of farming peoples was limited by the availability of fish and game, as in Amazonia. However, African herders used domesticated cattle as a special form of tangible, reproducible, and mobile wealth that made social equality possible in spite of increases in population density and growth in the scale of society. East African peoples clearly demonstrate that people can live in settled villages, control and accumulate wealth within limits, and still enjoy the human advantages of life in small-scale tribal societies focused on the well-being of households. Tribal herders have designed sustainable cultures that maximize personal autonomy for men and women, while meeting the needs of society without producing extreme inequities in the distribution of social power. Even though their food production systems are very different from those that sustain Australian for-

agers and Amazon villagers, African herders also reject any form of centralized political power. The archaeological and historic record shows that tribal people lived successfully as herders in East Africa for nearly five thousand years, while making detailed changes in their lifestyle in response to changing circumstances over the centuries. Significantly, by keeping the politically independent unit no larger than small villages, relying on age-grade organization to maintain social solidarity, and distributing cattle in a way that maximized household equality, African herders achieved overall cultural stability at higher population densities and with larger societies than either Australian aborigines or the Amazon forest villagers. The fact that these people continue to maintain, modify, and reproduce these cultural systems shows that they serve individual self-interest very effectively. The key to their success was perhaps the inability of even the most aggrandizing power seekers to force people into supporting them against their will, because they could never gain monopoly control over crucial resources.

MAKING A LIVING WITH COWS

Cattle Herding and Tropical Grasslands

East Africa is part of the tropical savanna ecosytem, but it is topographically a highly diverse region (Figure 4.1). Much of the area occupied by the Nilotic pastoralists in Kenya and Tanzania straddles the equator along a zone lying 3000–7000 feet (914–2134 meters [m]) in elevation and consisting of arid plains and wetter, grassy uplands. Today this region includes some of the most famous game parks in the world, such as the Amboseli and Serengeti national parks in Kenya and Tanzania, respectively. It is also home to many tribal cultural groups involved in a wide range of subsistence economies.

The tropical savanna ecosystem is a grassland zone, which may have a few trees and shrubs,

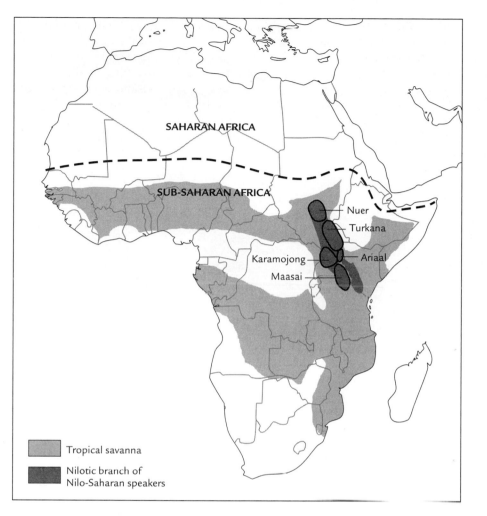

FIGURE 4.1 Map of savanna regions of Africa showing the Nilotic-speaking East African cattle cultures discussed.

separating tropical rain forests from arid deserts (Figure 4.2). Fire and grazing play an important role in maintaining and extending savannas. But savannas result primarily from climate, soil, and topographic conditions, especially a pronounced wet and dry season. In striking contrast to the diversity and stability of tropical rain forests, savannas are dominated by very few species and exist in an unstable, dynamic equilibrium. Drought cycles or changes in grazing pressure caused by livestock disease can rapidly change the inven-tory of plant species and shift the balance be-tween trees and grasses. Biological productivity in the savanna is high in relation to biomass, but plants are short-lived in comparison to rain for-est species. Nutrients are turned over, or cycled, much more rapidly in the savanna. There are proportionately more leaves and grass and less wood in the savanna, and the foliage is more palatable because it contains fewer resins and other chemical defenses. Extreme seasonal varia-tions in rainfall create periodic pulses of biological

FIGURE 4.2   Herding cattle in an African savanna.

productivity resulting in brief food surpluses that are best exploited by nomadic grazers (Bourliere and Hadley 1983).

Pastoralism in East Africa, like the savanna itself, exists along a rainfall continuum from wet to dry, showing greater dependence on animals and greater nomadism as rainfall declines. In areas where the average annual rainfall exceeds approximately 25 inches (650 millimeters [mm]) per year, people are likely to be village farmers, relying on grains such as millet, with livestock raising a minor subsistence activity. Where rainfall drops lower than 25 inches, pastoralism becomes increasingly attractive, nomadism increases, and people become more and more dependent on their animals, while farming becomes supplemental. In extreme cases, as with some Maasai groups, people may subsist almost entirely on animal products, although some may exchange animal products for grains from their settled neighbors.

The great advantage of domestic livestock is that they convert otherwise inedible plant mate-

rial into meat, blood, and milk for human consumption, in areas where farming would be at best a marginal activity. The use of domestic animals also permits dramatic increases in human population density over that supported in the same environment by foraging. East Africa can support up to 22,076 pounds (10,000 kilograms [kg]) of wildlife biomass per square kilometer (km^2) with some fifty species of large grazing mammals. This is easily double the biomass of game mammals in the Amazon. The Hadza of Tanzania, who forage in this hunter's paradise, take only a small fraction of the game and maintain themselves at typically low population densities of just 0.4 persons per square kilometer. The Maasai, their pastoral neighbors, support 2–6 people per square kilometer. Pastoralism permits precise control over reproduction and harvesting of the animals and leads to large increases in food production per unit of land. However, successful pastoralism is a complex, delicately balanced system that poses many difficult problems and

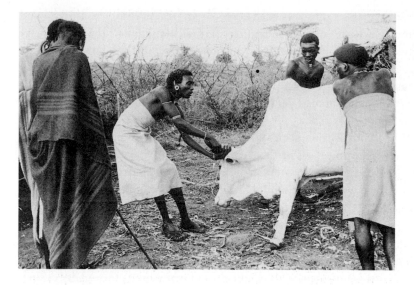

FIGURE 4.3 Samburu Maasai warriors preparing to slaughter a Zebu ox at a wedding. Hump-backed Zebu cattle may have been in Africa for 4000 years.

requires major adjustments in the organization of society and labor.

East African cattle peoples, operating within domestic-scale cultures, manage their cattle and relate to their grassland ecosystem in radically different ways from market-oriented ranchers operating within the commercial culture. The first objective of subsistence pastoralists is to extract the maximum food value from their animals for direct consumption as efficiently as possible, while emphasizing self-reliance and long-term security (Dyson-Hudson and Dyson-Hudson 1969). African cattle may appear scrawny in comparison with the hefty beef cattle of North American rangelands and feedlots, but range-fed African cattle do not require an enormous input of fossil fuel energy, and they are well adapted to survive seasonal drought and disease (see the box entitled "Cattle Carrying Capacity"). American cattle are raised with the least human labor possible. They must gain weight quickly so they can be sold for the maximum financial profit. They thrive on water pumped from deep wells; special food that is planted, processed, stored, and trucked to their feeding troughs and feedlots; and expensive antibiotics, growth hormones, and appetite stim-

ulants (see Chapter 12). Furthermore, American beef goes through a chain of processors, wholesalers, and retailers to be processed, packaged, advertised, stored, and marketed before being consumed. By contrast, no remote shareholders who did not participate in raising them profit from African cattle. African cattle are ritually sacrificed, butchered, and eaten by the same people who care for them.

THE PREHISTORY AND HISTORY OF AFRICAN PASTORALISM

Pastoralism, as a full-time specialization in domestic animals, probably has been practiced in Africa as long as anywhere in the world. Sheep and goats likely were brought into North Africa from the Middle East, whereas wild cattle may have been locally domesticated by 7000 BP or earlier (Smith 1984). The Zebu, or hump-backed cattle, apparently reached Africa from India about 4000 BP (Figure 4.3). Because the cattle, sheep, or goats have no known wild ancestors in sub-Saharan Africa, it is assumed that they were introduced to East Africa from elsewhere as domesticates.

Cattle Carrying Capacity

Comparative analysis of subsistence herders requires several types of data and concepts, which are outlined in Figure 4.A. Calculating the carrying capacity for herd animals and the number of people who could be supported by pastoralism is a deceptively simple theoretical problem. One need only know the amount of plant biomass that animals can consume in a given area each year on a sustained basis and the amount of human food that the herds can produce. The basic formula for estimating carrying capacity (CC) for African cattle is: CC = (AGNPP/.5)/C, where AGNPP = above-ground net primary productivity in kilograms of dry plant matter, the new plant biomass produced each year, and C = kilograms of cattle biomass, measured in TLUs, tropical livestock units of 250 kilograms, which is the equivalent of one cow. The number of people that can be supported by the cattle is (P) calculated as: P = CC/R, where R = the TLUs required for human subsistence per person per year.

In practice, none of these figures can be precise, and the formula is not so easily applied. This explains why there is so much professional disagreement over whether pastoralists are managing their herds rationally and maintaining the quality of their pastures. The primary problem is that AGNPP, the most critical value, varies dramatically in time and space in the pastoral zones. Successful pastoralists must plan for long-term, minimum carrying-capacity values, taking into account the frequency of droughts. Actual productivity rates of human food will depend on the particular mix of animals in use and the specific pattern of herd management.

Pastoralism first became established in East Africa in the central Sudan by 5400 BP and then in the arid zone of northeast Kenya by 5200 BP, where it was presumably introduced by early Cushitic-speaking peoples from Ethiopia (Table 4.1). Because of tsetse flies, the higher savannas of East Africa apparently were not occupied by pastoralists until 3300 BP, when changes in climate and vegetation made conditions more favorable. Shortly thereafter, by 2500 BP, Nilotic-speaking ancestors of the modern Maasai and Turkana peoples arrived (Ambrose 1984). Therefore, African pastoralism was a well-established human adaptation and can reasonably be considered a basic component of the savanna ecosystem.

Anthropologists often group the "cattle peoples" of East Africa into a single culture area stretching from Sudan to South Africa, but they are a diverse group of cultures organized at different scales of social complexity and united only by their common interest in cattle. The most famous cattle cultures, such as the Nuer, Dinka, Karimojong, Turkana, and Maasai, all belong to the Nilotic branch of Nilo-Saharan. (*Nilotic* also refers to the very tall physical type of Nilotic speakers.)

The Maasai may have been a distinct cultural group since at least the early 1600s, and were actively expanding their territories into what is now Tanzania by 1800 (McCabe 2003:103). Arab Muslim traders established themselves off the coast on the island of Zanzibar at about the same time, trading into the interior for slaves and ivory. The Arabs were followed in the mid-nineteenth century by European explorers and missionaries.

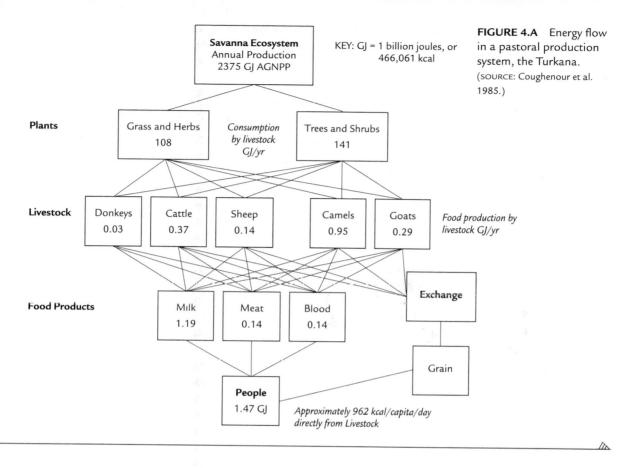

FIGURE 4.A   Energy flow in a pastoral production system, the Turkana. (SOURCE: Coughenour et al. 1985.)

KEY: GJ = 1 billion joules, or 466,061 kcal

European colonial governments were moving into place by the 1880s, followed by national independence in the 1960s.

The Cattle Complex: Obsession or Adaptation?

Historically, East African pastoralists have been seriously misunderstood by anthropologists, development planners, and conservationists. Many observers concluded that they irrationally overemphasized cattle in culturally determined ways, leading to overgrazing and poor-quality animals. American anthropologist Melville Herskovits (1926) apparently was the first to refer to the East African cattle area and to describe the Cattle Complex as an irrational cultural value on

cattle for nonutilitarian purposes. According to Herskovits, Cattle Complex peoples used cattle more for social and ritual purposes than for subsistence. Cattle were treated as wealth objects and sources of prestige. People rarely ate cattle; instead, they exchanged cattle at marriage, used them to settle disputes, and sacrificed them on ritual occasions. Besides these noneconomical uses, East Africans seemed to have an exaggerated and personal attachment to their animals. When range management professionals later found that pastoral cattle were underweight and less productive than their counterparts in the American West, they unfairly accused the pastoralists of overgrazing and blamed them for desertification, the process by which a savanna is converted to arid desert by overgrazing.

TABLE 4.1   PREHISTORY OF EAST AFRICA, 200,000–1000 BP

2000–1000 BP	Expansion of Bantu-speaking, iron-using village farmers
Pastoral Neolithic in Kenya (5200–2500 BP)	
2500	Southern Nilotic speakers from southern Sudan enter highlands as mixed farmer/pastoralists with livestock, millet, and sorghum
3300	Modern climate and vegetation established
	Savanna pastoral Neolithic in highlands
5200	Savanna pastoral Neolithic introduced in lowlands by Cushitic speakers bringing domestic livestock and ceramics
Saharan Pastoralism (8000–4000 BP)	
4000–5400	Domestic livestock and ceramics in central Sudan
7000–8000	Local domestication of cattle in Sahara
	Domestic sheep and goats reach North Africa from Near East
***Homo Sapiens* Foragers (200,000–40,000 BP)**	
200,000	Middle Stone Age; core tools, flake points, scrapers

SOURCES: Ambrose (1984), Clark (1984), Phillipson (1985), Smith (1984), and Wendorf and Schild (1984).

British anthropologist E. E. Evans-Pritchard conducted one of the first and most detailed studies of a cattle culture among the Nuer of Sudan between 1930 and 1936. This study (Evans-Pritchard 1940), which became a classic in ethnographic literature, showed the social, ritual, and emotional value of cattle but also demonstrated their utilitarian function.

Evans-Pritchard called the Nuer "pre-eminently pastoral." He reported that they considered themselves herdsmen above all else and only grudgingly resorted to farming when they didn't have enough animals. They looked contemptuously on people without cattle, as he discovered on his arrival in Nuerland, when the Nuer refused to carry his baggage. He found that they had "the herdsman's outlook on the world" and considered cattle "their dearest possessions." Cattle were ornamented and named, and their genealogies were remembered. Boys received an "ox-name" at birth, men were addressed using names that referred to their favorite oxen, and women were named after the cows they milked. And, to Evans-Pritchard's dismay, they always talked about their animals:

I used sometimes to despair that I never discussed anything with the young men but livestock and girls, and even the subject of girls led inevitably to that of cattle. Start on whatever subject I would, and approach it from whatever angle, we would soon be speaking of cows and oxen, heifers and steers. (Evans-Pritchard 1940:18–19)

For Evans-Pritchard, this "pastoral mentality" took on the appearance of an "over-emphasis," a "hypertrophy of a single interest." As further indication of Nuer obsession with cattle, he pointed to the "linguistic profusion" of cattle terminology. He found ten terms for describing cows of one solid color and hundreds of possible permutations of terms based on combinations of white with various patterns and associations with natural objects. Further Nuer terminological distinctions are based on horn shape, ear cropping, and age and sex categories. In all, the Nuer had thousands of ways of describing cattle and composed poetry and songs using their names. A. B. C. Ocholla-Ayayo (1979) has listed 125 terms applied by the Luo, Nilotic neighbors of the Nuer, to cattle anatomy, both internal and external, covering bones and internal organs in great detail (Figure 4.4).

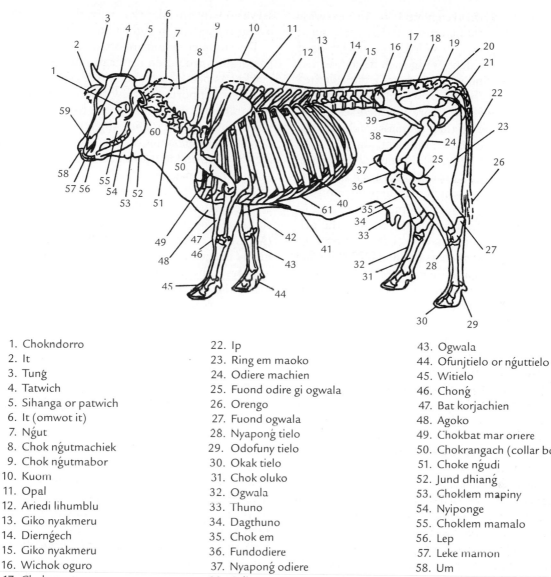

1. Chokndorro
2. It
3. Tuṅg
4. Tatwich
5. Sihanga or patwich
6. It (omwot it)
7. Nǵut
8. Chok nǵutmachiek
9. Chok nǵutmabor
10. Kuom
11. Opal
12. Ariedi lihumblu
13. Giko nyakmeru
14. Dierṅgech
15. Giko nyakmeru
16. Wichok oguro
17. Chokoguro
18. Choktie ip
19. Oguch dhiang
20. Ringsarara
21. Dhokisonga

22. Ip
23. Ring em maoko
24. Odiere machien
25. Fuond odire gi ogwala
26. Orengo
27. Fuond ogwala
28. Nyapoṅg tielo
29. Odofuny tielo
30. Okak tielo
31. Chok oluko
32. Ogwala
33. Thuno
34. Dagthuno
35. Chok em
36. Fundodiere
37. Nyapoṅg odiere
38. Odiere
39. Chokbam
40. Nǵede
41. Pinyich
42. Bat korachich

43. Ogwala
44. Ofunjtielo or nǵuttielo
45. Witielo
46. Choṅg
47. Bat korjachien
48. Agoko
49. Chokbat mar oriere
50. Chokrangach (collar bone)
51. Choke nǵudi
52. Jund dhiaṅg
53. Choklem mapiny
54. Nyiponge
55. Choklem mamalo
56. Lep
57. Leke mamon
58. Um
59. Chok um
60. Tiend it
61. Chokagoko

FIGURE 4.4   Approximately half of the 125 anatomical terms applied to cattle by the Nilotic-speaking Luo (Ocholla-Ayayo 1979).

Evans-Pritchard recognized that this extreme interest in cattle had a utilitarian basis. He noted that the Nuers' flat, clay-soiled, seasonally flooded environment was deficient in such basic raw materials as stone and wood and was a difficult area to grow crops, but it provided excellent pasturage. The Nuer therefore lavished seemingly extravagant care on their animals, such that the cattle enjoyed a "gentle, indolent, sluggish life" (Evans-Pritchard 1940:36). He described the virtually symbiotic relationship between the Nuer and their cattle, in which each depended on the other. The Nuer extract an impressive array of material resources from cattle. Milk is the primary product, and it may be consumed fresh or sour, or processed as cheese. Blood is drawn from veins in the neck and then boiled or allowed to coagulate and roasted in a block. An animal ordinarily is slaughtered only for ritual purposes, but then it is butchered and the parts distributed. Dung is a critical fuel for cooking, and dung fires help drive off biting insects. Dung is also used as a construction plaster, as well as for medicinal and cosmetic purposes. Cattle urine is used in cheese making and tanning, while skin and bones have many uses in the manufacture of various artifacts such as containers and ornaments. Without cattle and their products, life would be very difficult in Nuerland.

Pastoralists have been widely accused of irrationality for supposedly raising far more poor quality animals than they need for mere subsistence in order to achieve the prestige and social value of large numbers of cattle. They have been accused of overstocking their ranges and degrading their environments, thus contributing to desertification. This is sometimes seen as a classic tragedy of the commons situation, a destruction of a communal resource by self-interested individuals as described by biologist Garett Hardin (1968). East African grazing lands are common properties, but they are not the kind of unregulated open access system that Hardin imagined. The tragedy of the commons interpretation overlooked the fact that African herders act as a community to regulate grazing by individual herders (McCabe 1990). Herders practice seasonal con-

servation in an adaptive way that minimizes overgrazing (Ruttan and Mulder 1999).

Development planners often recommend that pastoralists would do better to raise beef for the market as private ranchers. Actually, little firm evidence supports the view that domestic-scale pastoralism is inherently prone to overstocking, while abundant evidence suggests that outside development pressures do contribute to overgrazing (Homewood and Rodgers 1984). Domestic-scale subsistence pastoralists operating outside of the market economy are unlikely to find any conflict between individual self-interest and their social responsibility to maintain range quality (McCay and Acheson 1987). Rainfall, which is highly irregular, not the total number of animals, appears to be the primary determinant of range condition over the long run (McCabe 2003). Herd size appears to fluctuate up and down, maintaining an average level in response to droughts and disease.

Whether or not African pastoralists are self-conscious conservationists, their traditional subsistence practices include important limiting factors that reduce the likelihood of overgrazing. First, the subsistence needs of a household determine herd size, and the labor supply and the declining feeding efficiencies that arise as herds grow set its upper limits. Second, in the absence of trucks, pumps, and deep wells, the frequency that animals must be watered and the distance they can travel between grazing areas and water severely limit grazing during the dry season.

African cattle under traditional nomadic pastoralism do appear to be of lower quality when compared with U.S. beef and dairy cattle. African animals convert less of their forage into human food and produce less body weight because the frequent droughts cause animals to channel more of their energy into biological maintenance than into meat production. They must adjust their metabolisms to cycles of periodic thirst and starvation followed by recovery (Coughenour et al. 1985, Western and Finch 1986). Low production is thus a long-range adaptation to severe environmental constraints. As mentioned previously, U.S. cattle achieve their high biological output thanks to a

all our assumptions & judgments are confused by our imagination & experience.

significant fossil fuel energy subsidy, which is not counted in these calculations but which is required to produce and distribute tractors, farm chemicals, feed, and agricultural research.

Pastoral Subsistence: Meat, Blood, and Milk

To design a reliable food system based on domestic animals, a subsistence herder must solve several problems: which animals to use, what food products to produce, how many animals to herd, what age and sex categories to maintain in the herds, when to slaughter, when to time breeding, how to feed and water the herd, and how to protect the herd from disease and predators. Whereas hunters let nature take care of most of these matters, herders must constantly attend to the needs of their animals.

Most East African pastoralists are considered, and consider themselves, to be cattle peoples because of the dominant cultural role they assign to cattle, but they actually depend on several functionally distinct domesticates, including cattle, camels, sheep, and goats. Cattle play major social, ritual, and subsistence roles while providing important material products. Camels become increasingly important as rainfall declines or pastures become overgrazed. The small stock (sheep and goats) may provide more of a household's meat requirements than cattle and can be a significant source of milk. Cattle are not as efficient as goats at meat production, so cattle are rarely slaughtered except ritually, although they are eaten when they die naturally. Small stock also are useful to speed recovery after a serious drought because they reproduce more quickly than cattle. Reliance on animal domesticates makes for a situation that is the reverse of the protein limitation situation in Amazonia. East African pastoralists have an abundance of protein but have some difficulty producing adequate carbohydrates and calories except where they can grow grain or obtain it by barter with neighboring farmers.

Complementarity between domesticates is a striking aspect of pastoral systems. Maintaining mixed herds of large and small grazers and browsers makes for more efficient utilization of available forage and, like Amazonian gardens, makes maximum use of the diversity of the natural ecosystem. As grazers, cattle and sheep feed primarily on grasses and herbaceous vegetation; as browsers, goats and camels rely on woody shrubs and trees. Utilization of diverse domesticates also helps level out seasonal fluctuation in food production: Camels often produce milk year-round, cows produce only during the wet season, and sheep and goats produce most milk during the dry season.

The diverse animal products that pastoralists consume also have the advantage of complementarity, and they maximize sustainable subsistence yield. Rather than emphasizing meat production, which obviously represents a onetime use of an animal, herders are concerned primarily with milk production. Milk maximizes biological efficiency because the calories in milk can be produced four times more efficiently in terms of energy costs than the calories in meat. Blood and milk can be produced without harm to the animal, and they complement each other in that blood is a major source of iron and can be drawn from animals that are not producing milk. This is especially important for cows when their milk production drops during the dry season. The importance of milk production in herder diets is shown by the remarkable fact that the Karimojong derive one-third of their total caloric requirements from their cattle, 88 percent of which is in the form of milk, with meat representing only 8 percent, and blood 4 percent of cattle dietary component (Little and Morren 1976). These figures show that cattle peoples are really dairy farmers.

Traditional herding is a labor-intensive activity. Individual herds may be subdivided to better reflect the abilities and requirements of different types of animals. Herds are moved seasonally to take advantage of the best pasture. In some areas this may involve **transhumance**, or herd movement into higher or lower environments. Pastoralists manage their herds to maximize the number of

---

transhumance Seasonal movements of livestock to different environmental zones often at different elevations, or latitudes.

female animals to keep milk yields and growth potential high. Given the natural mortality rates of cattle and their reproductive biology, a herd is unlikely to contain more than about 30 percent fertile cows, and only half of these will be producing milk.

Although the production of milk per animal under pastoral nomadism is lower than on American dairy farms, pastoral milk is more concentrated, and its nutritional value is 30 percent higher than that of commercially-produced milk. Given the archaeological record of pastoralism in East Africa and the incredible resilience of the system under the impact of colonial invasion and recent forces for change, traditional herders seem to be operating quite rationally. Their herding strategies contribute to the long-range survival of their families in a challenging environment.

Herding continues to be an important way of life, even as population growth, shrinking grazing lands, development programs, and restrictive government policies force herders to raise food crops and engage in the commercial economy to save their cattle. The Maasai described the situation in the 1990s: "I cultivate to avoid selling my cattle." "Life is now expensive, there is a demand in the family for food, education, and medical care, and the livestock are not enough to fulfill these life requirements" (McCabe 2003:106).

DAILY LIFE IN EAST AFRICA

East African cattle cultures are an ideal place to examine the relations between men and women in the tribal world, and the degree of personal freedom and social equality that tribal life makes possible. Just as there was an anthropological myth of irrational herders obsessively attached to their cattle, until recently many anthropologists mistakenly believed that African pastoralism, and indeed pastoralism generally, was naturally, and totally, a male-dominated enterprise. Male domination meant that men were the owner-managers of the cattle, that pastoral societies were gerontocracies directed by the old men, that men controlled patrilineages that structured the entire

social system and defined the pastoral identity of their cultures. The implication was that women were totally subordinate in "status" to men and culturally inferior, if not completely irrelevant.

These misleading interpretations should not be surprising, because just as outsider men have had difficulty fully understanding Australian aboriginal society, it has been difficult for male anthropologists to view African societies from a woman's perspective. The existence of male bias in fieldwork is clearly demonstrated in the following comment by a leading ethnographer of the Samburu Maasai who declared, "Samburu is essentially a man's society and *from the male point of view* women are inferior and politically uninfluential" [italics added] (Spencer 1965:3). Although Australian foragers, Amazon villagers, and African herders all appear to fit the model of a tribal male supremacy complex, this interpretation is at best incomplete. We may suspect that how men describe their societies is likely to reflect male ideology, rather than the realities of domestic life. A further difficulty, just as we saw with the problem of understanding violence in Amazonia, was the historical influence of the commercial world and colonialism, which disrupted domestically organized systems of social power in ways that consistently disadvantaged women. Nevertheless, there is an apparent contradiction between tribal cosmologies that portray men as culturally superior and the ideals of complementary opposition between men and women that also seems to characterize these societies. Gender equality can exist in the tribal world, in spite of contrary ideologies, because the household is the primary social institution, and the household is created and maintained by an age- and gender-based division of labor.

The following sections describing the Nuer and Maasai will demonstrate that, just as in tribal Australia and Amazonia, in African herding societies men and women play complementary, but not totally equitable, roles within the household, where they share a common interest in producing children who will become successful adults. Both men and women shape the direction of their society and culture, but this does not mean that

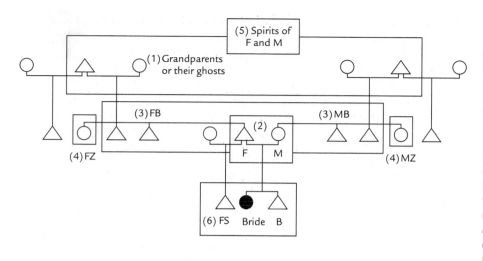

FIGURE 4.5 Order of precedence of claimants on Nuer bride-wealth cattle: (1) grandparents or their ghosts; (2) father (F) and mother (M); (3) father's brother(s) (FB) and mother's brother(s) (MB); (4) father's sister(s) (FZ) and mother's sister(s) (MZ); (5) spirits of father (F) and mother (M); (6) brother(s) (B) and half-brother(s) (FS). (SOURCE: Evans-Pritchard 1951.)

they share equal social status. The reality of gender relations in any society is seldom easily understood or explained. As will be shown, in African herding societies even women repeat myths that describe, and offer explanations for, the subordination of women to men. Women also practice and perpetuate rituals such as female circumcision, that outsiders, as well as some members of the culture, may consider oppressive.

Age and gender inequities show that preexisting cultural patterns are not always totally consistent and may not always benefit everyone equally. We may assume that the apparent injustices that an individual experiences will tend to balance out through the life cycle. However, culture may constrain individuals to accept inequity and personal pain and suffering as natural and unavoidable. Unjust cultural practices can be difficult for individuals acting alone to successfully challenge and change, even when alternative ways of life are almost always possible.

Nuer Society: Bride-Wealth, Lovers, and Ghosts

Apart from the obvious utilitarian value of their cattle, the Nuer say that the "supreme value" of cattle came from their use as **bride-wealth,** which is the basic requirement for establishing a fully legitimate household (Evans-Pritchard 1951:96).

(We will avoid the use of the term *legal* to refer to marriage or household in this context because it implies formal law, supported by courts and an enforcement structure that does not exist in Nuer society.) Nuer marriage involves rights over cattle and women and their children and is an agreement between the families of the bride and groom (see the box entitled "How Do Nuer Men View Women?"). It requires a lengthy series of negotiations, public and private ceremonies, and transactions, which are not complete until children are born to the couple. Because Nuer marriage is so complex and involves so many different rights, it is an ideal case from which to examine the meaning of marriage, family, gender relations, and household as cross-cultural concepts.

The process of Nuer marriage is initiated by preliminary talks between the two families in order to specify the animals that can be transferred. The bride's family can demand cattle for six different categories of claimants by order of precedence: the bride's grandparents or their ghosts, the bride's parents, her uncles, her aunts, the spirits of her father and mother, and her brothers and half-brothers (Figure 4.5). Ideally,

bride-wealth Goods, often livestock, that are transferred from the family of the groom to the family of the bride in order to legitimize the marriage and the children of the couple.

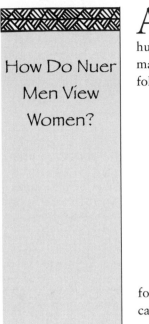

How Do Nuer Men View Women?

Anthropologist John Burton (1980) asked several Atuot (Nuer) men and women to respond to this question: "What are the relations of a wife and husband, and how do they come to quarrel?" He felt that their answers closely matched what he observed. Mayan Akuot, a father of six children, answered as follows:

> In our land, it is for a woman to give birth to children. Women are not good or bad—they are in between. Their badness is that even if you are married with one hundred cows, she may still leave. Even if you cultivate much grain, she may still leave you. This is because some women have no heart. If it is a good woman she will bear many children. If there were no women, how would all the people be here? She is the one who created the land. There is the wife of the black people, of the animals, of the cows, of the fish—all of them have this land. If it were not for women, how would people be so many? Women are good—they make children and food and beer. The woman has the land. If a man stays in this land without a woman, he will not go ahead [that is, his progeny will never be realized]. (Burton 1980:717)

These comments show that men are well aware of their dependence on women for the essentials of food, beer, and descendants. A man must be married, or he cannot be successful.

some forty head of cattle ultimately are transferred to the bride's father, who is then obligated to distribute them to each of the claimants on his side of the family and to the bride's mother's family. In a typical distribution, twenty animals would go to the bride's immediate family, with her father getting the largest share, and ten animals would go to each set of uncles and aunts (Figure 4.6). Each category of claimant receives a specific number and type of animal. For example, the bride's full brother can receive three cows, two oxen, and one cow with its calf, seven animals in all. In the negotiations, animals are promised by name to specific people.

The preliminary negotiations are formalized in the betrothal ceremony, which is the first public marriage ritual. Betrothal is marked by the sacrifice and distribution of an ox by the bride's father to the groom's family. The first installment of bride-wealth cattle also is transferred to the bride's father. Several weeks later, at the wedding ceremony, negotiations are finalized and more cattle transferred, but the transfer and the marriage are not considered official until a later con-

summation ceremony with its own series of rituals. After this, the groom's family can demand compensation in the event of his wife's infidelity, but the couple does not establish a joint homestead until after their first child is weaned. Until then, the wife remains in her parents' homestead, and her husband is a visitor who must maintain a ritual distance from his in-laws.

Once completed, the "ordinary" Nuer marriage creates a simple nuclear family household based on husband, wife, and child. Such a household draws its subsistence from his herd and from the wife's garden. The homestead contains a *byre* (a cattle barn) and its *kraal* (corral), a cooking hearth, and a small sleeping house for the wife. In a polygynous marriage, each wife has her own house. Several such homesteads belonging to a group of brothers or a father and his sons might cluster around a common *kraal* as a composite homestead.

Many other domestic arrangements are possible (Figure 4.7). For example, a woman, especially if she were infertile, might become a "husband" and have children by marrying another woman

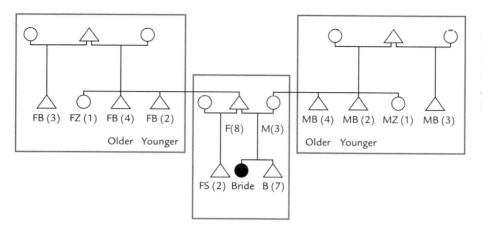

FIGURE 4.6 The distribution of Nuer bride-wealth cattle; the numbers in parentheses indicate the number of cattle received. (SOURCE: Evans-Pritchard 1951.)

who then takes a male lover who becomes the biological father, or **genitor**, of the female husband's children. In this case, the female husband is the legitimate father, or **pater**, of the children, as well as the husband, and her family transfers cattle as bride-wealth to the family of her wife. In a "ghost marriage," someone marries in the name of a sibling or other relative who has died without having completed a marriage and who thus has left no descendants. In all such cases, cattle are transferred to the bride's family, while the deceased, male or female, becomes the pater; the stand-in relative lives with the wife as "husband" and genitor but has no rights over the children. **Levirate** marriage, in which a man marries his deceased brother's wife, resembles ghost marriage except that the dead husband was already married and the bride-wealth had been transferred. The original, now dead, husband is still considered the husband, and the brother who stands in his place has less control over his wife's children than the "husband" in a ghost marriage.

Women have considerable freedom in Nuer domestic arrangements, even though all marriages are officially arranged by the families involved. Instead of remarrying, widows sometimes live with lovers, who may father children by them. However, the original legitimate family, established by bride-wealth, remains intact, and her children will be filiated to her original husband, who is always their pater. Evans-Pritchard (1951) called such ar-

rangements "widow concubinage." In some cases, a woman may move in with a lover while she is still married. She will be a "married concubine," and again her children will all be filiated to her husband because of the bride-wealth.

For the Nuer, the concept of paternity, or "belonging to," is far more important than biological parentage or the details of domestic arrangements. Paternity is established by bride-wealth cattle, thereby providing one with claims to cattle that may, in turn, be used for bride-wealth. Marriage also links one to a set of ancestor ghosts and spirits that must be ritually acknowledged. Maintaining such claims is more important than whether a "father" is living or dead, male or female, or with whom one's mother cohabits.

The use of bride-wealth, such as cattle, to formalize marriage has so many ramifications throughout the culture that some anthropologists recognize societies based on bride-wealth and those based on **bride-service** as distinctive societal types (Collier 1988). These two marriage systems create different culturally defined systems

genitor The biological father of a child.

pater The culturally legitimate, or sociological, father of a child.

levirate A cultural pattern in which a woman marries a brother of her deceased husband.

bride-service The cultural expectation that a newly married husband will perform certain tasks for his in-laws.

FIGURE 4.7   Nuer forms of marriage. (SOURCE: Evans-Pritchard 1951.)

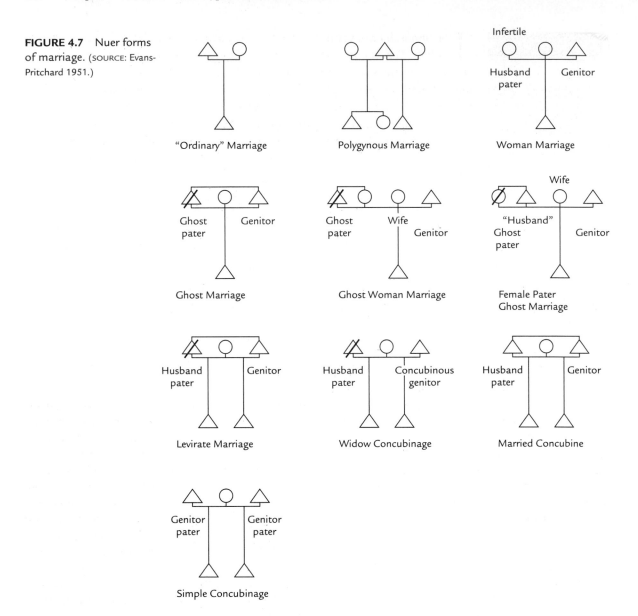

the social statuses of husband, wife, parent, and child. The social importance of bride-wealth cattle also gives a man more of a vested interest in the marriages of his brothers and sisters than he might have in a bride-service society.

Bride-wealth has sometimes been called *bride-price* by anthropologists, who may even refer to wife markets, but these terms are better avoided because they imply purchase and incorrectly sug-

of domestic relations, organizing the inequalities of age and sex in different ways. Young men in bride-service societies, such as in aboriginal Australia and Amazonia, do not incur long-term debt obligations when they marry and need only hunt or provide other services to their in-laws during the early stages in their marriage. In bride-wealth societies, the exchange of bride-wealth valuables between male "heads" of families sharply defines

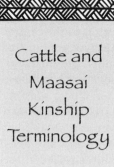

Cattle and
Maasai
Kinship
Terminology

The importance of cattle in marriage exchanges is also reflected in kinship terminology. For example, the Maasai kinship system places kin from different generations into the same category (Figure 4.B), because as a group they all have an
interest in the bride-wealth cattle they received from Ego's father's kin when Ego's
mother married. From Ego's perspective, this makes the members of mother's patrilineage a single group. They are all like mothers or mother's brothers (Radcliffe-
Brown 1941). Note that in the Nuer example in Figure 4.6, the bride's father and
her brother (MB to her son) are the major recipients of the bride-wealth cattle.

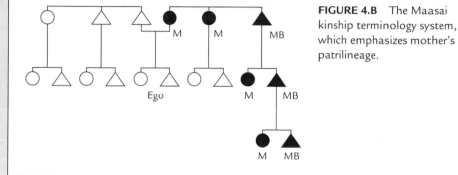

FIGURE 4.B The Maasai kinship terminology system, which emphasizes mother's patrilineage.

gest that women are chattels in cattle societies. With the Nuer, this is certainly *not* the case because women have the final say over whom they marry. It would be foolish for a father to force his daughter into a marriage against her wishes because bride-wealth cattle would have to be returned in the event of a divorce before children were born to the marriage. There are, however, inequalities of age and gender built into the system. The marriage transaction gives a man, or a woman acting as a man, the right to establish paternity, to demand cattle as an indemnity for adultery, and to claim cattle when his wife's daughters marry. Men in this system sometimes explicitly equate women with cattle because, when women are "given" in marriage, they bring cattle in exchange (see the box entitled "Cattle and Maasai Kinship Terminology").

The Status of Women in East African Pastoral Society: Ideology vs. Reality

In describing East African cattle peoples, ethnographers who followed Evans-Pritchard repeatedly

described patrilineages as the essential organizational basis of society, yet they also knew that the most important social connections were actualized through women and that it was primarily women who managed and reproduced the daily affairs of the household and were principally responsible for nurturing children. Patriarchy as an ideal social structure implies that men are naturally the exclusive "heads" of "their" households, whereas the reality of life in the tribal world is that there is no single ruler. Husbands and wives are partners in the cooperative project of producing and socializing children and transmitting culture to the next generation. The routine division of labor gives men and women complementary rights and responsibilities in their respective spheres of action, but this is not a hierarchy with a single authority. Extraordinary decisions are typically made jointly. The organization of domestic life maximizes the autonomy and independence of men and women, giving both control over the conditions of their daily life.

The difference between the ideology of how the social system is designed and how it actually operates is a paradox that anthropologists have long recognized. For example, Evans-Pritchard (1940:139–140) suggested that even when the Nuer traced descent through women, this did not challenge the validity of the patrilineal model. The patrilineal Turkana were said to have patrilineages composed of the descendants of a grandmother (Gulliver 1955:151). In reality, sons inherit movable wealth in the form of cattle from their mothers. Each of a man's wives holds and manages property for their respective sons. Schneider (1979:111) is explicit about this, stating "paradoxically, the wealth a man inherits comes from his mother's household, the product of her labor and management. In a sense, a man really inherits from his mother . . ."

The misleading emphasis on men gaining rights over women through the transfer of cattle obscures other important dimensions of gender relations in these societies. For example, when Nuer boys are initiated into manhood by receiving deep scars across the forehead known as *gaar,* they are no longer allowed to milk cows or cook food. These prohibitions signify the complete dependence of adult men on women for their food. Initiated men also can no longer drink milk directly from a cow, and instead are expected to nurture cattle by herding (Holtzman 2002). Nuer women can withhold food and beer to punish their husbands. This is a sensitive issue for men (see the box entitled "How Do Nuer Men View Women?"). Women might also influence their husband's political status by not cooking for his guests, or they might use food to influence whether or not men go on raids, or make peace.

The ideology of male owner-managers of cattle obscures the reality that the primary economic purpose of cattle raising is milk production, and this process is entirely controlled by women. Women also produce and control numerous other cattle by-products such as clothing and bedding made from cow hides, and fuel and mortar from dung. In reality, both men and women hold diverse, overlapping rights over animals, and to say that men exclusively own cattle would be misleading. Furthermore, women own and con-

trol their houses, hearths, and all domestic household articles, as well as all cooked food. The term "hearthhold" calls attention to the centrality of the domestic space that women control, and the crucial role that women play in maintaining, and reproducing African pastoral households (Hodgson 2000:12–13). Where seasonal nomadism is important, the matrifocal hearthhold is the family's fixed center. A woman manages the animals that her husband allocates to her sons. Women also may contribute to the household economy by gardening, foraging, trading, and by their services as healers and midwives.

In approaching gender relations, anthropologists often describe two separate realms of social action, the political sector controlled by men and the domestic sector controlled by women. The Nuer example shows that domestic and political realms are closely interconnected in the tribal world. Some authorities have suggested that women's domestic roles are "encompassed" by men's presumably more powerful and public and political activities (Rosaldo 1974), whereas women manipulate in the background using their perhaps not fully legitimate power (Ortner 1996: 142). However this is conceptualized, the Nuer case shows that women's control over the domestic sphere gives them influence over the entire society. From this perspective, tribal politics are really about men negotiating among themselves over the distribution of the goods and services that only women can provide, or that women actually control (Collier 1988).

In addition to questions of differences between men and women in ownership and use of livestock, there are also age and gender differences in labor expenditures. Time allocation studies of the Ariaal, a Maasai-related people in Kenya, show that men and women work seven to ten hours daily, respectively, at household, livestock, and manufacturing tasks (Fratkin 1989). This is a higher and less equitable workload than enjoyed by aborigines and Amazonian peoples, and reflects the extra burden of livestock as well as the age and gender division of labor. Because they take the largest share in livestock tasks, un-

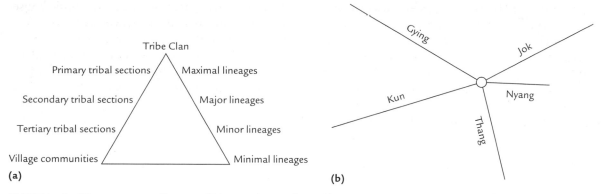

FIGURE 4.8   The segmentary lineage of Nuer society as derived by (a) Evans-Pritchard (1940) and (b) the Nuer themselves.

married males from age twelve to thirty-four rest less than three hours a day, whereas women rest nearly six hours and married men more than eight hours. Furthermore, workloads are lighter in richer households with more cattle, because caring for small stock is more labor intensive. Women also welcome co-wives who share the work.

Understanding Nuer Descent Groups

Evans-Pritchard devised an ingenious model to describe the political organization of Nuer society. The Nuer, with a population of some 300,000 in the 1930s, were said to be organized by clans, lineages, and territorial groups into an **acephalous**, or headless, political system, which operated in the absence of formal political offices (Evans-Pritchard 1940). The clans and lineages were descent groups that recruited members exclusively through males by means of patrilineal descent, or **filiation.** In Evans-Pritchard's scheme, the highest descent-based unit was the clan, which was composed of maximal, major, minor, and minimal lineages. These units corresponded to the territorial units, with the tribe at the top and primary, secondary, and tertiary tribal sections down to the village community at the lowest territorial level (Figure 4.8a).

As the figure shows, this system can be represented in a tidy diagram, but the Nuer themselves

may well understand it differently, as Michel Verdon (1982) suggests. The Nuer apparently have no term in their own language for clan or lineage; when Evans-Pritchard pressed them for lineage affiliations, they did not understand what he wanted to know. He was able to obtain names for lineage segments, but these were merely the names of particular ancestors. When he asked the Nuer to draw their lineages, they came up with lines radiating from a center, not the branching trees and pyramids that he preferred (Figure 4.8b). He also observed that "lineages" did not, in fact, form discrete localized groups. That is, the members of a lineage often did not live in the same village, nor were they strictly patrilineal. He found that lineages often incorporated children filiated through women or through adoption.

Despite the inconsistencies, Evans-Pritchard (1940) declared that clans and lineages appeared on ritual occasions when people made sacrifices to their ancestors, when groups mobilized to settle disputes, or when groups conducted raids. Such ephemeral descent groups acquired their own reality in the anthropological literature—especially

acephalous A political system without central authority or permanent leaders.

filiation A parent–child relationship link used as a basis for descent-group membership.

in the work of British functionalists in Africa, where they became standard descriptive devices, and in major comparative studies. However, regardless of whether the Nuer linguistically identify clans and lineages, they do divide their society into nested levels of inclusiveness, based on their assumptions about relations to ancestors and territory. Perhaps most importantly, they successfully organize large numbers of people without central political authority.

When it became obvious that the natives were not very concerned with the purity or even the existence of their descent groups, some argued that descent was simply "ideology." Sahlins (1965) observed that different ideological models of descent organization could be projected onto the same arrangement of people. A given group might, for example, consider themselves to be patrilineal, matrilineal, or even bilateral, without making any changes in individuals. Descent thus became a cultural fiction that people adopted for whatever purpose.

The anthropological conception of lineages, and clans grew out of nineteenth-century evolutionary theories that viewed them as stages on the way to statehood, according to Adam Kuper (1982). A clan-based society was thought to represent an evolutionary advance over societies organized only by families, but because they were still based on kinship or biological descent, clan societies were considered to be more "primitive" than territorially organized states. Lineages and clans were seen as equivalent to corporate legal entities that, like business corporations, existed in perpetuity apart from their individual members. However, in case after case, critical examination showed that clans and lineages did not form consistent, culturally recognized units. East African pastoralists do remember ancestors, and they marry outside of specific categories of kin; but, like Australian aborigines, they seem not to organize themselves into descent groups. Instead, their lives are organized around politically autonomous villages, households, and overlapping networks of kinship. The Nuer categories that Evans-Pritchard called **patrilineages** have also

been described as interest groups of individuals sharing claims in cattle (Verdon 1982). Ranked descent lines may be traced to elite persons in hierarchically organized societies; in such cases, "royal" or "noble" clans and lineages may be culturally significant, but such is not the case with the Nuer, or the other African pastoralists considered here.

Politics in Headless Societies: Leopard-Skin Chiefs and Stock Associates

Although the Nuer do not distinguish descent groups, many other peoples, such as the Maasai, do have named clans, and all East African tribal peoples use genealogical and residential proximity to structure their intergroup relations without resorting to political hierarchy. All of these societies face important organizational problems in the world beyond the village, because cattle raiding is a constant threat and temptation, and the total social universe is much larger, denser, and potentially more dangerous than in Australia, or much of Amazonia. For example, government census figures for 1955–56 listed some 460,000 Nuer (Southall 1976) living in an area of some 25,000 square miles (65,000 square kilometers). This was more people than the entire population of aboriginal Australia and in a much smaller area. People who live closer together are also likely to believe themselves to be more closely related, and Nuer men mobilize their kinship connections to conduct raids or organize defense. Kinship connections, whether real or fictive, make possible a form of order without permanent, formal leaders and without government. This is ordered anarchy, organized by what anthropologists have called a **segmentary lineage system** (Sahlins 1961). This is the familiar situation where geographic distance corresponds to social distance. In the tribal world, people living close together believe themselves to be related by common descent, and they align themselves as segments in opposition to more distant segments.

These are acephalus societies that maximize individual freedom. It was Nuer rejection of central authority that most impressed Evans-Pritchard about the Nuer. He called them "proud and individualistic" and declared:

> Their attitude towards any authority that would coerce them is one of touchiness, pride, and reckless disobedience. Each determines to go his own way as much as possible, has a hatred of submission, and is ready to defend himself and property from the inroads of others. They are thus self-reliant, brave fighters, turbulent and aggressive, and are extremely conservative in their aversion from innovation and interference. (Evans-Pritchard 1940:41)

This picture of Nuer individualism and autonomy is historically accurate. They resist "innovation" because their social system serves their interests. The Nuer resisted repeated punitive raids by the British colonial government in the Sudan, and have engaged the Republic of the Sudan in a civil war since the early 1980s. The key feature of the Nuer segmentary system is that political alliances form according to the affiliation of individual combatants. Thus, for example, if a conflict developed between two villages, members of other villages would not join in; but if someone stole a cow from another district, then neighboring villages might form a temporary alliance against the perceived common enemy.

Evans-Pritchard (1940) described a political system with increasing levels of violence as social distance increased. Within a village, men might fight with clubs, but serious disputes would be settled quickly. Between villages, men might fight with spears, and blood feuds were possible, but cattle could be accepted as compensation for homicide. Raiding for cattle routinely occured between more distant groups of Nuer villages, which Evans-Pritchard designated as tribes but which were probably shifting alliances of adjacent villages. Women and children and granaries were spared in "intertribal" raiding, but they might not be spared in raids against non-Nuer groups such as the Dinka, even though they developed from a common culture.

FIGURE 4.9 A Nuer leopard-skin chief. The individuals serve as mediators rather than as political leaders.

Conflicts seemed to arise primarily over cattle, either from cattle raiding or from disputes over unpaid bride-wealth transfers. Homicides could lead to feuds between kin groups, which could lead to further vengeance killings as in Amazonia, but among the Nuer there was a mechanism for mediation. Specific individuals, whom Evans-Pritchard (1940) called leopard-skin chiefs, served as mediators and attempted to persuade the conflicting parties to settle the dispute by means of compensation in the form of cattle transfer (Figure 4.9). Leopard-skin chiefs were respected as

patrilineage A lineage based on descent traced through a line of men to a common male ancestor and sharing a joint estate.

segmentary lineage system A tribal political system in which there are no permanent leaders, and instead individuals align with groups according to their assumed genealogical distance.

Tribal Ethnic Identities: Who are the Nuer and the Maasai?

A careful reader of Evans-Pritchard's *The Nuer* (1940) might be surprised to learn that the Nuer do not call themselves "Nuer." They are "Nath" or "Naath." In a footnote, we find that "the word 'Nuer' is sanctioned by a century of usage" and is what the Naath are called by the Dinka, and by all other outsiders, we might add. The Dinka, in turn, call themselves "Jieng." In both cases, just as with the Asháninka and Matsigenka, the words *Naath* and *Jieng* mean "people" (Southall 1976). Because there is no permanent Nuer political entity, it follows that there is no Nuer "tribe." Indeed, anthropologist John Burton declares, "Such ethnic designation as 'Nuer' and 'Dinka' . . . are at best marginally indicative of observable interethnic relations and associations" (1981:157). The only consensus, apparently shared by the Nuer and the Dinka and their observers, is that the Nuer raid cattle from the Dinka.

The absence of fixed boundaries between Nuer and Dinka frustrated British administrators for years. The Nuer and Dinka freely intermarry, and cattle move between them as booty and as bride-wealth. Someone might grow up as a Dinka and be initiated into adulthood as a Nuer. There are other rituals that convert adult Dinka into Nuer. Indeed, the two apparent ethnic categories share so many cultural traits that in mixed camps, they may tell each other apart most easily by referring to physical differences in their cattle. As Burton observes, "They are first of all pastoralists rather than antagonistic representatives of supposedly pure ethnic groups. . . . Ethnicity therefore moves on the hoof" (1981:160, 161).

John Galaty (1982) examined the problem of ethnic identity from the viewpoint of another Nilotic people, the Maasai of Kenya and Tanzania. According to Maasai ethnosociology (how a society views its own cultural identity), the Maasai are speakers of the Maa language who belong to any of a number of named tribal sections of a single Maasai "nation," which has no formal political organization. The term *Maasai* literally means "I will not beg" and is a frequently used polite expression associated with the dominant Maasai values of bravery and arrogance. In their self-designation, Maasai also call attention to the beads that are featured in their dress and, most prominently, to their association with cattle. In their own eyes, the Maasai are "people of cattle." However, as the term *Maasai* is used, it has multiple meanings that shift depending on context. Galaty has represented this as a series of three nested triangles of three sets of contrasting identities, based on distance from a central Maasai identity (Figure 4.C). In the widest context (triangle A in the diagram), Maasai speakers see themselves as pastoralists distinguished from other people who emphasize hunting or farming for their subsistence. Non-Maasai-

ritual practitioners and as mediators, but they were not chiefs with political authority. In his mediator role, the chief was expected to threaten to curse a reluctant party with supernatural sanctions but, in fact, had no coercive power.

Although cattle are a major cause of conflict, they also provide an incentive for reducing conflict. Intervillage feuding would disrupt bride-wealth transfers because wide extension of incest restrictions, which reduces confusion in bride-

speaking pastoral peoples, such as the Somali, may be considered "Maasai" in deference to their herding and are treated with special respect. At a second level, encompassing all Maasai speakers, there are specific categories based on dominant economy, such that Maasai who hunt are called *Torrobo,* those who farm are *Ilkurrman,* and "other Maasai" herders are *Iloikop.* Thus, at this level, common descent from mythical Maasai ancestors is invoked to verify one's Maasai identity even when herding is not practiced. Closest to the center, Maasai blacksmiths are *Ilkunono,* diviners are *Iloibonok,* and ordinary herders are called *Ilomet* by the blacksmiths and diviners. Because the specific meaning of Maasai and the nine related social categories are so dependent on the context in which the terms are used, the confusion experienced by colonial-era Europeans when they attempted to elicit East African "tribal" names is understandable. They were looking for discrete, territorially based, politically organized "tribes," led by "chiefs" with whom they could sign treaties, and that they could "administer" as colonial dependencies.

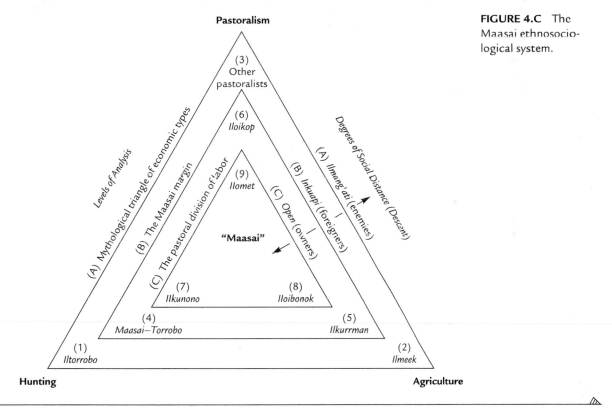

FIGURE 4.C The Maasai ethnosociological system.

wealth transfers, means that villages are usually exogamous. This divides the loyalties of people who might feel obligated to support one another in blood feuds as co-villagers, as close kin, or as claimants to bride-wealth cattle. It is thus in virtually everyone's self-interest to keep feuding to an absolute minimum. By crosscutting village membership in this way, domestic-scale societies create what has been called the peace in the feud (Gluckman 1956).

Bigman Wealth and Power in Herding Societies

The crucial economic condition that makes herding societies egalitarian is that cattle, the principle economic resource, are mobile and reproducible. Whereas in Australia and Amazonia natural wealth exists as wild game and plants, in herding systems it is found in the form of movable, reproducible wealth in animals, whose care and reproduction humans control directly. Beyond their immediate subsistence uses, men and women who are acting as men use cattle as currency to store social credits and debt obligations, and in this way can expand their personal imperia, but only within limits. The striking contrast with hierarchical societies that have chiefs, governments, and social class is that tribal herders seldom exchange labor service with non-kin and do not pay tribute. Instead all production is organized within households. Men make balanced exchanges of cattle, and in this respect treat each other as equals. As Schneider (1979:193) explains this, herders maintain relative equality between households by "setting up wide-ranging, crosscutting, balancing bonds between people which keep anyone from obtaining a monopoly of wealth which can be turned to creating hierarchy." Moving cattle between households also makes them available to people who need them for household consumption and thereby minimizes material poverty.

The nature of cattle in a tribal setting makes it difficult for any one person to control either the means of production (all the cattle), or to create unequal exchanges with dependent clients in order to concentrate coercive power within a personal imperium. Cattle are tangible wealth, or capital, and although they have the ability to multiply, they can only do so within natural, biological limits. Cattle are also mobile, which makes them vulnerable to theft and other hazards. For these and other reasons, herd size fluctuates unpredictably. This contrasts with intangible financial capital, such as dollars in account books in the commercial world, that individuals can accumulate and concentrate seemingly without limit.

Individual men use cattle to establish exchange relationships with other men that extend and supercede kinship relations. Every man extends his personal imperia beyond his close circle of kin by loaning cattle to more distant kin, to affines, and to friends to whom he is otherwise unrelated. These exchanges effectively distribute cattle for people to use, so that even poor households can subsist and cattleless men can borrow bridewealth. Anthropologists have called people who share cattle in this way "stock associates" (Gulliver 1955, Schneider 1979:192–203). Loans of cattle are long-term, deferred exchanges that carry the expectation of continuous repayment, and in this respect resemble Amazonian trading systems. Significantly, a Turkana man referred to his stock associates as "my people" (Gulliver 1955:198). One particularly powerful man had 28 stock associates (3 agnates, 12 affines, and 13 friends) scattered over an area of some 4,800 square miles (1,240 square kilometers).

African herders are ideal capitalists in the sense that they can maximize their economic freedom, having no political rulers to regulate their economic activities. Herders enjoy an equality of opportunity that allows for wide variation in outcome, but produces little extreme poverty. For example, detailed livestock figures for an Ariaal village of 38 households and 187 people in 1976 show that half (19) of the households were "rich," one-third (12) had sufficient animals, and only 18 percent (7) were "poor" (Fratkin and Roth 1990). This reverses the social hierarchy found in the politically centralized imperial world where there was typically only a very small wealthy elite, a small maintenance level, and the majority were poor. Calculated in TLUs (tropical livestock units) per person (see the box entitled "Cattle Carrying Capacity"), rich households had the equivalent of more than 9 cattle per person, and the poor had fewer than 4.5. The richest household had the equivalent of 205 cattle (22 per person) and the poorest only 2 (0.8 per person). The richest households were often polygynous. They were also better able to survive and recover from droughts. A poor man might work as a herder for a richer man in exchange for cattle, or he might seek wage labor in towns. In the past those who were unable to herd became foragers or farmers.

Men with the largest herds may be widely respected as "bigmen." Herd size is determined by a combination of a man's age, his personality, his network of kin and associates, as well as the number of fertile cows in his herd and the vagaries of fortune. A particularly successful Maasai man might have 12 wives and 60 children, suggesting a local herd of 300 cattle, but this is probably an upper limit for any man's domestic establishment.

Nuer Spirits, Symbolism, and Sacrifice

The religious beliefs of African pastoralists such as the Nuer and Maasai are primarily expressed in life cycle rituals or during crisis events, such as drought and disease, and often feature the sacrifice of animals. The cosmologies of African herders often deal with gender issues and show striking similarities with Amazonian cosmologies (see the box entitled "Turkana Household Symbolism and Cosmology").

The most basic distinctions in Nuer cosmology are made between Spirit and Creation, or between the immaterial and material worlds, which exist in complementary opposition (Beidelman 1966, 1971). When people show proper respect (*thek*) for these distinctions, their lives can normally be expected to go smoothly; misfortune occurs, however, when these categories intrude on each other, either in natural events or due to immoral human actions involving natural categories or human society. Failure to observe incest restrictions, for example, can bring illness. Confusion of categories causes ritual pollution, or contamination by "dirt," as "matter out of place" (Douglas 1966: 35). Sacrifice and ritual can restore the previous order by mediating between the opposing principles of Spirit and Creation.

In Evans-Pritchard's (1953) analysis of the Nuer concept of Spirit (his translation for the Nuer word *Kwoth*), he described a hierarchy of spirit manifestations ranked from high to low and with distinctions based on their location and social associations (Table 4.2). He thought that all of these different spirits were simply different "refractions" of a single unitary Spirit concept. The highest level is called God and is considered to be a pure spirit who is located in the sky and is associated with humanity in general. Genealogically, he may be referred to as father, but his involvement with human affairs is indirect. The air spirits occur at a lower level, in the atmosphere, and are represented by charismatic religious specialists known as prophets who are thought to communicate directly with these spirits. They may help warriors prepare themselves spiritually for cattle raiding and may be instrumental in organizing relatively large-scale military expeditions. Lower-level spirits may be manifest in animals and objects and are associated with kin groups and individuals. There are many ritual specialists including earth priests, cattle priests, and grass priests, to name a few, and a wide range of curers and diviners, all of whom maintain special relationships with these spirits. According to T. O. Beidelman's (1966, 1971) analysis, Nuer religious specialists demonstrate their association with Spirit by assuming the ambiguous characteristics of confused categories. Prophets have long hair and beards, wear clothing, and appear unkempt, when ordinary Nuer would be unclothed, clean-shaven, and neat. They accomplish their role as mediators between Spirit and Creation because they partake of both categories and thus are in a position to realign them. When anyone performs a ritual sacrifice, he, in effect, helps restore the cosmic order.

The preferred sacrificial animal is an ox (a bull, castrated at maturity), and every sacrifice is called an ox even when a sheep or goat is used. Because cattle are slaughtered only on ritual occasions and because herds are managed for maximum growth potential and milk production, it is reasonable on strictly utilitarian grounds that male animals would be sacrificed. However, Beidelman (1966) argued that oxen are chosen for sacrifice because of their close symbolic association with men and because oxen are male animals but sterile—thus, in an ambiguous category, making them ideal mediators between Spirit and Creation. Nuer cows are equated with women. Nuer women are

Turkana
Household
Symbolism
and
Cosmology

The Maasai myth of women originally owning cattle in the form of wild animals is the African equivalent of the Amazonian myth in which, in the beginning, women have culture and lose control to men. In the Maasai myth women allow their children to neglect their herds, and men take over the animals so they can claim to be the main providers for the household. This story combines the cultural ideology that men are said to "own" the cattle with the reality that women care for children and manage the household.

Terms used by the Turkana to describe different aspects of the household and related symbolic associations outlined by Vigdis Broch-Due (2000) help to demonstrate the primacy of domestic processes and the prominent role of women in African pastoral societies. The Turkana term *ekol,* "umbilicus," conceptually denotes the household as a space belonging to a woman within the extended family compound. *Awi,* both "belly" and "paternal family," refers to the containing space of the domestic compound and represents the early phase of the domestic cycle, based on an old husband and his young wife. As the household matures and children marry, the founder's widow will become the senior household member. Each *ekol* within the compound is fenced off by a brush windbreak and contains a woman's private cooking hearth, and structures for shade and sleeping. Conceptually, *ekol* also refers to her children and the animals that she cares for, as well as her descendants, or house-line.

Drinking milk, both mother's milk, and cow's milk, and eating butter, blood, and meat together make people related as kin, because kinship is based on shared substance. The Turkana emphasis on maternal functions is made explicit by their reference to a cow and calf as mother and child, and a mother as a "milking cow." Like a woman, a cow founds an *ekol,* or house-line. Turkana society is biologically constructed by common blood and milk from matrifiliation, and socially by livestock, from patrifiliation, or agnatic connections. Patrilineages require the flow of livestock between men to establish paternity.

In herder cosmology, nature is wet and soft, as in Amazonia, and culture is hard and dry. Children are born soft and wet, and they dry and harden as they mature. Old people are hard and dry. The four directions—east, west, and up (north) and down (south)—also have life cycle and sexual associations as in many cultures. A woman's cow's milk container is a prominent sexual symbol of her fertility, with its round, womblike base and phallic neck. Sexual imagery is seen in other comparisons between people and livestock. Cattle are creations of grass and water, as people are creations of semen and blood. Cooking in ceramic pots is a cultural act that makes people human, and a woman's round clay cooking pot is another prominent sexual symbol.

TABLE 4.2   THE NUER CONCEPT OF SPIRIT *(KWOTH)*

Spirit Type	Location	Social Association	Manifestation	Genealogy	Rank
God	Sky	Humanity	Pure spirit	Father	Aristocratic
Air spirits	Air, clouds, breezes	Political movements, raiding	Prophets	Upper: God's children Lower: God's grandchildren	—
Totemic spirits	Earth	Kinship groups	Animals	Children of God's daughters	Dinka-like
Nature spirits, fetishes	Earth, underworld	Individuals	Things	Children of daughters of air spirit	Foreigners

SOURCE: Evans-Pritchard (1953).

allocated cows from bride-wealth, and women may be named after the cows that they milk. Men have ox names and a favorite ox, which is "initiated" with cuts on its horns that duplicate the scars that young men receive at their initiations. Young men marry after their initiation, but their oxen (technically bulls until that point) are then castrated. Beidelman stresses the parallels between marriage and restrained sexual morality for men and castration as moral domestication of the animal. When men are called bulls it means that they are seen as aggressive and troublesome.

Even with the ethnographic reports of high gods, priests, and prophets for cattle pastoralists, these ideological systems are essentially egalitarian. There is no codified religious system and no fraternity of religious specialists. Spirit possession is available to anyone. Individuals retain a brief identity after death in relation to cattle and children, but there is no ancestor cult. Any man can perform sacrifices, and the political roles that prophets and leopard-skin chiefs play are strictly limited. These roles do not give them control over strategic resources or allow them to extract labor or tribute. At least one especially charismatic nineteenth-century Nuer prophet gained enough influence to convince people to erect a dirt-mound pyramid shrine, but he was unable to convert it into permanent political power or an enduring ancestor cult.

The Maasai Age-Class System

The Maasai pastoral system has remained viable even after years of colonial rule, cycles of drought and disease, persistent penetration by the market economy, and political control by the modern independent states of Kenya and Tanzania. African pastoralism has proved to have remarkable resilience, not only to the natural environment but also to the wider political economy surrounding it. The Maasai demonstrate that a domestic-scale culture based on subsistence herding organized at a family level can maintain a high degree of social equality and autonomy while coexisting with larger-scale social systems. Anthropologist Paul Spencer (1988) argues that perhaps the principal reason for the success of Maasai pastoralism is not the pervasiveness of "cattle complex values," but the personal rewards offered by the **age-class system** common to many East African cattle peoples.

age-class system A system in which individuals of similar age are placed in a named group and moved as a unit through the culturally defined stages of life. Specific rituals mark each change in age status.

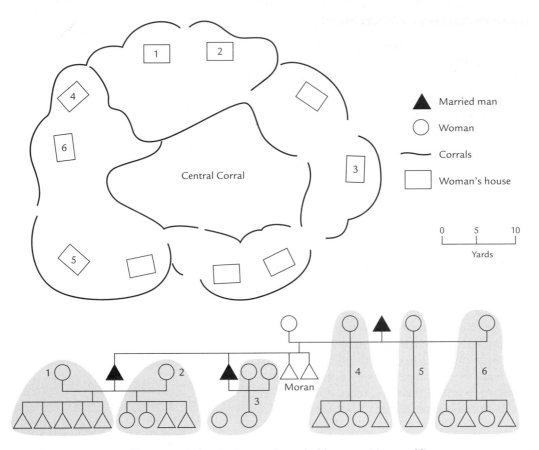

FIGURE 4.10   A Maasai homestead, showing houses, household composition, and livestock corrals. (SOURCE: Spencer 1988.)

Maasai pastoralism, in its ideal form, represents the extreme in subsistence dependence on herding by African cattle peoples. As described by Spencer, the Maasai system depends on three critical social roles: the elders, who control normal herding activities; the wives, who do the milking and take care of the animals within the domestic compound; and the *moran*, unmarried warriors who until recently raided for cattle. The Maasai settlement pattern resembles the Nuer pattern described previously. Family herds are managed by the male heads of households, which are ideally polygynous. A man's married sons live in the same homestead compound, with their individual corrals grouped around a common corral (Figure 4.10).

As is frequently the case with polygynous societies, women marry at a very young age, whereas men marry significantly later. This arrangement makes polygyny possible and makes it the prerogative of the older men, as in aboriginal Australia. With the Maasai surveyed by Spencer (1988), only 16 percent of the young men ages 18–25 years were married, and none polygynously, whereas 60 percent of the men over 40 (ages 41–70 years) had more than one wife. Polygyny offers direct advantages to the herd manager because it increases his labor force and allows him to subdivide responsibility for his animals.

The age-class system, with its associated rituals, helps balance the social stresses created by

TABLE 4.3   MAASAI AGE GRADES

Grade	Age*	Features
Senior elder	50+	Religious and ritual power, charisma of old age assumed
Great Ox Ceremony—Precedes Son's Initiation		
Junior elders	35–50	Incest avoidance of daughters of the age class, not expected to fight, have power to curse, sponsor new age class
Olngesher Ceremony—*Moran* Become Elders, Age Class United and Named		
Senior *moran*	20–35	Preparation of elderhood, may marry, meat and milk avoidance lifted
Eunoto Ceremony		
Junior *moran*	15–20	Wear red ochre, braid hair, dance with girls, have distinctive spears, perform ritual rebellion, form *manyata* warrior village, avoid meat and milk
Initiates	12–15	Age mates begin to associate, distinctive regalia
Circumcision Ceremony		
Boyhood	10–12	Earlobes cut and stretched, work as herdboys
Childhood	0–10	Naming, lower incisors removed

SOURCE: Spencer (1965, 1988).
*Age intervals overlap because the actual age of specific individuals in a particular grade will vary widely.

polygyny and patriarchy. Life stages and generation levels are marked by a series of rituals that occur throughout an individual's lifetime (Table 4.3). Step by step, prepubescent children are named, their heads are shaved, their lower incisors are removed, and their ears are pierced and stretched. Each ceremony indicates increasing maturity. Removal of the lower incisors, for example, means that a young boy is old enough to herd livestock near the homestead, but he does not go far afield with the animals until he is old enough to tolerate large incisions in his ear lobes. A calf is ritually slaughtered at the first stage of adulthood, but this must occur after the father has been ritually inducted into his status as a full elder by having an ox slaughtered and after the mother has ritually completed the process of her marriage. The spacing of these two ceremonies thus marks a generation. Ceremonies surrounding initiation make the initiation process a ritual re-

birth, and the initiate symbolically becomes a dependent child. Initiation itself is marked by genital mutilation—clitoridectomy for girls and circumcision for boys. Shortly after the operation, girls are led to their new husband's homesteads as brides, and boys move through other ceremonies that ritually separate them from their status as children and prepare them for *moran*-hood. Only males participate in the age-class system.

Age class refers to the group of people who are promoted together through the same sequence of **age grades,** or culturally designated stages (Bernardi 1985). Thus, for example, males of roughly the same age move as a group sequentially through a series of subgrades from boyhood, to warriorhood (or the *moran* grade), to elderhood,

age grade A culturally defined stage of an age-class system such as childhood, adolescence, parenthood, and old age.

and, finally, to retirement. Age classes are named, and the members of each class carry a distinct style of hand-forged iron spear and form a fraternity (Larick 1986).

Each tribal section independently operates its own age-class system. A new class is formed roughly every fifteen years under the sponsorship of the elders, who are two classes ahead of them, or approximately thirty years their senior, and who will serve as patrons of the new class. The recruitment period for each class is ritually closed by the elders in the class immediately senior to it. Each class is, in effect, forced up the age-grade ladder by the demands of the youths below who do not want to be the last to join a class that is about to advance. Late recruits experience a foreshortened time period in the favored warrior grade. The extended time during which a given age class can recruit means that there will be a relatively wide spread of ages within a given class; some Maasai set up junior and senior subsets within a single class, granting each different privileges and moving each subset through their own ritual stages of maturation. When the youngest subset of a class enters the grade of elderhood, the entire class assumes a single name.

The highlight of the entire age sequence is the *moran* grade, which young men enter after going through ceremonies that ritually separate them from their natal families. As *moran,* they become the warrior protectors of their communities; at the same time, however, these young men form their own egalitarian communities of age mates united by special bonds of loyalty and shared experience. Freed from domestic routines and still unmarried, the novice *moran* are expected to dress in special finery, wear their hair in braids, dance and display, and carry on with young girls. Traditionally, they conducted raids to capture cattle and defended the local herds against raiders and lions. The most important privilege of the *moran* is the few years they spend in segregated warrior villages, known as *manyat* (singular, *manyata*), which are set up to defend individual districts. The *moran* flaunt their independence and live the communalistic ideals of *moran* brotherhood in their *manyat.* The supreme ideal of the *manyata* is represented by individual warriors, known as "diehards," who pledge themselves to die in combat rather than retreat (Figure 4.11).

To establish a *manyata,* the *moran* conduct raids on their parental homes and carry off their mothers and small herds of cattle, sometimes against the protests of their fathers. As Spencer (1988) points out, this is clearly a ritual rebellion against the fathers. The *manyat* villages of the *moran* are organized around egalitarian and communalistic principles in direct opposition to the age hierarchy and individualism of the domestic homestead.

The midpoint of *moran*-hood is ritually marked by an extended ceremony known as *eunoto,* which begins five years into the grade and initiates a ten-year series of steps leading to elderhood. After this ceremony, a *moran* may be expected to marry. In the *eunoto,* the *manyat* villages are disbanded, and the combined age class is formally launched. This ceremony involves a spectacular display of massed warriors that even attracts fee-paying European tourists and film crews.

Although many ceremonial phases of the Maasai age-class system incorporate ritualized rebellions against parental authority, the excesses of the *moran* are held in check, and they are guided through the maturation process by their elder patrons, who maintain ultimate control by their power to curse their charges. It could certainly be argued that the age-class system constructively channels the otherwise potentially disruptive energies of young men who grow up as subservient herdboys and must wait at least ten years before they can marry. Spencer (1988) suggests that the age system diverts the stresses that are inherent in the family system away from the senior male household heads to elders in general. In some respects, the *manyata* phase places the *moran* in what Arnold van Gennep (1909) would call a **liminal phase.** It is a rite of transition in which the *moran* are ritually suspended in the space between being herdboys and elders.

FIGURE 4.11   Maasai warriors.

The age-class system is functionally related to incest avoidance and marriage practices in a mutually reinforcing way. Spencer (1988) points out that Maasai incest restrictions are more elaborated toward daughters and mothers-in-law than mothers and sisters. This is apparently because a system of age-class exogamy operates in which the men of one age class marry the daughters of the men in the class senior to them, rather than marrying the daughters of their own age mates. The age classes thus are linked by marriage alliances, such as might operate between exogamous clans. This reinforces the respect that must be obtained between junior and senior classes if the age-class system is to survive, because the junior class members will find their fathers-in-law in the senior class their wives would be the daughters of 45- to 50-year-old senior men, who might have married at 30, and could have 15- to 20-year-old marriageable daughters. Age-class exogamy thus means that men will tend to marry much younger women, thereby creating the age differential that makes frequent polygyny possible.

The persistence of the Maasai as a society up to the present day is evidence of the importance of their age-class system. It is significant that while the population of Kenya as a whole has recently experienced extremely high population increases that threaten the economic viability of the entire country, settled farming groups are growing at twice the rate of the Maasai and other pastoralists (4 percent versus 2.2 percent or less). Isaac Sindiga (1987) suggests that the traditional Maasai practices of polygyny, postpartum taboos on sexual intercourse, and prolonged lactation, which are all linked to patriarchy and the age-class system, are significant child-spacing and fertility-dampening factors.

Women do not become elders, but they clearly do have a stake in their society and work to maintain the system, especially as they grow older. Senior wives may welcome polygyny because it

---

liminal phase An ambiguous phase of ritual transition in which one is on the threshold between two states.

Maasai Women

In the film *Maasai Women* (1974), anthropologist Melissa Llewelyn-Davies, who speaks the Maasai language and has years of research experience with the Maasai, engages several Maasai women in a free-ranging discussion about their experiences as women. In their own words, these Maasai women define and accept as a given the gender roles of their culture. Women milk cows, bear children, and build their own houses. A woman "has nothing." Women care for animals and have milking rights but no ownership rights over them. Men make the decisions about herds. Yet in this discussion with a sympathetic and knowledgeable nonnative woman, the Maasai women are quick to place their own cultural roles in a positive light. Clitoridectomy (female circumcision), which is strongly condemned by international feminists, is defended as something "we've always done." One woman explains, "It is something God began long ago. A girl wants to hurry up and be circumcised. It is a very good thing." When Llewelyn-Davies asks if the initiate is happy about the experience, she is told emphatically that she is "very happy" because the girl will then be thought of as a woman and will be able to marry soon.

Female circumcision may not be fully supported by all Maasai women, regardless of what they say about it. It may not even be a functionally irreplaceable part of their culture. In this case, women themselves may feel compelled to perpetuate customs that may not be in their best interests.

In the film, the women tell Llewelyn-Davies that although they accept arranged marriages to old men, they are not always happy about it and may select young warriors as lovers even though their husbands would be angry if they found out. When Llewelyn-Davies raises the possibility of women being jealous over young co-wives in this polygynous society, a Maasai woman declares:

> We're not jealous like you Europeans. . . . To us a co-wife is something very good because there is much work to do. When it rains, the village gets mucky and it's you who clears it out. It's you who looks after the cows. You do the milking, and your husband may have very many cows. That's a lot of work. You have to milk and smear the roof and see to the calves. . . . So when you give birth and it rains, who will smear the roof if you have no co-wife? No one. Who will clear the muck from the village? No one. So Maasai aren't jealous because of all this work.

However, the film also shows women greeting new co-wives with open, "ritualized" hostility.

It is a hard life, but there are rewards. After a girl's initiation, a group of women in the film sing,

> Listen God to what suits women. It suits us to prepare charms for the initiates, to be busy with our children's circumcisions, to have celebrations, which are lavish in honey beer and milk and meat and butter. It suits us when our sons go out herding. It suits us to sit resting in the shade. It suits us when we suckle children. God, nursing mother, remember what suits us.

lightens their domestic routine (see the box entitled "Maasai Women"). Women themselves perform the clitoridectomy, and they accept it as a precondition of marriage. Divorce is an option, especially early in an unhappy marriage. After women have children, they gain more autonomy, and because they marry young, they usually outlive their husbands. Abused wives may appeal to the elders for help; men who commit serious offenses against women may be perceived as a threat to all women; they may be assaulted and beaten and have their cattle slaughtered by a large group of enraged women acting in a publicly sanctioned role as enforcers of community morality. Women also conduct their own rituals of rebellion against male authority.

The underlying principle of male age classes is that every male enjoys the same potential to be a warrior, marry, raise a family, officiate at rituals, and so on, and these potentials are realized in orderly sequence by virtue of his membership in an age class in which these rights are jointly shared. Conflicts do arise in the system, but they occur primarily over the timing of promotions. Political struggle takes place between groups, not individuals. Political power thus is widely distributed and strictly regulated. The system is not simply a gerontocracy with power concentrated at the top.

SUMMARY

East African cattle peoples have developed a highly successful cultural system that makes effective use of a difficult environment. They have created a society in which men and women and young and old share different responsibilities for supporting and reproducing households, society, and culture. The presence of cattle and other domesticated animals makes it possible for African pastoralists to support much higher population densities and larger societies than the Australian aborigines and Amazonian forest peoples. However, this is not always an advantage, because work loads increase and people's personal lives are more highly regulated. Like all tribal societies, there are no formal political leaders or governmental structure, and kinship remains the primary organizing principle. There are permanent villages, but herds and young men are mobile. Raiding is focused on capturing cattle rather than revenge killing of men and capturing women as in Amazonia, and young men must spend ten or more years with age mates in the status of warrior herdsmen before they can marry. The social roles of married men and women are less equitable than in aboriginal Australia and Amazonia. Women work harder than men and cannot ordinarily own and manage livestock or engage in politics, although they do have use rights to animals for subsistence purposes. Ideologically, women are in the contradictory position of being socially marginalized yet highly valued. However, women control domestic life, because they own their houses, beds, and hearths. Most importantly, women give men descendants to maintain their patrilines, and in polygynous households a man's mother is the source of his cattle inheritance.

Cattle are central to household subsistence and the primary means for men to pursue their individual self-interest beyond the household. However, their use of cattle as individually owned, movable, reproducible wealth makes it possible for more wealth differences to emerge than in other tribal societies. There are practical upper and lower limits on the size of household herds, but most households are wealthy enough in livestock to enjoy a comfortable margin to protect them from the effects of droughts, epidemics, and raids.

STUDY QUESTIONS

1. Describe the subsistence uses East African pastoralists make of their cattle.
2. What are the most critical limiting factors to which African pastoralists must adapt?
3. Why is it difficult to determine how many cattle African pastoralists actually need and to establish the carrying capacity of the range?

4. Describe the marriage process for the Nuer, including the concepts of bride-wealth, household, husband, wife, pater, and genitor.
5. How does the Maasai age-class system relate to
gerontocracy and patriarchy, and how does it contribute to the resilience of Maasai society?
6. Describe the social and ritual uses of cattle in East
Africa.
7. Describe the social power available to women in
herding societies.
8. What conditions work to maintain social and economic equality between households in herding
societies?

SUGGESTED READING

EVANS-PRITCHARD, E. E. 1940. *The Nuer: A Description of
the Modes of Livelihood and Political Institutions of a
Nilotic People.* New York and Oxford, Eng.: Oxford University Press. The most famous early ethnography of East
African cattle people; vividly describes their dependence
on cattle, emphasizing ecological relationships.
SPENCER, PAUL. 1988. *The Maasai of Matapato: A Study of
Rituals of Rebellion.* Bloomington and Indianapolis: Indiana University Press. An excellent modern ethnography
that focuses on social organization, life cycle, and ritual.

Independent Amazonian tribal peoples typically enjoy a healthy, vigorous life, relatively free of disease.

5

Body, Mind, and Soul: The Quality of Tribal Life

Learning Objectives

After studying this chapter you should be able to do the following:

1. Explain the difficulties involved in determining whether or not there are differences in the cognitive abilities of peoples in different cultures.
2. Explain why commonly used racial categories are not scientifically meaningful.
3. Explain why the concept of racial purity is not scientifically meaningful.
4. Evaluate the linguistic hypothesis that people speaking different languages live in different perceptual worlds.
5. Explain how shamanism, and other beliefs and practices related to the supernatural may benefit individuals.
6. Evaluate the quality of life experienced by people in the tribal world, making specific comparisons with people in the commercial world.

PRONUNCIATION GUIDE

Andean and Amazonian terms in this chapter are variously derived from Spanish, Portuguese, Quechua, and numerous tribal languages. Their most common pronunciation can be approximated by English speakers using the following orthography and sounds:

Key
a = a in father
o = o in go
ay = ay in day
ee = ee in beet
oo = oo in food
y = y in you
• = Syllable division
/ = Stress

cholo = [cho / lo]
criollos = [cree • ol / yos]
mestizo = [may • stee / so]
Quechua = [kaych / wa]
Xavante = [sha • van / tay]

The thoughts, beliefs, and health practices of people living in tribal cultures raise many important, intriguing, and critical questions related to cross-cultural understanding. The basic issue is how to evaluate the mental, emotional, and physical well-being of tribal peoples in order to assess the overall success of their cultures. This is an important problem because welfare intervention programs undertaken on behalf of tribal peoples by missionaries, government educators, and health workers often assume that these people must be ignorant and backward. Members of wealthy industrial nations easily equate hospitals, schools, and sewage treatment plants with health and intelligence and look down on any society lacking these facilities. Such ethnocentric views are reinforced by the seemingly bizarre and irrational elements in tribal shamanism, witchcraft, and magic. Whereas earlier chapters showed these aspects of religion and ideology within their cultural context, this chapter considers their significance for individuals.

We will review some of the classic interpretations of tribal religion and "primitive mentality" by such historically prominent anthropological theorists as Edward Tylor, Sir James Frazer, Franz Boas, Lucien Lévy-Bruhl, and Bronislaw Malinowski, along with the more recent views of Claude Lévi-Strauss and C. R. Hallpike. Because racist beliefs have clouded many views of tribal peoples, we will review the facts of human biology to affirm the fundamental unity of humankind, before considering the issues of language and culture, religious practice, and health. We will place special emphasis on Australian and Amazonian examples because full cultural context has been established in previous chapters.

THE MENTAL ABILITIES
OF TRIBAL PEOPLES

Just as any attempt to understand another culture is colored by the biases of one's own culture, the way anthropologists have historically understood the mental abilities of tribal peoples was shaped by their theoretical preconceptions about human biology and how human cultures are constructed and how they work. Modes of anthropological explanation have changed over time like fashions, often reflecting changes in national politics and changes within the global culture itself. Historically, the most misleading and damaging anthropological theories were those that assumed that biological differences made some human groups inferior. Equally damaging were theories that assumed not only that cultural evolutionary progress was inevitable, but that it was always progress, in the sense of human improvement. This left little room for evaluating the achievements of small-scale tribal culture in a positive light.

Prior to 1945, when the modern colonial era ended, biological explanations of cultural difference were still closely linked with European notions of cultural superiority. This was racist because it equated cultural differences with racial differences and always judged tribal peoples to be inferior. In extreme cases, such biological determinism took the form of **social Darwinism,** applying competitive natural selection and survival-of-the-fittest theories of biological evolution to entire cultures. Social Darwinists concluded that the peoples and cultures that European colonists were destroying were culturally and biologically "unfit" and therefore doomed to disappear. They viewed small-scale cultures as living fossils representing the earlier stages of evolutionary development beyond which Europeans had presumably advanced. This ethnocentric approach is illustrated in Chapter 1 by Staniland Wake's 1890s description of aborigines as backward children. Such extremely derogatory representations of tribal peoples led to insensitive colonial policies that accelerated the disintegration of tribal societies under the pressure of European conquest. Ethnocentric ethnography was rejected as unscientific by British functionalist anthropologists such as Radcliffe-Brown, Malinowski, and Evans-Pritchard, who by the 1930s began to assist colonial administrators by describing tribal societies and cultures as organism-like systems. Functionalists warned that even tribal cultural beliefs and practices that seemed disgusting or bizarre to Europeans could be shown to have "functions," or social purposes, and that indiscriminate colonial interference could have unintended negative consequences.

Collective Representations and Primitive Mentality

The rapid European colonial domination of Africa, which was in full swing by the late nineteenth century, made it imperative for the new European administrators and petty colonial officials to understand the peoples that they were attempting to control. Because it was so difficult for foreigners to predict the behavior of natives, it was widely believed that native thought processes were inferior to those of Europeans. And because explicitly racist evolutionary theories were used to justify colonialism, Europeans readily assumed that people living in tribal societies must be physically and culturally underdeveloped and therefore childlike in their thinking.

The approach of American anthropologists to the understanding of cultural differences was profoundly influenced by Franz Boas who, during his years at Columbia University from 1899 to 1937, trained many of the researchers who became the most prominent anthropologists of the twentieth century. Boas was a German immigrant with a Jewish heritage, and he emphatically opposed any theories of racial superiority, or that attributed cultural differences to racial type. Boas rated Euro-American civilization as the highest human cultural achievement, but he believed that there were no significant differences in basic mental faculties between "uncivilized primitives" and "civilized" peoples. In his book *The Mind of Primitive Man* (1911), he easily refuted a list of presumably inferior mental features that were widely attributed to tribal people, including their supposed inability to inhibit their emotions, their shortened attention spans, and their limited powers of original thought. Boas found that natives were impulsive and improvident when it was culturally appropriate but showed remarkable re-

straint when necessary. He noted that the supposed inability of natives to focus their attention was most likely to be reported by frustrated ethnographers who found it difficult to get reluctant informants to answer a long series of irrelevant questions. Likewise, within their own cultural context, natives showed plenty of creativity. Boas certainly acknowledged differences in forms of thought between tribal and civilized peoples, but these he attributed to social, or cultural, differences, not racial factors. He concluded that tribal peoples simply classified experiences differently and merged concepts in ways that appeared peculiar to us.

British anthropologist E. B. Tylor (1871) argued in *Primitive Culture* that seemingly bizarre tribal religious beliefs and rituals developed out of what he called **animistic thinking,** in which intellectually curious people attempted to explain dream experiences and death by attributing a detachable animating soul to people, animals, plants, and "inanimate" objects. Tylor felt that the soul concept was the basis of all religion, shamanism, and witchcraft and that tribal people arrived at it by logical mental processes, which were basically like our own. Sir James Frazer elaborated this intellectualist approach in *The Golden Bough* (1900) when he identified the laws that he thought underlay magical practices. His **law of sympathy** held that things such as hair, which were once part of someone, could still influence that person even after they were separated. Therefore, a man's hair clippings

---

social Darwinism A political philosophy that treats other societies, and in some cases the poor and weak within one's own society, as biologically and culturally inferior and therefore "unfit" for survival.

animistic thinking The soul concept used by tribal individuals as an intellectual explanation of life, death, and dream experiences; part of Tylor's theory of animism as the origin of religion.

law of sympathy Frazer's explanation for the logic underlying magic, sorcery, and shamanism. He thought that tribal peoples believed that anything ever connected with a person, such as hair or blood, could be manipulated to influence that person.

might be used by shamans to harm him. Tribal people may not recognize Frazer's "law of sympathy," but they do see a metaphorical relationship between substance and person. In this case the shaman can use the shared belief in invisible connections between biological substance and an individual to influence that person, just as in our society, where DNA analysis of a detached bodily substance can be used as legal evidence. DNA is invisible to most of us, yet we believe in its existence and use this belief to influence people. Like Tylor, Frazer argued that primitives were crude logicians who thought like Englishmen but simply made mistakes.

French positivist philosopher Lucien Lévy-Bruhl was one of the first scholars to systematically examine the thought processes of tribal peoples with the practical purpose of showing how they differed from those of "civilized" peoples. He applied the concept of **collective representations,** or group ideas, developed by French sociologist Emile Durkheim. According to Lévy-Bruhl (1923, 1926) collective representations, like culture in general, are emotion-laden thoughts, or ideas, that are shared by the members of a specific society and transmitted across generations. These thoughts are collective in that they are not the unique property of specific individuals, and therefore they cannot be understood according to the principles of individual psychology. He insisted throughout that primitive mentality was not inferior and that natives were not childlike; their thinking was simply different. However, this point was easily overlooked when he referred to primitive mentality as "prelogical," not "illogical," and when he declared that the collective representations of "undeveloped peoples" could not be understood by studying the categories and logical principles used by "adult, civilized, white man" (1926:13). Lévy-Bruhl agreed with Boas that thought was culturally conditioned, but he emphatically departed from Boas, as well as from Tylor and Frazer, by declaring that the mental processes of "primitives" are distinctively different and can be understood only by their own "laws." He rejected animist, intel-

lectualist explanations because they were based on individual, not collective, thought.

The most critical aspect of primitive thought, Lévy-Bruhl argued, was that it assumed a "mystic" reality—it was based on a socially conditioned belief in imperceptible forces. This was **prelogical thinking,** based on a **law of participation,** under which contradictions were ignored and something could be two things at once. Thus, primitives saw nothing contradictory in a shaman being a man and a tiger at the same time. Of course, all peoples have this ability. For example, Christians, who may be members of political- and commercial-scale cultures, have no apparent difficulty considering Jesus Christ to be both a man and a god.

Lévy-Bruhl declared, "Primitives perceive nothing in the same way as we do" (1926:43), even though their brains and their senses are the same as ours. In primitive thought, according to Lévy-Bruhl, the causes of natural events like disease and accident might be sought in what we would call the supernatural. Physical causes were irrelevant in collective representations, even though individuals were certainly logical enough to know when to come in out of the rain and could successfully manage their daily affairs. Prelogical natives formed concrete impressions that they felt and lived emotionally, whereas civilized people worked with abstract, conceptual thought. In his own contradictory terms, Lévy-Bruhl suggested that primitive thought was thus "concrete," whereas civilized thinking was abstract and conceptual.

Despite the difficulties Lévy-Bruhl experienced in grappling with cross-cultural understanding, he correctly observed that barriers to emic understanding (meanings internal to a given culture) were in a sense insurmountable. Translation problems are critical because categories are seldom precisely the same even when superficial resemblances exist. For example, traditional exchange objects, which often are called "money," are not actually money as it exists in a market economy. Although the difference in meaning may not be accurately characterized as that between concrete and abstract, Lévy-Bruhl was correct in calling for in-depth linguistic knowledge because it is perfectly possible to have a minimal speaking knowledge without really being able to think in another language.

After Lévy-Bruhl, anthropologists largely abandoned efforts to examine the mental world of tribal peoples until the 1960s, when another French anthropologist, Claude Lévi-Strauss (1966), elaborated his structuralist approach to the mental processes underlying tribal culture. Lévi-Strauss questioned the entire distinction between abstract and concrete words by relating it to differences in level of attention and interest, not to differences in method of thought. Lévi-Strauss argued that tribal people, like civilized people, use many abstract words and pursue objective knowledge about the environment for its own sake. People name things, not simply because these are objects of immediate utilitarian interest, but because they find it aesthetically pleasing to impose order on the world through careful observation and cataloguing. Such attention to detail was well illustrated in our previous discussion of the ethnoecological knowledge of Native Amazonians and the Dreaming maps of Australian aborigines. According to Lévi-Strauss, it is this common drive for order that underlies all human thought and that makes unfamiliar thought patterns understandable.

Lévi-Strauss did not find it particularly mystical that people identify with totemic animals. Natives are not confused by a law of participation into thinking that they are their totems. There is no contradiction in holding empirical and emotional knowledge about a single object. Instead of speaking of a prelogical mentality, Lévi-Strauss maintained that magical thought, or what he preferred to call **mythical thought**, differs from formal scientific thought in method and purpose, but not in logic. Mythical thought is scientific in that it produced the important technological developments of the Neolithic, such as domestication, pottery, and weaving. However, the "Neolithic paradox" for Lévi-Strauss is the difficulty in explaining why technological

development seemingly stagnated after the scientific achievements of the Neolithic until the establishment of formal science. To resolve the paradox, Lévi-Strauss argued that there are two distinct but opposite types of scientific thought, each equally valid and neither a stage in the development of the other: the **science of the concrete**, which is based on perceptions and signs, and formal science, which works with concepts. Here he uses the term "science" in the sense of a systematic ordering of observations and ideas to help people define and understand reality. The science of the concrete as applied in the tribal world is not directed toward creating new technology to change the physical world directly; it is concerned with shaping perception. In that respect, it resembles the use of visual images in the contemporary film and video media.

Mythical thought works with a culturally limited set of signs, including significant images and events, which it orders into structured relationships that provide aesthetic satisfaction while helping people understand reality (Figure 5.1). Lévi-Strauss is here referring to the structured sets of logical associations and complementary oppositions that are so characteristic of myths and the ritual beliefs and practices that are related to them. These were discussed in some detail in the Amazonian cosmology examined in

collective representations Ideas, or thoughts, and emotions common to a society as a whole, especially in reference to the supernatural.

prelogical thinking Lévy-Bruhl's characterization of the collective representations of tribal peoples, which he thought reflected concrete thought and a mystic reality unique to domestic-scale cultures.

law of participation The assumption that a thing can participate in or be part of two or more things at once; identified by Lévy-Bruhl as the principle underlying his concept of prelogical thought.

mythical thought Lévi-Strauss's term for the thinking underlying myth and magic; logically similar to scientific thought but based on the science of the concrete and used to serve aesthetic purposes and to solve existential problems.

science of the concrete Levi-Strauss's term for thought based on perceptions and signs, images, and events, as opposed to formal science based on concepts.

FIGURE 5.1   The Pokot, East African pastoralists, dancing to celebrate a male initiation ceremony. Ritual activities like these are rich in symbolic associations, connecting mind, body, and soul.

Chapter 3. Formal scientific concepts remain as close to natural reality as possible. They are derived from structured theories and hypotheses and are used to expand the total cultural inventory and to make changes, or create events, in the external world.

Cross-Cultural Intelligence Testing

Anthropologist C. R. Hallpike (1979) carried on Lévy-Bruhl's argument that "primitives" think differently from civilized peoples. Primitives, for Hallpike, are the rural illiterate and unschooled, as well as the members of the domestic-scale societies dealt with in Chapters 2–4 of this book. Their

thinking is not actually different from our own—it is merely incomplete and less developed. Hallpike uses the developmental stages devised by Swiss psychologist Jean Piaget to describe the acquisition of cognitive abilities by children in order to catalogue the cognitive abilities of tribal adults. Hallpike's interpretation is that the majority of primitive adults are incapable of adult thought. They are mentally equivalent to seven-year-old European children, but because they are grown up, they are, in effect, retarded. Such retardation, Hallpike argues, is caused by the absence of schools and literacy.

Hallpike cites a variety of psychological tests performed on "primitives" to support his conclusions. These tests seem to show that primitives cannot verbally sort objects into classes by obvious differences, cannot sort the events of a narrative into a logical sequence, cannot grasp the argument of simple syllogisms, and so on. Hallpike makes a careful point-by-point comparison of primitive thought with our presumably more developed formal thought and finds primitive thinking profoundly inadequate.

Hallpike's theories are vulnerable on a number of issues (Shweder 1982, 1985). In the first place, Piagetian stage theory has come under increasing attack by developmental psychologists who stress that the boundaries between the stages are not as sharp as once thought. Young children may be quite capable of "higher" thinking at much earlier ages than previously believed; they may simply not often use these abilities and may have difficulty verbalizing about them.

Hallpike's developmentalist view is in opposition to both *universalist* and *relativist* approaches to thought. In the universalist view (represented by Lévi-Strauss), the mental processes that people use to construct classification systems are a human universal shared by all peoples. The relativist position would emphasize the priority of language in the development of thought, suggesting that individuals do not invent their own mentalities but take on the mental processes that their language hands them. Such a view is not incompatible with a universalist interpretation to the extent that linguistic universals are recognized.

Separating what people actually know from what they claim to believe is not easy. For example, Europeans are often seen as relying on the presumably culturally specific Cartesian dualism that treats mind and body as separate things, as well as such familiar dualisms as biology and culture, nature and nurture, subject and object, etc. In contrast, it is claimed that tribal peoples do not distinguish between the biological facts of life and the cultural construction of kinship. However, many dualist distinctions may actually be human universals. In the United States developmental psychologists devised a simple test and found that before the age of seven American children do not distinguish between birth (nature)

or parenting (nurture) as a source of an individual's mental or physical traits, and they do not differentiate between mental (mind) and physical (body) traits. Rita Astuti (2001) applied the same test to the Verzo of Madagascar, and found that, although Verso children like American children did not make these distinctions, most adults had no difficulty differentiating both mind/body and nature/nurture dualisms to solve the logical problem of predicting whether an adopted child would resemble its adoptive or biological parents. Remarkably, the Verzo adults were *cognitive* dualists in these matters even though *culturally* they appeared to disregard these "Cartesian" distinctions. The conclusion is that what people say may not always reflect what they think. This may seem obvious, but much cultural theory takes cultural narratives at face value as representative of underlying cognitive processes.

Failure to identify higher cognitive skills in children or "primitives" may tell us more about deficiencies in testing techniques and our concepts of cognition than about their thought processes. Many cross-cultural psychologists have questioned the validity of applying test procedures developed in one culture to people in an entirely different culture, especially where there is no practical context, content, or experience for the procedure or any familiarity with the concept of an intelligence test. Language is an obvious barrier in cross-cultural testing, and even when interpreters are used and in-depth interviews attempted, questioning will still be an impersonal, out-of-context ritual, which subjects likely will treat as irrelevant, if not as an unwelcome invasion of their privacy. Test subjects also may be quite justified in objecting to testing because it has often had practical implications for people and has seldom been carried out as pure science. For example, early in the twentieth century, the Stanford-Binet IQ test was extensively used in the United States to identify the "feebleminded" and to influence policies concerning immigration, eugenics, education, institutionalization, and military service (Gould 1981).

The most significant differences in thought patterns between the members of tribal societies and urban peoples in the commercial world probably do relate to cultural differences in lifestyle. For example, the pervasive influence of advertising and television may produce very unusual modes of thought about the real world. Such differences would not reflect individual mental development or the absolute superiority of one culture over the other. Perhaps the most serious problem with earlier attempts to assess the cognitive abilities of peoples living in small-scale societies is that they have focused on a rather narrow, culture-specific concept of pure intelligence. Surely, intelligence must mean more than scores achieved on a test that might relate to academic achievement or some other performance in commercial societies.

Cross-cultural psychologists J. W. Berry and S. H. Irvine (1986, Irvine and Berry 1988) stress that for test scores to be meaningful, the tests must be conducted within the cultural and ecological context of the people being assessed. They categorically reject the validity of tests that are applied outside the culture for which they were originally devised. Taking a firmly cultural-relativist position on cognitive ability, Irvine and Berry have formulated a **law of cultural differentiation,** which states:

> Cultural factors prescribe what shall be learned and at what age; consequently different cultural environments lead to the development of different patterns of ability. (Irvine and Berry 1988:4)

They prefer to speak of cognitive abilities rather than "intelligence" because there is no agreement on a global theory of human intelligence. Few researchers have even asked, What does intelligence mean to a particular people? Too often, intelligence testing has shown what people do not do but has not examined the cognitive skills, or the "practical intelligence," that is required for the successful performances of everyday life. In the following section, we consider this kind of intelligence for Australian aborigines.

Anthropologist Jack Goody (1977) points out that the use of written language allows people to store and manipulate information in unique ways. This makes it easier for literate peoples to make lists and arrange ideas in matrices to reveal complex relationships, but does not change the cognitive functions of the human mind. Information technologies such as writing and computers, however, are tools that help elites concentrate social power in larger-scale social systems.

The Cognitive Abilities of Australian Aborigines

The European invaders of Australia were convinced of the intellectual inferiority of aborigines from the very beginning. The first formal test of the cognitive abilities of aborigines was conducted in 1915 using the Porteus Maze Solving Test, which could be taken by illiterates. S. D. Porteus (1917) first applied his maze test to a control group of forty-two delinquent and criminal European Australian boys to make sure the test would identify a lack of foresight, prudence, and general mental deficiency, which he assumed would accompany social deviancy. When he applied the test to twenty-eight aboriginal children at a mission, he discovered that they actually performed better than the European delinquents and criminals, but he attributed this to the assumed rapid physical maturation of aborigines. He argued that aboriginal mental development occurred rapidly and then stopped. Unshaken in his belief in the racial inferiority of aborigines, he concluded that by early adolescence, "the common racial characteristics of indolence, shiftlessness, and lack of foresight become apparent" (Porteus 1917:38).

Psychological testing in Australia, as elsewhere, was used by the state to diagnose mental health, educational problems, and vocational potential; thus, for aborigines, the tests had significant implications. During the period from 1960 to 1980, as the government became increasingly concerned with the social problems of aborigines, some 280 separate cognitive studies were conducted on aborigines (Klich 1988). This research often yielded contradictory results. Considerable debate ensued over whether the diagnosed aboriginal "inferiority" was due to culture or genes, but the prevailing view that aborigines were somehow mentally inferior seemed unshaken. For example, Piagetian tests applied to aborigines showed performance levels consistently lower than the European standard. Because the aboriginal environment was assumed to be the problem, some researchers concluded that aboriginal children should be removed from their retarding environments so that they could develop "normally" (see reviews by Keats and Keats 1988 and Klich 1988).

A modern study of aboriginal mentality by psychoanalytic anthropologist Arthur Hippler (1978) took a Freudian twist and ethnocentrically attributed assumed aboriginal mental deficiencies to "inferior" child-rearing practices. Hippler rejected racist explanations but explicitly retained the biased evolutionist position that peoples can usefully be ranked by cognitive and emotional ability according to a Euro-American standard. As a self-styled "psychocultural evolutionist," Hippler believed that all people are born with equal mental potential but that primitive cultures stifle this potential by faulty child rearing. Following a modified Piagetian-stages approach, he argued that primitives are developmentally retarded and thus as adults allow the magical fantasies of childhood to cloud their perception of the real world. According to Hippler (1977), primitives practice an "infanticidal and abandoning" evolutionary stage of child rearing, which is so cruel and inconsistent that children are unable to repress their sexual impulses and childish fantasies and are thus unable to reach their cognitive potentials.

Hippler paid a brief visit to aboriginal communities in Arnhem Land where he administered Rorschach inkblot tests and concluded that the Yolngu people were "impulse-ridden, sexually anxious, jealous and fearful." They had difficulty separating fantasy from reality. They lacked imagination, were impulsive yet rigid, and had cognitively "lesser" capacities than Western norms. He considered sacred sites to be a "cultural pathology" because they overvalued land forms. In remarkable detail, he pointed out the shortcomings of Yolngu child rearing, which he felt accounted for their cognitive problems.

Australian anthropologists who were familiar with the Yolngu people were outraged by Hippler's assessment, both theoretically and substantively, and found it a totally unfounded distortion (Hamilton 1979, Reser 1981). They had no difficulty presenting respectable and convincing evidence based on in-depth field experience to refute Hippler's ethnocentric stereotypes. In response, rather than defending his specific interpretations, Hippler (1981) reiterated his view that traditional culture was "incredibly repressive" and argued for the complete abandonment of cultural relativism.

Belatedly, researchers began to examine the cognitive skills that aborigines actually used in their daily lives and found that they consistently rated higher than Europeans. For example, aborigines excelled on visual memory and spatial tests, which were skills that served them well in route finding, tracking, hunting, and gathering (Klich 1988). Earlier anthropological observers also had been impressed by the superior visual acuity and observational abilities of aborigines; but in line with their racist and evolutionary biases, they devalued them as instinctive survival skills and "lower" mental functions. D. Lewis (1976) found that aborigines routinely kept detailed mental track of the topographic features that they passed when traveling across country that to him seemed virtually featureless. In random tests in which he used a compass, Lewis found that aborigines could point with great precision in the direction of sacred sites that were 77 or more miles (200 km) away. Such accuracy required them to constantly update a mental map of their movements, and they were able to do this even in unfamiliar country. These spatial abilities

law of cultural differentiation A statement of the cultural relativity of cognitive ability or basic intelligence. It assumes that no single culture-bound test can adequately test cognitive ability because different cultures produce different cognitive abilities in individuals.

are well supported by the aboriginal language and the Dreamtime cosmology. A European would have rated as feebleminded in such a test.

RACISM

In this section, we briefly review the principal scientific findings of physical anthropology and archaeology demonstrating the common origins of humanity, the genetic basis of human unity and diversity, and the failures of recent attempts to explain economic performance in genetic terms.

The archaeological record confirms that for at least the past 30,000 or so years, all *Homo sapiens* populations have shared the same biological capacity to produce rich, linguistically based cultures. This means that all peoples have the same overall human potential. About two million years ago, our closest humanlike fossil ancestor, *Homo erectus,* moved definitively in the human direction. *Homo erectus* did not look fully modern— they had thick skulls with receding foreheads and chins and heavy brow ridges and jaws—but their brains approached modern size. Even more significantly, *Homo erectus* used culture to adaptive advantage. They probably made fires, built shelters, lived in caves, and used relatively sophisticated stone tools for butchering and woodworking. It also seems likely that they had some form of "protolanguage" (Bickerton 1990) to propel these cultural developments, thus making it possible for *Homo erectus* to spread beyond Africa to Europe and Asia perhaps one million years ago. This began the evolutionary process of humanization that simultaneously produced human culture and physically modern *Homo sapiens.*

Fossil evidence and DNA analysis of contemporary peoples suggest that physically modern humans can be traced to a common origin in Africa some 200,000 years ago. By perhaps 100,000 years ago a genetic mutation that produced the physical ability for human speech may have occurred (Enard et al. 2002). It is reasonable to conclude that humans have been a species with great variation in body form (polymor-phism), as well as considerable genetic diversity, since the very dawn of humanity.

Facts of Life and the Culture of Race

Popular racial classifications are primarily *cultural* constructions, not biological realities. For example, the five categories—black, white, American Indian–Alaskan Native, Asian–Pacific Islander, and Hispanic—used by the U.S. Census in 1980 and 1990 were culturally produced legal fictions that had no scientific validity. Culturally defined racial categories mix legal citizenship and ethnicity with naive assumptions about skin color and blood, but they ignore the genetic facts of life. For example, the U.S. government follows a blood quantum rule and recognizes "American Indians" as legal tribal members only if they can demonstrate ancestry of at least one-fourth "full blood." But "full blood" is itself a legal fiction based on previous tribal enrollments. Thus, "American Indian" is legally declared to be a biological category. Similarly, an American with a single black grandparent is likely to be classified "black." The underlying myth of such racial categories is that genetically "pure" races exist. Nazi attempts to "purify" an Aryan super-race during World War II were equally misguided and caused enormous human suffering.

For the 2000 census, the U.S. government continued to employ the concept of race, although after consulting with the American Anthropological Association they declared that officially "race" was not intended to be a biological or anthropological definition. Race would now be whatever respondents on the census form thought it was, and could include race as biology, national origin, and sociocultural affiliation. The form first asked about "Hispanic origin" and then offered six categories for people to self-identify their race as White *alone;* Black or African American *alone;* American Indian and Alaska Native *alone;* Asian *alone;* Native Hawaiian and other Pacific Islander *alone;* and Other race *alone.* The census added another category for those who claimed more than one race. From an anthropological perspective, all of this was an unsatisfactory compromise, because it still left the false impression that there were six or more races that could be biologically defined.

In Latin America, there are many racial classifications that explicitly reflect culture rather than biology. For example, in Andean Peru, individuals who look exactly alike will self-identify and be called (1) *indios* (Native American Indian), if they wear distinctive Indian clothing and speak Quechua (an indigenous language); (2) *cholos,* if they are small shopkeepers fluent in both Quechua and Spanish; or (3) *mestizos* or *criollos* if they are more affluent Spanish speakers. The cultural basis of these categories is demonstrated by the ability of individuals to move from one to another depending on their success in the market economy.

Human racial classifications are scientifically inappropriate for several reasons. Humans constitute a global, polymorphic, continuously interbreeding population. For the past 30,000 years, no peoples, other than a handful of tiny populations on remote islands, have been isolated long enough to produce more than a relatively small genetic distance from any other human populations. Therefore, any scientific classification of people into genetic populations must necessarily be an arbitrary exercise based on variations in gene frequencies. The U.S. Census categories cannot be validated scientifically with gene frequency tests. A careful observer could distinguish thousands of "races" based on particular traits.

The human genome consists of 23 pairs of chromosomes, carrying 50–100,000 genes, each represented by unique segments of DNA (see the box entitled "Human Genetics Glossary"). The genetic information encoded in the sequences of the four DNA nucleotides (A, C, G, T) in human chromosomes provides virtually infinite potential for human diversity. Human geneticist Luigi Cavalli-Sforza (Cavalli-Sforza and Cavalli-Sforza 1995:255) notes that it would take some 3000 volumes of 300 pages each to print the ACGT codes making up the 3 billion nucleotides of the human genome.

Many genetic differences between peoples do have important health implications, but these real differences do not have any relation to popular racial stereotypes. For example, the blood

sickle-cell allele found originally in certain West African tropical forest populations provides resistance to malaria. Another allele, present in descendants of herding peoples, produces lactase, an enzyme that digests lactose, or milk sugar. People lacking this allele can suffer from lactose intolerance. Knowing that someone was categorized as an "Asian–Pacific Islander" would not be a reliable predictor of lactase deficiency, and knowing that a person was categorized as "black" would not identify the sickle-cell allele.

Geneticists and anthropologists (Cavalli-Sforza and Cavalli-Sforza 1995; Cavalli-Sforza, Menozzi, and Piazza 1994; Krantz 1980) sort human genetic variation into two broad types: classical adaptive traits and neutral polymorphisms. Classical traits are highly visible features, such as skin, hair and eye color; body build; and the shape of the face. These traits are the basis of popular racial stereotypes, but they are not discrete variables. They are produced in complex ways by the interaction of multiple genes, and they vary continuously among individuals and populations, as shades of skin color along a gradient from light to dark. For example, populations can be described using fine distinctions in average skin reflectivity along a scale of 1 to 100. Classical traits are actively selected for by climate, and they often correlate with latitude. For example, darker—rather than lighter—skin, eyes, and hair provide better protection from intensive solar radiation. Natural selection, the differential survival of various phenotypes under differing environmental conditions, means that populations that are not closely related may come to resemble one another in classical traits if they move into similar environments. Blood types, proteins, enzymes, and mitochondrial DNA provide a rather precise way of establishing human descent groups, but these traits are not readily observed without sophisticated testing techniques.

Family Trees and the Myth of Racial Purity

The complexity of actual genetic relationships among peoples, in contrast to simplistic racial

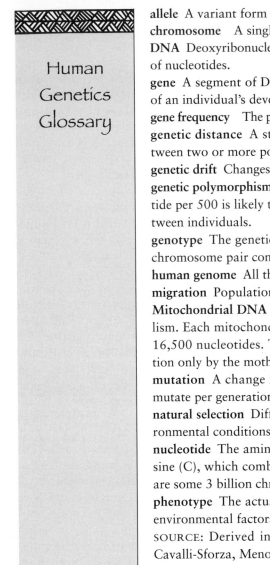

Human Genetics Glossary

allele A variant form of a gene, produced by mutation.

chromosome   A single strand of DNA; twenty-three pairs in humans.

DNA Deoxyribonucleic acid. A long double-helix molecule composed of a sequence of nucleotides.

gene A segment of DNA producing a particular protein controlling some aspect of an individual's development.

gene frequency   The percentage of individuals in a population with a particular gene.

genetic distance A statistical measure of the difference in gene frequencies between two or more populations.

genetic drift Changes in gene frequencies caused by random factors.

genetic polymorphism Multiple alleles for a particular trait. On average, 1 nucleotide per 500 is likely to vary, between the same chromosome in a given pair or between individuals.

genotype The genetic composition of an individual, including each half of each chromosome pair contributed by each parent.

human genome All the genetic material that makes up an individual.

migration Population movements that can produce changes in gene frequencies.

Mitochondrial DNA Mitochondria are cellular structures that drive cell metabolism. Each mitochondrion possesses its own small chromosome containing some 16,500 nucleotides. This mitochondrial DNA is transmitted to the next generation only by the mother's egg cell.

mutation A change in a nucleotide. On average, 1 in 200,000,000 nucleotides mutate per generation.

natural selection Differential survival of varying phenotypes under differing environmental conditions, producing changes in gene frequencies.

nucleotide The amino acids adenine (A) and guanine (G), thymine (T) and cytosine (C), which combine in a sequential chain to form the DNA molecule. There are some 3 billion chromosomal nucleotides in each half of the DNA molecule.

phenotype The actual expression of genetic traits in an individual as shaped by environmental factors.

SOURCE: Derived in part from Cavalli-Sforza and Cavalli-Sforza (1995) and Cavalli-Sforza, Menozzi, and Piazza (1994).

---

stereotypes, is illustrated by human family trees based on sophisticated genetic testing. Although enormously complex, Allan Wilson and R. L. Cann's (1992) family tree of 182 diverse individuals (based on mitochondrial DNA) ultimately connects everyone to a common African ancestress. Cavalli-Sforza and his associates (1994) have produced a global family tree for forty-two local populations based on 120 neutral allele frequencies (Figure 5.2). These populations were pooled from a much larger sample of nearly 2000 "indigenous" populations whose ancestors presumably were living in the same location before AD 1500. Branches in this diagram reflect the major

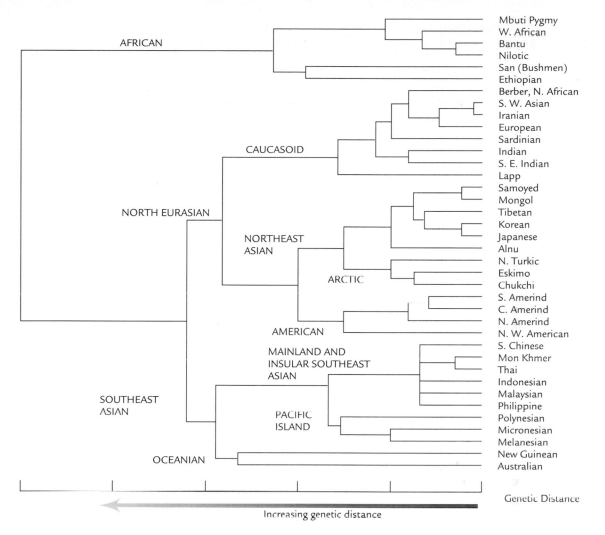

FIGURE 5.2   Global family tree based on a genetic analysis of 142 allele frequencies in forty-two populations. (SOURCE: Cavalli-Sforza et al. 1994, Figure 2.3.2.A.)

population movements of the past 30,000 years up to AD 1500, including the pioneer occupations of the major land masses and the migrations associated with domestication and cultivation. The Cavalli-Sforza tree also roughly corresponds to major language classifications and, like Wilson and Cann's tree, suggests a common African origin for humanity. For example, the branches of the human family tree show that Nilotic-speaking African herding peoples are closely re-

lated to their Bantu-speaking agricultural neighbors, because they are short offshoots from a common branch. Both of these African populations are more distantly related, through four branches, to North Eurasians and Southeast Asians. Likewise, South Amerind-speaking Amazonian peoples in the North Eurasian branch are more closely related to Australian aborigines in the Southeast Asian branch, than either are to African peoples. However, all contemporary peoples are of the same age, because all share a common African ancestor, a *Homo erectus* more than a million years ago.

Popular racial classifications fail because they falsely assume purity and stability of genetic inheritance. Not only is racial purity improbable, it would be extremely maladaptive. All the processes of biological evolution—including mutation, genetic drift, migration, and natural selection—are constantly changing the genetic composition of every population. The genetic characteristics of populations are not discrete bundles of features; they overlap in complex ways, and the frequencies of particular genes vary gradually along geographical gradients. By AD 1500, many local populations had the necessary stability for natural selection to produce superficial adaptations in skin and body form to regional climates. However, since 1500, the dramatic increases in migration and travel and the demographic disturbances initiated by the emerging global commercial culture have introduced tremendous genetic diversity into formerly indigenous populations. Any person is likely to have ancestors drawn from many formerly indigenous gene pools. For example, someone born in 1975 theoretically would have 510 ancestors, assuming 25-year generations and counting back eight generations to great-great-great-great-great-great-grandparents born in 1775. Counting back nineteen generations to AD 1500 would include more than a million ancestors! Only extremely naive racists could pretend that each and every one of their ancestors came from the same discrete gene pool.

Race, IQ, and Economic Achievement

Several recent authors have used racial categories and notions of racial inferiority, citing IQ test scores, to explain different levels of economic achievement in the United States. The modern argument began with an article by Berkeley, California, educational psychologist Arthur Jensen (1969), who claimed that black IQs averaged 15 points lower than white IQs, that this difference was primarily genetic, and that it explained poor

academic achievement by black children. Psychologist Richard J. Herrnstein (1971) quickly pushed these misleading conclusions to another level, arguing that IQ, economic achievement, and social standing were all significantly determined by genetics.

Anthropologists, biologists, and geneticists promptly refuted Jensen's and Herrnstein's theories as unscientific (Bodmer and Cavalli-Sforza 1970, Cavalli-Sforza and Feldman 1981, Gould 1981), but they reappeared 25 years later in the 1994 bestseller *The Bell Curve: Intelligence and Class Structure in American Life,* co-authored by Herrnstein and political scientist Charles Murray. This time the term *ethnic* often replaced the more emotional *race,* but the underlying genetic argument has remained unchanged. At its starkest, *The Bell Curve* argues that blacks have inferior genes for basic intelligence and so score poorly on IQ tests; thus, they are unable to attain the high-paying jobs that lead to economic achievement in America. Crime, welfare dependency, and broken homes are all portrayed as inherited-IQ problems. This argument requires the improbable assumption that American society is structured to reward people strictly on the basis of their genetic endowment. The "cognitive elite" are successful, good citizens primarily because their genes are superior. The obvious policy implication is that federal money for social services would be wasted on the poor because they are too genetically inferior to improve.

Critical reviewers of *The Bell Curve* again have pointed out the numerous logical and scientific flaws in this racist argument (Cavalli-Sforza and Cavalli-Sforza 1995, Kamin 1995, Marks 1995). Anthropologists' exasperation with this revival of "pseudo-scientific racism" led to a resolution at their 1994 annual meeting declaring that biologically defined "races" were "meaningless and unscientific as a way of explaining variation (whether in intelligence or other traits)" (*Anthropology Newsletter* 1995).

It is both arrogant and ethnocentric to assume that the designers of IQ tests know what human intelligence is and that they can measure it for all people. IQ scores are cultural products that measure a relatively narrow range of cognitive skills, skills that have only recently been elevated in status in commercial-scale culture. There are many human intellectual qualities, such as wisdom and creativity, that IQ does not measure.

Herrnstein and Murray maintain that 60–70 percent of IQ is genetically determined, yet the heritability of intellectual qualities of whatever sort cannot be accurately separated from cultural factors, and especially from parental influences. Luigi and Francesco Cavalli-Sforza (1995:280) suggest that only 33 percent of an IQ score might be attributable to genetic inheritance. Furthermore, the racial classifications underlying arguments of racial inferiority are as problematic as the IQ scores themselves. Given that "blacks" and "whites" are cultural categories that do not represent discrete gene pools, it is meaningless to attribute black/white IQ differences to genetics.

Attributing differences in economic success to IQ scores confuses correlation with causation. How can Herrnstein and Murray be so certain that genetics, and not poverty, causes low scores? It is more reasonable to speculate that people who are enculturated in impoverished households and communities with poorly equipped schools and fewer cultural resources will exhibit both lower IQ scores and lower economic achievement. Physical anthropologist Jonathan Marks (1995) points out that an earlier American impoverished underclass from central and southern Europe—including ancestors of present-day Italian Americans, Polish Americans, Czech Americans, Jewish Americans, and so on—was branded as genetically inferior by the "cognitive elites" of the time (to use Herrnstein and Murray's invidious and arrogant term), but they and their descendants successfully raised their IQ scores and joined the overclass. It is self-serving and disingenuous for elites to deprecate the intellectual abilities of the underclass. The primary forces shaping human destiny are now cultural, not biological. The cultural organization of social power, not genetics, is the primary determinant of human well-being.

LANGUAGE AND CULTURE

A major point of theoretical debate in anthropology is between the extreme relativists, who insist that each culture can only be understood in its own terms, and those who are more interested in comparison and seek cultural universals or stages of development. This debate was introduced in Chapter 1 with the emic/etic distinction and was discussed again in the first section of this chapter. In this section, we view the issue from the perspective of language. The goal here is to assess the tendency of people who speak different languages to see the world in fundamentally unique ways and then examine the ways in which linguistic classification is constrained by the limits of the physical world. Linguistic and ethnoscience material on biological classification systems and color terminologies will help to illuminate these intriguing questions.

Linguistic Relativity and the Sapir-Whorf Hypothesis

The relativist view of language, as it developed in American anthropology under Franz Boas and his student Edward Sapir, was a direct response to the extreme Eurocentric evolutionary schemes that were developed by nineteenth-century linguists who maintained that Indo-European languages were the most highly evolved in the world. German linguist Max Müller constructed a scale of linguistic evolutionary development based on an earlier grammatical classification of languages into isolating, agglutinating, and amalgamating types. The most primitive types were called *isolating* because they were thought to use words that were unaltered roots. *Agglutinating* languages made composite words from previously isolated roots, and *amalgamating* languages, such as Indo-European, changed the meaning of words by inflection. In Müller's scheme of evolutionary progress, the appearance of amalgamating languages corresponded to the rise of civilization in the Near East and thus was identified with civilization and progress, whereas more primitive languages were associated with nomadism.

As non-Indo-European languages became better known, it quickly became apparent that Müller's evolutionary scheme had little empirical foundation. Using Native American languages, Boas argued that with language, as with mentality generally, there was no basis for ranking into higher and lower stages of evolutionary progress. Although Boas recognized many specific differences in languages, he felt that all were equally capable of expressing complex ideas and did so as the need arose. Boas also implied that linguistic categories were characterized by a certain arbitrariness. For example, he observed that although many hues of color could be distinguished, a given language might name only a few, and in ways that were not readily translatable into the color terms of another language (Boas 1911). Ruth Benedict (1934) adopted this position when she argued that each culture was built from behaviors arbitrarily selected from the spectrum of possible behavior. Edward Sapir, a linguistic student of Boas, and Sapir's student Benjamin Whorf carried these ideas further and implied that linguistic categories defined the reality that the speakers of a given language perceived. In effect, the speakers of different languages live in different perceptual worlds. This general view that language somehow shapes perception became known as the **Sapir-Whorf hypothesis,** although Sapir and Whorf never formulated their views as a single testable hypothesis (Kay and Kempton 1984).

Color Classifications and Folk Taxonomies

The most famous examination of the issues implied by the Sapir-Whorf hypothesis was the comparative analysis of color terms by Brent Berlin and Paul Kay (1969). These researchers collected color terms from speakers of twenty widely diverse languages by placing a transparent sheet over a chart of 329 color chips arranged by degree of hue and brightness. Native speakers were asked to mark with a grease pen the focal point of each color term or the chip that best

represented it, as well as the total range of chips to which each term could refer. Basic color terms could not be composites or narrowly applied, so terms like *blue-green, pinkish,* and *apple red* were excluded.

The researchers found that among all the languages, only eleven basic color terms were recognized (*white, black, red, green, yellow, blue, brown, purple, pink, orange,* and *gray*), and there was remarkable agreement on the focal points of each term (Figure 5.3). This was a surprising blow to those who felt that color terms were not constrained by nature. But even more surprising was the discovery that the set of terms used by any particular language was limited and to a certain extent predictable. Although, in theory, there were 2048 possible combinations of the 11 basic color terms, only 22 sets or combinations actually occurred. Furthermore, these combinations could be grouped into seven stages, which implied an evolutionary sequence because they appeared to correspond to levels of cultural complexity (Figure 5.4).

By searching the literature, Berlin and Kay (1969) expanded their sample to include ninety-eight languages and confirmed their original findings. No language had fewer than two color terms, and these two were *black* and *white* (see the box entitled "An Aboriginal Color System"). When there were three terms, *red* would be added to *black* and *white*. Next, *green* and *yellow* were added in either order, then *blue* and *brown* in sequence. Finally, *purple, pink, orange,* and *gray* would be added in any order. Languages associated with tribal cultures had fewer color terms than those spoken by commercial societies. Presumably, the increase in color terms was in response to increased cultural needs, but the precise sequence of color terms could not be explained beyond the possibility that they represented levels of distinctive physical contrast, which were perceptual universals.

The search for universals in linguistic classification and their possible evolutionary implications quickly expanded to other domains. Berlin and his associates turned their attention to ethnobiology and established a hierarchy of folk

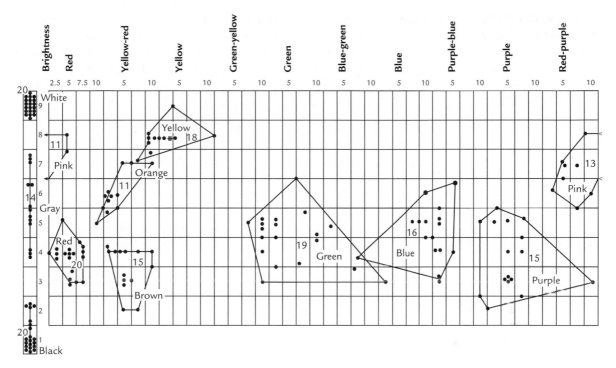

FIGURE 5.3 Normalized foci of basic color terms in twenty languages. Numerals appearing along the borders of the chart refer to the Munsell system of color notation, distinguishing hue, brightness, and color strength. Numerals appearing in the body of the chart refer to the number of languages in the sample of twenty that encode the corresponding color category. The smallest possible number of lines are used to enclose each color area. (SOURCE: Berlin and Kay 1969.)

FIGURE 5.4 Developmental sequence for the acquisition of basic color terms. (SOURCE: Berlin and Kay 1969:4.)

taxonomic terms that appeared to resemble the color term sequence (Berlin 1972; Berlin, Breedlove, and Raven 1973).

In an inferred developmental sequence of plant taxonomies, a language first acquires generic terms, such as *oak* and *pine*, before differentiating between them with specific terms, such as *black oak*, or generalizing by adding a few life-form terms, such as *tree*. Varietal terms are most likely to be applied to cultivated plants.

Cecil Brown (1977) suggested that six globally distributed life-form terms for plants—*tree, grass, herb, "grerb"* (grass and herb), *bush,* and *vine*—were added to a language in a predictable sequence, like basic color terms (Figure 5.5). The six life-form

<hr>

Sapir-Whorf hypothesis Suggests that one's view of the world is shaped by language, such that the speakers of different languages may live in different perceptual worlds.

An Aboriginal Color System

That any culture could function with no more than two basic color terms is difficult to imagine, but an Australian aboriginal example of such a system shows how feasible it is. Based on their fieldwork, Rhys Jones and Betty Meehan (1978) have provided a detailed description of the use of color terms by the An-barra aborigines of Arnhem Land. They found two basic terms in use as adjectives: -*gungaltja* (light) and -*gungundja* (dark). Only a few of the very lightest colors were called -*gungaltja*—just 10 percent of the Munsell chips used by Berlin and Kay (1969), including bright red. All objects could be described using these two terms. For example, storm clouds, the sky, granite, and aborigines were "dark," while other clouds, the sea, sandstone, newborn babies, Europeans, and sunsets were "light." Four mineral pigments were used as paints and were distinctively named: white clay, black charcoal, red ochre, and yellow ochre. These pigments are very ancient in Australia and have great symbolic significance. Objects painted with these pigments, or that resemble their color, could be described in reference to the pigment. Thus, a sunset might be described as "light, red ochre present within it," but such restricted use would seem to disqualify such pigment terms for recognition as basic color terms as defined by Berlin and Kay. A gray-green-colored, waterborne algal scum was also treated as a paint pigment term. The restricted nature of pigment terms was apparent as well from the fact that each belonged to a specific moiety, whereas the basic color terms, *light* and *dark,* had no moiety affiliation. Many plant dyes were in use, and dyed objects were described by reference to the specific plant used, but such terms were not generalized further. In recent years, the Anbarra have readily applied English color terms to the brightly colored European objects that have entered their region.

terms could in theory occur in sixty-four different combinations. However, in a survey of 105 languages, Brown found that only eleven patterns actually occurred, and these could be grouped into six stages. A language might have no life-form terms, or it might only recognize the *tree* life form. In Stage 3, a single life-form term was added, *"grerb,"* which might refer to either grass or herbs, or both. By Stage 6, all six life-form terms would be recognized. The first three stages of development thus used no more than two life-form terms and were thought to be associated with tribal societies.

Brown (1979a) infers that the actual sequence of life-form terms reflects the universal tendency for classification to be based on simple binary oppositions and the fact that biological groupings share natural features that make them conspicuous to human perception.

This analysis has interesting implications for the debate about "primitive mentality." Increased abstraction coincides with a general devolution in knowledge of nature as cultural scale increases. Terms seem to disappear from the bottom of the taxonomic hierarchy as increasingly urbanized and industrialized people become less directly dependent on nature. It is not uncommon for individuals in tribal societies to able to name 500–1000 plants, whereas urban people may know barely 50–100 plants. Based on detailed linguistic reconstructions within specific language groups,

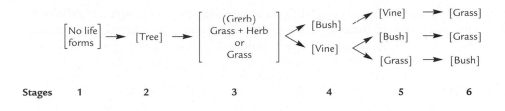

Stages	1	2	3	4	5	6

"Grerb" is realized as *herb* when *grass* is encoded at Stage 5 or 6.
Herb refers to herbaceous plants excluding grasses.

FIGURE 5.5   Lexical-encoding sequence for folk botanical life forms (showing three possible paths for adding life-form terms). *"Grerb"* is realized as *herb* when *grass* is encoded at Stage 5 or 6. *Herb* refers to herbaceous plants excluding grasses. (SOURCE: Brown 1977.)

Brown (1979b) infers that life-form terms have been added largely within the past 2000–4000 years in step with the increase in political complexity, while use of generic terms has sharply declined.

The methods and assumption of color terms and folk taxonomy research have been questioned (Hun 1985, Randall and Hun 1984). Saunders (2000) argues that basic color terms and the evolutionary sequence may be the product of the research method itself, which presumably sifted out ambiguous responses to produce a predetermined outcome (Saunders 2000). Nevertheless, the consensus seems to be that color terms are genuine cultural universals (Hardin & Maffi 1997). They are a challenge to strict cultural relativists, who maintain that cultures can define physical reality in completely arbitrary ways. But cultural determinism still can be seen to operate. Marshall Sahlins (1976a) argued that cultures systematically make symbolic use of the natural distinctions that people can most readily perceive in color, just as natural sounds are used for linguistic purposes. Berlin and Kay (1969) pointed out that languages add new color terms in a way that maximizes the efficiency of perceptible contrasts, which parallels the order in which children learn to articulate phonemic distinctions as they acquire speech. However, as Sahlins stressed, even given that color differences are naturally perceptible, it is still important to ask what cultural uses, or meanings,

are made of these differences. What was important for Sahlins when new color terms are added is the new relations between terms, the new meanings, that become possible.

Sahlins observed that Stage 1 color terms, which distinguish only two colors, light and dark, are used for simple dualistic symbolic oppositions, such as between life and death, male and female, or sacred and profane. The addition of red creates a mediated opposition in which red can variously be opposed to either dark or light, like the ambiguous jaguar mediating between the complementary opposites of male and female in Chapter 3. The further addition of either green or yellow in Stage 3 creates a pair of analogous opposition, as in the familiar $a : b :: c : d$ pattern. These perceptual structures can be created using jaguars, caimans, and anacondas, as well as with colors, and they can then be made to carry a variety of cultural meanings.

MAGIC, BELIEF, AND THE SUPERNATURAL

Shamanism and Psychopathology

Shamans are part-time religious specialists and healers who personify the most extreme elements of so-called primitive mentalities and magical thinking in tribal societies. Early missionaries often called shamans witch doctors, attributing their supernatural powers to the devil, and confronted them as enemies of Christianity. Government authorities often disapproved of shamans because they sometimes used their powers within the community to organize resistance to government programs and because shamanistic curing practices frequently were considered to be contrary to modern medical science, if not actually dangerous. Even anthropologists have had difficulty being objective about shamans. For example, Alfred Kroeber, a prominent Boas-trained anthropologist, suggested in the 1948 edition of *Anthropology,* long a standard textbook, that modern civilization's rejection of shamanism and related beliefs was a measure of scientific progress. He observed that people in our own society recognize as abnormal or insane anyone who talks to the dead or who thinks they can turn into a bear, whereas "backward people" consider such behavior socially acceptable and even admirable. Kroeber regarded shamanism as a psychopathology and emphatically declared:

> When the sane and well in one culture believe what only the most ignorant, warped, and insane believe in another, there would seem to be some warrant for rating the first culture lower and the second higher. Or are our discards, insane, and hypersuggestibles perhaps right and the rest of us wrong? (Kroeber 1948:298)

It is important to recognize, however, that shamanism is based on concepts about the supernatural that are useful, not irrational. Pascal Boyer (2000:196) suggests that people remember and pass on supernatural concepts that are important to them socially. The mental skills that people apply to the supernatural are the same skills they use in dealing with each other, and they involve close attention to human perceptions, beliefs, and desires. Shamans use shared beliefs about the supernatural to reinforce the moral dimensions of human behavior, thereby helping people be more confident that others will cooperate with them. Using, or "believing in" supernatural concepts does not mean that people accept the supernatural as natural, but they do find belief in the supernatural to be useful. The supernatural beliefs

that people universally recognize as "religious" are related to morality, commitment, group identity, ritual, and individual experience. Such concepts generally involve supernatural "persons," or objects believed to have humanlike minds, but that behave in extraordinary ways.

Shamanism does involve a striking collection of phenomena, including various trance states, magical flight, and spirit possession (Peters and Price-Williams 1980), all of which may be difficult to understand outside of the cultural context in which they occur. Shamans induce trances using rhythmical chanting, dancing, deprivation, and psychoactive drugs. Anthropologist Michael Harner (1980), who conducted popular workshops and seminars on shamanism, demonstrated that under the proper conditions, virtually anyone can induce such trance states. Shamanism may well be tens of thousands of years old, judging from parallels between the distinctive lines and grid patterns scratched on European cave walls during the Ice Age and similar designs characteristic of rock art associated with shamans in many parts of the world. Some researchers infer that these are images that tribal shamans see with their mind's eye during trance states. In ecstatic trance, shamans contact the otherwise invisible spirit world and perform amazing feats, including the magical killing of enemies and transformations into animals. Using their spirit helpers to cure, shamans massage their patients and dramatically suck out intrusive objects thought to be the causes of illness (Figure 5.6); or they shoot invisible darts into the bodies of enemies to harm them. Australian aboriginal shamans reportedly have killed people simply by pointing a bone in their direction.

I was impressed by the cultural reality of Amazonian shamanism while I conducted a routine residence pattern survey in an Asháninka village. I was surprised to encounter a man who maintained a separate house from his wife. It is common for young unmarried Asháninka men to build separate houses, but this case was unusual enough for me to question further. I discovered that this man was a powerful jaguar shaman who could

FIGURE 5.6 Zaparo shaman blowing tobacco smoke on patient, Conambo River, Ecuadorean Amazon, 2003.

cure people and transform himself into a jaguar to magically attack his enemies. He explained to me matter-of-factly that it sometimes upset his wife when he became a jaguar at night, so he often slept in his own house.

Asháninka shamans are called "tobacco-eaters," after the bamboo tubes they carry containing a thick, tarlike tobacco paste that is licked from a stick to help induce shamanistic visions. Jaguar shamans are widely respected and feared by the Asháninka, and their exploits are well known. I heard accounts of someone shooting an intruding jaguar at night and then discovering that he had killed a shaman. Another incident demonstrated the social context of shamanistic curing. My Shipibo field assistant developed a chronic leg infection that refused to heal. He consulted a shaman who attributed the problem to the otter spirit, which had been sent by another villager who was a personal enemy of my assistant. The cure was effected when the two reached a reconciliation.

Many observers have questioned the authenticity of shamanistic performances, pointing to incidences in which the shaman does not seem to be in a genuine trance or when a curer has hidden in his mouth the object that he intends to suck from his patient. Deliberately hidden objects of this sort simply add drama to the curing performance. Some shamans may indeed pretend to be in trance, but most suspicions of fraud may be due to a misunderstanding of the nature of shamanism, especially the fact that shamanistic trances often differ from other forms of spirit possession. A shaman typically is in a "lucid trance" or a "waking dream" in which he communicates with both the spirits and his audience, and he will usually be able to remember the events later. This is not the same as pathological hysteria, and it does not mean that the shaman becomes totally dissociated. The shaman trance is a temporary reduction of normal reality testing in which dream images are treated as if real within a specific cultural context and are then used for social purposes (Peters and Price-Williams 1980).

The psychopathological view of shamanism by anthropologists was in favor for a long time. For example, Julian Silverman (1967) emphasized the parallels between acute schizophrenics who behave in bizarre fashion and shamans who experience cognitive disturbances, or altered states of consciousness, as an apparent reaction to a major personal crisis involving guilt or failure. In Silverman's view, like Kroeber's, the most significant difference between schizophrenics in our society and shamans in tribal societies is that schizophrenics find no social support for their behavior, and it is consequently maladaptive, whereas shamans are culturally accepted. Thus, in this view, shamanism can be considered a therapeutic psychological adjustment to a psychopathology.

The connection between schizophrenia and shamanism is also implied in the authoritative *Diagnostic and Statistical Manual of Mental Disorders (DSM-III)*, the guidebook published by the American Psychiatric Association (APA) for use by clinicians. According to *DSM-III*, "magical thinking" is seen "in children, in people in primitive cultures, and in Schizotypal Personality Disorder, Schizophrenia, and Obsessive Compulsive Disorder" (APA 1980:363). The belief that the members of domestic-scale cultures are sick and childlike dies hard!

The clinical concept of schizophrenia has been refined considerably since Silverman's analysis was published, and even using the definition of schizophrenic disorders contained within *DSM-III*, striking differences between schizophrenics and shamans now seem evident. The DSM-IV (2000) Glossary of Technical Terms (Appendix C) defines "magical thinking" as "the erroneous belief that one's thoughts, words, or actions will cause or prevent a specific outcome in some way that defies commonly understood laws of cause and effect." The definition adds: "Magical thinking may be a part of normal child development." However, the revised *DSM-IV* (2000) entry for "Schizophrenia" advises clinicians to take cultural differences into account, because even "bizarre delusions" are not always easy to identify. In fact, "In some cultures, visual or auditory hallucinations with a religious content may be a normal part of religious experience (e.g., seeing the Virgin Mary or hearing God's voice)." As Richard Noll (1984) points out, attributing shamanistic experiences to an altered state of consciousness implies out-of-control hallucinations

and other paranoid delusions that we tend to view negatively but that, in fact, are not characteristic of shamanism. Noll speaks of the **shamanic state of consciousness (SSC)**, which he distinguishes from the altered state of consciousness (ASC) as it is usually recognized. The ASC of the schizophrenic is obviously maladaptive. It comes unbidden, and the schizophrenic hears uncontrollable mocking voices, whereas the shaman can enter the SSC virtually at will, remains aware of his state, sees visions, uses them for socially beneficial purposes, and then freely returns to his normal consciousness. A successful shaman achieves a balance between his spiritual experiences and the demands of everyday life, but there is no reason to view the SSC as a psychopathology.

Aboriginal Voodoo Death and Culture-Bound Syndromes

Anthropologists and medical researchers have been fascinated by reports of mysterious deaths and illnesses in tribal societies that are culturally attributed to supernatural causes and that have not always been readily explainable in purely physical terms. A prime example from aboriginal Australia are cases of so-called voodoo death, such as the bone pointing referred to previously, in which people are killed by sorcery. The long-established anthropological interpretation of such incidents was that the victim died from shock, caused by intense fear of death combined with an absolute belief in the reality of sorcery (Cannon 1942). More extensive observations by medically trained individuals clarified both the physical and cultural basis of such deaths. Harry Eastwell (1982), who conducted periodic psychiatric clinics in aboriginal communities in Arnhem Land between 1969 and 1980, treated thirty-nine patients for a variety of physical and emotional symptoms that he called "fear of sorcery syndrome." In nearly all cases, some specific event—such as the death or illness of close kin, interpersonal conflicts, or a ritual violation—led to suspicions of supernatural danger. Patients showed the typical symptoms of extreme fear: bulging eyes, di-lated pupils, sweating, agitation, and sleeplessness. Two of the patients died, one with an abnormality of the adrenal glands, which may have made him more vulnerable to stress, and the other from kidney and heart failure.

Because so few deaths actually occurred in these cases, Eastwell began to suspect that more than merely fear was involved in voodoo death. This suspicion was further supported when two patients thought to be dying from sorcery were found to be severely dehydrated and were saved by prompt medical intervention. Additional analyses of the process of dying experienced by elderly aborigines revealed a regular cultural pattern in which both dying person and kin decide that death is imminent and mutually facilitate the process—the dying person refuses to drink and the kin withhold water so that death by dehydration occurs within 24–48 hours.

The parallels between aboriginal patient-assisted euthanasia and voodoo death are striking. In both cases, the actual mechanism of death is probably dehydration, but it occurs because the patient and the community agree that the patient is dying. Water is withheld at the same time that wailing and formal funeral rituals are begun. It is believed that only the totemic spirit animates the dying person, and it does not need to drink. At death, this spirit returns to the ancestral well.

Psychiatrist John Cawte (1976) describes another Australian culture-bound syndrome, *Malgri,* from the Wellesley Island aborigines in the Gulf of Carpentaria. In this case, violation of ritual restrictions on keeping land foods and seafoods separate causes local totemic spirits to afflict a person with severe abdominal swelling and pain. The condition apparently is not fatal, and sufferers usually respond to specific ritual treatment. To observers trained in psychoanalysis, *Malgri* suggested hysterical "displacement" of oedipal conflicts, but Cawte felt that it was more understandable as part of the totemically regulated system of territoriality based on the Dreaming. He noted that *Malgri* was most likely to affect people outside of their own estate territories, and the most dangerous spirits were those

controlling the richest resource zones, where foraging pressure was the greatest. Furthermore, *Malgri* did not occur on the nearby mainland, where population densities were lower and resources thus less critical.

The Healing Power of Myth and Symbols

Medically trained observers generally agree that shamanistic healers can successfully treat people suffering from a variety of psychiatric complaints, such as *Malgri,* using ritual techniques. Native curers may also be adept at treating injuries and illnesses with herbal remedies that have empirically identifiable chemical properties. Researchers further concede that shamanistic rituals may involve important psychotherapeutic techniques including the power of suggestion, the restructuring of social relations, catharsis, and the stimulation of neurochemicals (Dow 1986).

Whatever the specific healing mechanism might be, James Dow suggests that shamanistic ritual works because culturally defined symbols are manipulated to influence the body–mind relationship by helping people to alter their self-perceptions. Symbols, whether they involve totemic spirits or psychoanalytic concepts such as guilt and repression, are drawn from cultural myths that condense important truths about the human experience in society. For psychotherapy to succeed, the patient and practitioner must establish a working relationship, and the shaman may facilitate this through what Dow calls the "shamanic paradox." That is, the patient must suspend any disbelief about the validity of the empirically unbelievable supernatural powers claimed by the shaman—he must implicitly believe in the authenticity of the therapeutic process before it can be effective. When the patient fully participates in the curing

shamanic state of consciousness (SSC) An interpretation of the shamantic trance phenomenon that distinguishes it from the altered state of consciousness of schizophrenics. A shaman may enter and leave the SSC at will, remains aware of his surroundings, and uses the SSC for socially beneficial purposes.

process, through belief or the suspension of disbelief, he may be able to reevaluate his own experiences and gain control over his feelings. These therapeutic principles help explain the persistence and apparent success of many ritual symbols.

Australian material (again from Arnhem Land) illustrates the effectiveness of symbols. In this area, the central Dreamtime myth, which is reenacted in a major series of rituals including circumcision ceremonies, concerns the Wawilak sisters, two Dreaming ancestors who created the local cultural landscape during their Dreamtime travels. The myth details the creative activities of the Wawilak sisters and recounts how they lose ritual power to men when they are swallowed by the Rainbow Serpent, who is attracted when the sisters' menstrual blood contaminates the snake's pool. The Wawilak sisters, and women in general, are associated with the fertile dry season. The Rainbow Serpent rising up to eat the Wawilak sisters has obvious male associations and creates the widespread flooding of the lowlands during the Arnhem Land wet season (Figure 5.7).

The Wawilak myth parallels the sacred flute myths found in Amazonia and deals with the same classic issues of life and death, reproduction, and gender roles. Although the Wawilak ritual complex does not directly involve shamanistic curing, according to the analysis of Nancy Munn (1969), participants in the rituals consciously identify with the characters in the myth, and as they enact it they convert their personal fears of death into more positive outcomes and satisfying images of health and community well-being. For example, circumcision of a boy is metaphorically compared to the swallowing of the sisters, only in this case he is ritually reborn. In other ceremonial reenactments, women happily avoid being eaten by the serpent. Bloodletting conducted in connection with circumcision ceremonies is equated with the menstrual blood of the Wawilak sisters and is converted to ritual use as body paint, thus transferring symbolic strength and actual positive feelings to the participant. As one aboriginal man explained,

FIGURE 5.7   Rock painting of the Rainbow Serpent, an important mythic figure central to ritual performances that strengthen community well-being in many areas of northern Australia.

It makes us feel easy and comfortable and it makes us strong. It makes us good. . . .We have that . . . strength from that blood. It goes inside when we put that blood on. (Munn 1969:195, citing Warner 1958)

Interpreting the meaning of many other specific practices that we identify as "magical" because we assume they have no empirical basis is equally challenging. Michael Brown (1984) has examined ritual songs that the Aguaruna of the Peruvian Amazon use to improve their hunting, especially when they go after spider monkeys with blowguns. The songs may be sung before a man goes hunting or sung silently as the hunt is in progress, and they contain complex allusions to myths and images of hunting success. Brown argues that the Aguaruna consider these songs to be as instrumental for their hunting success as the technical quality of their blowguns and stalking skills. In his view, the Aguaruna are right because these "magical" songs help them focus their energy on the hunting task. They alter their internal mental states, giving them confidence, in the same way that ritual symbols can have a psychotherapeutic effect. This line of argument is similar to Bronislaw Malinowski's functionalist theory that magic helps people deal with the uncertainties that lie beyond the limits of their technical capabilities.

HEALTH AND NUTRITION IN TRIBAL SOCIETIES

Many well-meaning people who are neither racist nor unusually ethnocentric may mistakenly assume that tribal peoples must have a low quality of life because their sanitation standards seem lower and they lack the advantages of modern medicine. This is not a simple issue, because public health programs and modern medicine associated with the commercial world have improved life expectancy for many people; nevertheless, independent tribal societies typically enjoy a high quality of life as long as they are not negatively affected by outsiders. Perhaps what tribal peoples have, and what we have lost, is an equitable distribution of social power, giving everyone the feeling of control over their daily lives. Tribal peoples living in autonomous, tribal cultures seldom experience material impoverishment. In this section, we consider specific evidence on tribal health and well-being bearing on these important questions.

Myth and Reality of the "Noble Savage"

Most early visitors to undisturbed tribal societies were impressed with the health and vigor of the peoples they saw. These first impressions likely were basically accurate, but they were confused and embellished with unnecessary pronouncements about morality and human perfection that became the myth of the "noble savage." For example, some of the first Europeans to visit Brazil reported that the Indians "naturally follow goodness" and "live together in harmony, with no dis-

sension" (Hemming 1978:15). From such glowing descriptions, it was easy to conclude that "savages" were superior human beings living idyllic lives in Eden-like innocence. The comfortable nudity of most Native Amazonians that astonished Europeans certainly contributed to this noble savage image.

Most anthropologists have been careful to disassociate themselves from such noble savage romanticism. Members of tribal societies clearly are no more superior or inferior as individual human beings than any other group of humans. Tribal peoples can be selfish and cruel. They quarrel and kill one another, just like people who live in cities. Tribal culture is also not perfect. Tribal societies are not perfectly egalitarian, nor are they perfectly balanced with nature. And dietary and medical practices, as well as many aspects of tribal culture, may sometimes be harmful, as Robert Edgerton (1992) emphasizes. It is not unusual for tribal therapy to conflict with accepted practices in the medical community. For example, I witnessed a snake-bite victim being treated with herbal hot compresses, which would have accelerated the spread of the venom. Individuals must sometimes pay high personal costs for tribal membership, as people must to live in any human society. Nevertheless, generally good health and vigor seem to be two advantages of life in tribal cultures for those who reach adulthood.

Evidence for the overall high quality of life in relatively independent tribal societies appears in a report by geneticist James Neel (1970). This is the same James Neel who was falsely accused of crimes against humanity by journalist Patrick Tierney (2000) as discussed in Chapter 3, but Neel's record of humanistic concern for the Yanomami is clear. Neel summarized the findings of eight years of biochemical and health research among Native Amazonians, carried out by an interdisciplinary team of more than a dozen researchers using sophisticated techniques. Neel reported that, in general, they found the Xavante, Yanomami, and Makiritare, whom they examined in Brazil and Venezuela, to be in "excellent

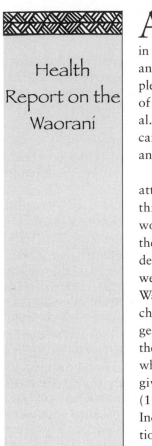

Health Report on the Waorani

A detailed assessment of the health status of the Waorani of Ecuador, a Native Amazonian group, was conducted in the field by a seven-person medical team in 1976. At that time, the Waorani were living independently as manioc gardeners and hunters and maintained only limited contacts with outsiders. In all, 293 people received thorough medical exams. On the positive side, more than 95 percent of the sample appeared to be "very robust" and in "excellent health" (Larrick et al. 1979). There was no malnutrition, no obesity, no high blood pressure, and no cardiovascular disease. Everyone had excellent eyesight, with no color blindness, and no one was deaf.

There were some negatives: Many children had scalp infections, but these were attributed to contacts with outsiders; some two-thirds out of a sample of sixty-three people showed evidence of light intestinal parasite infestation; two old women had pneumonia; three people were blind in one eye due to accidents; and there were many scars from spears and jaguar and peccary bites. Six people were described by the Waorani themselves as mentally deficient, and most of these cases were readily attributed to head injuries, fevers, or genetic defects. Surprisingly, the Waorani of all ages had high rates of dental decay. Only 5 out of the 230 people checked by the dentist were found to be completely free of cavities. It was suggested that such exceptionally high cavity rates were due to the unusual fact that the Waorani, unlike most Amazonians, consumed their manioc drink unfermented, while it still had a high sugar content. Although no estimate of mortality rates was given, it appears that many adults died in violent conflicts. Like James Neel's (1970) report, the Waorani study attributed much of the excellent health of the Indians to the high quality of their diet, low population density, and relative isolation from outside diseases.

physical condition" (see the box entitled "Health Report on the Waorani"). Infant and childhood mortality rates were higher than in fully industrialized countries, but the general pattern of life expectancy was better than in colonial India at the end of the nineteenth century.

Neel concluded that these tribal peoples were well adjusted to the viruses, bacterial diseases, and internal parasites naturally occurring in their territory. The Yanomami and Xavante were found to have twice the levels of gamma globulin, the blood protein containing infection-fighting antibodies, found in civilized populations. Yanomami babies are born with a high degree of natural immunity acquired from their mothers and maintained by prolonged breast feeding. Yanomami infants then quickly develop additional immunities because they are continuously exposed to all the local pathogens. The most significant diseases, including malaria and measles, were assumed to be post-Columbian introductions to which people were not yet well adjusted. Neel inoculated a group of Yanomami to protect them from an ongoing measles epidemic, but Tierney questioned his motives and suggested incorrectly that he used an improper vaccine.

Rebecca Holmes found that, by international standards, the Yanomami could be classified as malnourished because by age their heights and weights are too low (Holmes 1995). However, the obvious vitality of the Yanomami suggests that such measures are inappropriate in their case.

Holmes suggests that small stature actually may be an adaptive genetic response, allowing people to be well nourished as tribal villagers in the rain forest. The implication is that outside intervention that changed their lifestyles to improve their health would probably be counterproductive.

Theoretically, there are many reasons the quality of life should be high in tribal societies. The most important are their generally low population densities and relative social equality, which help ensure equal access to basic subsistence resources so that everyone enjoys good nutrition. Furthermore, low densities and frequent mobility significantly reduce the occurrence of epidemic diseases, and natural selection—in the absence of antibiotics, immunizations, surgery, and other forms of medical intervention—results in a population with high levels of disease resistance. Healthy people are those who survive. Tribal societies, in effect, maintain public health by emphasizing prevention of morbidity rather than treatment. The healthiest conditions likely exist under mobile foraging and pastoralism, whereas there might be some health costs associated with the increased densities and reduced mobility of settled farming villages.

Dental Health and Tribal Diets

Health researchers have increasingly recognized that the typical diet found among tribal subsistence foragers and farmers, which is low in fat, salt, and refined sugars and high in fiber and various beneficial nutrients, is actually an ideal human diet. Skeletal evidence suggests that archaeologically, the shift from foraging to farming frequently was accompanied by a decline in overall health and human nutrition (Cohen 1989). Significant epidemiological evidence suggests that many forms of cancer are associated with relatively recent dietary changes related to food marketing, processing, and storage, such as salting, pickling, and refining, and to dramatic increases in consumption of fat and simple carbohydrates or refined sugars (Cohen 1987). Of course, foods eaten by self-supporting subsistence peoples are also free of the contaminants and additives that are introduced into industrially produced foods by the chemicals used in agriculture and in processing.

Perhaps the first scientific evidence that tribal peoples could be shown to be physically superior to "civilized" peoples appeared in an article published in 1894 in the *Journal of the Royal Anthropological Institute* by Wilberforce Smith, who compared the teeth of Sioux Indians with those of typical Londoners. Smith became interested in this problem while conducting a survey of the teeth of his fellow Englishmen, which he found to be disastrously decayed. He knew that the skulls of prehistoric European "savages" invariably contained healthier teeth than contemporary peoples and decided to find out if modern "savages" also had healthy teeth. Taking advantage of the appearance of Buffalo Bill's Wild West Show in London, he obtained permission to examine the teeth of ten Sioux men, roughly ages 15–50. He found that all had "massive admirably formed teeth, evenly ranged." They were well worn, but none were decayed, and no molars were missing. He concluded, "Their teeth alone proved them to have led the life of genuine savages" (1894:110). By comparison, the younger portion of the 300 Londoners whom he also examined had half as many usable pairs of opposed molars as the Sioux of the same age category, while Londoners ages 35–45 had some 80 percent fewer paired molars than the older Sioux.

When Smith (1894) presented his findings in a lecture before the Royal Anthropological Institute, he displayed a dental cast made from a member of his own family, which showed the terrible condition of a typical Londoner's teeth alongside the skull of an average "savage" showing beautifully preserved teeth. To test the possibility that the remarkable health of the Sioux's teeth was because they were exceptionally robust and healthy people, Smith did a comparison check of the teeth of twelve men of the regiment of Horse Guards from the Royal Household Cavalry, who would have been in superb physical condition. He found that the cavalrymen had teeth that were only a "trifling degree better preserved" than the average Londoner's.

Smith correctly concluded that the lack of dental decay and tooth loss observed in tribal peoples was due to increased tooth wear, which kept the teeth clean and polished. He attributed the increased wear to the consumption of less cooked and less refined food, to the absence of knives and forks, which meant that more chewing was required, and to the presence of grit or "dirt" in the food. It was later learned that the absence of refined carbohydrates also contributed to healthy tribal teeth. The reduced tooth wear of contemporary peoples who eat industrially processed foods is also likely related to the common problem of impacted molars, as Grover Krantz (1978) has observed. People eating coarse foods wear down not only the grinding surfaces of their teeth but also the sides of their teeth, which creates enough jaw space to accommodate the third molars when they erupt. When there is no significant wear, these "wisdom teeth" often must be extracted.

The association between traditional dietary patterns and healthy teeth was documented more systematically in a series of field studies conducted by American dentist Weston Price (1945) between 1931 and 1936. Price visited some of the most traditional peoples in Amazonia, East Africa, Australia, and the Pacific and found that tooth decay and periodontal disease were virtually absent among self-sufficient peoples but steadily increased as these same peoples adopted the food patterns of industrial societies.

In 1956, shortly after Price's dental research, T. L. Cleave, a doctor in the British Royal Navy, used medical data on tribal peoples to isolate a single feature in the diets of industrialized peoples that caused what he called the "saccharine disease," a wide-ranging complex of conditions including tooth decay, ulcers, appendicitis, obesity, diabetes, constipation, and varicose veins. Like both Smith and Price before him, Cleave (1974) was impressed by the fact that tribal peoples did not suffer from many of the common ailments of civilization. Thus, he attempted to find the special conditions that made tribal peoples healthier. His primary finding was that the traditional foods of tribal groups were consistently

much higher in dietary fiber than the highly refined complex carbohydrates consumed by industrialized peoples. High-fiber diets speed the transit time of food through the digestive system, thereby reducing many common diseases of civilization. It took many years for his findings to be incorporated into popular nutritional wisdom in the industrial world, but now high fiber, along with low fat and low salt, is widely accepted as an important component of a healthy diet.

Clifford Behrens (1986) provides some insights into how traditional classification systems are related to the maintenance of a high level of nutrition in tribal diets. Behrens found that the Shipibo of the Peruvian Amazon grouped their most preferred foods into two main emic categories, which he called "not-wild and cooked" and "wild and cooked." The Shipibo placed garden products such as plantains, maize, and manioc, which are high in carbohydrates, in the first category, and fish and game, which are high in protein and fat, in the second. The Shipibo considered their diet adequate only when it contained a balance of foods drawn from both categories. They accurately identified garden foods as the source of the energy needed for daily activities, while they felt that fish and game were needed for long-term health and growth.

Tribal Life Expectancy and Quality of Life

At a special symposium on the health of tribal peoples, held at the CIBA Foundation in London in 1976 and attended by more than two dozen specialists, it was concluded that self-sufficient tribal groups were generally healthy, and it was recognized that intervention by outsiders, even when well intended, could seriously undermine existing balances (CIBA 1977). However, Betsy Lozoff and Gary Brittenham (1977) found that some important tribal health "paradoxes" remained unanswered: (1) How is population growth regulated? (2) If foragers are well nourished, why are they physically small? and (3) If disease rates are low, why is tribal mortality high? These studies may seem out of date, but these issues may never be fully resolved, because only small, refugee-like tribal groups had escaped the negative impacts of the commercial world by the late twentieth century. The invasion and destruction of the tribal world is discussed in more detail in Chapter 14.

We still cannot fully answer these apparent paradoxes. Population regulation is a critical issue because maintaining a stationary population seems to be a key to relative balance between resources and quality of life. Population stability at constant, low-density levels also seems to be a general, but not invariable, characteristic of tribal groups. More recent interpretations suggest that fertility-limiting cultural mechanisms, such as prolonged lactation and postpartum sex taboos, were probably more important population regulators than raiding and infanticide, but the evidence is incomplete. High mortality due to raiding and infanticide would imply a reduced quality of life because it would lower average life expectancy. Yet, from a functionalist perspective, it might arguably increase life quality for the survivors by promoting stability between people and resources.

There are some troubling and probably unanswerable philosophical issues involved in the preceding paradoxes. Although tribal peoples in general are often smaller and slighter than Europeans and appear to have shorter life expectancies, how does one decide that a given stature or life expectancy should be an appropriate cross-cultural measure of well-being? Some evidence suggests that very low birth weights or relatively low infant weight gain or growth rates may be associated with higher infant mortality rates. Some researchers also argue that small stature may indicate poor nutrition, especially in densely populated tribal areas (Dennett and Connell 1988). However, taller and longer may not always be better, especially if taller or longer-lived people experience a reduced quality of life within their particular cultural and environmental setting.

Estimating the life expectancy of tribal populations is an inherently difficult task because there are few reliable data that unambiguously represent fully independent populations. Many widely cited demographic profiles of tribal peoples are actually inferences based on paleodemographic techniques of questionable validity. Life tables, such as those used by insurance companies to show the probability of someone surviving to a given age, have been drawn up for various tribal and prehistoric populations and generally show a significantly lower life expectancy for tribal peoples than for contemporary industrial populations (Table 5.1). Demographers often calculate life expectancy at age 15 for populations where infant and childhood mortality may be high. This means for example, that Northern Territory aborigines with a life expectancy of 34 years at age 15 could expect to live on the average to 49. Of course, a few might live significantly longer. The figures compiled by Fekri Hassan (1981) in Table 5.1 yield an estimated average life expectancy at age 15 for 7 ethnographically known foraging groups, including 3 from Australia, of only 26.4 years. By comparison, the figure for European Americans

TABLE 5.1   ESTIMATED AVERAGE LIFE EXPECTANCY OF PREHISTORIC AND TRIBAL POPULATIONS

Population	Life Expectancy at Age 15
Upper Paleolithic	16.9
Catal Huyuk (Neolithic)	17.0
Neandertals	17.5
Natufians (Mesolithic)	17.5
Angamgssalik Eskimo*	19.2
Aborigines (Groote Eylandt)*	23.3
East Greenland Eskimo*	23.5
Birhor (foragers, India)*	24.0
England (fourteenth century)	25.8
Baker Lake Eskimo*	27.7
Aborigines (Tiwi)*	33.1
Aborigines (northern territory)*	34.0
European Americans (1986)[†]	61.3

SOURCE: Hassan (1981:118).
*Ethnographically described foragers; average life expectancy = 26.4 years.
[†]Data from Wright (1990:225).

in 1986 was 61.3 years at age 15; however, 26.4 years was higher than the figures estimated for several archaeological populations and was higher than in fourteenth-century England.

Although tribal life expectancy appears to be lower than that of modern industrial populations, this should not be surprising because life expectancy has made dramatic increases only within the past two centuries. Tribal peoples compare favorably with many preindustrial groups. However, all demographic estimates for tribal peoples must be used cautiously. Only figures based on reliable census records can be accepted at face value. There are significant sources of bias and uncertainty in demographic research on tribal populations (Bocquet-Appel and Masset 1981).

Anthropologists have long known that tribal lifestyles were conducive to good health, but that conclusion, and its corollary that the commercial world promoted unhealthy lifestyles, was confirmed by an international panel of health experts convened by the United Nations in 2002 to make recommendations on the prevention of chronic noncommunicable diseases such as obesity, diabetes, cardiovascular disease, cancer, dental disease, and osteoporosis. These are precisely the diseases that are either nonexistent or occur at very low rates among independent tribal peoples, yet they accounted for 60 percent of global mortality in 2001. The infrequency of these diseases in the independent tribal world is partly because they become more frequent with advancing age, and tribals may not live long enough to develop these conditions. However, tribals show lower rates of these diseases than other populations at the same age. Furthermore, many of these conditions now occur in children and are becoming more frequent in middle-aged adults in the commercial world. The panel produced a major technical report that directly linked "the growing epidemic of chronic disease" to specific unhealthy dietary and lifestyle changes associated with "industrialization, urbanization, economic development and market globalization" (UN, WHO/FAO 2003:1). The market-driven "nutrition transition" from healthy traditional diets to unhealthy diets based on high "value added" processed food commodities was clearly the central problem (Drewnowski and Popkin 1997, Popkin 1998). According to the WHO report, commercial diets high in salt, sugars, and saturated fats, including processed vegetable fats with trans-fatty acids, all of which are now known to promote chronic disease, have "swept the entire world," swiftly replacing "traditional" diets that were high in fiber, complex carbohydrates, and natural fats known to be beneficial. The panel stressed that the harmful effects of these diet changes were amplified by the reductions in physical activity promoted by mechanization, motorized transport, and sedentary lifestyles. Significantly, the report concluded that traditional diets based on whole grains and unprocessed fruits, nuts, and vegetables were "particularly protective of health, and clearly environmentally sustainable. Much can be learned from these." (UN, WHO/FAO 2003:101)

SUMMARY

This chapter demonstrates the difficulties of making meaningful cross-cultural quality-of-life comparisons of mental ability and health. It should make anyone cautious of simple stereotypes about tribal peoples as "underdeveloped." Although tribal individuals have the same basic intellectual and perceptual abilities as people in larger-scale cultures, their collective view of the world as reflected in myth, religion, and linguistic classification differs in significant ways that may be related to cultural scale and the absence of writing. However, when viewed from a relativistic and culturally sensitive position, tribal peoples are no more irrational, ignorant, or childish than people anywhere.

Tribal peoples have tremendous stores of culturally transmitted knowledge about the world around them, and their religious beliefs are perpetuated because they work effectively and because their validity is reinforced by the experience of daily life. This position must be spelled out clearly because some anthropologists have suggested that developmentally, tribal peoples are children who do not use adult logic and have difficulty separating fantasy from reality. Others have argued that tribal religious practices such as shamanism are the product of psychopathology.

Formal schooling and institutionalized medicine clearly are not the only route to understanding and health. Not only are there inherent problems in data collection on these issues, but there are dangers in generalizing from individuals to groups and major problems in deciding what standard of comparison can be used. The evidence suggests that although infant mortality rates appear to be high and life expectancy low relative to those of urban industrial populations, tribal peoples are generally free of infectious disease and nutritional deficiencies and avoid many of the dental problems and degenerative diseases that are so common in other populations. The most conservative conclusion is that tribal peoples show no basic differences in their mental abilities, even though they lack writing. The average tribal person would appear to enjoy a healthy vigorous life, relatively free of disease.

STUDY QUESTIONS

1. Explain the views that each of the following took on the nature of "primitive" mentality: Boas, Tylor, Frazer, Lévy-Bruhl, Lévi-Strauss, and Hallpike.
2. In what respects are popular American racial categories cultural constructions rather than biological realities?
3. Why are popular racial categories unscientific? What genetic processes make racial purity a misleading concept?
4. How do human descent groups based on selectively neutral traits compare with populations defined by environmentally selected genetic traits?
5. Explain the cultural context of *Malgri*.
6. Use the Wawilak myth to illustrate the effectiveness of symbols.
7. Why are cross-cultural tests of cognitive ability difficult to apply and interpret?
8. Critique the psychopathological explanation of shamanism.
9. What conditions of tribal cultures contribute to health?

SUGGESTED READING

CAVALLI-SFORZA, LUIGI LUCA, AND FRANCESCO CAVALLI-SFORZA. 1995. *The Great Human Diasporas: The History of Diversity and Evolution.* Reading, Mass.: Addison-Wesley. A useful overview of the migrations of peoples and their effects on genetic diversity.

COHEN, MARK, AND GEORGE ARMELEGOS (eds.). 1984. *Paleopathology and the Origins of Agriculture.* Orlando, Fla.: Academic Press. A collection of essays on the health consequences of the transition to agriculture.

EATON, S. B. BOYD, MELVIN KONNER, AND MARJORIE SHOSTAK. 1988. *The Paleolithic Prescription.* New York: Harper & Row. An examination of the health aspects of forager dietary patterns that applies them to contemporary society.

HARNER, M. J. 1980. *The Way of the Shaman.* New York: Harper & Row. A "how-to" manual that can be used by anyone interested in experimenting with the shamanistic experience.

PART TWO

THE IMPERIAL WORLD
The End of Equality

The tribal world was the only world until perhaps 7500 years ago when the first aggrandizing individuals succeeded in concentrating political power to form chiefdoms. This was the beginning of a global cultural transformation in which very quickly a handful of ruling elites successively constructed large, complex chiefdoms, kingdoms, city-states, and empires in favorable locations worldwide. These were large societies, numbering up to 100 million people, and they created totally different living conditions from the tribal world. The most important difference was that most people in the imperial world were subjects, not rulers. In contrast, tribal people enjoyed maximum freedom and personal autonomy. Tribals were in charge of the conditions of their daily lives. Imperial subjects were dependents. They were forced to pay taxes and tribute, and their lives might be expended at the whim of the emperor. Many subjects were literally slaves. The living conditions of most subjects were probably significantly lower than in the tribal world. Imperial societies are totalitarian systems, ruled by the head of a single family, who typically assumes supernatural powers. Imperial societies are large, complex, and expensive to maintain. They also degrade ecosystems, and collapse frequently. It is difficult to explain how such societies were ever developed.

The following four chapters first describe Pacific islander societies as representative chiefdoms, and then explore the problem of state origins with a case study on Mesopotamia in the ancient Near East. The Inca Empire represents a New World civilization. Imperial China, Hindu kingdoms, and the Mughal Empire represent Old World Great Tradition Civilizations. Chapter 10 examines why imperial societies are so prone to collapse.

Pacific Islanders: The Ranked Chiefdoms

Micronesian islanders

Learning Objectives

After studying this chapter you should be able to do the following.

1. Explain the physical challenges facing the first people to explore and settle the Pacific islands, and describe the cultural solutions that they used.

2. Define and distinguish between the three ethnogeographic regions of the Pacific: Melanesia, Polynesia, and Micronesia.

3. Explain how we can be certain that the ancestors of the Pacific Islanders originated in Asia, not South America.

4. Describe the main components of Pacific Islander subsistence and compare with Amazonian systems.

5. Explain the ways in which life in Pacific island chiefdoms makes demands on people that conflict with the moral systems that characterize the tribal world.

6. Evaluate the Pacific Islander evidence for the theory that growth is an elite directed process that concentrates social power and diffuses the costs.

7. Using Pacific Islander examples, describe the conditions that facilitated the construction of complex chiefdoms, and weigh the evidence for alternative causal explanations.

8. Describe the distribution of social power in Hawaii under King Kamehameha in 1819.

9. Describe the main features of Pacific Islander religious belief and practice in comparison with those of the tribal world.

10. Describe how absolute size of island societies is related to cultural organization and the distribution of social power.

11. Compare gender relations in island societies with gender relations in the tribal world.

PRONUNCIATION GUIDE

The pronunciation of Hawaiian and other Pacific Islander words in this chapter can be approximated by English speakers using the following orthography and sounds:*

Key

a = a in father	h = h in hat
o = o in go	y = y in you
ai = i in ice	• = Syllable division
e = e in bed	/ = Stress
i = i in bit	' = glottal stop, resembles
ee = ee in beet	the stop in English
oo = oo in food	between Oh-Oh

ahupua'a = [a • hoo • pu / a ' a]
ali'i = [a • lee /' ee]
kahuna = [ka • hoo / na]
Kamehameha = [ka• me / ha • me / ha]
kanaka = [ka • na / ka]
kapu = [ka • poo /]
konohiki = [ko • no • hee / kee]
Kumulipo = [koo • moo • lee / po]
Lapita = [la • pee / ta]
Makahiki = [ma • ka • hee/ kee]
maka'ainana = [ma • ka '/ ai • na • na]
mana = [ma / na]
moku = [mo / koo]
ohua = ['o • hua]
Ulithi = [you • li / thee]

*Source: *Hawaiian Dictionary* by Pukui and Elbert 1986:xvii–xviii, and *Ulithi: A Micronesian Design for Living* by William A. Lessa 1966.

The vast Pacific region, known as Oceania, was successfully explored and colonized by Austronesian-speaking voyagers, who spread out from their earlier footholds in the western Pacific, beginning about 3500 years ago. By 1000 BP, virtually every habitable Pacific island supported thriving societies. When Europeans began to arrive in significant numbers in the nineteenth century, they found the Pacific Islanders, except for those in New Guinea, organized into chiefdoms, or small kingdoms. Pacific cultures were perched on the "great divide" between tribes and states, displaying much of the social equality and equilibrium of tribal societies, yet maintaining a pervasive concern with **rank**. Pacific Islanders have simple forms of social stratification and are important examples of the way politicization divides people based on differing access to wealth and power. From a human perspective, pervasive social stratification is perhaps the most important feature of the imperial and commercial worlds.

Remote from the centers of power in the industrializing world and offering relatively few resources to attract outsiders, many Pacific islands maintain much of their traditional cultural system today. They also offer ideal material for examining the contrasts between tribes and states and for understanding the development of political-scale cultures. Given the severe environmental constraints of small islands, Oceania also offers an important place to examine the relationships between population, culture, and resources. The archaeological evidence suggests that Pacific island societies were already chiefdoms when they began their migration into the Pacific from Island Southeast Asia. Therefore, this chapter will highlight the scale-related contrasts between tribal and chiefdom societies and focus on how chiefdom societies were organized, how they developed on different Pacific islands, but not on how chiefdoms originated. Chapter 7 will examine the origins of Mesopotamian chiefdoms from tribal societies, and their further development into city states and empires.

OCEANIA: LIVING IN THE ISLAND WORLD

Searching for Paradise: From High Islands to Low Coral Atolls

In the popular imagination, the reef-fringed, palm-shaded islands of the Pacific are paradises. In reality, many Pacific islands have no drinking water, no soil, and virtually no native plants or animals, and they may be subject to devastating typhoons. Furthermore, without a chart, they are difficult to find in the first place. Exploring and successfully colonizing the Pacific world was one of the greatest human adventures, and it is surely a tribute to the courage and ingenuity of generations of Austronesian-speaking peoples who accomplished this feat roughly a thousand years ago.

The Pacific Ocean covers roughly one-third of the earth's surface. Excluding Hawaii and New Zealand, most Pacific islands are very small, and many are uninhabitable. There are some 10,000 islands scattered across a vast area of ocean, with a total land area of only 4,500 square miles (12,000 square kilometers). The average island is barely more than a square mile of land, and island groups are separated by immense ocean distances. It is 8,000 miles (12,800 kilometers) from Easter Island at the eastern end of Polynesia to Palau in Western Micronesia. There are 2,000 Micronesian islands averaging a third of a square mile spread over an area the size of the continental United States.

Following the original distinctions drawn in 1832 by French geographer Dumont d'Urville (1790–1842), Oceania customarily is divided into three ethnogeographic regions: Melanesia, Polynesia, and Micronesia (Figure 6.1). Melanesia ("black islands") originally was distinguished from Polynesia on ethnocentric and racist grounds. The early European explorers were more comfortable with the Polynesians because they were lighter skinned

---

rank Social position in a status hierarchy.

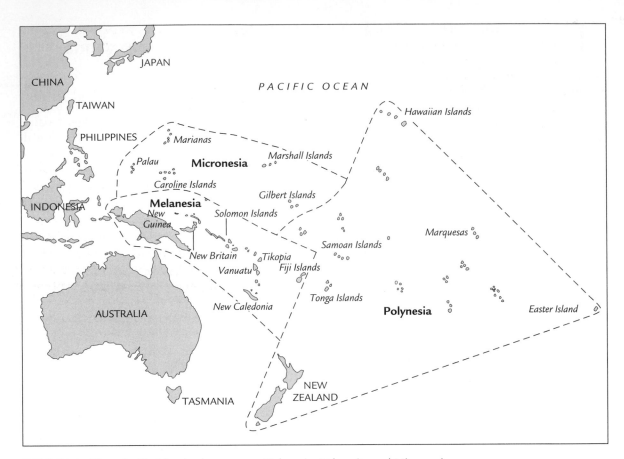

FIGURE 6.1   Three Pacific island culture areas—Melanesia, Polynesia, and Micronesia—with the principal island groups and cultures discussed in the text.

and more hierarchically organized and were seen as attractive, friendly, and almost civilized (Thomas 1989). By contrast, the relatively dark-skinned Melanesians were associated with Africans and were viewed as savage, tribal, and hostile, and even as cannibals and headhunters. In reality, however, the boundaries between Melanesia, Micronesia, and Polynesia were not that sharp, either biologically or culturally, as we will see.

Melanesian islands are predominantly large, mountainous islands formed on the Indian continental plate. They derive their rich and varied terrestrial ecosystems from their close proximity to the Southeast Asian mainland and Australia. The true oceanic islands, which make up most of Polynesia and Micronesia, are either the above-water tops of volcanoes or coral that was formed in the shallow waters on undersea volcanic slopes (Figure 6.2). Hawaii, New Zealand, and Easter Island form the corners of the vast Polynesian triangle. Polynesia ("many islands") contains many high volcanic islands, most of which lie south of the equator. The islands of Micronesia ("tiny islands") are primarily very small islets of coral sand that form on the reefs that fringed ancient, now submerged volcanoes. Before the arrival of Europeans, the two largest cultural areas, Polynesia and Micronesia, which will be the focus of this chapter, together contained a population estimated at 700,000 people (Oliver 1989).

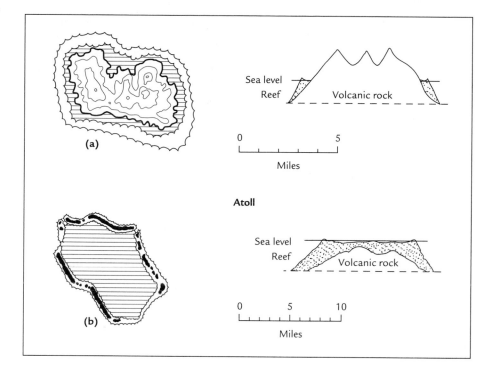

Sea level
Reef   Volcanic rock

0   5
Miles

(a)

Atoll

Sea level
Reef   Volcanic rock

0   5   10
Miles

(b)

FIGURE 6.2 Examples of island types. (*a*) Rarotonga, a high, reef-rimmed volcanic island; (*b*) Penrhyn, an atoll. (SOURCE: Cumberland 1956.)

Many factors affect the habitability of islands. Generally, large, high, volcanic islands, such as those found in Melanesia and Polynesia, contain relatively more land resources than the small coral islands of Micronesia. High islands will support a larger human population and are likely to have several zones of natural vegetation, rich soils, and flowing freshwater. However, there may be significant environmental differences between the moist windward side of these islands and the dry leeward side, which is sheltered from the rain by the mountains. There is also a general decline in biological diversity with increasing distance from the Asian mainland and Australia. For example, only a few reptiles, rats, and bats are native to the oceanic islands and the most remote islands have only a few seabirds. Unless human colonists brought animal domesticates with them, animal protein could only be obtained from marine life. Similarly, few if any edible plants occurred naturally on the smaller islands, and a reliable source of carbohydrates in the form of domesticated plants had to be introduced.

Perhaps the most critical limiting factors are related to climate and the absolute size of an island. The tiny coral islets might be no more than 6–8 feet (2–3 meters [m]) above sea level and lack flowing freshwater. But if they are at least 350 feet (107 m) in diameter, they might support an underground layer of freshwater, which forms when rainwater percolates through the porous coral and sand and mixes only gradually with the denser seawater beneath. Many islets support a small freshwater or brackish swamp in the center, but they depend on rainfall that is regionally variable and erratic, so that in some places serious droughts can occur. The freshwater supply of small atolls may also be temporarily destroyed by typhoons, which can wash saltwater completely over low islets. Despite all these limitations, an islet as small as 0.25 square miles might sustain 200 people, given the appropriate technical skills, as long as they maintain contacts with neighboring groups who can be relied on for support.

Speculation on the origin of the Pacific Islanders began as soon as outsiders encountered them. But in the absence of solid linguistic, archaeological, and biological data, many fanciful and mutually exclusive theories were devised (Howard 1967). Some theorists deprecated the navigational skills and cultural creativity of Pacific Islanders, believing that only ancient Egyptians could have settled the Pacific (Perry 1923, E. Smith 1928). In 1947, Norwegian adventurer Thor Heyerdahl drifted on a balsa-log raft westward with the winds and currents across the Pacific from South America to prove his theory that Pacific Islanders were Native Americans. Contrary to these theorists, however, the overwhelming evidence of physical anthropology, linguistics, and archaeology shows that the Pacific Islanders came from Southeast Asia and were sufficiently skilled as navigators to sail against the prevailing winds and currents (see the box entitled "The Origin of the Pacific Islanders"). Table 6.1 outlines the prehistory of the Pacific Islands and adjacent Island Southeast Asia.

The basic cultural requirements for the successful colonization of the Pacific islands include the appropriate boat-building, sailing, and navigating skills to get to the islands in the first place; domesticated plants and gardening skills suited to often marginal conditions; and a varied inventory of fishing implements and techniques. It is now generally believed that these prerequisites originated with peoples speaking Austronesian languages and began to emerge in Southeast Asia by about 7000 BP. The Proto-Austronesian culture of that time, based on archaeology and linguistic reconstruction, presumably had a broad inventory of cultivated plants including taro, yams, banana, sugarcane, breadfruit, coconut, sago, and rice. Just as important, the culture possessed the basic foundation for an effective maritime adaptation, including outrigger canoes and a variety of fishing techniques effective for overseas voyaging.

Contrary to the arguments of some that much of the Pacific was settled by Polynesians accidentally marooned after being lost and adrift at sea, it seems reasonable that this feat was accomplished by deliberate colonization expeditions that set out fully stocked with food and domesticated plants and animals. Detailed studies of the winds and currents using computer simulations suggest that

drifting canoes would have been a most unlikely means of colonizing the Pacific (Levison, Ward, and Webb 1973). These expeditions likely were driven by population growth and political dynamics on the home islands, as well as the challenge and excitement of exploring unknown waters. Because all Polynesians and Micronesians and many Melanesians speak Austronesian languages and grow crops derived from Southeast Asia, all these peoples most certainly derived from that region, and not the New World or elsewhere.

Glottochronology: Word Tracks Across the Pacific

The general picture of the settlement of Oceania seems to conform well with linguistic reconstructions based on **glottochronology,** which suggests that most modern Austronesian languages emerged within the past 5000 years (Figure 6.3). Glottochronology assumes that all languages lose words from a common core vocabulary at a constant rate historically documented for Indo-European languages (Gudschinsky 1956). The core vocabulary is a list of 100–200 words for cultural universals such as body parts and geographic features. The years since two languages separated from a common ancestor are calculated from the percentage of cognates identified in the core vocabulary. **Cognates** are words that are recognizably derived from a common source in a parent language, and thus their frequency is assumed to be a measure of their separation time. To cite a Polynesian example, Table 6.2 lists the words for *deity, chief,* and *taboo* in Tikopian, a member of the Samoic branch of Nuclear Polynesian, and Hawaiian, an Eastern Polynesian language. The words in both languages obviously are similar enough to be considered cognates, implying a common ancestry, even though their speakers live more than 3000 miles apart.

Languages sharing more than 80 percent cognates are considered to be dialects of the same language and are assumed to be separated by no more than 500 years. In theory, relationships as remote as 10,000 years might be suggested on the basis of extremely low percentages of shared cognates.

The Origin of the Pacific Islanders

By about 5000 BP, Austronesian-speaking peoples began to expand toward the Pacific islands, first into Taiwan and the Philippines and then along coastal New Guinea. By 3000 BP virtually all of Melanesia and much of Micronesia were occupied, and the Proto-Polynesians had established a firm foothold in Fiji, Tonga, and Samoa on the western edge of what would become Polynesia.

Some of the best archaeological evidence for the sequence of colonization in the Pacific is based on the discovery of a distinctive red, stamped, and incised pottery style, known as Lapita (Figure 6.A), and associated domesticated plants and fishing technology. Lapita peoples ultimately were derived from the Proto-Austronesians of Island Southeast Asia. But they appear to have developed their distinctive style in the New Britain area off of eastern New Guinea about 3600 years ago before spreading through the closely spaced chain of Melanesian islands to New Caledonia (Kirch 1985). The crossing of the 528 miles (850 km) of open ocean between Vanuatu and Fiji, which took place about 3250 BP, judging by the appearance of Lapita pottery in Fiji at that time, was a major achievement that set the stage for expansion into the rest of the inhabitable Pacific. The 1000-mile (1600-km) crossing between Samoa and the Marquesas in central Polynesia, which took place approximately 2000 years ago, was a logical continuation of the earlier voyages of discovery. Even longer voyages from the Marquesas to Hawaii, Easter Island, and New Zealand followed shortly thereafter.

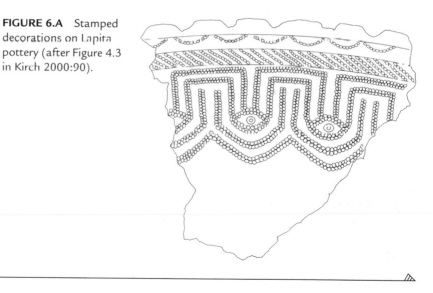

FIGURE 6.A Stamped decorations on Lapita pottery (after Figure 4.3 in Kirch 2000:90).

Islander Survival Skills: Outrigger Canoes and Navigation

Canoes and navigation were a vital part of Pacific island culture. Not only did they make discovery and colonization possible, but they were necessary

glottochronology A method of estimating the relative date at which related languages separated from a common ancestral language, by calculating the percentage of cognates shared between the related languages.

cognates Related words that are found in more than one language and that were derived from a common protolanguage.

TABLE 6.1   PREHISTORY OF THE PACIFIC ISLANDS, 250,000 BP–AD 1778

AD 1778	Captain James Cook lands in the Hawaiian Islands
AD 1522	Ferdinand Magellan expedition crosses the Pacific
Polynesian Expansion (3600 BP–AD 800)	
800 AD	New Zealand settled
400 AD	Easter Island settled
300 AD	Hawaii settled
2000 BP	Marquesas settled
3250 BP	Lapita pottery in Fiji
Proto-Oceanic Expansion (5000 BP–3600 BP)	
5000 BP	Outrigger canoes enter Oceania
	Proto-Oceanic maritime specialization
Proto-Austronesians (15,000 BP–5,000 BP)	
7000 BP	Domestication of banana, sugarcane, breadfruit, coconut, sago, rice; fishing technology
9000 BP	Taro and yams horticulture in New Guinea
***Homo sapiens* Foragers (60,000 BP–15,000 BP)**	
60,000 BP	Ancestral Australian and Papuan Foragers in Sundaland
Homo erectus in Java (1.5 million BP to 250,000 BP)	

SOURCES: Bellwood (1980), Kirch (1985, 2000), Oliver (1989).

for making a living and maintaining communication between islands. Seagoing Micronesian outriggers, which were routinely used to cross more than 300 miles (483 km) of open ocean, were only 25 feet (8 m) long, whereas the huge double-hulled Polynesian canoes used in overseas colonization were nearly 100 feet (30 m) long and could easily accommodate supplies for an extended voyage. Canoes were designed to be extremely seaworthy and, unlike rafts, were highly maneuverable and could be propelled by both sail and paddles. The most widely distributed canoe type was the outrigger, which in Micronesia was usually constructed from a carved breadfruit-log hull with wooden planks lashed on the side. The outrigger was a wooden float suspended approximately half a hull length off the windward side of the canoe and counterbalanced by a platform suspended off the lee side (Figure 6.4). The outrigger was oriented so that the float would be lifted by the wind on the sail. When the float dipped into the water, it pulled the canoe back into the wind. The great advantage of the outrigger was that it maximized speed and stability without a deep keel (to counterbalance the sail), which would impede passage over the reefs surrounding most Pacific islands.

The addition of an outrigger posed many design problems that traditional canoe builders solved in very sophisticated ways. The hull had to be asymmetrical in cross section, and its overall contours were shaped within very narrow tolerances to achieve a balance between seaworthiness, speed, and maneuverability (Gladwin 1970). Only a few specialists had the necessary skills to direct construction of such a complex craft. The bow and stern of the outrigger were reversible, and when a major change in direction was made, the sail was shifted from end to end to keep the float facing the wind.

The navigational techniques that allowed Polynesian explorers to maintain a steady course across vast distances in search of islands are still being practiced by a few skilled navigators on some of the most isolated Micronesian atolls. Thomas Gladwin's (1970) research on the atoll of Puluwat revealed the main features of the system. Gladwin found that Micronesian navigation was based on an elaborate body of formal knowledge, both empirical and mythical. A few titled specialists, known as master navigators, controlled the system and offered formal instruction to aspiring navigators. Out of the island population of 400 people, only 6 men were considered master navigators. Successful navigation depended on the ability to sail a steady course on a specific bearing while keeping a mental record of the distance traveled, for days or weeks at a time, at night, during storms, across changing currents, and in unfamiliar waters. The key to the system

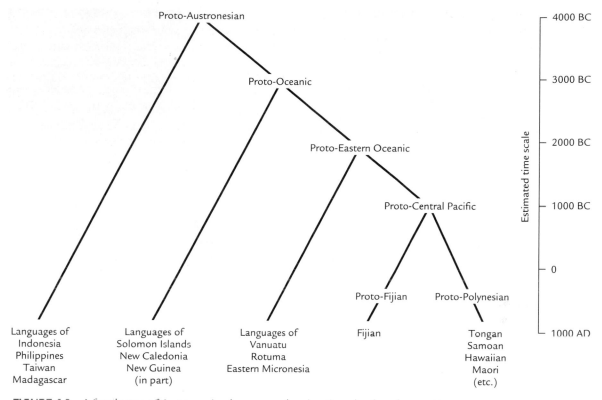

FIGURE 6.3 A family tree of Austronesian languages showing time depths of separations for the Oceanic branches. (SOURCE: Kirch 1985:62.)

TABLE 6.2   COGNATES BETWEEN TIKOPIAN AND HAWAIIAN LANGUAGES OF NUCLEAR POLYNESIAN

Word	Tikopian (Samoic Outlier)	Hawaiian (Eastern Polynesian)
Deity	*Atua*	*Akua*
Chief	*Ariki*	*Ali'i*
Taboo	*Tapu*	*Kapu*

SOURCES: Firth ([1936] 1957), Malo (1951), and Ruhlen (1987).

was a star chart with thirty-two named bearing points based on the rising and setting points of specific stars (Figure 6.5). For each route traveled, a navigator had to commit to memory a unique sequence of bearing stars.

The navigators on Puluwat routinely sailed between 26 islands using 110 different routes. To follow a given bearing, the navigators needed to know what stars would be observed en route, and they kept careful track of wave patterns and weather conditions. There was little margin for error on a long voyage because small atolls were only visible for 10 miles (16 km) at sea and so might easily be missed in passing. And even upon arrival, the navigator had to find narrow passes through treacherous reefs.

Navigators were greatly respected, high-status individuals. Canoes were treated with great care. They were stored in special canoe houses to prevent them from becoming waterlogged, and the lashings and caulking might be replaced every 2 years.

FIGURE 6.4
Micronesian outrigger.

Long-distance voyages also depended on a reliable system of food storage. Whole coconuts were a ready, storable source of food and drinking water, but there were elaborate ways of processing other important staples such as breadfruit, pandanus palm fruits, and taros so that they could be stored indefinitely without canning or refrigeration (Schattenburg 1976). Micronesians had at least four different ways of preserving breadfruit, involving grating, pounding, soaking, fermenting, cooking, and sun drying. In one method, peeled slices of raw ripe breadfruit were soaked for 1½ days in the lagoon, fermented for 2 days on the ground, then squeezed and stirred with fresh water for 3 more days to convert them to dough. When the dough was shaped into slabs and sun-dried, it could be stored for up to 2 years before being reconstituted by soaking again in water (Murai, Pen, and Miller 1958).

Breadfruit is more nutritious than potatoes and is rich enough in calories and vitamins to supply virtually all daily food requirements when supplemented with fish and coconut. Because many of the cultivated plants in the Pacific are grown from cuttings, special techniques were developed for transporting them. Patricia Schattenburg (1976) reported that when the root balls of delicate young breadfruit trees were wrapped in rotted coconut husks, bound with dried leaves, and bundled in woven baskets, they were protected from saltwater.

Fishing and Gardening: The Island Technological Base

Pacific island subsistence is similar to that of Amazonia in that it is based on two rather distinct systems: (1) fishing and gathering of marine animals to provide protein, and (2) gardening to produce the bulk of dietary calories. According to the usual gender division of labor, men do the fishing and heavy gardening work while women gather marine animals and do the daily garden cultivating and harvesting. Three crop zones, which on small islands are often arranged in concentric zones according to altitude and proximity to the ocean, include orchard crops, dry crops, and wet crops. The orchard crops are the bread-

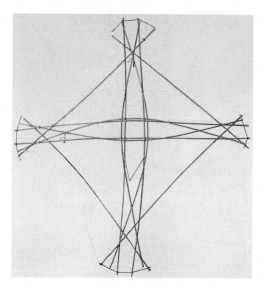

FIGURE 6.5 Stick figure from the Marshall Islands, used to teach the fundamentals of the Micronesian star chart.

fruit trees and the relatively salt-tolerant co-conuts and pandanus palms that can grow near the beach (Figure 6.6a). All of these trees provide food as well as raw materials for canoe building, house construction, and basketry. On the smaller islands, they are the only significant sources of wood and fiber. The subsistence importance of coconuts is indicated by the fact that Polynesians name seventeen different stages of nuts accord-ing to their edibility (Handy and Handy 1972). Micronesians specialize in producing a fermented drink from the sap tapped from the unopened flower stem.

The dry gardens produce sweet potatoes, yams, and bananas, but the extent of such gar-dens is severely limited by soil conditions and rainfall, especially on the smaller coral islands and atolls. On many of these islands, soil other than coral sand is virtually absent, and humus must be created and maintained by a continuous process of mulching. Throughout much of the Pacific, the most important food plants are the taros, members of the arum family *(Araceae),* known as aroids (see the box entitled "Taro" and Figure 6.6b).

The productivity of taro and its subsistence importance are indicated by data obtained by William Alkire (1965) on the Micronesian atoll of Lamotrek in the central Caroline Islands. In Lamotrek, approximately 200 people live on a 0.25-square mile (158-acre or 64-hectare) islet. Alkire estimated that taro supplied approxi-mately three-fourths of the average 2 pounds (0.9 kg) of plant food consumed daily by adults on the island. An estimated 500,000 taro plants grew on the island, with some 15,000 per acre in the 58 acres of the island's swampy interior. An-nual consumption was only about 20 percent of the total crop, but even if most of the plants were slow-growing swamp taro, the consumption rate still would have been well below potential pro-duction. However, if typhoons swept saltwater into the swamp and destroyed the crop, recovery would take at least 3 years.

Taro-based subsistence was a time-consuming female task on Lamotrek. During the half of the year when breadfruit was not being harvested, Lamotrek women worked over 2 hours a day in the taro swamp, cultivating and harvesting. Taro processing took nearly an additional 3 hours a day. Breadfruit harvesting and processing re-quired about 3 hours a day in season.

Fishing was a primary male activity through-out the Pacific. Alkire (1965) found that on an average day, nearly one-fourth of the male popu-lation of Lamotrek would be out fishing. Men typically spent over 5 hours fishing at a time and brought back about 9 pounds (4 kg) of fish. Vir-tually every major fishing technique was used, including traps, nets, spears, and hook and line. Fish were also raised in fish farms—rock-lined pools in tidal shallows—where they were fed and allowed to reproduce.

Coral reef ecosystems cover less than 0.1 per-cent of the globe, but they produce some 10 per-cent of the world's fish and support many other traditionally important food animals, such as sea turtles, and edible marine invertebrates, such as shellfish. Estimates for sustained productivity of these rich coral reef zones range as high as 22 tons (20 metric tons) of fish per square kilometer of reef

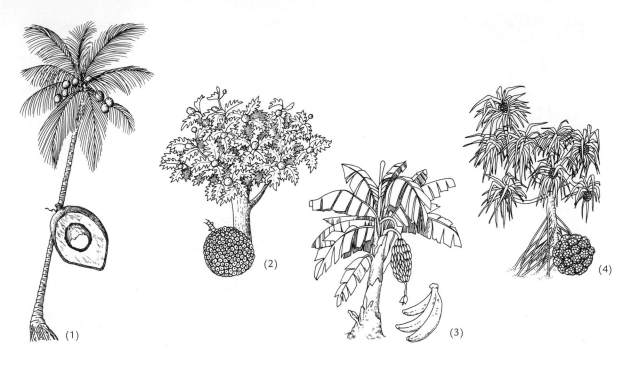

(a)

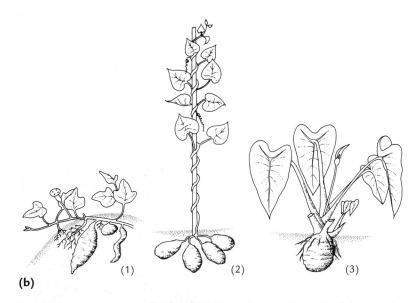

(b)

FIGURE 6.6 Primary Pacific island subsistence crops (*a*) orchard crops: (1) coconut palm, (2) breadfruit, (3) banana, and (4) pandanus palm. (*b*) Root crops: (1) yam, (2) sweet potato, and (3) taro. (SOURCE: Based on Oliver 1989:186, 191.)

Taro

The arum family includes many familiar leafy tropical ornamentals, such as the philodendron. The edible aroids grow large heart-shaped ears and are sprouted from cuttings. They produce starchy corms and bulbous underground stems and are highly productive, but they require large amounts of relatively fresh water. The true taro, *Colocasia esculenta,* is sometimes grown in terraced, irrigated ponds on high islands. It can be planted at any time and is harvested within a year, but it does not store well, either in the ground or after harvest. Another important aroid, *Cyrtosperma,* the swamp taro, produces a more fibrous corm. It takes 3 years to reach full maturity, but it can be harvested over a longer period, allowing it to be stored in the ground, and it keeps for about 2 weeks after harvest. It is the preferred taro in much of Micronesia, where it is grown in the swampy center of small coral islands where freshwater reaches the surface. Another aroid, *Alocasia macrorrhiza,* or giant taro (elephant ear), grows under drier conditions, but its corms require special processing to remove irritating crystals.

per year (Kenchington 1985). This would be enough for 110 people. The availability of animal protein is clearly not a limiting factor for most Pacific Islanders. In comparison, the mammal protein produced in a square kilometer of tropical rain forest would support only one person per year.

The amount of specialized knowledge that successful fishing required was most impressive. Many important marine ecozones were exploited in different ways. Atolls, for example, included at least five broad marine zones (Knudson 1970): the lagoon in the center of the atoll, shallow waters, deep waters along reef edges and coral heads, intertidal reefs and flats, and the open ocean. Pacific Islanders themselves recognized many finer distinctions. The shallow waters, reef edges, and lagoons generally were the most intensively exploited zones, where nets, traps, and weirs could be used most effectively (Figure 6.7). According to a study by Don Rubinstein (1978), the people of Fais, in the Carolines, named four broad marine zones and thirteen subzones ringing their 1-square-mile (2.6-km^2) raised coral island. They located specific fishing areas by reference to some sixty submerged coral heads, which were individually named, and they identified eleven lines radiating from the island and aligned with named features on shore and at sea.

FIGURE 6.7 In Micronesia, fish are frequently taken in traps.

Phil Lobel (1978) found that the Gilbertese Islanders in Kiribati have names for 254 fish species, 95 marine invertebrates, and 25 fish anatomical features.

Marine biologist Robert Johannes (1981) has documented the knowledge employed by native fishermen on Palau in Micronesia. A critical element in organizing Palauan fishing activities was keeping careful track of the seasons. For this purpose, the Palauans utilized a 12-month lunar calendar that allowed them to predict with considerable precision changes in wind, weather, and waves and the movements and breeding patterns of many pelagic fish, turtles, and seabirds. Palauans understood how ocean currents were deflected by islands and reefs, and they knew where specific fish would concentrate seasonally in relation to the eddies and calm places (Figure 6.8).

A profusion of fishing gear and techniques reflected an understanding of the specific feeding habits, life history, and anatomy of many different fish species. The curiously incurved shell fishhook, so widely used in the Pacific, works more effectively than the standard barbed steel hook, which Europeans assumed to be superior. The traditional shell hook is designed to slide to the corner of the fish's mouth after a light tug and then to rotate, penetrating and locking securely in the fish's jaw (Johannes 1981).

PACIFIC ISLAND SOCIETIES: LIVING WITH INEQUALITY

Understanding Pacific island chiefdoms requires a brief review of the evolutionary background of human society. Early hominids shared ancient primate social instincts with their chimpanzee relatives that made it possible for both chimps and humans to live in very small, intimate family groups of 25 to 50 individuals. Such small societies depended on direct physical contact, interpersonal cooperation, mating, grooming, and simple dominance hierarchies. The evolution of fully modern humans living in tribal societies of 500 or more people required new, culturally transmitted, so-

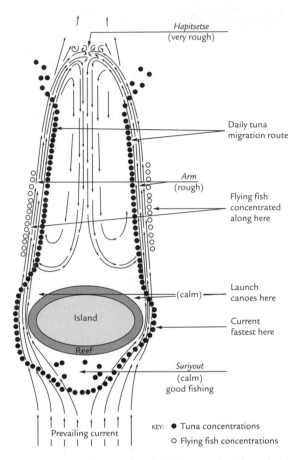

FIGURE 6.8   Micronesians in Palau use their knowledge of ocean currents to locate fish. (Source: Based on Johannes 1981, Figure 3.)

cial instincts for morality and ethnocentrism, and the cultural construction of social identity based on kinship, marriage, and exchange (Read 2000, Richerson and Boyd 1998, 1999).

Prototribes developed by means of a coevolutionary process of natural selection operating on the genetics of individuals and cultural selection operating on the shared beliefs and practices of organized human groups. Individuals most likely to reproduce would have been those who could live cooperatively in a successful group. The cultural meanings and behaviors that people transmitted to their children and to society at large were those that favored individual survival and reproduction, and that also favored group survival in competition with other human groups. People were morally compelled to seek group approval, and they had to believe that their own society was superior to all others (Alexander 1987). For this kind of evolution to work, all individuals and the tribe as a whole had to succeed.

Thus, morality and ethnocentrism became powerful forces for social equality, and they made it difficult for any individuals to concentrate social power in personal imperia that were conspicuously larger than average. In view of the apparent success of tribal constraints against concentrated social power, the evolution of larger, less egalitarian chiefdoms and states has been called a "grand series of experiments at the expense of the social instincts" (Richerson and Boyd 1999:265).

Elite-Directed Cultural Transformation in Polynesia

Pacific island societies were strikingly different from any of the tribal groups we have examined thus far. Before the invasion of the commercial world, Pacific Islanders lived in politically centralized chiefdoms that were often orders of magnitude larger than tribes, and they were ruled by elites who enjoyed special privileges. The size difference matters enormously. Chiefdoms were not simply tribes grown larger. Chiefdoms required social transformations that conflicted with the human predilections for personal freedom and equality that defined the tribal way of life. The natural laws of scale meant that when tribal societies grew larger, unless they segmented, rulers had to radically transform the culture in order to prevent social disintegration. Why this was so is explained in the box "A Matter of Scale: The Political Transformation of Tribes into Chiefdoms." These larger chiefdom societies so restricted human freedom and apportioned benefits so unequally and were so out of step with the lifestyles and personalities familiar to tribal people, that they could only have been sustained with coercive institutions directed by the principal beneficiaries of this enormous cultural transformation.

The world's earliest known chiefdoms existed in Mesopotamia 7500 years ago (see Chapter 7). Their appearance was so sudden and so recent that they had to have been the product of cultural rather than biological change. It seems likely that they were constructed when a combination of circumstances made it possible for power-seeking individuals to enlarge their personal imperia beyond the constraints typically imposed by tribal societies. Chiefdom organization did not originate independently in Polynesia. The proto-Austronesian peoples who settled the Pacific brought simple chiefdoms with them from Southeast Asia. However, the processes involved in the transformation of tribes into chiefdoms, which are explored in Chapter 7, are similar to the transformation from simple to complex chiefdoms, which occurred in the Pacific. Any culture must be reproduced by people in a continuous process, but this is more difficult in chiefdoms where the benefits are not equally shared. Less privileged members of chiefdom societies must be forced to make the best of their inferior positions, or they are persuaded by elite-manipulated symbols to imagine that they are not actually disadvantaged. The central organizational problem that rulers must repeatedly solve is that people naturally don't like to be commanded by others, and they don't like social inequality unless they are at the top.

The discovery and settlement of the Pacific islands by Polynesians involved a dynamic process of population growth and subsistence intensification. On several of the largest islands, elites used cycles of competitive feasting and warfare to construct complex chiefdoms with highly unequal social classes (Kirch 1984:13–15). This was an elite-directed politicization process, in which a handful of people successfully manipulated the legitimizing power of cosmology to create political economies that compelled the majority of society to support elite self-interested growth projects. When the scale of Polynesian societies increased, social power became more concentrated in the hands of the chiefs, and most people lost control

A Matter
of Scale:
The Political
Transforma-
tion of Tribes
into
Chiefdoms

In the tribal world most human interaction, as we have seen, took place between the members of households and between the members of nearby households in a village or band. A 5-person household forms a very small network in which there are only 10 possible interactions between all the individual members, and these can be handled easily by the institutionalized distinctions of age and gender. In a village of 50 people there are suddenly more than 1,000 possible human interactions, according to the mathematics of network law $I = P*[P–1]/2$, where I = interaction and P = population). Thus, when the population increases by 1 power of 10, possible human interactions multiply by 2 powers of 10 (Figure 6.B). This growth creates significant new sources of interpersonal stress and conflict, but the problem is vastly greater at the tribal level where with 500 people there are more than 100,000 human interactions possible. A typical Polynesian chiefdom of 5000 people would have more than 12 million possible interactions, and a small kingdom encompassing 300,000 people in all of the Hawaii islands, nearly 20 billion.

The solution to the intensified stress of tribal society was the addition of organizational complexity in the form of new cultural institutions, such as moieties, lineages, and clans, myths, and rituals but not powerful rulers. Robert Carneiro (1967) examined 100 small-scale societies and found that as societies grew, the number of organizational traits approximated the square root of the population. By these calculations we would expect the Hawaii kingdom of 300,000 people to be an order of magnitude (tenfold) more complex than a tribal society (Figure 6.B). The additional complexity was primarily in the addition of specialists to manage the political economy and new ideological institutions to persuade people of the legitimacy of the king's authority.

Population size is an important variable because size constrains decision-making processes. In a social group of 150 or fewer people, virtually everyone can participate in decisions; but in a society of 500 or more, public decision-making is likely to be controlled by the adult men. A consensual village head might be able to informally coordinate up to 500 household heads within a local group of 2500 peo-

over the natural and cultural resources they needed to meet their basic needs.

The colonization of unoccupied Polynesian islands would have favored very rapid initial population growth, with founder populations potentially doubling within a single generation up to natural and cultural limits. However, cultural forms of population regulation were as important as natural limits, and continuous growth was not inevitable. Even at 2 percent annual growth, doubling in 36 years, a founder population of 25 would

have grown to more than a trillion people within 1234 years. Polynesians settled the Pacific over 3500 years, and island population did not regularly crash. On some islands it took a long time for limits to be reached. For example, the archaeological record shows that over 1400 years Hawaii's population may have reached 800,000 before Europeans arrived in 1778 (Kirch 1984, 2001:170, Stannard 1989). By then they were probably approaching overall carrying capacity for their intensive, hand-powered subsistence technology. It

ple, but a formal political elite is necessarily required to manage larger settlements. Five hundred is a crucial number because the limits of human memory and information-processing ability make it difficult for people—including chiefs—to keep track of more than that number of items in any domain (Kosse 1990).

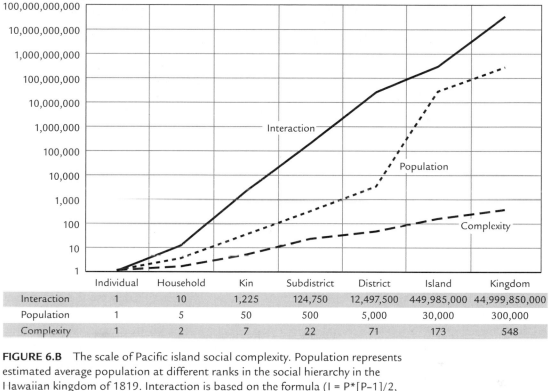

	Individual	Household	Kin	Subdistrict	District	Island	Kingdom
Interaction	1	10	1,225	124,750	12,497,500	449,985,000	44,999,850,000
Population	1	5	50	500	5,000	30,000	300,000
Complexity	1	2	7	22	71	173	548

FIGURE 6.B   The scale of Pacific island social complexity. Population represents estimated average population at different ranks in the social hierarchy in the Hawaiian kingdom of 1819. Interaction is based on the formula ($I = P*[P-1]/2$, where I = interaction, and P = population. Complexity is the square root of population, based on Carneiro (1967).

took global commercial trade and an enormous input of fossil fuels to push Hawaii's population to 1.2 million people by the year 2000.

As island populations grew larger, people modified and sometimes degraded the natural ecosystems by creating artificial plant communities. Many unique native birds were exterminated in the process (Steadman 1995). Growth also meant that people had to work harder, steadily intensifying their subsistence activities by developing irrigation systems and fish ponds to produce more food from a very limited space. Similar subsistence intensification growth trends also characterized the neolithic and were familiar to tribal peoples, but in the islands the human outcome was different, because power-seeking chiefs took advantage of the stresses of population growth to expand their personal imperia. Tribal peoples were apparently able to maintain lower limits on the size of their societies and seldom felt compelled to transform the internal structure of their societies. Generally, when growing tribal populations segmented, they did so simply by dividing into two or more identical, small-scale groups. Rather than segmenting and remaining the same, Polynesians apparently felt compelled to accept greater inequality, hierarchy, technological change, and specialization in order to meet chiefly demands for greater production and organizational complexity to integrate society at a higher scale. The underlying constraint was that islands filled up quickly and were so small that it was difficult for people to separate and move apart to maintain their independence. People had invested too much effort to easily move away.

The power and authority of the chiefs was the most remarkable feature of Polynesian societies. Most significantly, much of production was stimulated by the demands of chiefs, who had a vested self-interest in promoting technological intensification so that more commoners could supply more tribute. In the tribal world every household controlled their own productive resources, and stopped production when their needs were met. However, in Polynesia the chiefs controlled access to productive land, and there were many people who performed specialized economic activities, such as canoe making or craft production, or who became full-time chiefs, or priests. Specialists had to be supported by the common people who actually worked the land. The chiefs used the supporting ideological concepts of ranked descent lines, mana, tabu, and sacrifice to the gods as the key organizing principles of Polynesian societies. These elements were present at least on a small scale from the very beginning of the colonization of the Pacific (Kirch 1984). The religious basis of Pacific island status systems appeared most conspicuously in the related concepts of *mana* and *tabu* (taboo), or *tapu*. **Mana** has been variously defined as an impersonal supernatural force, or power, which could manifest itself in people, objects, and spirits. Cognate terms occur throughout the Pacific, and the *mana* concept has close parallels in many parts of the world. It is sometimes referred to as animatism to distinguish it from the more elementary belief in souls, or animism.

Mana was inherited with chiefly rank, and its presence was demonstrated in the chief's objective ability to control his followers. A chief with powerful *mana* could give goods to his subjects in exchange for their labor services, and he could influence nature as an agent of the gods. Thus, in a circular fashion, the hereditary elite demanded respect because they had *mana,* and the presence of *mana* was expressed in the respect that they received. The elite could possess various degrees of *mana,* while commoners might have none. The Polynesian term **tabu,** usually translated as "forbidden actions," refers to a wide range of ritual avoidances that lower-ranked individuals must observe as an acknowledgment of the sanctity of elite status. Deference toward chiefs included such things as bowing, keeping one's head below the chiefs' head, using special "respect language," and making special offerings.

Chiefly prerogatives might also be marked by special forms of dress, badges, housing, and foods, which accrued to the chief by birth to the status; but perhaps more important were the claims that a chief could make into land, labor, and goods, as an expression of his personal power. Polynesian status inequality also appeared in honorific titles that were applied to outstanding warriors and to a variety of individuals, including priests and craftsmen, who displayed special skills. These individuals, especially if they were already elites with *mana,* were important challenges to chiefly authority.

Chiefdoms and the Politicization Process

Chiefdoms were a radical transformation of life in the tribal world where local bands and villages were politically autonomous and economically self-sufficient. This "first transcending of local autonomy in human history" was the great social divide between egalitarian and nonegalitarian societies, and it occurred only within the past 7500 years when the first villagers surrendered their political autonomy to chiefs from other vil-

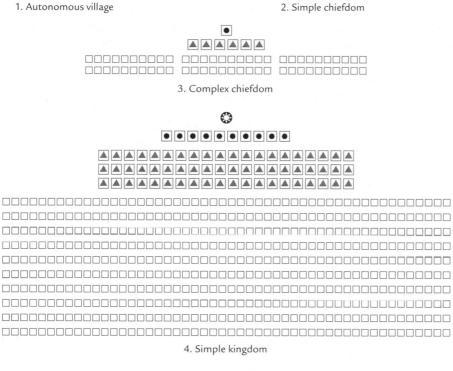

FIGURE 6.9 Levels of political complexity, from autonomous village to kingdom.

1. Autonomous village

2. Simple chiefdom

3. Complex chiefdom

4. Simple kingdom

KEY: □ 500 villagers   ▲ District chief   ● Paramount chief   ✸ King

lages (Carneiro 1981:37–38). The defining feature of chiefdoms was that chiefs styled themselves as superior human beings, and were able to establish dynasties and transmit their advantageous position to their descendants. Chiefdoms were the first step in the politicization process that ultimately allowed power-seeking rulers to build kingdoms, city-states, states, and empires. A chief directing a simple chiefdom might have political authority over 10 local village heads and bigmen and perhaps command 5000 people (Figure 6.9). A more enterprising chief might use military force to gain another tenfold increase in social power by pulling several district chiefs under his leadership, creating a complex chiefdom of 30,000 people or more. From there it would be a short step for a power-driven ruler to conquer his neighbors and bring several complex chiefdoms together to

form a simple kingdom that could draw tribute from hundreds of thousands of commoners.

It is not easy to explain the successes of political power-seekers, because the benefits of the politicization process are enjoyed by only a very small proportion of society, whereas most people are burdened by reduced social status, higher taxes, warfare, and insecurity. Concentrated power disproportionately improves the chief's quality of life and genetic fitness while diminishing the fitness of others. Power also can be used coercively to

mana An impersonal supernatural force thought to reside in particular people and objects. In the Pacific islands, *mana* is the basis of chiefly power.

tabu Actions that are forbidden under the sanction of supernatural punishment. *Tabus* may be imposed by chiefs and are supported by chiefly *mana*.

threaten or otherwise manipulate cultural choices so that people are persuaded to lend their support to the chief. As William Durham (1991:211) notes, "cultural evolution is an intrinsically political process." The emergence and persistence of chiefdoms is an example of the imposition of cultural patterns by a power elite, rather than free choice by the population at large. Chiefdoms are produced by biased cultural transmission that actually works against the humanization process for most households. Politicization is the first step in an evolutionary process that rewards a powerful, self-interested minority for promoting cultural ideas that support runaway growth harmful to others.

Politicization requires growth. Power seekers must mobilize household labor, warriors, technology, trade, and religion in their growth projects. Politicization works because as growth occurs, political leaders become a mathematically smaller proportion of society and their power steadily increases. Elites are thus naturally rewarded for developing cultural ideas that remove the barriers to growth. Marshall Sahlins (1958) pointed out that the power of Polynesian chiefs increased simultaneously with economic productivity as measured by the size of the networks in which food was redistributed, the frequency of redistribution, and the number of specialists who were not directly involved in primary food production, and who were therefore supported by "surplus" production.

The concept of environmental or social **circumscription** offers the most attractive explanation for understanding why people accepted chiefly rule (Carneiro 1981). Here the argument is that in times of stress or crisis, living with even oppressive rulers may sometimes not seem as bad an alternative as the risks of immigration. Circumscription, or "social caging" (Mann 1986), occurs when geographic or environmental barriers in combination with social circumstances and historical contingencies prevent villagers from easily escaping threats of political domination. Often the crucial contingency is armed conflict driven by status rivalry, or power struggles between chiefs fighting to control narrowly cir-

cumscribed intensive food production zones and productive populations. Villagers in conquered territories would have little choice but to pay tribute to a high chief unless flight were possible. The exploration and settlement of Polynesia was probably driven by people escaping political crises, but not everyone could leave, and the risks of failure were high.

The Polynesian Chiefdoms: Elementary Aristocracies

Polynesian chiefdoms were **aristocracies** in which a small elite directed the activities of people living in more than a single village. In Polynesian cosmology, as presented in origin myths and ritual, a Polynesian high chief symbolized the entire society before the gods. The chief was treated like a god, often called a god, and sometimes claimed to be a god. In a real sense the chief was the principal human agent in society (Sahlins 1985a, 1985b). This was reflected in a chief's use of the pronouns "I" and "my" to refer collectively to everyone on the island, and in the fact that Polynesian mythic histories invariably recounted the actions of chiefs and detailed their lengthy genealogies. As Sahlins expressed it, "The king encompasses the people in his own person, as projection of his own being" (Sahlins 1985b: 214–215). This would be unimaginable in the tribal world and literally made the well-being of one person and one family line more important than the well-being of everyone else.

As chiefdoms, many Polynesian societies were organized into segmentary, or "conical" descent groups based on an ideology of a patrilineal descent system resembling Nuer segmentary lineages, but centered on the chief. Like the Nuer system, the segments, or branches of Polynesian conical descent groups were associated with territorial units, but unlike Nuer tribal segments, in Polynesia the segments were ranked and under the control of a titled leader, who directed production and collected tribute for higher authorities. The striking difference in Polynesia was that everyone and every line of descent was ranked by social status relative to everyone else by their genealogical distance from the founding chiefly ancestor. The underlying principle was a belief in the "inherent superiority of a line of descent" (Goldman 1970:xvi). The top chief was the senior member of the senior descent line.

Typically there were five ranks in the Polynesian social hierarchy, from bottom to top as follows: (1) the household, (2) local kin group under a senior head, (3) subdistrict under a lesser chief, (4) district under a paramount chief, and (5) an islandwide high chief (Figures 6.B, 6.9). A few Polynesian societies such as Hawaii and Tonga were exceptionally large, multi-island polities, representing a sixth level of social complexity. They were small kingdoms ruled by especially powerful chiefs who could be called kings. All social levels were connected into a single command structure that was effectively headed by one person's imperium. In comparison, a tribal society had only a very weak authority structure at the local kin group level.

The Polynesian ranking system was based on the hierarchy between ancestor and descendent, and on **primogeniture**, order of birth within a family, with firstborn ranking highest. This was reflected symbolically in the familiar logical equation: father : son :: older brother : younger brother :: chief : commoner (Kirch 1984:34).

Chiefs used this ranking to encompass the entire society. At the bottom, men imagined every household to be a miniature chiefdom, as described by Sahlins:

> Like the great chief in his domain, the father is in his own house a sacred figure, a man of superior *mana,* his possessions, even his food, guarded by tabus against defilement by lesser familial kinsmen. Polynesians know innately how to honor the chief, for chieftainship begins at home: the chief's due is no more than elaborate filial respect. (Sahlins 1968:64)

This was an exaggerated "filial respect," and scale effects enormously magnified its human outcome when chiefs managed to project it to the entire society.

Anthropologists often describe "chief" as an **ascribed status** in contrast with "bigman" in a tribal society, which is said to be an **achieved status** (Sahlins 1963). This suggests that tribal bigmen were self-made leaders, who constantly had to reward their supporters to verify their position, whereas Polynesian chiefs simply received their titles and *mana* (power) at birth. In reality, there was considerable ambiguity in how Polynesian chiefs acquired their "inherited" titles and demonstrated their *mana.* Furthermore, chiefs who misused their authority, or who proved too weak, could be deposed by rivals. Thus, in Polynesian practice the distinction between achieved and ascribed status was often blurred. Ideally, the key to success for both bigmen and chiefs was their ability to organize lavish feasts, give gifts to influential supporters, and provide other chiefs with services such as defense. Chiefs operated on a much grander scale than tribal bigmen.

Chiefdoms are a systems of **social status,** a scale of human worth, that gives advantages to a few households. Irving Goldman defined a status system as:

> the principles that define worth and more specifically honor, that establish the scales of personal and group value, that relate position or role to privileges and obligations, that allocate respect, and that codify respect behavior. (1970:7)

In this definition, status is equated with honor. Status systems are found in all societies; but,

---

circumscription Carneiro's explanation for the development of political centralization—that villagers may be forced to surrender their autonomy if they are unable to move away from authorities because of geographic barriers or neighboring societies.

aristocracy A political system in which a small, privileged elite rule. This is a rule by the "best."

primogeniture Preferential treatment to a couple's firstborn offspring or oldest surviving child; may be a basis for establishing social rank.

ascribed status The social status that one is born into; includes sex, birth order, lineage, clan affiliation, and connection with elite ancestors.

achieved status Social position based on a person's demonstrated personal abilities apart from social status ascribed at birth.

social status A position that an individual occupies within a social system; defined by age, sex, kinship relationships, or other cultural criteria and involving specific behavioral expectations.

where age, sex, and personal characteristics are the only status criteria, as in most tribal societies, relative equality and balance are likely to prevail.

Chiefs portray themselves in a benevolent public role as the generous feast givers. Anthropologists call this "**redistribution.**" However, this was not the same as an Asháninka big man throwing a beer party, because chiefs grew more powerful by converting freely given offerings into forced tribute and diverting public goods to private benefit. Furthermore, commoners did not need chiefs to redistribute resources to them, because subdistrict territorial divisions radiated out from the center of the island like the slices of a pie, crisscrossing all ecozones, so that ideally each subdistrict could be self-sufficient. In larger scale societies commoners were excluded from feasts, whereas chiefs lived in ostentatious luxury (Kirch 2001). Chiefs regulated production and maintained the social hierarchy by controlling the ritual calender, thereby setting everyone's seasonal schedule for all major productive activities such as planting and fishing. Chiefs also used their power to make particular places tabu to prevent people from exploiting them. Such tabus often directly benefitted the chief rather than society as a whole. Commoners benefitted from the chief's military defense activities only because the aggressive wars that chiefs waged to expand chiefly imperia made life more dangerous for everyone. The only clear way the entire society benefitted from chiefs was when they distributed food from their storehouses in the event of natural disasters. In the event of crisis such redistribution may have been crucial for group survival, but village level food storage was a reasonable alternative.

Rivalry between older brother and younger brother was an inherent feature of Polynesian ranking systems based on primogeniture, and it was common for younger brothers to usurp the position of their superior. The complexity of the ranking system, and the degree of inequality was related to the scale, or total population of society. Pukapuka, the smallest Polynesian island with only 500 people, was the same scale as an Australian tribe and showed only ceremonial distinctions between chief and commoner. However, as societies grew larger, chiefs were able to compel commoners to contribute to chiefly feasts and construction projects. In Hawaii, with the population conservatively estimated at 300,000 people, there were enough chiefs for them to form an in-marrying group that claimed control over all the land and titles. This made the chiefly elite a distinct ruling class, distinguished from the commoners by degree of social power.

Although these societies were often called "patrilineal," Polynesians could claim descent from an ancestor through both male and female links, and they are therefore sometimes called ambilateral (Latin *ambo,* "both"). Because it was so important for Polynesians to establish a connection with high-ranking ancestors, it is reasonable to describe their social system as ascent-based rather than descent-based. As Sahlins describes it, "Hawaiians . . . do not trace descent so much as *ascent,* selectively choosing their way upward, by a path that notably includes female ancestors, to a connection with some ancient ruling line" (Sahlins 1985a:20). In addition to its utility in establishing rank, an ambilateral, ascent-based system is especially useful in island societies where access to land is crucial, because a person could claim land from both his mother's and his father's descent groups.

The extent to which chiefs could elaborate and concentrate their personal command over primary producers differed from island to island with the scale of society and differences in the cultural organization of power (Goldman 1970). The most powerful chiefs on larger islands emerged from intense struggles with competitors. The victors in these status rivalries organized and directed the construction of increasingly elaborate stone temples, house platforms, and fortifications. With larger scale populations, chiefs were able to stratify society into distinct **social classes** of nobles and commoners. **Social stratification** is based on differential access to natural resources and cultural capital. Such developments are conspicuously absent in the tribal world and are the foundations from which, under the right historical circumstances and environmental conditions, aggrandizing individuals were able to create ever larger personal imperia. There were probably only a few places in the world where chiefdoms were originally formed independently and then spread as organized societies into other regions. In only six places were chiefdoms then transformed into states and empires (see Figure 1.8). When militant chiefdoms invaded neighboring tribes, tribals sometimes felt compelled to organize their own chiefdoms in self-defense, causing chiefdoms to spread far beyond the few areas where aspiring elites managed to construct them independently.

The following ethnographic case studies will examine Tikopia to represent simple chiefdom and Hawaii as an example of a complex chiefdom that was transformed into a small kingdom early in the nineteenth century.

Tikopia: A Traditional Small Polynesian Chiefdom

Tikopia is 3 square miles (4.6 km²) of land, a miniature high island dominated by the jagged rim of an extinct volcano surrounding a crater lake. It is occupied by one of the best-described traditional Polynesian cultures, thanks to the detailed monographs published by Raymond Firth (1957, 1967, 1975). Tikopia is a Polynesian outlier situated well inside Melanesia, some 1200 miles (2000 km) west of Samoa and Tonga in western Polynesia. In 1928, Tikopia was inhabited by 1200 "healthy and vigorous natives," and Firth considered them "almost untouched by the outside world" although European explorers had landed on the island in 1798.

Archaeological research revealed 3000 years of continuous occupation of Tikopia, presumably initiated by Austronesian-speaking peoples carrying Lapita-like pottery (Kirch and Yen 1982). In their excavations, Kirch and Yen recovered 35,000 bones representing 85 different types of animals, 2204 pounds of shells, and thousands of artifacts. The record was complete enough to provide a reasonably clear picture of the human impact on Tikopia's ecosystem. The first settlers

found a pristine environment teeming with wildlife. The island was covered with rain forest, and the crater lake was then a saltwater bay or lagoon. During the early centuries of settlement, the wild protein resources were decimated. Harvests of fish, shellfish, and sea turtles rapidly declined in volume and diversity and increasingly were augmented by domestic pigs and chickens. At least one wild bird, the megapod, a chicken-like scrub fowl, was locally exterminated, whereas, according to local tradition, sea turtles apparently were protected by *tapu*.

Continuous slash-and-burn cultivation gradually led to severe deforestation that had the effect of enlarging the land base by some 40 percent at the expense of the reef zone, through infilling by eroded materials from the volcanic slopes. This greatly extended the gardening areas on the west end of the island but also cut off the lagoon, turning it into a lake, thus further reducing marine resources. Over the centuries, the inhabitants gradually abandoned shifting cultivation in favor of a system of permanent gardens and selectively planted domesticated forests. Tikopian arboriculture created a multistoried, multispecies forest orchard of useful trees and shrubs that replaced virtually all of the natural forest on the island. It also stabilized the slopes and dunes and helped buffer the damaging effects of typhoons. At the same time, according to their own accounts, the Tikopians decided to eliminate pigs, thereby reducing demands on their gardens because pigs, although they contributed protein, competed directly for garden produce.

As severely restricted environments, small islands such as Tikopia should be excellent testing

redistribution A form of exchange in which goods, such as foodstuffs, are concentrated and then distributed under the control of a central political authority.

social class A group of people in a stratified society, such as elites and commoners, who each share a similar level of access to resources, power, and privilege.

social stratification A ranking of social statuses such that the individuals of a society belong to different groups having differential access to resources, power, and privileges.

FIGURE 6.10 Map of Tikopia districts, villages, and temples.
(SOURCES: Based on Firth [1936] 1957 and Kirch and Yen 1982.)

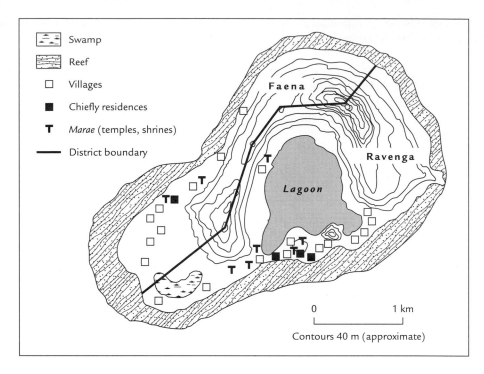

grounds for cultural ecological theory. However, it is difficult to discuss carrying capacity and balance with resources on Tikopia because the relationship between people and resources is not simple. Since 1929, the resident population has fluctuated between about 1000 and 1700. Population growth historically was regulated by numerous cultural means, including ritual sanctions, abortion, and infanticide, and by emigration. Firth reported that celibacy was required of younger brothers. Traditional history, verified by archaeology, records that bloody intergroup conflicts, exterminations, and expulsions of whole groups occurred a few centuries ago and were attributed to land conflicts. However, this cultural interpretation may have been a rationalization for what was actually a rivalry between competing chiefs. Furthermore, serious food shortages occurred after hurricanes hit the island in the 1950s. Direct and indirect human action has improved the island's agricultural potential, but there has been no effort to intensify agricultural

production through terracing or irrigation. The island continued to be virtually self-sufficient as recently as the mid-1970s.

The 1200 people living on Tikopia in 1928 were organized into two districts, or "sides," divided by the crater rim. Faena was on the (sheltered) lee side and Ravenga on the windward (Figure 6.10). There were some twenty-five named villages concentrated in the lowlands near the western and southern shores. Districts and villages acted as individual units in ritual and economic activities, although they were crosscut by descent-based groups that formed the status hierarchy and organized land tenure.

Each village consisted of a row of named hereditary house sites with attached orchards or garden sites. Houses were accompanied by canoe sheds and ovens. The houses themselves contained the graves of their former owners aligned along the "sacred" inside half of the house, facing the beach. This made each house, in effect, a temple, and long abandoned houses of important

KEY:

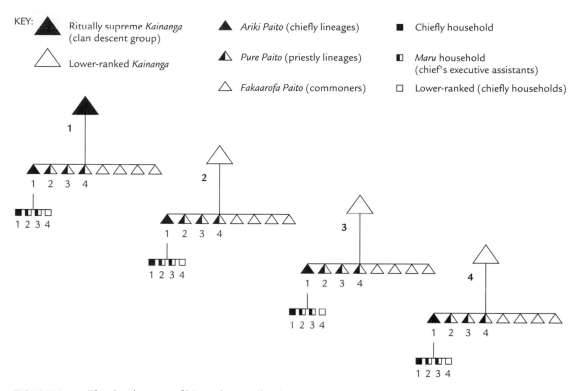

FIGURE 6.11 The ritual status of hierarchy on Tikopia. (SOURCE: Based on Firth 1936.)

chiefs were marked by upright slabs of stone and were recognized *Marae*. They served as important temples and sites for major rituals. Land was so important that virtually every part of the island was under some form of ownership, which was inherited patrilineally. Boundaries between gardens were carefully demarcated, and every feature of the island was named. Even the lake and reef zones were under chiefly jurisdiction.

The status system, as described by Firth, was the key to understanding most claims of ownership and explained most personal interaction. Every person was assigned a position in the status hierarchy, which was organized into units at four distinct levels: household; *Paito,* or lineage; *Kainanga,* or clan; and the entire island community (Figure 6.11).

At the highest level, the islandwide ritual community was presided over by a single chief, or

Ariki, who controlled an elaborate series of rituals founded by the ancestral deity of the chief's descent group. These rituals, known as "the work of the gods," promoted the welfare of the entire island, ensuring productive gardening and fishing.

At the second level were four named descent groups, or *Kainanga,* which were ranked by order of ritual precedence and ranged in size from 89 to 443 people (Figure 6.11). Firth called these groups clans, and they claimed patrilineal descent from founding tutelary deities (supernatural entities guarding specific descent groups) enshrined at specific clan "temple" sites. However, the clans were neither localized nor exogamous and only indirectly owned land of their constituent lineages and households. Membership recruitment was usually by patrifiliation, but it was also possible to marry in, as when a stranger would be adopted after marrying the chief's daughter. Each *Kainanga* had its own chief, named for his *Kainanga,* and participated as a unit in the island-wide "work of the gods." The *Kainanga* were linked in pairs for ritual food exchanges, and the chief of each *Kainanga* also had ritual responsibility for the fertility of one of four major food plants: taro, coconut, breadfruit, and yams.

At the third level, the *Kainanga* segmented into individual, named patrilineages called *Paito,* or houses. The primary property-holding unit, these groups averaged about forty persons each. There is no question about the cultural reality of these clan and lineage groups. Regardless of how the rules of rank or recruitment worked, Tikopian culture had names for these groups, and they had clearly defined functions. The highest ranked *Paito* (lineage) in a *Kainanga* (clan) supplied the *Ariki* (chief) for that *Kainanga.* Below the *Ariki Paito,* chiefly lineage, were high-ranking lineages, *Pure Paito,* that supplied ritual specialists, or priests, known as *Pure.* Lower-ranked *Paito* were *Fakaarofa Paito,* commoner lineages, whose relative order was irrelevant.

The lowest-level unit was the individual nuclear family household, although polygyny, especially among higher-ranked people, might extend the size of this unit. The husband was the ritual head of the family. The rank of the household was determined by his seniority within the lineage, the seniority of its lineage within the clan, and the ritual precedence of the clan. Relative rank within the *Ariki Paito,* chiefly lineages, was most critical. The households most closely related to the chief supplied the assistants, or *Maru,* who helped carry out his directives.

The authority of the chiefs was derived from their religious position as hereditary representatives of important ancestral deities who were responsible for the welfare of the land. Clan chiefs held titular control over all the lands owned by the members of their clan. Chiefs were sometimes called upon to settle territorial disputes and could impose *tabus* to restrict use of local resources under certain conditions. It was as-

sumed that they worked for the community's benefit, and they seem to have been genuinely respected. They often owned more land than other individuals, but this only helped them fulfill their ritual responsibilities. Chiefs might claim ritual ownership of the freshwater springs near their villages, but they did not deny community access. Wealth in land was generally independent of rank, and even commoners could be richer than chiefs. Land ownership did not mean exclusive use; upon request, individuals were often allowed to plant or harvest resources from land they did not own in return for a token gift of food. There were no landless classes.

A visiting Australian aborigine would have been overwhelmed by the density and permanence of the population on Tikopia and by the degree to which people manipulated the environment for productive purposes. But the aborigine also would have understood many features of Tikopian culture. As in any tribal society, kinship was certainly the most important organizing principle of domestic life on Tikopia, and households were largely self-provisioning units that worked cooperatively with kin-related households in the local settlement. Tikopian villages were similar in size to aboriginal bands, but the villages were circumscribed by their neighbors and were much less independent than the mobile bands. The belief that mythical ancestral beings continued to influence human affairs would have been familiar to the aborigine, but the sanctity of specific descent lines linked to the gods and the pervasive ranking of social units would have seemed strange. Even stranger to the aborigine would have been the islandwide authority carried by the Tikopian hereditary title *Ariki* and the extreme deferential behavior accorded the person of *Ariki* status. This calls to mind Firth's summary of the chief's politicized role on Tikopia, which has no parallel in tribal societies:

> the chief has been shown to be the most important single human factor in the economic life of the Tikopia. Not only does he play a part as a producer within his immediate household, but by initiative

and example he gives direction to the productive work of the community; he is titular owner of the most valuable property of the members of his clan; he imposes far-reaching restrictions on production and consumption and in many important activities he acts as a focal point in the processes of exchange and distribution. ([1965:231] 1975)

Hawaii: From Kinship to Kingship

The Hawaiian Archipelago is extremely isolated from the rest of Polynesia, and indeed from everywhere else. The major inhabited Hawaiian islands are high, volcanic islands and very large for Polynesia. Hawaii, the largest, contains 6500 square miles (10,458 km^2) of land, more than all the rest of Micronesia and Polynesia combined, with the exception of New Zealand. Such large, high islands trap considerable rainfall on their windward sides, which are often sharply eroded into steep, narrow valleys, and they support a wide variety of plant communities, from deserts to wet mountain forests with many endemic species.

The reef zones are smaller than might be expected because of the relative youth of the larger islands; furthermore, much of the shoreline is inaccessible because of the steep cliffs. Rainfall and soil are critical variables for crops, yet they are very unevenly distributed. Only restricted windward valleys offer the alluvial soils, abundant rainfall, and flowing streams most favorable for the cultivation of Polynesian crops (Kirch 1985).

In comparison with Tikopia, the most obvious difference in Hawaiian subsistence patterns is in the elaborate complexes of ditches and terraced and irrigated pond fields for taro cultivation, as well as the extensive area devoted to permanent dry-field cultivation. Kirch (1985) also emphasizes that the Hawaiians developed true aquaculture, in which fish were raised on a large scale in special fish ponds constructed on reef flats.

The irrigation systems have the most interesting theoretical implications because many theorists have speculated that control of irrigation systems was the primary route to state formation

for all the world's great civilizations. Hawaiian irrigation systems were well developed by Polynesian standards. As a significant form of agricultural intensification, they helped produce the surplus that supported the elites, but the construction of these systems seems not to have required either technical specialists or large labor forces (Earle 1978).

Hawaiian oral and documentary history, and archaeology show that over some 250 years, from approximately AD 1550 to AD 1792, a succession of 25 high chiefs, primarily members of a single dynasty, gradually gained political control over the six major districts of the island of Hawaii (Kirch 1984:253–255). This ruling elite steadily expanded the administrative structure, elaborated the religious system, and constructed an intensive production system of fish ponds, terraced garden fields, irrigation systems, stone walls, ditches, trails, and demarcated land parcels. They financed these developments by monopolizing the production of food staples, and wealth objects (Earle 2001). This was an intentional project of imperial expansion and infrastructure development that facilitated growth that quadrupled the population and quickly transformed the nature of Hawaiian society. Such growth made it possible for a handful of elites and their families to live luxurious super-successful lifestyles, while the majority lost control over the conditions of their daily life, were subjected to demeaning restrictions, and were compelled to work harder than ever before. Previously, Hawaiians had lived for more than a thousand years with relatively low intensity subsistence in relatively small chiefdoms that minimized the human effects of rank and status differences.

In comparison with the small number of people that anyone could command in the tribal world, the scale of Hawaiian chiefly power is astounding. Kamehameha I (1758–1819) (Figure 6.12), twenty-fifth in the dynasty, commanded a personal imperium of 7000 to 15,000 warriors for his interisland conquests. By 1792, he successfully took full control of Hawaii and the

FIGURE 6.12 Statue of Hawaiian chief Kamehameha, who united rival chiefdoms.

neighboring island of Maui. Then, in 1795 he conquered Lanai, Molokai, and O'ahu. In 1809 he negotiated the takeover of Kaua'i, and was thus able to rule all of the Hawaiian islands, with a total population of some 300,000 people. This became the largest politically centralized society in the Pacific world, and roughly equivalent in scale to the entire population of aboriginal Australia.

Hawaii's rulers organized the islands in typical Polynesian structure, but by the time Kamehameha's imperium encompassed all of the islands, he had effectively created a small kingdom, which was an order of magnitude larger than an island-wide chiefdom. Kamehameha was a king. The chiefly rulers divided each island *(moku)* into districts (also *moku*), and subdistricts *(ahupua'a)*

commanded by their respective chiefs *(ali'i)*. Each subdistrict chief used land managers *(konohiki)* to allocate land parcels to the commoners and to collect tribute in labor and goods. The largest islands such as Hawaii, Maui, O'ahu, and Kaua'i were subdivided into five to six districts each, and each district was subdivided into an average of thirty subdistricts (Hommon 1986). This administrative bureaucracy may have supported a total of some 100 high chiefs and priests, 900 subdistrict chiefs, and 1800 land managers, as well as 32,500 retainers and dependents (Table 6.3).

Chiefs tried to enlarge their personal domestic establishments, or extended households, as much as possible. Hawaiians called this group *ma*, "the people of, or associates of someone," and it was the core of a personal imperium. It included family members *('ohana)*, and retainers *(ōhua)*, as well as dependent specialists. Chiefs expanded their power network through marriage alliances and gifts to other chiefs. Commoners, *(maka'ainana)*, "the people of the land," correctly considered the chiefs to be outsiders who "eat the land." This was clearly the case because the paramount chief claimed ownership over all the land, and allocated it through the administrative structure to lower level chiefs and landlords who allocated parcels to commoners to cultivate as tenants.

In viewing growth in the scale of Hawaiian society as an elite-directed process, it is important to consider how social power was distributed. A careful reconstruction of Hawaiian society suggests that there were about 3000 elite households, about 5 percent of all households. Because the elite had larger families and were closely intermarried, the elite and their close kin may have constituted a subset of some 23,000 people, or just under 8 percent of the total population of 300,000 in AD 1778. Elite households probably included another 32,000 people as retainers. Furthermore, the elite lived lavishly, were feasting constantly, and the highest chiefs were distinguished by their corpulence. In one phase of a temple ritual 1440 pigs were consumed (Kirch 2001:177). In contrast to the custom on Tikopia,

TABLE 6.3   THE SOCIAL STRUCTURE OF THE HAWAIIAN KINGDOM, ESTIMATES FOR 1809

	Households	Family	Retainers	Average	Persons
King	1	50	950	1,000	1,000
Paramounts	4	25	75	100	400
District Chiefs	30	15	50	65	1,950
High Priests	70	15	50	65	4,550
Ahupua'a Chiefs	900	10	25	35	31,500
Konohikis	1,800	7	2	9	16,200
Commoners	48,880	5	—	5	244,400
	51,685				300,000

the Hawaiian elite excluded commoners from their feasts. Elite households with their retainers may have consumed about one-fourth of total production.

Kamehameha's reward for imperial conquest was that he enlarged his domestic establishment to an order of magnitude greater than those of other chiefs. He supported a court of perhaps a thousand people (Linnekin 1990:100). There were more than a dozen categories of **specialists** who were directly attached to the chief's personal household, including political advisors, military experts, architects, astrologers, food handlers, robe masters, priests, masseurs, keepers of his images and paraphernalia, and servants to whisk away flies and stand over him as he slept, in addition to miscellaneous "hangers-on." As symbolic fertilizing father of the entire society, Kamehameha had sexual access to all commoner women, although he had only 8 wives (Valeri 1985:150). His primary residence at Kamakahonu on the island of Hawaii was a walled compound of 27,000 square meters containing his sleeping and cooking houses, houses for his wives, storehouses, and his temple, the *Ahuena heiau*, which has been preserved and restored. Chiefly households supported from 30 to 100 people in their imperia including retainers, servants, wives, and family. Polygyny was typically only a prerogative of the nobility, because commoners did not have access to enough land to support a large family. A chief's residential com-

plex of stone platforms covered approximately 1000 square meters (Kirch 1985:160). In comparison, an Asháninka house was only 50 square meters. Hawaiian houses and temples were simple wooden structures on stone platforms. The largest construction was a 300-meter defensive stone wall, which was nearly 4 meters tall with a volume of 5864 cubic meters (Kirch 1985:164). It might have weighed 15 million kilograms. Building it would have required an enormous human effort. Associated with this site was a temple that housed the remains of paramount chiefs, but there were no monumental royal tombs.

The Hawaiian elite were able to support their inflated domestic establishments because they effectively controlled all the natural resources as well as the built infrastructure on the islands. Kamehameha held for his personal use approximately a million acres, a quarter of the land area of all the Hawaiian islands (Linnekin 1990:8). High chiefs held 10,000 acres, other chiefs 1500 acres, administrators 75 acres, whereas commoner households were allocated an average of three acres (Linnekin 1990:204–205). The elite may have retained nearly 90 percent of the developed land for their own use. The elite drew

---

specialist An individual who provides goods and services to elites in hierarchically organized societies. Such a specialist does not produce his or her own food but is supported from the surplus that is politically extracted by central authorities.

their daily subsistence from extensive and highly productive irrigated taro pondfields, and dryland gardens that they controlled directly. They also consumed food sacrifices offered at temples, as well as tribute collected from the commoners. The chiefs controlled the 449 artificially constructed fish ponds that were capable of producing more than a thousand tons of fish annually (Kirch 1984:180–181, 1985:211–214). This would have supplied more than 5,000 people with half a kilogram of fish per person, per day, annually.

High Chiefs, Gods, and Sacrifice

The Hawaiian elite created an exclusive religious system that served their interests well. It kept food and goods flowing to them, and kept the commoners subservient. For the elite, the most important features of Hawaiian cosmology were the Kumulipo creation myth and the annual ritual drama of the Makahiki in which the divine king *(ali'i akua)* appropriates the gifts of the fertility god Lono and assumes the qualities of the war god Kū. These interconnected cultural elements were the ideological centerpieces of a centrally directed religion based on gods, divine kings, sacrifice, and military conquest. The Kumulipo was a composite of sixteen genealogical chants in 2,102 lines that was recited by a genealogical specialist attached to the royal household. Chanting the Kumulipo affirmed the noble lineage of a new paramount chief and connected him, as a divine king, with the gods at the center of the entire cosmos (Beckwith 1951). Kingship incorporated everything—up and down, land and sea, and everyone in the kingdom.

Like spirit beings in the tribal world, Hawaiian deities *(akua)* were mental constructs given multiple forms. People materialized them as anthropomorphic images, as humans, plants and animals, and as natural phenomena (Valeri 1985). As in tribal cosmologies, the principle beings were symbolically coded by color, cardinal directions, plants, animals, seasons, and function. For example, the war god Kū was red, up,

east, right, mountains, and war. The fertility god Lono was black, leeward, clouds, rainy season, gourds, pigs, dry land farming, and fertility. The deities modeled idealized human types, and they were reproduced in people's minds by the act of ritual sacrifice. Because deities were hierarchically ranked and were identified with particular ranks and individuals, their respective rituals affirmed the structure of society with privileged chiefs at the top and defined proper behavior. These religious beliefs mystified in that they obscured the daily reality of human exploitation, and they legitimized chiefs as naturally superior human beings. The cosmology made extreme social inequality seem perfectly natural, inevitable, and irresistible. The relative ease with which people abandoned the entire system makes it clear that their religion was an elite construction, designed by and for the elite. When circumstances changed, the king abruptly abolished the practice of sacrifice and *tabu* in 1819, shortly after the arrival of Europeans. This was soon followed by the adoption of Christianity, especially by elite women, who thereby increased their social power relative to the chiefs.

The king had virtually all the attributes of divinity. He was a perfect, exemplary human, closest to the gods, and was the only one who, with his high priests, could mediate between society as a whole and the most powerful gods. Kings were descended from the gods, and were formally turned into gods by their own funeral rituals. Kings shared with gods the attribute of encompassing the cosmos, and like gods they were defined by incestuous marriage with a full or classificatory sister. Succession was invariably fratricidal and incestuous, with one brother killing the other, sacrificing him to the gods, and marrying his sister (Valeri 1985). The king kills his rival brother and loves his sister, thereby demonstrated his divinity and producing a divine heir. Only the king could consecrate a human sacrifice, which was another extreme expression of his divine power. Like gods, kings were also represented by transcendent symbols, like rainbows, stars, and the sky. They could be addressed as *kalani* ("heaven") or *kalaninui* ("great heaven"). Kings were assumed to be free of desire, because they had everything, and they could not show emotion. Thus they remained immobile and were carried on a litter. Kings also demonstrated their divine powers by remaining out of sight, invisible to commoners, and by their possession of the *kapu moe,* the prostration *tabu.* This *tabu* forced everyone to lie flat on the ground in their presence. Lower ranked chiefs had the *kapu noho,* which required inferiors to sit in their presence. The highest chiefs were so *tabu* that people had to prostrate themselves on the ground even if only his personal possessions were carried by. Special retainers ran ahead carrying a special staff signaling the *tabu,* and they shouted a warning to people to prostrate themselves. Chiefs sometimes traveled at night to minimize the inconvenience that the *tabus* created. No one could allow his or her shadow to fall across to chief or any of his personal possessions, including his house. No one, other than his immediate retainers, was allowed to approach closer than 12 feet (4 m) to the chief's back. When the chief ate, everyone in his presence had to remain on their knees.

The paramount chiefs had life-and-death powers over their subjects, including lower-level chiefs. They could kill them or expel them from their land at will. They apparently sometimes did so, although not all chiefs were considered to be abusive and oppressive. Infractions of *tabus* were strictly enforced by burning, strangulation, or stoning. Sometimes, people who violated seemingly minor *tabus* were put to death. John Papa Ii (1983), who became a personal attendant to high chief Liholiho, described a case in which three men were caught eating coconuts with women while a major ritual for the general welfare was being performed at the paramount chief's temple, or *luakini heiau* (Figure 6.13). Because there was a general *tabu* against men and women eating together and against women eating coconuts, the three men were seized and sacrificed along with pigs on the altar before a row

of images of the deities (Ii 1983). Human sacrifices of this sort apparently only took place at the temples of paramount chiefs and on special ritual occasions.

On Tikopia, it was understood that the deities might be angered if rituals were neglected or improperly performed and might even take a human life as a sacrifice (Firth [1940] 1967). But it would have been unthinkable for a chief or any of his priests to carry out such an act themselves. Clearly, the high chiefs of Hawaii enlarged upon an underlying Polynesian belief that chiefs were descended from the gods, and they assumed the role of gods themselves.

The Kumulipo creation myth recognized an explicit interdependence between man and gods. The gods make people, and people make the gods as divine images and in ritual. The Hawaiian gods, like Dreamtime beings, and Amazon spirits, were transcendent, nonempirical concepts. They existed in people's minds and in the material objects that embodied them, and they worked because their existence reinforced proper action. Hawaiian cosmology was more highly structured and formalized than tribal cosmologies because Hawaiians had a professional priesthood. Their cosmology assumed that ultimately everyone's well-being was determined by rituals performed by higher ranking individuals. This supernatural mediation superficially resembled the role of shamans in tribal society, but it was hierarchical and exclusive, and the benefits flowed unequally.

The primary form of Hawaiian ritual was the sacrificial consecration of some offering to a deity. Priests *(kahuna)* performed the sacrifices, and guarded, fed, and cared for the gods, and maintained their temples. Priests were possessed by and effectively belonged to the gods to whom they were sacrificing. High priests who officiated in chiefly temples were themselves chiefs and received land rights in return for their temple services. Sacrifices were accompanied by prayers detailing the intent of the ritual. The god ate the essence, and those attending the ritual ate the remainder. Sacrifice reproduced the social hierarchy because

FIGURE 6.13 The Hawaiian *luakini heiau,* or paramount chief's temple, where human sacrifices were performed.

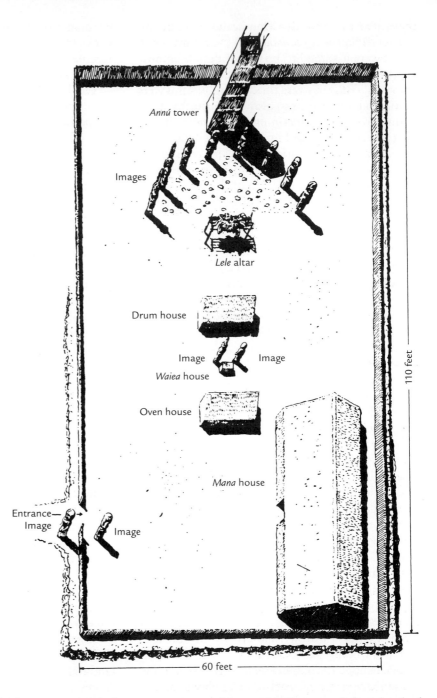

one only sacrificed to the gods that corresponded to one's own social position.

The Makahiki Ceremony was a complex ritual cycle that annually renewed both kingship and natural fertility. It involved the king and his entourage making a circuit around the island of Hawaii, collecting tribute, living off the land, and conducting a series of feasts, ritual license, and mock combats. It lasted for months and was coordinated to end with the winter solstice and the end of the rainy season, marking the beginning of the growing season, and the return of the Pleiades, and the sun. Thus the king was implicitly associated with the sun and fertility. In the final Makahiki rituals, the fertility god Lono is killed in the form of a human sacrifice at the king's personal temple *(luakini heiau)*. The king then appropriates the earth's fertility for human benefit, and reinstalls himself as the representative of the war god Kū.

Hawaiian Daily Life: Commoner Men and Women

Commoners *(maka'ainana),* who constituted 92 percent of Hawaiian society, were objectively disempowered by their limited access to productive land, and by their exclusion from the religious and genealogical sources of status. Land was a portion of divine nature, and the higher one was situated in the land ownership chain, the closer to divinity. Inferior social status made it difficult for most people to make a living. Women were further disadvantaged by their symbolic inferiority. The elite monopoly and extravagance made land a scarce resource. Commoners, who actually worked the land, were at the bottom of a chain of land holders that ran all the way to the king, who held all the land as his divine prerogative. Commoners were marginalized as tenants who cared for land belonging to the chiefs. Use rights had to be legitimized by a gift of the first fruits to the landowner chief. Land rights were held for life, could not be further subdivided, and were normally transmitted to the senior son, or more likely to a senior grandchild. Only couples holding use rights were able to establish households, produce children, and maintain long-term marriages. If juniors were unable to implement claims to land elsewhere, they attached themselves as dependents *(kanaka)* to a chief and/or remained unmarried. Fortunately, Hawaiian society allowed a remarkable degree of sexual freedom, and young and landless commoners readily engaged in informal relationships (Linnekin 1990).

Below the commoners were the *kauwa* (sometimes called slaves), a despised category of hered-itary outcasts. There were also special terms for vagrants, beggars, and the landless. In comparison, Tikopian commoners did not form a powerless class; Tikopia had no outcasts, beggars, or landless, and Tikopian chiefs remained relatively inconspicuous and unassuming.

The differences in wealth and power between the Hawaiian elites and the commoners were so extreme that it is appropriate to call them social classes. The most conspicuous class markers were the lavish and magnificent feathered short capes, long cloaks, leis, helmets, and whale-tooth necklaces, which only the elite could wear (Figure 6.14).Chiefs were accompanied by bearers of 20-foot (6-m) poles topped with brilliantly feathered banners as insignias of rank (Feher 1969). Because as many as 10,000 birds might have been required to produce a single feathered cloak, it had major ostentatious value (Earle 1987).

The classic understanding of the relation between men and women in Polynesia was summarized in the structural formula [men : women :: sacred : profane :: pure : impure]. This resembled the negative symbolic position of women in Amazonian cosmology where women were associated with sickness and death. In Hawaii female symbolic spiritual inferiority was reflected in food taboos and female exclusion from temple sacrifice, but was contradicted by the ideology of bilateral descent, in which high rank was inherited through women (Linnekin 1990). The *kapu* system called for a rigid separation of men and women. They could not eat together according to the restrictions of *'ai kapu,* the eating tabu. Men did all the cooking, but there were separate earth ovens and separate eating houses for men and women. Women could not enter temples or the men's house. Women were not allowed to eat the most prized, highest status foods, including pork, coconut, and bananas, that were also prime articles of tribute to chiefs and sacrifice to gods.

Officially, violations of these taboos were punished by death, with offenders sacrificed to the gods, although such extreme penalties were more likely to be applied to commoner women. This gave men life or death power over women, but the highest-ranking chiefly women were apparently

FIGURE 6.14
Hawaiian feather work.

immune from punishment, and they could kill men for breaking *tabus*.

Gender relations in daily life were quite different from how they were symbolically conceptualized. Hawaiian women actively subverted the *tabu* system when they could, and clearly viewed it differently from the high-ranking men (Linnekin (1990:24). Significantly, the entire *kapu* system and the temple cults were overthrown in 1819 at the instigation of high-ranking chiefly women (Linnekin 1990:11). Even though women in general were symbolically *noa*, "*kapu* free, profane, or common," women chiefs held the highest *kapu* ranks, and profane women made the fine mats and tapa cloth that were used in the sacrificial rituals that high-ranking men needed to confirm their high status. This situation resembles the gender complementarity that was common in the tribal world, and suggests that it would be misleading to label the status of Hawaiian women simply as high or low in relation to men.

In Hawaii constructing a personal imperium depended on a person's ability to manipulate kinship networks, real or fictive, to elevate their social rank in an ideologically acceptable manner (Linnekin 1990). Anyone who could trace a genealogical connection to the king within at least ten generations was considered noble, but commoners were forbidden to track their genealogies beyond grandparents. However, in reality, parents could improve the genealogical rank of their children by hypergamy, marrying a higher-status person. Women actively sought high-ranking husbands for their daughters. Men also tried to marry higher-ranking women. Realistically, succession to high rank was always contentious because both men and women often had children by multiple partners. Furthermore, because filiation could be claimed bilaterally, through either male or female links, there were many opportunities for establishing noble links. As soon as a person's claim to high genealogical status was recognized by the king, it became real.

In such a competitive society, with power so highly concentrated, it is not surprising that commoners, men or women, did not always endorse the system. When chiefs extracted too much they risked creating open dissatisfaction, and greed and extravagance were often the official justification for a younger brother to usurp power.

Daily life at the village level was not differentiated by hereditary status rankings, and social relations were basically egalitarian (Linnekin 1985: 44). After the *kapu* system and temple cults were abolished in 1819, the core ideology that remained seemed characteristic of the equality of the tribal world. In the 1960s researchers found village Hawaiians more interested in nurturing human relationships than in accumulating material wealth. They measured success by the social relationships that people could construct and maintain, not by material wealth accumulated. People disapproved of public displays of economic success (Gallimore and Howard 1968:10).

Two-Headed Children and Hawaiian Kinship

Hawaiian family structure and the kinship terminology had unusual features that were directly related to the extreme concentration of social power in the noble class. Hawaiians practiced virtually all forms of marriage: **polygyny, sororal polygyny, polyandry, fraternal polyandry, levirate,** and **sororate,** and they moved in and out of marriage easily (Linnekin 1990:121–125). Commoners were not allowed to marry anyone called brother, sister, son, or daughter, but this was the preference among the nobility, because such close marriages preserved their high rank.

Hawaiian kinship terminology was a generational system in which everyone in ego's generation was called brother and sister, everyone in the parents' generation was mother and father, and so on (Figure 6.15). The terms *kaikua'ana* and *kaikaina* mean older and younger sibling of the same sex. This system, which was used by nobles and commoners, reflected the *punalua* co-spouse relationship, in which plural spouses, or spouses and spouses' lovers treated each other like siblings and their offspring like their own children. Two men married to one woman or a woman's husband and her lover would call themselves brothers. A child that had two fathers in a

punalua relationship was called *po'olua*, a "two-headed child" (Sahlins 1992:198). The advantage of this arrangement was that it made it easier to consolidate kin and reduce land fragmentation.

Regardless of the kin terms they used, Hawaiians distinguished "true" kin from classificatory kin. How the system worked in practice is illustrated by the following commentary from a Hawaiian in the 1960s:

> Kealoha is my brother's child. Of course my brother isn't really my brother as both he and I are hanai [adopted] children of my father. I guess my father isn't really my father, is he? I know who my real mother is but I don't like her and I never see her. My hanai brother is half Hawaiian and I am pure Hawaiian. We aren't really any blood relation I guess, but I always think of him as my brother and I always think of my father as my father. I think maybe Papa is my grandfather's brother . . . so I don't know what relationship Kealoha really is though I call her my child. (Howard 1968:92)

The reality that chiefs appropriated much of the land forced commoner families to limit their household reproduction to the minimum replacement level. Commoners exchanged children and land in order to piece together enough usable parcels of otherwise scattered productive land to reproduce the household. This process focused on grandparents *(kupuna)* who adopted their grandchildren, who were favored like chiefs, and inherited the ancestral estate. The grandparents were the ancestors, and the term *kupuna* also means ancestor. Their descendants who lived on the land were recognized as consanguines. The descendants of grandparents were considered

---

polygyny A form of marriage in which a man may have more than one wife.

sororal polygyny When a man marries two or more women who are sisters.

polyandry When a woman marries two or more men.

fraternal polyandry When a woman marries two or more men who are brothers.

levirate When a woman marries her deceased husband's brother.

sororate When a man marries his deceased wife's sister.

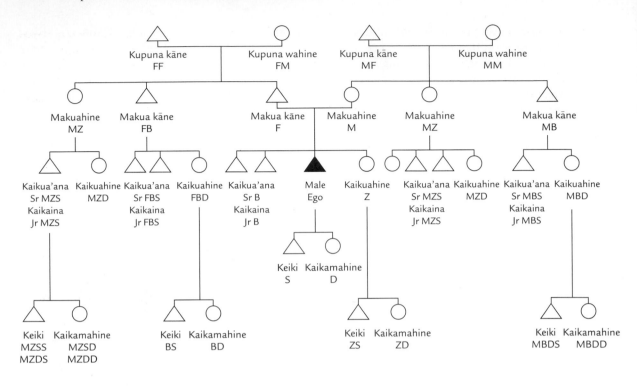

Note: Kāne = "male," Wahine = "female." Kaikua'ana = older same sex sibling; Kaikaina = younger, same sex sibling. Source: Linnekin 1985:91.

FIGURE 6.15   Hawaiian kinship terminology.

"true" kin. By adopting grandchildren as their own children, otherwise unrelated people were converted into consanguines, now related through shared grandchildren. This allowed people to hold together pieces of land that might otherwise be dispersed. Noninheriting youths who could not form households, enjoyed the "freedom of the dispossessed" by devoting themselves to pleasure-seeking (Sahlins 1992:202). Fertility-limiting practices such as abortion and infanticide were probably common among the landless population. This situation was not a result of "population pressure" on limited material resources. Land existed as a "natural" resource, but, because of the existing **political economy** it was simply not culturally available to everyone who needed it for household reproduction

(Sahlins 1992:200-201). The political economy controlled by the Hawaiian elite had effectively subordinated the **subsistence economy.**

SUMMARY

The Pacific islands presented formidable obstacles to successful human occupation because they were so widely scattered and were often very small and resource-poor. They were settled by skilled Austronesian-speaking farmers, sailors, and navigators who originated in Southeast Asia about 6000 years ago. The farthest reaches of Polynesia were settled during a period of approximately 1000 years ending by 800 A.D. with the settlement of New Zealand.

The societies of Polynesia and Micronesia represent a major contrast to the domestic-scale societies of Australia, Amazonia, and East Africa examined in earlier chapters. Pacific island societies were characterized by a great concern with rank, and they developed permanent political and economic structures above the level of local village communities. These island societies were chiefdoms that elevated certain high-ranking individuals to permanent leadership positions as chiefs. The example from the Polynesian island of Tikopia showed that chiefs in small chiefdoms coordinated ritual and economic activities between villages, but they had relatively little power and so there were no social classes. On larger islands, such as Hawaii, political struggles between chiefs led to the formation of powerful chiefdoms. These societies became divided by class into the elites, who extracted tribute from the commoners, who produced food and wealth objects. The highest-ranking chiefs claimed the supernatural power of deities and gained life-and-death control over lower-ranked people. Some of the Hawaiian chiefdoms were complex enough to be considered protostates, or small kingdoms.

The ethnographic evidence shows that the larger Polynesian societies were highly inequitable societies in which not everyone could enjoy the sociability, material prosperity, security, and participation in expressive culture that would be the essential elements of the universal "good life." In some cases it was difficult or even impossible for everyone to form successful households. Most people, especially women, were also restricted by various demeaning *tabus,* and their lives could literally be sacrificed by rulers. However, except for the landless, there is little indication that the majority suffered physical poverty. It is possible that most people accepted their inferior social status as natural and did not feel exploited, although in comparison with tribals, Polynesians clearly had much less control over the conditions of their daily life. For the majority, the human cost of supporting a tiny nobility was the increased workload of tribute payments, reduced access to the cultural sources of social power, reduced access to natural resources, and increased insecurity of tenure. It is possible to imagine island cultural systems that could have distributed social power more equitably and maximized human freedom.

STUDY QUESTIONS

1. Characterize and distinguish between each of the following cultural areas: Polynesia, Melanesia, and Micronesia.
2. Discuss the physical constraints limiting settlement on Pacific islands, characterizing the cultural response.
3. Discuss the role of status rivalry, irrigation, redistribution, environmental circumscription, and economic productivity in the development of Pacific island chiefdoms.
4. How have linguists reconstructed the history of Austronesian migrations by analyzing word lists?
5. What special navigation skills do Pacific Islanders use for long-distance voyaging? What problems are posed by the unusual design of outrigger canoes?
6. What are the most important island crops? What do they contribute to the diet and what makes them especially suited to the island environment? What is the division of subsistence labor? What special skills does fishing require?
7. How are Pacific chiefs different from Amazon headmen? What is the cultural basis of islander ranking systems?
8. How is Tikopian society organized? What is the role of the chief? How would an Australian aborigine view this society?
9. What is a political economy and how does it contrast with a subsistence economy?
10. How does the power of Hawaiian chiefs and the organization of Hawaiian society compare with

---

political economy A cultural pattern in which centralized political authority intervenes in the production and distribution of goods and services.

subsistence economy Production and distribution carried on at the local community level, primarily for local consumption.

the Tikopia? What environmental factors are related to these differences?

SUGGESTED READING

FIRTH, RAYMOND. [1936] 1957. *We the Tikopia: A Sociological Study of Kinship in Primitive Polynesia,* 2nd ed. New York: Barnes & Noble. The basic ethnographic description of Tikopia, with an emphasis on social organization.

FIRTH, RAYMOND. [1940] 1967. "The Work of the Gods." In *Tikopia,* 2nd ed. London: Athlone Press. Describes in detail the system of ritual feasting on Tikopia.

FIRTH, RAYMOND. [1965] 1975. *Primitive Polynesian Economy.* Reprint. New York: Norton. An analysis of the subsistence economy and distribution system on Tikopia.

KIRCH, PATRICK VINTON. 2000. *On the Road of the Winds: An Archaeological History of the Pacific Islands Before European Contact.* Berkeley: University of California Press. Excellent overview of the prehistory of the Pacific.

The Inca imperial resort of Machu Picchu

7 Ancient Empires in Two Worlds: Mesopotamia and the Andes

PRONUNCIATION GUIDE

Andean terms in this chapter are derived from Spanish and Quechua. Their most common pronunciation can be approximated by English speakers using the following orthography and sounds:

Key

a = a in father	ee = ee in beet
o = o in go	oo = oo in food
ay = ay in day	• – Syllable division
ai = i in ice	/ – Stress
e = e in bed	

aclla = [ak / la]
altiplano = [al • tee • pla / no]
ayllu = [ay / yoo]
ayni = [ai / nee]
camayo= [ca • mai / o]
ceque = [say / kay]
Chan Chan = [chan / chan]
Chimú = [chee • moo /]
Cuzco = [cooz / co]
huaca = [wa / ka]
llama = [ya / ma]
mita = [mee / ta]
orejones = [or • ay • ho / nays]
panaqa = [pa • na / ka]
puna = [poo / na]
Quechua = [kaych / wa]
quipu = [kee / poo]
Tawantinsuyu = [ta / wan • teen / soo • yoo]

Learning Objectives

After studying this chapter you should be able to do the following.

1. Compare the ancient Mesopotamian and Andean empires and Pacific island chiefdoms, highlighting the most important points of contrast related to scale of society.

2. Define the state and civilization in comparison with tribes and chiefdoms, and discuss the relationship between size of society, cultural complexity, and the distribution of social power.

3. Evaluate the theory that civilizations originated as an elite-directed process designed to concentrate social power, rather than as a natural, inevitable evolutionary process.

4. Use evidence from Mesopotamia and the Andes to assess the interconnections between technology, long-distance trade, population, environment, and human decision-making in the development of large-scale complex societies.

5. Describe and compare the four social ranks of Ur III and the Inca empire, referring to social function, the distribution of social power, and costs and benefits.

6. Describe and compare the religious system of Ur III and the Inca empire.

7. Evaluate the evidence for tyranny, oppression, and exploitation in Mesopotamian and Andean civilizations.

Although many Pacific island chiefdoms crossed the "great divide" from the social equality of domestic scale societies into rank- and class-based social systems, a major gulf separates these island cultures from the larger-scale states and empires to be considered in this chapter. The rulers of early states created monumental temples, pyramids, palaces, and cities that have been hailed as major achievements and attributes of civilization. However, these impressive constructions clearly depended on pervasive social inequality, and these states were characterized by an inherent instability not found in domestic scale cultures. The politicization process that rulers used to construct **city-states** and conquest empires represented a major departure from the domestic-scale cultural patterns that had sustained humanity for so long. The rise of centralized state political power is perhaps the greatest anthropological mystery of all. Although no explanation is completely satisfactory, it is clear that states were human constructions, designed by egocentric power seekers who were able to take advantage of unique circumstances that made it difficult for households and communities to escape the influence of elite power and circumstances that could support increases in cultural scale through intensified subsistence production.

The existence of civilizations, or societies with cities, governments, and elite-directed institutions and cultural patterns, is difficult to explain because civilizations make such costly demands on people and natural resources. Urban culture and the luxurious lifestyles of elite rulers in the imperial world placed unequal demands on the nonelite majority, and required vast and complex bureaucracies and armies as well as enormous expenditures of energy and materials. These developments separated ordinary people from direct control over the daily necessities of life. Because they were such large-scale systems, these urban civilizations also required complex institutional structures that tended naturally to concentrate social power in the hands of a wealthy aristocratic oligarchy, because the poor majority were either unable or unwilling to demand and implement democratic control and a more equitable distribution of costs and benefits. All of the civilizations examined in this chapter, and in Chapters 8 and 9, were despotic political systems that showed remarkable cultural parallels. This suggests that rulers were following similar human solutions to similar problems, but there is no reason to consider these parallel developments to have been the inevitable unfolding of any preordained evolutionary pattern.

The contrasts between tribal cultures and state civilizations are so extreme, and the comparative disadvantages of state civilizations for all but the elite minority are so obvious, that explaining how states originate and function as cultural systems continues to be a major theoretical challenge for anthropology. Understanding the full implications of urban civilization for the long-term future of humanity is also a critical issue. It is important to remember that urban civilization has existed for only 5000 years and could be considered a very shaky experiment when its short span and record of chronic collapse are compared with the 60,000-year record of tribal foraging cultures in Australia. In this chapter, we will review the issues surrounding urban civilization within the context of two major civilizations from different parts of the world: the Sumerians of Mesopotamia and the Inca of Peru.

ANCIENT CIVILIZATIONS AND THE TRIUMPH OF STATE POWER

Civilization is about social power. The cities, writings, monuments, and artwork that identify civilization give certain people massive and historically unprecedented power over others. The principal function of civilization is to organize overlapping social networks of ideological, political, economic, and military power in ways that differentially benefit privileged households (Mann 1986). Civilization gives some households institutionalized coercive power to permanently control property in ways that reduce the material opportunities of other households. This coercive use of social power would baffle tribal peoples because it overrides the humanization process that equally provided for everyone's material needs in tribal cultures. Simple chiefdoms, such as in Tikopia, introduced differential ranking between individuals, but rank was not used to deny anyone the right to satisfy material needs. Politicization was the cultural process that elites used to institutionalize social inequality in the state, but it is difficult to explain why people allowed this to happen. Civilization is unlikely to develop directly out of tribal cultures because tribal peoples self-consciously refused to grant anyone permanent, coercive social power over other households. Tribal war leaders and village heads are temporary and have no coercive authority; ideological power is open to everyone; and there are no cultural incentives for depriving anyone of life's necessities.

Tribal leaders were community servants who served at the will of the community and did not found dynasties. In the imperial world political elites managed to split society into a tiny elite managerial sector and a commoner working sector where the majority produced the goods and services that the elite disproportionately enjoyed. The elite also organized the structure of society so that their high status positions could be passed on to their own children, making it possible for them to create dynasties. In effect, the aristocracy transformed the commoner majority into domesticated cattle, forcing them to surrender their freedom and political and economic equality in order to sustain a hereditary power elite (Adams 1988).

The centralization of political power is the most important underlying feature of civilization because it is functionally connected with many other "civilized" traits; this, in turn, suggests that explanatory theories that focus on political power will be most productive. Before treating the issue of the origin of civilization, let us consider in more detail the functionally interconnected organizational features and cultural traits that are most closely related to the concentration of social power in the hands of rulers and that have figured prominently in definitions of civilization.

State Bureaucracy and the Structures of Elite Power

Probably the most useful definitions of the state cite the presence of government institutions, or bureaucratic hierarchies, often characterized as having a monopoly on the legitimate use of force. Thus, kings, courts, and judges, concentrated in an urban center and supported by temples, treasuries, writing systems, police forces, and armies, might be considered the essential features of states. Such formal institutions are uniquely important developments because they have explicit goals, such as the preservation of the social order, and they can legitimately be analyzed in functional terms. Perhaps most importantly, institutionalized state power historically has tended to enclose people within "social cages" (Mann 1986) and to make it difficult for them to escape from exploitative relationships. States operate within bounded territories and create fixed societies and ethnic groups where previously there were highly flexible, domestic-scale societies that allowed people to shift allegiances in ways that deprived would-be despots of power.

None of the ancient state societies were democracies in which rule was directly exercised by all of the people. Political societies of 2500 people are the approximate upper limit for consensus decision-making, or direct participatory democracy, which requires face-to-face interaction. It is difficult but not impossible to hold larger communities together, and most known larger societies have formal political leadership, elite rulers, and social classes. Sociologist Max Weber (1968:942) attributed elite rule to the "law of the small number," pointing out that it is easier for a few to organize against opposition and keep secrets. Elites are likely to act in their self-interest, and they may resort to physical coercion and ideological domination to enforce their decisions.

---

city-states Politically organized societies based on the intensive exploitation of landless workers in the local area.

There are exceptional archaeological examples of large villages or towns, or integrated communities that were larger than 2500 people but show little evidence of government and social classes, such as the Anasazi in the American Southwest (Plog 2001), the prehistoric Lillooet in interior British Columbia (Hayden 1995), Neolithic villages in the Middle East such as Abu Hureya (Moore, Hillman, and Legge 2000), and Bronze Age Cyprus (Keswani 1996). It is possible to have social complexity without hierarchy and extreme inequality. These atypical larger societies were probably *heterarchies* in which individuals were ranked on multiple dimensions, rather than hierarchies with a single dominant ranking system (Crumley 2001). There are many pathways to social power not all of which lead inevitably to the state and despotic rulers. The alternative of heterarchy will be examined in Chapter 15.

Deciding who should rule, how rulers should be controlled, and how a society's wealth should be distributed was the persistent problem of social power that plagued all civilizations in the ancient imperial world, and is a continuing challenge for all people today. Representative democracy is seen as an ideal government by many in the contemporary world, but it was rare in ancient civilizations. Greek philosopher Aristotle equated democracy, rule by the people, with rule by a poor majority, and felt that it was unlikely to endure because popular democratic leaders, or demagogues, would threaten the interests of wealthy elites. Thus, he thought that either tyranny, absolute rule by a king, other forms of monarchy, or some form of oligarchy, rule by the few, would be the most likely political system. Monarchs and oligarchs would constitute an aristocracy and would rule because they were the most virtuous, meritorious, or wealthy.

In order for rulers to increase the number of people they commanded in their personal imperia, and thereby gain more social power, they needed to increase the scale of society and the complexity of the total cultural system. Initially growth in scale and power occurred together, with positive feedback between the two, but once power becomes firmly established it becomes easier for elites to independently promote growth. Elites created growth by calling into being new organizational forms, new social beliefs and symbols, and in some cases new technologies. These new cultural features were functionally interconnected, and rulers tended to add them in a predictable sequence. Rulers could increase social scale through in-place growth by constructing social hierarchy. This kind of growth in social scale did not require growth in overall population, but it did require that more people become integrated into a larger society. Thus, growth in scale and growth in power occurred simultaneously. When rulers had the institutional structures in place to create and maintain a political economy, they could encourage growth in population by demanding more labor from people. When taxes and tribute replaced kinship reciprocity, it gave people an incentive to increase the size of their families to ease the new burdens. Elite-directed subsistence intensification increased total food production, making it possible to support more people in the same territory.

Figure 7.1 illustrates how increases in cultural complexity allowed aggrandizing individuals to concentrate social power in their personal imperia. This scalogram displays the presence or absence of fifty culture traits among fifteen societies, including three Australian foragers, three Amazon villagers, two African herders, four Pacific island societies, and three empires (Mesopotamia, the Inca, and China). The fifty traits were sifted out of a list of hundreds of organizational traits, because they proved to be generally cumulative and most strongly reflected increasing cultural complexity and culture scale (Carneiro and Tobias 1963). The scalogram shows, for example, that if a society had a city of 10,000 people or more it would also be likely to have all forty-one traits lower on the list, because these traits were functionally related to urbanization. This means that the presence of large cities is a useful defining feature of civilization.

These rankings demonstrate that the eight societies drawn from the tribal world were very similar in complexity and in the modest scale of the largest personal imperia that they supported.

Cultural Scale:
- B = Band
- T = Tribe
- C = Chiefdom
- K = Kingdom
- E = Empire

Personal Imperia: Maximum number of people commanded by most powerful individual.
- xk = tens of thousands
- ck = hundreds of thousands
- m = millions
- xm = tens of millions
- cm = hundreds of millions

Group labels: **EMPIRES**; **PACIFIC ISLANDER CHIEFDOM/KINGDOMS**; **TRIBAL WORLD** (African Herders, Amazonians, Australians).

Trait	Tasmanians	Murngin	Walbiri	Mundurucu	Ashaninka	Kuikuru	Nuer	Maasai	Marquesans	Fiji	Tahiti	Hawaii	Inca	Mesopotamia	China
Markets															1
Temple exacts tithes														1	1
Two or more cities													1	1	1
Empire													1	1	1
City of 100,000+													1	1	1
Sedentary merchants														1	1
Papermaking															1
Arch used in construction													1	1	1
City of 10,000+													1	1	1
Full-time architects or engineers													1	1	1
Full-time painters or sculptors													1	1	1
Code of laws													1	1	1
Monumental stone architecture													1	1	1
Calendrical system													1	1	1
Census taken													1	1	1
State inspectors													1	1	1
State regulation of commerce													1	1	1
Sumptuary laws												1	1	1	1
Royal treasury												1	1	1	1
Roads connecting settlements												1	1	1	1
Royal court												1	1	1	1
≥ 3 levels of territorial administration											1	1	1	1	1
Monarchy										1	1	1	1	1	1
State/church employs artisans											1	1	1	1	1
Military conscription												1	1	1	1
Towns of 2,000+												1	1	1	1
Taxation in kind									1	1	1	1	1	1	1
Corvee									1	1	1	1	1	1	1
Ruler bestows land, slaves, or rank									1	1	1	1	1	1	1
Political leader appoints officials									1	1	1	1	1	1	1
Temples									1	1	1	1	1	1	1
Special deference to political leader									1	1	1	1	1	1	1
Administrative hierarchy										1	1	1	1	1	1
Full-time craft specialists									1				1	1	
Ruler grants audiences									1	1	1	1	1	1	1
Supraprovincial organization									1		1	1	1	1	1
Full-time retainers for political leaders									1			1	1	1	1
Death penalty							1		1	1	1	1	1	1	1
Full-time political leader							1	1	1	1	1	1	1	1	1
Craft production for exchange							1		1		1	1	1	1	1
Judicial process								1	1	1	1	1	1	1	1
Domesticated food sources predominant						1	1	1	1	1	1	1	1	1	1
Craft specialization							1	1	1	1	1	1	1	1	1
Social stratification						1	1	1	1	1	1	1	1	1	1
Communities of 100 people+						1	1	1	1	1	1	1	1	1	1
Peacekeeping machinery						1	1	1	1	1	1	1	1	1	1
Social segments above family		1	1	1	1	1	1	1	1	1	1	1	1	1	1
Formal political leadership				1	1	1	1	1	1	1	1	1	1	1	1
Trade between communities			1	1	1	1	1	1	1	1	1	1	1	1	1
Special religious practitioners		1		1	1	1	1	1	1	1	1	1	1	1	1
Cultural scale	B	B	B	T	T	T	T	T	C	C	K	K	E	E	E
Cultural complexity	0	2	2	4	4	7	8	12	21	22	26	29	46	48	49
Personal imperia	5	25	25	25	25	25	75	75	xk	xk	xk	ck	xm	m	cm

FIGURE 7.1 Scalogram of 15 societies by cultural scale, cultural complexity, and size of personal imperia. (SOURCE: Adapted from Carniero & Tobias 1963, with modifications.)

The four Pacific island chiefdoms and the Hawaiian kingdom were significantly more complex than tribal societies, and they supported personal imperia that were orders of magnitude larger than any in the tribal world. The even more enormous gains made by the Mesopotamian, Inca, and Chinese emperors stand out clearly, but this expansion in elite power required at least seventeen additional traits beyond the Pacific Islanders, including bureaucratic inspectors, census takers, laws, and a hierarchy of urban places.

The scale leap from Pacific island chiefdoms to empires with millions of tax-paying subjects was costly because of the added expense of cities, information management systems, and social control, as well as the increased need for defense as society's total stock of tangible wealth increased. The big organizational problem was coping with the vast increase in potential social interaction, with inequality magnifying sources of discontent. As shown in Chapter 6, Figure 6.B, the Hawaiian king had to deal with tens of billions of potential human interactions, but in 1911 the Chinese emperor directed a vast society where 125 quadrillion (12.5 with 15 zeros) social interactions were possible. This required enormous bureaucratic complexity and a corresponding loss of personal freedom for millions of people. The **bureaucracy** that top rulers constructed to administer these vastly larger-scale societies also defined a class structure because rank in the bureaucracy determined access to the benefits that rulers accumulated and distributed.

Weber (1968:942) called bureaucracy an institutionalized form of domination in which rulers with "authoritarian power of command" impose their will on others. Bureaucratic rule is structured by a hierarchy of officials under a top ruler. In the ancient world bureaucratic rule was often based on patronage and nepotism, but ideally a bureaucrat operates like a machine, without regard for human feeling and emotion. Bureaucracy is an advantage for top rulers, but it creates special problems for people. To be effective, bureaucrats must ultimately surrender their will, and their conscience, to dictates of their superiors (Hummel 1987:2). There is always a top ruler in a bureaucracy, but lower level bureaucrats may in turn be despotic rulers in their own spheres of control.

Evidence for elite direction of the cultural development process in the imperial world can be seen in the steady concentration of social power in elite hands as rulers increase the scale of society. This is a natural function of the mathematics of scale and bureaucratic hierarchies. To demonstrate how this works, Figure 7.2 graphs ruling hierarchies in five hypothetical societies arranged by increasing scale from tribe to empire. The lines show the number of rulers, officials, leaders, or heads by the number of people they command in each society, representing their personal imperia. Each slanted line represents a model society, and each point on the lines is a ranked position in that society's social power hierarchy. Each line extends from self-rule by a single person to a five-person household, and then multiplies each rank by ten to produce the next higher level. For example, a tribe has just four social power ranks, each with its own "ruler": single person, five-person household, fifty-person kin group, and five-hundred-person village. In this simulated tribal society there are only two positions above household head, the kin group head and village head, and only eleven "rulers," (one village head, and ten kin group heads). The high degree of human freedom and economic equality in tribal societies meant that tribal "rulers" had very limited coercive power over their personal imperia.

In the typical administrative hierarchies of the chiefdoms, kingdoms, and empires illustrated in Figure 7.2, elite power becomes mathematically more concentrated by powers of ten, in direct proportion with increases in social scale. Ruling elite households always represent the top 1.1 percent of society, not counting their retainers. Growth in scale benefits the elite, because it promotes the top ruler and increases the total number of rulers at lower levels in the hierarchy. However, the top ruler actually receives a disproportionate increase in power, even when the overall power distribution remains constant. This is because the top

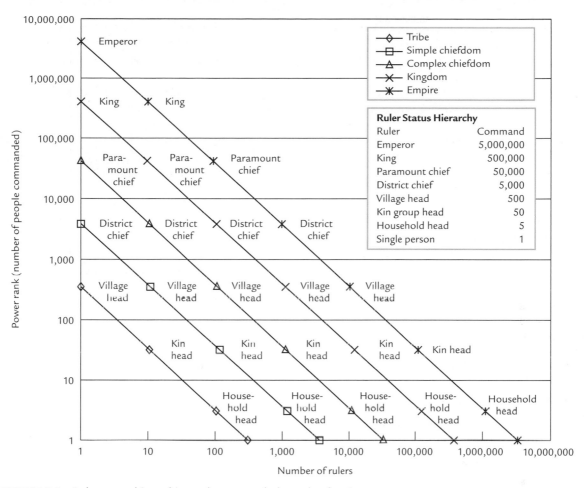

FIGURE 7.2   Ruler status hierarchies and power ranks by scale of society.

ruler's household is always number one, not a fixed percentage of society, and it therefore becomes a declining proportion of all households even as growth magnifies its social power tenfold (Figure 7.3). This power bonus gives the top ruler a powerful incentive to promote more growth.

Figure 7.2 shows that beyond the tribe, when rulers construct a ruling bureaucracy to manage larger-scale societies, they divide society into elite and commoner social classes comprised of increasing numbers of rulers collectively commanding more and more people. More powerful rulers can maintain ever larger household establishments and can support more and more luxurious lifestyles.

The power of kings and emperors is three and four orders of magnitude greater, respectively, than the power of village heads. Such rulers can be designated "super-elites," because they command hundreds of thousands and millions of people.

These civilizations were all directed by urban based rulers who produced broadly similar **Great Tradition** religious ideologies and elite status

bureaucracy A centralized command and control social structure with officials arranged in an administrative hierarchy.

Great Tradition The culture of the elite in a state-organized society with a tradition that is usually written, and not fully shared by nonliterate, village-level commoners.

FIGURE 7.3 The concentration of social power in the top ruler by scale of society.

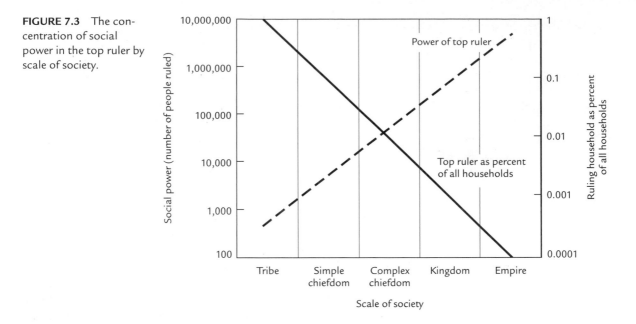

markers to legitimize their superiority and to help them extract material support from the poor majority. Anthropologists distinguish between city-states and **village-states** to identify two different elite strategies for integrating ancient empires (Maisels 1990). The rulers of city-states intensively exploited landless commoners who lived in urban and suburban neighborhoods as dependents on urban institutions and urban elites. The rulers of village-states extracted small amounts of labor from vast numbers of self-sufficient peasant villagers, who often lived far from cities. Villagers maintained their own more egalitarian **Little Tradition** cultures that had obvious roots in the tribal world. Mesopotamian city-states and the Inca Empire are ideal examples of a city-state and village-state respectively, whereas the elites who directed imperial China (Chapter 8) and Hindu India (Chapter 9) drew on a mix of Great Tradition ruling strategies.

Explaining State Origins: Natural Growth or Quest for Power?

Many theorists speak of states as social organisms that simply "emerge," or arise and grow following a natural evolutionary process in a predetermined sequence. In this view, the process may be set in motion by a prime mover, such as population growth, and then it is fueled by further developments. Often this is described as people solving human problems, and the cultural system that "emerges" is a machine of functionally interconnected parts following its own logic. For example, the invention of farming may have been a response to an environmental crisis. Farming is then said to have "caused" population pressure, which in turn caused irrigation and conquest war, which produced tribute and slaves, which led to greater productivity and more inventions. This treats state development as a progressive, presumably beneficial, process that inevitably unfolded as human creativity increased and populations grew.

Taking an evolutionary approach, anthropologist Julian Steward (1949) observed that civilizations in Peru, Mesoamerica, Mesopotamia, Egypt, and China all developed independently along similar **multilinear evolutionary** lines. He stressed the regularities in this process, noting that these early civilizations all developed in arid, or semi-arid environments, where irrigation could support dense populations. Steward thought that irrigation was the key technology that promoted population growth, and that elites were needed to manage the irrigation system. Historian William McNeil (1987:31) simplified this into a sequence in which farmers produced a surplus thereby "freeing" others to develop specialized skills and new ideas ". . . until society as a whole became sufficiently complex, wealthy, and powerful to be called 'civilized.'"

There is considerable merit in such explanations, but they are incomplete and misleading. Even when the sequence and the functional interconnections are historically accurate, they do not adequately *explain* why people actually did these things, because other perhaps better solutions to human problems are always possible. Functionalist, evolutionary explanations also obscure the role of elite decision-making, minimizing the negative human consequences of social transformation and making the process appear too natural and logical. The problems that ancient civilizations solved were primarily the problems of elites seeking to maintain and expand their powers. Structurally, civilizations are greatly enlarged chiefdoms, and they can best be explained in reference to the politics of circumscription and social caging described in Chapter 6. In this view, rulers took advantage of crisis situations in order to force people to accept the elite's self-interested solutions.

Explanations that make technology a prime mover disregard who calls technology into being and who directs its use. Inventions don't just happen, and civilization does not need to wait for the right inventive genius to appear. Earlier, equally creative people invented neolithic technology, which included farming, in a creative process that everyone participated in, because it helped solve everyone's subsistence problems. The Neolithic Paradox referred to in Chapter 5, questions why Neolithic peoples, who were obviously so creative, failed to invent irrigation, writing, cities, kingship, and social class. The paradox is resolved by recognizing that as long as tribal societies functioned as their creators intended they saw no advantage in radical social transforma-

tions that would empower rulers, and make everyone else pay the taxes and bear the risks.

There are some general benefits to state organization. As with chiefdoms, rulers may collect and store food surpluses, then redistribute them to the population to prevent famine. For example, the Romans used a free grain "dole" to maintain the urban poor, but this sort of welfare disguises the social inequalities that make welfare necessary. Karl Wittfogel (1957:126), who experienced the "benefits" of life in a Nazi concentration camp, observed that when pirates keep their ship afloat they are not being benevolent to their captives. Despotic rulers can be expected to maximize their own benefits, but too much exploitation would be counterproductive.

The strongest evidence for intentional elite-direction of state development, in addition to their mathematical increase in social power as shown above, is the unmistakable material payoff appropriated by the rulers. This is clearly seen in the increasing size of domestic establishments at higher levels in the social hierarchy. For example, in the ancient Egyptian city of el-Amarna, built by King Akenaten in about 1350 BC, the average floor space of 75 percent of houses measured 69 square meters (Kemp 1989:298–300), whereas the houses of the top 25 percent averaged in the hundreds of square meters, and they occupied over half of the total residential space. If King Akenaten's 20,000-square-meter palace is included, the elite share rises to 63 percent. In fourth century AD Rome, a city of a million people, fewer than 2,000 were wealthy enough to live in mansions, whereas 98 percent of the empire of 50 million people remained poor.

village-states Politically centralized societies based on an urban administrative and ceremonial center drawing their support from self-sufficient peasant villagers scattered over a vast region.

Little Tradition Ritual beliefs and practices followed by nonliterate commoners, especially rural villagers who are part of a larger state-level society.

multilinear evolution Steward's theory that, given similar conditions, cultures can develop independently along similar lines. For example, he argued that irrigation agriculture led to state organization several times.

FIGURE 7.4   Map of the Middle East showing the Fertile Crescent, Mesopotamia, and major archaeological sites referred to in the text.

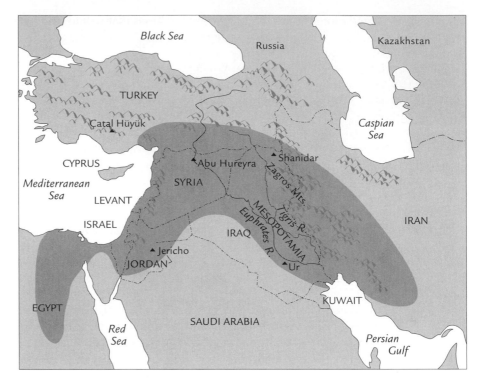

A similar picture of wealth concentration appears in ancient Greece, where nearly a third of the population were slaves, and the top 4 percent of free households held more than half of all private wealth (Goldsmith 1987:16–33). In ancient empires generally larger households meant larger kin networks, larger personal imperia, and improved reproductive fitness for men. The number of a ruler's wives and concubines increased by orders of magnitude from tens in small chiefdoms, to hundreds in larger chiefdoms and small kingdoms, to thousands in empires (Betzig 1986, 1993).

Clearly, there can be no single explanation for such a complex phenomenon as state organization. It will perhaps be most useful to move to specific case studies. The following sections will examine some of the archaeological evidence for the development of Mesopotamian civilization within the larger context of Near Eastern prehistory and environment, as well as a comparative view of Andean civilization.

The Mesopotamian World of Two Rivers: Heartland of Cities

The "fertile crescent" in the Middle East is a remarkable culture area where several of the most significant social transformations in human prehistory and history first took place. This is a 1500- (2414 km) mile-long area curving from the mouth of the Tigris-Euphrates rivers at the head of the Persian Gulf, stretching northwest across modern Iraq, adjacent parts of Iran, southern Turkey, and through Syria, Lebanon, Jordan, and Israel, to the lower Nile Valley in Egypt (Figure 7.4). This environment offered people both unique opportunities and special challenges. Major rivers traversed arid deserts in Mesopotamia, and elevation changes in the surrounding

TABLE 7.1   MESOPOTAMIAN PREHISTORY AND EARLY HISTORY

539 BC	Persian invasion destroys Mesopotamian civilization
1000–539 BC	Neo-Babylonia, Neo-Assyria, Iron Age 　King Nebuchadnezzar II (604–562 BC) 　Metal coins (650 BC)
1500–1000 BC	Middle Babylonia, Middle Assyria, Late Bronze Age
2000–1500 BC	Old Babylonian, Old Assyria, Middle Bronze Age 　City of 100,000 (1600 BC) 　King Hammurabi (1792–1750 BC) 　Ninlil-zimu family in Nippur (1970–1720 BC)
3000–2000 BC	Early Bronze Age 　City of 30,000 (2250 BC) 　Ur III - King Ur-Nammu, empire (2112–2004 BC) 　Sargon the Great (2334–2279 BC), first empire 　Palaces as military-political centers (2800 BC) 　Semitic-speaking Akkadians arrive (2900 BC) 　Early dynastic, Sumerian city-states (3000–2350 BC)
4000–3000 BC	Uruk 　Writing (3100 BC) 　Temple centers, walled cities (3500 BC) 　Sea level stabilizes (4000 BC)
5000–4000 BC	Ubaid 　Urban centers of 1,000–1,500 　Chiefdoms, clay seals 　Sea level and climatic instability (5500–4000 BC)
11,000–6,000 BP	Neolithic (Upper Euphrates River) 　Abu Hureya farmer-herders (8,300–7,000 BP) 　Abu Hureya forager-farmers (11,000–8,300 BP) 　Optimum precipitation (12,000–6,000 BP) 　Early Holocene, warmer & drier (10,000–8,300 BP) 　Younger Dryas, cooler & drier (11,000–10,000 BP)
20,000–11,000 BP	Epipaleolithic 　Abu Hureya foragers (11,500–11,000 BP) 　Optimum warm, moist climate
100,000 BP	Modern humans

Note: Dates are rounded and approximate.

uplands created diverse belts of steppe vegetation, dry woodland, and upland forests, all rich in diverse plant and game resources. All of these ecosystems were in a dynamic, shifting balance with global and regional climate. People have been repeatedly forced to adjust to unpredictable environmental crises over the millennia since modern humans first lived there at least 100,000 years ago. This was where tribal peoples first domesticated wild plants and animals (11,000 BP) and where elites first constructed chiefdoms (7000 BP), city-states (3500 BC), and empires (2334 BC). Table 7.1 summarizes the chronology of these major cultural events and related environmental changes. The shift in dates from BP (before present) to BC (before the Christian era) marks the beginning of writing and the shift from prehistory to history.

Mesopotamian city states are especially noteworthy because they were one of a handful of "pristine" civilizations, created in-place, presumably independently of any other states, and they have been heavily researched by specialists from many fields. This makes them an ideal case study for investigating the causes and consequences of the origins of civilization. Before examining life in Mesopotamian city-states, this section reviews the archaeological background and shows how and why a few elite individuals were able to gain control of the urbanization and politicization processes and direct the cultural transformations that created these first civilizations.

The contrast between the consensus response of tribal peoples to environmental changes in the ancient Middle East and the autocratic response of power-seeking elites highlights important differences between the tribal and imperial worlds. These different responses demonstrate that political centralization was not inevitable, but under some circumstances aspiring elites could force the majority to accept their domineering leadership. Village life and farming are often hailed by historians as the first steps toward civilization, but creating the Neolithic was a different process from building cities. The Neolithic resulted from democratic choices that people made freely, and everyone benefitted equally. People individually adopted farming and herding, freely opting to gradually intensify their subsistence practices as the best response to changing circumstances. Autonomous Neolithic villages were also enormously successful. People lived in them for millennia without going on to invent civilization (see the box entitled "Before Civilization: Abu Hureyra, 4000 Years of Tribal Village Autonomy").

Archaeologist Charles Redman (1978a, 1978b) offered one of the most comprehensive explanations for the origin of Mesopotamian civilization using an elaborate flow chart and complex systems analysis that expand on and refine Steward's earlier explanation (Figure 7.5). In Redman's analysis the development process began with an empty, but potentially productive, niche that was colonized by people using irrigated agriculture. Redman then identified five crucial variables: A. population growth, B. specialized food production, C. the "need" to import raw materials, D. warfare, and E. the existence of social stratification and administrative elites, and showed how they were connected to form positive feedback loops that worked together to accelerate state development. The natural dynamic of the evolving system then quickly produced civilization. This interpretation is a helpful starting point, but it makes environment and technology the primary causes, and would seem to make human agency irrelevant. It now appears that the development process was not so natural and mechanistic. A different interpretation of Redman's diagram shows that elites actually decided how the system evolved. It was the elite, not society as a whole, who decided to tax people, go to war, monopolize food storage, direct trade, and so on. The elite solution was not the only human alternative. Furthermore, particular technologies such as irrigation did not by themselves cause civilization to "emerge."

Redman's analysis and circumscription theory suggest that warring chiefdoms and states were "natural" institutional responses to population growth and resource shortages, but it is striking that this undemocratic solution was the last choice. Migration to more favorable areas was the first choice when population growth, arid conditions, and crop failure made village life difficult. Displaced villagers sometimes turned to pastoral nomadism. When migration was not possible, some villages began to manage communally stored village foodstuffs using seals and tokens made by impressing marks into soft clay. This simple information technology was in public use by 9000 BP. It did not require writing or political centralization, and helped make sure that village leaders could individually identify and fairly distribute stored surpluses in large sedentary communities coping with resource stress (Frangipane 2000). These solutions were clearly designed to help the entire society, whereas many cultural features of

Before Civilization: Abu Hureyra, 4000 Years of Tribal Village Autonomy

The Neolithic processes of sedentarization and domestication are best documented archeologically at Abu Hureyra (Moore, Hillman, and Legge 2000). This settlement mound was situated in an unusually rich and diverse region on the Euphrates River in Syria, some 400 miles upriver from Baghdad. Tribal people founded the village of Abu Hureyra 11,500 years ago, near the end of the Epipaleolithic (Mesolithic) and occupied it virtually continuously for 4500 years. Abu Hureyra was a remarkable human achievement and a tribute to the resilience of tribal life. It existed as a tribal village for a thousand years longer than the Mesopotamian city-states and empires that followed.

Initially, the area near Abu Hureyra was so rich in wild food plants and game that people were able to construct a small permanent village of semi-subterranean houses. Within a few hundred years the village grew to some 300 people who began to build timber and reed houses. They were able to secure a diverse and resilient diet for 500 years by relying entirely on herds of wild gazelles and other wild animals and more than 250 wild plant species, especially wild rye. During the 2500 years from 11,000 BP to about 8500 BP, people gradually changed their subsistence from wild to cultivated plants, bringing rye and other grains, legumes, and flax under cultivation, while still foraging and hunting part time. They probably took this momentous technological step because cooler and drier conditions pushed favorable vegetation zones out of reach, thereby reducing their supply of plant staples, especially the grains that made sedentary life possible. Domestication was an obvious solution. Wild rye plants that produce tough, easily harvested grain heads that are also easily husked, and yield plump, soft grains occur naturally in wild rye populations. By selectively harvesting and cultivating these preferred plants, people could have produced solid stands with these desirable genetic traits within 200 years. Cultivation increased their workload, but it allowed people to produce more food in a given area of land, which meant they could remain in their village as wild foods disappeared. People turned to cultivation because there were no easier resources open to them, and they did not want to abandon their village.

After they adopted farming, the settlement grew to 2500 people by 9000 BP. Within a few more centuries, people began to live in densely packed mud-brick houses. When the wild gazelle herds declined they began keeping sheep and goats and quickly domesticated them. By 8000 BP the population had doubled, peaking at an amazing 5000 people. Remarkably, Abu Hureyra crossed the social scale threshold usually associated with tribal equality, yet remained integrated for another 2000 years without leaving any trace of invidious social ranking. People cooperated in economic activities, made ceramics, used cattle as draft animals, and probably had formal leaders, but they built no temples and apparently refused to construct a chiefdom. They obtained exotic materials such as obsidian and marine shells from more than 100 miles (160 kms) away. A combination of resource depletion and increasing aridity probably forced people to finally abandon the settlement. The neolithic village of Çatal Hüyük in Turkey also grew large and avoided social stratification (Mellaart 1967, Todd 1976).

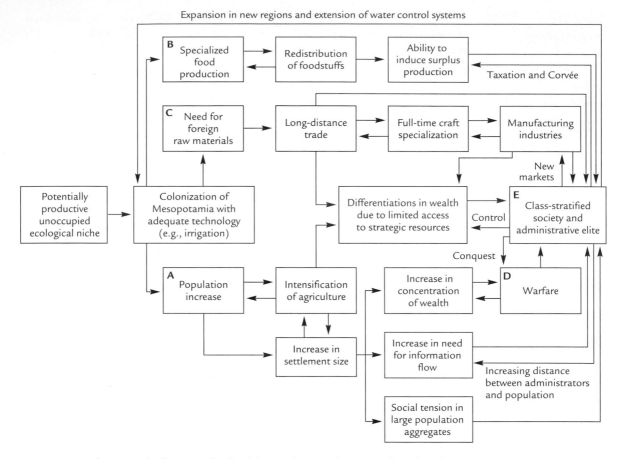

FIGURE 7.5   The network of positive feedback loops that may have contributed to the growth of the Mesopotamian state. (SOURCE: Based on Redman 1978a, 1979b.)

chiefdoms and states were self-serving institutions designed by elites to sustain centralized power itself (Flannery 1972).

The first chiefdoms, temples, and small administrative hierarchies didn't just happen. They were constructed by opportunistic elites during the Ubaid Period (5500–3800 BC). Southern Mesopotamia (Sumer) was first colonized by Neolithic peoples. This occurred before 5000 BC when conditions still favored dry-land farming. The first settlers avoided irrigation, and lived successfully in small villages for some 2700 years as fluctuating sea levels kept the river systems unstable. After 5000 BC, shifts in global climate brought on dangerously unpredictable droughts and flood-

ing, and produced catastrophic crop failures that turned many people into refugees, forcing them to concentrate in a few larger settlements where stored food was still available (Hole 1994).

Refugees became dependent laborers for those fortunate few householders who had managed to survive multiple environmental crises by relying on small irrigation systems that didn't fail. The continuous arrival of refugees caused these larger settlements to grow into small towns of 2000 people surrounded by villages of a few hundred people. These towns became the centers of Ubaid chiefdoms, which may have encompassed 5000 people. Town founders became chiefs and developed temples as community grain storehouses

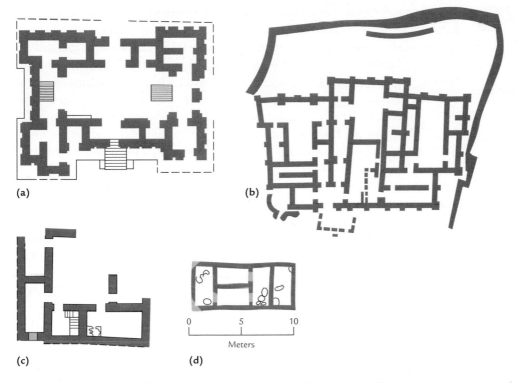

FIGURE 7.6   The scale of Mesopotamian structures. (*a*) Ubaid Temple, (*b*) Ubaid Great House, (*c*) Nippur Great House, (*d*) Neolithic House (Abu Hureyra).

that attracted hungry refugees. Temples contained altars and offering tables, and the chiefs used markings on clay proto-tablets to help them collect, store, and manage food surpluses. Managing temples allowed elites to skim off surplus for personal benefit, permitting them to live on a somewhat higher material level than commoners. Chiefs lived in the center of town in houses as big as temples, three to four times larger than commoner houses (Figure 7.6). Elite houses may have been occupied by the same elite family for generations, and supported large families and dependent workers. However, material differences between elites and commoners were not yet extreme.

Ubaid chiefs relied on staple finance to maintain their power, in contrast to the Hawaiian chiefs and the Inca emperors who used both staple and wealth finance. The Ubaid elite controlled the water, land, and labor needed for irrigation-based food production, but they did not abuse

their power. They relied on religious ideology, ritual, and offerings to legitimize their control, and there is no evidence for warfare, political instability, or elite-directed long-distance trade to secure high-status wealth objects (Stein 1994). Ubaid chiefdoms seem to have been very peaceful societies focused on temple rituals. The conspicuous absence of status markers made it easier for people to limit elite rivalry and avoid the runaway growth described in Redman's model that later produced the first empires. This made the Ubaid chiefdoms remarkably durable, relatively small-scale societies that lasted virtually unchanged for 1500 years. They spread by replication, rather than conquest, from Sumer into nonirrigated dry-farming areas in upper Mesopotamia.

When the sea level stabilized by 4000 BC, circumstances abruptly changed. Irrigation became more reliable, and the most successful chiefs moved to create larger-scale societies by further

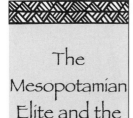

The Mesopotamian Elite and the Rewards of Leadership

Because they boasted of their achievements, we have the names of specific rulers and a written record of the cultural changes that they imposed in order to continually increase the scale of Mesopotamian society. Sargon the Great founded the first Mesopotamian empire (2334–2279 BC), and shortly thereafter King Ur-Nammu founded the Ur III dynasty (2112–2004 BC), creating a regional empire of some five million people centered on the capital city of Ur (McEvedy and Jones 1978:150). The Ur III rulers started out in command of the small city-state of Ur. King Ur-Nammu and his son Shulgi turned it into a multinational empire and a family dynasty that dominated the entire Mesopotamian plain and neighboring areas for four generations (2112–2004 BC).

Shulgi consolidated his father's territorial conquests by instituting a series of administrative "reforms" according to a "master plan" that he carried out over a ten-year period. Shulgi's reforms involved making himself a god, establishing a standing army and scribal schools, and improving the temple household system, the bureaucracy, the legal code, and the taxation, writing, weights and measures, accounting, and calender systems. He brought all the temples under government control and created a system of "crown land" as part of his personal royal household and the industrial enterprises operated by the central government (Steinkeller 1991). All of the social transformations implemented by this family defined the major institutions of Mesopotamian civilizations for the next twenty-five centuries.

The Ur III kings divided their empire into some 25 provinces, each centered on a formerly independent city-state. They may have incorporated some 25 cities of 10,000 or more, 48 towns of 2,000 people, and more than 1000 villages into their system of tribute and taxation. The largest city probably approached 100,000

intensifying production, acquiring exotic materials, and waging conquest war in order to make themselves kings. The first city-states were in place by 3500 BC during the Uruk Period (4000–3000 BC) marking the beginning of Sumerian civilization. The Sumerian elite directed centralized economic systems and distributed rations to workers who produced high-status wealth objects. Scribes were soon keeping administrative records in cuneiform on clay tablets, making Sumerian the world's first written language. By 3000 BC urban centers reached 10,000 people and, including local villagers, may have reached 100,000 people.

Uruk-period elite initiated a fundamental transformation of society. The Sumerian elite not only controlled food production, but they organized the mass production of ceramics, and shifted textile production from domestically produced linen to large-scale workshop production of woolen textiles (McCorriston 1997). In Neolithic villages women controlled textile production, growing their own flax in small domestic plots, making linen, and weaving in the home. In the city-states, dependent women attached to the temples wove woolens, and men tended large herds of sheep on institutionally owned pastures. The elite then used the woolen goods for long-distance trade. By about 3500 BC there were Uruk colonies on the upper Euphrates in Syria for the acquisition of exotic raw materials such as wood and metals that the elite needed to build cities and to serve as status-marking wealth objects (Oates 1993).

people. In an empire of this scale there were positions for more elites, and the emperor could live much more extravagantly than ever before. At 3000 square meters Shulgi's personal temple palace was 10 times larger than a 300-square-meter Ubaid chief's house. The four main temples in the city of Ur were more than 100 times larger than an Ubaid temple. The elites who directed the temples and the top political leadership were no doubt a few closely interconnected families. The gap between rich and poor in Ur's residential district is shown by the contrast between the "meanest and shoddiest" one-room, nine-square-meter house, and a nearby three-story, sixty-room mansion of 1500 square meters, which was no doubt occupied by a very high-ranking elite (Woolley and Moorey 1982:204). The houses of the poorest in Ur were smaller than standard housing in the tribal world, and are an objective indicator of poverty.

The personal payoff for lower-level elites in Mesopotamian empires is demonstrated by the extraordinary success of the Ninlil-zimu family in Nippur (1970–1720 BC). Clay tablets show that this family dominated both the city of Nippur and the family's neighborhood for nearly 200 years (Stone 1987). Their carefully constructed family house was more than twice the size of ordinary houses, and was occupied by six generations of the Ninlil-zimu family. The family was probably the largest property owner in the city and held several important official titles, including some of the most prestigious temple offices. The family owned at least three houses, as well as fields and orchards on the edge of the city. A single block of undeveloped urban property, twice the size of their residential neighborhood, remained in the family for at least 150 years. The family also received substantial gifts of property from the king, owned slaves, and employed laborers.

Multiple city-states belonged to the same interaction network, sharing a common language and religion, and collectively constituted a single civilization. Private ownership of land by individual households was a key feature of Mesopotamian city-states, and it fostered a class system based on unequal access to landed wealth. City-state governments were in the hands of privileged citizens, who were rewarded by expansion (see the box entitled "The Mesopotamian Elite and the Rewards of Leadership").

Making a Living in Mesopotamian City-States and Empire

Daily life in Mesopotamian civilization can be reconstructed from the floor plans of excavated houses, inscriptions describing ancient property transfers, and clay tablets containing household inventories (Maisels 1990). Mesopotamian society was designed to serve elite patrilineal households whose large private landholdings were cultivated by their retinues of dependent laborers. The residential core of the urban centers contained large household compounds, each controlled by a senior household residing in a large central hall. Junior extended-family households and dependent nonkin lived in small, individual household apartments arranged along the side of the main hall and in detached outbuildings. Dependents held reduced titles to land or were totally landless. Household archives show that these compounds were large economic enterprises managing people, land, grain, food, livestock, and craft products. The heads of these private "great-house" economic units formed the citizens of the Mesopotamian city-state. They also ran the temples and the city government.

Barley Rations, Cylinder Seals, and Social Power in Ur III

The Ur III empire (2112–2004 BC), constructed by the kings of the Ur-Nammu dynasty, consisted of a core area centered on the principle city-states in the Tigris-Euphrates irrigated zone and a peripheral area of tributary provinces. Core and periphery were combined into a single state finance system in which rulers extracted taxes to support the royal family and their corporate establishments (Steinkeller 1991). The core economic sectors were the royal domain, the temple domain, and the private sector. The royal domain included vast tracts of farm land, irrigation systems, pastures, and workshops under the emperor's direct control that supported households of his extended family, the military, and the central administrative bureaucracy. The temples were corporate institutions run as great households by governors (ensi) who were connected to the royal family by ties of kinship, marriage, or patronage. The heads of temple establishments also managed workshops and controlled large tracts of land and herds. The poorly documented private sector consisted of private households headed by private individuals operating as independent landholders, farmers, herders, craftsmen, and merchants.

Individuals and households situated in all of these sectors were connected by a flow of materials and services mobilized by the taxation system known as bala, in which individuals of all ranks were required to deliver specific quantities of livestock, grain, craft products, or other materials, and various kinds of labor service to higher authorities. Various bala taxes were levied according to the products available in particular areas, and in the case of personal income or property taxes, according to an individual's rank and land holdings. Bala goods were transported

to distribution centers and passed through the bureaucracy to final consumers.

Initially, there were three broad social ranks in the early Mesopotamian city-states with the city governor, or king (lugal), at the top, administrative officials in the middle, and ordinary people at the bottom. The rank of officials was reflected directly in their salaries, land allotments, and the cylinder seals issued by authorities (Winter 1991). Specialists carved designated inscriptions and images into short stone, bone, or metal rods that were then pressed and rolled across wet clay to make impressions. After the clay dried any alterations in the inscriptions could be readily detected. Seals functioned much like identity cards or badges. They attested to one's official authority and responsibility and were used by civil, military, and temple officials, and by wealthy private individuals to certify personal business transactions. Each seal carried the personal name of the holder, his family name, and title. For the highest officials, especially ensi (civil governor or temple head), šagina (military general, controlled crown lands), and sukkal-mah (chancellor, the highest civil official under the king), the seal bore standardized images of a presentation scene showing the bearer standing in the presence of a seated king to receive the seal, or being led to the king by a deity (Figure 7.7). Additional inscriptions glorified the king and connected the official with him. The wives of high officials also had personal seals depicting presentations from goddesses, not the king, that were probably used to manage domestic business. The seals of merchants show by the absence of royal presentation images that they were ranked below top administrators.

The Ur III proliferation of seals used by high ranking bureaucrats corresponds with Ur-Nammu's transformation of city-states into empire, the deification of the king, and the increasing need to use written documents to manage information in a larger-scale society. It is significant that at this time the king appears on seals in a position formerly occupied by a god, reflecting the divine king as emperor ranking over the governors of

FIGURE 7.7 Seal issued by Ur III Emperor Ur-Nammu, seated, to a governor, lead by a deity (Winter 1991:90, Plate 1a).

FIGURE 7.8 Ur-Nammu's transformation of Mesopotamian city-states into the Ur III Empire (adapted from Winter 1991:76, Figure 1).

other formerly independent city-states. The divine king emperor headed a society now expanded into four ranks with parallel political, military, and ideological (temple) power structures (Figure 7.8). Third-level officials such as overseers, managers, and scribes carried seals presented to them by second-level officials. Merchants were generally third-rank because there were apparently no organized markets in Mesopotamian society, although the most important merchants worked directly for the royal household. Long-distance trade was directed by the elite, who also controlled the extraction and distribution of all social surplus production.

Analysis of seal inscriptions and tablets shows that high offices often remained within the same family and were bequeathed from father to son, attesting to the existence of private dynasties that paralleled the royal dynasties. For example, the

highest office of the Temple of Inanna in Nippur remained in the same family for at least five generations (Zettler 1991:109). It is likely that the same individuals and families held multiple titles that connected them to different sources of power in palace, temple, the military, and private business. The power elite were a tiny hereditary aristocracy, and there may have been little upward social mobility.

There may have been as many as 500,000 urban nonfood-producing people in the Ur III empire, including elite households and specialists (Waetzoldt 1987). Given the agricultural production system, it can be estimated that 90 percent of the population lived at the subsistence level and engaged directly in agricultural labor (Hunt 1991). Most other people were nonfood producers working as low-level managers, craft workers, and domestics servants. Ordinary people in the lowest rank faced an insecure existence because they controlled little productive property, and unless they were full-time temple or palace employees or were attached to a large private household, their subsistence was always uncertain. Many employees, especially women, received less than the official annual ration of 720 liters *(sila)* of barley per year for one adult man (see the box entitled "The Mesopotamian Ration System).

The Ur III emperors managed a nonmonetary, nonmarket economy. There were no coins, but exchange values were fixed by the ruler. Barley was a universal medium of exchange, and even land was valued according to the amount of barley it could produce. Three hundred liters of barley (one *gur*) was exchanged for eight grams of silver (one *shekel*). One ox was worth ten shekels, and a sheep one shekel. Low-level managers and administrators received only a few thousand liters of barley a year, which was barely enough to meet the official minimum subsistence level of 1680 liters of barley per year for a six-person family (Waetzoldt 1987). This meant that most people survived by putting all family members into wage labor, but at any time misfortune could force householders into indentured servitude, or they might even have to sell themselves, or a family member into slavery.

Inequality was pervasive throughout Mesopotamian society. The system was skewed toward the top even for professionals living above the subsistence level. For example, in the largest temples the wage structure shows that 120 managers received an average annual income of 4775 liters of barley, whereas 4 upper administrators averaged 30,000. The top official received a regular salary of 60,000, and he was allocated enough land to produce an additional net gain of nearly 18,000 liters of barley, which would have raised his income to the level of 100 minimum wage workers at 720 liters for an adult man (Waetzoldt 1987).

The Mesoptamian elite constructed a society in which they oppressed and exploited the commoners to enhance their own lifestyles. This was *oppression* because the elite overpowered the majority with cultural institutions, beliefs, and practices that maintained unequal access to productive land and labor. It was exploitation because the labor of those with reduced access to resources sustained the well-being of the elite few who owned or controlled their land and labor (E. Wright 1997:9–13). Most people did not own land, and were forced to either rent, or work as dependents of the landowners.

The four social ranks of imperial Mesopotamia were broadly related to differences in property ownership and employment, which determined an individual's ability to successfully maintain a family. Some people owned property but did not engage in production. Others owned property and worked their land alongside nonowning workers, whereas the majority worked for others, and did not own productive property. The latter category included people who were variously called captives, slaves, serfs, or "helots" (Diakonoff 1987, Klengel 1987). Slaves were themselves property, but were not always readily distinguished from indentured laborers.

Members of the royal household were the largest land owners. The king, his spouse, and their children individually owned crown estates and allocated use rights to others. Members of the royal family hired workers as household domestic labor and as general laborers. Second-rank officials owned property in their own names, held large allotments of crown land in exchange for service, and received large salaries as state officials. This made it possible for them to rent additional property and hire labor. Third-ranked people held smaller allotments and received smaller salaries.

The **social product,** or aggregate income of the empire, was sufficient to securely support the entire Mesopotamian population at a culturally defined decent standard of living, but in reality only the top one percent of society was actually prosperous and secure. Measured as grain production,

social product The value of the aggregate annual production of a society, measured either as production or consumption.

The
Mesopotamian
Ration
System

The early Mesopotamian city-state was populated by a large number of full-time urban specialists, who included priests, scribes, overseers, and artisans. All these people were supported by monthly allotments of rations, which in Sumerian were called *Se-ba* (*Se* means "barley"; *ba* means "distribution"). According to I. J. Gelb's (1965) analysis of the textual evidence, standard rations included *Se-ba, I-ba* (oil), and *Sig-ba* (wool) in standardized units according to a set formula specifying the amounts that people would receive by age and sex. For example, barley was distributed by the *sila,* a volume measurement equivalent to 0.85 liter (L). Men normally received 60 *sila;* women, 30; boys, 25; girls, 20; and infants, 10 (Table 7.A). The rations were probably generous, and people no doubt bartered the surplus to fill other basic needs. According to figures used by Johnson (1973), 1 L of barley contained 829 grams (g), and 100 g of barley produced 350 calories (cal). The average adult ration of 45 *sila* would have provided 3698 calories per day. Barley was the most important subsistence staple, but it probably accounted for only 66 percent of people's average caloric consumption, the balance being supplied by animal products, fruits, and vegetables. Thus, people probably consumed directly only about half of their barley allotments. The oil ration was generally animal fat, although sometimes it might have been sesame oil, and it was used for consumption and in ritual anointings. Besides barley, oil, and wool distributions, there were also irregular distributions of wheat, bread, flour, and cloth. Standard rations were sometimes replaced with equivalent substitutes, such that 1 *sila* of oil could replace 2 *sila* of barley. On ritual occasions or to specific categories of people, there were also supplemental distributions of meat, dairy products, beer, wine, fish, dates, fruits, and vegetables.

observance of rituals were rewarded with special foods. Christmas?

TABLE 7.A   RATIONS IN MESOPOTAMIA BY AGE AND SEX

	Se-ba (Barley) (*sila*/month)*	I-ba (Oil) (*sila*/year)	Sig-ba (Wool) (ma-na/ year)†
Men	60	4	4
Women	30	4	3
Children	—	1.5	1.5
Boys	20–30	—	—
Girls	20	—	—
Infants	10	—	—

SOURCES: Gelb (1965), Johnson (1973), Kramer (1963).
*Sila = 0.85 L, 705 g of barley.
†Ma-na = 500 g.

the annual social product must have approached the equivalent of some 1.8 billion liters of barley, assuming one million farmer households producing an annual average of 1882 liters (1246 kilos). This was *net* production after deductions for loss in storage, transport, and seed and yielded a 10 percent margin above the official subsistence minimum of 1680 liters. This margin was not really a "surplus," because in autonomous Neolithic tribal villages where production was approximately at the same level, people themselves would have invested any social product above minimum consumption needs in feasting and alliances, or they stored it as security against misfortune. Under the empire, rulers extracted this "surplus" as a tax, as a sacrifice to the gods, their temples, and the divine king, or as tribute from conquered people. However legitimized, this extraction left producers with virtually no security margin.

A 10 percent tax may seem insignificant. It was less than the 15 percent inevitably lost in production and distribution in ancient agricultural systems. However, this estimate is an average that assumes every household was taxed equally. In reality, the most productive land was taxed most heavily, and in some provinces rulers extracted up to 50 percent of the barley crop for the *bala* (Steinkeller 1991:23, note 29). Given the scale of the empire, the tax in the Ur III empire allowed the royal family of perhaps only 500 people to control the social distribution of 188 million liters of grain produced by a million worker households. The cost of extracting, moving, and storing this much grain was a further burden that the tax itself subsidized. This subsidy covered both direct administrative and managerial costs, as well as the costs of the temple and legitimizing temple ritual. There were probably more than 11,000 nonfood-producing administrators and managers, in addition to troops, and other full-time specialists. In addition to the grain, which was produced in irrigated fields near urban centers and transported by boat, more than 30,000 head of livestock were annually driven to a distribution center

near the city of Nippur to be allocated to temples, the military, and elite individuals (Zeder 1994). Many of these activities were unproductive costs, because they were needed to maintain and reproduce the social system itself, and did not directly provide consumption goods for most households. The tax system was a **scale subsidy** that supported a social system at a scale that would not otherwise have been sustainable. The rulers also forced nature to subsidize their empire, because intensive flood plain irrigation in the Mesopotamian environment steadily caused an accumulation of salts that steadily degraded the soil.

Table 7.2 offers a provisional sketch of the distribution of social power in the Ur III empire, making reasonable assumptions about agricultural production, numbers of people in different ranks, and their income and wealth, based on tax records, land allotments, salaries, and wage or ration rates, the structure of the bureaucracy, and the size of temple establishments (Hunt 1991, Steinkeller 1991, Waetzoldt 1987, Winter 1991, Zettler 1991). The ranking of personal imperia as super-elite, elite, maintenance, and poor corresponds to the four ranks of Ur III society, and represents the relative well-being of households according to their social power. Higher-ranked imperia command more wealth and income, as well as other people. Maintenance-level imperia command enough resources to meet basic needs, whereas poor often must borrow to survive. Elites have more than enough to comfortably maintain themselves, and can promote growth. Table 7.2 dramatically demonstrates how growth in scale can disempower and impoverish most of society, even as a tiny elite are disproportionately benefited. Super-elite royal households could have supported an average of nearly 350 extra-household adult laborers at the annual wage ration of 720 barley liters. A thousand top administrator households could have supported 80 laborers, and 7 extra-household adults. Their larger, more secure household establishments gave the elites and their children improved life chances. At the broad base of the social pyramid, in good times 99 per-

TABLE 7.2   UR III IMPERIA BY WEALTH, INCOME, AND SOCIAL RANK, 2000 BC

Rank	Households Population	Wealth	Average Household Income (barley liters)	Imperia
Emperor, Divine King	1 — 50	Royal Domain 13,000 hectares Royal Temple-Palace, workshops	9,000,000	**Super-Elite** 0.01% of population
Extended Royal Family	100 —— 500	Land, Temples, Mansions, Slaves, Livestock, Grain, Silver	250,000	
Royal Officials Chancellor, Governors, Generals, Top Administrators	1,000 ——— 5,000	Land, Mansions, Slaves, Livestock, Grain, Silver	60,000	**Elite** 0.1% of population
Managers, Mayors, Top Specialists, Large Landowners, Merchants	10,000 ———— 50,000	Land, Mansions, Slaves, Livestock, Grain, Silver	5,000	**Maintenance** 0.99% of population
Independent Farmers, Herders, Low Wage Urban Workers, Low Wage Rural Workers, Indentured Workers, Slaves	1,000,000 ————— 5,000,000	Use Rights	1,680	**Poor** 98.9% of population
Totals	1,011,110 households 5,055,550 persons	2.5 million hectares of irrigated cropland	1.8 billion barley liters social product	188 million barley liters social surplus

Note: The emperor's income represents his command over an estimated 10,000 civil and religious officials, and troops, and 5,000 women in royal temples and workshops.

cent of the population would have had a bare minimum to support 2 adult household members and 3 children.

Cuneiform Writing, Law, and Justice

As the administrative bureaucracy in the Mesopotamian city-states grew, the requirements for information storage increased dramatically. The earliest written inscriptions appeared about 3100 BC in a pictographic script found in the city

scale subsidy Social support in the form of taxes or tribute for activities that promote growth in scale, or that maintain a larger-scale society when benefits are inequitably distributed.

of Uruk and involved economic control functions such as bookkeeping of receipts, expenses, and goods. By 2400 BC, Mesopotamian writing had become a well developed cuneiform system (Nissen 1986). The word *cuneiform* (*cunei* means "nails") refers to the distinctive nail shape produced when a stylus with a triangular cross section is pressed into a soft clay tablet at an angle. The early pictographs represented the names of naturalistically portrayed objects, but this limited and cumbersome system was readily improved by simplifying the pictographs into abstract forms and giving some of them phonetic meanings (Figure 7.9). The basic cuneiform system was used throughout the Near East by the Sumerians, Babylonians, Assyrians, and Persians over a 2000-year period.

A scribal school, the *edubba,* became institutionalized as a formal means to standardize the writing system and to produce the professional body of scribes needed to write and archive the great masses of clay tablets required for routine administration. Students memorized some 2000 different cuneiform signs by copying standard texts that often consisted of word lists. These academic exercises provide useful insights into the degree of specialization and scale of wage differences at the beginning of civilization. For example, one word list contained a ranking of one hundred professions and titles and is a power of ten increase over the level of specialization in Hawaii. The writing system developed rapidly over a period of about 150 years (Nissen 1986) and then became very stable. It was a medium for sacred temple literature, epic poetry, and royal decrees, but the bulk of the material concerned mundane administrative matters and domestic accounts. Numeration was based on a sexagesimal (60s) system with place values, but it also used a numeral for 10. There was no concept of zero, but complex mathematical calculations—such as multiplication, square roots, and area problems—were still accomplished.

Rulers used writing to publically endorse the formal structures of society and their concept of official justice. For example, King Hammurabi's

(a)

(b)

FIGURE 7.9   Mesopotamian writing. (*a*) Clay tablet inscribed in an early Mesopotamian writing system. (*b*) Characteristic nail-shaped cuneiform writing representing the number thirty.

(1792–1750 BC) famous "law code," engraved on a stone monument, was a collection of legal cases, or conflict situations, along with his own corresponding "just" decisions (Johns 1926). These cases took into account the social positions of men and women, young and old, aristocrat and commoner, free and slave, and demonstrated the king's awesome life or death powers over his subjects. Punishments varied from monetary fines to mutilation and death, but the king's justice always took into account the relative social status of those involved. Personal injuries to servants or the poor were compensated with silver, but if an aristocrat was injured, it was an eye for

FIGURE 7.10   The central Ziggarat (temple tower) of Ur, built around 2000 BC.

an eye. If the poor were unable to pay a fine, they could be killed. Punishments could be severe and seemingly arbitrary. Theft might bring death, and a man who struck his father might have his hand chopped off. However, many of the judgments on business disputes would seem reasonable by modern business law, and decisions on divorce and inheritance often protected the rights of women and children.

Mesopotamian Religion in the Service of the Ruler

Like the Hawaiian king, the Mesopotamian king headed a divine cult, built and maintained the temples, appointed officials, and coordinated the ritual calendar. He assumed the role of a fertility god, Dumuzi or Tammuz, in an annual temple ritual in which he "married" a woman representing the fertility goddess Ishtar, reenacting a divine wedding. This ritual symbolically gave the king power over natural fertility throughout the land, just as it did with the Hawaiian king in the Makahiki ceremony. Rulers were probably exceptionally fertile, producing many children. Although Mesopotamian marriage was typically monoga-

mous for succession to royal titles, matings were polygynous. Rulers had children by their concubines and nourished them with wet nurses in their extended domestic establishments (Betzig 1993).

Each city belonged to a founding god drawn from the rich Sumerian pantheon and contained temples dedicated to it. The Sumerian word for temple, *ebitum,* meant "house," so the temple was the god's house, and the temple personnel existed as the god's caretakers. The visible focal point of major Sumerian cities was the *ziggurat* (an Akkadian word for "temple tower"), a stepped pyramid of clay bricks built as a shrine to the city's deity.

The Ziggurat of Ur, the best-surviving example, was completed during the third Sumerian dynasty, around 2000 BC. It is one of the best preserved early ziggurats. The base platform was 200 feet by 150 feet (61 m by 46 m) and 50 feet (15 m) high. Two other levels were built on top of this, and they were topped by a small shrine to the moon god Nanna, so that the total height was at least 70 feet (21 m) (Figure 7.10). Because the ziggurat was built on an elevated terrace, the whole structure must have been an imposing sight rising above the surrounding plain. The ziggurat was part of the *Temenos* (Greek for "sacred ground"), a sacred enclosure containing a major temple to Nanna, other shrines, storehouses, courtyards, and quarters for temple personnel (Woolley and Moorey 1982). At this time, Ur was a walled city of some 321 acres (130 hectares) that might have contained 25,000 people.

The spiritual head of the Sumerian temple bore the title *En,* and he or she resided in an elaborate complex within the *Temenos,* called the *Giparu.* The temple administrator was titled *Sanga,* and there were many other named temple or priestly offices. The temple claimed ownership of at least three named categories of land:

1. *Nigenna,* whose produce directly supported the temple
2. *Kurra,* used to support those who worked *nigenna* land
3. *Urulal,* lands that could be farmed by temple personnel for their own use, in exchange for a share of the produce

Thus, the temple administration, besides conducting major religious activities, managed the farmland, collected and stored grain, and paid out rations to laborers. This arrangement must have reflected the structure of elite private households. The temples also took in dependents, but they were public institutions, and their grain surpluses were probably available in times of shortage.

Secular rulers apparently rose to prominence as military leaders in conflicts with neighboring city-states. As kings (*lugal,* literally "bigman"), they founded dynasties, built palaces and temples, raised armies, maintained the city walls, and were buried in royal tombs. In 1927–1928, Sir Leonard Woolley discovered some of the most spectacular art treasures of the ancient Middle East in the royal tombs of Ur. A series of royal burials dating to the Early Dynastic period were unearthed in a cemetery just beyond the *Tenemos* wall (Woolley 1982). The burials contained a treasure trove of grave goods, including lyres decorated with golden bull heads (Figure 7.11), gold and silver weapons, jewelry, and headdresses.

FIGURE 7.11   A lyre decorated with a golden bull's head from the royal tombs of Ur.

Most remarkable was the discovery that the royal personages were accompanied in death by an entourage of soldiers and retainers, in full regalia, along with wagons and oxen. One tomb contained seventy-four additional people, including four male guards, four female musicians, and sixty-four women of the royal court in ceremonial dress. Woolley and Mooney (1982) infer that many of the sacrificed attendants may have taken poison in a mass suicide ceremony as part of the royal funeral. Human sacrifice on this scale certainly attests to the strength of the religious system, as well as to the despotic power of the temple–palace complex. It makes the occasional human sacrifice associated with the Hawaiian temple cults seem almost trivial by comparison.

In Mesopotamian religion, the god *Utu* was the sun and the sun's numinous power, all at the same time. The gods thus represented the indwelling power of specific natural phenomena. Mesopotamian religion was highly **polytheistic** because there were a multitude of situations in which the numinous could be experienced. People could invoke numinous power by building temples and shrines as sacred dwellings for deities, by performing rituals, or by making images (Jacobsen 1976).

During the 4000-year span of Mesopotamian culture, three different metaphors of noumenal, supernatural power existed. The earliest and most persistent metaphor was of the immanent power of specific nature deities. By the Early Dynastic, gods began to be called "rulers," just as human rulers began to take power in the emerging city-states. By the second millennium BC, during the Old Babylonian period, personal gods began to appear who were concerned with the security of individuals.

The earliest Mesopotamian deities, as revealed in a series of engravings and lyric poems preserved in clay tablets, were nature gods concerned with fertility. Initially, these deities were depicted in the form of the natural objects they represented, but over time they were gradually given more human form. Prominent among them were the gods associated with specific cities and expressing the power of economically important natural resources, such as *Enki* the water god, *Nanshe* the fish goddess, and *Dumuzi*, who was concerned with livestock and the date palm. The most important annual rituals, no doubt performed at the temple, involved a sacred wedding, in which nature deities as bride and groom perpetuated the return of fertility in the spring and mourned the decline and death of fertility in the fall. The temple deity and associated storehouse were direct embodiments of nature's fertility.

By the third millennium BC, deities were referred to as "Lords" or "Masters" and mirrored the actions of human rulers. People were now impressed by the awe-inspiring energy and majesty of the noumenal beings, not simply their life-sustaining powers of fertility. The major city gods assumed new roles as spiritual estate managers, judges, and warriors. This sequence of development shows that religion, as part of a culture's **superstructure**, changes in response to changes in the **structure**, the social organization and political economy. This functional interconnection is further verified by the statistical association between the presence of high gods and hierarchical political structures found in an extensive sample of world cultures (Swanson 1960).

The new Mesopotamian deities obviously reflected the rising importance of political rulers in the emerging city-states of the Early Dynastic. For example, Jacobsen (1976) showed that *Ningirsu,* god of life-giving spring thunderstorms and floods and titular deity of the city of Girsu, was head of a twenty-one-deity pantheon of gods who staffed his temple and supervised his estate. Counted as deities were a high constable, a steward, a chamberlain, two musicians, seven handmaidens, a councilor, a secretary, two generals, two herdsmen, a plowman, a fisherman, and a general manager of natural resources. These deities had their human counterparts who directed human laborers in service to *Ningirsu.* Whereas the original nature deities had no functions beyond their immanent qualities, the new ruler-gods could make demands on people, and their wills were transmitted through dreams and signs that had to be interpreted by diviners.

The entire Mesopotamian cosmos was hierarchically arranged, with deities holding titles and

polytheism A religious system based on belief in many gods, or deities.

superstructure The mental, ideological, or belief systems, as expressed in the religion, myths, and rituals of a culture. According to Harris's cultural materialist theory, superstructure is shaped by the structure.

structure The social, economic, and political organization of a culture, which is shaped by the technological base, or infrastructure, according to Marvin Harris's cultural materialist theory.

offices. There were seven primary gods, who determined the fate of other gods and humans, and some fifty "great gods," along with a vast multitude of lesser deities, who collectively met as a formal assembly of gods. City deities such as *Ningirsu* served the higher-ranking deity *Enlil,* Lord of the Wind and primary executive god. The water god *Enki,* Lord of the Soil and Owner of the River, was credited not only with establishing the seasonal regime of the Tigris-Euphrates system but also with placing various deities in charge of a number of recognized occupational specialties such as farming, brickmaking, architecture, and weaving. *Enki* made *Utu,* the sun god and god of justice, responsible for boundary maintenance. Even the creation myths were brought in line with the realities of the political system. By the second millennium BC, the primary Mesopotamian creation epic, known as *Enuma Elish,* was a lengthy account of how the god *Marduk* became the permanent king of the universe and all the basic elements of the Mesopotamian cosmic politics were in place.

THE INCA EMPIRE IN THE LAND OF FOUR QUARTERS

The Inca were situated 3500 years later in time than the Ur III empire and 8500 miles away in a different hemisphere, but the two empires were remarkably similar in design and purpose. The Inca rulers commanded an empire of twice as many people as in Ur III, but most importantly, both empires were directed by royal dynastic families and noble aristocracies. Both empires were based on the concept of divine kingship, and both were four-ranked societies where 97 to 99 percent of the population labored at a bare subsistence level to provide luxury and security for a few special people at the top. Temples and rituals in both empires celebrated the cult of the divine king and legitimized totalitarian rule as part of nature.

Andean and Mesopotamian empires were both nonmarket, command political economies designed to extract resources from a subsistence-level commoner majority. Elite rulers directed development projects that intensified agricultural production, which was the basis of their wealth and power. State bureaucrats managed massive food surpluses, and directed specialists in the production of wealth objects that were exclusively disposed of by the aristocracy. Royals lived in palaces, surrounded themselves with hundreds and even thousands of military retainers, servants, wives, and concubines, and maintained vast private estates that they transmitted to their children. Like the Ur III emperors, the Inca lords lived luxuriously in a royal capital, but the Inca lived off tribute labor extracted from village commoners scattered over a vast territory, unlike the Mesopotamian nobility who extracted taxes primarily in grain and livestock or other goods. The Inca moved labor about to produce the food staples and wealth objects that they needed to support imperial religious institutions and their administrative bureaucracy. In apparent contrast to the Mesopotamian empire, most Andean villagers held land communally and were highly self-sufficient in basic subsistence.

The Inca organized some nine million people (Cook 1981:114) into the following four social ranks according to their differential access to religious power, natural resources, food, wealth objects, status, and control over other people: (1) a tiny super-elite of a few hundred royal households closely related to the emperor; (2) a noble elite of some 6000 distantly related Inca upper level administrators and non-Inca local rulers; (3) 60,000 lower level managers, and skilled specialists; and (4) two million commoner households from diverse ethnic groups, most working part-time for the state to pay their labor service tax. A few commoners were full-time, low-level, state workers supported by surpluses drawn from the Inca warehouses.

The Inca rulers integrated their vast imperial territory and population by appealing to a powerful ideology of common kinship and a shared participation in cults dedicated to the sun and moon, the divine king and queen, and diverse local shrines. Rulers portrayed their empire as a greatly extended, divincly ordained chiefdom where everyone was properly situated in ranked descent groups within a single giant genealogy, with the divine monarch at the top. Commoners were offered supernatural rewards and token material gifts in exchange for their labor tribute. This created the illusion of a fair reciprocal exchange, as if the empire was simply a very large egalitarian tribal society. However, the social reality was profoundly unequal.

Andean Environment and Prehistory

The Inca empire, which reached its peak between AD 1476 and 1532, was the last in a series of imperial cultures that developed independently in the Andean region of South America beginning approximately 4000 years ago (see Table 7.B and the box entitled "Before the Inca: Moche and Chimú Lords"). This last pre-Columbian empire extended over an area of some 380,000 square miles (mi^2) (984,000 square kilometers [km^2]), covering the Andean regions of modern Ecuador, Peru, Bolivia, and the northern Andes of Chile and Argentina (Figure 7.12). Estimates of its population range from 6 million to 32 million people. The Inca empire was a village-state that rivaled the Roman empire in scale, yet it was maintained without wheeled vehicles, writing, or draft animals by the effective mobilization of a vast labor force, within the framework of an elaborate bureaucracy that was ordered and sustained by a compelling religious system.

The dominant geographic feature of the Andean region is the Andean mountain chain. Because the Andes run north and south, they form a barrier to global winds and currents, blocking westward-flowing moisture from the Atlantic and creating one of the world's driest deserts in the rain shadow along the coast of Peru and Chile. A series of narrow, short valleys descend from the Andes to the Pacific and offer significant irrigation potential not unlike that offered by the Mesopotamian floodplain. An additional advantage of the Andean region is that the cold,

upwelling Peru current lifts rich nutrients toward the ocean surface from the deep offshore trench and thereby supports one of the world's richest marine fisheries. Unfortunately, during an unpredictable phenomenon called El Niño, the Peru current is replaced by warmer water that disrupts the ecosystem, destroying marine life and causing rains and flooding.

The bulk of the Andean population occupied the *altiplano,* the high plateau, at elevations from 12,000 feet (3658 m) to over 16,000 feet (4877 m). The mountains are an inhospitable place for farmers because soils are thin, freezes can occur at any time, and droughts are frequent. The treeless vegetation, called *puna,* supports only the hardiest grazers such as the native camelids, the guanaco and vicuña. Llamas and alpacas, domesticated members of the camel family, were valued for their meat and wool, and as pack animals they were capable of carrying up to 100 pounds (45 kg). Dried llama dung was an important fuel on the treeless *altiplano,* and, as fertilizer, it helped keep thin mountain soils productive. Another important domesticate, the guinea pig, lived on kitchen scraps and was eaten. The potato was the primary highland subsistence crop because it was highly nutritious, tolerated frost, was readily stored, and could be grown at elevations of up to 14,000 feet (4267 m). Andean farmers developed some 3000 varieties of potatoes, selecting for differing tuber qualities and environmental tolerances (Brush, Carney, and Huaman 1981). Another important early highland domesticate was quinoa, which also grows well under the harsh conditions of the *altiplano* and produces a protein-rich, grainlike seed. Some 200 varieties of quinoa were developed.

Inca cities were administrative centers, populated by bureaucrats and their servants, whose existence depended on sustaining a power network that extended throughout the Andean region. Why independent villagers would support the empire is difficult to explain, because the empire apparently gave them few material benefits. As in Mesopotamia, Andean civilization was an improbable development that depended on certain

For at least 6000 years Andean peoples were mobile foragers, hunting wild gua-
naco and vicuñas in the high mountains, and gathering plants and sea food on
the coast (Lanning 1967). Probably as an adjustment to postglacial environmental
changes by about 5000–6000 BP, foragers began to settle and domesticate potatoes, llamas and alpacas in the highlands (Wheeler 1984), and began living in
coastal fishing villages cultivating cotton and gourds. Chiefs may have successfully
organized the first large coastal settlements as early as 4000 BP, even before pottery was in use, or maize was cultivated (Mosely 1975, Quilter and Stocker 1983).
Rulers may have developed irrigated agriculture in desert river valleys by 3000 BP
in order to protect their power in response to warm El Niño ocean currents that
damaged the fisheries (Table 7.B).

The basic elements of the Andean cultural tradition were firmly in place 3000
years ago. These included state-level political organization, intensive agriculture
based on maize and potatoes, high-altitude llama pastoralism, monumental architecture, religious shrines, urban centers, and elaborate ceramics and textiles. Pre-
Inca Andean peoples were masters at metallurgy, weaving, and ceramics. Andean
peoples worked copper, gold, bronze, and silver, using a variety of techniques, including lost-wax casting, to produce elaborate jewelry and simple implements
(Figure 7.A). Textiles, including tapestry and embroidery, were highly developed
and, along with jewelry, became important markers of status.

The Inca elite were latecomers who followed cultural patterns, including bureaucratic forms of administration and details of technology and ideology practiced by their immediate predecessors, the rulers of the Moche (AD 100–700) and
Chimú kingdoms (AD 700–1465) on the north coast of Peru. Pre-Inca civilizations
are less well known than the older Mesopotamian civilizations, because they left
no writing, and their tombs were systematically looted over the centuries. Fortu-
itously, in 1987–1990 Peruvian archaeologists discovered three Moche royal

TABLE 7.B   ANDEAN PREHISTORY, 14,000 BP–AD 1532

AD 1476–1532	Inca empire
AD 1000–1476	Chimu state on north coast
AD 600–1000	Middle Horizon, Moche kingdom, Tiahuanaco, and Huari empires
1400–2200	Mochica and Nazca regional coastal states
2200–2800	Early Horizon; Chavin; metallurgy
2900–3500	Initial Ceramic period, city-states or advanced chiefdoms; ceramics, irrigation, population growth
3500–4000	Late (Cotton) Pre-Ceramic chiefdoms; maize, manioc
5000	Sedentary coastal fishing villages; domestic-scale farming of cotton, gourds, beans, squash
5800	Domesticated potatoes in highlands
6000	Domestic llamas and alpacas
6000–14,000	Mobile foragers and hunters

SOURCES: Burger and van der Merwe (1990), Lanning (1967), and Wheeler (1984).

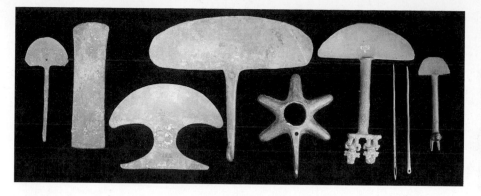

FIGURE 7.A Inca bronze tools and implements, which reveal that Andean peoples were accomplished metallurgists.

FIGURE 7.B Moche lord in full regalia, a reconstruction based on the remains found in the royal tombs of Sipán.

tombs with their treasures intact at the site of Sipán, near Chiclayo (Alva and Donnan 1993). These burials provide a remarkable glimpse of the material wealth that defined social power in the Andean world before the Inca. Tomb One contained a large wooden casket with the body of a high-ranking Moche warrior priest bundled together with an amazing array of wealth objects, including 1137 ceramic pots in a single offering cache. There were ten banners and a tunic covered with plates of gilded copper, six shell and copper-beaded pectorals and armbands, numerous gold nose and ear ornaments, finely wrought gold and silver necklaces, gold scepters, gold face masks, several gold and feathered headdress ornaments, ceremonial knives, silver back plates, and silver sandals (Figure 7.B).

The well-preserved Chimú capital city of Chan Chan may have had a population of 30,000 people, making it one of the largest cities in the pre-Columbian New World. The city was dominated by ten walled royal compounds built as residences for successive Chimú kings (Day 1982). Following the Andean custom of split inheritance, when a Chimú king died he retained his divine status, and was buried in his own compound with a treasure trove of wealth objects. The deceased king's compound and properties were managed by his close relatives as a religious shrine, and his political successor became the next divine king. Split inheritance kept wealth and power concentrated, but it also gave the new king an incentive to expand the scale of society to build a new estate. This custom was one of the driving forces behind the rapid growth of the Inca empire.

Each Chimú royal compound contained a palace, temples, tombs, courtyards, wells, control posts and audience chambers, and storehouses stocked with wealth objects. These were exclusive places, surrounded by adobe walls 9 meters tall, and up to 5 meters thick. Access into their interiors was through one narrow door and labyrinthine halls. The social inequality in Chan Chan resembled conditions in the Mesopotamian city of Ur and is apparent in the relative magnitude of residential structures. The royal compounds were as large as 221,000 square meters—1785 times larger than commoner houses. Lower-class specialist workers were crowded into small, unwalled compounds of only 125 square meters each, with limited access to water, and containing workshops rather than wealth-filled storehouses.

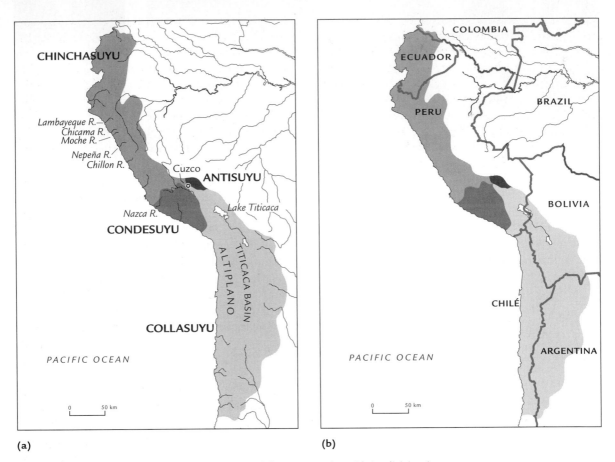

FIGURE 7.12 (*a*) Map of the Andean region and the Inca empire with its division into four quarters: Chinchasuyu, Antisuyu, Condesuyu, and Collasuyu; (*b*) map of the same region with today's nation's territories. (SOURCE: Figure 7.12a based on Conrad and Demarest 1984.)

environmental and cultural circumstances. The Andean cultural tradition was in place 3000 years ago. The cyclical record of state growth and collapse suggests that tribal agricultural village life, not the state, was the optimal human adaptation for the Andean world. Like their predecessors, the Inca were able briefly to exploit a particular combination of distinctive Andean cultural principles and an agricultural system based on a unique mix of domesticated crops and animals that could thrive in the harsh conditions of the high Andes.

Like the Hawaiian and Mesopotamian kings, Andean rulers expanded their social power by

asserting a symbolic connection between themselves, the fertility of nature, and the general well-being of society. They claimed to be divine kings with legitimate claims on all the land, resources, and labor within their reach. This was reflected in their control over monumental constructions, irrigation systems, and urban spaces. They also controlled the ritual calendar and the procurement and processing of crucial raw materials such as marine shells, copper, gold, and silver that symbolized their power. Aggrandizing Andean elites were able to construct empires by dominating existing trade routes, taking advantage of regional differences in the value of goods, manipulating cultural traditions of kinship reciprocity and religious belief, and exploiting diverse ethnic groups. The Inca rulers controlled access to raw materials such as gold, silver, and copper from the Andes, marine shells from Ecuador, and tropical plants such as coca from the Amazon. They used these goods to command labor and to convert them into even more valuable wealth objects in a seemingly endless cycle of self-reinforcing accumulation. The Andean elite used imperial military expansion to gain permanent control over the sources of the raw materials needed to produce the prestige goods and gifts that sustained their power. As in Mesopotamia, control over long-distance exchange systems allowed Inca rulers to steadily expand their individual personal imperia by accumulating exotic wealth objects and giving them to their political supporters. Those individuals who gained the most then used their wealth and political power to command large labor forces to build the large-scale terracing and irrigation projects, cities, roads, and temple complexes that allowed them to integrate a large-scale society.

One of the most important sources of Inca power was their monopoly over the exchange of Peruvian copper for shells of *Spondylus,* the thorny oyster, a marine mollusk from Ecuadorian coastal waters (Hornborg 2001:65–87, Paulsen 1974). The Inca called the *Spondylus* shell *mullu,* and made them into valuable beads. *Spondylus* shells were considered to be "daughters of the sea," symbolizing water and fertility, and they were food for the gods. *Spondylus* was also remarkable for its seasonal toxicity and because it appeared off the Peruvian coast only during El Niño events.

Trading Peruvian copper for Ecuadorean *Spondylus* shells was an unequal exchange that disproportionately benefitted the Inca, because the shells were symbolically more valuable to the Inca than were copper blades for the Ecuadoreans (Hornborg 2001:65–87). Ecuadorean elites used coppers as bridewealth and funerary valuables, whereas *Spondylus* helped the Inca elite accumulate wealth and command vast supplies

of corvée laborers for elite-directed work projects. Those who did the actual work of diving for shells, and mining and smelting copper got less than the elites who commanded their labor, because their labor was underpaid relative to the value of the goods to command more labor. The system was based on ritual and symbolic values that obscured the underlying material inequity and was designed by elites primarily to serve their personal needs for power.

The immediate beginnings of the Inca dynasty can be traced to a small Quechua-speaking chiefdom in the region of Cuzco in approximately AD 1200. The rapid expansion of the Inca empire, which began in 1438 under Pachacuti, joined together preexisting regional states, chiefdoms, and domestic-scale communities into a centrally managed system. The ultimate ideological foundation of the empire was the religious belief in the supreme divinity of the Inca ruler, who was the sun god personified. The Inca's identity with the sun had a literal reality, given the vast energy resources at the ruler's disposal in the form of enormous quantities of foodstuffs stored in state warehouses scattered throughout the empire. The Inca state also supported large numbers of full-time craft specialists, part-time corvée laborers, and military personnel. Over a 60-year period, the state financed innumerable monumental building projects, constructed and maintained a vast road network (Hyslop 1984), and developed large-scale agricultural projects. These impressive activities ultimately depended on maintaining the loyalty of villagers, who cared first and foremost about the day-to-day well-being of their domestic households.

Potatoes, Maize, and Gold: Foundations of the Empire

The material foundation of the Andean empire was in the hands of the self-sufficient villagers who operated a highly productive, intensive agricultural system based on communal land and complementary labor exchange. Without an effective subsistence sector, there would have been

TABLE 7.3   PRODUCTIVE ZONES IN THE ANDEAN VERTICAL ECONOMY

Zone	Altitude*	Subsistence Production
Puna— alpine	14,000+ feet (4267+ meters)	Grazing of llamas and alpacas on wet and frosty alpine pastures
Puna/Jalka— subalpine	11,000–14,000 feet (3353–4267 meters)	Potato cultivation in dry, frost-prone zones
Kichwa— temperate	7000–11,000 feet (2134–3353 meters)	Maize and beans
Tropical	Lowest	Tropical crops such as manioc, avocados, coca, and papayas

SOURCES: Brush (1976) and Murra (1972).
*Elevations of each zone vary from north to south in the Andes and are only approximate.

no part-time labor force to sustain the Inca elite. The community-level Andean agricultural system was a major achievement in which egalitarian villagers cooperated to increase agricultural production in an otherwise hostile environment by draining and ridging fields in low areas, terracing steep hillsides, and creating and maintaining irrigation canals. Community leaders managed a technically sophisticated sectoral fallow system in which each sector, or plot of land, was rotated through a 5–15-year production cycle of carefully selected annual crops and grazing fallow periods that maximized yield while maintaining long-term soil fertility. In successive years, specific crops were sequentially planted to take advantage of the particular qualities of a dozen or more distinct environmental zones that were available to the community. This system served everyone. Each household received enough land to sustain itself in exchange for participation in cooperative labor projects that collectively maintained the system (Hastorf 1993).

The highly successful village-level subsistence sector has been characterized as a vertical economy because households and villages exploited resources in different ecological zones at different elevations, rather than depending on trade or market exchanges. The extremely steep Andean topography often meant that several sharply dif-

ferent environments would be within a village's reach. Four major zones, in descending elevation order, produced grazing, potatoes, maize, or tropical crops (Table 7.3).

Andean political centralization is not explained by population pressure or the adaptive advantages of exchange, specialization, or irrigation management because these could be effectively handled by relatively egalitarian local communities without coercive hereditary rulers. Archaeological evidence suggests that ambitious local leaders shrewdly manipulated the power vacuum left by the collapse of the Huari and Tiahuanaco empires to increase their personal power, turning local intercommunity rivalries into aggressive conquest warfare. People were forced to move into large, fortified towns for defense, and they accepted increasingly centralized authority as the best of a bad bargain in a threatening world (Hastorf 1993).

Agricultural work was intensified when large, walled settlements had to be formed, but people resisted inequality. For example, during the century before the Inca conquerors arrived, all households in the fortified settlements of the Upper Mantaro valley had access to land and metal goods, and everyone farmed. Community leaders were distinguished only by their larger, wealthier households. For political centralization to emerge, preexisting Andean cultural principles, which fostered community balance, kinship reciprocity, and social equality, had to be subverted to first create and then perpetuate coercive power structures and elite privilege (Hastorf 1993).

The Inca state was a nonmarket political economy based on "supply on command" rather than the "supply and demand" of a market economy (La Lone 1982). The state economy was functionally divided into a staple economy and a wealth economy (D'Altroy and Earle 1985). The **staple economy** was concerned with the production and storage of potatoes and other primary foodstuffs to provision the army and the vast numbers of full-time state employees. Maize was an important crop used to brew *chicha* beer, which state officials provided to part-time laborers in ritual feasts in exchange for their labor (Murra 1960). The **wealth economy** involved the state-directed production of luxury goods such as gold and silver jewelry, featherwork, and fine textiles, which were status markers used to reward the ruling class. Gold symbolized the sun god and was a marker of the Inca nobility. Wealth objects also bought the loyalty of local village leaders turned Inca bureaucrats; these bureaucrats, backed by the coercive power of the Inca state and army, facilitated the extraction of the labor tax.

Under the Inca, specialized laborers in full-time service to the state were called *camayo (camayoc)*, with an additional designation to specify their duty. For example, there were *llama camayo*, who herded llamas; *coca camayo*, who raised coca; *chacara camayo*, who farmed; and *pukara camayo*, who garrisoned frontier fortresses (Rowe 1982). The *mitima (mitmaq)* were members of ethnic groups who were relocated as colonists to work on large-scale agricultural projects. Commoner women might also become *acllas*, or "chosen women," who worked full-time to produce high-status textiles known as *kumpi*. *Acllas* might also be married to the *yanacona*, commoners who served the nobility. Nonspecialist commoners were called *suyu runa*, "people of the quarter," and were subject to periodic labor service, known as the *mita*.

Royal Lineages and Chosen Women

The Inca empire was known as *Tawantinsuyu*, or the land of four parts. It was directed from the capital of Cuzco, at the center of the named quarters: *Antisuyu* covered the tropical lowlands; *Chinchasuyu*, the north coast and highlands; *Collasuyu*, present-day Bolivia; and *Condesuyu*, the south coast (Figure 7.12a). Each quarter was directed by a member of the royal family and was subdivided into provinces, also ruled by the nobility. The eighty or so provinces were further subdivided into paired *suyus*, or moieties, which were ranked as upper and lower, and contained *ayllus*, or localized kin-based groups. Territorial units were defined in part by the individual *huacas*, or cult shrines, for which they were responsible, reminiscent of how Australian aboriginal estate groups, or clans, were responsible for Dreamtime sacred sites. In theory, productive lands were owned by the Inca state, temples, and local communities. Much land was centrally administered, but, as in Mesopotamia, the line between temple and state was not always clear, and newly elevated local elites administered many locally controlled estates. The empire was apparently not as monolithic as it might appear.

Much of the rural population was also organized as a labor force into a formalized hierarchy of workers in units that were subdivided alternately into units of two and five. The largest unit was the *hunu*, which contained approximately 10,000 workers. It was divided into two units of 5000 called *piska* (five) *waranqa*. Each *piska waranqa* contained five *waranqa* units of 1000 workers. The *waranqa*, in turn, were divided into two units of 500 called *piska pachaka*, which, in turn, contained five *pachaka* units of 100 workers (Figure 7.13).

---

staple economy The state-controlled production, storage, and distribution of subsistence staples, such as potatoes and maize in the Inca case, to support nonfood-producing specialist groups and to provide emergency aid.

wealth economy The state-controlled production, storage, and distribution of wealth objects that support the status hierarchy.

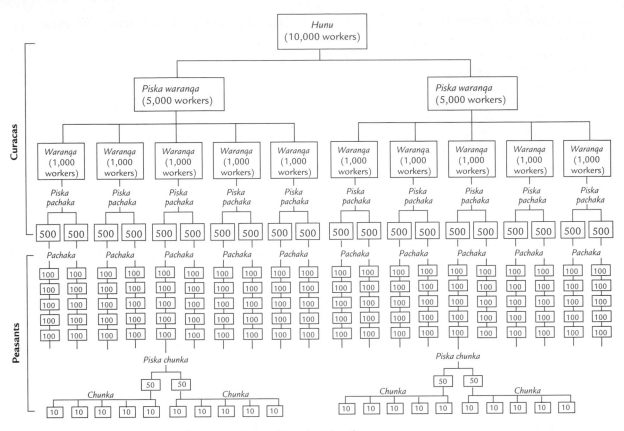

FIGURE 7.13   The Inca bureaucratic system of organizing the labor force.

This bureaucractic system was closely connected with the *quipu* recording system (see the box entitled "The *Quipu:* An Andean Information Storage System"). Decades after the Spanish conquest, local native leaders were still able to describe the system in detail, and the Spaniards immediately recognized its utility as a census and control mechanism.

Superimposed on the hierarchy of territories and labor units was a hierarchy of offices and social classes and a variety of named occupational specialties and ethnic groups. Social status was defined by a dress code and associated privileges and duties. The Inca god-king was personally sacred in the same way as the Hawaiian rulers. He likewise married a full sister and was the head of the *Capac Ayllu,* or Inca royal family, which consisted of a central patriline and nine ranked **cognatic lines,** or side branches, which were also designated *panaqa* (D'Altroy 2002:89–90). The members of the royal *ayllu* constituted the nobility, the highest social class, and were the most powerful officials in the bureaucracy. The Spaniards called them *Orejones,* or "big ears," because they were privileged to wear enormous gold earplugs and distinguished headgear. Their social status was finely ranked by genealogical distance from the Inca king.

The Inca bureaucracy sustained an amazing concentration of social power that primarily benefitted a tiny minority. Figure 7.14 shows the approximate number of individuals who would have occupied the various administrative positions in the system, and the number of taxpayers that they might have commanded at each level. Taxpayers commanded was only an indirect measure of social power, because the product of the *mita* tax was passed up the command chain. However, officials were materially rewarded by the emperor according to their position in the hierarchy. Goods produced by *mita* labor filled the Inca storehouses, and were ultimately distributed by the top Inca rulers. Central Andean Inca storehouses had the capacity to store 320,000 cubic yards (244,283 cubic meters) of goods (Levine 1992:139). The Inca used these vast resources to finance their military campaigns and to support their administrators and specialists, but they also diverted much of the surplus into their personal household establishments. The most visible evidence of private use of Inca wealth was the series of great family estates that stretched for 100 kilometers along the upper Urubamba-Vilcanota river valley from Machu Picchu to beyond Cuzco. The "city" of Machu Picchu (Figure 7.15) was actually only one of several private family retreats built by Pachakuti Inka. The primary estate of Inca Huayna Capac (AD 1493–1525) at Yucay is especially well documented (Niles 1999). It covered some 27 square kilometers of land, and included developed roads, bridges, agricultural terraces, special gardens, private hunting parks and lodge, a palace compound, and towns and housing for some 2000 support households. This project required construction parties of 150,000 workers, and included rerouting the Urubamaba River, filling in swamps, and removing hills (Niles 1999).

The Inca emperors commanded armies totaling perhaps 200,000 men (D'Altroy 2002:216–217), and used force to expand the empire and to make sure that everyone supported the system. Officials could impose severe punishments for offenders who committed forbidden acts (Moore 1958). They were especially concerned with theft, prescribing death for taking even small articles belonging to the Inca or the temples. Hunting in the Inca's game park, moving boundary markers, disobeying a *curaca* rank official, or fleeing from a work assignment, were all punishable by death. Poor job performance could bring public

whipping, or beating with stones. Traveling without permission, changing residence, or hiding from the census taker were all punishable offenses. Clearly, commoners paid a heavy cost in personal freedom for life under Inca rule.

According to the analysis of R. Tom Zuidema (1990), the marriage of the Inca king to his sister was a cultural statement that symbolically used kinship categories and marriage form to dramatize the hierarchical nature of Inca society. All those men within the royal *ayllu* in Cuzco who could claim descent from the Inca king belonged to *ayllus,* which were ranked in several ways. Descent was calculated back five generations to a mythical founding Inca king-ancestor, yielding a six-ranked generational system. The ruling Inca's direct line was considered to be a straight line, or *ceque,* and its members were most highly ranked, whereas those who belonged to a branch *ceque,* sister's-sons lines, were treated either as high-ranking "sons" with Inca mothers or as low-ranking "nephews" with non-Inca mothers. These categories may also be distinguished as "older" and "younger" sons, with older being superior. Men of the highest genealogical rank, and thus closest to the ruling Inca, were called lords and were associated with eagles; the most distant were called "skunks" and "stinkers," thus emphatically spelling out their relative social worth, even though they were all superior to commoners.

Depending on the genealogical depth of their closest link to the royal *ceque,* these men might be actual grandsons, great-grandsons, and so on of the founding Inca ruler. Those called nephews were the children of the Inca's dozens of secondary non-Inca wives. Sons became administrators over the upper moiety of Cuzco, and nephews were placed in charge of Cuzco's lower moiety. Sons were associated with ruling lords, and younger sons or nephews were servants or priests and sometimes played ritual feminine roles.

cognatic line A descent line that is traced to a common ancestor and that need not rely on exclusively male or female links.

The *Quipu:* An Andean Information Storage System

A social system as complex as the Inca empire required an effective system of information storage. Instead of writing, the Inca used a highly specialized information system based on bundles of knotted cord known as *quipus* (*quipu* means "knot" in Quechua), which closely paralleled the structure of the Incan bureaucracy as depicted in Figure 7.13. The *quipu* was a complex symbolic system of signs for recording statistical information by category of object. The signs were provided by a series of strings or cords, with multiple branches off the top and bottom of a central cord. Besides varying in position, individual pendant cords could vary in color, direction of twist, and ply. Even multicolored cords were used, such that hundreds of color combinations could be produced. Subsidiary cords could be attached at several places to create subcategories. Quantity was recorded using three different knot types and a decimal positional system employing a zero concept. *Quipus* were "written" to and "read" by a class of professionals known as *quipu camayo*, who must have resembled Mesopotamian scribes (Figure 7.C). The highly specialized knowledge involved in the use of the *quipus* has been described in detail by Marcia and Robert Ascher (1981).

The *quipu* is a good example of the many ways that cultures can be functionally integrated. The Aschers (1981) point out that *quipus* reflected many aspects of Inca aesthetics and other features of the culture that gave it a uniquely Inca ethos. For example, the Inca were concerned with spatial relationships, symmetry of pattern, portability of objects, methodical and repetitive design, and an overall conservatism, which can be seen in the Inca political system, architecture, ceramics, and textiles. On a much larger scale, the *ceque* system, which related *ayllu* social groups and *huaca* sacred places within a larger political whole, represented the same cultural reality.

A *quipu* might contain several thousand cords, but each cord occupied a specific place, oriented vertically along a horizontal axis. Like cloth, *quipus* were highly portable and based on spatial relationships. A *quipu* could be designed to

Who the men of the royal *ayllu* were permitted to marry revealed their rank along a continuum from extreme endogamy to maximum exogamy, with marriage to the closest kin demonstrating the highest rank. The marriage of the king to his sister represented the highest degree of endogamy and was reserved for the highest-ranking person. Marriage to a full sibling might seem maladaptive because of the possibility of genetic defects in the offspring, but such matings were not common. Furthermore, close inbreeding will also enhance beneficial traits. Individuals ranking immediately below the Inca were permitted to marry half-sisters and parallel cousins. Third-ranking individuals could marry cross-cousins. Finally, people more than five generational ranks removed from the ruling Inca married non-kin, thereby reflecting maximum exogamy.

Zuidema (1990) shows that women of the royal *ayllu* were placed in six ranked *aclla* (chosen women) categories based on age grades that were associated metaphorically with an invidious ranking based on physical appearance. These age–beauty ranks apparently corresponded to the genealogically based male ranks, such that women of high-ranking genealogical standing relative to

represent different levels of the Inca bureaucracy and could record the quantities of goods such as various types of cloth, crops, and animals that were moved and stored, as well as the numbers of soldiers and workers of different types. It was an ideal device for keeping track of *mita* service and goods stockpiled in storehouses.

The Aschers (1981) emphasize the close parallels between Sumerian writing and the *quipu* and argue that *quipu* makers were, in fact, writing. The *quipu* could be read verbally, and the act of tying knots was tactilely and visually comparable to using a stylus in clay or a pencil on paper. Furthermore, both systems recorded information in the service of the state.

FIGURE 7.C An Inca *quipu* specialist (*quipu camayo*) reporting to the Inca emperor as illustrated by Felipe Guaman Poma in 1613.
(SOURCE: Guaman Poma de Ayala, Felipe. 1980. El primer nueva corónica y buen gobierno. Mexico, D.F.: Siglo Veintiuno.)

the ruling Inca were assigned to high-ranking *aclla* age grades. Those women who, because of their genealogical rank, were assigned to the most prestigious *aclla* group at approximately 20–24 years of age were considered "most beautiful" and remained in that category for life. They were never supposed to speak to men and performed ritual services in the most sacred shrines. Women of lower genealogical rank were selected for lower-ranked *aclla* age grades as they grew older, and they carried out lower-level ritual duties. For example, the three lowest *aclla* grades were joined at ages 35, 40, and 50, and these women wove textiles of increasingly lower quality and social worth. At age 35, an *aclla* could make very fine cloth for ritual use in the most important *huacas,* whereas women who became *acllas* at 50 years of age were commoners who made the most ordinary textiles such as belts and bags.

Below the nobility were *curacas,* officials who were in charge of decimal units down to the *pichaka* (100s) level. These Inca appointees held positions that became hereditary offices. Leaders of lower-level units were commoners. The highest non-*curaca* status was that of *yanacona,* who worked as retainers to the nobility. Raised as

FIGURE 7.14   Distribution of Inca rulers by number of taxpayers, 1500 A.D.

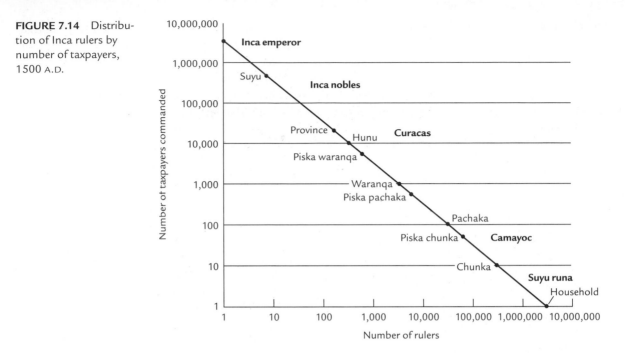

children in royal households, they were trained to become servants and attendants in the palaces and temples. Sometimes they were rewarded with *Orejon* status.

The decimal-based hierarchy was well suited for labor mobilization, which was a primary and self-serving state function. For example, if a *hunu* (10,000) level *curaca* needed to draft 1000 laborers, they could be readily assembled from the bottom up, if one man from the *chunka* (10) level was sent up the hierarchy. A typical labor assignment that was documented for four *waranqas* (4000 men) showed nearly half the men assigned to permanent assignments as *camayo* craft specialists, in the military service, and as *yanacona*. The other half served on rotating *mita* in the mines, on construction projects, and as soldiers and carriers (Julien 1982).

Inca Cosmology: The Universe Is Order and Sharing

The Inca bureaucracy was based on traditional Andean cosmology and conceptions of spatial order and reciprocity, of which the Inca rulers were quick to make use. The concept of four quarters still organizes the space around rural Andean villages (Urton 1981). Conceptually, the quarters are derived from the great cross in the sky formed by the Milky Way as it shifts its position relative to earth between 6 PM and 6 AM. This sky cross defines a center and divides the night sky into quarters that people imagine projecting to the ground. Each village contains its own center, called *chawpi* in Quechua, and the individual quarters, or *suyus,* are usually grouped into upper and lower divisions. Imaginary lines, like the descent lines, called *ceques,* radiate from the village center toward sacred points situated on the mountain skyline and along the way align with specific shrines or *huacas.*

Zuidema (1990) found that there were forty-two *ceques* in Cuzco, radiating as vectors or lines of sight toward the horizon as viewed from the main temple. There were 328 *huacas* located along the *ceque* lines. The *ceques* divided the province of Cuzco into territories, which were assigned to specific *ayllus, suyus,* and moieties.

FIGURE 7.15 View of the Inca "city" of Machu Picchu, which was actually a private family resort built by Pachakuti Inca (emperor from 1438 to 1471).

This system was integrated with a ritual calendar established by astronomical observations in which special rituals were performed sequentially at specific *huacas* on certain days of the year. The most important of these rituals concerned agricultural activities. The two most basic principles underlying the interaction among households within the village community and among households and nature and the Inca state were *ayni* (reciprocity) and *mita* (a turn or a share) (Earls and Silverblatt 1978). *Ayni* referred to the exchange of services between a variety of entities and was considered essential to the orderly operation of the cosmos. It applied to marriage ex-

changes, food and drink given for communal labor within the village, gifts of drink to the earth mother at harvest, and water cycling between earth and sky. Labor service to the state was also *ayni* and was rewarded by ritual *chicha* (maize beer) distributions. *Mita* added temporal order to *ayni*. *Mita* referred to crop rotation, calving seasons, human generations, and an individual's share in labor service to the state. *Ayni* and *mita* were thus ritually sanctioned as part of the natural order.

The divine right of the Inca to rule was supported by the Inca nobility's origin myth, which recounts how the first Incas conquered the indigenous

FIGURE 7.16 An Andean model of the place of people, culture, and the flow of energy in the cosmos, based on a plaque in the Inca temple in Cuzco. (SOURCE: Based on Earls and Silverblatt 1978.)

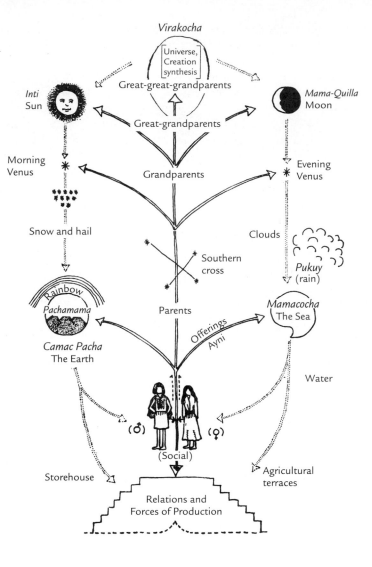

inhabitants of the valley of Cuzco. This event is commemorated in the annual rituals that mark the first planting of maize and the harvest. These elaborate ritual events were presided over by the Inca ruler himself and by the nobility. Because no one in the empire could plant or harvest before these rituals were performed, they gave the Inca effective power over nature, in effect naturalizing their rule (Bauer 1996).

Figure 7.16 presents a native view of Andean cosmology based on a representation appearing in the temple of the sun in Cuzco, the imperial capital. To provide ideological support for a supreme ruler, the Inca elevated the creator deity, *Virakocha,* and the celestial sun god, *Inti,* to dominant positions above the pantheon of local mountain, earth, and lake deities that connected local communities with their territories. The cosmological model employs the Andean concept of *yanantin,* or balanced oppositions, and presents a parallel hierarchy of divinities, showing male and female aspects. It clearly reflects the central elements of the state hierarchy, even to the detail of depicting *ayni* relationships and showing the state storehouse *(collqa),* terraced agricultural land, and a domestic couple as the foundation. This cosmological system shares some features with the Amazonian tribal cosmology (see Figure 3.14) discussed earlier, with which it is no doubt historically connected, but the Inca message is that giving labor to the state is part of the natural order.

Before the Inca took power, ordinary people in local communities had direct, gender specific access to the supernatural forces of nature. Parallel lines of men and women provided kinship access to the resources households needed to maintain and reproduce themselves (Silberblatt 1987). The goddesses and gods gave people their life, and people reciprocated by worship and sacrifice expressed in local shrines and cults. The goddess *Pachamama* was the earth mother, an embodiment of procreative forces equivalent to the Hawaiian god *Lono,* except that *Pachamama* was a female image of earthly regeneration. *Pachamama's* daughters were also goddesses and included *Saramama* (maiz), *Axomama* (potatoes), *Cocamama* (coca), *Coyamama* (metals), and *Sañumama* (clay). For example, *Saramama,* the mother of corn, was embodied in special stalks of corn that produced more ears than normal, or unusually well-formed ears of corn, or kernels of a unique color. Belief in the power of *Saramama* and associated practice was literally true in that venerating and replanting particular plants with outstanding qualities was genetic engineering that produced new varieties.

Gods of sky and mountains embodied masculine political forces. *Illapa, Intillapa, Chuquiilla, Catuilla,* god of thunder and lightning, provided rain, hail, clouds, and storms, and god of conquest. As embodied in political conquest, the thunder god, *Illapa,* was seen as the conquering hero ancestor of a dominant local chief and his descent group. Appropriately, male family heads maintained mountaintop shrines dedicated to Thunder. The ancestors of a local *curaca* were sons of *Illapa.* Mountain gods are still recognized in the southern Andes as *Wamanis,* where they accurately embody the natural forces that control springs and glacial meltwater.

Gods and goddesses were always defined in a particular context, or relative to other deities, acting in a dialectic. *Pachamama* paired with Thunder, *Illapa,* so that *Illapa's* rain could combine with *Pachamama's* fertility. Appropriate seasonal rituals and sacrifice helped fix respect for these supernatural deities in the community culture, and symbolized human reciprocity for the powers of nature. The Inca emperor made himself an embodiment of the sun god, *Inti,* redefined as the conquering god, like the Hawaiian war god *Kū. Inti* was symbolized by gold, "sweat of the sun." This kept the local chiefs in power, but made them subservient. Likewise, the emperor's wife became the embodiment of the moon goddess, *Mama-Quilla,* claiming control over water, fertility, and everything feminine. Like the association between *Inti* and gold, *Mama-Quilla* was symbolized by silver, "tears of the moon."

Huanaco Pampa: An Inca City

All elements of Inca society are shown diagrammatically in the layout of Huanaco Pampa, a representative Inca city (Figure 7.17). Huanaco Pampa was a planned city, built about AD 1475 as an administrative center. It covered 0.8 square miles (2 km^2) and was situated at an elevation of 12,471 feet (3801 m) in a prime potato-growing region. The city contained a special platform where the Inca ruler could lead public ceremonies, and a residence where he could be accommodated on royal visits. There were elite residences, barracks for rotating *mita* laborers, and great halls where they were entertained at ritual *chicha*-drinking feasts. The *aclla,* or chosen women, were securely sequestered within a walled compound (Morris and Thompson 1985). The city's primary function must have been warehousing great quantities of food, judging by the 30,065 cubic yards (yd^3) (23,000 m^3) of space in storehouses devoted to potatoes and

FIGURE 7.17 Layout of the Inca administrative city of Huanaco Pampa: a 0.8-square-mile (2-km^2) planned city at 12,471 feet (3801 m), built around 1475; the Spanish took over in 1539. It had 4000 structures and 10,000–15,000 residents. (SOURCE: Based on Morris and Thompson 1985.)

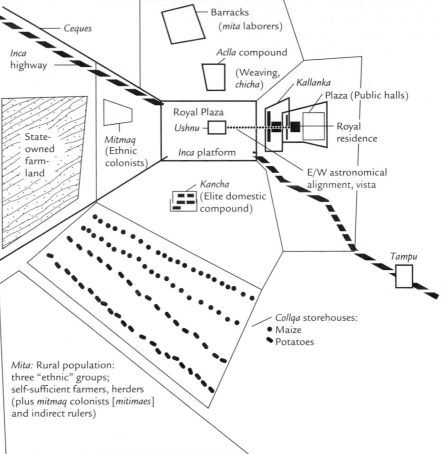

18,301 cubic yards (14,000 m^3) for maize. The potato storehouses alone could have supplied more than 50,000 workers a year with a pound (0.5 kg) of potatoes a day, which is more than the average daily consumption of potatoes by rural Andean peoples today (Orlove 1987). Additionally, the stored maize could have been used to brew vast quantities of *chicha* beer.

Some authorities consider food storage to be the most important functional advantage of state organization in the Andean region (D'Altroy and Earle 1985, Isbell 1978). The state storehouses could have served to average out environmentally determined fluctuations in food production, which occurred both seasonally and from year to year with *El Niño*–related events and unpredictable droughts and frosts. Large-scale storage might have raised the overall carrying capacity of the region. This food–energy averaging interpretation tends to support the redistributive social benefits theory of state origins, and many observers have described the Inca system as a great socialist welfare state. The Inca state could equally well be considered despotic and totalitarian because individual freedom was constrained by how wealth and power were distributed. The state moved whole communities at will and imposed a national language. The real advantage in expanding the scope of national control was that it increased the power of the privileged elite.

SUMMARY

The ancient agrarian civilizations examined in this chapter and in Chapters 8 through 10 demonstrate that elite-directed cultural development was neither natural nor inevitable. They were also not progressive societies, if progress is measured as widely shared improvements in human well-being. These civilizations were the outcome of particular decisions made by a few individuals who were uniquely positioned to take personal advantage of historical circumstances to advance their self-interest.

The most striking parallels between Mesopotamian and Andean civilizations is that both were despotic, four-ranked societies, ruled by divine kings who claimed control over the forces of nature and could demand unquestioned servitude from everyone. These imperial civilizations produced impressive artistic, architectural, and technical achievements, but their rulers perpetrated exploitation, oppression, and violence within their societies, and waged wars of aggression against neighboring peoples. These imperial cultures had highly productive economies that created tremendous wealth, but their rulers distributed economic benefits in extremely unjust ways that left the majority at or below the margins of subsistence. Social inequality was strongly demonstrated by differences in the size of household establishments. Such unequal outcomes reflect concentrated social power and suggest that these imperial cultures were indeed being directed by their principal beneficiaries. It seems reasonable to consider such cultures to be unjust, even if they were successful as cultures in the sense that people supported and reproduced the system. Rather than marveling at the impressive "achievements" of imperial societies, we might instead ask why they failed to serve human needs more broadly.

STUDY QUESTIONS

1. In what way is centralized political power a fundamental element of "civilization" as it is usually defined?
2. What are the most useful defining features of ancient agrarian civilizations?
3. Discuss the explanations that have been proposed to account for the gradual process of plant and animal domestication in the Near East.
4. What unique environmental circumstances or "crises" were implicated in the adoption of domestication, and the growth of urban centers, chiefdoms, and the state in ancient Mesopotamia?
5. Describe the role of religion in the early Mesopotamian city-state. Make specific comparisons with religion in the Inca state.
6. What was the role of record keeping, and how was it carried out in ancient Mesopotamia and in the Inca empire?
7. Distinguish between wealth economy and staple economy, and show how each operated in the Inca empire.
8. Compare Inca cosmology with the cosmologies of aboriginal Australia and tribal Amazonia, and interpret the differences in reference to social structure.

SUGGESTED READING

ALVA, WALTER AND CHRISTOPHER B. DONNAN. 1993. *Royal Tombs of Sipán.* Los Angeles: Fowler Museum of Cultural History, University of California. Describes the discovery and excavation of the best unlooted tombs known from Peru.

ASCHER, MARCIA, AND ROBERT A. ASCHER. 1981. *Code of the* Quipa: *Study in Media, Mathematics, and Culture.* Ann Arbor: University of Michigan Press. Explains how the *quipu* was used to encode information.

BAUER, BRIAN S. 1998. *The Sacred Landscape of the Inca: The Cusco Ceque System.* Austin: University of Texas Press. Monographic treatment of *huacas* and *ceques,* and their connection with the Inca royal descent groups.

D'ALTROY, TERRENCE N. 2002. *The Incas.* Oxford: Blackwell. A comprehensive overview of Inca civilization.

KRAMER, SAMUEL NOAH. 1967. *Cradle of Civilization.* New York: Time-Life Books. A well illustrated, popular description of Mesopotamian civilization by a respected scholar.

MORRIS, CRAIG, AND DONALD E. THOMPSON. 1985. *Huanaco Pampa: An Inca City and Its Hinterland.* London: Thames & Hudson. Uses archaeological analysis to describe an Inca city.

NILES, SUSAN A. 1999. *The Shape of Inca History: Narrative and Architecture in an Andean Empire.* Iowa City: University of Iowa Press. Provides a detailed view of Inca emperor Huayna Capac's estate at Yucay.

REDMAN, CHARLES L. 1978. *The Rise of Civilization: From Early Farmers to Urban Society in the Ancient Near East.* San Francisco: Freeman. Presents a complete overview of the origin of Mesopotamian civilization.

WOOLLEY, SIR LEONARD. 1982. *Ur "of the Chaldees."* London: Herbert Press. A detailed account of the royal tombs of Ur by the original discoverer.

8

Inside the Forbidden City, an Imperial palace-temple complex in Beijing.

The Chinese Great Tradition

Learning Objectives

After studying this chapter you should be able to do the following.

1. Compare the basic organization of Chinese civilization with the civilizations of ancient Mesopotamia, the Andes, and Hawaii, identifying parallel developments and points of contrast.

2. Explain how tribal leaders could use shamanism, clans, and lineages to transform tribes into chiefdoms and states and make themselves divine rulers.

3. Identify common patterns underlying the origin of chiefdoms and states in China, Mesopotamia, the Andes, and Hawaii.

4. Explain how religious, or moral, belief and practice helped the Chinese nobility integrate the empire, focusing specifically on the Confucian Great Tradition.

5. Distinguish between Great Tradition and Little Tradition cultures in China, referring to their respective distinctive features, and explain how and why each is reproduced. Relate each of these cultures to the hierarchy of urban places.

6. Describe how labor-intensive preindustrial Chinese agriculture was able to support 500 million people, making comparisons with capital-intensive U.S. production systems, and land-extensive shifting cultivation system in tribal Amazonia.

7. Describe the distribution of social power in village-level China in comparison with tribal villages, and explain why Chinese poverty might be attributed to exploitation rather than overpopulation.

8. Describe the formation and structure of Chinese families and households, and discuss how the dynamics of domestic life shape the relations between men and women, young and old.

In this chapter and Chapter 9, we will examine the great cultural traditions of China, India, and Islam. All are important area-study specializations that anthropology shares with history and geography. Because these cultures continue to shape the lives of well over half of the contemporary world's peoples, understanding them is essential to understanding world cultures. Traditional China is the largest imperial state to survive into the twentieth century on a preindustrial base. With a population that probably numbered 400 million people by 1850, China is a dramatic example of an empire based on moral authority and a superintensive agricultural system using human labor. Yet it was also the largest early literate civilization, with cities and a monetary economy continuously in place for more than 2000 years. Chinese villagers, as a taxpaying rural peasantry, provide a sharp contrast with the egalitarian, politically autonomous tribal villagers of Amazonia seen in Chapter 3.

THE CHINESE VILLAGE-STATE: MANDATE OF HEAVEN

In China, the elite-directed politicization process produced a village-state civilization, which began with the Shang dynasty, perhaps as early as 2000 BC, and continued with only minor change up to 1949, when the People's Republic was established. As with Andean civilization, under the village-state mode of production, the persistence of Chinese civilization required self-sufficient villagers to support the royal capital and the ruling class with taxes, tribute, and labor. The villagers did so in the belief that the divine monarch would, in turn, keep the cosmos in order, thus ensuring the good life in the villages. Chinese cities were political and ceremonial centers where the elites and their retainers lived. They were sustained by the labor and surplus production extracted from the villages. The Chinese state was thought to function like an enormous village based on patrilineages, ancestor worship, and kinship-based reciprocity. Village life revolved around subsis-

tence farming, the performance of rituals centered on nature deities and patrilineal ancestors, and the daily obligations of kinship and community. The ritual observances and sacrifices by the villagers were mirrored by similar rituals conducted in the royal capital for the benefit of the entire kingdom. Rulers were divinely appointed and held power as a "mandate from heaven" as long as they promoted village welfare and maintained order in the kingdom.

"Chinese" is not a single language, although there was a proto-Chinese common ancestor language. The predominant Chinese languages are all classified as Sino-Tibetan and are spoken by more than a billion people. Sino-Tibetan includes 8 modern Chinese languages and more than 200 other languages scattered throughout southern and eastern China, Tibet, the Himalayas, and Burma. (Japanese, Korean, and Mongolian are grouped in the Altaic language family, which also includes Turkish and Ainu [Ruhlen 1987].) The long use of a common writing system by speakers of related languages that are mutually unintelligible has led to the unfortunate use of the term *dialect* to refer to what are actually distinct languages. Chinese written characters are logographic—they refer to entire words and can retain their meaning with different pronunciation, in different languages. According to linguists, dialects must be mutually intelligible variations of a single language.

In China, the term *Han* is applied to all speakers of Chinese languages. Standard Chinese, or Mandarin, is spoken in northern China, and official Chinese is based on the Beijing dialect. All Sino-Tibetan languages are based on monosyllable words, and most are tonal—that is, the tone of a syllable constitutes a phonemic distinction, which makes a meaning difference in words.

The Nature of Early Chinese Civilization

China is a vast subcontinental area of 3.6 million square miles (mi^2) (9.5 million square kilometers [km^2]), approximately the same size as

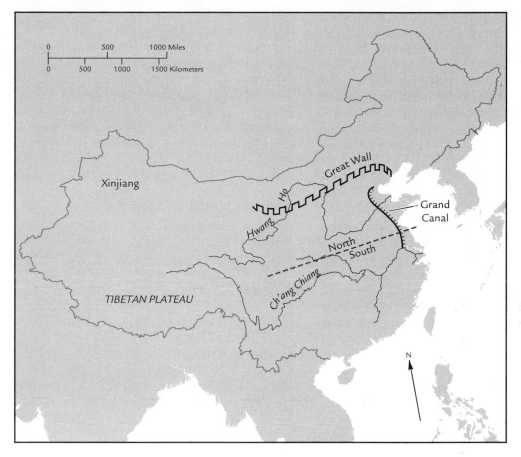

FIGURE 8.1   Map of the major rivers and regions of China.

the United States. In the south, China reaches into the tropics; in the north, it reaches the subarctic. Much of the eastern half of the country, including the Tibetan Plateau and the Xinjiang (Sinkiang) region, is mountainous, relatively barren, and inhospitable and will not be treated in this chapter. Eastern China is divided into a northern temperate zone and a southern subtropical zone, with a dividing line running midway between China's two great rivers, the Hwang Ho (Huang He), or Yellow River, in the north and the Ch'ang Chiang (Yangtze), or Long River, in the south (Figure 8.1). The great Chinese agrarian civilizations developed on the rich alluvial soils along the lower reaches of these two rivers,

primarily in the relatively flat plains and lake areas of the North China Plain at elevations below 650 feet (200 meters). The temperate Hwang Ho zone was the center of millet and wheat production, while the warmer and wetter Ch'ang Chiang tropical zone was the main rice-producing area. Collectively, these grains were the primary foods.

Marvin Harris (1988) characterizes traditional China as an agromanagerial state resembling the Inca state. The Chinese **peasantry** was

peasantry Village farmers who provide most of their own subsistence but who must pay taxes and are politically and often, to some extent, economically dependent on the central state government.

subject to large-scale conscript labor service but, in theory, received emergency aid from the state in times of scarcity. The peasantry was also subject to the local elite, who extracted taxes and rents. A contrast can be drawn between this type of peasantry and European **feudalism,** in which serfs were granted hereditary rights to use land in exchange for payment of rent and military service to local lords. Chinese peasants were potentially subject to exploitation by both local elites and the central government, although the peasant was allowed relative freedom to relocate and upward mobility was possible.

The institutionalization of **ancestor worship** by the Shang state had important consequences that helped set the future direction of Chinese civilization (Keightly 1990). With ancestor worship, the king was the central religious figure who served as his own priest, and the kingdom was in effect a **theocracy.** All lineage heads also worshiped their ancestors, and the whole kingdom was integrated as a single great politicoreligious family, leaving little room for conflicting loyalties. Ancestor worship, especially involving lavish mortuary gifts and human sacrifice, emphasized the permanence of the social hierarchy and kinship structure. There was no difference between the secular and the sacred, there was no ambiguity in the system, and everything was assumed to work as long as everyone followed their hierarchically structured kinship–ritual obligations. The virtual deification of the ruler in Chinese civilization closely resembled the status of rulers in the Ur III and Inca Empires, as well as in the Hawaiian kingdom.

Ancestor worship was thus a "strategic custom" that provided the foundation for the later elaboration of the concept of *hsiao,* or **filial piety.** In Mesopotamia, by contrast, there was a distinct priesthood, although temple and palace were not always in harmony, and the clan and lineage system was not institutionalized. Even though one can speak analytically of social classes in early China, the emic view of the social system was kinship-based, and the dominant

FIGURE 8.2   The Great Wall of China, constructed along the northern frontier during the Ch'in dynasty, 215 BC.

value was family harmony. This certainly must have minimized the potential for conflict that the grossly unequal flow of resources might otherwise have generated.

Wealth and power in the Chinese system derived from control of the labor force, as in Inca Peru. A vast conscript labor army was mobilized for the construction of the 1400-mile (2250 km) Great Wall along the northern boundary of China (Figure 8.2) during the Ch'in dynasty (approximately 215 BC). Significantly, the major river valleys run east and west and thus remain in broadly similar ecological zones, reducing the importance of trade and providing little incentive for the development of a merchant class (Keightly 1990). The Grand Canal, only one of many monumental water development projects, linked the Ch'ang Chiang in the south with the Hwang Ho in the north by AD 610, providing a major boost to trade.

Chinese cities contained temples and palaces and were walled like Mesopotamian cities, but there were important differences. Chinese cities were intentionally designed to symbolize the emperor's central position in the universe. The city was a great square, aligned with the four cardinal directions, with the palace in the center, presumably aligned with the North Star on the earth's central axis. The world was literally thought to pivot about the emperor (Wheatley 1971, Wright 1977). In contrast to the Mesopotamian city-state, Chinese cities were not economically self-sufficient, but depended on their immediate hinterlands for basic subsistence. They were not economic centers, but were designed to reproduce the political and ideological infrastructure.

The imperial system of Chinese government was an expansion of the earlier Shang system, and it remained in place with variations in detail until 1911, when the last emperor was removed from power. Historian Jack Dull (1990) distinguishes four stages in the development of Chinese government: patrimonial (1766–221 BC), meritocracy (221 BC–AD 220), aristocracy (220–906), and gentry (960–1911) (Table 8.1). Over the centuries, the political structure varied with cycles of civil war and conquest, with fluctuations in the strength of the central government versus regional kingdoms, and with shifts in the importance of local families. Important changes also occurred in the system of recruitment to political office. The patrimonial stage will be described in the next section using the Shang example. The rulers of the Chou dynasty, which overthrew the Shang, elaborated the concept of the mandate of heaven *(t'ien-ming)* as the formal legitimation of dynastic rule. Chou kings called themselves "The Son of Heaven" to emphasize that their rule was a mandate from heaven. This

led to the related concept of the "bad last emperor" because a dynasty could end only when the mandate of heaven was withdrawn due to the emperor's misconduct.

The Ch'in rulers, who ushered in imperial rule in 221 BC, called themselves *Huang-ti*, literally "august god" usually translated as "emperor" because their kings were not considered to be gods. The imperial bureaucracy under the Ch'in was territorially structured and more elaborate than the familial organization of the Shang, presumably because the former patrimonial system could not deal with the increased scale of empire. The emperor had three officials and nine ministers who ran the central government. The hinterland was divided into forty-two commanderies *(chun),* subdivided into prefectures *(hsien);* each territorial unit had an imperially appointed administrator, an inspector, and a police chief. Imperial officials were "outsiders," prohibited from operating within their home territories to minimize opportunities for corruption. Regional governments developed their own large bureaucracies with many positions that, in theory, were filled by local individuals who were promoted on the basis of merit; thus, this entire period was characterized as a meritocracy. The constant struggle against corruption led to the creation of provinces as a higher-level political unit, whose officials could oversee the commanderies.

During the aristocracy period, recruitment to the bureaucracy was dominated by membership in a nine-level hereditary hierarchy of social status.

feudalism A political system in which village farmers occupy lands owned by local lords to whom they owe loyalty, rent, and service.

ancestor worship A religious system based on reverence for specific ancestors and sometimes involving shrines, rituals, and sacrifice.

theocracy State government based on religious authority or divine guidance. The Chinese emperor was the highest civil and religious leader.

filial piety *Hsiao,* the ritual obligation of children to respect their ancestors, and especially the duty of sons to care for shrines of their patrilineal ancestors.

TABLE 8.1   CHINESE EMPIRES, 1766 BC–Present*

Modern China (AD 1912–)	1949–	People's Republic of China
	1912–1949	Republic of China
Gentry China (AD 960–1911)	1644–1911	Ch'ing dynasty: civil service exam abolished (1905); last Chinese monarchy
	1368–1644	Ming dynasty (Chinese rule)
	1272–1368	Yüan dynasty (Mongol rule)
	960–1279	Sung dynasty: civil service exam established; invention of movable type; Confucian-scholar officials
Aristocratic China (AD 220–906)	618–907	T'ang dynasty
	610	Great Canal built
	265–420	Tsin dynasty
Meritocratic China (221 BC–AD 220)		Han dynasty: paper invented (AD 105); Buddhism introduced (AD 65); Confucianism
	202 BC–AD 220	established as state orthodoxy (141–87 BC)
		Ch'in dynasty: imperial rule; hereditary rule abolished; written language standardized;
	221–206 BC	Great Wall built
Patrimonial China (1766–221 BC)		Chou dynasty: iron; cavalry; mandate of heaven established; written laws; era of Confucius (551–479), Mencius (371–289), Hzun Tzu (298–238); followed by Warring States (403–221)

SOURCES: Chang (1986) and Dull (1990).
*This is not an exhaustive list of all Chinese kingdoms and empires. Only the most prominent are included, corresponding to the major phases in political development. Precise dates used by different authorities do not always agree, and there are gaps in the sequence and in the historically overlapping empires.

Recruitment during the gentry period was based on the examination system, which became highly elaborated and allowed more social mobility than under the aristocracy. Prospective bureaucrats took highly competitive examinations in the Confucian classics. There were three exam levels: provincial, national, and imperial (palace). The system was potentially open to anyone who could gain admission to the government schools. Only two to three percent passed their preliminary exams and were permitted to take the palace exam; after passing the palace exam, the person was rewarded with entry to elite or gentry status and a position in the bureaucracy. The examination system, which was ultimately controlled by the emperor, reduced the potential conflicts be-

tween local aristocratic families and the central government and gave more people an interest in maintaining the system.

High Shamanism: The Emergence of the Shang Dynasty

The earliest Chinese states appeared by approximately 2000–1000 BC out of a Chinese co-tradition, or interaction sphere (see the box entitled "The Prehistoric Origins of Chinese Civilization"). Like the Andean cultural tradition, the Chinese co-tradition contained elements that are still prominent features of Chinese culture and directly preceded the first Chinese urban civilizations. In the politicization process, towns became administrative and ritual centers, chiefs became kings who founded dynasties, simple writing systems were developed, and the production of crafts and specialized wealth objects was greatly expanded. This was the beginning of the period of initial Chinese civilization, which historians refer to as the Three Dynasties—the semimythical Hsia, the Shang, and Chou.

Shang (1766–1045 BC) is the earliest well-described civilization of early dynastic China, thanks to extensive excavations carried out since 1928 by Chinese archaeologists at An-yang, a major Shang center north of the Hwang Ho in Henan (Honan) province (Figure 8.3). An-yang was a sprawling urban complex centered on a palace–temple complex of elaborate wooden buildings constructed on low platforms of stamped earth (Figure 8.4). The center was surrounded by residential areas, cemeteries, and specialized workshops (Chang 1980). The graves of nobles and commoners were clearly distinguished by the quality and abundance of grave goods. In addition, rank was indicated by the better quality of the dentition in higher-status individuals. This suggests that social stratification operated such that the nobility enjoyed better nutrition than commoners (Fried 1983).

One of the most spectacular aspects of An-yang was the royal cemetery where eleven Shang kings and their consorts were buried. The royal tombs were wood-lined pits, up to 59 by 52 feet (18 by 16 m) at the top and 98 feet (30 m) deep, which were entered by four long excavated ramps oriented to the four compass directions. It is estimated that some 7000 working days may have been required in their construction (Chang 1986), but even more labor was invested in the treasure trove of bronze and jade grave goods.

Most royal tombs were looted over the centuries, but in 1976 an unlooted tomb belonging to Fu Hao, wife of a Shang king, was found to contain 440 bronzes, 590 jades, and many other bone, stone, ivory, and ceramic objects, along with 16 human sacrifices and 6 dogs. Similar to royal tombs at Ur, the An-yang royal burials and palace foundations were often accompanied by human and animal sacrifices. Whole chariots with horses still in harness were buried. One An-yang tomb contained 111 human skulls, and more than 600 people were sacrificed in the construction of a single Shang building (Chang 1980). Such large-scale sacrifices clearly foreshadowed the recently uncovered 7000-man life-size terra-cotta army buried with the first Ch'in emperor about 210 BC (Figure 8.5).

Historians sometimes imply that early Chinese states evolved directly from tribes, suggesting a certain inevitability and naturalness to the process. However, tribes are not miniature states waiting to grow. Aggrandizing leaders must first transform tribal societies into small chiefdoms by persuading people to make them rulers and to accept hereditary social ranks and unequal access to resources. The archaeological record suggests that, in China, just as in Mesopotamia and the Andes, this politicization process occurred over a period of some 2000 years in only a few places and under unique circumstances.

The elite-directed transformation of tribes into chiefdoms and chiefdoms into expansive kingdoms changed conditions in the neighboring tribal world. The new rulers transformed tribal societies under their control into **ethnic groups,** freezing their boundaries, and imposing formal identities and cultural markers to make them easier to control. This imperial process changed formerly independent tribal peoples into peasants that retained distinctive linguistic or cultural characteristics. On the periphery of their territories, imperial rulers sometimes designated ethnically distinct "tribes" as political dependencies, allowing them to retain more autonomy than peasants. Such tribes were permitted to run their own village-level affairs, but they still paid taxes or tribute.

Even though Chinese urban civilization emerged some 1500 years later than Sumerian city-states,

ethnic group A dependent, culturally distinct population that forms part of a larger state or empire and that was formerly autonomous.

The Prehistoric Origins of Chinese Civilization

China is famous for the site of Zhoukoudian (Chou-k'ou-tien), west of Beijing (Peking), where fossils of the early hominid *Homo erectus*, dating to the Lower Paleolithic at approximately 1 million–200,000 BP (before the present), were discovered in the 1930s. *Homo erectus* began to look more like *Homo sapiens* beginning about 200,000 years ago (Table 8.A), and fully modern peoples were clearly present by at least 25,000 BP. The pre-Neolithic of China is not well known, but this Late Pleistocene–Early Holocene period from about 12,000 to 9000 BP seems to mirror some of the general trends seen in other parts of the world, with foraging peoples steadily intensifying their subsistence activities. This trend is suggested, for example, by the appearance of microlithic tools—small, thin pieces of sharp stone, often a fragment of a long blade, which may be mounted on a shaft.

Wild rice and millet, which became the foundation of Chinese civilization, are spread through a wide zone from the Ganges region of India to southern China. Millet, which includes several grasses producing small round seeds, was being cul-

TABLE 8.A   PREHISTORIC AND EARLY HISTORIC CHINA

BC	
2000–1000	Early Chinese States
	Writing 1400 BC
	Shang Dynasty (1766–1045 BC)
3000–2000	Lung-shan Culture, social stratification, complex chiefdoms, towns, metallurgy, ancestor cult
5000–3000	Yang-shao Culture, clans, lineages, ranking, simple chiefdoms
7000–5000	Regional Neolithic Cultures, early farming villages, ceramics
BP	
12,000–9000	Epipaleolithic, foragers, modern climate
50,000–12,000	Upper Paleolithic, modern *Homo sapiens*
200,000–50,000	Middle Paleolithic, archaic *Homo sapiens*
1 million to 200,000	Lower Paleolithic, *Homo erectus* in Zhoukoudian caves

SOURCE: Chang (1986).

urbanization in China apparently occurred independent of outside influences (Wheatley 1971). There was no colonial expansion from Mesopotamia into China that might have led to the founding of urban centers, nor was there any obvious borrowing leading to the introduction of economic, religious, or political influences from

Mesopotamia that might have indirectly stimulated cultural development. Borrowing can occur if the *idea* for some cultural trait, rather than its direct transfer, inspires its development in another culture.

The Chinese state was apparently constructed by political elites who gained control of the reli-

tivated in the Hwang Ho river basin by 6000 BC, and rice in the lower Ch'ang Chiang region by 5000 BC, only a few centuries after their Neolithic counterparts in the Near East. Domestication in East Asia may have followed a path similar to that of the Near East (Bellwood 1985). The wild ancestral rices and millets may have expanded during favorable climatic conditions in the Early Holocene. The availability of very rich and predictable resources may have encouraged mobile foragers to sedentarize, which resulted in gradual population growth. Subtle climatic changes might have threatened the natural supply of the wild grains and encouraged people to turn to intentional cultivation, selecting plants that produced larger, more numerous seeds that ripened at the same time and stuck together when harvested. This is the same process that probably occurred in the Middle East, as illustrated at Abu Hureya (see Table 7.2). T. T. Chang (1983) suggests that domestication may have occurred independently in China, at the limits of the natural range, where conditions would have been marginal and selection pressures most severe.

Early farming villages developed into seven regional cultures scattered throughout northern and southwestern China (Chang 1986). These apparently were tribal scale, basically egalitarian cultures, with a wide range of domesticates, including millet, pigs, dogs, chickens, and water buffalo. People used stone sickles, mortars and pestles, and ceramics, including a three-legged pot, or *ting,* which later became such a prominent shape in bronze. The period from approximately 5000 to 4000 BC was characterized by steadily increasing cultural complexity, growing diversification, and emerging social ranking, as in the Mesopotamian and Andean regions. Status differences in burials appear in the Yang-shao culture in the lower Hwang Ho plain suggesting that by 4000–2000 BC, simple chiefdoms had emerged. The larger mobilization of labor implied by the monumental constructions and craft specialization in Lung-shan and later Shang cultures suggests the transformation of simple chiefdoms into complex chiefdoms or small kingdoms. The expanding regional cultures had begun to influence one another such that a pan-Chinese culture could be distinguished on the basis of shared art styles, burial practices, and inferred common religious beliefs involving shamanism and ancestor worship. The best example of this period is the Lung-shan culture (3000–2000 BC), which showed the first bronze work, divination based on scapulimancy (divination using animal bones), elaborate burials, craft specialization, and large villages fortified with walls of stamped earth.

gious system and used it to increase their political power, creating self-reinforcing growth in wealth and power that allowed them to turn towns into cities, and expand a complex chiefdom into a kingdom (Chang 1983, 1986). This suggests that what people believed about the invisible world of the supernatural may have been more important politically than the technology that they used to make a living. Clearly, elites can use the superstructure of a culture to direct cultural growth and development.

The religious foundation of Chinese civilization can be called high shamanism because it was a direct elaboration of the shamanistic communication

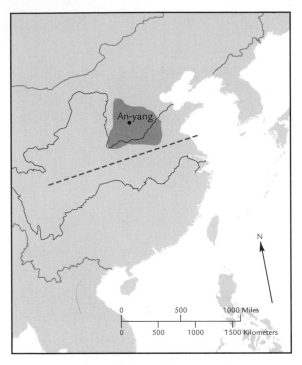

FIGURE 8.3   Map of Shang China, 1766–1045 BC.

with spirits that characterizes tribal cultures (Chang 1983, 1986). The official cosmologies of early dynastic China incorporated concepts of a stratified universe connected by a world tree, animal intermediaries, and transformations. The critical difference, however, was that unlike Amazonian or Australian shamanism, Chinese high shamanism involved highly exclusive communication with specific ancestors and deities who were sources of wisdom and supporters of the social hierarchy. Communication with the ancestors was by means of **scapulimancy,** which was conducted by full-time ritual specialists (see the box entitled "Early Chinese Scapulimancy").

This interpretation rejects theories of state formation that rely on economic determinants as prime movers. Early Chinese kings may not have gained their positions merely because they controlled irrigation systems, trade, or the means of production, or because certain social classes gained control over strategic subsistence resources. Chang notes that no significant change in Chinese agri-

culture preceded state formation. Bronze was an important technological innovation, but it was used to manufacture ritual paraphernalia, weapons, and chariots, which provided both religious and military support for elite political power. Early Chinese leaders succeeded in turning themselves into rulers by their skillful manipulation of both ideological and material systems.

Shang Society

At the center of the Shang social hierarchy was the king, who was a member of the royal lineage *(wang tsu),* within the ruling clan *(tsu),* a patrilineal descent group that was not strictly exogamous. In many ways, the Shang system shows striking parallels to the organization of the Inca royal *ayllus,* but the differences are obvious enough that no direct connections need be posited. The Shang royal lineage was apparently divided into ten ritual units named after the celestial signs naming the ten days of the week and structuring the ritual calendar (Chang 1980). These units were arranged in two groups between which the kingship alternated according to specific rules of succession, with the alternate group serving as the king's councilors. The royal court contained the king's many wives or consorts, princes, and at least twenty categories of titled officials, such as priest, prime minister, and diviner. The court and its dependents must have been large, because individual kings are known to have had up to 64 wives and 120 diviners (Chang 1980).

The political power of Shang rulers is shown by the standing armies of up to 10,000 men that they commanded, and there are reports of some 30,000 war captives being taken in a single campaign. The army was organized into 100-man foot companies, with three companies to a regiment, and chariot companies of 5 chariots and 15 men, with 5 companies to a squadron. Troops were armed with bows, bronze halberds, knives, and shields. Rural towns were also organized as militia units and could supply thousands more troops if needed. Military force was an important means of expanding the state and maintaining internal order.

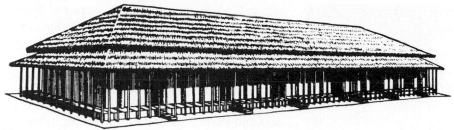

(a)

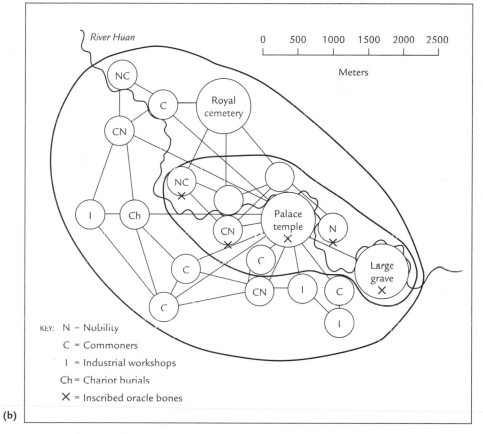

(b)

KEY: N = Nobility
       C = Commoners
       I = Industrial workshops
       Ch = Chariot burials
       X = Inscribed oracle bones

FIGURE 8.4   Shang civilization, early dynastic China (1766–1045 BC). (*a*) Reconstruction of a wooden palace building; (*b*) structural model of the An-yang urban network during the Shang dynasty. (SOURCE: Chang 1980:130, Figure 38.)

Law, in its formal sense (see the box entitled "The Law and the State"), supported the Shang social hierarchy, as in ancient Sumer, although no Shang law codes survive. Early historical texts referring to this period and fragmentary Shang records indicate that a well-developed court sys-tem must have existed. Subordinates were obli-gated to obey their rulers, and lawbreakers were

scapulimancy Divination by interpreting the pattern of cracks formed in heated animals' scapula or turtle shells.

FIGURE 8.5   A view of the life-sized ceramic troops buried as part of the royal tombs of the first emperor (Ch'in dynasty) over a unified China about 210 BC.

whole land. By means of his diviners and through proper ritual, prayer, and sacrifice, the king could persuade his dead ancestors to appeal to the high god on behalf of the whole community.

The status and prestige of Shang royalty was further affirmed by the symbols of royalty: banners, battle axes, and bronze pots of particular size and shape, bearing specific decorations and inscriptions. Royal objects were often decorated with stylized animals such as tigers, which reinforced the king's religious role, because animals also served as supernatural messengers in Shang mythology.

The Shang state, like the Inca empire, was divided into four quarters, oriented to the compass directions. Away from the capital, which was the political, economic, and ceremonial center, the hinterland population lived in walled towns *(yi)*, ruled by lords. The king claimed formal title to all the kingdom and was responsible for its welfare, but the lords personally managed it to maintain and increase the power of the royal lineage. New towns were centrally planned and built as a unit by ranked lords to whom the king granted a clan name, town land, a title, ancestor tablets, and appropriate ritual paraphernalia. The townspeople constituted the working class or peasantry *(ch'ung-jen)* and were organized into ranked patrilineages *(tsu)*. Because numerous pictographic lineage names depict various economic activities, lineages may have been occupationally specialized. War captives *(ch'iang)* were at the very bottom of the social pyramid (Figure 8.6) and served as laborers; they also were probably the primary source of human sacrifices, because divination records list more than 7400 such victims (Chang 1980).

Modern Chinese scholars, following Marxist terminology, often refer to Shang as a slave society, whereas Western writers refer to a "free" peasantry. Probably only the war captives were slaves in a formal sense, but the bulk of the population enjoyed few of the benefits of their own labor. Even their semisubterranean housing symbolically separated them from the elite, who resided on stamped-earth platforms.

harshly punished by various forms of shackling, mutilation, and execution. Rulers were obligated not to be too oppressive; if they failed, they faced supernatural punishments such as natural disasters or overthrow by a rival.

The underlying religious basis of the Shang state was the assumption that the king was the exclusive channel, via his personal ancestors, to *Ti*, the high god, who was responsible for the welfare of the entire population and the fertility of nature. The king was a key node in a supernatural communication network. He called himself "I, The One Man" or "I, The Unique One," assuming absolute power as the parental authority over the

Early Chinese Scapulimancy

The basic technique of divination by scapulimancy involves interpreting the pattern of cracks that develops in a heated piece of flat bone, such as a scapula or turtle plastron (lower shell). In Shang China, scapulimancy was used to guide the conduct of official business in the royal court and was carried out by specialists at the request of the king (Chang 1980). A royal representative would submit an official yes or no question to the diviner—for example, asking whether a proposed military campaign would be successful. The diviner would then apply heat to a specially polished, grooved, and notched bone, usually a turtle plastron or water buffalo scapula. The preparation helped direct the cracking into a center-line crack with intersecting side cracks. The angle of the side cracks and other details were then interpreted by an official prognosticator, who came up

FIGURE 8.A
Inscribed turtle plastron used in Chinese scapulimancy.

with an answer to the question. Each piece of cracked bone was inscribed by an official archivist with signs and pictographic characters, recording the date, name of the inquirer, question, answer, and final outcome (Figure 8.A). These bones were then archived for future reference. Some 100,000 inscribed oracle bones have been recovered from An-yang, and they have provided detailed insights into the organization of Shang society.

It is difficult to see what benefits, other than protection, the peasantry derived from the Shang state. Goods and services flowed to the center to support the army and the royal court, although some wealth returned as rewards to the lords ruling the towns. Writing was not concerned with recording economic transactions but dealt only with divination records and the identification of clans and lineages. There was no market system or trader class. Kinship obligations and religious duty were the primary foundations of the social structure, which basically resembled a large Hawaiian chiefdom.

Confucianism and Liturgical Government

Confucianism is a Western label for what the Chinese themselves referred to as *ju-chia,* "family of scholars." It is a scholarly tradition and moral order, based on the humanistic teachings of Confucius (K'ung-Fu-tzu, 551–479 BC). Confucianism was not a religion as such, but it became a virtual state cult because it advocated filial piety and perpetuation of the ritual and political traditions of the Chou dynasty, which was at the core of Chinese civilization.

Confucianism taught that social order was based on virtue that came from ritual performance, beginning with household-level ancestor worship and moving up the hierarchy to the emperor. Confucius—whose teachings were preserved in the "Analects"—and other major teachers who followed, such as Mencius (Meng-tzu, 371–289 BC) and Hzun Tzu (298–238 BC), sought to promote practical ideals of good government, citizenship, and domestic life that would preserve a stable system of social inequality.

The Law and the State

Law, if broadly defined as social control, is a universal (Hoebel 1968). However, significant differences exist between social control in tribal societies—where basic equality and low population density reduce internal conflict to levels that kinship roles can easily manage—and that in politically organized societies. Imperial societies face more difficulties. Anthropologist Leopold Pospisil (1972) identifies four attributes of law:

1. *Authority:* the ability to enforce a decision
2. *Intention:* the assumption that legal decisions will be applied universally
3. *Obligation:* specific rights and duties for different categories of people
4. *Sanction:* punishment for lawbreakers

These attributes can be recognized in the conflict-resolution mechanisms of some tribal societies. Law as a formal concept, however, is most appropriately applied to larger-scale, ranked-and-stratified societies and especially to politically organized states, where it serves a critical social-control function. States have courts, judges, and formally codified laws, which may be written. The authority of a king comes from his executioners, the palace guard, and the standing army. Legal codes specify what a ruler can demand of his subordinate subjects and what the subjects can expect from their rulers.

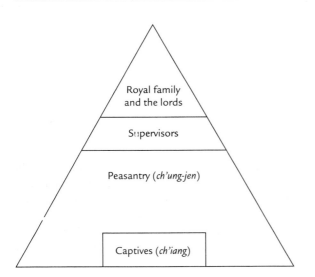

FIGURE 8.6 Social hierarchy of the Shang state.
(SOURCE: Chang 1980:231, Figure 60.)

Confucianism was institutionalized by 124 BC with the creation of an imperial university focused on the five classics:

1. The *I Ching,* "Book of Change," is concerned with divination according to the principles of Confucian ethics and yin-yang complementary oppositions.
2. The *Shu Ching,* "Book of Documents," spells out the ideals of statecraft to be followed by the "Sage King" and all bureaucrats.
3. The *Shih Ching,* "Book of Songs," contains Confucian poetry.
4. The *Li Chi,* "Book of Rites," specifies the formal duties and rituals between social classes, kin, and husbands and wives.
5. The *Ch'un-ch'iu,* "Spring and Autumn Annals," deals with dynastic history (Wei-ming 1990).

Confucianism constituted the Chinese **Great Tradition**—elite culture, or high culture—because it was propagated by the literate elite and was directly involved with official ritual and the maintenance of the bureaucracy. Under Confucian ideals, which remained important until modern times, Chinese society was divided into a class system that was very similar to that of Shang times, but increased population resulted in more extreme social inequality.

The Confucian Great Tradition represented the power of the emperor in the form of great

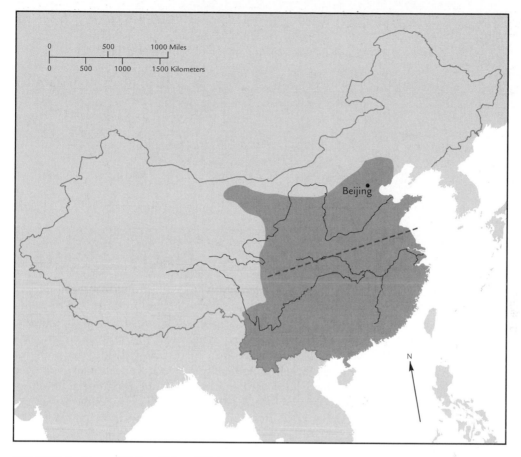

FIGURE 8.7   Map of Ch'ing China, 1900.

palaces, temples, rituals, literature, and artworks, which collectively must have inspired feelings of awe and subordination in the commoners. This elite culture, together with the literate and institutionalized elements of Taoism and Buddhism, receives most attention from Western historians and students of comparative religion, art, and literature. However, commoners, who constituted 98 percent of the population, were only passive participants in the Great Tradition; they also maintained their own **Little Tradition,** or popular culture. (The Chinese Little Tradition will be examined in the section on village life.)

By the end of the Ch'ing dynasty, under the Manchu rulers (AD 1644–911), some 700 people belonged to the emperor's clan at the top of the hierarchy (Figures 8.7 and 8.8). Perhaps 40,000 more were part of the formal administrative bureaucracy. Beneath this group were four social classes: (1) scholars *(shih),* (2) merchants *(shang),* (3) artisans *(kung),* and (4) farmers *(nung).* The 7.5 million or so scholar-bureaucrats were part of the privileged elite *(kwei)* gentry, who controlled local affairs and enjoyed many special privileges (Stover and Stover 1976).

Great Tradition   The culture of the elite in a state-organized society with a written tradition that is not fully shared by nonliterate, village-level commoners.

Little Tradition   Ritual beliefs and practices followed by nonliterate commoners, especially rural villagers who are part of a larger state-level society.

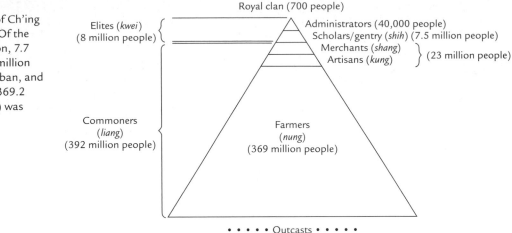

FIGURE 8.8

The structure of Ch'ing society, 1900. Of the total population, 7.7 percent (30.8 million people) was urban, and 92.3 percent (369.2 million people) was rural.

Royal clan (700 people)

Elites (*kwei*)
(8 million people)

Administrators (40,000 people)
Scholars/gentry (*shih*) (7.5 million people)
Merchants (*shang*)
Artisans (*kung*)   } (23 million people)

Commoners
(*liang*)
(392 million people)

Farmers
(*nung*)
(369 million people)

• • • • • Outcasts • • • • •

The elite were set apart by special dress and their rigid adherence to Confucian ideals, linguistic forms, and ritual. In all, elites and their families may have totaled 8 million by 1900, perhaps less than 2 percent of the total population (Michael 1964, Wolf 1969). Some authorities distinguish between three elite subgroups: (1) the upper gentry, who were entitled to formal offices in the bureaucracy, (2) scholars who did not qualify for high office, and (3) nonscholars who derived elite status from independent economic or political power (Eastman 1988).

The bulk of the population, which may have grown to some 400 million by the mid-nineteenth century, constituted the commoners *(liang)*, who were primarily farmers with very small landholdings. At the very bottom were outcasts, such as bandits and prostitutes.

Confucian concepts of formal ritual and etiquette, or *li*, regulated social conduct and helped people feel good about their social station. Leon Stover and Takeko Stover (1976) have characterized the Chinese system as **liturgical government,** or "culturalism," arguing that Confucianism created a form of moral nationalism that held the empire together in the absence of overt political or military force. According to the Stovers, the emperor occupied the ritual center of the world, where he held lavish state rituals and established

a formal ritual calendar. The emperor lived a leisurely life of conspicuous consumption, defining and legitimizing the cultural ideal for the elite. In this view, which was probably accurate only during certain historical periods, the emperor was a politically weak figurehead who supported himself from local tribute, the imperial monopoly on the Grand Canal connecting north and south China, the salt tax, and foreign trade. The emperor's primary political role was to award scholarly degrees and official appointments and to maintain overall peace and security.

The local nobility and elite had virtually full political and economic autonomy in the countryside. Because they earned only token salaries, they supported themselves by extracting taxes and rents from the peasantry. The provincial elite returned little material support to the center but acknowledged the superior status of the imperial court by following the centrally issued ritual calendar and by observing the *kowtow (k'ou-t'ou)*, or ritual prostration. Whenever an official received a message from the emperor, the official was required to bow to his knees three times, rapping his forehead against the floor three times for each bow. This was a small cost to pay to support a high culture that quieted the peasantry with the sayings of Mencius and Confucius that "inequalities are in the nature of things" (Mencius) and that one should "seek no happiness that does not pertain to your lot in life" (Confucius) (Stover and Stover 1976:166, 170).

The *Li Chi,* "Book of Rites"

The Confucian classic, the *Li Chi,* was compiled during the Han dynasty in the first century BC by Confucian scholars. It specified details of dress, diet, ritual, and interaction between all ranks, offices, and kinship categories. The Inca state was no doubt guided by a similar cultural code; however, in the Inca case, the details were part of the oral tradition and were not compiled in a formal book. The *Li Chi* provides a remarkable inside view of the the cultural minutiae of the Chinese Great Tradition. For example, for state rituals during the first month of spring, the *Li Chi* specifies the alignment of stars; the day names to be used; the deities, animals, and musical notes, numbers, and tastes; the temple room in which sacrifices are to be offered by the emperor; the bells on the royal carriage; the type of horse drawing the carriage; the color of flags on the carriage; the color of the emperor's robes; and the type of jade ornaments on his cap. According to the *Li Chi,* the emperor is also supposed to eat mutton and wheat from vessels carved to represent sprouting plants, during the first month of spring (Legge 1967).

In excruciating detail, the *Li Chi* prescribes deference behavior between officials of different rank. For example:

> All (officers) in attendance on the ruler let the sash hang down till their feet seemed to tread on the lower edge (of their skirt). Their chins projected like the eaves of a house, and their hands were clasped before them low down. Their eyes were directed downwards, and their ears were higher than their eyes. They saw (the ruler) from his girdle up to his collar. They listened to him with their ears turned to the left. (Legge 1967, vol. 2:17 [Bk. 11, sec. 3, pt. 1])

The respective contributions of individuals, families, officials, and the emperor to harmony are described as follows:

> When the four limbs are all well proportioned, and the skin is smooth and full, the individual is in good condition. When there is generous affection between father and son, harmony between brothers, and happy union between husband and wife, the family is in good condition. When the great ministers are observant of the laws, the smaller ministers pure, officers and their duties kept in their regular relations and the ruler and his ministers are correctly helpful to one another, the state is in good condition. When the son of Heaven [the emperor] moves in his virtue as a chariot, with music as his driver, while all the princes conduct their mutual intercourse according to the rules of propriety *[Li],* the great officers maintain the order between them according to the laws, inferior officers complete one another by their good faith, and the common people guard one another with a spirit of harmony, all under the sky is in good condition. All this produces what we call (the state of) great mutual consideration (and harmony). (Legge 1967, vol. 1:390–391 [Bk. 7, sec. 13])

When everyone does their duty, the living are fed, the dead are properly buried, and the ancestral spirits are taken care of.

Taoism and Buddhism

Taoism and Buddhism are other important religious and philosophical systems that were part of the Chinese Great Tradition. Both had literate components and shared many elements with Confucianism, but they did not enjoy the official support the state gave Confucianism.

Most prominently, Taoism shares with Confucianism a concern with the *tao,* or "way," which could be identified with the "way of heaven" and all the cosmic forces, as well as with one's social and ritual duty. However, unlike Confucianism, which is strongly secular, Taoism is a mystical religious system that appealed to disaffected commoners and contained messianic elements that sometimes mobilized the peasantry to oppose the

liturgical government The use of ritually prescribed interpersonal relations and religious, moral authority as a primary means of social control in a state-level society.

established political order. Taoism traces its origins to Lao-tzu (Lao-tze), a religious sage and contemporary of Confucius, who wrote the primary sacred text of Taoism, the *Tao-te Ching.* As a formal religious institution, Taoism has its saints and divinities, diverse sects and schools, and is represented in temples throughout China. There are full-time Taoist priests, who are celibate and live in monasteries. Taoist thought has been an important influence on both Confucianism and folk religion.

Buddhism reached China from India by AD 65, during the Han dynasty, and simply added another literate temple-monastic system and enriched the Chinese pantheon. It ultimately shaped the Taoist and Confucianist traditions and was absorbed into the folk religion, adding concepts of hell, sin, *karma,* and judgment.

DAILY LIFE IN VILLAGE CHINA

Farmers of Forty Centuries

U.S. Department of Agriculture soil scientist and agriculture professor F. H. King (1911) visited China and Japan during the first decade of the twentieth century to learn how these "farmers of forty centuries" could support dense populations and still maintain soil fertility after so many years of permanent agriculture. King found that Chinese farmlands were being cultivated so intensively that they directly supported 1783 people, 212 cattle or oxen, and 399 pigs per 1 square mile (2.6 km²), nearly thirty times the comparable human density for the United States at that time. He attributed the success of Chinese agriculture to favorable climate and soils and choice of crops, along with labor-intensive multicropping, intertilling, and terracing and highly efficient use of water and organic fertilizer. He estimated that some 200,000 miles (321,800 km) of major canals supported rice cultivation. Soil fertility was maintained by composting, reclamation of canal mud, manuring, and extensive application of night soil,

or human waste. Soil and subsoil were sometimes carried to the village to be mixed with compost and then returned to the field. King credited the Chinese with judiciously rotating legumes in their gardens to improve fertility, even though Western scientists failed to understand their nitrogen-fixing role until 1888. Most of all, King was impressed with the Chinese economy of resource use:

> Almost every foot of land is made to contribute material for food, fuel or fabric. Everything which can be made edible serves as food for man or domestic animals. Whatever cannot be eaten or worn is used for fuel. The wastes of the body, of fuel and of fabric worn beyond other use are taken back to the field; before doing so they are housed against waste from weather, compounded with intelligence and forethought and patiently labored with through one, three or even six months, to bring them into the most efficient form to serve as manure for the soil or as feed for the crop. (1911:13)

Prerevolutionary China's 500 million people were supported by very small farms, usually of less than 5 acres (2 hectares), which were concentrated on just 8 percent of the land. As the Stovers (1976) noted, the Chinese agricultural strategy was to apply human labor intensively to the lands that would yield the greatest return per acre. They argued that, in a sense, Chinese agriculture was a capital-maintaining, labor-absorbing, intensive hand-gardening system, in which the real crop was human beings. People were produced in the smallest possible space at the lowest energy cost.

In parts of southwest China where the population is low, rice is grown by shifting cultivation in clearings in forested uplands. Rice seeds can also be broadcast onto plowed fields, but the highest yields are obtained when seedlings are grown in nurseries and transplanted by hand into specially prepared diked fields (Figure 8.9). This is very intensive and highly skilled work. Carefully regulated irrigated flows of river water maintain a delicate ecosystem with the essential nutrients, fungi, and bacteria that produce maximum rice yields. Although transplanted rice brings the highest returns, it requires large, precisely

FIGURE 8.9
Chinese wet-rice agriculture, a highly labor-intensive system that produces enormous per-acre yields on a sustainable basis.

timed labor inputs for uprooting seedlings, replanting, and harvest and thus is impractical unless population is high and landholdings small (Hanks 1972). I have observed intensive rice replanting in the Philippines by wage laborers on vast commercial estates using chemical inputs, as well as by tribal Ifugao villagers on steep hillsides. The Philippine Ifugao fully appreciated the ecological complexity of their terraced paddy system. Given an appropriate labor force and small landholdings, villagers do not consider capital-intensive technological innovations such as mechanization to be an advantage. Thus, not surprisingly, virtually all of the seventy-seven farm implements described in traditional Chinese agricultural manuals published since AD 1313 were still in use in the mid-twentieth century (Perkins 1969).

The productivity of labor-intensive Chinese agriculture is remarkable. In 1940, researchers investigated a village of 611 people, which they called Luts'un, in central Yunnan province in south China (Fei and Chang 1945). They found that when multi-cropped, a standard 2688-square-foot (250-m^2) unit of land (called a *kung*) pro-

duced 821 pounds (372 kilograms [kg]) of rice and beans per year, yielding approximately 1.147 million kilocalories (kcal) of food. This assumed good-quality land and an input of 152 hours of human labor (Table 8.3). This is more than 60 times the per-acre productivity from industrially grown American rice in 1975, which required enormous inputs of chemical fertilizers, pesticides, and fossil fuels. The Chinese production system yielded a return of 50 kilocalories of food energy for each kilocalorie of human labor expended, whereas the American rice was grown at an energy deficit because of the energy cost of the fossil fuels expended.

The Chinese subsistence system is effective because it makes limited use of draft animals or animal protein (Stover and Stover 1976). The Chinese diet is typically vegetarian, with only 2–3 percent of the caloric intake derived from meat (Eastman 1988). Only chickens, ducks, and pigs, which are scavengers, are raised to be consumed. They can also be fed rice hulls and bean stalks, whereas large draft animals are costly to feed, especially if valuable cropland is devoted

TABLE 8.3   THE PRODUCTIVITY OF CHINESE INTENSIVE AGRICULTURE (KCAL/*KUNG*/YEAR), LUTS'UN, KUNMING, 1940

	Picuals	kg/year	kcal/kg	Total kcal
Rice, hulled	3.8	192	3600	691,200
Broad beans	2.6	130	3380	439,400
Green beans	1.0	50	320	16,000

Total kcal produced: 1,146,600
Input: 20.3 days × 7.5 hours × 150 kcal = 22,837
Output–input ratio: 50.2 to 1

Comparison with U.S. Rice Production

	kg/Acre	kcal/Acre
U.S., 1975		
Hulled rice	828	298,080
Luts'un, 1940		
Multicrop	5952	18,345,600

SOURCE: Fei and Chang (1945:70, Table 12).
NOTES: The caloric value of "waste" by-products such as bean stalks, rice hulls, and straw, which are used as animal feeds, are not included. 1 *picual* = 50.1 kg; 1 *kung* = 250 m² of land, 40 *kung* = 1 hectare, 16 *kung* = 1 acre; 1 *kung* of labor = 1 person day of labor, 7.5 hours; 1 hour of labor = 150 kcal expended.

to raising animal food. In some areas, fish ponds were also a significant source of food.

Immiseration, Overpopulation, and Exploitation

With periodic wars and famines, the population of China fluctuated between 30 and 60 million people during most of the first millennium AD, jumping to 100 million by AD 1100, then moving steadily upward (Figure 8.10). The most dramatic change was the fivefold increase that began after 1400, during the Ming dynasty, and approached 500 million by the end of the Ch'ing dynasty in 1911. By 1975, China's population reached 800 million, and, by 1990, it exceeded 1 billion. Several factors have been proposed to explain the Ming–Ch'ing increases, including a prolonged period of peace and stability; improvements in health, such as the development of smallpox vaccinations in the sixteenth century; the introduction of new food crops from the Americas; and a

global warming trend that improved agricultural conditions (Eastman 1988).

Although population growth had fundamentally changed the scale of Chinese society by 1900, the culture remained basically the same, and many observers argued that the Chinese peasantry was undergoing a steady Malthusian **immiseration,** or impoverishment. The English demographer Thomas Malthus (1766–1834) theorized in his famous *Essay on the Principle of Population* ([1798] 1895) that populations naturally increased faster than their food supply and were limited by the misery that ensued when poverty set in. However, the Chinese case demonstrates that cultural factors significantly shaped how Malthusian pressures were felt. By 1900, China's population was ten times larger than during the 2000-year period between 1000 BC and AD 1000, when the basic cultural system of a stratified, agrarian state was established, with a ranked bureaucracy extracting taxes, rents, and labor from the peasantry.

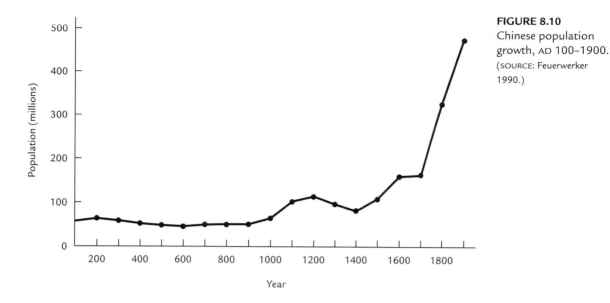

FIGURE 8.10
Chinese population growth, AD 100–1900. (SOURCE: Feuerwerker 1990.)

Large-scale migration out of the lower Hwang Ho and Ch'ang Chiang floodplains, as well as further agricultural intensification during the Ch'ing dynasty, helped the standard of living keep up with population growth. Pioneer expansion into the forested and hilly autonomous tribal areas of south and central China, and into Taiwan and Manchuria, accounted for a significant portion of the population increase. Large-scale deforestation and erosion accompanied this expansion, resulting in drastic changes in the Chinese landscape. Farmers tended to cultivate smaller plots more intensively. Maize, potatoes, and sweet potatoes from the New World complemented existing crops and certainly increased productivity. The fragmentation of plots was accelerated by the Chinese practice of giving each son an equal division of the family land. There were also incentives for population growth. Patriliny and ancestor worship provided strong cultural reasons for having sons; indeed, Confucian ideals stressed the importance of maintaining the lineage. Furthermore, agricultural intensification depended on greater and greater inputs of human labor, as discussed previously.

It is difficult to demonstrate the extent to which conditions for the peasantry deteriorated significantly with population increase. Albert Feuerwerker (1990) argues that per-capita economic productivity peaked during the Sung dynasty (AD 1000) and that there was no significant change in the basic standard of living until after 1900, despite population increase. However, other researchers point to a steady reduction in the urban proportion of the population and the increasing fragmentation of land as evidence of overpopulation (Chao 1986). Kang Chao also argues that population growth prevented an early industrial revolution in China, even though China in AD 1000 was technologically more advanced than Europe, because there was no incentive to produce labor-saving machinery.

Lloyd Eastman (1988) suggests that immiseration was a myth because the lot of the peasantry had always been poor, although conditions

---

immiseration Malthusian impoverishment, a declining standard of living attributed to continuous population growth on a limited-resource base.

reached a low during the political and economic upheavals of the 1930s and 1940s. However, the fact that the population continued to increase suggests that, contrary to Malthusian predictions, conditions did not become absolutely intolerable. Perhaps the most important factor underlying the pervasive impoverishment of the peasantry was the operation of a highly nonegalitarian market economy in which most of the population were subsistence farmers. The class structure in which a small elite controlled most of the best farmland kept the poorest classes at a permanent disadvantage. Peasants paid rent even to use "communally" owned clan land, and privately owned plots were often only tiny inheritances. Cash cropping to pay for land was risky and could undercut subsistence production.

The extent of social inequality at the household level in village China by 1940 is clearly shown in the data collected by Hsiao-Tung Fei and Chih-I Chang (1945), which revealed three social classes in the village of Luts'un. At the top was a landowning leisured class that managed its land to produce enough subsistence and cash crops to ensure a minimum standard of living for the least effort. Men in this group often refused to engage in any agricultural labor and spent their time relaxing and smoking. The "middle" class was composed of owner-tenants who had to rent additional land to farm in order to produce a slim subsistence margin. At the bottom was the landless class—those who had to survive by hiring out their labor and purchasing basic necessities. In Luts'un, 41 percent of the farmland was owned by 15 percent of the households, and 31 percent of the households were completely landless. Nearly half of these nonlandowning households were too poor to even rent land. The distribution of rich and poor in Luts'un was the opposite of that seen among East African cattle herders and mirrored the inequalities in the imperial society, but with a much smaller gap between rich and poor.

Energetics analysis (comparing annual input and output ratios, and energy flow patterns between a modest landowning household in Luts'un

village and a landless household) dramatically illustrates the physical dimensions of this social stratification (Bodley 1981b). The sample households differed in size, with five individuals in the landholding family and only two in the landless household. The landowning household controlled only 27 *kung* (1.6 acres [0.65 hectares]), which placed it in the lower range of the landowning class, but it still enjoyed a comfortable standard of living. When the caloric value of rice was used as a cash equivalent, the landed household showed a potential per-capita food consumption five times that of the landless household. On a per-capita basis, it also consumed more than four times the goods and produced at more than twice the energy efficiency of the landless household. The wealthy household had enough savings to last it for one year and was able to support pigs with its garden waste. The poor household was able to purchase only enough rice to meet its minimal caloric requirements and had difficulty meeting its protein needs. There was little left over for housing, clothing, fuel, or medical needs. Significantly, the poor household paid enough in rent and taxes to support two additional people, and this was actually more than was paid by the wealthy household. Inequality of this magnitude could not have existed in an unstratified tribal village.

It would seem appropriate to call the Chinese system exploitative, at least by late Ch'ing times, if *exploitation* is defined as the unjust or improper use of a person for someone else's benefit. In Marvin Harris' (1988) view, exploitation exists if the lower class is deprived of basic necessities relative to the upper class and if the upper class derives luxuries from the lower class yet refuses to redistribute its wealth. By this definition, exploitation was probably a frequent social problem in Chinese civilization. Confucian teaching explicitly condemned such abuse of the peasantry because it was not good government, and Buddhist and Taoist sages spoke against it. However, inequities of wealth and power were inherent features of the Chinese state. Whether the Chinese peasantry conceived of themselves as an oppressed social class in an emic sense is another matter. From a social scientist's etic perspective, social classes existed in China for at least 4000 years, but the powerful ideology of ancestor cults and Confucianism made such inequality seem part of the natural order of things. Furthermore, the examination system always held open the possibility of upward mobility.

The Chinese Village System

The daily life of the Chinese peasantry was centered on the highly self-sufficient village, which probably contained an average of 400–500 people, approximately the same number as in Australian "tribes" or the largest Amazonian village communities. Unlike these tribal societies, which maintained essentially horizontal interaction links with structurally similar neighbors, however, Chinese villages were the lowest rural units in an organizational hierarchy ultimately linking them to the imperial center. This system of social, economic, ritual, and political ties linking the literate elites of the Great Tradition and the peasantry of the Little Tradition has been called the **folk-urban continuum** (Redfield 1941). Cultural elements of the Great Tradition are most prominent in the urban capitals and decline steadily as one moves toward smaller towns and villages, where the Little Tradition becomes strongest.

In China, G. William Skinner (1964) found that villages group themselves around local centers, which he calls standard market towns, in order to most efficiently exchange their produce for the limited range of goods and services that they cannot produce themselves. Villagers were usually self-sufficient in food, but they purchased such items as lamp oil, candles, incense, needles, soap, and matches and occasionally made use of blacksmiths, coffin makers, medical practitioners, scribes, and ritual specialists.

Skinner (1964) found that an average of eighteen villages were arranged about a standard market town within an area of some 19 square miles (50 km²), such that the most distant village was only about 3 miles (5 km) from the center, although where population density was low, the

most remote villagers might need to walk 5 miles (8 km) to town (Figure 8.11a). Markets were held in adjacent market towns according to a regular schedule, following the lunar calendar, that divides the month into three 10-day "weeks." A typical cycle meant that a market would be held in the same town every 5 days; thus, an itinerant peddler or specialist could visit a different market every day and thereby greatly increase his potential customers. This system made it possible to efficiently sustain a very large and dense rural population without a costly and fuel-intensive transportation technology such as developed in industrial Europe and North America.

Skinner (1964) argued that the villages using a standard market town constituted the basic unit of the Chinese Little Tradition, or folk society. These 7000 or so people formed a relatively discrete social network that regularly interacted on market days and was united by ties of kinship and marriage. They thought of themselves as a group; shared details of dress, ritual, and dialect; and sometimes even used their own system of weights and measures. The market town was where the villagers paid their rents and taxes; it also contained religious shrines, and teahouses where the members of secret societies and mutual aid societies could meet. With its varied specialized functions, the market town often served as the power base of a single large lineage or clan, whose various members might be localized in villages within the market district.

An average of six standard market towns were grouped in hexagonal territories around an intermediate market town where the local gentry conducted much of their business (Figure 8.11b). Intermediate market towns were often enclosed by walls and contained a temple to an urban deity. They might serve an overlapping area of 135 square miles (350 km²) containing 50,000 people and were connected, in turn, with a central

folk-urban continuum Robert Redfield's concept of a gradual distinction between the Little Tradition culture of rural commoners and the Great Tradition culture of the urban elites in a political-scale culture.

FIGURE 8.11 Chinese market towns grouped about higher-level central places. (*a*) Map view of towns and the road network; (*b*) a diagrammatic view on a hexagonal grid (numbers represent market days in 10-day weeks). Note that (*a*) and (*b*) show the same urban places. (SOURCE: Skinner 1964.)

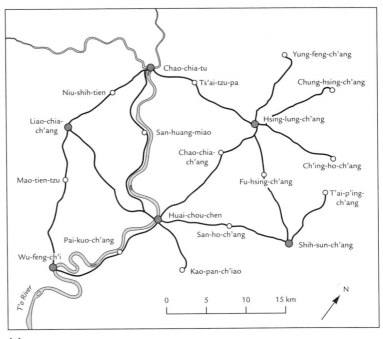

(a)

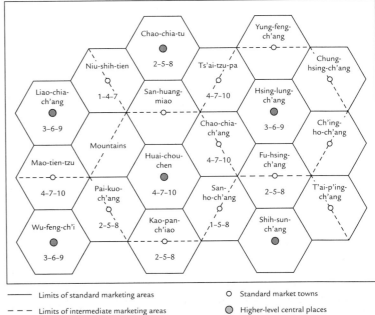

(b)

market town, where the lowest-level officials of the official bureaucracy were located. People maintaining connections between intermediate or central market towns likely were literate elites, whereas most peasants never left their local market districts.

In theory, Chinese social organization was based on the patrilineal *tsu,* usually translated as either "clan" or "lineage." These genealogically defined units were segmented, localized, property-holding groups, with a specific surname and clan temples or halls, where tablets dedicated to specific clan ancestors were kept. Villages or towns might be dominated by a single clan, with lineage segments occupying specific blocks. There might also be written genealogies of remarkable depth. For example, a village of 1100 people examined in Guangdong (Kwangtung) province in 1957 contained members of two clans. The dominant clan preserved ancestor tablets back forty-two generations to the founding of the village in AD 1091 (Freedman 1966).

There are conflicting interpretations of how Chinese descent groups were organized and how they functioned. Francis Hsu (1963) probably presented an incomplete picture when he described the "clan" as a large extended family, which forms a warm, peaceful, mutually self-contained unit. Freedman (1966) called the same descent group a "lineage" and stressed that it was characterized by both internal conflict and harmony, similar to the Nuer system of segmentary opposition. Freedman speculates that Chinese lineages may have gained special importance as landholding groups when lineage members cooperated in the development of local irrigation systems for wet-rice agriculture or formed self-defense groups on the frontiers of pioneer settlement.

Village Cosmology and the Little Tradition

In their daily lives, the commoners directly perpetuated shamanistic cultural traditions that

FIGURE 8.12   Yin-yang.

were rooted in the Neolithic past, underlying both the Great and Little Traditions. Commoners practiced a folk religion that drew freely on elements from formal Confucianism, Taoism, and Buddhism. Part-time Taoist priests, who did not live in the monasteries, were often called on as ritual specialists to perform at marriages, funerals, and curing ceremonies. The most prominent cultural elements shared by elites and commoners included the basic family system, with its emphasis on patrilineal descent lines and the ancestor cult, and basic cosmological traditions. The lowest-level deity, who operated at the household level, was the stove, or kitchen, god, who symbolized the domestic unity of the family. The stove god represented the bureaucracy and could report directly to the god symbolizing the emperor in the supernatural bureaucracy (Wolf 1974).

Complementary opposition, a prominent element in Australian and Amazonian cosmologies, was also a basic feature of Chinese popular culture. Complementarity was represented in Chinese cosmology by the yin-yang concept, symbolized in Figure 8.12. Yin is female, passive, dark, and cool, and is associated with earth, winter, valleys, tigers, and the color orange. Yang is male, light, and hot, and is associated with heaven, summer, mountains, dragons, and the color blue. The yin-yang concept was formalized by the Great Tradition during the early dynasties and combined with other philosophical features such as the concept of the five elements—metal, wood, water, fire, and earth—which were connected in a transformation cycle emphasizing balance, harmony, change, and continuity. According to five-element philosophy,

> Water produces Wood but overcomes Fire
> Fire produces Earth but overcomes Metal
> Metal produces Water but overcomes Wood
> Wood produces Fire but overcomes Earth
> Earth produces Metal but overcomes Water
> (Chai and Chai 1967:lxviii)

The five elements were correlated with colors, directions, musical notes, and periods of Chinese history to produce an elaborate, often occult, cosmology. Color symbolism has also been important in Chinese popular culture. White, considered the color of mourning, was associated with the west, and the east was blue-green. Red was auspicious and south, black was north, and yellow was associated with the emperor (Rawski 1987).

This popular belief system has sometimes been called a correlative cosmology because it provided a framework that helped elites and commoners alike structure their daily lives in proper alignment with the cosmic forces to guarantee prosperity. Concern for proper alignments was reflected in the layout of cities, temples, tombs, and houses; in the timing of ritual events; in the selection of mates; and in the seating of guests. Specialists in *geomancy* (divination by examining the spatial relationships of lines and figures) took cosmic forces into account when they studied the topographic details of a particular locality to select the most auspicious location for houses and graves. Correlative cosmology also influenced popular medicine, diet, and astrology.

Domestic Life and the Role of Women

Given the patrilineal descent system, the ideal Chinese nuclear family would produce many sons who would bring their wives to live in their father's house, or at least to his village. This would increase the strength of the lineage and ensure its perpetuation. Wealthy families could also add new members by adoption. Maurice Freedman (1966) described two broad types of Chinese families by size. The ideal was a large family containing two or more married sons, often called a joint family. The small family was either a nuclear family with no married sons or a stem family with only a single married son. Joint families were likely to be relatively wealthy, and they could form large lineage segments, whereas small families were usually poor members of disappearing lineages. The male members of Chinese families, large or small, held joint property, which was usually divided equally.

Western observers often regard the position of women in Chinese society negatively. Sons were said to be preferred over daughters and women did not own lineage property. Favoring sons over daughters meant that in imperial China infant girls would be more likely to die from neglect or infanticide than boys. Furthermore, a child bride was dominated by her mother-in-law. Such domination, which reinforced the control of the extended family by the elders, was reflected in the common practice of adopting a girl into the family for the son to marry (A. Wolf 1968). Marriages were often arranged, and even though monogamy was the pattern, concubinage occurred, divorce was difficult, and widow remarriage was discouraged. Upon marriage, a woman was virtually absorbed into her husband's family. Marriage was so essential for women that if they died unmarried, their spirits could be married later in a pattern reminiscent of Nuer ghost marriage.

Footbinding produced small, stunted feet, leaving many women virtually crippled. This practice demonstrated a man's affluence because it meant that his wife did not do heavy domestic work. But footbinding was apparently not limited to the elite. It was thought to make women more attractive, but it also supported the ideal of wifely virtue by making it more difficult for women to venture unattended from the home (Ebrey 1990).

This picture of female subordination is incomplete. Freedman (1979) points out that Chinese women bring a sizable endowment of domestic articles and personal wealth with them when they marry. A woman can also manage her husband's share of the family estate, and she owns her private earnings. Although new daughters-in-law may be treated harshly, they will become mothers-in-law in turn. As a wife, a woman has important responsibilities in domestic rituals, and her tablet will rest in her husband's ancestor hall (see the box entitled "The Meaning of Chinese Kinship Terms").

The House of Lim: Chinese Marriage, Family, and Kinship

The intimate realities of a Chinese joint family and its stresses and strains as a common domestic unit are sensitively documented in a remarkable ethnography, *The House of Lim*, by Margery Wolf (1968), wife of anthropologist Arthur Wolf. The Wolfs lived for two years (1959–1960) with the Lim family (a pseudonym) while they studied daily life in a small farming village they called Peihotien (Hai-shan) on the Tamsui (Tahan) River in northern Taiwan, fifteen miles southwest of Taipei. The Lim family was part of a large patrilineage whose Hokkien-speaking ancestors had migrated to Taiwan from Fukien province in adjacent mainland south China about 1770.

The House of Lim was the wealthiest family in the village. The Lims had realized the Chinese ideal with their three-generation joint family of fourteen people living as a single domestic unit, under one roof, with one kitchen. The household occupied a walled compound enclosing a large rectangular brick house with a central courtyard. The Lim family jointly owned the house, five acres of farmland, a small cement-bag factory, and a dozen pigs. They worked together, sharing their common economic resources under the general management of the senior male of the Lim patrilineage, Lim Chieng-cua. The joint family contained two branches (Figure 8.13):

1. Lim Chieng-cua, his wife, Chui-ieng, and their six unmarried children.
2. Lim A-bok, Lim Chieng-cua's deceased brother's son, with A-bok's wife, A-ki, their two unmarried children, his mother, Lim A-pou, and his younger unmarried brother.

Lim A-bok managed the farm while his mother took care of the pigs. The two wives, Lim Chui-

ieng and A-ki, shared the cooking on a five-day rotation. Everything seemed to run smoothly in the family, but beneath the surface there was considerable tension between the two branches of the family, between spouses, and between parents and children. Many interpersonal problems seemed related to the practice of adoptive and arranged marriages. The family head, Lim Chieng-cua, had refused to marry his foster sister and then agreed to a marriage with Chui-ieng, arranged by her foster parents. Chui-ieng was not happy with her marriage, especially when her husband took on a mistress. She berated him and threatened to leave, and he violently assaulted her. One of the family's adopted daughters turned to prostitution after she was given to another family but remained unmarried.

Lim A-pou had been adopted into the family as an infant, but her foster brother took a second wife after marrying her. Lim A-pou was considered a "little daughter-in-law" *(sim-pua)*, because she was selected to later marry her foster brother. Her husband's new wife was a love match. *Sim-pua* marriages were not prestigious, but they were very practical because they saved expensive bride-wealth expenses. They accounted for nearly half the marriages in Peihotien, but this practice has now completely disappeared in Taiwan. The preference for sons over daughters is a strong incentive for giving away daughters in such adoptions. In China, where patrilineages are so important, sons are the best old-age insurance. Furthermore, giving away infant daughters saves the expense of raising a "useless" daughter, who would require a dowry. One woman bluntly told Margery Wolf,

> Why should I want so many daughters? It is useless to raise your own daughters. I'd just have to give them away when they were grown, so when someone asked for them as infants I gave them away. Think of all the rice I saved. (1968:40)

The downside of such arrangements is that marrying someone with whom you have grown up does not make for a healthy marriage. Arthur Wolf's (1995) later analysis of the Chinese material

The Meaning of Chinese Kinship Terms

Chinese kinship terminology is complex because of the great diversity of terms that can be employed, but careful linguistic analysis reveals an orderly system that reflects the organization of Chinese society. In his study of the kinship terms used in Guangdong province by male speakers of Toishan, a Cantonese dialect of south China, John McCoy (1970) listed sixty-nine different terms used in indirect reference to kin and some fifty-three terms used in direct address. Table 8.B presents a simplified list of thirty-five selected terms drawn from this list in Mandarin, but representing only terms used by males for five generations of consanguineal kin, excluding affines. The Chinese terms appear in column 2 in phonemic linguistic notation. The terms are also written using Chinese characters to represent each syllable. Column 1 describes the terms using the abbreviated primary kin terms introduced in Chapter 2 (two new abbreviations are O, which means "older," and Y, which means "younger").

The genealogical distribution of the kin terms is diagrammed in Figure 8.B, which is keyed to the kin term numbers used in Table 8.B. Close inspection shows the importance of the male descent line and relative age, which is a very ancient pattern in Chinese culture. For example, FB's children (numbers 8, 9, 10, and 11) are terminologically distinguished from all other cousins because they could share surnames as members of ego's patrilineal descent group, the *tsu*, which existed during the Shang dynasty nearly 4000 years ago. Cross-cousins were not distinguished from parallel cousins, and no cousins were typically considered marriageable. Mates normally had different surnames and were unrelated, and probably even unacquainted.

Older or younger age relative to ego is distinguished for everyone in ego's generation and for male siblings of ego's male lineal kin in higher generations. Concern with relative age reflects the increased ceremonial responsibilities of older siblings in carrying out the duties of *hsiao*, filial piety, and the preferential treatment that they might receive in many areas, including inheritance.

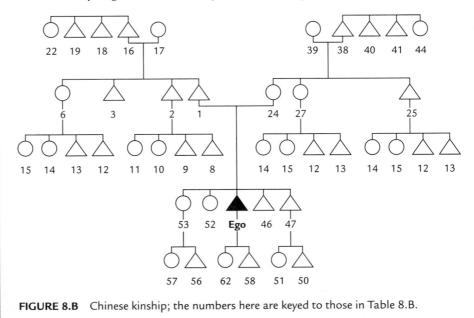

FIGURE 8.B Chinese kinship; the numbers here are keyed to those in Table 8.B.

Lineal relatives, who are ego's direct ancestors and descendants, are distinguished from all collateral relatives, who are off to the side. This distinction is important because it is lineal kin who must care for the elderly, play specific roles in mourning, and conduct ancestor rituals, all expressions of *hsiao*. Thus, an understanding of the meaning of Chinese kinship shows how important Chinese cultural patterns are enacted at the domestic level.

TABLE 8.B CHINESE KINSHIP TERMINOLOGICAL SYSTEM (MANDARIN LANGUAGE)

O = older; Y = younger
B = brother; Z = sister
F = father; M = mother
S = son; D= daughter

Description*		Chinese Term
1. F	父亲	Fu Qing [fù·tsīng]
2. FOB	伯父	Bo Fu [bó·fù]
3. FYB	叔父	Shu Fu [shū·fù]
6. FZ	姑母	Gu Mu [gū·mǔ]
8. FBOS	堂兄	Tang Xiong [táng·shōng]
9. FBYS	堂弟	Tang Di [táng·dì]
10. FBOD	堂姐	Tang Jie [táng·jěi]
11. FBYD	堂妹	Tang Mei [táng·mèi]
12. FZOS, MZOS, MBOS	表兄	Biao Xiong [bǐao·shōng]
13. FZYS, MBYS, MZYS	表弟	Biao Di [bǐao·dì]
14. FZOD, MBOD, MZYD	表姐	Biao Jie [bǐao·jěi]
15. FZYD, MBYD, MZOD	表妹	Biao Mei [bǐao·mèi]
16. FF	祖父	Zu Fu [tzǔ·fù]
17. FM	祖母	Zu Mu [tzǔ·mǔ]
18. FFOB	伯祖父	Bo Zu Fu [bó·tzǔ·fù]
19. FFYB	叔祖父	Shu Zu Fu [shū·tzǔ·fù]
22. FFZ	姑祖母	Go Zu Mu [gū·zǔ·mǔ]
24. M	母亲	Mu Qing [mǔ·tsīng]
25. MB	祖父	Jiu Fu [jìu·fù]
27. MZ	姨母	Yi Mu [yí·mǔ]
38. MF	外祖父	Wai Zu Fu [waì·tzǔ·fù]
39. MM	外祖母	Wai Zu Mu [waì·tzǔ·mǔ]
40. MFOB	外伯祖父	Wai Bo Zu Fu [waì·bó·tzǔ·fù]
41. MFYB	外伯祖母	Wai Shu Zu Fu [waì·shū·tzǔ·fù]
44. MFZ	外姑祖母	Wai Gu Zu Mu [waì·gū·tzǔ·mǔ]
46. OB	家兄	Jia Xiong [jiā·shōng]
47. YB	胞弟	Bao Di [bāo·dì]
50. BS	侄	Zhi [tzí]
51. BD	侄女	Zhi Nu [tzí·nǔ]
52. OZ	家姐	Jia Jie [jiā·jěi]
53. YZ	胞妹	Bao Mei [bāo·mèi]
56. ZS	甥子	Sun Zi [sūn·tzí]
57. ZD	甥女	Sun Nu [sūn·nǔ]
58. S	子	Zi [tzí]
62. D	女儿	Nu Er [nǔ·é]

*The numbers in this column are keyed to kinship terms in Figure 8.B.

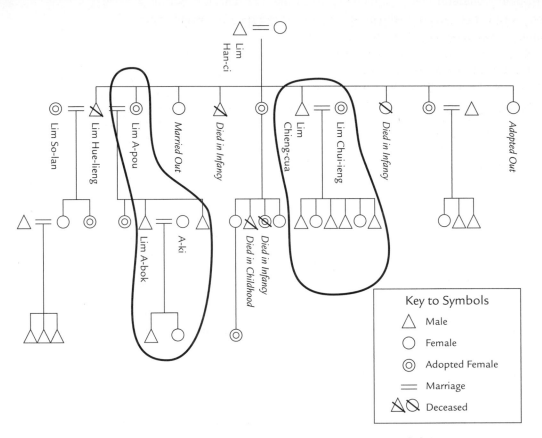

FIGURE 8.13 Two branches of the House of Lim in a Taiwanese village, 14 people living under one roof and sharing one kitchen (Wolf 1968).

seems to confirm Edward Westermark's theory in his *History of Human Marriage* (1922) that people who are raised together from infancy are likely to develop a sexual aversion to one another. Such aversion is especially likely in the Chinese case in which the couple actually called each other "brother" and "sister" before they married. Wolf found that Chinese marriages to adopted daughters showed lower fertility and higher adultery and divorce rates than other marriages.

The obvious insecurity of the women of the Lim household was reflected in frequent bickering between them, especially over work loads and the allocation of economic resources. Shortly after the Wolfs completed their fieldwork, the

Lim family divided their property and set up a separate stove and kitchen for Lim A-bok and his branch of the family. The two households continued to live in the same house and worshiped at the Lim family altar in the guest hall where the ancestral tablet was kept, but they no longer formed a joint family.

SUMMARY

The Chinese Great Tradition began to develop some 7000 years ago as a gradual transformation of the domestic-scale Neolithic farming cultures that had developed in the great river valleys of China 2000 years earlier. Their foraging ancestors can be traced to at least 15,000 BP in the same region. Many of the distinctive features of Chinese civilization were in place by the time of the Shang dynasty, which began nearly 4000 years ago and continued with only minor modifications until the last emperor was overthrown in 1911. Chinese civilization provides an important perspective on the debate over state origins because, in this case, control of religion by the political elite seems to have played a critical role in both the origin and long-term continuity of the state system. Chinese emperors were not deities, but they ruled with the mandate of heaven, and the political order has been described as a liturgical government based on moral authority backed by military force. Ancestor worship and the associated concept of filial piety were key elements in this system, especially at the domestic level. The entire ideology was expressed in a complex correlative cosmology based on complementary oppositions such as yin-yang and symbolism drawn from the five elements, which were correlated with colors, music, compass directions, and calendrical rituals.

Chinese agriculture was a gardening system powered by human labor on small family farms, operating within a highly efficient village system that provided basic subsistence needs to a very large and dense rural population at a minimal energy cost. This labor-intensive system is a significant contrast to the industrial farming, fossil fuel system described for the United States in Chapter 12.

Chinese culture tended to encourage large families and population growth, but the intensely hierarchical system kept living standards extremely low for most of the population. Chinese domestic life was structured around the patrilineage and extended family, which were dominated by men. The importance of males, relative age, and the patrilineage is reflected in Chinese kinship terminology.

STUDY QUESTIONS

1. Identify, define, or discuss the following Chinese ideological concepts: Confucianism, Taoism, five classics, five elements, filial piety, *li*, mandate of heaven, august god, yin-yang, stove god, ancestor tablet, and *kowtow*.
2. Discuss the following political concepts within the Chinese context: meritocracy, patrimonial, aristocracy, and gentry.
3. Discuss the following aspects of subsistence intensification using Chinese examples: multicropping, intertillage, permanent agriculture, labor intensive, capital intensive, and population density.
4. How does the Chinese state fit within the various theories of the origin of the state?
5. Discuss problems with the concepts of exploitation, immiseration, and Malthusian overpopulation, using Chinese material.
6. Discuss the role of ancestor worship as a central integrating device in Chinese culture.
7. Show how the components of descent line, relative age, lineal and collateral, sex, and generation are significant in Chinese kinship terminological systems.

SUGGESTED READING

CHANG, KWANG-CHIH. 1986. *The Archaeology of Ancient China*, 4th ed. New Haven, Conn.: Yale University Press. An authoritative overview of Chinese prehistory.
ROPP, PAUL S. 1990. *Heritage of China: Contemporary Perspectives on Chinese Civilization*. Berkeley: University of California Press. An interdisciplinary collection of articles on China including such topics as Confucianism, the origin of Chinese civilization, and the development of government, economy, and family.
STOVER, LEON N., AND TAKEKO STOVER. 1976. *China: An Anthropological Perspective*. Pacific Palisades, Calif.: Goodyear. A wide-ranging analysis of Chinese culture.
WHEATLEY, PAUL. 1971. *The Pivot of the Four Quarters: A Preliminary Enquiry into the Origins and Character of the Ancient Chinese City*. Chicago: Aldine. Examines the physical organization of Chinese cities through time in relation to worldview and cosmology.

9

Great Traditions: Hinduism and Islam in South Asia

Hindu temples symbolize the importance of religious belief in South Asia.

Learning Objectives

After studying this chapter you should be able to do the following.

1. Explain the relationship between language, Great Tradition, and political organization in South Asia and neighboring geographic regions, and make specific cultural comparisons between Hinduism, Buddhism, and Islam.

2. Compare the major stages of South Asian cultural development in comparison with developments in Mesopotamia, China, and the Andean region.

3. Outline the major cultural organizational features of Hindu kingdoms and empires in comparison with Mesopotamia, China, and the Andean region.

4. Make specific comparisons between ancient Hindu social organization, gender relations, and religious belief and practice, and these cultural features in other ancient civilizations and contemporary national societies.

5. Compare the rank distribution of social power in the Thai Kingdom and Akbar's empire, considering the household differences from top to bottom.

6. Outline the defining features of the Hindu caste system, and describe how food, marriage, and service transactions encode caste identity, explaining how Hindu cosmology and ritual practice support the rank order of Hindu society.

7. Compare the Islamic and Hindu Great Traditions, referring to their origin and development, and how they structure society and shape the practices of daily life.

8. Describe the status of women in South Asia, referring to underlying cultural understandings and basic practices in both Hindu and Muslim traditions.

Most of the Hindu words in this chapter are from Sanskrit. Their approximate pronunciation for English speakers are as follows:

Key

a = *aw* in h*aw*k	j = *j* in *j*oke	d = softer than
ā = *a* in f*a*ther	ch = *ch* in *ch*arm	in English
o = *o* in g*o*	sh = *sh* in *sh*e	t = softer than
e = *a* in f*a*te	oo = *oo* in f*oo*d	in English
ee = *ee* in b*ee*	ai = *i* in *i*ce	

dharma = [dar´/ ma]	rasa [ra / sha]
kshatriya [sha / tree • ya]	jajmani [jaj • mā/ nee]
vaisya [vai / shya]	harijan [ha • ree / jan]
sudra [shoo / dra]	Siva [shee / va]
jati [jā / tee]	kacha [kā / chā]
varna [var / na]	pakka [pā / kā]
darsan [dar • shan/]	arthasastra [ar • ta • sha / stra]

280

One-third of the contemporary world's people identify themselves as either Hindus or Muslims. These two Great Traditions arose independently more than 1000 years ago and are culturally distinct, but both are centered on formal religions with sacred texts. These religions provide charters for a hierarchically organized society and regulate the smallest details of daily life, including family structure, gender relations, and diet. Europeans, as members of the Judeo-Christian Great Tradition, have been both fascinated and repulsed by Hindus and Muslims for centuries, but they have consistently misunderstood them. In this chapter, we focus primarily on classical Hindu civilization, especially the relationship between religion and society, and show how the ancient culture is reflected in modern India. The South Asian culture area is emphasized because it is the homeland of the Hindu Great Tradition and because Muslims and Hindus have coexisted here for 800 years. This area is examined again in Chapter 13 in relation to contemporary issues of poverty and economic development.

THE SOUTH ASIAN CULTURE AREA

Languages, Geography, and Prehistory of South Asia

The South Asian culture area covers modern Pakistan, India, Nepal, Bhutan, Bangladesh, Burma, and Sri Lanka. It is a complex mix of languages and culture types, with more than one billion people occupying an area less than two-thirds the size of the United States. South Asia is centered on the Indian subcontinent and is predominantly a Hindu and Muslim region, with important Buddhist elements as well as many coexisting tribal cultures.

Most South Asian languages belong to one of three major language groups: Indo-European, Dravidian, and Sino-Tibetan (Figure 9.1). India alone recognizes fifteen official languages, including four of the twelve most populous languages in the world: English, Hindi, Urdu, and Bengali. Many other languages are spoken within the political boundaries of the country. The last three languages are members of the Indic branch of Indo-European, related to ancient Sanskrit, and are spoken by some 600 million people in the densely populated Indus Valley of Pakistan and the Gangetic Plain of India. Dravidian languages are spoken in southeastern India and Sri Lanka. They are presumed to have preceded the Indo-European languages in India and are spoken by many tribal groups. Sino-Tibetan languages are spoken in the Himalayan region, in Burma, and by many tribal peoples in extreme eastern India and Bangladesh.

The cultural Great Tradition with which people identify may be associated with a particular language. There are perhaps 60 million Buddhists in South Asia, primarily in India, Burma, and Sri Lanka, and some 200 million more in East Asia (Figure 9.2a). Buddhists are most likely to be speakers of Dravidian or Sino-Tibetan languages. Furthermore, many Dravidian and Sino-Tibetan peoples are tribal peoples who do not identify with any Great Tradition. The largest cultural group in South Asia is composed of some 700 million Hindus centered in India, Bangladesh, and Nepal, who are primarily speakers of Indic languages. At its peak, the Hindu Great Tradition expanded into Southeast Asia as far as Java and Bali in what is now Indonesia (Figure 9.2b). Approximately 300 million Muslims live in Pakistan, Bangladesh, and India. South Asian Muslims are predominantly speakers of Urdu and Bengali. There are more than 800 million Muslims worldwide, including some 170 million in Malaysia and Indonesia and more than 200 million in Africa and the Middle East (Figure 9.2c). The Islamic Great Tradition, although originated by speakers of Arabic, a Semitic language, is now practiced by more Indic speakers in South Asia than Arabic speakers in the Middle East. Furthermore, because not all Arab speakers are Muslim, the common stereotype that equates Muslim with Arab is misleading (compare Figures 9.2c and 9.2d).

FIGURE 9.1
Map of South Asian languages and geography.

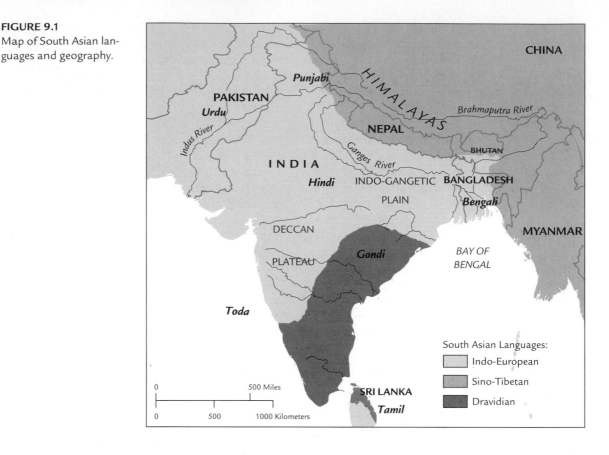

The South Asian subcontinent (Figure 9.1) extends more than 2000 miles (3218 kilometers [km]) east to west and north to south, encompassing many sharply different environments. Because of this diverse expanse, cultures of very different scale have been able to interact with one another over the millennia while retaining their essential autonomy. South and central India lie within the tropics, while north India extends well into the temperate zones. Tropical rain forest is found along a narrow coastal strip of western India, Sri Lanka, and the hill tribe areas of Bangladesh, eastern India, and Burma. Much of southern India is an arid upland dominated by the Deccan Plateau, which was not conducive to intensive agriculture and sheltered many Dravidian-speaking tribal peoples.

India is separated from China and Central Asia by the Himalayan–Hindu Kush mountains, which form the southern boundary of the vast Tibetan Plateau and contain the world's highest mountains and the largest permanent snowfields outside the polar regions. The 1500-mile (2414-km) east–west trend of the massive Himalayan range creates an enormous rain shadow to the north and funnels tropical monsoonal rain from Southeast Asia onto the rich soils of the low Gangetic Plain, making it a highly productive agricultural zone. The Himalayas are the source of the Indus, the Ganges, and the Brahmaputra rivers, which annually carry tons of fertile Himalayan soil to the Indo-Gangetic Plain. The Indus Valley, where Indian civilization began, lies on the opposite end of the Iranian plateau from Mesopotamia, which it ecologically resembles. The Indus Valley is an arid alluvial plain, bordered by mountains. The Indus, like the Euphrates, is a silt-laden, down-cutting river, ideally suited to

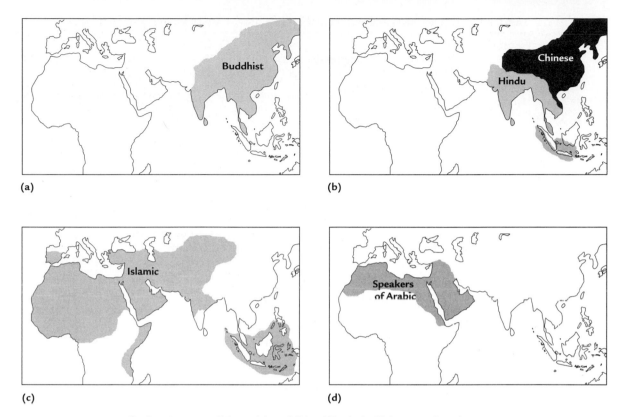

FIGURE 9.2 Maps of Asian Great Traditions: (*a*) Buddhist, (*b*) Hindu (light screen) and Chinese (dark screen), (*c*) Islamic, and (*d*) speakers of Arabic.

floodplain agriculture yet frequently changing course.

Significant changes in the South Asian environment may have affected cultural development in ways that are still not understood. Changes in sea level and alluvial deposition on the floodplain have altered the area of prime agricultural lands. The Himalayas are still being pushed up by the northward-moving Indian continental plate colliding with the Eurasian plate, and this has happened rapidly enough to modify regional climate during the period of human occupation. Since the Lower Paleolithic, in some areas of India the climate has been both wetter and drier than at present (Allchin and Allchin 1982).

South Asia is not as well known archaeologically as the Near East, but cultural developments seem to have followed a similar pattern in both

areas. The Lower Paleolithic is well represented by Acheulean hand axes and choppers found throughout India (Table 9.1). The Middle Paleolithic flake tools and Upper Paleolithic blade tools are also well represented. Archaeologists working in South Asia refer to cultures based on microlithic tools, foraging, fishing, and nomadic herding as Mesolithic. This adaptation began during the Early Holocene, about 12,000–8000 BP, and continued in various parts of the subcontinent into the twentieth century.

The South Asian Neolithic also went through a pre-Ceramic phase of initial farming villages at about the same time as in the Near East (10,000–7000 BP) and a full ceramic Neolithic (7000–5500 BP), which includes paint-decorated pottery. Because the earliest South Asian farming villages are known from the Indus region and the eastern

TABLE 9.1   HISTORY AND PREHISTORY OF SOUTH ASIA, 1 MILLION BP TO AD 1971

Post-Colonial
1971	Pakistan and Bangladesh partitioned
1947	India and Pakistan partitioned
1947	Indian independence

British Colonialism
1818–1947	British Empire of India
1757–1947	British rule Bengal
1600–1873	British East India Company

Muslim India 1192–1818
1526–1761	Mughal Empire
1556–1605	Akbar the Great

Classic Hindu India 600 BC–AD 1192
350–100 BC	Mauryan Empire (Arthasastra, Dharma Sastra, Code of Manu)
563–483	Buddha (Siddhartha Gautama), founder of Buddhism
900–300	Upanishads compiled

Vedic India 1600–600 BC
1600	Indo-European migrations

Harappan Civilization 2600–1900 BC
Cities, writing, temples, trade

Chiefdoms 4600–3500 BC

Neolithic India 8000–5500 BP Domestic wheat, barley, livestock

Mesolithic 12,000–8000 BP Foraging, hunting, early domesticates

Upper Paleolithic 18,000 BP Blade tools

Middle Paleolithic 200,000 Flake and core tools

Lower Paleolithic 1 million BP Acheulean hand axes and choppers

SOURCE: Allchin and Allchin (1982) for prehistory.

edge of the Iranian plateau in Baluchistan, it is inferred that developments here were perhaps part of the same process that occurred in the Near East, especially given the similarities in ecological setting.

EARLY HINDU CIVILIZATION

Origin of the Hindu Kingdom

Harappa, the earliest South Asian civilization, may have arisen independently in the Indus Valley (see the box entitled "Harappan Civilization: The Earliest South Asian State"). A clear break seems to have occurred between Harappa and the later Hindu civilization centered on the Gangetic Plain, which is attributed primarily to Indo-European-speaking Aryan pastoralists.

Sometime around 1600 BC, Indo-European-speaking peoples apparently moved from the Iranian plateau to the Indus plains. These were the Aryans, who were probably seminomadic pastoral people, speaking an early form of Sanskrit and organized in chiefdoms. These Aryans should *not* be confused with the imaginary north European "Aryan" superrace of Hitler's Nazi Germany and neo-Nazi racist political ideology. The Aryans of ancient Asia and the Neolithic settlers of Europe may well have had common ancestors in Southwest Asia some 8500 years ago

Harappan Civilization: The Earliest South Asian State

After 3500 BC, the agricultural potential of the Indus floodplain began to be realized, and the settled population began to increase. Between 2800 and 2500 BC, small, walled urban sites appeared, and highly uniform ceramic styles over a wide area, together with further evidence of long-distance trade, indicate that a socioeconomic interaction network had developed. Over the next several centuries (approximately 2500–1500 BC), Harappan civilization flourished throughout the Indus region. This was the earliest state-level culture in South Asia.

Harappa, at the upper end of the Indus floodplain, and Mohenjo-Daro, in the lower, were major urban centers, both built according to a similar plan. Mohenjo-Daro may have had a population of 35,000 people. It contained an elevated brick-walled citadel with a large ritual bath, grain storehouses, and probably a temple. Near the citadel was a separate, lower, and much larger grid cluster of brick buildings, which were residences and workshops. Houses had bathrooms complete with drains that emptied into what appeared to be a public sewer system. The diversity of house plans and the presence of single-room barracks suggest differences in social class or wealth, but no royal tombs have been found, and the Harappan elite remain anonymous.

The Harappans produced finely crafted utilitarian objects in bronze and copper, as well as jewelry and beads in gold, silver, and semiprecious stones. Because the floodplain lacked mineral resources, they maintained extensive trade contacts throughout India and as far as Central Asia and Mesopotamia. Standardized sets of weights and measures and numerous incised seals, resembling those from Mesopotamia but bearing unique Harappan markings, are further indications of the importance of trade (Figure 9.A). The Harappan language is unknown, and its unique writing system has never been successfully deciphered, but there does not seem to have been a developed literary tradition. Terra-cotta figurines and inscriptions of earth mothers, horned men, bulls, composite animals, and human-animals have been interpreted to be cult objects and forerunners of important Hindu deities such as Siva and Parvati. The Harappan civilization apparently collapsed completely around 1500 BC for reasons that are not well understood, as will be discussed in Chapter 10.

FIGURE 9.A An incised steatite Harappan seal with undeciphered script from Harappa.

and may belong to the Indo-European language family, but otherwise they were different peoples.

The Aryans portrayed in the Vedas were cattle herders probably organized as warrior chiefdoms, who fought with the earlier, presumably Dravidian-speaking, peoples whom they encountered. Some historians believe that the Aryans may have contributed to the collapse of the Harappan civilization, but this is difficult to establish (see Chapter 10). The Aryans settled initially in the Punjab and between the Indus and Ganges rivers, the region that was identified in the Vedic texts as Brahmavarta, the Aryan heartland. They then expanded steadily eastward into the fertile Gangetic Plain, such that by 600 BC they effectively occupied the entire region and were becoming increasingly sedentary and stratified. Over the next four centuries, classical Indian civilization became fully established, with cities, writing, states, empires, and the Great Traditions of Hinduism and Buddhism that continue to shape Indian culture to the present day (Table 9.1).

Hindu civilization has its roots in the religious hymns and verses preserved in the Vedas, especially the four Samhita Vedas compiled as oral texts between 1500 and 1000 BC. Pre-Aryan peoples, including members of the Harappan civilization, certainly contributed to what was, in effect, a second period of state formation, urbanization, and civilization in South Asia. The rise of early Hindu civilization between approximately 600 and 200 BC seems to have been primarily a political process that does not easily fit the Mesopotamian, Andean, or Chinese models of state origin examined previously. Hindu civilization developed after the Aryan invaders conquered the earlier tribal residents of the Ganges region and incorporated them into larger-scale centralized polities, whose rulers then began to war against one another. Because the Ganges, as an incised river, was a difficult source of irrigation water, early Gangetic states were not hydraulic societies; that is, they were not directed by rulers who also controlled irrigation works. Furthermore, because significant increases in population density took place only after political centralization, neither population pressure nor environmental circumscription could have been important causes of state formation. However, because Hindu civilization incorporated some elements of Harappan civilization and may also have been indirectly stimulated by contacts with Mesopotamian and Persian civilizations, it should not be considered an example of strictly pristine state development.

In his investigation of the development of Indian civilization, archaeologist George Erdosy (1988) focused on urbanization in the central Ganges region, viewing "the containers of those institutions that are required for the maintenance of increasingly complex and inegalitarian societies" (1988:5).

Tribal societies did not need cities because small villages were self-regulating. Cities were places where the instruments of social control could themselves be developed and controlled, such that their appearance signals the arrival of state-level organization.

Erdosy (1988) surveyed settlement patterns at intervals covering the period from 1000 BC to AD 300, looking for changes in the size, distribution, and function of settlements that might serve as clues to changes in cultural complexity. During the first 400 years, up to 600 BC, only two types of settlements could be distinguished: (1) numerous small villages of perhaps 275 people and (2) a small center of 1600 people, which was in a position to control the flow of imported mineral resources. Even in the absence of clear archaeological evidence of rank, this two-level settlement hierarchy suggests that simple chiefdoms existed at this time on the Ganges Plain (Figure 9.3a), but the institutions of social control must have been primarily religious and relatively unspecialized.

After 600 BC, an obvious change in political organization occurred, perhaps as high-ranking Aryans sought to enhance their control in the region. A functionally diversified, four-level settlement hierarchy emerged, clearly indicating the emergence of a state (Figure 9.3b). The largest settlement within the study area became a small fortified city of perhaps 8000 people. It contained material evidence of formal administra-

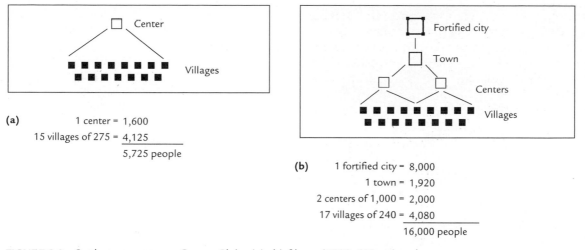

(a)

1 center = 1,600
15 villages of 275 = 4,125
―――――――
5,725 people

(b)

1 fortified city = 8,000
1 town = 1,920
2 centers of 1,000 = 2,000
17 villages of 240 = 4,080
―――――――
16,000 people

FIGURE 9.3   Settlement patterns, Ganges Plain: (*a*) chiefdoms (1000–600 BC) and (*b*) early states (600–350 BC).

tive, economic, and religious functions, in the form of coins, beads, sculptures, and iron slag. After 350 BC, the Ganges Valley settlement hierarchy, as archaeologically detected, successively revealed the presence of the kingdoms and empires of early classic Hindu civilization, which have also left their own historical record.

Hindu rulers merged political and religious power in their persons, and were the center of a "circle of kings" (Hagesteijn 1989). This was a radiating network of kings, little kings, and lords, all ranked relative to each other, and linked in a chain of personal **patron**-client relationships reaching to the village level. Each ruler commanded his own *chakra* (circle of power). This was a personal imperium, a fluctuating entourage of clients, kin, affines, dependents, or servants, all of whom were individually linked to the ruler by ties of patronage, but may not have been otherwise related to each other (Hanks 1975). These elite imperia crosscut other social categories based on ethnicity, kinship, religion, or **caste**, and made it possible for rulers to create and manipulate society and culture to their personal advantage, although rulers vied with each other for the loyalty of their followers and dependents. Operating as patrons, kings gave gifts

and offered protection to lesser lords in exchange for loyalty and tribute. Lesser lords cultivated similar patron-client relations with villagers, offering them protection from oppressive taxation, but still extracting their labor and produce. Similar patron-client relations were also acted out between people and the gods in temples, and between husband and wife in households. Throughout, loyalty, devotion, or worship was expressed by means of gifts of food, goods, or service. This very personal use of power meant that individual rulers and dynasties could easily remain in control whether the Great Tradition was predominately Hindu, Muslim, or Buddhist.

Kings were invariably insecure because they were seldom powerful enough to command unquestioned authority throughout their realms. Therefore they portrayed themselves as divine and channeled much of their resources into staging dramatic ritual performances to demonstrate

---

patron A Spanish term for someone who extends credits or goods to a client who is kept in a debt relationship.
caste An endogamous, ranked, occupationally defined group, known as *jati* in India, and based on differences in ritual purity and impurity.

FIGURE 9.4   Statue of the Hindu god Vishnu, depicted with a *chakra,* (circle of power) in his hand.

of kings throughout Southeast Asia into tribal areas occupied by Dravidian, Sino-Tibetan, and Austronesian speaking peoples. However, chiefdoms and kingdoms were not irreversible social formations. In upland areas where shifting cultivation was practiced, often only fragile chiefdoms could be constructed, and then only temporarily. For example, in twentieth century Sino-Tibetan–speaking Burma, an enterprising tribal headman could, with effort and under the right circumstances, turn himself into a chief, local lord, or small king, and form a small, fortified temple center (Leach 1964). Transformation from headman to chief required an especially productive resource base, skillful manipulation of marriage exchanges, and the ability to sponsor large feasts, ritually sacrifice cattle, support an expanded household, and build a network of supporters. Such success was a conspicuous demonstration of personal merit, potency, or spiritual virtue like Polynesian *mana,* except that in the Burmese case power could be achieved (Kirsch 1973). A chief might then become a client-vassal to a Hindu-Buddhist king who occupied a larger, walled center with a temple and palace. In addition to the Hindu kingdoms in South Asia, between A.D. 500 and 1400 perhaps a hundred small temple centers, and some twenty-four large centers were formed in Southeast Asia (Hagesteijn 1989).

Kautilya's Hindu Kingdom: An Emic Political Model, 250 BC

The ideal organization of the early Hindu state is precisely detailed in Kautilya's Arthasastra, a written manual on ancient Indian statecraft. The Arthasastra is attributed to Kautilya, a minister in the Mauryan empire in 250 BC, but was probably written by several people in the early centuries AD. It is a composite treatise on political science for kings and aspiring kings, written with candor, cynicism, and insight. As a manual for public administrators, it resembles the Confucian classics, but instead of professional ethics and ritual, the Arthasastra advocates the use of coercive power backed by the army, the police,

their power. They represented the kingdom as a *mandala* (circle model of the Hindu universe), with concentric rings centered on Mount Meru, the axis of the world and center of the universe in Hindu mythology. Hindu kings might claim the title *cakravartin* "world ruler," and their power was symbolized by the *chakra* shown in representations of the Hindu god Vishnu (Figure 9.4). Behind the legitimizing ideological framework lay military power, control over land, control over people, and a revenue collecting bureaucracy.

The first Hindu rulers used invasion and conquest to construct their kingdoms, but power-seeking individuals quickly spread Hindu circles

the courts, and covert state security agents. The Arthasastra may be taken as a portrayal of the ideal structure and function of a hypothetical Indian kingdom during the early centuries of classic Hindu civilization. As an emic view, composed by elite political professionals, it may not be an accurate picture of any specific kingdom, and the ideal rules may not have been followed. However, the general system as described provides a useful model for comparison with the organization of tribes and other state systems.

The Arthasastra offers insider views on the use of state power for the king's personal advantage. It is filled with practical advice on palace intrigue—complete with how-to examples of the use of spies, sex, poison, and deception for political assassination—and ways to test the loyalty of government officials. In the Arthasastra, religion was simply another self-conscious tool of statecraft. Kings were advised to use rituals and pilgrimages as excuses to raise revenue. It was even proposed that omens, such as spirits speaking in trees, be deliberately staged to stir up fear so that people would increase their religious donations.

The difference between political leaders in Indian kingdoms such as this and tribal leaders who might also use deception and treachery to personal advantage was simply that tribal cultures limited political power. Tribal leaders did not have standing armies, police forces, and secret agents at their disposal. They could not personally control the availability of basic subsistence goods to thousands of households. Tribal peoples feared and avoided those who abused their limited powers and thereby denied them control. Peasant villagers living in a world of rival kingdoms were pawns for the ruling kings, who tried to keep the levy just below the point at which disaffected villagers would join an enemy kingdom.

In 500 BC, there were some eighteen large kingdoms in northern India centered on the Gangetic Plain (Erdosy 1988). According to the Arthasastra, an ideally organized kingdom would have been divided into four districts, each containing 800 villages dominated by a fortified city, with smaller cities, towns, and centers hierarchically arranged to facilitate administration and the flow of revenue. The government officials in two cities would have administrative responsibility for 400 villages each, officials in four towns would control 200 villages each, and some eighty local centers would each be responsible for very specific census taking, tax collecting, and police work in 10 villages within the district (Figure 9.5). Such an arrangement closely corresponds to the archaeological record, and suggests that a kingdom might have contained some 1.6 million people, with perhaps 143,000 people, 9 percent of the total population, living in cities of more than 2000 people (Table 9.2).

A kingdom of 1.6 million people would have been much more amenable to management by direct political power than the 50–500 million people living in the vast Chinese empire, or the later Hindu-Muslim Mughal Empire. Mughal, also spelled Mogul, refers to the Mongol origin of the first Muslim dynasty in India. Traditional China and early Hindu India make an interesting comparison because they were both pre-industrial, agrarian civilizations, yet there were significant cultural differences. As shown in Chapter 8, China relied primarily on ethical principles, ritual, moral authority, and patrilineal descent groups to maintain social order. Hindu India, in contrast, used the moral authority of religion to support an endogamous caste system and relied on coercive political authority to a significant degree. Although patrilineage, clan, and filial piety were primary integrating principles in China, and caste was primary in India, diverse forms of lineage and clan were also important in many areas of village India. Military power backed up the moral order in both cultural systems. In India, kings built a succession of empires that peaked with Akbar the Great's (1542–1605) empire of 110 million people. Akbar's empire was so large that military mobilization was a dominant preoccupation and absorbed much of the imperial social product.

The territory of an Indian kingdom was relatively small. The total population of 1.6 million required total territory of approximately 34,749

FIGURE 9.5
Settlement hierarchy
within a specific Hindu
kingdom, 250 BC.
(SOURCE: Shamasastry 1960
[Arthasastra].)

Palace

Fortress

2 cities

4 towns

80 centers

800 villages

square miles (90,000 km²), 186 miles (300 km) on a side. In comparison, the 500 million people of the Chinese empire at its height were spread over a territory of 3.4 million square miles (9 million square kilometers). It is not surprising that Chinese civilization came to rely so heavily on moral authority.

The approximate social composition of a hypothetical Hindu kingdom suggests that a surprisingly small elite maintained absolute power. There may have been fewer than 150 salaried elites in the top administrative ranks, barely 50,000 retainers, bureaucrats, specialists, and merchants who paid taxes in cash, and perhaps 275,000 farm householders. Most of the population, probably about 85 percent, lived in farm households, which supplied basic subsistence for the other 15 percent. State-supported craft specialists did produce consumer goods for the villagers, but much of their production directly supported the state.

The Arthasastra gives a detailed picture of the revenue system and basic administrative structure of the Hindu kingdom. State-controlled wealth was concentrated in the capital and in district fortresses. An underground royal treasury vault contained gold, jewelry, coins, and precious textiles. Special storehouses held grain and other products, which were collected as taxes in kind or produced on crown land. Farmers paid an average grain tax of 16 percent, which was raised to 25–33 percent under emergency conditions. There were also village taxes, temple taxes, gate taxes, sales taxes, income taxes, tolls, fines, and excise taxes of various sorts. Some villagers submitted to corvée labor or military inscription in place of the grain tax.

Although there were no vast canal systems or irrigation works in ancient India, large armies were mobilized for frequent wars, and royal construction projects and defensive works required large labor forces. For example, Erdosy (1988)

TABLE 9.2   POPULATION OF MODEL HINDU KINGDOM, 350 BC

Number per District	Population in Each*	Total
Fortified city (1)	20,000	20,000
Cities (2)	3,500	7,000
Towns (4)	2,000	8,000
Centers (80)	1,000	80,000
Villages (800)	350	280,000
Total district population		395,000
4 Districts = 1,580,000		
Capital city = 35,000		
Kingdom total = 1,615,000		
Urban population (cities over 2000 people = 143,000 (8.8%)		

SOURCES: Erdosy (1988) and Kautilya's Arthasastra (Shamasastry 1960).
*The Arthasastra states that villages ranged in size from 100 to 500 families. Erdosy estimates 3.5 persons per family and average villages of 240 people, assuming 160 people per hectare of archaeological site. Thus, villages of 350 people represent the lower range for the Arthasastra figures but are higher than predicted archaeologically.

estimates that construction of the 49-foot (15-m)-tall earthen ramparts stretching for 3.7 miles (6 km) around a fortified city would have engaged 20,000 workmen for 250 days.

The state regulated commercial activities, mining, forestry, herding, and craft production to extract the maximum feasible revenue (Figure 9.6). Even prostitutes were licensed and paid a monthly income tax. The supply of marketable consumer goods was centrally controlled. Only the Brahmans, who formed the religious elite, and frontier villages and state-supported colonization projects were exempt from taxes. A collector general attached to the royal palace was responsible for all revenue collection received from district and village tax collectors. There was also a high-ranking tax commissioner and a tax inspector, who used covert means to monitor the flow of revenue. Detailed bookkeeping was carried out at all levels, and all government expenses were further monitored by the central accounts office.

Many diverse functions were carried out in the fortified city, especially if it was also the capital. As described in the Arthasastra, the city was divided into twelve major sections, where specific categories of people were expected to live and where specific activities and buildings were to be located (Figure 9.7). Each of the four *varna*, or "colors," representing the four ranks of Vedic society—Brahman, Kshatriya, Vaisya, and Sudra—was assigned specific quarters within the city, grouped together with appropriately ranked economic activities. These social categories will be discussed in more detail in the later section dealing with caste.

The *varna* were the early form of the caste system. During this early period of Hindu civilization, they were already associated with endogamy, relative purity, and occupation. For example, the Sudra, in the lowest-ranked *varna*, were assigned to the city's west quarter, where leather-working, an especially spiritually polluting activity, was carried out. The royal palace occupied one-ninth of the city and was to be located just north of city center, opening onto the sections occupied by Brahmans, jewelers, and the divine king. Merchants and high-ranking specialist crafts were located in the east quarter together with government ministers and the Kshatriya.

Law in the Hindu Kingdom

The legal system in the Hindu kingdom upheld the authority of the state and the *varna* social system, which gave ritual priority and economic

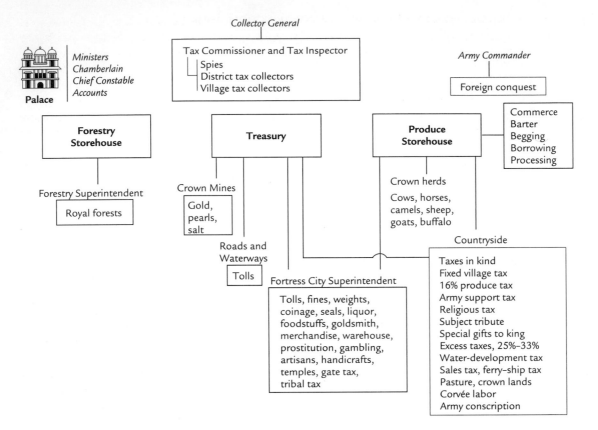

FIGURE 9.6   State finance in a Hindu kingdom, 250 BC.

FIGURE 9.7
Functional diversification within a fortified Hindu capital, 250 BC.
(SOURCE: Shamasastry 1960 [Arthasastra].)

KEY:
C = Craft specialist residences
D = Guardian deities

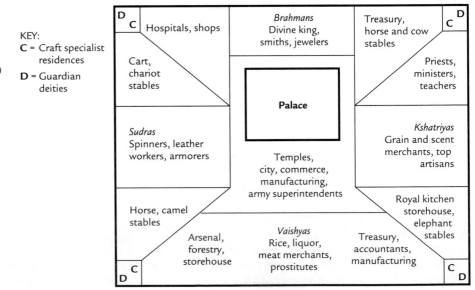

advantage to the upper ranks. Furthermore, fines imposed by the court were a source of state revenue and enforced the tax system. Law was based on tradition, or customary law, and on *dharma,* or sacred religious law, which resembled *li* in the Chinese system. Both *dharma* and *li* referred to duty, morality, and proper conduct; however, where *li* emphasized duty to emperor, ancestors, and family, *dharma* laid out different moral requirements for each *varna* and for individuals at different stages of the life cycle. Furthermore, the Hindu king was clearly a political ruler.

All law in the Hindu kingdom was ultimately vested in the king, who was assisted by his political ministers and priestly authorities on *dharma.* According to the secular authors of the Arthasastra, the king's traditional law had legal priority over *dharma,* and the king was expected to use the state's power and physical punishment to "maintain both this world and the next" (Shamasastry 1960 [Bk. 3, chap. 1]).

Laws were explicitly designed to support the *varna* system and provided a quantified measure of the relative worth of each rank. For example, one could be fined for causing a Brahman to violate one of his food taboos, and a Sudra could be burned alive for committing adultery with a Brahman woman. Brahmans were generally immune from taxes, fines, and punishments. The fine for selling a Brahman child into slavery was four times as severe as when the victim was a Sudra. The sons of a Brahman woman were to inherit four shares of their Brahman father's estate, but only one share if their mother was a Sudra. Twenty-four different terms existed to describe the conditions of birth according to the *varna* of the parents. Stanley Tambiah (1985) demonstrates that the caste system itself was generated by the legal classification and rank ordering of all the logically possible types of marriage between people in different *varna* categories.

There was a broad three-level scale for fines in pana, the basic monetary unit, ranging from under 100 to 1000 pana. According to the government's salary scale, the highest officials were paid 24,000–48,000 pana a year, midrange offi-

cials earned 1000–12,000 pana, and the lowest retainers earned just 60 pana. Those unable to pay fines could substitute an equal number of lashes or body parts according to a scale of equivalent values. A thumb was worth 54 pana; a right hand, 400 pana; and both eyes, 800 pana.

Verbal abuse or insults were scaled according to whether they were true, false, or sarcastic. For example, calling a blind man "blind" was true abuse, but telling a blind man that he had beautiful eyes was false abuse. Generally, the fine was doubled if the victim was in a superior *varna* and halved if the victim was inferior (Table 9.3). More precise rank distinctions could also be made if one's profession was insulted, with the severity of the fine increasing by three for each increase in the victim's relative rank and decreasing by two for lower-level ranks.

The legal severity of physical assault was measured along a graduated scale of violence taking into account both the objects used and the body areas struck. The Hindu scale added relative rank. Throwing mud on a low-ranking person's feet was a minor offense (0.5 pana), whereas throwing feces on a high-ranking person's face was a very serious offense (96 pana). The most serious cases involved extreme differences in rank. Although striking with a hand or leg was normally a moderate offense, the Arthasastra declared "that limb of a Shudra with which he strikes a Brahmin shall be cut off" (Shamasastry 1960 [Bk. 3, chap. 19]).

To convince people of the "omniscient power of the state," the Arthasastra advocated routine use of undercover agents, entrapment, arrest on suspicion, torture to elicit confessions, severe punishment, and public display of criminals. Workers who failed to produce on time or who fled their workshops were fined. Theft of a minor commodity from a home or shop was punished with public humiliation, but theft of an object of one-fourth the value from the government could bring banishment. Taking any government property worth more than 8 pana, spreading rumors, letting out prisoners, or using government documents without authorization could mean death.

TABLE 9.3   LEGAL FINES (IN PANAS) FOR VERBAL ABUSE, INSULT, AND ASSAULT
IN RELATION TO *VARNA* IN THE HINDU KINGDOM, 350 BC

Verbal Abuse	Victim's Rank		
	Equal	Superior	Inferior
Valid	12+	6	0.5
False	12+	12	3
Sarcasm	12+	24	6

	Victim's Rank			
Insultor	Brahman	Kshatriya	Vaisya	Sudra
Brahman	12	10	8	6
Kshatriya	15	12	10	8
Vaisya	18	15	12	10
Sudra	21	18	15	12

	Below Navel*		Above Navel		Head	
Assault	Inferior†	Superior†	Inferior	Superior	Inferior	Superior
Throwing mud	0.5	6	3	12	6	24
Spitting	3	12	6	24	12	48
Throwing feces	6	24	12	48	24	96

SOURCE: Shamasastry (1960 [Arthasastra]).
*Target.
†Rank.

Insulting the king was punished by cutting out the offender's tongue. The most severe punishment, burning alive, was reserved for those spreading disorder in the countryside.

Power and Scale in the Thai Kingdom and Mughal Empire

Remarkably, the distribution of social power by rank that can be inferred from Kautilya's model kingdom corresponds closely to the ethnographically documented power structure of the Hindu-Buddhist Thai kingdom in 1851 under the Chakri dynasty (1782–1932), and the much larger Hindu-Muslim Mughal Empire in 1605. These examples demonstrate the power concentrating effects of growth in the scale of society, and also show that similar social structures can be supported by diverse ideological systems.

Growth in scale produced an astounding concentration of power for Akbar, the Mughal Em-

peror. The 110 million subjects commanded by Akbar were 2 orders of magnitude more numerous than the 4 million commanded by the Thai king, and the 1.6 million in the early Hindu kingdom. These scale differences were reflected in the size of ruler households and the magnificence of their lifestyles.

The social distance from top to bottom in these societies was staggering, but not fundamentally different from that seen in Ur III, the Inca Empire, and imperial China. For example, in 1851 the Thai kingdom was divided into three broad, but finely ranked social classes: nobles, commoners, and slaves (Table 9.4). The king assigned every household head a *sakdina* (dignity) rank of from 5 to 100,000 *sakdina*, whereas his own *sakdina* was "infinite" (Bodley 2003:37–44). Each *sakdina* was worth 0.4 acres of cultivable land, the amount a water buffalo could plow in a day. Ninety-five percent of the households were at the maintenance level or below with an average of 25

TABLE 9.4   THAI HOUSEHOLDS BY CLASS, RANK, TITLE, AND IMPERIA, CHAKRI DYNASTY, 1782–1932

Classes	Titles	Sakdina Ranks	Households	Dependents	Imperia
Nobles 0.2%	Universal Monarch Lord Buddha, Great Ruler, Lord of the Land, Lord of Life	infinite	1	225,000	Super-Elite 0.2%
	Royal Family and Top Officials, Crown Prince, Prince	range 100,000–5,000	500	average 500	
	Nobles Lesser Royalty	range 5000–400	1000	50	Elite 5%
Commoners 75%	Petty Officials	range 50 300	36,000	7	
	Labor Supervisors	25	120,000	0	Maintenance 45%
	Freemen	15	242,500		
	King's Men, Servants	10	200,000		
	Poor, Beggars				Poor 50%
Slaves 25%	Slaves bond slaves, criminals, captives	5	200,000		

SOURCES: A. Rabibhadana (1969), Poumisak (1987), H. G. Quaritcha Wales (1934).
Note: Perhaps another 100,000 people were living as monks.

or fewer *sakdina*, but 50 percent were objectively poor with only 10 *sakdina* or less, making them vulnerable to servitude. In contrast, the *sakdina* of the ordinary elite ranged from 400 to 5,000, and on the average may have supported households of 50 persons. At the top, King Mongkut maintained a personal household of 9000 wives, concubines, slaves, and retainers in a 100 hectare (247 acre) walled palace compound, at the center of a city of 50,000 people. Mongkut officially produced 82 children from 35 mothers. Life in the Thai royal court and harem was described in detail by the English woman Anna Leonowens (1870, 1953), who spent six years as a tutor in Mongkut's palace.

The Thai kingdom was large enough that in addition to the royal dynasty, other high-ranking elites were able to perpetuate their personal imperia as dynasties. For example, just four nonroyal families were able to maintain cross-generational control over the six top ministries. One family held power from 1782 to 1886 (Wyatt 1968).

Akbar's empire was so large that in 1605 he in effect commanded twenty percent of the world's people (Goldsmith 1987:94–122). If Akbar's empire is counted together with the empire of his contemporary, the emperor of Ming China, then just two men commanded half of the world's people. They converted their social power into extraordinary personal luxury. The quantitative details of Mughal India during Akbar's reign are thoroughly documented in a text, the *Ain-i-Akbari* compiled in the 1590s by one of Akbar's ministers Abu Fazl (Blochmann 1939). The record shows

FIGURE 9.8   The royal palace complex in the Akbar's capital city of Fatehpur-Sikri, 1588.

that at least 18 percent of the empire's national product of R 650 million (R = rupees, 1 rupee = 11 grams of silver) was appropriated by Akbar and his top 1672 nobles (Goldsmith 1987:106–107). This R 108 million financed the government and elite luxuries. Akbar's annual expenditure on his personal household was approximately R 20 million, or 3 percent of the empire's total annual product. This may seem like a small amount, but given that an average villager household subsisted annually on the equivalent of R 20, Akbar's personal consumption was a million times greater than minimum subsistence. About two-thirds of government income was used to support the military establishment, including the maintenance of Akbar's personal guard of 90,000 men, but a great deal was spent on extravagant luxury. Akbar maintained a harem of 5000 women, and on hunting expeditions traveled with an entourage of more than 2000 men, 500 camels, and 100 elephants. This suggests that this was a practical ceiling for the size of harems and personal households, but palaces could be multiplied, and treasure could also be expended on art, monumental constructions, and other displays. In 1570 Akbar commanded the construction of the lavish city of Fatehpur-Sikri, as an entirely new walled royal capital and palace complex, complete with harems, audience halls, mosques, residences, gardens, waterworks, and tombs (Brand and Lowry 1987). The city was an architectural splendor, but Akbar and his elite clients only occupied it from 1572 to 1588, when it was completely abandoned (Figure 9.8).

HINDU IDEOLOGY, SOCIETY, AND CULTURE

Caste and Orthodox Hinduism: The Brahman View of *Dharma*

Hindu civilization is most widely known for its caste system with its emphasis on hierarchy and on ritual **purity** and ritual or spiritual pollution, which continues to be a major fact of life in India. The caste system assumed its basic form in the Hindu kingdoms during the last centuries BC, as described in the preceding section. The term *caste* is an English version of the Spanish and Portuguese word *casta,* meaning "race," "breed," or "family." The corresponding Indian term is *jati,* "birth" or "breed," which emphasizes that caste membership is assigned by birth; each caste is ideally an endogamous group. At its most general level, caste has been defined as a society "made up of birth-ascribed groups which are hierarchically ordered and culturally distinct. The hierarchy entails differential evaluation, rewards, and association" (Berreman 1979:73).

By this definition, caste could also describe race relations in the United States in the 1950s (Berreman 1960) and the positions of blacksmiths in East Africa. French anthropologist Louis Dumont (1970) took a more intellectualist approach, describing Indian caste as an ideological system of categories based on (1) hierarchically ordered social groups, (2) detailed rules of separation, and (3) a division of labor. The four *varna*—Brahman, Kshatriya, Vaisya, and Sudra—can be considered the most general castes, but castes are continuously segmented into many localized subcastes, which form finely ranked regional systems. The members of subcastes claim descent from a common founder and identify an original group specialty—such as herding, farming, blacksmithing, or weaving—even though it may not always be practiced.

Many scholars view caste as the defining symbol of Hindu society, but this is an incomplete understanding. What we know about "traditional" Hindu society and culture, including how we understand caste, is a product of centuries of conquest and empire building, and the selective transmission and creation of cultural knowledge. Hindu society is based on a continually evolving moral system that has been under construction for centuries. A tiny elite of Hindu intellectuals first recorded its features in ancient Sanskrit texts, but over the centuries various political and economic rulers, as well as ordinary people have continually reshaped the Hindu cultural system into a tool for their self-interest. However, in this cultural process the elites, because of their dominant position, have been most influential, and have been able to define the system's boundaries. This is the exercise of **cultural hegemony**. Most recently, from 1757–1947 British colonial rulers were the dominant influences on Hindu society. In asserting their rule over a vast and diverse society, they used laws, maps, and the census, backed by military and economic power, in ways that made caste the dominant social fact of Indian society. In the process they deposed Indian political rulers, and transformed the caste system (Cohn 1996, Dirks 1989, 2001). Before British rule, as the previous discussion of Kautilya's Hindu kingdom shows, kings, as political rulers, were the dominant agents in society, not the Brahman priests.

The caste system is supported by Hindu ideology. Modern Hinduism is a complex blend of beliefs and practices originating in the Vedic period, and carried on in a formal, "Great Tradition" way by Brahman priests who follow rituals based on the sacred Vedic texts. A central feature of Hinduism is belief in *samsara*, an endless cycle of death and rebirth experienced by the human soul. This is reincarnation, or transmigration of the soul, and is closely connected with the concept of *karma*, the belief that what a person did in a previous existence determines the conditions of one's future existence. This explains one's position in the caste system, and holds out the possibility of being reborn in a higher caste. It also focuses attention on the importance of following proper ritual behavior, which is the only means of finding salvation from *samsara*. For Brahmans, ritual purity as prescribed in the Veda is also required for approaching the supreme lord Brahman. Ritual pollution, or impurity is caused by any behavior proscribed by the Vedic texts, and requires ritual purification.

Caste organization and related concepts of ritual purity have a significant bearing on aspects of Hindu marriage and family life. Caste endogamy, the requirement that one marry within the caste, helps define caste boundaries, but subcastes are often further subdivided into exogamous lineages

---

purity Ritually superior status; a category in logical opposition to impurity.

cultural hegemony Preponderant influence, or authority, by an elite in the production and reproduction of a society's moral order and associated cultural beliefs, symbols, and practices.

and clans. Marriage between different subcastes is often characterized by **hypergamy,** in which low-rank women marry equal- or higher-ranked men. This practice may severely limit choices for women in high-ranked subcastes, whereas downmarrying men (**hypogamy**) are unlikely to experience difficulty.

Marriage is one of the most important Hindu rituals. It involves great expenditure by the bride's family and extreme concern for ritual purity and status. Normally, all marriages are arranged by the families of the prospective bride and groom. Chastity is a ritual requirement, especially for the highest castes, and is related to infant marriage, prohibition on divorce and widow remarriage, and the practice of *sati,* or widow self-immolation, in which a "virtuous woman" throws herself on her husband's funeral pyre to be transformed into a goddess. Many of these practices are followed only by the strictest Brahman subcastes, which adhere to the severest requirements for ritual purity. It must also be stressed that marriages did not always conform to the expected patterns, but when they didn't, a loss of ritual status could occur.

Dumont (1970) maintained that the three basic aspects of caste—hierarchy, separation, and division of labor—can all be reduced to the single principle of the opposition of pure and impure. The pure are defined as superior, and impure castes are impure because of their association with impure occupational specialties. **Impurity** for Hindus means a loss of status and is caused by association with "polluting" organic products and biological events such as birth, puberty, menses, and death. In tribal societies, such events may put individuals temporarily at supernatural risk, but Hindu ideology permanently associates particular social groups with impure biological events or organic products. The Hindu system is a logical reversal of the practice common in chiefdoms in which the chief is considered to be endowed with sacred power *(mana),* which makes him dangerously *tabu* to lower-ranked individuals, but in India it is lower ranked individuals who endanger higher ranks.

The most extreme form of pollution could be transmitted by mere physical contact. This kind of impurity applied to members of the lowest Sudra castes, who were handlers of dead animals and human waste. They might also eat meat, including beef. Europeans called them untouchables, because any contact with such persons required some form of ritual purification such as sprinkling with water. In India, untouchables are sometimes called Harijans, or "God's children," or "exterior castes." They are exterior because they are often excluded from many public activities due to their ritual disabilities. Untouchability was officially declared illegal by the Indian constitution of 1949 and by Pakistan's constitution of 1953, but it continues to be an important social phenomenon.

The mythical charter for caste is found in the *purusha* myth, an account of creation contained in the Dharma Shastra of Manu (Buhler 1886, Burnell and Hopkins 1884; see also the box entitled "The *Purusha* Myth"). According to this account, Lord Brahma, the creator god, "for the prosperity of the worlds" created the four *varna*—Brahman, Kshatriya, Vaisya, and Sudra—from his mouth, arms, thigh, and feet, respectively (Buhler 1886 [Manu 1:31]). Separate duties were assigned by the creator to each *varna.* The Brahmans (Figure 9.9) were the "Lords of Creation" and the perpetual incarnation of *dharma* (sacred law). They were the priests, teachers, sacrificers, and receivers of gifts, who, because of their "superiority and eminence of birth," were entitled to "whatever exists in the universe" (Buhler 1886 [Manu 1:88–100]). The Kshatriya were to be protectors of the people and took political roles as rulers and warriors. The Vaisya were responsible for cattle herding, farming, and trade. The Sudra were to serve the top three *varna,* "without grudging." Similarly, only the top three were allowed to participate in a series of initiation rites that allowed them to be considered "twice-born," and only the twice-born could request the Brahman priests to perform sacrifices.

There are thousands of castes throughout modern India, and many different ways of group-

The *Purusha* Myth: A Mythic Charter for *Varna* and Caste

"But in order to protect this universe, He, the most resplendent one, assigned separate (duties and) occupations to those who sprang from his mouth, arms, thighs, and feet.

To Brahmans he assigned teaching and studying (the Veda), sacrificing for their own benefit and for others, giving and accepting (of alms).

The Kshatriya he commanded to protect the people, to bestow gifts, to offer sacrifices, to study (the Veda), and to abstain from attaching himself to sensual pleasures.

The Vaisya to tend cattle, to bestow gifts, to offer sacrifices, to study (the Veda), to trade, to lend money, and to cultivate land.

One occupation only the lord prescribed to the Sudra, to serve meekly even these (other) three castes." SOURCE: Buhler (1886 [Manu 1:87–91]).

FIGURE 9.9
A high-caste Brahman priest studying a sacred text.

ing and ranking them. It is common, particularly in census-taking, to group them by *varna* ranks, but caste clusters, castes, and subcastes may be distinguished.

Hindu building manuals prescribe a physical layout of house and temple that supports the caste

hypergamy Marriage to someone of higher rank. For example, Hindu women may marry men of a higher subcaste.

hypogamy Marriage to someone of lower rank.

impurity Low ritual status attributed to association or contact with polluting biological events or products.

FIGURE 9.10

South Indian Brahman house layout with supporting gods and Foundation Man (after Moore 1989, Figures 1 and 3).

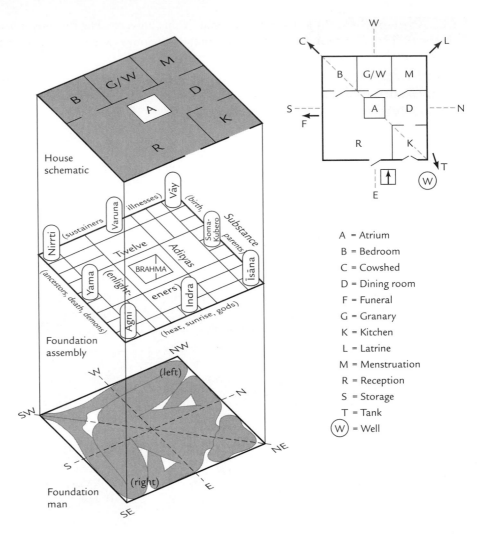

A = Atrium
B = Bedroom
C = Cowshed
D = Dining room
F = Funeral
G = Granary
K = Kitchen
L = Latrine
M = Menstruation
R = Reception
S = Storage
T = Tank
(W) = Well

system and the social hierarchy. Figure 9.10 shows the formal architectural plan of a Brahman's house in South India based on a sixth-century text, which outlined a model for domestic houses that was still followed in the twentieth century (Melinda Moore 1989). Rooms are aligned with the cosmos, including the cardinal directions. The house literally builds on the body of a mythic Foundation Man, who supports Brahma, the primordial solar creator god, Brahma's twelve attendants, the enlighteners, and an outer array of gods and demons each associated with particular human concerns such

as birth, death, illness, and ancestors. The sun rotates from east to west, and the north-south axis is associated with birth and death cycles respectively. The arrangement of the deities in concentric rings of 1, 4, 8, and 32 portrays a rank order that naturalizes hierarchy. This rank order is also reflected in the sequential order of domestic space with the atrium as the center of the house, and the rooms, the veranda, the compound, and the outside ranked in descending order of exclusivity. The rooms of the house are also functionally aligned with the Foundation Man so that the kitchen corresponds with his mouth, his genitals with the bedroom, and his impure left hand with the latrine.

Food, Eating, and Caste in Hindu Culture

Caste membership may be defined in a very general way by occupational speciality and by endogamy, but food rules are also very important. Certain caste groups are distinguished by strict vegetarianism, avoidance of domestic pigs and fowl, abstinence from alcohol, or the eating of pork or beef. At the village level, caste membership is also defined by the commensal hierarchy, according to which castes give or accept specific categories of food or water from each other or smoke together (Mayer 1970).

Hindu intellectuals made ideas about food a central element in their esoteric cosmological texts. The food circulation model presented in Figure 9.11 was abstracted from ancient texts and contemporary ethnographic observation by R. S. Khare (1976a). It is remarkably similar to the Andean cosmology (see Figure 7.16). There is an explicit flow of energy and materials, and a hierarchical structure in both cosmologies. Hindu cosmology distinguishes material and spiritual existence, and assumes a three-ranked cosmos with a natural base, divided into organic and inorganic sectors; a human level in the middle, distinguishing individual and social group; and a supernatural level at the top, distinguishing human ancestors and gods. This is the same as the familiar anthropological analytic framework of infrastructure, structure, and superstructure.

Food moves through the Hindu cosmos in four interconnected cycles, each more inclusive, as follows: (1) through the body of an individual person; (2) ritual exchanges between individuals and groups; (3) symbiotic and spiritual links between the gods, people, and nature; (4) from primordial material to spiritual order. The physical and cultural existence of food is variously degraded, regenerated, and degenerated in these cycles from inorganic to organic, from pure to

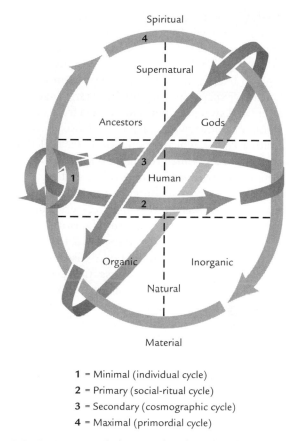

1 = Minimal (individual cycle)
2 = Primary (social-ritual cycle)
3 = Secondary (cosmographic cycle)
4 = Maximal (primordial cycle)

FIGURE 9.11   A Hindu cosmology based on food cycles (Khare 1976). (SOURCE: R. S. Khare 1976. *Culture and Reality: Essays on the Hindu System of Managing Foods.* Simla: Indian Institute of Advanced Study, page 136, Figure 3.)

impure, and from impure back to pure. As a natural category "food" may exist as food *(anna)*, leftover garbage *(jūthā)*, or excrement *(gū)*. In the supernatural order food offered to the gods becomes *prasād*, and can be eaten by everyone, but other forms of food necessarily encode social status and rank.

If village-level food transactions are viewed as a ranking game, then an individual player may win a point, or dominate, in any transaction between unequal partners in which he gives food to the other player, but loses points when he receives food (Marriot 1968). The act of giving food can establish dominance, whereas receiving can establish subordination. Relative caste ranking in a community is the net score (wins minus losses) from a series of such transactions. Raw food stuffs, *sīdhā*, such as grain, flour, and sugar are given back and forth among the members of all castes, except the very lowest castes, such as hunters and sweepers, who can receive from everyone, but can only give to each other. Cooked foods are either *kacha*, which is commonly rice boiled in water, or *pakka*, which is fried in oil. Kacha foods are highly restricted by purity rules, and the way in which they are distributed makes fine distinctions in rank between givers and receivers. For example, anthropologist McKim Marriot (1968) was able to sort the 166 families and 24 castes in a North Indian village into 12 ranks based on their *pakka, kacha*, and garbage transaction scores.

Within their households, orthodox Brahman Hindus make an important ritual distinction between cooking and serving areas, and maintain separate storage areas for uncooked and cooked food (Khare 1976a). The storage area is inside the house near the worship area, or in the pure end of the house as shown in Figure 9.10, and must be kept far from the impure waste disposal area. The cooking area is compared to the most sacred area of a temple. It is an exclusive space where only the cook is allowed. The serving area is less exclusive. The serving and eating area may itself be subdivided into three ranked subzones by degree of purity and exclusiveness. The cooking and serving areas become impure when eating is over and leftovers and cooking vessels must be cleaned in a separate washing place. Members of the lowest caste deal with the final waste, but a higher caste does the washing. The food area is ritually cleaned by low caste workers twice a day after each of the two daily meals. All visible specks of dirt must be removed from floor, hearth, utensils, or furniture, and the wall freshly plastered with cow dung to return these areas to their original high rank. The important point is that the high caste person requires the services of a lower caste person to restore his own high ritual status. The cook must be either a Brahman or the highest ranking person in the household, and in a state of ritual purity. Purification requires complete bathing in water and wearing freshly hand-washed clothing.

Kacha and *pakka* foods must be kept separate, because *pakka* foods become *kacha* when they come in contact with *kacha* food. A cook may not taste food as he cooks because that would make it "eaten" food, thereby polluting the entire meal. Food is polluted by contact with saliva. Offering food to the deity and keeping the fire going help it retain its pure state. Men eat before women, and a husband eats separately from his wife. In preparation for his meal, a senior man would be ritually purified by bathing and would wear only a hand-washed loincloth and sandals. He would wash his hands and feet, gargle, and sprinkle water on his head before seating himself on the floor in the eating area, on a spot where water had been sprinkled. Women servers would be veiled in his presence. Before eating, he would offer a food sacrifice to the fire, then he would eat in silence, and after eating he would touch the empty plate three times, thanking the food god. Then he would again wash his hands and feet, because eating makes one impure. He might leave food on his plate for his wife.

Village-Level Caste and Exploitation

From 1954 to 1956, anthropologist Adrian Mayer (1970) studied caste relations in the village of Ramkheri in the Malwa district of Madhya Pradesh in central India. Ramkheri was a relatively large village with 912 people belonging to 27 different castes. The castes were grouped by mutual consent into 5 groups and 11 ranks, with the Brahmans at the top and five untouchable castes at the bottom. Groups of castes at a similar rank tended to be localized in distinct quarters of the village. An interdependent division of labor, called the *jajmani system,* operated between the castes, with certain castes, such as barber, carpenter, blacksmith, potter, tanner-shoemaker, and sweeper, providing communitywide services. For example, the sweeper caste was responsible for cleaning latrines and disposing of dead animals—highly polluting functions that benefited everyone. In exchange for their services, caste members received foodstuffs according to a regular schedule. Some caste members, such as farmers and tailors who sold their products in town, were paid in cash for their goods by their fellow villagers.

All castes could draw water from the village well except the Harijan, who used their own wells and even washed their clothes and bathed at a separate place in the stream. The Harijan were expected to avoid the village temple and stood in the background during community meetings.

In the case of Ramkheri, the caste system had obvious implications for social stratification. Mayer (1970) found that the high-caste individuals owned more and tended to be more prosperous than low-caste people. However, wealth differences were not extreme and were partly attributed to expectations about relative occupational abilities. The economic advantages enjoyed by the upper castes were to some extent offset by the mutual advantages provided by the caste division of labor, and people appeared to accept their traditional occupations as a religious duty. Basic Hindu beliefs in *karma* and reincarnation support such acceptance by implying that one's *karma* (deeds or action) in life reflects previous existences and shapes one's future lives. The next life might be more pleasant.

Researchers in other areas described more extreme wealth inequities between castes. For example, Gerald Berreman (1979), who worked in the Himalayan foothills of Uttar Pradesh in 1957–1958, found that the Rajput and Brahmans enjoyed what M. N. Srinivas (1959) called "decisive dominance" in the region. Jonathan Parry (1979), who worked in the Kangra district of Himachal Pradesh in 1966–1968, also found that the highest castes received the best education, owned the most land, and held the best jobs.

The conspicuous inequality inherent in the caste system has led Western observers to focus on its economic component and to see caste as an exaggerated form of social stratification and rank, perhaps designed by the Brahmans for

their own benefit. Dumont (1970) acknowledged that there is an important material dimension to caste but suggested that exclusive emphasis on this aspect is ethnocentric and obscures the native view in which caste forms a rational intellectual system. Dumont argued that it is most useful to examine caste as a "state of mind." He did not claim that mental facts cause the caste system—rather, they make it intelligible.

British anthropologist J. H. Hutton, in his classic study of caste (1963), identified the functionalist advantages of caste at several levels. He argued that it provides individuals with employment, a pattern for living, and personal security. The individual castes also function as self-reproducing corporate groups. They provide for themselves many services that the state might otherwise be required to supply. Hutton further argued that the caste system contributes to Indian national stability by creating a "plural society" capable of absorbing diverse groups into a single cohesive whole. Hutton was also critical of the inequities of caste—especially the disadvantages that women suffered under it—but as a functionalist, he cautiously concluded that it is too central to Hindu culture for reform-minded government administrators to attack directly.

The Hindu caste system is an extreme form of institutionalized inequality, which, as Berreman (1979) argued, arose in the process of state building by the Aryan invaders of India. Many castes are historically known to have been distinct tribal groups that were absorbed into expanding Hindu kingdoms. In the process, the hierarchical ranking of kin within tribal societies was replaced by the hierarchical ranking of castes within the state system, which was actually an incipient form of social stratification. The new ranking system helped to secure the advantageous position of the political elites by making the former tribal groups dependent and divided against themselves.

Regardless of how it may be described in intellectualist or functionalist terms, or how it may be understood emically, the caste system is a form of oppression and exploitation that benefits certain elite groups at the expense of other groups. Ultimately, it is political power that perpetuates the system. As Berreman observed,

> Poverty and oppression, whether rationalized by criteria of race, ethnicity, caste, or class, are endured not because people agree on their legitimacy, but because they are enforced by those who benefit from them. (1979:221)

Hindu Aesthetics: Divine Image and the Religious Power of Art

The caste system, with all its inequities, is closely identified with and supported by the Hindu religion. However, beyond the belief in spiritual reincarnation, Hinduism also provides important emotional compensations for those wishing to escape the very real material inequities of caste. As monotheists, Christians have great difficulty understanding the Hindu religion because, from a Christian viewpoint, it is based on the worship of "idols." Furthermore, the prominence of erotic themes in Hindu religious art blurs the Western distinction between the sacred and the profane, thus making Hinduism appear very profane. Closer inspection of Hinduism shows that it contains an aesthetic system that makes culturally distinctive assumptions about art, worship, and the relationship between secular and sacred. Hinduism uses religious art as a powerful tool for helping individuals at all levels of the social hierarchy to experience a feeling of contact with an ultimate, eternal reality that transcends their daily mortal concerns. Christianity may accomplish the same objectives through different means.

Two key Hindu concepts, *rasa* and *darsan*, draw attention to some of the most important contrasts between Western and Hindu notions of religion and art. Richard Anderson (1990) notes that early Hindu philosophers felt that art was an important enough component of Hinduism to be considered a "fifth veda" on a par with the principal sacred texts, but open to everyone, regardless of their *varna* level. Art in the Hindu context refers, first, to drama, poetry, music, and dance, all of which emphasize a temporal dimen-

sion, and, second, to painting, sculpture, and architecture, which are relatively static. According to classical Hindu scholars, art is supposed to be an unconscious vehicle for moral improvement and pleasure, which are assumed to be mutually reinforcing.

Rasa refers to the emotional pleasure that the experience of art can provide. Anderson (1990) shows that Hindu art is thought to be pleasurable because it helps people attain the most important goals of the Hindu good life: righteousness, spirituality, prosperity, and pleasure. It is this linking of pleasure with religion that offends some Christians, who at the same time would readily acknowledge that doing "good" should make one feel good. The Hindu concept of good merges the "sacred" goals of righteousness and spirituality with the "profane" goals of material prosperity and sensual pleasure. Thus, for Hindus, there is no contradiction in erotic religious art. The religious use of sensuality is even more obvious in Tantrism, which is a Hindu and Buddhist sect that uses food and ritualized sex as a form of religious meditation.

Rasa refers to the fleeting peak experience that art can inspire, as distinguished from religious meditation, which also has an important role in Hinduism. In a more mundane sense, *rasa* also refers to culinary flavor, spice, or relish. Scholarly definitions of *rasa* identify eight universal human emotions—happiness, pride, laughter, sorrow, anger, disgust, fear, and wonder—which may be experienced as *rasa*. Some Hindu authorities add tranquility as a ninth *rasa* emotion. Thus, religious art uses culturally specific symbols to manipulate emotion to help people feel good. As Anderson explains, art in the service of religion

> can sweep us away, transporting our spirits from the tedious cares and anxieties that besiege our daily lives. . . . It provides a means whereby we can transcend the sensory world around us and escape to a state of superior pleasure, practical betterment, and, ultimately, spiritual bliss. (1990:171–172)

Although Hinduism assumes the existence of one ultimate divine reality, it encourages great

Siva Iconography

Siva, or Shiva, the "Auspicious One," is one of the most prominent Hindu deities and illustrates the complexity of Hindu polytheism and iconography. Siva incorporates many universal complementary oppositions and ambiguities. He is a creator and a destroyer, a sensuous ascetic, benevolent and vengeful. He may be portrayed with multiple faces, three eyes, and four arms and sometimes as both male and female. He is often portrayed as a dancing figure in a ring of fire (Figure 9.B). Diana Eck provides a concise exegesis of this image:

FIGURE 9.B   Siva, in the form of Nataraja, the Lord of Dance, in a ring of fire.

> The flaming circle in which he dances is the circle of creation and destruction called *samsara* (the earthly round of birth and death) or *maya* (the illusory world). The Lord who dances in the circle of this changing world holds in two of his hands the drum of creation and the fire of destruction. He displays his strength by crushing the bewildered demon underfoot. Simultaneously, he shows his mercy by raising his palm to the worshiper in the "fear-not" gesture and, with another hand, by pointing to his upraised foot, where the worshiper may take refuge. It is a wild dance, for the coils of his ascetic's hair are flying in both directions, and yet the facial countenance of the Lord is utterly peaceful and his limbs in complete balance. Around one arm twines the *naga*, the ancient serpent which he has incorporated into his sphere of power and wears now as an ornament. In his hair sits the mermaid River Ganga, who landed first on Siva's hair when she fell from heaven to earth. Such an image as the dancing Siva engages the eye and extends one's vision of the nature of this god, using simple, subtle, and commonly understood gestures and emblems. (1985:41)

diversity in how this reality is culturally expressed and approached. Christianity, in contrast, is a very exclusive religion and recognizes relatively few images of divinity, such as the Father, Son, Holy Ghost, and the Virgin Mary.

Darsan refers to religious "seeing." For Hindus, viewing an image of the divine is in itself a form of worship or devotion (Eck 1985). It is expressed in pilgrimages to sacred places, in the special reverence for Hindu holy persons, and in the attention given to religious art, sculpture, temples, and shrines. Religious seeing, as Diana Eck (1985) points out, is a two-way process. The Hindu deity must "give" its image, and the ob-

server must receive it. Hindu polytheism is expressed in a vast variety of religious images, which may be called icons when they take on a definite form—for example, as a representational painting or sculpture (see the box entitled "Siva Iconography"). Often Hindu icons combine animal and human shapes with multiple arms, heads, or eyes to indicate different aspects of the deity. They are aniconic images when they are nonrepresentational, "formless" shapes, such as colored stones or a flame. Hindu religious images are not empty idols to Hindus; they are simply different forms or manifestations of the divine. Divine images are divine, and they focus the mind on the

FIGURE 9.12 A richly costumed spirit dancer preparing to leap into a mound of white-hot coals to demonstrate the purity of his devotion to a particular Hindu deity.

divine. Hindu devotion is expressed through the offering of humble gestures, flowers, food, and water or other special gifts, chants, and hymns to the divine images (Figure 9.12).

As in Amazonia, Hindu supernatural practices are based on metaphors, chains of association, and complex multiple meanings for the same symbols. Sex, fertility, and eroticism are especially prominent themes in Hindu representations of the deities Siva, his wife Parvati, and their children Ganesh and Murukan (Good 2000). In Hindu iconography Siva is represented by a round topped, phallic shaped stone column *(linga,*

linkam) with an iconographic vulva *(yoni)* at its base representing the goddess Śakti (power, or female power), or Parvati. The combined *linga* and *yoni* represent the union of male and female as the basis of existence. Active gods are incomplete without female energy. This is similar to Australian and Amazonian concepts of complementary opposition. Siva's first son Ganesh is depicted with an elephant head because he was generated directly by Parvati. Siva beheaded him out of jealousy and Ganesh took on the elephant head. Siva's second son Murukan was conceived in the normal way.

Temple worship is conspicuously a "rite of hospitality" for the deities, and enacts routine household duties that wives are expected to perform for husbands and guests (Good 2000). In south India, Tamil Hindus are devotees of androgenous deities representing gender balance and complementarity in marriage. Reenactments of divine weddings are prominent features of Hindu temple ritual. This affirms the belief that marriage as a combination of male and female principles is a source of social power, and helps define the social order. For example, every year the temple in Kalugumalai, in Tamil Nadu, south India, celebrates Siva's son Murukan's marriages with two very different daughters of Vishnu, each contributing to Murukan's multiple identity. In November local people celebrate Murkan's marriage with Vishnu's daughter Amutavalli. This connects Murukan with divine power, whereas in February they celebrate Murukan's marriage with Suntaravalli (Valli) who is associated with local tribals, forest, and agriculture. Significantly Tamils believe both of these marriages to be appropriate cross-cousin marriages, because for Murukan, Amutuvalli and Suntaravalli are MBDs, daughters of his mother Parvati's brother Vishnu.

Daily Hindu temple liturgical practice involves six daily "worship" services *(pūja)*, each involving unction (anointing as a symbol of consecration), decoration, food-offering, and lampshowing centered on divine couples who have their own connubial bedrooms in the temple. In these rituals divinities are represented either as separate entities or united as couples. These services give people opportunities to view images or "take darshan" of the divine at propitious times. The six phases in the Kalugumalai temple are bedroom lamp-offering at 5:30 AM, holy adorning at 6:00, festival worship at 8:00, the daily festival and the royal endowment at 11:00, the noon service, a lamp showing at 6 PM, and a "midnight service" and bedroom worship at 8:30.

Controversy over the Sacred Cow

Cattle sacrifice, which was central to the ritual system, was a monopoly of the Brahman priests during the Vedic period in India. As Hinduism and the caste system developed, cattle were treated as deities and became an important feature of the ritual purity complex. The five products of the cow—fresh milk, sour milk, butter, urine, and dung—were important purifying agents, whereas the consumption of a cow's flesh and leather working were polluting. According to the Dharma Sastra, cows were not to be disturbed or injured. The Arthasastra was blunt: "Whoever hurts or causes another to hurt, or steals or causes another to steal, a cow, should be slain" (Shamasastry 1960 [Bk. 2, chap. 29]). Under the influence of the *ahimsa* doctrine of nonviolence toward people and all animals, promoted by the Jains (adherents of Jainism, a major Hindu sect) and Buddhists since the sixth century BC this reverence for cows was carried to the point that special templelike homes were maintained to care for aged and abandoned cattle. The sacred status of the cow was increased by the arrival of the beef-eating Muslims and the British because cow reverence became a conspicuous marker of Hindu culture.

The Indian Sacred Cow Complex has been the center of a theoretical debate between anthropologists, economists, and geographers over whether Indians keep too many cows for primarily religious reasons. Anthropologist Marvin Harris (1965, 1966) argued that practical economic choices by poor farmers were more important determinants of cattle practices in India than strictly religious considerations.

Harris (1965, 1966) was responding to numerous assessments by Indian public officials and development experts that Indians wastefully maintained vast numbers of useless cows because of irrational religious beliefs. Much of the criticism was over the poor quality of many of the animals and the quantity of fodder that they consumed. Harris challenged this interpretation, arguing that it was based on irrelevant market-economy cash accounting. He emphasized that the relationship between people and cows in India was more likely to be symbiotic. Cattle subsist on the byproducts of the grain production system, which they in turn help sustain. He suggested that ecological pressures encouraged the maintenance of seemingly unproductive cattle, as well as the ideology of *ahimsa,* which supports the practice.

Harris (1965, 1966) maintained that the most important contribution of Indian cattle was their support of the grain-based subsistence system as draft animals and through the production of dung for fuel and fertilizer. Bullocks pulling plows and carts help produce and transport the grain that supplies 80 percent of the calories people consume. For most peasant families, tractors would be prohibitively expensive to purchase and operate, and a pair of bullocks is an absolute necessity. There appears to be an actual shortage of traction animals during periods of intense plowing activity, which is determined by the annual cycle of monsoon rains. Furthermore, Harris argued, up to half of the cow dung may be used as a domestic cooking fuel, while the remainder serves as fertilizer. Considering the volume of energy involved in a country as densely populated as India, this resource would be very costly to replace with commercially produced fossil fuels. Harris concluded that

it should be obvious that without major technical and environmental innovations or drastic population cuts, India could not tolerate a large beef-producing industry. This suggests that insofar as the beef-eating taboo helps discourage growth of beef-producing industries, it is part of an ecological adjustment which maximizes rather than minimizes the calorie and protein output of the productive process. (1966:57)

The Cattle Complex of India resembles the East African Cattle Complex in that in both cultures cattle play a central role in the material infrastructure, the social structure, and in the ideological superstructure, but there are important cultural contrasts. Indian cattle are managed primarily to produce male traction animals, yet the direct production of animal protein remains an important secondary outcome. At 413 pounds (187 kg) of milk a year, average milk production of Indian cattle is less than half that of East African cattle (1606 lb [728 kg]) and 8 percent of an intensively managed U.S. dairy cow (5000 lb [2265 kg]). However, even this relatively low production rate represents a significant contribution to the animal-protein intake of the Indian population. It is also important to remember that beef is consumed in India by Muslims, Christians, and members of the untouchable castes who can afford it, and cattle are an important source of leather, which is produced by the untouchables.

Harris (1965, 1966) agreed that cattle can be environmentally destructive and are part of the problem of increased human pressure on resources. But he still argued that poorly fed, relatively inefficient cattle can nevertheless be advantageous to individual poor farmers.

Indian cattle are malnourished during the dry season, but when their services as draft animals are most required, they rebound when grazing improves with the monsoons. Like their East African counterparts, they tolerate drought conditions better than larger breeds, and they rebound more quickly. Free-ranging cattle feed themselves at public expense and no doubt, in some cases, at the expense of wealthy farmers and landlords; thus, they may play a role in wealth redistribution where great economic inequality exists.

The origin of the Sacred Cow Complex has been debated. Harris (1966) proposed that it may have begun in the Ganges Valley by 1000 BC when population pressure resulted in decreased farm size and made cattle more valuable as draft animals. The religious taboo on killing cattle thus came about so that people would not be tempted to slaughter them for food and thereby threaten their agricultural system. Simoons (1979) argued that the ban on killing cattle may have been proposed by the early Hindu kingdoms in order to secure a surplus for the expanding urban centers, thus benefiting the elite rather than the peasants. This is in agreement with Harris's view that the prohibition on cattle killing was part of an "imperial cult" that supported the elite and is not incompatible with the view that the ban also benefited the peasants.

At the village level, evidence supports rational herd-management practices by farmers as well as decision making based on religious principles (Freed and Freed 1981). People do say that they protect cows as an act of worship, and there is no reason to doubt their sincerity. At the same time, as Harris observes (1988), from an etic point of view, Indians selectively starve unwanted calves, while emicly they claim that all calves must be protected.

On balance, the controversy has drawn attention to the economic value of seemingly useless cows, but it also demonstrates the difficulty of positively determining why people do what they do. The sacred cow case does affirm the importance of religious belief. For example, as Simoons (1979) pointed out, many low-caste groups have stopped eating beef in order to avoid the ritual stigma of pollution and thereby enhance their social standing. The relationships between belief and actions are complex, and the best analysis would take a holistic ethnographic approach.

WOMEN IN SOUTH ASIA

South Asian women, whether under Hindu or Islamic Great Traditions, are clearly at a cultural disadvantage in comparison with men. This disadvantage is based on myth and religious ideology recorded in sacred texts and is expressed in ritual and physical separation between men and women, whereby men take leadership roles and enjoy relatively greater freedom outside the household. In this section, we will review the cultural-historical background of Islam to facilitate comparison with the Hindu Great Tradition. Then we will consider the position of women under both cultural traditions.

The Islamic Great Tradition

Striking parallels exist between the rise of Islam as an expansive state system and the development of Hindu civilization. Both cases are examples of secondary state formation from a pastoral tribal base in response to the influence of preexisting states. In both cases, a complex interethnic conquest state was integrated by means of a literate Great Tradition ideological system. It is remarkable that both traditions came to coexist in India even though the two systems were incompatible on fundamental issues of belief.

In contrast to Hinduism, the details of the founding of Islam are well known. Islam is a revealed religion, transmitted in Arabic directly by Allah to his messenger, the Prophet Muhammad (AD 570–632). God's message is recorded as sacred scripture in the *Qur'an* (Koran) and is augmented by the *hadith,* or traditions surrounding the Prophet. Islam, which in Arabic means "surrender," refers to the need of the Muslim (believer) to surrender to the will of Allah, the one God. The fundamental articles of faith are encompassed by the Five Pillars of Islam:

1. Recitation of the Shahadah, confession of faith: "There is no God but Allah and Muhammad is his Prophet"
2. The performance of five daily prayers
3. The giving of alms *(zakkat)*
4. Observance of the fast of Ramadan
5. Pilgrimage to Mecca (the *hajj)*

Muhammad was a member of the Quraysh, a sedentarized north Arabian Bedouin tribe that controlled the Red Sea trade from Mecca, which was already an important ritual center. Muhammad's religious visions began in about 610; by the time of his death in 632, he had succeeded in uniting all the Bedouin tribes of Arabia into a religious state based on the new faith. The pre-Islamic Bedouin tribes were relatively egalitarian, patrilineal segmentary systems, led by popularly supported "chiefs" or *shaykhs* (sheiks), who led raids, settled disputes, and enjoyed some prestige but were still considered "first among equals." An essential element in this tribe-to-state transformation was the replacement of tribal and kinship loyalties with membership in the Umma, the Islamic community, which created a united front by suppressing the blood feud that had characterized intertribal relations throughout Arabia (Lewis 1960).

The Umma was a nascent religious state, united by common belief and military opposition to unbelieving outsiders as expressed in the *jihad,* or holy war. Under Islam, the Prophet Muhammad was accepted as the divinely appointed head of state. However, Muhammad did not specify how his successor, the caliph, was to be selected. Conflict over the succession resulted in a sectarian split between the Sunnites, who believed they were following the *Sunna* (the Prophet's collected sayings) in selecting the caliph, and the Shi'ites, who favored keeping the imam (foremost of the community) in the Prophet's closest line of descent and recognized their own line of imams. The caliph or imam, as the leader of the Islamic state and chief defender of the faith, was expected to lead prayers at the Friday service in the mosque. He was also responsible for settling disputes, collecting taxes, and organizing the *jihad* against unbelievers.

After the death of Muhammad, a period of rapid military expansion began that brought the Mesopotamian region—much of Persia, Egypt, and North Africa—under Islamic control by 700. Next, Muslims entered Spain and began to raid northern India. Conquest was a major source of state revenue, whether directly as battlefield booty or as tribute or tax in agricultural production. During the expansion of Islam, unbelievers with literate sacred scriptures—such as Jews, Christians, and, by extension, Hindus—were granted protection as peoples of the book as long as they acknowledged Islamic political authority and paid their taxes. Small Islamic kingdoms, or sultanates, were established in India by 1200, and from 1526 to 1761, the Islamic Mughal empire ruled over most of the Indian subcontinent. Although the Mughal rulers generally tolerated Hindu practices, there were many areas of conflict between the two Great Traditions, as illustrated by the modern partitioning of British India into Muslim Pakistan and Hindu India in 1947.

The Islamic state was based on the *shari'a,* which, like *tao* in Chinese, means "path" or "road." Like the Hindu concept of *dharma, shari'a* is God's law as outlined in the Koran and the *Sunna* or the *hadith* accepted by the Shi'ites (Levy 1962). Islamic law is a detailed prescription for all areas of life, specifying whether individual acts are required, forbidden, recommended, disapproved, or permitted. Islam, like Hinduism, constitutes a complete social system and has had a profound influence over preexisting cultural practices whenever Islamic states have been established.

Women in Islamic Society

Any discussion of Islamic social practices must begin with a careful disclaimer acknowledging the great diversity of practices in specific countries and regions, at different historical times, between urban and village settings, and between different social classes. Furthermore, the Koran itself is interpreted in many different ways. However, certain principles do stand out. According to fundamentalist Islamic interpretations, women are generally viewed as morally and legally inferior to men. They are to be protected by their husbands and close male kin and are to stay out of public life. In several respects, in comparison with men, Muslim women are at a legal disadvantage by many interpretations of Islamic law. Daughters inherit less than sons. Women are permitted only one spouse at a time, whereas men may have up to four wives as long as they can provide for them and treat them fairly. Muslim women are expected to marry only other Muslims, whereas men may marry unbelieving peo-

ples of the book. It is more difficult for a woman to obtain a divorce. Furthermore, modesty and male honor often require female seclusion (discussed in detail in the following section).

Many observers stress that Koranic law actually represented an improvement in the position of women over the common practice of pre-Islamic times. Women's rights in marriage, divorce, inheritance, and property ownership are specified in ways that no doubt increased their security.

A modern expression of Islamic gender roles is a common tendency toward gender segregation in education and employment. Labor migration by men for extended periods, leaving wives to maintain the household, is a common pattern. Women are less likely to work outside the home than men, and when they are employed as professionals, women tend to work with other women as teachers or doctors. Both high-status and low-status positions in the complementary occupational pairs—such as doctor–nurse, principal–teacher, executive–secretary, which are commonly seen as male–female sets in Western industrial countries—are more likely to be filled by men in Islamic countries (Papanek 1982).

When they address Western audiences, and especially Western feminists, Muslim female social scientists often stress that many of the cultural patterns that Western women take as evidence of Islamic oppression of women are misunderstood in ways that perpetuate the view that Muslim women are passive and ignorant, if not inferior. For example, Leila Ahmed (1982) argues that Westerners usually describe the harem entirely in male terms, as an institution for confining and controlling women to provide men with secure sexual access to multiple wives. The harem system does segregate women from men; Islamic women themselves, however, recognize that such segregation need not be oppressive in itself. Ahmed notes that the word *harem* is derived from the Arabic word *haram,* meaning "forbidden." She suggests that it is women who forbid males to enter exclusively female space. The harem is a gathering place for women where they can freely discuss and ridicule men and the world of men. It is also a place where a feminist critique of Islamic society can take place. Many Western women, isolated in nuclear families, do not enjoy such freedom. Thus, although Islamic women are in many ways discriminated against by their societies, seeing specific Islamic social institutions in entirely negative terms can be misleading. According to Ahmed,

> to believe that segregated societies are by definition more oppressive to women, or that women secluded from the company of men are women deprived, is only to allow ourselves to be servilely obedient to the constructs of men, Western or Middle Eastern. (1982:531)

It must be remembered, however, that the harem is part of a larger Islamic society, which is controlled primarily by men.

Female Seclusion: The Purdah System

The practice of *purdah*, the veiling and seclusion of women, is a conspicuous South Asian cultural pattern, shared by Hindus and Muslims alike, and is related to the institutionalization of gender inequality shared by both cultures. *Purdah* means "curtain" or "veil" and refers to the physical separation of the living spaces used by men and women, as well as the actual veiling of a woman's face and body. This is a South Asian variation of the harem of the Arab Islamic world. The concept of *purdah* is also commonly extended to refer to types of avoidance or deference behavior practiced by women, including not looking at or speaking to certain people. Adherence to *purdah* restrictions is related to specific factors such as employment, education, social class, politics, and religion. Some Muslim sects have abolished or intensified seclusion by decree. Western observers often denounce *purdah* as another example of male oppression, but, like the harem, it plays an important functional role in the culture and is supported by many of the women who practice it.

In the strictest form of *purdah,* a woman must remain completely within the confines of her

FIGURE 9.13   An Indian Muslim woman wearing *burqa.*

home throughout her adult life. Within a large house, there may be women's rooms and entrances that outside men cannot use, and special screens and partitions may be set up to hide women from view. In some cases, seclusion of women extends to otherwise public buildings and public transportation. Although there is considerable variation in the degree to which veiling is practiced, in extreme form, a Muslim woman in *purdah* can leave the seclusion of her home only when wearing the *burqa,* a full length garment covering head and body (Figure 9.13).

Purdah is based on the interconnected principles of *separate worlds* for men and women, and *symbolic shelter* for women (Papanek 1982).

The principle of separate worlds is expressed in a sharp division of labor and workplace and in the corresponding economic interdependence between men and women. The principle of symbolic shelter is founded in the belief that women are especially vulnerable in a hostile outside world and therefore must be kept sheltered at home. The outside danger from which women need protection is the threat of uncontrolled sexual and aggressive impulses. The underlying assumption seems to be that people need close external supervision to control themselves; thus, *purdah* restrictions physically remove women from possible harm. Papanek suggests that Hindus and Muslims may view the dangers to women somewhat differently, with Hindu women seen as potential temptresses and Muslim women seen as potential victims, but either way they need to be protected. The dependency of women and supremacy of men are as deeply rooted in Hindu culture as they are in Islam. In certain details, the Hindu version of *purdah* has been influenced by Islamic traditions, but the principles of symbolic sanctuary existed prior to Islam in India. For example, Manu, in the Dharma Sastra, declared the following laws for women:

> No act is to be done according to (her) own will by a young girl, a young woman, or even by an old woman, though in (their own) houses. In her childhood (a girl) should be under the will of her father; in (her) youth, of (her) husband; her husband being dead, of her sons; a woman should never enjoy her own will. She must never wish separation of her self from her father, husband, or sons, for by separation from them a woman would make both families contemptible. She must always be cheerful and clever in household business, with the furniture well cleaned, and with not a free hand in expenditure. But him to whom her father gives her, or (her) brother with the father's consent, she must obey alive, and dead must not disregard. (Burnell and Hopkins 1884:130–131)

Papanek (1982) stresses another important dimension of symbolic shelter: Women are "status demonstrators" for their husbands. The Muslim concept of *izzat,* family "honor" or "pride," ex-

tends to the modesty and virtue of a man's wife, sister, and daughter. Of course, the reverse is not the case; that is, a woman's status is not determined by the virtue of her husband, brother, or father. This is the famous double standard that also has a long history in Western civilization. The observance of *purdah* is an expression of modesty, social solidarity, and family respectability. The importance of feminine virtue is emphatically demonstrated by the ideal of Sita, the heroine of the Ramayana, one of the best-known Hindu myths (see the box entitled "The Ramayana").

Anthropologist Manisha Roy (1975), a Bengali woman, has carefully documented how the experience of growing up in the Hindu extended family creates culturally conditioned expectations for women that are often unfulfilled. The popular Hindu myths, which stress the ideals of romantic love and self-sacrificing devotion to the husband, conflict with the realities of arranged Hindu marriages and generate psychological frustration for women. A woman's husband often turns out to be an emotionally remote protector who is close to his wife only when he relates to her as mother of his children. Upper-class, urban Bengali women are able to find some compensation for the frustrations in their domestic lives by developing a long-term relationship as a devoted disciple of a guru outside the extended family, but this is only possible after their children are grown.

There are significant differences between the way Muslim and Hindu women in South Asia practice *purdah*. For example, Muslim women are secluded from all outside men, whereas Hindu women are secluded from all male affines, especially from their husband's kinsmen (Papanek 1982, Vatuk 1982). The Hindu pattern has been described in detail by Doranne Jacobson (1982), based on her research in the Bhopal region of central India. In this area, a Hindu woman remains fully veiled before virtually all male affines in her husband's joint family. She must also be partially veiled before many of the senior women in her husband's joint family. However, when she visits her natal village, she is virtually free of *purdah* restrictions.

The Ramayana: A Hindu Mythic Charter of Feminine Virtue

The Ramayana is one of the most popular Hindu myths, dating to 300 BC, during the early classic period of Hindu civilization. This epic romance is a part of the cultural identity of all Hindus. It is frequently recited in dramatic performances and is required reading in Indian schools. It presents a compelling role model of the ideal Hindu wife.

Briefly stated, the Ramayana (the Romance of Rama) tells the story of Rama, an incarnation of Vishnu, who weds the beautiful Sita, the heroine, after passing a heroic test. However, he is cheated out of his place as heir to his father's throne and banished to a 14-year exile in the forest. Out of devotion to her husband, Sita follows her husband into exile, even though he urges her to stay behind. Later, Sita is treacherously abducted by an evil king who wants to marry her, but she rejects his advances and is imprisoned. Meanwhile, her husband, Rama, recruits an army and rescues her, but he suspects that Sita was unfaithful to him during her imprisonment and forces her to pass an ordeal by fire to prove her loyalty before accepting her back. Rama takes his rightful place on the throne of his kingdom with Sita as queen. When his subjects gossip that Sita really was unfaithful after all, Rama sends her away again to the forest, where she raises his twin sons. When Sita sends his grown sons back to him, he invites her to return but insists that she again prove her virtue. She has, of course, been completely faithful and totally devoted to him throughout her ordeal, but this time she accepts his rejection and asks the earth to swallow her up. This is a fitting gesture because in the myth she was born from the earth.

Before examining the possible functions of *purdah*, it is important to consider the emic view. Women who practice *purdah* often attribute their adherence to feelings of shame, shyness, or embarrassment, and they relate it to parallel concerns for honor and respect. Their enculturation, especially through internalization of the heroic role models provided by mythic figures such as Sita, makes it an internal response that does not require outside sanctions. As Jacobson reports, "Most secluded women, too, pride themselves on their strict observance of purdah" (1982:96–97). This emic view supports the symbolic sanctuary interpretation, but women also recognize that *purdah* can be a marker of elite status because only economically well-off households could afford to observe it fully.

Many functions of *purdah* have been proposed, and it seems clear that it does not represent a simple conspiracy of males to oppress women. *Purdah* also restricts men and imposes responsibilities on them. It creates dependency between men and women because a woman who cannot leave her home must rely on her husband, children, or servants to perform outside errands, such as shopping. A man, in turn, might not do domestic chores such as cooking and cleaning. It has been suggested that Hindus might use *purdah* to reduce the danger of female ritual pollution and to safeguard the purity of caste endogamy (Yalman 1963). The most direct function of *purdah* is that it helps sustain the integrity of the patrilineal extended or joint family, which is the most viable minimal social unit in stratified state societies based on plow agriculture (Boserup 1970, Jacobson 1982). This system requires careful control of small parcels of land and support from neighboring families and seems to work best with unambiguous lines of authority, a strict division of labor, and a maximum of domestic tranquility.

Purdah imposes social distance between men and women and intensifies their respective role differences. *Purdah* also minimizes the possibility for potentially disruptive incidents of adultery, both within and outside the extended family, and supports the common pattern of arranged marriages. Unmarried girls who are secluded in their homes are unlikely to find lovers to marry who might undermine established community alliance networks. In Muslim societies, marriage may be arranged between patrilateral parallel cousins (a man marries FBD), which helps to concentrate lineage resources and furthers a woman's seclusion by making even her affines relatively close kin.

In Jacobson's view, *purdah* has played a vital cultural role:

> However inimical such a system may be to the ideals of Westerners, urban-educated South Asians, or even to the preferences of a certain number of veiled women themselves, there can be no doubt that arrangements of this kind have allowed hundreds of millions of people to live—and sometimes even to prosper—over the course of several centuries in various corners of the earth. It should also be acknowledged that for many fortunate women, sequestered life in bustling and affectionate family units has provided security and satisfaction. Only as alternative family structures become economically feasible or necessary are male-dominated societies undergoing alteration in the direction of allowing females to assert their individuality in any but limited circumstances. (1982:84–85)

Bride Burning: Dowry Deaths in Modern Hindu India

In recent decades, Indian newspapers have increasingly reported on new brides who were burned to death in unexplained grease fires in their kitchens. It is generally understood that in these cases, the bride has been murdered by her husband after he has extorted as much dowry as possible from her family. The murderer is then free to seek more dowry "gifts" from a new bride.

In their analysis of this problem, anthropologists Linda Stone and Caroline James (1995) estimate that 2000 or more dowry deaths occur every year in India. Stone and James suggest that some of the cause of this violence against women is found both in traditional Hindu culture and in recent changes related to commercial-scale culture. Hindu culture provides many incentives for a woman's family to arrange marriage for their daughters and to give large dowries. In traditional India, it was not acceptable for a woman to be unmarried, even if widowed, as the traditional custom *sati* demonstrated. Divorce is seen as dishonoring the family. Furthermore, with the cultural ideal of hypergamy, a Hindu bride and her parents are considered to be gifts from social inferiors. This places them in a subservient position relative to the groom's family, making them vulnerable to harassment and demands for higher dowry payments. Dowry payments reflect the reduced economic value of women in cultures in which plow agriculture, which is a male domain, is the dominant economic activity. Dowry payments are also associated with private land ownership and wage labor in agrarian civilizations. Bride-wealth is more common in tribal cultures, such as in East Africa, where women are valued for both their subsistence and their reproductive roles.

The emergence of a consumption-based middle class in modern India has inflated dowry payments. Traditionally, the Hindu dowry involved household articles that were produced directly by the bride's family. Modern dowry payments may include large amounts of cash and expensive consumer goods such as televisions and refrigerators that are beyond the financial means of many middle-class Indians. It is significant that bride burning is primarily an urban, middle-class phenomenon. Frustrated consumer aspirations are a powerful motivation for these murders.

"Sita," who survived an attempted bride burning, told Caroline James that she brought a lavish dowry of $8000 along with 500 saris, jewelry, a television, a freezer, furniture, and kitchenware, but this was not enough to please her husband's family. Sita overheard her mother-in-law telling her husband, "Leave this woman and we will get another one; at least the other party will give us more and better dowry than what these people have given us. What her parents have given us is nothing. Moreover, this girl is ugly, and she is dark" (Stone and James 1995:128). Sita woke up one night to find that her husband had doused her with kerosene, but she escaped when he couldn't find a match.

Stone and James (1995) note that in traditional Hindu India, women were not likely to be subjected to such violence because female fertility was highly valued as the means of perpetuating the patrilineage. A woman's ability to produce sons gave her significant domestic power and security. It is probably not a coincidence that bride burnings have emerged just as fertility rates in India have begun to decline, especially in urban areas, where children are more likely to be an economic burden. The vulnerability of women is further increased in the modern urban setting because, relative to men, they can contribute little to household income in the wage economy. The status of women is higher in tribal cultures than in traditional agrarian civilizations, especially when the commercial culture transforms domestic economies.

SUMMARY

The Hindu civilization of South Asia is a literate Great Tradition with significant cultural continuity over the past 3000 years. The earliest South Asian Neolithic cultures were probably participants in the domestication process that occurred throughout Southwest Asia during the Early Holocene period. The Harappan civilization of the Indus Valley was the earliest South Asian state and probably had some connections with Mesopotamia. Hindu civilization arose in the Ganges region after the collapse of the Harappan civilization. Hindu culture apparently drew on some Harappan cultural elements but was primarily derived from the Indo-European-speaking Aryans who invaded South Asia from the west about 1600 BC.

The early Hindu kingdoms were a by-product of the Aryan conquest and the incorporation of the preexisting tribal cultures of the subcontinent. Classical Hindu kingdoms, as described in the Arthasastra, were organized around a complex government bureaucracy based on secular political power backed by a formal legal system with fines and physical punishments for offenders. It also relied on a religious system that divided society into four ranked groups, or *varna*. The dominant structure of Hindu society up to the present time is the caste system, which assigns everyone to a ritually ranked endogamous occupational group. This generates great social inequality, but it is justified and supported by Hindu religious beliefs that emphasize religious duty, the hope of reincarnation at a higher level, and the opportunity for people at all social levels to enjoy transcendental contact with the divine. Hindu religious beliefs also provide ritual protection for cows, which are an important source of fuel, food, and traction power for poor people who might otherwise have great difficulty supporting themselves.

Women are placed in inferior positions relative to men by both the Islamic and Hindu Great Traditions. These cultures rigidly separate men's and women's worlds in a way that supports the continuity of male-dominated extended families. Men occupy dominant roles in both their own families and the larger society. Women gain greater power as they grow older, and they benefit in certain ways from culturally prescribed separation. But women in modern India have been increasingly the targets of violence. Bride burning is related to the demand for high dowries and the difficulty women have contributing financially in a male-dominated wage economy.

STUDY QUESTIONS

1. Discuss the cultural significance of the following South Asian language groups: Indo-European, Dravidian, Sino-Tibetan, Hindi, Bengali, and Urdu.

2. Describe the basic social structure of the early Hindu kingdom. How did early Hindu kingdoms use direct political power to maintain and extend the state?
3. Compare and contrast the organization of the state in China and Hindu India.
4. How did the Hindu legal system reflect the inequalities of Hindu society?
5. Describe the basic structural features of the Hindu caste system, distinguishing it from class and clan.
6. In what way was ritual purity a central feature of Hindu culture?
7. Distinguish between *varna, jati,* Brahman, Kshatriya, Vaisya, and Sudra. Discuss the economic correlates of caste, and weigh the arguments that it served positive social functions or was exploitive.
8. In what ways does the Hindu Sacred Cow Complex have positive adaptive functions? What are the arguments for the religious explanations of the Sacred Cow Complex?
9. Describe the position of women according to fundamentalist Islamic principles.
10. Distinguish between the Islamic and Hindu cultural context of *purdah,* referring to the principles of separate worlds and symbolic shelter. What are the functionalist explanations of *purdah?*
11. Contrast the basic features of Islam and Hinduism, placing each system in its appropriate cultural-historical context.
12. Discuss how bride burning is related to modern Indian economics and the status of women.

SUGGESTED READING

ALLCHIN, BRIDGET, AND F. RAYMOND ALLCHIN. 1982. *The Rise of Civilization in India and Pakistan.* Cambridge, Eng.: Cambridge University Press. An archaeological overview of South Asian prehistory and the early development of Harappan and Hindu civilization.

BASHAM, A. L. 1954. *The Wonder That Was India: A Survey of the Culture of the Indian Sub-Continent Before the Coming of the Muslims.* London: Sidgwick & Jackson. A widely respected basic textbook on South Asian history and culture.

ECK, DIANA L. 1985. *Darsan: Seeing the Divine Image in India.* Chambersburg, Penn.: Anima Books. An in-depth treatment of the visual aspects of Hindu religion.

PAPANEK, HANNA, AND GAIL MINAULT (EDS.). 1982. *Separate Worlds: Studies of Purdah in South Asia.* Delhi: Chanakya Publications. An interdisciplinary collection of papers on the seclusion of women in South Asia.

TYLER, STEPHEN A. 1986. *India: An Anthropological Perspective.* Prospect Heights, Ill.: Waveland Press. An anthropological overview of many aspects of Indian culture with an emphasis on linguistic and cognitive categories.

Mesopotamian civilization collapsed after
3500 years.

10

The Breakdown
of States

Learning Objectives

After studying this chapter you should be able to do the
following.

1. Explain what happens to people and culture when
   politically organized societies break down.
2. Compare politically organized societies and tribal
   societies in reference to their vulnerability to collapse.
3. Compare the process of collapse in Mesopotamian,
   Harappan, and Andean civilizations and identify the
   likely causes.
4. Identify the principal scale thresholds that limited the
   scale of ancient empires.
5. Identify the system processes that limit the scale and
   durability of large cultural systems, including diminishing returns, sunk-cost effects, institutional functions and
   costs, and Parkinson's law.

A recurrent issue in Chapters 6–9 is how to explain the increases in social complexity that culminated in social stratification, state political organization, and Great Tradition civilizations. The origin of the state has been a central research problem in anthropology for many years; but much less attention has been devoted to the equally important issue of the continuity of states and the reasons for their frequent collapse. In this chapter, we consider the breakdown of states, which also forces us to reconsider theories of cultural development and the nature of the state itself. History has shown that states are unstable entities, prone to collapse from internal conflict and external invasion. Considering the multiple, interconnected potential threats to which states are vulnerable, it is remarkable that they ever arose in the first place. The failure of deterministic origin theories to satisfactorily account for all cases suggests that state formation is not an entirely predictable process. Similarly, the frequent collapse of states helps demonstrate that cultural evolution is not a straight line in one direction. It is also not irreversible, and not inevitable, despite persistent popular beliefs in "progress."

THE VIABILITY OF THE STATE

The Concept of Collapse

Our primary concern here is understanding the process by which states and empires decompose into smaller political units. This kind of system collapse must be distinguished from the fall of particular dynasties and their replacement by other sets of rulers. Changing dynasties is a major topic for historians but will not be treated here, except when the change represents a major cultural discontinuity. The focus of this discussion is the fate of ancient, precapitalist systems, because additional dynamics influence states in the modern world system; these new factors will be explored in Chapters 11–15.

In dealing with dynamic cultural and biological systems, defining when an entity ceases to exist and when it has changed into a different system is always a problem. Processual continuity—the continuation of dominant cultural processes such as urbanization, or continuity in long-established cultural practices such as writing systems, or government despite change in dynastic leadership—is the most useful criterion for determining when a cultural system has survived (Rappaport 1977b). But some ambiguity will always remain, and arbitrary judgments must be made about whether a particular culture, state, or civilization has been extinguished. The issue in this chapter is those conspicuous cases in which governments collapse and cities are abandoned. We will also consider a related but distinct issue: the less common problem of the total disappearance of particular Great Traditions.

Like any cultural system, a civilization is composed of the individuals or societies that perpetuate it, as well as the technologies, organizational patterns, and ideological systems that maintain it. States can break down while the population continues to transmit significant elements of the culture. The total disappearance of a people with their language and culture is an unlikely event, except when modern states have exterminated tribal peoples and cultures as a policy of national expansion (see Chapter 14).

It is important to ask, what changes when states collapse? The fall of states is not just an inconsequential change of political regimes; it also carries important human and environmental costs. State systems are based on social inequality and exploitation, but they do provide vital social services for very large populations. In ancient civilizations, the ruling elite had a clear vested interest in maintaining a large, productive population because people were the main source of state revenue and the troops used to extract booty from other states, to extend the boundaries of the state, or to defend the state against aggressors. People under state control may resent paying taxes, but, like it or not, their personal security depends on government institutions, like the police, the law, the courts, and the army. The state provides famine relief and promotes capital-intensive agricultural development. The state also develops and maintains the communications system and public services required for commerce and foreign trade. Living standards may be drastically reduced during periods of extreme political instability, as trade and marketing networks break down, and many people may be killed when social control mechanisms disappear or foreigners take over. Collapsing states may deplete valuable nonrenewable resources and leave behind seriously degraded ecosystems.

The Vulnerability of Inequality and Political Hierarchy

Although no culture can claim perfect functional integration, focusing on the issue of collapse makes it clear that large-scale, politically centralized societies are significantly more precarious than small-scale tribal societies. States are more complex systems with more pieces and more things to go wrong. However, this is not just a quantitative matter. Tribes cannot break down because there is no tribal political structure to collapse. Villages and bands undergo continuous reorganization and can be dissolved at any time with no particular impact on the larger society and culture. By contrast, large regional states break down into local kingdoms or city-states, which, in turn, may further split into chiefdoms or autonomous villages and bands.

States are especially vulnerable to collapse because they contain social classes based on major inequities in wealth and power. States create special-interest groups and give them a reason to risk bringing the whole system down in order to improve their own position. A limitation on the number of political offices generates perpetual rivalries. Inequalities of wealth and power may be the most critical defining feature of states and the single most important cause of their breakdown. The creation of wealth requires revenue,

but revenue extraction by taxation is a doubly risky state function. State authorities will seek as much revenue as possible, but if they demand too much, the peasantry may rebel. Too high a rate of revenue extraction also forces people to intensify their subsistence activities, which will increase the pressure on natural ecosystems.

Unequal concentrations of wealth—whether in the form of luxury goods, stored food, or labor-intensive construction projects—appear to be functional prerequisites for state organization; their presence, however, also causes dangerous instability. Warehoused food is required to support nonfood-producing specialists and to sustain dense populations that might be threatened by fluctuations in production. Luxury goods are necessary status markers and rewards for political service. Storehouses are prime targets for looters from both within and without a particular state, and their defense requires expensive walls and standing armies. The unequal distribution of luxury goods also makes police forces and court systems necessary.

Creating and defending state wealth is a primary reason for costly military campaigns against neighboring states. The maintenance of a full-time officer corps, palace guards, and frontier garrisons are permanent military expenses, and specific campaigns in which large numbers of peasant soldiers are mobilized can be extremely costly. Military expenditures may be the largest category in many state budgets and create constant pressure for potentially destabilizing increases in revenue extraction.

In comparison with a cultural universe occupied exclusively by tribal cultures, states introduced a qualitatively different cultural dynamic into any regional system. Whereas chronic feuding was endemic in tribal systems, territorial conquest was a permanent characteristic of states. Tribal raids and blood feuds did not require permanent leaders or a standing professional army and thus were not incentives for increased production. However, the appearance of states in a non-state area stimulated trade and raiding by tribal groups against the state. This sometimes pushed tribes into political developments leading to wealth inequality and tribal instability.

STATE SYSTEMS THAT FAILED

In the following sections, we will examine possible causes of political collapse and the relationship between collapse and the continuity of particular civilizations or Great Traditions. Examples are drawn from the cultures that were discussed in previous chapters. In Mesopotamia, foreign invasion definitively terminated 3500 years of cyclical state building and collapse. Mesopotamian civilization disappeared a few centuries later. Harappan urban civilization collapsed after approximately 1000 years but contributed significantly to later cultural developments in India. Andean civilization was characterized by perhaps 4500 years of processual continuity, punctuated by frequent collapse of individual states and empires, until it was halted by foreign invasion. In the Andes, however, even though the Spanish conquerors destroyed Andean civilization as an independent, politically centralized cultural system, indigenous Andean peoples still maintain and reproduce many cultural practices at the village level, including the language and important features of subsistence, social organization, and ideology. China, which is not examined in this chapter, also demonstrated nearly 4000 years of processual continuity, even though individual states and dynasties repeatedly collapsed. In China, the foreign invaders were absorbed by the Great Tradition, which persisted despite political change. These cases show the complexity of the issue of political collapse and the fate of civilizations. Cultural continuity clearly is stronger than political structure.

Mesopotamia: The End of a Great Tradition

If state organization began in Mesopotamia with the Uruk period in 4000 BC and if the Persian conquest of Babylonia in 539 BC marked the end of the distinctively Mesopotamian political system, then the Mesopotamian political system based on the state lasted for approximately 3500 years, and the Mesopotamian civilization ended some 500 years later in AD 75, when the last cuneiform document is known to have been written (Yoffee 1988a). After that time, no recognizable Mesopotamian language, economy, or belief system persisted, although certain specific cultural connections can still be traced in succeeding civilizations. This raises the question of whether Mesopotamian culture or civilization can be considered an entity. Yoffee defines Mesopotamian civilization as

> that fragile, but reproducible, set of cultural boundaries that encompass a variety of peoples, political and social systems, and geographies marked as Mesopotamian and that, importantly, include the idea of a political center. (1988a:44).

Mesopotamian civilization clearly was a complex, multiethnic system, incorporating peoples speaking different languages, practicing different subsistence activities, and worshiping different gods. The written tradition and related religious beliefs gave the civilization great continuity. The Mesopotamian political system was based on a network of city-states, which at various times were combined into regional states or empires. There were constant power struggles between the rulers of different cities, and cities were abandoned or relocated after military defeats or changes in the course of major rivers. Dynasties were replaced following foreign invasions or internal conflicts.

The Sumerian King List shows how unstable the political situation was in Mesopotamia. The list is an official written record of the sequence of individual kings, together with their capital cities, who were entitled to rule over the Mesopotamian empire. The list begins in approximately 2900 BC in the Early Dynastic and continues through the last Sumerian dynasty in approximately 2000 BC. The list creates the fiction of perfect continuity, with a single ruler always in control of the entire region; thus, it cannot be accepted as literal his-

TABLE 10.1   SEQUENCE OF DYNASTIES RECORDED IN THE SUMERIAN KING LIST, 2900–2000 BC

City	Source	Rulers	Cause of Loss	Putative Duration (years)
Eridu	Heaven	2	City abandoned	64,800
Badtibira	Transfer	3	City abandoned	108,000
Larak	Transfer	1	City abandoned	28,800
Sippar	Transfer	1	City abandoned	21,000
Shuruppak	Transfer	1	Flood	18,600
Kish	Heaven	23	Battle	24,510
Eanna	Conquest	1	Transfer	324
Erech	Transfer	12	Battle	2,310
Ur	Conquest	4	Battle	177
Awan	Conquest	3	Battle	356
Kish	Conquest	8	Battle	3,195
Hamazi	Conquest	1	Battle	360
Erech	Conquest	3	Battle	187
Ur	Conquest	4	Battle	116
Adab	Conquest	1	Battle	90
Mari	Conquest	6	Battle	136
Kish	Conquest	1	Battle	100
Akshak	Conquest	6	Battle	99
Kish	Conquest	7	Battle	491
Erech	Conquest	1	Battle	25
Agade	Conquest	11	Battle	197
Erech	Conquest	5	Invasion	30
Gutians	Conquest	21	Battle	91
Erech	Conquest	1	Battle	7
Ur	Conquest	5	Battle	108
Isin	Conquest	14	—	203

SOURCE: Kramer (1963).
NOTE: This is the "official record," the given length of particular dynasties.

tory. The time span attributed to individual dynasties is purely metaphorical, and the list is an incomplete emic view, idealized for political purposes. Nevertheless, it provides a glimpse of the kind of upheavals that must have characterized the Mesopotamian scene.

The list names 146 rulers in twenty-six dynasties over the 900-year period (Table 10.1). This suggests an average of just 6 years per king and 35 years per dynasty, and the dynastic turnover is invariably attributed to military defeat. Some authors (Jacobsen and Adams 1958) have pointed out that overirrigation under state management may have played a role in the abandonment of

southern Mesopotamian cities and the collapse of the third Ur dynasty, which effectively marked the end of the Sumerian period. In this scenario, overuse of irrigation water inadvertently elevated the water table, causing subsurface saltwater to contaminate the soil and damage crops. Identifying such an ecological factor as a sole cause of collapse would be misleading, however, because underlying political factors caused the mismanagement of the irrigation system and created the demand for increased production.

Foreign invaders, or "barbarians," such as Amorites, Kassites, and Gutians, have sometimes been credited with bringing down Mesopotamian states. However, as Yoffee (1988a) observes, Mesopotamian civilization incorporated different ethnic groups that actually contributed to its persistence. It was only when the Persian invaders from a still larger empire conquered Mesopotamia that the established political system, and later the entire civilization, was brought down. Previous breakdowns did not prevent the city-states from being regrouped into regional states.

Thus, in the Mesopotamian case, we see a cultural tradition that maintained itself for a very long time despite chronic political instability. In the end, Mesopotamian civilization was superseded by a more powerful regional civilization, within what had become a western Asian world system based on extensive tributary empires. Mesopotamian civilization apparently was so weakened when it lost its central position within the local world system that it was unable to recover from a routine dynastic collapse. The world system concept will be discussed in more detail in Chapter 11.

Harappa: Deurbanization and Cultural Continuity

By 1500 BC the cities associated with the Harappan civilization in the Indus Valley had been abandoned, perhaps 1000 years after their founding. Without the cities, the state also disappeared, along with the writing system. The best-known cities of Harappa and Mohenjo-Daro (Figure 10.1) apparently were rebuilt several times during that period, but the civilization ultimately succumbed to a process that has been called deurbanization (Gosh 1982). Deurbanization is the reverse of the urbanization process and implies a breakdown of political authority at the top. The population of cities dwindles; fewer full-time specialists, craftsmen, and administrators are needed; and long-distance trade in luxury goods ceases. Judging by the steady decline in the quality of housing, which is archaeologically documented, the city of Harappa seems to have turned into a slum before it was completely abandoned (Possehl 1977).

The cause of the demise of the Harappan civilization has been a long-standing mystery because there is no documentary account of the event. However, three different explanations have been posed: (1) destruction by foreign invasion, (2) natural destruction by Indus floods, or (3) exhaustion of the resource base through overuse. The foreign invasion theory typically cites the Aryans as the principal villains and the skeletons piled in the streets of Mohenjo-Daro as evidence of conquest and massacre. However, on close inspection, this interpretation seems weak. The Aryans did have a warrior tradition, but as noted previously, their arrival cannot be correlated precisely with the fall of Harappan civilization. Furthermore, no hard evidence supports an invasion at either Harappa or Mohenjo-Daro.

The famous massacre is probably a myth, according to archaeologist George Dales (1964), who directed excavations at Mohenjo-Daro in the 1960s. The thirty-five skeletons were found in six different groups, and the deaths may not have occurred at the same time; this suggests that most were probably intentional burials. Two bodies may have inadvertently been buried on top of a much older street, which may have fed the "bodies in the street" myth. There is no evidence of weapons or destruction to fortifications to indicate an assault ever took place, nor is there evidence that the "victims" died of traumatic injury (Kennedy 1982). Bandits might have killed some people who remained in the city after it was abandoned for other reasons.

Perhaps the most dramatic single-cause explanation of Harappan collapse is the theory developed by Dales (1965, 1966, 1982; Dales and Raikes 1968) and his associate hydrologist Robert Raikes (1964, 1965): A series of great floods caused the cities to be abandoned. This theory suggests that Harappan civilization was destroyed not by the normal fluctuation in the Indus seasonal flood regime but by catastrophic tectonic uplift and associated earthquakes and flooding. Uplift below Mohenjo-Daro caused perhaps several gigantic earth dams to block the flow of the

FIGURE 10.1
Mohenjo-Daro, one of the two urban centers of the Indus Valley civilization, which collapsed about 1500 BC.

Indus, flooding out the settlements immediately upstream and then drowning them in a sea of mud. Earthquakes throughout the region would have destroyed other settlements and disrupted trade. Repeated attempts to rebuild or move the major cities ultimately failed. Dales summarized this natural disaster view as follows:

> Flooding was the principal enemy of the Mohenjo-darians, and of all the Harappan period inhabitants of the lower Indus Valley. Bands of raiders from the nearby Baluchistan hills could well have taken advantage of the chaotic conditions following the floods, but they were apparently not the cause of such conditions. (1965:14)

The Dales–Raikes flood theory has been rigorously attacked by other researchers. H. T. Lambrick (1967) found insufficient geophysical evidence that an earth dam over 100 feet (30 meters [m]) high and more than 30 miles (48 kilometers [km]) long had formed across the Indus. He also argued that the sediment deposits in the Harappan cities could be accounted for in other ways. Gregory Possehl (1967) also challenged the physical evidence for the dam and further argued that even

if Mohenjo-Daro was so destroyed, that would be an insufficient explanation for the destruction of the entire civilization. Flooding was, after all, a normal problem along the Indus, and Possehl agreed that Mohenjo-Daro itself may have been repeatedly flooded out and rebuilt. Instead of flooding, Possehl favored the ecological argument that the Harappan civilization collapsed because of resource depletion.

Possehl cited conjectural evidence assembled by Walter Fairservis (1967) to suggest the level of resource demand posed by a city the size of Mohenjo-Daro. Based on data from contemporary Indus Valley villagers, Fairservis estimated that Mohenjo-Daro may have contained 41,250 people. The total population would have required at least 22,715 acres (9200 hectares) to supply 384 pounds (174 kilograms [kg]) of grain per person per year. The necessary bullocks for plowing (one bullock plows 8 acres [3 hectares]) would require a herd of 8755 cattle and another 3097 acres (1254 hectares) just to grow 25 percent of the fodder. Vast additional grazing lands would be required, but deforestation to supply building materials and fuel must have degraded much of the surrounding territory.

Disregarding the specific causes of the breakdown of the urban phase of Harappan civilization, it is likely that it was largely expressed as a steady economic decline over a period of perhaps 200–300 years, with a reduction in the production of luxury goods (Rao 1982). Because, as some have suggested (Miller 1985), Harappa may have been less socially stratified than other ancient civilizations, the deurbanization transition may have been relatively smooth, with considerable cultural continuity. A recognized post-Harappan archaeological culture suggests that the Harappan peasantry maintained much of the earlier culture and folk tradition and that significant cultural elements must have been reflected in the second urbanization that took place in the Ganges by 600 BC, culminating in the Hindu Great Tradition (Allchin 1982).

Like Mesopotamia, the Harappan case might also be considered an example of the local discontinuity of progress. However, the lengthy temporal gap between the fall of Harappa and the rise of classical Hindu civilization makes it difficult to argue that Harappa was outcompeted by a more "progressive" civilization. India provides numerous other examples of the rise and fall of states. After Harappa, over the centuries between 500 BC and AD 1970, sixty-two large regional states have successively arisen and collapsed in India (Figure 10.2).

Andean Civilizations: Fragile Empire, Robust Culture

The Inca empire is as famous for the manner in which it collapsed as it is for its great size and wealth. The vast 380,000-square-mile (mi^2) (984,200-square-kilometer [km^2]) empire, which may have encompassed 32 million people, was brought under foreign control within less than 5 years. Much of its wealth was subsequently extracted to benefit the even larger Spanish empire, whose capital was more than 5000 miles (8045 km) away. Even more remarkable was the fact that only 180 men made up the conquering Spanish army. The Inca empire was, in fact, a very fragile political superstructure that had grown rapidly following the long-established tradition of Andean civilization. The basic nature of Andean civilization, and the way political power developed and the empire expanded, helps explain the relative fragility of these complex systems, as well as their underlying cultural continuity. The following analysis is based largely on the work of Geoffrey Conrad and Arthur Demarest (1984).

The most critical factor underlying the dynamics of the Inca state was the ideological emphasis on ancestor cults. By AD 1000, ancestor worship as practiced by the kingdoms along the Peruvian coast began to assume forms that would set the stage for Inca expansion. A key cultural pattern related to the ancestor cult, one that the Inca shared with the north coast Chimu state, has been called split inheritance by Conrad (1981). Both the Chimu and Inca kings were worshiped as divinities after they died; even in death, they continued to hold title to the vast wealth that they had accumulated during their reigns. The office of kingship was inherited by the deceased ruler's principal son, but his other heirs were made trustees of the royal mummy and the deceased's treasury.

As in China, the Andean ancestor cult also must have functioned to reinforce the legitimacy of the rulers. More importantly for empire building, however, the added feature of split inheritance forced the newly installed ruler to engage in military conquest to build the personal wealth that would become the basis for his own ancestor cult. Thus, an ideological pattern provided a clear motive for state expansion in the Andean area.

The Inca system of ancestor worship is well described in the ethnohistoric material recorded immediately after the Spanish conquest. It reveals the same functional connections between kinship, land, and political power that characterized Chinese ancestor worship. In the Inca case, as described by Conrad and Demarest (1984), the mummified bodies of the dead became sacred objects, or *mallquis,* and specialist diviners, known

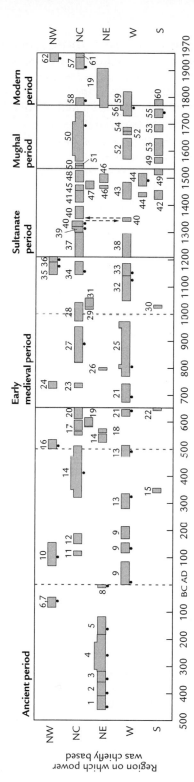

KEY: • *Time of Apogee of Power*

Region on which power
was chiefly based

1. Haryankas	10. Kusanas
2. Saisunagas	11. Ksaharatas
3. Nandas	12. Kardamakas
4. Mauryas	13. Vakatakas
5. Sungas	14. Guptas
6. Northern Sakas	15. Pallavas
7. Indo-Parthians	16. Southern Hunas
8. Mahameghavahanas	17. Maukharis
9. Satavahana	18. Later Guptas

19. Early Kalacuris	28. Paramaras
20. Pusyabhutis	29. Candellas
21. Calukyas of Vatapi	30. Colas
22. Greater Pallavas	31. Kalacuris
23. "Varmans" of Kanyakubja	32. Calukyas of Kalyani
24. Karkotas	33. Caulukyas (Solankis)
25. Rastrakutas	34. Gahadavalas
26. Patas	35. Cahamanas
27. Gurjara-Pratiharas	36. Ghurids

37. Mamluks	46. Cajapatis
38. Yadavas	47. Sharqis
39. Khaljis	48. Lodis
40. Tughlugs	49. Tuluvas (Vijayanagara)
41. Saiyyids	50. Mughal
42. Sangamas	51. Surs
43. (Vijayanagara) Bahmanis	52. Adil Shahis (Bijapur)
44. Ahmad Shahis	53. Qutb Shahis (Golkonda)
45. Khaljis (of Malwa)	

54. Sivaji	
55. Nizam-u-Mulk (Hyderabad)	
56. Peshwa	
57. British	
58. Sindhia (Gwali)	
59. Bhonsle (Nagpu)	
60. Mysore	
61. Republic of India	
62. Pakistan	

FIGURE 10.2 Major powers of the Indian subcontinent, 500 BC–1970 AD

(SOURCE: Schwartzberg 1977.)

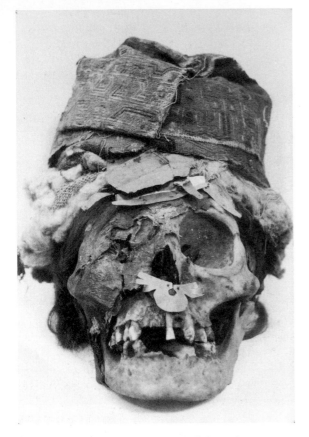

FIGURE 10.3 Richly decorated skull from the pre-Inca Nazca culture, used by a cult of the dead, a prominent feature of Andean civilization.

as *mallquip-villac,* communicated with the ancestors through these mummies (Figure 10.3). The concept of *huaca,* shrine or sacred object, links the related concepts of *mallquis* (mummy), *ayllu* (descent group), and the kinship term *vilca* (great-grandfather or great-grandson, which also means ancestor). All these terms were used interchangeably. Furthermore, there are specific associations between specific ancestors and specific shrines. As in China, the well-being of the descent group was thought to depend on the proper ritual respect being accorded the *huaca* and mummy. In pre-Inca times, individual *ayllu* groups cared for their own mummies and *huacas.* Women wove

special textiles for funeral rituals, and *ayllu* members cultivated specific plots to support the relatively small-scale ceremonies that were part of *ayllu*-level ancestor worship.

Split inheritance provided a major ritual function and guaranteed material support for a branch of the Inca royal lineage whose head might otherwise try to claim the title of Inca. The Inca royal mummy cult was a conspicuous feature of the state religion and, as such, was certainly not a lowly consolation prize. The mummies were identified with the manifestation of the solar or sky deity who founded the Inca dynasty, and thus were key legitimizing symbols of the state. They also were identified with specific natural forces and therefore could ensure the welfare of the general population.

When the Spaniards arrived, the mummies of at least five earlier rulers in the Inca dynasty, dating back as far as Viracocha Inca, who died in 1438, were being maintained in the Coricancha, the main temple in the capital city of Cuzco (Figure 10.4). Each mummy was treated as lavishly as it had been in life. It was attended by its descendants, who served it as retainers and formed a corporate descent group, known as *panaqa.* *Panaqa* members were the Orejones, the Inca hereditary elite, who occupied the highest offices in the Inca bureaucracy. The *panaqa* was a special type of *ayllu,* a royal court focused on the deceased ruler who was treated as a *huaca.* The members of the *panaqa* paraded the mummy for important ceremonies, sacrificed food and drink to it, and managed its property.

The Inca system of split inheritance promoted imperial expansion because a ruler's personal wealth was derived from the production of his personal landholdings and the *mita* labor service that he could call up from his domain. The king needed to control land because labor service had to be rewarded with food and drink as discussed in Chapter 7. All his personal royal estate remained with the *panaqa* of each ruler and significantly reduced the resources available both for the state as a whole and for succeeding rulers. Therefore, the newly installed king was obligated to

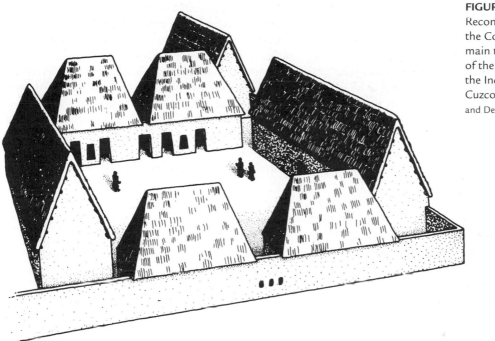

FIGURE 10.4
Reconstructed view of the Coricancha, the main temple and center of the state religion in the Inca capital of Cuzco. (SOURCE: Conrad and Demarest 1984.)

expand the total territory of the empire to finance the government and build his own wealth in food surpluses and subjects to support his *panaqa*.

Apparently, the institutionalization of split inheritance and the royal mummy cult, which began under the rule of Pachakuti Inca in 1438, gave the Inca rulers a decisive advantage in their struggles with their neighbors. However, Conrad and Demarest (1984) argue that continuous expansion quickly proved unsustainable. Within less than a century, the empire reached its maximum extent (see Figure 7.12). Beyond the limits of the familiar Andean environment, the Inca armies floundered at the edges of the Amazon rain forest, while further extension north or south along the Andean chain was hampered by communication difficulties. Administrative costs soared. The well-endowed *panaqa,* led by their mummy kings, were a constant challenge to the authority of the living Inca ruler, because they were headed by men who were brothers of former or current emperors and who would always be potential usurpers. There were also problems

with rebellious ethnic groups that were forcibly incorporated into the empire.

Even with no more frontiers open to easy conquest, the practice of split inheritance continued to push the elite to increase production. But now this meant confiscating prime land from the citizenry, increasing the labor tax to support the mummy cult, and mounting large-scale and costly agricultural development projects on marginal lands subject to chronic crop failures. A further response to increasing economic pressures was the use of *yanacona* retainers and the *mitima* colonists as fulltime agricultural laborers in service to the state and the nobility. Contrary to long-established Andean tradition, these changes made the rulers less obligated to maintain their reciprocal ties with the peasantry, and they undermined village self-sufficiency.

The final crisis began when the death of the Inca ruler Huayna Capac in 1525 resulted in controversy over the succession between two of his sons: Huascar, who assumed the throne in Cuzco, and Atahuallpa, who controlled the army. By this time, the economic deterioration of the empire had become so serious that Huascar attempted to abolish the royal mummy cult in an effort to stabilize the situation. However, this move threatened the position of the *panaqa* elite, and they joined with Atahuallpa in a civil war against Huascar. Atahuallpa won but was treacherously taken captive by the Spanish in 1532 before he could consolidate his victory.

Historians can cite many reasons for the remarkable success of the Spaniards, but above all else, they simply had lucky timing. They were veterans with steel swords, metal armor, guns, and horses, who were at first thought to be supernatural beings. The Inca population was being seriously disrupted by epidemic European diseases that reached Peru in 1524, 8 years ahead of the Spaniards (Dobyns and Doughty 1976). However, despite these material and psychological advantages, the empire would not have fallen so easily if internal contradictions had not prepared the way. In the Inca case, split inheritance and a special form of ancestor worship seems to have caused a frenzied period of self-destructive expansion that drove the empire to collapse within less than 100 years. Huascar's reforms might have worked, but it was already too late. The empire was hopelessly divided against itself and simply fell apart. The Spanish forces were met by a peasantry that no longer had any vested interest in supporting the Inca mummies, the Inca elite, or the living emperor.

The Spaniards succeeded in destroying the last of the royal mummies by 1559, and although a fragmented Inca government remained in the hinterland until 1572, Inca civilization was effectively destroyed when the Spaniards occupied Cuzco in 1533. The Andean cultural tradition—including subsistence practices, social organization, material culture, and beliefs—continued with little significant change at the village level. The Spanish conquerors replaced the Inca elite and turned the Inca labor tax into a harshly exploitative system that further impoverished the countryside. The Andean peasantry kept their

language and culture, but they were forcibly incorporated into the emerging world system dominated by Europeans. The Spanish treatment of Atahuallpa was symbolic of the transformation. He was taken captive and held for ransom. To gain his release, he amassed a treasure of more than 13,000 pounds (5889 kilograms [kg]) of gold and 26,000 pounds (11,778 kg) of silver—three times the treasure that Cortez took from Mexico—but he was killed and the treasure went to Spain (Dobyns and Doughty 1976).

THE LIMITS OF PROGRESS

Growth Thresholds and Scale Limits in Ancient Empires

The quest for political power was the primary cause of cultural development and growth in the imperial world. Rulers intent on expanding their political empires inevitably confronted scale limits in the number of people commanded, the size of territory ruled, and the number and size of cities. Depending on circumstances, when scale thresholds were reached, any imperial society was forced either to stabilize at a given size, disintegrate and fall back, or else its rulers resorted to some cultural innovation to move beyond the limits.

Three broad scale trends have characterized the political history of the world since the creation of the first politically centralized societies 7,000 years ago: (1) decline in the number of independent political units, reflecting the increasing concentration of political power (Carneiro 1978b); (2) increase in the scale and power of the largest polities (Taagepera 1978a, 1978b, 1997); and (3) increase in the number and size of cities (Chandler 1987, Fletcher 1995). These trends are correlated with order of magnitude increases in global population, and technological intensification, in addition to the increases in overall cultural complexity that were examined in Chapter 7 (see Figure 7.1).

In 1000 BC most of the world was still tribal and there were probably fewer than 100 million people and some 600,000 autonomous polities, primarily small, fully independent bands and villages (Carneiro 1978b). Arguably, with so many small polities this was the maximum level of human political freedom that the world has ever enjoyed. Since that time there has been a relentless concentration of political power. By AD 500, as political empires expanded, global population had reached nearly 200 million, but the number of political units had declined to only 200,000. By AD 2000 there were only 188 nation states in the United Nations, and they controlled virtually all of the world's 6 billion people. This made most of humanity bystanders in the power struggles among rulers.

The growth of political empires may appear to follow "the inexorable laws of history" (Boas 1945:100). However, empires don't simply happen, they are constructed by rulers pursuing wars of conquest. Surely war is not inevitable, and it is likely that if decision-making were democratic, and if the costs and rewards of war were equitably distributed, war would be replaced by diplomacy as a means of conflict resolution. The empires of history were totalitarian societies, in which one man could decide to wage war against his neighbors. Successful military conquest made further conquests more likely as the balance of power shifted in favor of the victor and led to a rapid proliferation of military technology from bronze to iron armaments to cavalry and spoked wheels. By about 500 BC, armaments reached a firepower and lethality threshold that was not exceeded until after AD 1600 when Europeans gained the financial resources to make effective use of gunpowder and mobile cannon, causing the theoretical killing power of individual weapons to soar by orders of magnitude (Dupuy 1979:7).

As their military capabilities increased, rulers became "macroparasites," preying on other people by pillage, organized robbery, violence, and threats of violence (McNeill 1982). Rulers continued to expand their empires by conquest

until they outran their bureaucratic capabilities, or they reached physical limits determined by military logistics (Naroll 1967). For example, in 1600 it would have taken Akbar's armies a month to move the 1000 miles from their capital of Fatehpur Sikri to the frontier with Burma. Even the size of field armies was limited by the provisions they could carry. Alexander the Great's Macedonian army of 65,000 men, and 3000 animals consumed an incredible 280,000 pounds (127,272 kilograms) of grain per day for men and animals, and this imposed severe constraints on their ability to move and remain integrated (Engels 1978, Table 1). Before the fossil fuel era, the total armed forces of even the largest empires never exceeded a few hundred thousand men, and most were much smaller. The difficulty of projecting military control over a large empire explains why Great Tradition religions became so important as a means of social control, and why rulers encouraged agricultural development to increase population density.

There were also severe limits on the development of large urban centers. Before 3000 BC the largest cities were usually under 10,000 people, because rulers could command few resources. Large cities required extensive exchange networks and transportation infrastructure. Before fossil fuels, industrial capitalism, and electronic communication, the largest urban places generally contained only a few hundred thousand people, and seldom, and then only briefly, exceeded a million people (Fletcher 1995).

When viewed from the perspective of millennia, the changes in the territorial scale of polities as empires grew larger are dramatic (Figure 10.5), and they required major cultural changes that occurred in phases. In the absence of a developed bureaucracy and communication technology, the first simple chiefdoms were limited in size to roughly the 2500 square kilometer (965 square miles) area that the chief could personally visit within half a day's travel (Spencer 1990:7). Until military technology and bureaucracy could be improved, the number of people that rulers could

FIGURE 10.5
Combined average territorial size of the world's three largest political empires, 3000 BC to 2000 AD (after Taagepera 1978a:115, Figure 1).

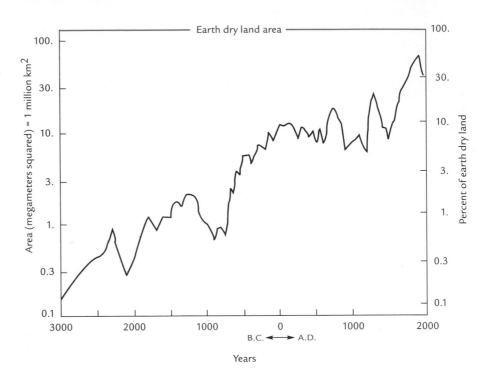

command depended on the productivity of intensive agriculture. The early Mesopotamian city states commanded some 50,000 square kilometers of territory, and Ur III may have reached 675,000 square kilometers. With steady cultural development by AD 1450 the Ming China empire was able to control 6.5 milllion square kilometers of territory. Given a continuation of these growth trends it is possible to project a time when a single government would rule the world, based on the trend toward political concentration since 7000 BC. Using different approaches, anthropologist Raoul Naroll (1967) thought there would be a 50 percent chance of world government by AD 2200. Others project dates ranging from AD 2300 to 3800 (Carneiro 1978b, Marano 1973, Taagepera 1997:487). However, diminishing returns to technological and organizational intensification suggest that it will be too costly for a single imperial power to ever rule the world by political means, or military force. The limits of state power are clearly demonstrated by the

record of history showing that over 5000 years half of all large polities remained large for only 130 years, and few lasted more than 200 years (Taagepera 1997). This is shown in the peaks and valleys of the curve on Figure 10.5.

Diminishing Returns and Breakdown

The Mesopotamian and Harappan examples raise questions about the explanatory value of both environmental factors and foreign invasion as sole causes of the breakdown of states. It would be surprising if environmental problems were the primary cause of state collapse because, according to some theories of state origin, states arise to help alleviate resource deficiencies (Tainter 1988). The case for the collapse of food production systems as a cause of political breakdown is especially hard to make because cause and effect is difficult to establish from archaeological evidence. Furthermore, complex state-supported production systems would almost

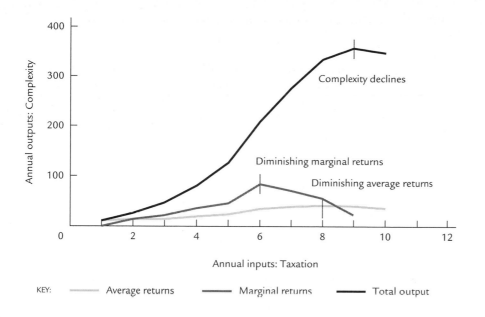

FIGURE 10.6
The principle of diminishing returns.

certainly be abandoned in the event of political breakdown.

Environmental imbalance is only one example of a more general problem of **diminishing returns,** which affects virtually all state functions and most human endeavors (Tainter 1988). Technological or organizational changes that increase or maintain cultural complexity will eventually experience diminishing returns, and "collapse" will occur when the cost of maintaining cultural complexity becomes prohibitively expensive.

Diminishing returns apply to three conceptually distinct outputs, or products: **marginal returns,** average returns, and total output. Each output behaves somewhat differently, but marginal returns are most sensitive to the prognosis for the system. When marginal returns decline, more and more effort must be expended for less and less of whatever is being produced, whether it be food or cultural complexity. A decline in marginal returns means that average returns are also likely to decline soon. Even though total output might continue to increase for a time, it, too, will experience a decline. Figure 10.6 shows diminishing returns on a scale of cultural complexity in relation to increases in tax revenues for

a hypothetical state. This example arbitrarily assumes that average returns in complexity would increase for each added unit of revenue up to 8 units and would then decline steadily. Such a decline would be due to rising inefficiency and corruption, as the bureaucracy became more cumbersome. In this case, marginal returns begin to decline when revenue inputs reach 6, but total complexity declines only when inputs reach 9. Thus, an inattentive ruler interested in rapid state building might be tempted to raise taxes too high by disregarding the warning sign of diminishing marginal returns.

Agricultural Intensification

The primary problem for the ruler of a state is how to increase the production of food staples,

diminishing returns The situation in which output values will decline as effort is increased in any production system.
marginal returns The increase in the total output produced by the additional input; in subsistence production, the additional amount above what was produced the previous year, resulting from the increased effort.

TABLE 10.2   DIMINISHING RETURNS IN AGRICULTURAL INTENSIFICATION

Subsistence Type*	Input/Hectare (in thousands of kcal)	Average Return (in kcal)	Total Output (in millions of kcal)	Marginal Return (in millions of kcal)
Forest fallow	24	72	1.7	—
Bush fallow	250	68	17.0	15.3
Short fallow	475	62	29.0	12.0
Annual crop	700	56	39.0	10.0
Multicrop	912	50	45.8	6.8

*Forest fallow system is based on estimates for Amazonian shifting cultivation of manioc (30,000 lbs [13,590 kg] of manioc/acre/year for 1606 hours/year), 25-year fallow. Multicrop system is based on the Chinese village of Luts'un (see Chapter 8). Data for the intermediate systems are based on extrapolations from the Amazonian and Chinese data. Bush fallow assumes hoe cultivation on an 8-year rotation. Short fallow assumes plow cultivation on a 2-year rotation.

which can be taxed to finance growth in the non-food-producing sector of the population. There are two immediate ways to increase agricultural productivity: (1) by increasing the number of peasant farmers and/or (2) by increasing the amount of land farmed. Either approach, however, will ultimately require technological changes because of diminishing returns on labor. Danish agricultural economist Ester Boserup (1965) has argued that intensification of food production typically follows a predictable sequence of diminishing returns, involving shortened fallow periods, increased effort per unit of land, and technological change. People must work harder for a smaller return for their effort in order to increase the total production per unit of land.

The typical agricultural intensification sequence would begin with a shifting-cultivation production system, such as the Amazonian example presented in Chapter 3. This is a **forest fallow system** because a plot must be allowed to return to forest before it can be recultivated, in order to maintain soil quality. Productivity per unit of labor input with shifting cultivation is relatively high, but the output per unit of land is very low when the forest is counted as part of the production system. The forest fallow system can, in theory, remain stable if no additional demands arise from population increase or political pressure to extract a surplus. When increases are required, this can be accomplished by shortening

the fallow period and thereby putting more land into production at a given time. The problem with this is that secondary forest is brushy and requires more work to clear than primary forest, thus increasing the labor input. As the fallow period is shortened further, hoes will be needed to dig out the weeds and composting may be required to maintain soil fertility. When the fallow period is reduced to one year, a plow and draft animals will be needed to turn over the grass sod, which has replaced the forest.

The data presented in Table 10.2 and shown graphically in Figure 10.7 are largely conjectural, but they make more concrete the abstract principle of diminishing returns in agricultural intensification. Because documenting the intensification process for a single culture through time would be difficult, these figures were generated using an Amazonian shifting-cultivation system and a Chinese irrigated rice-growing village to define extreme points along a straight-line continuum. The intermediate values were simply extrapolated. Calculations of this sort are imprecise because the underlying data are estimates subject to sampling error and because the different systems themselves may not be strictly comparable. For example, not all the potential production of a shifting-cultivation system is ever harvested, and a garden plot may continue to be productive to some degree as it goes through the fallow process. Also, different estimates would generate

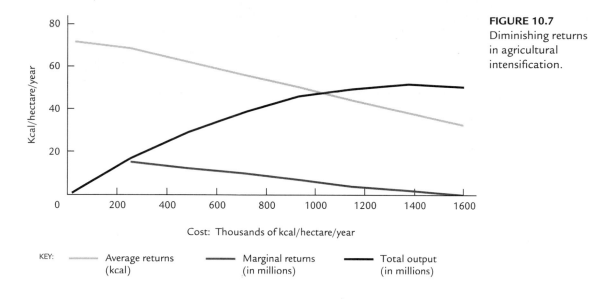

FIGURE 10.7
Diminishing returns
in agricultural
intensification.

KEY: Average returns (kcal)   Marginal returns (in millions)   Total output (in millions)

different curves. Nevertheless, the figures demonstrate the magnitude of difference between land-extensive systems, which make little demand on labor, and highly intensive systems, which require a very large labor force.

These figures also help explain why extensive systems are more likely to be found with smaller-scale egalitarian cultures. It could certainly be argued that people would not willingly move to the more intensive system, which clearly increases work loads, unless they were pushed by population growth or political pressure. Political factors, such as taxation, are probably the most important determinants of agricultural intensification because, when a ruler extracts a steadily increasing "surplus" from a peasantry with a fixed land base, the only way for the peasants to reduce their rising labor costs is to raise a larger family and divide the work load. Thus, the population will tend to grow, but it is important to note that the underlying cause is the *political policy* of the state, not the inherent tendency of population to rise. In previous chapters, it was argued that diminishing returns in subsistence might provide a cultural incentive for limiting family size in tribal cultures where individual households are free to set their own production goals.

State Institutional Functions and Costs

As a state system develops, a series of new problems arise, each of which offers further areas in which costs rise and returns diminish. The state has institutional responses to the special problems it creates, but each response requires further increases in the number of nonfood-producing specialists and includes additional capital costs and maintenance costs. The states' institutional responses themselves generate new problems that call for new institutional solutions, in a continually expanding positive-feedback system with steadily diminishing returns.

Figure 10.8 illustrates some of these complex interconnections. The key functions that the state must support if it is to survive are staple production, wealth production, maintenance costs, technology, coordination, storage, transport, information, social control, defense, and conquest. The specialists carrying out specific functions—corvée laborers, artisans, and so on—are shown on the left in the figure, opposite the functions

forest fallow system A system of cultivation in which soil nutrients are restored by allowing the forest to regrow.

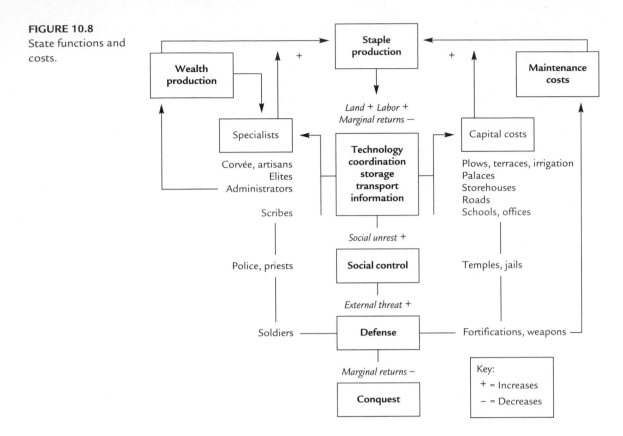

FIGURE 10.8
State functions and costs.

they serve. The physical constructions, or capital costs—palaces, irrigation systems, storehouses, and so on—are shown on the right. State functions, institutional responses, and new problems are arranged in the diagram along a vertical axis in a general developmental sequence from top to bottom.

The most critical state function, increasing staple-food production, is met at first through taxation, which forces the peasantry to put more land into production, shortens fallow periods, and encourages larger families. However, increased pressure on land and labor generates the problem of marginal returns as the soil is depleted and cultivation becomes more difficult. The state must then finance a series of technological changes in order to apply more and more labor to each unit of land. Full-time artisans are needed to manufacture new tools such as metal

hoes and then plows. Eventually, large drafts of corvée labor must be mobilized to build terraces and irrigation canals. These developments themselves require increased production of food staples and more administrative elites to coordinate their activities and to collect and store the revenue. Palaces, storehouses, roads, and offices also must be constructed and maintained. But the increased taxes and social inequality will generate social unrest, calling for social control functions provided by priests and police, temples and jails. A successful state with large storehouses and wealthy palaces will tempt neighboring states to invade; therefore, soldiers, weapons, and fortifications will be needed for defense functions. Eventually, as marginal returns decline in all areas, territorial expansion and looting through conquest will become an attractive means of perpetuating the system.

TABLE 10.3   STATE FINANCE IN THE EARLY DYNASTIC CITY-STATE OF UR, MESOPOTAMIA

Capital Construction*	Total Cost (5 years)	Annual Cost
Irrigation canals	1,544,825	308,965
Storehouses	500,000	100,000
Palace	965,515	193,103
Ziggurat	2,395,310	479,062
City wall	500,000	100,000
Total construction costs	5,905,650	1,181,130

1,181,130	Total annual construction costs
+ 253,500	500 workmen × 507 kg of grain per year
+1,102,000	5800 citizens × 380 kg of grain per year × 50% famine reduction
2,536,630	Subtotal 1
+ 380,495	Subtotal 1 × seed grain (15%)
2,917,125	Subtotal 2
+ 729,281	Subtotal 2 × storage loss (25%)
3,646,406	Total annual cost

$$\text{Annual production} = \text{hectares} \times \frac{\text{kg of grain}}{\text{hectare}}$$

$$2,400,000 = 6000 \text{ hectares} \times \frac{400 \text{ kg of grain}}{\text{hectare}}$$

$$\text{Revenue} = \text{annual production} \times \text{tax rate (25\%)}$$
$$600,000 = 2,400,000 \times .25$$

SOURCES: Data for capital construction costs from Erdosy (1988) and Wheatley (1971). Estimates for storage, seed, population, and grain production from Wright (1969) and Adams (1981).
*Capital construction costs are expressed in kilograms of grain required to supply a workman's official barley ration of 60 *sila*/month, 507 kg/year (see Chapter 7).

Table 10.3 gives some indication of the relative cost of state functions. Like previous estimates, these figures are largely conjectural, but they illustrate some of the constraints with which ancient rulers had to contend. This example shows the possible costs of capital construction in an early Mesopotamian city-state such as Ur. The values represent kilograms of barley, which was the basic ration used to pay laborers. With a combined population of perhaps only 5800 people, the small city of Ur and its support communities would have needed to draft large numbers of temporary laborers from outside to complete these projects within a short time. If the canals, storehouses, palace, ziggurat, and city walls were all built within 5 years as Table 10.3 assumes, more than 11,000 construction workers would have been needed each year. Shortening construction time would have been difficult.

Given potential grain production in the 14,815 cultivated acres (6000 hectares) surrounding Ur and a tax rate of 25 percent, grain stores would have to accumulate for 6 years to finance each year of construction. In the meantime, losses in storage would take an increasing toll. It would take the state 2 years simply to accumulate enough surplus grain to supply half the annual subsistence needs of its regular citizens in the case of a crop failure.

Because the capital costs of state functions are relatively high, they would probably only be taken on as they became absolutely necessary. Construction projects would probably be carried out in the order listed, with technological improvements in agricultural production coming first. Large-scale temple construction and expensive royal tombs would probably be later elaborations designed to reduce social unrest by lending greater religious legitimacy to the state apparatus.

Any increases in nonfood-producing elites or other government specialists would add to the state's financial burden. However, as C. Northcote Parkinson (1957) showed, bureaucracy exhibits an inherent tendency to expand, even as total output declines. According to Parkinson's law, administrative staffs will expand at a predictable rate of 5.75 percent a year, regardless of the actual work produced. This is because overworked officials prefer to add at least two subordinates rather than divide their work with a potential rival. At the same time, the added officials increase the work load because they slow the flow of information. The potential growth rate of bureaucracy thus vastly outstrips population growth and helps explain the diminishing returns that occur with increases in cultural complexity.

In 300 years a staff of 10 theoretically would expand to more than 192 million people. At the same time, the base population would expand from 250 to under 1.8 million people if it grew at 3 percent a year, which is a very high but possible rate. Such an outcome would, of course, be impossible because if the bureaucracy actually did increase at 5.75 percent a year, the system would collapse long before the demand for bureaucrats exceeded the total population. Tax revenues to support the nonfood-producing administrators could not be sustained by the dwindling farm labor force. In this case, collapse could occur without environmental deterioration.

SUMMARY

State breakdown, like the rise of states, is an over-determined phenomenon. That is, it can be caused by many different, often interconnected, factors, such that identifying the most important causes is often difficult. Because the state is a form of political organization, it could be argued that the best explanations for its demise will be political. However, as the examples demonstrate, specific environmental problems, ideological factors, and foreign invasion can all amplify the political weaknesses inherent in state organization. The best explanations in any particular case require detailed historical information. The most critical weakness of states is their vulnerability to diminishing returns in many important state functions.

STUDY QUESTIONS

1. What does state breakdown mean? How can it be identified? Use specific examples.
2. What were the most important growth thresholds that limited the scale of political empires, and how did rulers overcome these limits?
3. Relate the principle of diminishing returns and Parkinson's law to the problem of state breakdown. Include the following concepts in your discussion: diminishing marginal returns, average returns, and total output.
4. Explain how diminishing returns operate in agricultural production.
5. Critically discuss each of the following explanations for the demise of Harappan civilization: foreign invasion, floods, and resource depletion.
6. Why was the Spanish conquest of the Inca empire so easy?
7. What aspects of politically centralized societies make them more vulnerable to collapse than tribal societies?

SUGGESTED READING

LOWE, JOHN W. 1985. *The Dynamics of Apocalypse: A Systems Simulation of the Classic Maya Collapse.* Albuquerque: University of New Mexico Press. One of several interpretations of the Maya case.

PARKINSON, C. NORTHCOTE. 1957. *Parkinson's Law and Other Studies in Administration.* Boston: Houghton Mifflin. The classic study of why bureaucracy tends to expand and become unworkable.

TAINTER, JOSEPH A. 1988. *The Collapse of Complex Societies*. Cambridge, Eng.: Cambridge University Press. A nice review of explanations for collapse that includes many case studies and treats the Romans, Maya, and Chaco Couzon in detail.

YOFFEE, NORMAN, AND GEORGE L. COWGILL (EDS.). 1988. *The Collapse of Ancient States and Civilizations*. Tucson: University of Arizona Press. A collection of case studies by specialists covering Mesopotamia, the Maya, Teotihuacan, the Romans, and Han China.

PART THREE

THE COMMERCIAL WORLD
The Capitalist Global System

The commercial world is only a few centuries old yet at a global level it has transformed human societies, cultures, and the physical world much more dramatically and more rapidly than all ancient empires in the imperial world. Commercialization is a radical, revolutionary cultural process. The commercial world makes the success of business corporation and the accumulation of financial wealth more important human objectives than the need to maintain governments and households. The following chapters show that this massive cultural transformation has occurred in a way that is fundamentally similar to the construction of the imperial world. A very small number of elite decision-makers designed the specific capitalist cultural institutions, including the financial system of banks and stock markets, giant multi-national corporations, and the fiscal-military state that allowed the wealthiest investors to shape the entire world according to their needs. More financial capital has accumulated in proportionately fewer hands than at any time in the past. The human problem with these cultural developments is that in absolute numbers, the commercial world has generated more poverty, illness, and human suffering in a shorter time than any past civilizations. The process of accumulating financial wealth has also drawn down natural capital stored ecosystems and in fossil fuels at a rate that threatens the long term sustainability of the commercial world as a system.

Chapter 11 examines the distinctive cultural features of capitalism and the history of its European origins, as well as its impact on ordinary people, focusing on England. Chapter 12 examines the development of capitalism, democracy, corporate business, and factory food production systems in the United States, looking at both wealth and poverty. The next two chapters look at the impact of capitalist development on peoples who identify with cultural heritages derived from the tribal world, and on societies derived from pre-capitalist, Great Tradition civilizations. Finally, the last chapter assesses the limits of commercial growth and explores the prospects for further cultural development to sustain human societies and cultures beyond the present century.

11

Europe and the Commercial World

The switch to non-renewable fossil-fuel energy sources was crucial to the creation of the commercial world.

Learning Objectives

After studying this chapter you should be able to do the following.

1. Describe the differences in per capita and total energy use in the tribal, imperial, and commercial worlds. Explain how these differences are related to size of population and their significance for human well-being and cultural sustainability.

2. Describe the distinctive features of capitalism as a world system and mode of production and distribution, in comparison with tribal and precapitalist systems.

3. Describe the distinctive features of capitalism as ideology and cosmology in comparison with tribal and pre-capitalist systems, identifying points at which capitalist belief may conflict with reality.

4. Identify the crucial elite-directed cultural processes and the unique historical circumstances that produced capitalism and the commercial world.

5. Describe the increase in English poverty as the commercial world was developed, identifying the key causal factors, and make comparisons with household well-being in the tribal and imperial worlds.

6. Describe the evidence for elite-direction in the development of the British colonial empire.

7. Describe the evidence for elite-direction in the development of the postcolonial global commercial order since 1945.

In this chapter and Chapters 12–15, we look at cultural developments in the modern world as it has been shaped by commercially driven increases in the speed and volume of production and distribution associated with modern technology and by related changes in the organization of social power. Throughout the imperial world, economic power was controlled by political rulers, however, under the right set of circumstances, it became possible for entrepreneurs to build great commercial imperia that pushed beyond the limits of political power. In addition to the persistent problem of collapse, the most important problem with the ancient imperial world from the perspective of power-seeking individuals was that there were severe limitations on the absolute number of power positions in the political hierarchy. It also became increasingly difficult for aspiring individuals to gain entry to the upper ranks of power.

After the fall of the Roman Empire the initial foundations of the commercial world were gradually constructed by a handful of European merchants, financiers, and investors during the six centuries between approximately AD 1000 and 1600. Shortly thereafter, and well before the industrial revolution had gained momentum, virtually all of the crucial institutional structures of modern capitalism were quickly put in place including banks, business corporations, stock exchanges, and insurance companies. These financial institutions worked together as the heart of a global commercial system, which could operate independently of any particular government. The individuals who constructed the commercial world had no grand vision, and they could not have foreseen the consequences of their actions. They simply took advantage of the opportunities that they found. They expanded their personal economic power, concentrating the benefits of growth, and shifted the costs to society at large much as political rulers had done earlier.

Almost overnight, commercial interests became the primary influence on political systems, as well as on the daily life and well-being of people throughout the world. In this commercializa-tion process, world population increased nearly sixfold, from some 800 million people in 1750 to 6.3 billion by 2003, while per capita rates of resource consumption soared to unprecedented levels in the industrial centers. A few people became fabulously wealthy, a comfortably well-off middle class emerged, and millions of people sank into poverty. All societies and cultures are now interconnected within a single economically stratified global system of nation-states dominated by the directors of giant corporations, and dependent on the flow of finance capital. These dramatic cultural changes present a major challenge for anthropologists and other social scientists seeking to understand how and why they occurred and to evaluate their human impact. Technological changes, especially the adoption of mechanized mass production and the use of fossil fuels, were crucial factors in this transformation, but the human agents that directed these technologies and the underlying cultural changes were even more fundamental causes of this remarkable process.

Many people identify "free market capitalism" with human freedom, democracy, economic growth, and material prosperity. However, capitalism evolved and flourished in the absence of democracy, and it was not originally designed to produce prosperity or freedom for the mass of humanity. Freedom and democracy are a very recent, and not a necessary, historical convergence that may be only indirectly related to capitalism. It is unfortunately possible that continued economic growth in the commercial world may ultimately undermine freedom, democracy, and prosperity. The cultural transformations that produce growth in the scale of societies and economies are humanly directed, they are not inevitable and may not be "progressive" in the sense of benefiting humanity as a whole.

After examining the dominant features of this remarkable cultural transformation, this chapter presents ethnohistoric data on European cosmology, feudalism, peasant farming systems, specific mercantile capitalists, and the London poor in order to trace the development of commercialization.

CULTURE-SCALE PERSPECTIVES ON THE CONTEMPORARY WORLD

This chapter examines specific human-directed cultural changes that increased the scale of European societies and produced a commercially organized world system. This book argues that these changes were neither natural nor inevitable. This view contrasts sharply with popular explanations for the "inevitability" of cultural development as due to (1) *natural* population growth, (2) *natural* technological progress, and (3) *natural* economic progress. Given the relative stability of human population within tribal cultures and its sudden expansion under politically organized cultures, population growth likely is a culturally mediated process, not a natural constant. Furthermore, technology and economic organization clearly are cultural, not natural, phenomena.

In a popular book on the global economy, economist Lester Thurow (1996) used the geological principles of plate tectonics to explain how economic forces shape the world. This reflects common beliefs in the irresistible force of markets, but ignores human agency. A major assumption in this book is that economic growth is not a "natural" process. Rather, growth is the result of many individual decision makers seeking greater economic power in particular places.

Many of those who now design and direct commercial technology also maintain that technological change is natural. For example, Microsoft founder Bill Gates (1996:11) insists:

> No one gets to vote on whether technology is going to change our lives. No one can stop productive change in the long run because the market inexorably embraces it. . . . I believe that because progress will come no matter what, we need to make the best of it—not try to forestall it.

Individual decision makers use specific cultural institutions and cultural processes to promote or limit growth, and they guide cultural development in particular directions. In previous chapters, we saw that political rulers used population growth, technology, and economic organization to increase the scale of society, and thereby to enlarge their own social power. The disadvantage of this kind of directed culture change is that decision makers cannot know what the total consequences will be or how many will ultimately suffer or benefit. Gates (1996:10, 313) speaks optimistically of the revolutionary, even "seismic" effects of computer technology, assuring us that computers will change every aspect of our lives. But he acknowledges some unanswered, and troublesome, questions when he asks: "What will happen to our jobs? . . . Will the gulf between the haves and the have-nots widen irreparably?" These are serious questions, because, since AD 1600, commercially directed technological change plunged millions into poverty even as it elevated a few to great wealth and power.

The contemporary world is fundamentally different from everything that preceded it because it is dominated by *commercialization,* a new, untested cultural process that now supersedes both politicization and humanization. *Politicization,* the process that produces and maintains centralized political power, has become a secondary cultural process in the commercial world, maintaining the conditions of economic growth in support of the commercialization process. The world's dominant national and international institutions primarily are concerned with promoting perpetual growth in the commercial production, exchange, and consumption of goods and services.

This overwhelming focus on the accumulation and concentration of wealth, as an end in itself, is an extremely unusual cultural development. Neither wealth nor poverty exists in tribal cultures, where production occurs at the household level to meet the needs that households define. There is no cultural incentive for one household to accumulate more than any other or to produce beyond immediate needs. In ancient Mesopotamia, the Andes, imperial China, and Hindu India, wealth was used to maintain the politicization process—wealth accumulation was not an end in itself. In ancient civilizations, surplus production was extracted from the peasants to finance temples, irrigation works, and fortifications. Wealth maintained the infrastructure of state power, and wealth objects verified political rank, rewarded loyalty, and were buried in royal tombs and in mummy cults.

The infrequent rise and regular collapse of ancient states and empires suggest that they were not the most reliable human adaptations. Commercial culture is only a few centuries old, but it has already transformed and destabilized the world in unusual ways. Its cultural superiority remains to be demonstrated.

Human Needs and Culture Scale

By definition, tribal cultures were the only cultures to focus exclusively on satisfying basic human needs. Every household had access to the subsistence resources it needed and controlled its own production and consumption. Every household was, in effect, guaranteed what Paul Radin called the "irreducible minimum," an inalienable right to "adequate food, shelter and clothing" (1971: 106). Under political-scale cultures, the politicization process took some decision-making power and control away from households and communities; however, human labor power continued to be important, and labor still was required to fulfill the needs of most people. Enormous differences in social power, wealth, and status separated the social classes in ancient civilizations. The lower classes were certainly exploited, but relatively few people, usually outsiders, were enslaved and sacrificed. Most people were able to maintain viable households.

In the commercialization process, everything that people need for their well-being has been converted into a commodity to be sold for profit. State power is used to encourage people to become wage laborers—producing, purchasing, and consuming commodities rather than pursuing noncommercial subsistence activities. The inherent problem with this system is that millions of people no longer have access to basic subsistence resources and cannot earn a sufficient wage to purchase a decent living. Thus, millions are unable to provide for such basic needs as food, shelter, clean water, and pure air. Infant mortality rates soar, and malnutrition is now common. This kind of poverty makes the commercial world seem inhumane relative to both imperial and tribal worlds.

Energy and Population Growth in the Commercial World

The elite-directed cultural innovations and social transformations that produced the commercial world have led to vast, almost inconceivable, increases in energy consumption. In the precapitalist, imperial world, elites generated their social power from the relatively limited number of subjects that they could tax, whereas in the commercial world economic elites accumulate power by skimming profits from a growing volume of market transactions limited only by the availability of energy and materials, the scale of markets, and the human capacity to produce and consume. The revolutionary nature of the global transformation of production and consumption that accompanied commercialization can be readily seen in the changes in per capita energy consumption in different cultures over time (Figure 11.1). Foragers drew their energy only from food and firewood for an estimated 5000 kcal per capita per day. Tribal villagers using domesticated animals raised their daily per capita total to perhaps 12,000 kcal. In the imperial world, this level increased only modestly with the gradual addition of water and wind power to support urbanization. By AD 1400, on the eve of the revolutionary transformations brought about by the commercialization process, the additional use of small amounts of coal may have raised daily energy consumption in England to 26,000 kcal per capita (Cook 1971:136). However, by 1875, with commercialization well underway, increasing urbanization and industrialization fueled by expanded use of coal brought the English average to 77,000 kcal. The addition of fossil fuels can appropriately be called the **fuel revolution**. An even more revolutionary change in per capita energy consumption was brought about during

fuel revolution The large-scale adoption of fossil fuels such as coal and oil.

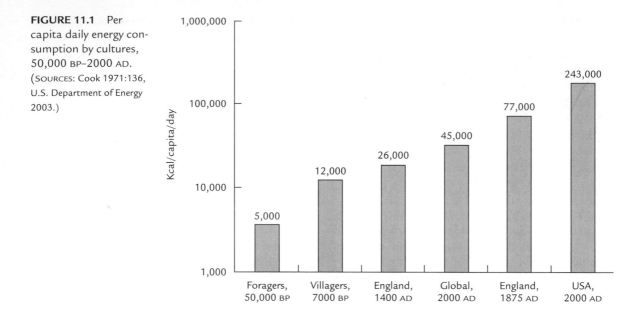

FIGURE 11.1 Per capita daily energy consumption by cultures, 50,000 BP–2000 AD. (SOURCES: Cook 1971:136, U.S. Department of Energy 2003.)

the twentieth century by the addition of petroleum, natural gas, and hydroelectric power. By the year 2000 Americans were consuming 242,870 kcal per capita per day (U.S. Dept. Of Energy 2003a, Table E1). Significantly, in 2000 the global average per capita energy consumption of 45,273 kcal remained lower than England in 1875, and much lower than the average in the United States. This was because global population had grown so large, and very high energy use was so concentrated in the wealthiest countries.

The increases in per capita daily energy consumption from 5000 kcal by foragers to 242,870 in the United States is only 2 powers of 10 and may not seem very significant, but commercialization also brought about a human demographic revolution, which dramatically elevated aggregate energy costs. Global energy consumption of primary energy (coal, natural gas, petroleum, electricity, geothermal, solar, and wind) exceeded 100 quadrillion kilocalories (398 quadrillion BTUs) annually by the year 2000 (Figure 11.2). Even one quadrillion (1000 trillion) is an inconceivably large number, but 100 quadrillion (10^{17}) is 4 powers of 10 greater than the aggregate of

the modest 14.6 trillion kilocalories consumed annually in the forager world.

Remarkably, 85 percent of global energy consumption in the year 2000 was in the form of nonrenewable fossil fuels, and 45 percent of fossil fuel energy was in the form of petroleum. One country, the United States, consumed 25 percent of total global energy. This degree of energy inequality and dependency on unevenly distributed nonrenewable fossil fuels creates enormous stresses in the global system. Increased consumption combined with population growth has totally transformed the relationship between human groups, and between humans and the physical and biological world of nature. Within a single century of growth fueled by fossil fuels, the commercial world has suddenly placed human sustainability in doubt for the first time in 200,000 years of human existence.

Global population in the precapitalist imperial world had apparently reached a threshold at about 360 million people in the thirteenth century AD (McEvedy and Jones 1978). Rather than continuing to grow, population actually declined somewhat as unfavorable weather, plagues, and

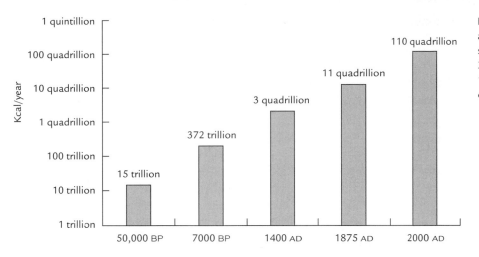

FIGURE 11.2   Global aggregate energy consumption, 50,000 BP–2000 AD. (SOURCES: Cook 1971:136, U.S. Department of Energy 2003.)

social and economic turmoil impacted the most densely settled areas of the world in the fourteenth century. This was similar to the environmental crisis produced by postglacial global warming in the early Holocene that contributed to the Neolithic and the formation of the first chiefdoms city-states. However, given historical circumstances in Europe by AD 1400, these multiple crises created unique opportunities for economic elites to promote commercialization and accumulate wealth. The weakness of political rulers during times of social and economic turmoil gave merchants, financiers, and large land owners a free hand, allowing them to expand their influence over markets, and making it possible for them to create personal power networks that connected sources of political and religious power. Economic elites were also wealthy enough to be insulated from economic crises, and were able to take advantage of new economic opportunities as they arose. At the same time elite-directed changes in the organization of production forced vast numbers of people into economic dependency in crowded cities. The unprecedented combination of economic growth, poverty, and urbanization for the first time caused population to increase at exponential rates. Population growth created abundant cheap labor and larger markets. Global population suddenly passed the billion mark by about 1804, with intercontinental

commercial transfers of food and materials drawing on pre-industrial agricultural technology. Rapidly accelerating growth since then saw global population double to 2 billion within 123 years by 1927, and double again to 4 billion within 47 years by 1974 (Figure 11.3).

Population growth in the commercial world has been directly subsidized by the burning of fossil fuels. For example, in the year 2000, most of the world's 6 billion people were heavily dependent on food produced by large scale factory farms. In addition to petroleum products farm machinery consumed, factory farms were consuming some 130 million metric tons of synthetically manufactured ammonia fertilizer (NH_3) produced at a cost of a quadrillion kilocalories of natural gas. Of course, primary agricultural production is only a small part of the energy cost of food in the commercial world.

THE NATURE OF CAPITALISM

Systems of Production and Exchange

The modern capitalist economy is radically different from all previous systems of production and exchange. The distinctive features of capitalism created the global political economy. The concept of *political economy* used in this book emphasizes

FIGURE 11.3 Global population, 50,000 BP–2000 AD.

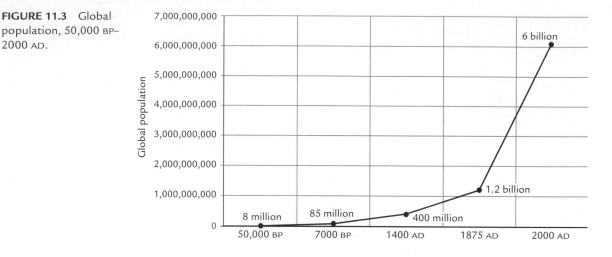

the fact that economics cannot be separated from politics. This means that the commercial world is as much about a social structure that is maintained by political power, as it is about a material infrastructure and an ideological superstructure. Capitalism is a particular property regime and an unequal distribution of wealth that is ultimately enforced by the coercive power of government. Capitalist economic organization uses social inequality to promote wealth accumulation and political expansionism on a scale unequaled in human history (Figure 11.4).

The concept of an economy existing apart from the rest of society began as a uniquely European cultural construction. All societies have cultural systems of production and distribution, but only Europeans came to believe that human well-being depended on having a *growing* economy. What Europeans call the *economy* is embedded within everyday household activities in tribal societies. It is helpful for comparative purposes to distinguish three different systems of production and distribution (Wolf 1982): kin-ordered, tributary, and capitalist.

Kin-ordered production characterizes the tribal cultures treated in Chapters 2–5. In these systems, kinship constitutes the culturally defined social categories around which productive activities are organized. Relationships between individuals established by marriage or family connections, real or fictive, determine the form of food producing and -sharing groups. In all systems that are ordered exclusively by kinship, production is primarily for direct consumption, or **use value,** rather than for **exchange value.** Small Pacific Island chiefdoms such as Tikopia have ranked descent groups, but production and distribution continue to be primarily based on kinship. However, large Pacific chiefdoms and the Hawaiian kingdom are tributary political economies in which the rulers command a significant portion of both production and distribution.

Tributary production characterizes the ancient civilizations described in Chapters 7–9. In these systems, the commoners, or peasantry, produced their own food, while the rulers supported themselves by extracting "surplus" production as tribute. Surplus extraction was exploitation whenever it reduced the security of the producers or lowered their standard of living. Title to land was often claimed by the state, but it was political power and ideology that compelled the peasantry to turn over surplus production to the state. The structure of surplus extraction was maintained by placing primary producers in subordinate status positions relative to the nonfood-producing elites. Much of the accumulated wealth went into maintaining status differences by means of the conspicuous display of luxury goods or the construction of awe-inspiring temples and funerary

FIGURE 11.4 The New York Stock Exchange, one of the central institutions of the capitalist market economy, which drives the commercial-scale world.

ritual. Bureaucratically organized tribute extraction often existed alongside long-distance, market-oriented exchange systems managed by merchants or traders. Developed market systems helped rulers acquire exotic luxury goods, but a fully commercialized distribution system would have undermined the status structure that supported the tribute system and would, in theory, have transformed it into a **capitalist production** mode.

The Uniqueness of Capitalism

Capitalism is by definition an ideology that gives priority to the "free market" and makes economic growth and perpetual capital accumulation the

most important human objective. In addition to thinking of capitalism as a belief system, commercialization (the production and maintenance of private profit-making business enterprise) is the dominant cultural process, and economic elites draw their social power from commercial transactions.

Under capitalism as a system of commercial production and exchange, land, labor, technology, money, raw materials, and goods and services are commodities to be bought and sold for a profit. The emergence of a monetary market for labor is a key distinguishing feature of capitalism, because wage labor reduced the self-sufficiency of the household far more decisively than did tribute systems. Political economist and theorist Karl Marx (1818–1883) argued that the labor market emerged historically when capitalists separated the peasantry from their land and other resources that constituted their means of production, thus compelling the peasantry to sell their labor to secure basic subsistence. Laborers came to constitute a social class characterized by their separation from the means of production. Land and tools became **capital,** which only a few owned, and basic products became **commodities** to be marketed. As a social class, capitalists, or the

---

kin-ordered production A mode of production organized at the domestic or kinship level and producing primarily for domestic use rather than exchange.

use value The value of goods produced for domestic consumption, usually within a kin-ordered mode of production.

exchange value The value of goods when used as commodities.

tributary production A mode of production in which products are extracted as surplus from a self-supporting peasantry and used to support the state.

capitalist production A mode of production in which a few people control the means of production and purchase the labor of those who could not otherwise support themselves.

capital Marx's term for land and tools as the means of production; also refers generally to accumulated wealth used for productive purposes.

commodities Basic goods that are produced for their exchange value in a market economy to generate profit to be accumulated as capital.

owners of capital, made a profit by appropriating surplus production above the costs of labor and capital. In this mode of production, the capitalist seeks to accumulate a surplus to increase profit. The surplus can be increased by depressing the wage of the laborers and by raising the level of technology. The interest of capitalists to increase their profits by keeping the labor wage low is opposed to the interest of laborers to increase their own share of the products of their labor. Individual capitalists also compete with one another to increase their profits. This incentive to increase profits, as well as the contradiction of interests between social classes, encourages economic elites to use their influence on political rulers to increase their social power. Elites lobby for government policies that direct public finance into infrastructure improvements and social institutions that will favor the development of capital intensive technologies, increased production, and the expansion of markets. Capitalists also tend to favor expansionist foreign policies that will gain them access to new sources of labor, markets, raw materials, and land to further their personal goals of wealth accumulation.

The Greek concept of economy described by the ancient philosopher Aristotle (384–322 BC) illustrates the contrasts between the imperial and commercial worlds. The Greeks took economy to mean household economy *(oikonomia)*. They did not think of "the economy" as something separate from daily life. They imagined a stable, **embedded economy,** much as in the tribal world, and they were not concerned with promoting economic growth. They tolerated, but stigmatized, merchants who engaged in money-making *(chrēmatistikē),* on the assumption that they sought unjust profits from unequal exchange. Greek society was to be composed ideally of relatively equal citizens. Wealth accumulation was suspect because it could lead to wasteful luxury and impropriety, but it could be a source of honor if devoted to public interests. In the ancient city state of Attica (Athens), two-thirds of all wealth was in buildings (33 percent) and

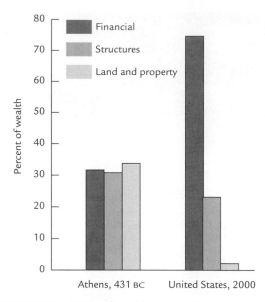

FIGURE 11.5   National wealth composition in ancient Greece and the United States.

coins (32 percent). The remainder was in farm land (22 percent), slaves (7 percent), and livestock and moveable goods (6 percent) (Goldsmith 1987:16–33). Slightly more than half of all Athenian wealth was in public hands. Equally remarkable, most public wealth was economically unproductive, and nearly one-fourth of this was in religious buildings and cult objects. In comparison, in the United States in the year 2000, most wealth was in financial assets (75 percent) and structures (23 percent), and land and all moveable assets together were only 2 percent of the total (Figure 11.5). In 1995, all U.S. governments—federal, state, and local—held only 11 percent of national wealth.

Aristotle advocated a production and exchange system that, in theory, was remarkably reminiscent of the "original affluent society" of foragers (Sahlins 1968). Aristotle felt that human wants were limited and that economic scarcity was not a problem. This ideal represents a view that is in direct opposition to the modern definition of a **disembodied economy,** which assumes limited means and unlimited wants. Aristotle's ideal city-state assumed a small community based on reciprocal exchange, self-sufficiency, and social justice. In this system, individuals were not supposed to make a profit at their neighbors' expense because this would lead to inequality that would threaten community solidarity. Aristotle accepted money as a medium of exchange but argued that too much market trade would undermine the good life, and he considered wealth accumulation to be contrary to natural law.

The commercial world is obviously superior at wealth building. In 431 BC, the total wealth of Attica could be estimated at the equivalent of a mere $807 million, or $2,522 per capita in a population of 320,000 people. This is based on converting the minimum annual household subsistence value of 275 Greek drachma into the equivalent of $1500 dollars, treated as universal income units for comparative purposes. In the year 2000 the aggregate wealth of the United States was $117 trillion (Statistical Abstract of the United States, 2001, Tables 690, 1163). This was an astounding 6 orders of magnitude greater than Greek wealth. Wealth was much greater in the United States, both in absolute quantity and in the amount per capita. U.S. per capita wealth was $414,374 for 282 million people (Figure 11.6). Furthermore, even though private wealth was highly concentrated in both cultures, the vast volume of total American wealth, as well as the greater proportion that was privately held, meant that America's wealthiest controlled vastly more absolute power than the wealthiest Greeks. Even more importantly, as capitalists, wealthy Americans use their wealth to produce more wealth.

Earlier noncapitalist societies did not institutionalize private property and had no organized markets for land, labor, and money. Production and trade were directed by political rulers, and people became wealthy because of their political power. Furthermore, people lacked the concept of economic freedom and were bound to their occupations. In contrast, "the capitalist employee has the legal right to work or not work as he or she chooses" (Heilbroner and Thurow 1987:12–14),

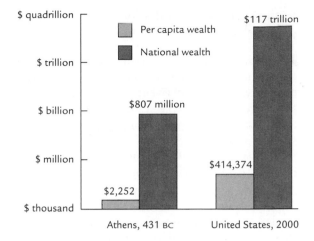

FIGURE 11.6 National wealth and per capita wealth in ancient Greece and the United States.

as well as the right to buy up farmland and turn it into a more profitable shopping center.

Heilbroner and Thurow (1987) consider capitalism to be "utterly alien" and a "volcanic disruption" in comparison to the "tradition and command" systems that preceded it. In their view, there were no "factors of production" in precapitalist societies, because "labor, land, and capital were not commodities for sale." Instead, these factors

are the creations of a process of historic change, a change that divorced labor from social life, that created real estate out of ancestral land, and that made treasure into capital. Capitalism is the outcome of a revolutionary change—a change in laws, attitudes, and social relationships as deep and far-reaching as any in history. (1987:15–16)

embedded economy An economy that can only be observed and understood within the context of the social, political, and religious systems of the culture.

disembodied economy The concept of an economy as something that can be understood apart from the rest of society and culture, especially with a capitalist mode of production.

Inequality and Instability in the Capitalist World System

The emergence of capitalism in sixteenth-century Europe led to a uniquely organized global world economy by the early twentieth century. Capitalism succeeded as a social system because it proved to be a more effective means of appropriating surplus production than the earlier tributary empires (Wallerstein 1974). Empires that used coercion to extract surplus were expensive to maintain and very fragile. Earlier noncapitalist states were, in effect, "homeostatic systems," in that they tended to rise and fall within certain limits set by their unstable political organization. In comparison with tribal cultures, the early states and empires functioned at a much higher density and total size, but they were still limited in absolute scale.

In the capitalist **world system,** expansion to the limits of the globe becomes theoretically possible because the system can function without a centralized state political authority. Individual states are needed only to maintain internal order, to enforce contracts, and to encourage the international market economy. The key to the success of capitalism was that the market economy provided incentives for technological improvements that increased productivity, while a world division of labor allowed costs and benefits to be unequally apportioned.

The emerging capitalist world system was a multilayered economic hierarchy divided into a European core, a southern European semiperiphery, and an eastern European and New World periphery. Each zone was defined by distinctive geography, political organization, economic production, and its form of labor control, but the zones were all linked to the center by **unequal exchanges** that contributed to **capital accumulation** in the **core.** The exploited lower classes were concentrated in the **periphery** and semiperiphery, where they were coerced to work as slaves and serfs for European managers. Conditions were somewhat less coercive for the tenant farmers in the semiperiphery. In the core, laborers worked for wages, and small farmers worked their own land, while merchants and industrialists profited enormously from their privileged positions as the prime beneficiaries of the unequal exchange.

It is important to note the distinctions between *world* and *globe* in this context. The world system initially did not encompass the globe; it began in Europe and expanded outward. Wallerstein (1974) distinguished four distinct historical phases in the development of the world system. It originated in an economic crisis that undermined European feudalism by 1450 and encouraged capital accumulation at the expense of the peasantry. The system was spurred on by the gold and silver extracted as booty from the New World and was consolidated as a system between 1640 and 1815. The Industrial Revolution, utilizing coal as a new energy base, facilitated further expansion that transformed the world system into a global system between 1815 and 1917. Since 1917, the system has consolidated further.

Wallerstein (1990) lists six destabilizing realities that characterize the modern world system:

1. A hierarchical division of labor
2. Periodic expansion and incorporation
3. Continuous accumulation
4. Continuous progress
5. Polarization of individuals and groups
6. The impossibility of perpetual growth

These characteristics imply critical contradictions in the system and have generated particular ideologies that tend to obscure the realities and help keep the system functioning.

The global division of labor integrates the world into a single production system based on exploitation and inequalities that paradoxically are supported by ideologies that stress universal values of peace and world order. Racist ideologies are also used to justify the disadvantaged position of peripheral groups, with economic rewards apportioned differentially according to the intrinsic merit and ability of different groups.

Since 1450, the world system has gone through cycles of expansion marked by the steady incorporation of external cultural groups into the periphery. This trend has been supported by the

FIGURE 11.7 A cotton mill in Lancashire, England, 1900. Factory workers in the industrial core of the global system worked long hours, but they were encouraged by their religious faith that hard work was the key to salvation and by their belief in continuous economic growth.

ideology calling for all peoples to be assimilated into a universal Western culture, on the assumption that other cultures were simply incapable of "advance."

Continuous capital accumulation is made easier when workers are persuaded by an ideology that extolls the virtues of hard work and competitiveness to overcome inequality (Figure 11.7). German social scientist Max Weber (1864–1920) was the first to point out that extreme Calvinist forms of Protestantism encouraged capital accumulation, in his famous book *The Protestant Ethic and the Spirit of Capitalism* ([1904–1905] 1930). According to Weber, German Calvinists believed that continuous hard work and self-denial were the best way to demonstrate that one was predestined for salvation. Such a belief was a religious endorsement for precisely the behavior that the new economic elite needed.

Capitalism tends to polarize people by steadily widening the gap between rich and poor.

However, such a reality is destabilizing. It is therefore vigorously denied by the world system's myth of the rising standard of living, which ignores population increase, health problems, onerous work loads, and negative environmental

world system An international hierarchy of diverse societies and cultures integrated into a single economic system based on unequal exchange that allows wealth to accumulate in the core.

unequal exchange Market-based exchanges in which one party is consistently able to accumulate a disproportionate share of the profit or wealth.

capital accumulation Expansion of wealth and the means of production that can be devoted to further production.

core The wealthy industrial countries at the center of the world system where the recipients of unequal exchange reside.

periphery Capital-poor areas that supply raw materials and labor to the core; this area was integrated into the early capitalist world system through conquest and coercion.

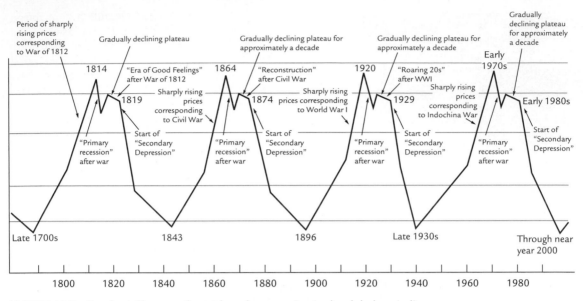

FIGURE 11.8 Kondratieff waves of growth and contraction in the global capitalist economy, 1790–2000 as projected by Mager (1987). This shows peaks at 1814, 1864, and 1920, followed by sharp drops (primary recessions), a short recovery, and then a long decline (secondary depression). The vertical axis is undefined and the curve impressionistic.

impacts, all clear indicators of a declining living standard. Core elites also exhort the periphery to greater "development" efforts, while implying that failure to achieve development must be due to racial or cultural inferiority.

The human problems that perpetual economic expansion creates are highlighted by the existence of Konratieff waves, or K-waves, of expansion and collapse, named after their discovery by Russian economist Nikolai Kondratieff in the 1920s (Kondratieff 1984, Mager 1987, Stoken 1993). These cyclical phenomena are also known as "long waves" and "price waves." They are long boom-and-bust episodes that seem to characterize market systems, and have been identified in ancient empires, and in medieval Europe, as well as in the modern world system (Fischer 1996). Waves resemble business cycles, but waves are longer, wider in scope, and less predictable. Waves begin with decades of prosperity, with economic growth, low interest rates, low prices, increased profits for investors, and higher wages

for workers. Prosperity is followed by decades of high prices, unemployment, increased poverty, and hardship. Kondratieff identified three long waves between 1790 and 1925 (Figure 11.8), accurately predicting the global economic depression of the 1930s (Kondratieff 1984). Theorists believe that military expenditures and wars may exert an important influence on wave phenomena (Goldstein 1988), but in the commercial world waves are too vast and complex to attribute to a single cause, or a single human decision maker.

Elites clearly have further concentrated their social power by moving beyond the constraints of nationally based political economies and creating transnational commercial empires based on capitalist market exchanges. This shift to transnational commercial empires has enormous significance for humanity, yet it has received remarkably little attention from anthropologists. Commercially organized, globally integrated cultures are important because (1) they are reducing cultural diversity at an unprecedented scale

(Bodley 1999), (2) they have increased the number of poor, and (3) they may be ultimately limited by the integrity of the biosphere itself or by the human ability to tolerate mass impoverishment.

THE EUROPEAN ORIGINS OF CAPITALISM

Western Cosmology and the Industrial Revelation

Marshall Sahlins (1996) points out that Judeo-Christian cosmology is apparently unique among cultural traditions because it attributes the evil in the world to a human act of free will, as recounted in the Book of Genesis. Western cosmology assumes that because of their original sin in the Garden of Eden, humans are inherently evil, and human misery is the natural punishment for this evil human nature. This gloomy cosmology derives from religious beliefs, but the underlying assumptions about human nature and economic scarcity seem to have permeated Western scientific and secular thought.

The European Enlightenment, which made riches a desirable goal, represented a change in thought that kept the underlying belief in original sin and human inadequacy intact. Material progress was assumed to be natural, although this view overlooked the contradiction that progress also increased human needs, leaving people perpetually unsatisfied. Commerce, industrial technology, and the science of economics are all seemingly designed to help people *reduce,* but never *overcome,* the inevitable scarcity that insatiable human nature implies. What Sahlins calls the *industrial revelation* is the sad realization that "in the world's richest societies, the subjective experience of lack increases in proportion to the objective output of wealth" (Sahlins 1996:401). In effect, economic growth must impoverish.

In Western cosmology, people are driven by natural law to seek pleasure and avoid pain. Society itself is thought to be the product of selfish individuals seeking self-satisfaction, just as the "laws" of market supply and demand, or "free trade," will give us the best distribution of economic goods. As we have seen in previous chapters, this view of human existence is strikingly different from the belief of tribal peoples that life is good and that they can provide for all of their material and emotional needs through their own efforts. Liberated and empowered by their culture, tribal peoples maximize individual freedom and personal autonomy and do not view society as a coercive force. By contrast, Western philosophers from Bishop Augustine to Thomas Hobbes, as well as many modern sociologists and anthropologists, consider society to be a coercive power structure. This view equates society with government and treats it as a natural response to a selfish, and thus dangerous, human nature. Sahlins even argues that the "invisible hand" theorized by Adam Smith (discussed later in the chapter) and the functionalism of anthropology and sociology can be derived from the understanding of Divine Providence found in medieval cosmology, in which whatever happens is God's, or society's, plan and will result in collective good. This natural law of the Enlightenment philosophers provided the foundation for economics, natural science, political science, and national constitutions.

The notion of a spiritual soul existing apart from the physical body is virtually a human universal, but only Westerners see body and soul in conflict. Medieval philosophers extended the mind/body dualism to humans and nature. They situated humans midway between animals and gods in a hierarchical "chain of being," giving humans the mortal bodies of animals and godlike intellects. Judeo-Christian notions that humans exist apart *from,* and with dominion *over,* nature prepared the way for capitalism by making it easy to objectify nature—that is, to treat natural objects as commodities. Such dualism and universal commodification is quite alien to virtually all other cultures, where even the concept of nature as distinct from the supernatural does not exist. The outcome of this Western cosmology of evil humanity, natural scarcity, insatiable wants, human separation from nature, and presumably perfect markets based on free trade, is that people are persuaded to believe that their culture evolved *naturally* to meet our human needs, not that it was designed by particular people to meet their particular needs.

Commercialization Under the Feudal Monarchs

The roots of the commercialization process were present in the rudimentary markets, trade structures, monetary systems, and craft specialization found in most ancient agrarian civilizations, but political rulers jealously regulated commercial activities to safeguard their personal power. It was in Europe in the centuries after the collapse of the Roman empire that merchants and commerce gradually became the dominant forces in cultural development. How this vast cultural change came about is an intriguing anthropological problem, because under the politicization process virtually all resources were officially controlled by church and state, a rigid social hierarchy became entrenched, and an apparent ceiling on economic growth was reached. The hereditary rulers were ambivalent about the rising commercial elite; they sought both to restrict their activities and to form alliances with them, establishing a pattern that still continues. The crucial point is that merchants gradually became the driving force of cultural development.

The Domesday Survey of England, conducted in 1086 for William the Conqueror shortly after the Norman Conquest, provides an excellent baseline for measuring the astounding cultural transformations eventually brought about by commercialization. Designed for tax purposes, the great Domesday Book enumerated every manor in the country and all the plows, land, and cattle, and ranked all adult males by social category. The survey dramatically reveals a remarkable concentration of social power and shows the limits of power under preindustrial technology with little commercial activity. More than 90 percent of the perhaps 2 million inhabitants were farm laborers living on the manors and dependent villages scattered over the countryside. A hierarchy

of centrally placed market towns existed, but the peasantry produced most of their own food and manufactured domestic consumer goods by working part-time as independent millers, iron smiths, potters, and weavers in the household, village, or manor. Only 12,000 people lived in London, the largest city. Overseas trade and much of the industrial activity centered on supplying luxury goods to the hereditary nobility, who probably numbered fewer than 40,000 people, counting men, women, and children—about 2 percent of the population. Political power and land ownership remained in the hands of the king and nobles. Forty percent of the land was controlled by thirty-two great landlords under Royal Charter, and much of the other productive land was held in manors under other subtenants. All landlords served as the king's representatives.

The bulk of the English population were serfs, who held use rights to small subsistence parcels in return for working two to three days per week for the lord of the manor and who provided various additional services, taxes, and payments. These small holdings were worked cooperatively under the open-fields system, which allowed the serfs to retain enough of the advantages of domestic-scale life to make serfdom bearable (see the box entitled "The Open-Fields System"). Almost 10 percent of the population were chattel slaves. Except for the nobles and a few wealthy burghers (townsmen) and clergy, most people had little control over the conditions that influenced their daily lives. Over the next 300 years, the bulk of the peasantry experienced steadily declining living standards, but conditions improved for the few landlords and merchants who gained access to the growing international market in wool. The English population increased threefold to some 6 million, with perhaps 15 percent living in the expanding urban centers (Miller and Hatcher 1995:396).

The manorial system had obvious limits, because a feudal land baron could effectively control only so many manors, but money was an inherently expandable form of wealth. Economic growth during this period is demonstrated by the dramatic forty-four-fold increase in the supply of royal coinage in circulation in medieval

England—from £25,000 in 1086 to £1,100,000 by 1320. Under constant promotion by the emerging merchant class, money steadily replaced barter exchange, greatly facilitated government finance, and made trade much more profitable. However, the serfs could barely participate in this kind of economic activity, because they did not control sufficient productive land. Small farmers were being forced below a comfortable subsistence level at the same time that money to pay taxes and buy essentials was becoming critical for survival. Under the existing social structure, modest technological improvements barely increased total agricultural production and brought few benefits to the peasants. Land that could have generated adequate subsistence was devoted to the production of wool for export, and was held in vast hunting preserves, horse pastures, and forests as a private luxury. By the fourteenth century, the social system was in crisis. Then disastrous famines and a series of plagues known as the Black Death reduced the population almost to the Domesday level.

Growth in medieval England clearly produced great wealth (see the box entitled "Richard Fitzalan: Medieval England's Richest Lord"). However, the *proportion* of the wealthholders at the top of the feudal hierarchy probably did not increase as economic growth occurred. Rather, the scale of society and the total amount of extractable wealth increased, making those at the top more powerful. Most of the newly wealthy merchants were probably already members of the upper class, whose numbers may have increased by 80,000 in this era. Before the Black Death struck in 1349, there were 3.6 million more impoverished peasants than at the time of the Norman Conquest. In the absence of culture change to produce a more equitable power structure, the growth in scale associated with commercialization left more people in England poor than wealthy.

The Financial Revolution and the Power of Money

Mass-production industrial technology did not have a major influence until the 1800s, but the basic institutional structures of capitalism, including joint stock corporations, securities trading, and investment banking, were firmly in place in Europe prior to 1700. Less savory cultural features such as monopoly, bribery, and market manipulation were also commonplace. In medieval Europe before the emergence of capitalism, commercial activities were strictly regulated by church and state in ways that discouraged the accumulation of money by private individuals. Prices were often fixed at what was considered to be a "just price." Moneylenders and the wealthy were looked down on, and there were sumptuary laws restricting luxury and gambling, as well as laws against usury (charging exorbitant interest rates). Profit-generating practices such as monopolies and reselling at a higher price were forbidden as "offenses against public trade." Money itself existed only as a relatively fixed supply of coins, and there were no banks. As merchants steadily increased interregional trade, and rulers began to wage longer and more expensive military campaigns, they began to adopt more flexible ways of conceptualizing and handling money. Money is symbolic as well as "real." Its primary function is to store obligations between people. It exists both as numbers recorded in accounts and in the form of circulating coin and currency. And money can exist in the imagination. Credit (from the Latin *credere*, "to believe") is based on belief in return payment and makes it possible to multiply and manipulate money in truly amazing ways. The concept of credit was a simple extension of the concept of contract, based on the distinction between possessions in hand and possessions one was due to receive. When credit, interest charges, banking, and paper money and securities all became culturally acceptable, a *financial revolution* occurred that made capitalism possible. This cultural transformation was as significant as the Neolithic revolution.

The Amsterdam Exchange Bank, founded in 1609, was perhaps the first major bank, and it was followed shortly by the Amsterdam Stock Exchange. The first bank notes, the forerunners of modern paper money and checks, were issued by the Bank of Stockholm in 1661. Paper bills of exchange and bank notes greatly facilitated

The Open-Fields System

For landlords, industrialists, and merchants to gain the labor and raw materials necessary to increase their wealth, they had to force the self-sufficient European peasantry out of the *open-fields system* of land use that had sustained them for millennia. Egalitarian peasant communities that relied on cooperative plow agriculture used the open-fields system primarily to meet their subsistence needs, not to produce marketable surpluses (Orwin and Orwin 1967, Seebohm 1905). This system helped individual farmers minimize the risk of crop failure in an unpredictable natural environment, where politics were uncertain and access to markets was limited (McCloskey 1976, Townsend 1993). It was easier for farmers to plow cooperatively, especially when not every farmer owned plows and full draft teams.

The open-fields system produced a patchwork of individually held strips of land, each roughly an acre in area and representing one day's work for a single plow team. Each farmer held use rights from his landlord to a *virgate,* a collection of perhaps 30 acres of land scattered in strips throughout the manor (Figure 11.A). This would be sufficient to allow him to cultivate half to meet the annual subsistence needs of his household, and keep half fallow to maintain soil fertility. A farmer's holdings were in scattered strips because this distribution made plowing most equitable and ensured that each farmer would have land of equal quality and distance from the village. The patchwork effect resulted because fields were plowed in blocks of *furlongs* (parallel plow strips), and the contour of the land determined the direction of plowing. As long as the cultivated area remained unfenced, it was open for common grazing after harvest. Every household also had access to common pastures, meadows, and woodlands beyond the cultivated fields for hunting, grazing, and gathering wood and materials.

The essentially tribal open-fields system predated the Romans and operated in various forms throughout medieval Europe, but it was incompatible with the demands of large-scale commercial agriculture. By the fifteenth century, English landlords began to find feudal tenure and the open-fields system ill-suited to the new opportunities presented by the emerging urban and international markets. Landowners increasingly fenced their holdings in order to raise great herds of sheep to supply the growing urban market for wool. In the process, self-sufficient tenants and smallholders were driven off the land. A second wave of enclosures in the eighteenth century was prompted by the adoption of new crops and more intensive production systems.

international trade, government and commercial finance, and capital investment. Economic growth quickly accelerated when enterprising bankers discovered they could lend out more money than they actually held in deposit. *Finance capital* is at the heart of capitalism, and money as a cultural symbol makes infinite economic growth seem deceptively possible.

A small network of individuals managed to accumulate wealth by acting within triangles connecting governments, militaries, and financial institutions. Political rulers borrowed from the

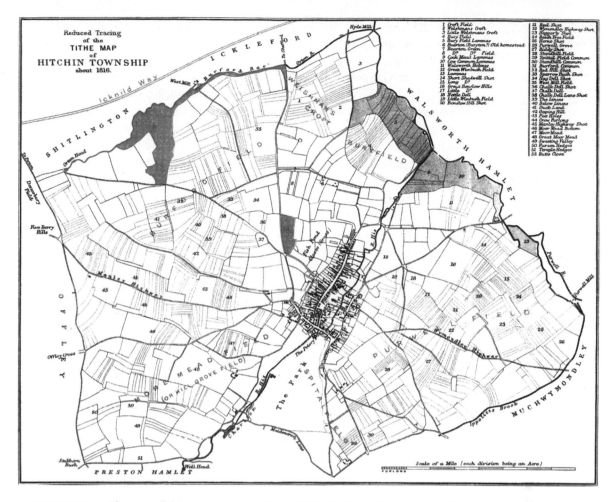

FIGURE 11.A The open-fields system of the village of Hitchin in 1816, showing individually held strips of land. The village is at the crossroads in the center, and the numbers refer to place names. (SOURCE: Seebohm, 1905.)

wealthy for military expenditures, and bankers sold the bonds back to the wealthy. This encouraged an arms race, but the investors, bankers, and military contractors all benefitted, and they shifted the cost to taxpayers. The investors were also the politicians who borrowed the funds, and

sometimes they were also the bankers. This arrangement created the "fiscal-military state" and clearly promoted economic growth (Brewer 1989, Carruthers 1996).

The financial revolution suddenly gave the wealthy a powerful means of influencing the

Richard Fitzalan: Medieval England's Richest Lord

The level of wealth and luxury that this emerging commercial system could support at the top of the social pyramid is illustrated by an enterprising fourteenth-century nobleman, Richard Fitzalan, the earl of Arundel and Surrey, then the richest private person in England. When he died in 1376, Richard had amassed capital of £72,245 in cash, property, and credits (Given-Wilson 1991)—three times the sum *in circulation* in 1086. Fitzalan owned multiple residences (Figure 11.B), vast estates, and 25,000 sheep. His fortune came from the sale of wool, metals, and livestock; from overseas investments; from loans to the king and other nobles; and from political favors. He was a capitalist who used his money to make money.

We can put Fitzalan's wealth and this early phase of commercialization in perspective. At the beginning of the politicization process in southern England in 3000 BC, the most powerful Neolithic chiefdom might have been able to mobilize the 1200 people a year to build a megalithic monument. By contrast, even as a private citizen, Fitzalan could support more than twice that number from his annual income, and more than ten times more from accumulated capital. His annual landed income alone was sufficient to support 2857 manor servants at the high grain prices of that time. And his total capital would have allowed him to hire 15,451 annual laborers.

FIGURE 11.B   Fitzalan's Arundel Castle.

course of cultural development to their own advantage. The popular wisdom that money is power is correct, but successful financiers did not need to be personally wealthy. Credit, and the newly created financial institutions allowed them to magnify their own power by using other people's money. Capitalism didn't just happen. Economic historians attribute the emergence of capitalism to rising consumer demand, but market demand came from people who could use money, not from the mass of the European population struggling to maintain themselves. The "demand" was for palaces, mansions, luxury goods, and military power to satisfy the aristocracy and to support their dependent servants, artisans, soldiers, and courtiers. The wealthy also demanded profitable new investments. These were the financial demands that created exciting opportunities for the most powerful merchants and financiers, who came to manage enormous accumulations of capital. A few prominent families such as the Fuggers in Augsburg (1367–1641), the Medici in Florence (1434–1737), and the Rothschilds in Frankfurt (1770–   ) were the principal financial architects of European capitalism (see the box entitled "Fuggers and Rothschilds"). These families, together with the owners and directors of a handful of banks and trading companies, such as the Bank of Amsterdam, the Bank of England, the British East India Company, and the Dutch East India Company, were the driving forces behind the accumulation, exchange, and marketing of money that began to increase the scale of culture and transform the world long before the Industrial Revolution.

European Marriage and Family

The system of kinship and marriage in medieval Europe was severely constrained by economic inequality. While European civilization was still predominantly agrarian, people needed access to individual landholdings before they could marry and establish a new household. Given the manorial system, land was in extremely short supply, and even a peasant's right to rent tiny parcels was a crucial inheritance to be safeguarded. Land rights were normally transmitted by inheritance to men, whereas women received a dowry of movable property or money upon marriage. This meant that men might not be able to marry until they were over 25. It also meant that many men and women could never marry, and they instead joined the religious monasteries as celibate monks or nuns.

British social anthropologist Jack Goody (1976: 14–25) pointed out that European marriage was characterized by class endogamy, in which the bride's dowry and the groom's inheritance had to be a good "match" for a marriage to take place, because inheritance and dowry served as rough measures of social standing. This meant that parents usually arranged marriages for their children within their own class, but at the same time people tried to marry up. Dowry thus helped the upper class keep their wealth intact. Dowry also made monogamy the preferred European form of marriage, because of the impossibility of sorting out multiple dowries within a single household. The European emphasis on female premarital chastity, chaperons, and arranged marriage may also be related to the importance of preventing lower-class men from marrying higher-class women and thereby diluting the family estate (Stone 1997:229–234).

Most European households were based on the small nuclear family, with peasant households averaging only 4.5 persons. On the manors, there were many single-person households, which would be unthinkable in the tribal world. There were no corporate descent groups, because impoverished peasants had too few resources to form a meaningful corporate estate. In this respect, European peasants were far poorer than people in most tribal societies, where everyone had access to an abundance of physical, social, and spiritual resources. In contrast to the peasants, the few upper-class Europeans often maintained large extended families and large households with many family members and domestic servants. As an extreme example, the French king, Louis XIV (reigned 1643–1715), maintained a household of 500 personal attendants. Family and kin were important to the aristocracy because they had vast corporate estates and wealth to pass on to the next generation. The English dukes, marquesses, earls, viscounts, and barons needed extensive genealogies to keep track of their complex kinship networks and inherited titles.

Fuggers and Rothschilds: Business Family Success Stories

The most successful early European capitalists accumulated great fortunes by forming family-owned business enterprises based on kinship and strategic marriage alliances. These corporate lineages became commercial dynasties that paralleled and were often intertwined with political dynasties (Ehrenberg 1928, Flynn 1941).

The German Catholic Fugger family created what became the richest and most influential business of the time. The Fugger enterprise began as a simple family-owned cotton and textile business in Augsburg, Bavaria, in 1367. The business expanded into the overseas spice trade, and eventually grew into a distinctly modern, diversified mining, trading, and banking business with branches and property throughout Europe. By the third generation in 1485, four Fugger brothers operated the company offices in Rome and Florence in Italy, in Innsbruck in Austria, and at their Augsburg headquarters. The Fuggers cultivated the patronage of the most powerful civil and religious rulers of the time and profitably financed wars and political intrigues, buying elections and offices, and loaning money to create profitable supporters. After 1500, the Fugger company gained monopolistic control over copper and silver mines and smelters in Austria and Hungary, which were then Europe's principal source for these metals. Benefiting from Spain's conquests in the New World, they developed mining interests in Peru and became involved in the African slave trade. By 1546, their fortune had grown to more than 5 million guilders. If converted to wheat at prevailing prices, this would have been sufficient to support 521,477 persons for a year—a thirtyfold increase in social power over Richard Fitzalan's record in 1376. The Fuggers' lucrative monopoly and behind-the-scenes manipulations of church and state generated labor

GROWTH AND POVERTY UNDER EARLY BRITISH INDUSTRIAL CAPITALISM

The Industrial Revolution and the Culture of Consumption

The most outstanding physical transformations accompanying the modern world system were dramatic increases in population and resource consumption, which began in England between 1760 and 1830. Immediately prior to the Industrial Revolution, world population growth was relatively slow, with a doubling time of approximately 250 years. However, with industrialization well established, the European population doubled in just 80 years after 1850, while the European population of the United States, Canada, Australia, and Argentina tripled between 1851 and 1900, thanks in part to large-scale immigration. Between 1851 and 1900, some 35 million people left Europe (Woodruff 1966).

This growth in population was accompanied by a shift in consumption patterns that marked a radical break with the relative stability of prior political-scale cultures. Capitalist economic growth requires continuous per-capita increases in consumption, which would inevitably deplete resources, at least in the core countries. For example, by 1850, England was unable to satisfy its needs

unrest, peasant revolts, protests from other merchants;
eventually led to national-
ization of their mining interests; and contributed to the
Protestant Reformation.

Much like the Fuggers,
the Rothschild family rose
from humble beginnings, in
the Jewish ghetto in Frankfurt in 1744, to create an
international banking dy-
nasty operated by brothers
from offices in Frankfurt,
London, Paris, Vienna, and
Naples by the 1820s (Fig-
ure 11.C). The family married carefully to increase

SOLOMON ROTHSCHILD, HEAD OF
THE VIENNA HOUSE.
ANSELM MAYER ROTHSCHILD, HEAD
OF THE PARENT HOUSE AT
FRANKFORT, 1812-55.
CHARLES ROTHSCHILD, HEAD OF THE
OLD HOUSE AT NAPLES.

FIGURE 11.C The Rothschild brothers, left to right
Solomon (1774–1855), Anselm Mayer (1773–1855),
Charles (1788–1855).

their power, sometimes practicing cross-cousin marriage to keep their growing
power and influence intact. Like the Fuggers, they maintained alliances with the
most powerful political figures of the time and were able control an enormous
flow of finance capital in the most profitable way. By the end of the tumultuous
nineteenth century, the Rothschilds had accumulated the world's largest private
fortune. Their descendants are now billionaire financiers.

---

for grain, wood, fibers, and hides from within its
immediate borders (Woodruff 1966). Newly industrializing countries initially secured more resources by expanding trade networks and colonial
territories to draw resources from throughout
the world. Equally important was the switch in
energy resources from the renewable, solar-driven
fuels, such as wood, wind, and water, and a reliance on traction animals and human labor, which
had characterized ancient civilizations, to the use
of nonrenewable fossil fuels, such as coal, to power
industrial machines. Many earlier civilizations
utilized a complex division of labor, assembly-
line mass-production techniques, and a wide variety of simple machines; however, their reliance

on renewable energy sources was compatible with
relatively stable consumption patterns.

Coal fueled the factories, ships, and trains of
western Europe and North America in the nineteenth century and prepared the way for the age
of oil. In the short run, use of fossil fuels allowed
the industrial, capitalist world system to consume global resources at unsustainable levels,
subsidizing otherwise impossible growth. Industrial civilization is unique in human history as a
culture of consumption (Bodley 1996). In such a
culture, economy, society, and belief systems are
geared to "nonsustainable levels of resource consumption, and to continual, ever-higher elevation of those levels on a per-capita basis" (Bodley

1996:65). Biologically, this is overconsumption, as ecologist Howard Odum explained:

> In the industrial system with man living off a fuel, he manages all his affairs with industrial machinery, all parts of which are metabolically consumers. . . . This system of man has consumption in excess of production. The products of respiration—carbon dioxide, metabolic water, and mineralized inorganic wastes—are discharged in rates in excess of their incorporation into organic matter by photosynthesis. If the industrialized urban system were enclosed in a chamber with only the air above it at the time, it would quickly exhaust its oxygen, be stifled with waste, and destroy itself since it does not have the recycling pattern of the agrarian system. (1971:17)

This biological imbalance in its urban centers and the pressure to increase consumption force the industrial civilization to be a global system because it would have difficulty sustaining itself in any other way.

The label *Industrial Revolution* that historians apply to this great cultural transformation overemphasizes the role of technological factors; but, as with the Neolithic, more than technology changed. It was not simply the inventive genius of a particular people that caused the Industrial Revolution. It was cultural changes in social organization and ideological systems that called forth technological innovation.

British historian T. S. Ashton (1969) argued that organizational and technological changes, rather than population growth, accelerated production during the Industrial Revolution in England. Increased production was initiated by organizational changes that brought more land into production and facilitated the adoption of technological changes, such as new crops and cropping systems. Like Adam Smith, Ashton argued that social inequality, perhaps even "injustice," was the key that encouraged the accumulation of capital that funded the technological innovations of the Industrial Revolution:

> It is generally recognized that more saving takes place in communities in which the distribution of wealth is uneven than in those in which it approaches more closely to modern conceptions of what is just. (1969:7)

Technological innovations are not chance discoveries. They involve repeated trial and error and are often based on combinations of previous inventions. This is a panhuman process, but it is accelerated by specific cultural conditions. Invention was especially encouraged by specialization and the complex division of labor that emerged with the first states, but the unprecedented pressures for perpetual growth in the emerging capitalist world system set in motion the positive feedback between technical innovation and capital accumulation that became the Industrial Revolution.

Historians identify the enclosure movement as an important organizational change leading to the Industrial Revolution. In Europe during the seventeenth and eighteenth centuries, the shift from village self-sufficiency to market-oriented agriculture was accompanied by the transformation of open communal pastures and woodlands into numerous enclosed, privately controlled plots dedicated to the production of wool, meat, and hides.

Many historians urge us not to dwell on the fate of the formerly self-sufficient villagers who were forced off the land and impoverished by the enclosure process, which was supported by government decree. These peoples were surely being victimized by industrial progress. But according to the ideology of capitalism, we should focus on "the constructive activities that were being carried on inside the fences" (Ashton 1969:20). The historical interpretation of this dispossession process is that it was used to increase agricultural productivity while reducing the rural population, in order to raise the national standard of living. Those who were pushed off the land were considered to be "free to devote themselves to other activities," which meant they could either become vagrants or accept poorly paid jobs in the newly appearing industrial factories in the cities.

The enclosure movement was only the beginning of a series of vast cultural disruptions that ultimately spread throughout the globe as the capitalist world system began its expansion. In the following section, we examine the second phase of this expansion process, using the production, distribution, and consumption of sugar as a specific case study.

Sugar Eaters and the World System

As European entrepreneurs began to accumulate capital they were well positioned to take advantage of the opportunities opened to them by new trade routes to Asia and the Americas. The infrastructure for British overseas commercial empires was formed in the few decades from 1575 to 1630 by a total of about 6,000 investors who formed 33 London-based joint stock companies to seek overseas profits. In a given year only some 2,500 investors, mostly wealthy merchants, landed aristocrats, and members of parliament were involved. Perhaps only a hundred men served as directors. These individuals funded the Virginia and Massachusetts colonies in North America, the British East India Company, and various colonies and outposts in Africa, eastern Europe, and elsewhere (Rabb 1967). Their decisions created modern colonialism and ultimately transformed the world.

Refined sugar, or sucrose, played a major role in the rise of British colonialism and the modern world system, contributing to the accumulation of capital and helping the English lower class adjust to their changed life conditions (Mintz 1985). During the Industrial Revolution, sugar was transformed from a rare European luxury before 1750 to a household necessity by 1850. In this process, the English subsistence system changed from its traditional reliance on a local, inexpensively produced complex carbohydrate, primarily wheat, to a system in which an imported, energy-intensive simple carbohydrate, sucrose, became a virtual staple for the lower and middle classes.

Sugarcane is a tropical plant that was probably domesticated in Melanesia by 8000 BC for its sweet sap. By 400 BC, it was being grown in India, where the earliest processed sugar is known to

have been prepared by at least AD 500. Muslims spread sugarcane growing and sugar processing throughout the Mediterranean region by AD 1000. In medieval Europe, sugar was treated as a spice and had many medicinal uses but was too scarce to be available to any but the most wealthy. Sugar was used in the royal court to prepare edible decorative works of art, which served as symbols of power and status. Such objects were a special expression of power because they could be conspicuously consumed as a valuable on a ritual occasion. By 1500, sugar decorations were an important part of ritual feasts throughout the upper classes, and within 200 years, such use had become common even among the middle classes as sugar became more readily available.

During the early phase of capitalist development in England, from approximately 1650 to 1750, sugar was the single most important product imported from its colonies. Produced by slave labor on plantations in the British West Indies, sugar supported a major trade triangle that contributed to the accumulation of profits in the capitalist core. Shipments of manufactured goods, such as cloth, tools, and iron shackles, moved from England to Africa; slaves were carried from Africa to the West Indies; and sugar was shipped from the West Indies to England, where it was further refined (Figure 11.9). Thus, sugar helped generate direct profits while providing a market for manufactured goods. In the process, millions of African slaves were forced to work 12-hour days, often while supplying their own provisions. After slavery was abolished in the British colonies in the 1830s, perhaps 50 million Asians, primarily from India, were carried to sugar-producing areas as contract laborers during the nineteenth century.

The number of individuals who profited handsomely from the sugar trade was very small. For example in 1688 there were only some 2000 capitalist merchants in England (King 1936), and in 1812 some 3500 eminent merchants and bankers (Colquhoun 1815). Between 1735 and 1784 just 4 prominent, interconnected, London-based merchant families and their 19 associates maintained

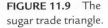

FIGURE 11.9   The sugar trade triangle.

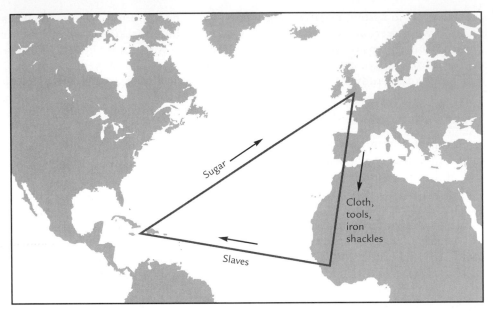

business properties and operations at every point in the sugar trade triangle (Hancock 1995). One of these men, Richard Oswald, "exported" some 13,000 slaves from his station in Sierra Leone to his Caribbean sugar plantations, and was also a major investor in the British East India Company. When Oswald died in 1784 he left a personal estate of £500,000, more than 10,000 times the prevailing annual subsistence wage.

Perhaps as important as sugar's role in the trade triangle was the energy boost and comfort it gave to the English working class who supplied the human energy for the Industrial Revolution. The large-scale introduction of energy-dense processed sugar to the diet at this time was the beginning of the unhealthy "nutrition transition" referred to in Chapter 5. Sugar was especially appealing because it was quickly metabolized and absorbed, yet it provided "empty" calories, lacking in minerals and vitamins, and left people craving more. Sugar's crucial role in industrialization developed gradually as the plantation system expanded to make sugar more available and as sugar proved to be an ideal complement to the tropical "drug foods" such as tea, coffee, and

chocolate, which began to reach England in the seventeenth century. These are all bitter, calorie-free, stimulating drinks that are sweetened by the addition of sugar. Tea had been imported from China by an English trading monopoly beginning in 1660, but it became the most popular English drink after tea plantations were established in British India by 1840. In combination with sugar from the British West Indies, tea from British India became cheaper than beer as a stimulating drink for the English working class.

As Mintz (1985) explains, sugar consumption by the English working poor grew in stages. It was used first with tea and then in rich puddings, which by the nineteenth century became a dessert course to end a meal. Sugar was combined with wheat flour in sweetened baked goods; by the end of the century, bread and jam became a meal, especially in households in which both parents were employed. At the national level, per-capita sugar consumption tripled from approximately 30 pounds (14 kilograms [kg]) per year in 1800 to approximately 90 pounds (41 kg) per year by 1900. By the 1970s, per-capita consumption seems to have peaked at about 115 pounds (52 kg). As a proportion of total caloric consumption, sugar rose from 2 to 14 percent over the course of the nineteenth century. Such an increase was possible because the price of sugar in England decreased by 50 percent between 1840 and 1870. Sugar became a relatively cheap source of calories and tended to supplement and replace more expensive grains, fruits, vegetables, meat, and dairy products.

The per-capita consumption figures mask the important role that sugar played in the diet of the working poor because actual rates varied by class and by age and sex within households. By 1850, sugar consumption by the English working class exceeded that of the upper class. Increased sugar intake was accompanied by a decline in bread consumption, from which some historians infer that more meat must have been eaten and nutrition improved. However, in most lower-class households, the working man ate the meat while his wife and children were left with the sugar as empty calories and were thereby systematically malnourished. This was justified by the householders because the husband had to remain in top physical condition to be an effective worker (Mintz 1985). This nutritional inequality, however, must have elevated infant mortality rates.

Sugar was especially important in the capitalist transformation of the world system because its capacity to stimulate perpetually increasing consumer demand neatly supported the endless-growth ideals of capitalism. Sugar became the first great consumer product. It was a substance of which people never seemed to get enough, and it proved that basic human needs could be culturally redefined and expanded as an instrument of national policy. Precapitalist economic theory held that most wage laborers were "target workers" who worked only long enough to satisfy their fixed needs. Alcohol consumption was potentially elastic, but alcoholics made poor workers. Sugar, on the other hand, made for contented workers.

England was converted into a nation of sugar eaters, at least in part, because such a change served the interests of individuals who were in a position to exercise political power (Mintz 1985).

Many of the early West Indian sugarcane planters were themselves members of Parliament; along with the investors who supported them and those in slaving, shipping, refining, and marketing, who benefited from sugar, they formed a significant interest group that influenced government policy. It is not surprising that sugar was issued to the inmates of English poorhouses or that a half-pint of rum made from West Indian molasses became an official daily ration of the British Navy in 1731 (an amount that was soon raised to a pint a day). The British government gained revenues from the sugar trade and indirectly subsidized the Caribbean planters by helping keep prices high. By the 1850s, the government shifted in favor of a free-trade policy to reduce the price of sugar and thereby increase the supply, thus making it more widely available.

The Invisible Hand and the Problem of Poverty

Adam Smith (1723–1790), Scottish philosopher, political economist, and founding father of capitalism, presented an insightful and remarkably frank, emic view of how the early capitalist market economy was theoretically expected to work. In his famous book *Wealth of Nations* (1776), Smith identified labor specialization and private ownership of land, together with the related emergence of landlords, manufacturers, laborers, rent, and profit, as the fundamental elements of a market, or "commercial," economy. In this system, landlords received their share of production as rent and advanced part to laborers as wages for their maintenance. Labor specialization in manufacturing required that manufacturers accumulate stock or capital, but it permitted dramatic increases in production. Wealth inequality helped make the system work.

Smith felt that most laborers "naturally" needed masters to maintain them between harvests and to carry out productive tasks. The relative poverty of laborers gave manufacturers and landlords a strategic advantage in any disputes over wages. Even though they were ultimately dependent on their laborers, most manufacturers and land-lords, with their larger stockpiles of wealth, could last more than one year if the laborers stopped working in order to enforce a demand for increased wages. Smith estimated that most laborers would not have enough stores to hold out more than one week without their wages.

Smith argued that as long as government did not intervene unduly, economic competition caused by people's natural desire for self-improvement would maintain orderly economic growth, as if by an **invisible hand.** Smith advocated that workers receive the lowest wage "which is consistent with common humanity" (1776:103). This minimum wage would be determined by the short-run maintenance needs of individual workers combined with approximately double that amount to provide enough for workers to reproduce. Smith did not quantify this amount precisely, but he assumed that a worker would support a wife and four children, only two of which would reach adulthood. According to Smith, a direct feedback operated between increasing demand for labor during times of economic growth and an increase in the labor supply, because wages would necessarily go up, which would mean that the poor could better support their children so that more would grow up to become workers. If there were too many workers, wages would go down, and the ensuing poverty would increase infant mortality, thereby reducing the number of workers and sending wages back up.

Smith thought that improved wages would increase production, because it would give workers hope and make them work harder. Thus, continuous economic growth (the "progressive state") seemed to be the most desirable condition, as Smith explained:

> It is in the progressive state, while the society is advancing to the further acquisition . . . that the condition of the labouring poor, of the great body of the people, seems to be the happiest and the most comfortable. It is hard in the stationary, and miserable in the declining state. The progressive state is in reality the cheerful and the hearty state to all the different orders of the society. The stationary is dull; the declining, melancholy. (1776:123)

As the industrial era began, despite Smith's optimistic view of the invisible hand, England's lower class was desperately squeezed between declining agrarian living standards in the countryside and abysmally low wages in the towns and cities. The growing money economy had already made poverty such a serious social problem that long before Smith's time, severe compulsion was required to force people to find employment, even at wages that would not provide adequate subsistence. Family life disintegrated when households could not support children and elders, and the state was forced to deal with the problem. The first poor laws, in 1531–1536, called for compulsory almsgiving and made willful unemployment a crime punishable by forced labor, mutilation, and death. Later creative variations called for whipping, burning, branding, slavery, hard labor in chains, and *then* death for repeat offenders. Reforms in 1601 called for placing paupers, such as widows and those physically unable to work, in poorhouses, while the children of the poor were to be apprenticed to masters in workhouses. But modest welfare subsidies intended to bring the working poor up to a subsistence level only encouraged employers to offer substandard wages.

The total increase in poverty in England from 1086 to 1812 is clear evidence that the economic growth process was directed by elites who were more concerned with elevating production and accumulating capital for their own benefit than in building the commonwealth to benefit society as a whole. Table 11.1 shows that both between 1086 and 1688, and between 1688 and 1812 the number of poor households increased at a faster rate than either maintenance or elite households. This negative social outcome came about because political rulers directed public funds into the military and infrastructure improvements to support commerce, rather than into public education, public health, or meaningful social welfare. At the same time the barriers to upward mobility were formidable for anyone not fortunate enough to be born wealthy or to marry wealth (Earle 1989). The poor were forced to spend most of their meager incomes on food, clothing, and hous-

TABLE 11.1   ENGLISH HOUSEHOLDS RANKED BY IMPERIA, 1086–1812

	Norman England, 1086	Stuart England, 1688	Georgian England, 1812
Super-Elite	182	187	4,937
Elite	6,900	31,400	128,824
Maintenance	24,000	480,000	1,021,395
Poor	275,079	879,000	2,413,625

SOURCES: Colquhoun 1815, King 1936, Roberts and Roberts 1980, Snooks 1993.

ing, and had nothing to invest. Wages for English workers gradually increased over the centuries (Lindert and Williamson 1982, 1983), but material conditions remained bleak, and during hard economic times between 1760 and 1800 and between 1830 and 1860 the average height of the poor actually shrank due to poor nutrition in childhood (Komlos 1998).

By the 1830s, conditions among the working class in England had deteriorated so badly that the government took further measures in an effort to minimize the damage. Officially, 1.4 million people, nearly 10 percent of the population, were receiving relief under the poor laws. But this was an incomplete reckoning of poverty, and the assistance provided was woefully inadequate. A massive report presented to Parliament in 1842 by Edwin Chadwick (1965) showed unequivocally that the poor were being forced to live in crowded and unsanitary conditions that contributed to contagious disease, high mortality, high fertility, and reduced life expectancy. For example, in Liverpool in 1840, health conditions were poor for everyone, but Chadwick found that laborers died at an average age of 15, whereas upper-class people died at 35. More people were dying from poverty than in England's many wars. Chadwick viewed this costly and unnecessary loss of life as a public health problem and advocated better sewage drainage and administrative changes. But many others called for drastic social reforms. The working poor understood that their basic problem was inadequate and irregular wages and the loss of control over their subsistence resources brought about by unbalanced industrialization. The Luddites who destroyed textile machines in 1811–1816 and the farm work-

ers who rioted against the new threshing machines in the 1830s were not opposed to technological progress as such; they simply did not want to surrender their economic autonomy (Noble 1993).

The London Poor

By the 1840s, immigration and internal growth had swelled the population of metropolitan London to more than 2 million people, but employment opportunities remained inadequate. The human degradation that accompanied London's rapid industrial development was most vividly portrayed by novelist Charles Dickens (1953), journalist Henry Mayhew (1968), and shipping magnate turned sociologist Charles Booth (1892–1903). Mayhew's pioneer ethnographic work was explicitly anthropological. Mayhew viewed the existence of such poverty in the midst of wealthy London as a "national disgrace." He was incensed that the British public knew more about distant tribes than they knew about the poorest Londoners, who were not even counted in the national census. He wanted "to give the rich a more intimate knowledge of the sufferings, and frequent heroism under those sufferings, of the poor." Mayhew spent years observing life on the streets of London and collecting life stories and personal accounts of hundreds of street folk, which he carefully recorded in their own words.

Most of Mayhew's ethnographic work was devoted to London's working poor, who comprised

invisible hand The capitalist belief that market forces, operating through supply and demand, will lead to continuous economic growth and benefit everyone.

Mud-Larks, Bone-Grubbers, and a Coster Lad's Story

Henry Mayhew thought that the most degraded workers in London were the collectors who wandered the streets searching for marketable refuse, such as cigar butts, bits of metal, rags, rope, lumps of coal, and bone and dog feces used in industrial production. Three pounds of bone fragments were worth a penny, and a good bone-grubber (Figure 11.D) could gather 6 pence (half a shilling) worth in a day—only a third of the 10 shillings that a costermonger might earn per day. Apples sold at 6 for a penny, and a 4-pound loaf of bread cost 4 pence. Fortunate bone-grubbers would spend 2 pence of their meager earnings on the most wretched lodging and have 4 pence left to spend on a little sugar, coffee, and a quarter loaf of bread. Mayhew interviewed other unusual collectors including old-wood gatherers, dredgers, sewer hunters, and mud-larks. He thought the condition of the latter was the most deplorable—they were reduced to scavenging trash from the river mud at low tide. He described them as follows:

> Among the mud-larks may be seen many old women, and it is indeed pitiable to behold them, especially during the winter, bent nearly double with age and infirmity, paddling and groping among the wet mud for small pieces of coal, chips of wood, or any sort of refuse washed up by the tide. These women always have with them an old basket or an old tin kettle, in which they put whatever they chance to find. It usually takes them a whole tide to fill this receptacle, but when filled, it is as much as the feeble old creatures are able to carry home. (Mayhew 1968, vol. 2:155)

Mayhew (1968, vol. 1:39) recorded the following life history from a 16-year-old coster lad. This illustrates the physical and emotional stress that misfortune caused economically marginalized families in nineteenth-century London:

> "Father I've heard tell died when I was three and brother only a year old. It was worse luck for us! . . . Mother used to be up and out very early washing in families—anything for a living. She was a good mother to us. We was left at home with the key of the room and some bread and butter for dinner. Afore she got into work—and it was a goodish long time—we was shocking hard up, and she pawned nigh everything. Sometimes, when we hadn't no grub at all, the other lads, perhaps, would give us some bread and butter, but often our stomachs used to ache with

a ragged assortment of some 50,000 self-employed street vendors, refuse collectors, performers, artisans, vermin exterminators, and manual laborers. The street vendors, or costermongers, survived by selling everything from fresh produce and flowers to old books, dog collars, live birds, secondhand clothes, and old glassware. Mayhew found the costermongers to be hard-working and honest, and he admired their resourcefulness. Children sold things on the street as soon as they could walk and talk; most children went un-

schooled and might be informally married by age 14. Costermongers had minimal economic reserves, but those who were fortunate and extremely careful with their meager funds might have precariously comfortable lives. Others lived in squalor and struggled to survive.

Because of their economic marginality, many costermongers were too poor to buy the carts, donkeys, and miscellaneous equipment needed for their work. Their low and erratic income made them easy prey for those immediately higher

the hunger, and we would cry when we was werry far gone. She used to be at work from six in the morning till ten o'clock at night, which was a long time for a child's belly to hold out again, and when it was dark we would go and lie down on the bed and try and sleep until she came home with the food. I was eight year old then.

"A man as know'd mother, said to her, 'Your boy's got nothing to do, let him come along with me and yarn a few ha'pence,' and so I became a coster. He gave me 4d. [pence] a morning and my breakfast."

THE BONE-GRUBBER.

[From a Daguerreotype by BEARD.]

FIGURE 11.D The London bone-grubber.

in the economic hierarchy. Annual rent for a simple handcart was more than twice the cart's value. At those rates, enterprising small-scale capitalists turned a modest investment in handcarts into a profitable business. One man amassed an economic empire of 150 handcarts, which he rented to the costermongers at exorbitant weekly rates for a tidy return. Hard-pressed costermongers were also an easy target for unscrupulous moneylenders and pawnshop owners. Interest rates were so outrageous that costermongers were forced to

pay £65 to borrow £25 during the year to buy their stock. Costermongers lived in specific neighborhoods and supported each other, even holding raffles to raise money for those in most distress. In good times, the average annual income of costermongers could provide a minimum living, but if a few days of bad weather depressed sales, thousands would face starvation. The lives of many of the street people were unbelievably bleak (see the box entitled "Mud-Larks, Bone-Grubbers, and a Coster Lad's Story").

Marx and Engels: *The Communist Manifesto*

Social revolutionaries Karl Marx (1818–1883) and Friedrich Engels (1820–1895) were both living in London and directly experienced the wretched social conditions described by Mayhew. Engels' book *The Condition of the Working-Class in England: From Personal Observation and Authentic Sources* (1845) was written to inspire a social revolution. Marx and Engels coauthored their famous *Communist Manifesto* in London in 1848. They conceptualized the human problems of commercialization as a class struggle between "two great hostile camps"—the bourgeoisie (capitalists) and the proletariat (workers). Their solution called for "the forcible overthrow of all existing social conditions," declaring in the famous last lines of the Manifesto:

> Let the ruling classes tremble at a Communistic revolution. The proletarians have nothing to lose but their chains. They have a world to win. WORKING MEN OF ALL COUNTRIES UNITE!

More specifically, Marx and Engels advocated worker control of government; the abolition of private property; government control of production, communication, and transportation; free education; and the elimination of social classes. Even though they considered material conditions to be the primary influences on social order, they believed that intellectual elites, like themselves, could organize the masses to purposively transform society. In order to achieve these goals quickly, they were willing to replace one form of totalitarian political power with another. They were also overly optimistic about the possibility of eliminating social classes, and considered further economic growth, or material progress, to be a solution rather than a problem in itself. Consequently, they did not solve the problem of how to more equitably distribute social power in very large-scale social systems. However, they clearly understood the importance of political economy, and they recognized the human problems of the commercialization process. Marxist political ideology has certainly shaped the course of modern history, but simply placing commerce under state control does not solve all problems of scale and power, as the experience of the Soviet Union demonstrated.

At the end of the nineteenth century, England's political leaders still lacked a clear picture of the scale of the country's social problems (see the box entitled "Marx and Engels: *The Communist Manifesto*"). London's population had now grown to 5 million people, and radical reformers claimed that 25 percent were impoverished. Successful London businessman Charles Booth thought this figure was an exaggeration, and in 1886, following Mayhew's lead, he set out to systematically count London's poor. Funding his own research, he picked the northeast quarter of the city, where nearly a million people lived, and spent the next 17 years methodically mapping income levels, occupations, and housing conditions—street by street, house by house, even room by room. To precisely identify the truly poor, he sorted his data along different dimensions using an eight-level scale, ranked A to H and color coded, black to yellow, by living

TABLE 11.2   LIVING STANDARDS AND SOCIAL CLASS IN LONDON, 1890

Living Standard	Class	Income	Housing	Number	Percentage
Poor	A (lowest)	Occasional	Very crowded	37,610	0.89
Poor	B (very poor)	Casual	Very crowded	316,834	7.53
Poor	C–D (poor)	Ill-paid	Crowded	938,293	22.29
Comfortable	E–F (working class)	Fairly paid	—	2,166,503	51.47
Well-to-do	G (middle class)	—	—	732,124	17.39
Wealthy	H (upper class)	—	—	17,806	0.42
Totals				4,209,170	100.00

SOURCE: Booth (1892–1903).

standard. At the bottom of the scale in Class A, coded black, were semicriminals, loafers, and occasional laborers, with minimal family life. On a Class A street, Booth found 200 households, containing probably 1000 people, living in forty four-story houses in a 2-acre (4.8 hectares) section of London near the British Museum. Entire families were crowded into single 8- by 8-foot, vermin-infested rooms. Fifty people shared a single outside toilet and water tap, drawing from a cistern. Most of these people found occasional work as market porters and costermongers, or they were unemployed. The "very poor" in Class B were characterized by "casual labour, hand-to-mouth existence, [and] chronic want." The "poor" in Classes C and D could find seasonal, or poorly paid work, which was "barely sufficient for decent independent life." Members of all "poor" classes lived in crowded housing with two or more persons per room and were at or below a poverty level of 21 shillings of weekly income. Working-class people in Classes E and F were regularly employed and "fairly" paid, and Booth considered them to be "comfortable." At the upper end, Class G, "well-to-do" families had one or two servants. In Class H were "wealthy" families, which kept three or more servants and lived in houses valued at £100 or more. In his final analysis, Booth discovered that more than 30 percent of London's population were poor by his own definition (Table 11.2). The radical reformers actually had underestimated the prob-

lem. The 1.2 million poor living in London in 1890 exceeded the entire population of the city in 1801, suggesting that a century of growth had produced an unusual sort of progress. The 18,000 wealthy constituted the top 0.5 percent of London society.

London's poverty in the 1890s was related to social conditions in the countryside. Rural land ownership had become so concentrated that an official inquiry was held in 1875, and for the first time the government published the names and holdings of all major landowners in a "New Domesday Book" (Bateman 1883). There were some 24 million people in England and Wales in 1875, in 4.8 million households; but fewer than 14,000 large landowners, who represented only 0.28 percent of all households, held nearly 75 percent of the land. This land tenure system distinctly resembled the Norman system of the original Domesday Survey. Ninety-five percent of households held less than 0.5 percent of all individually owned land. The smallholders represented 15 percent of the population, but their properties averaged less than a quarter acre each, certainly not enough to sustain a farm family.

The British Empire

By 1878, a political hierarchy in the global system was clearly established. More than half the world's land area was claimed by just four giant states and their related territories: Britain, Russia,

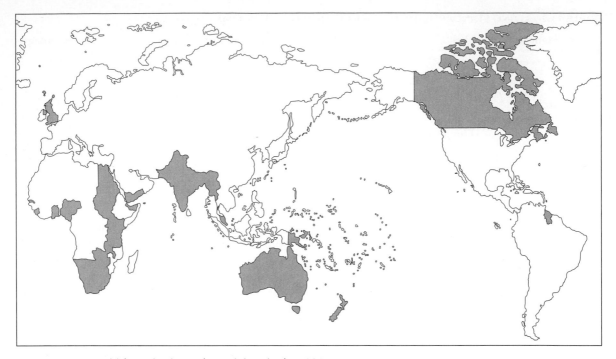

FIGURE 11.10   British Territories and Dominions in the 1930s

China, and the United States. Together with seven other colonial countries, these major states held claims over two-thirds of the world (Clark 1936). Most of Africa was still under the control of traditional kingdoms, chiefdoms, and tribal systems. Minor independent modern states had emerged in Latin America, but vast areas were still occupied by autonomous tribal groups.

Beginning in the 1880s, the major colonial powers scrambled to extend their political control over Africa and the Pacific, and by 1913 more than three-fourths of the world's land area was controlled by just thirteen countries.

Throughout the modern colonial period from 1800 to 1945, a single power, Great Britain, remained dominant. At its height in the 1930s, the British empire spanned the globe, encompassing roughly one-fourth of the world's land area and population (Figure 11.10). The British empire was primarily a loose federation held together by diverse political connections and the common British origin and English language of the ruling elites in each political unit.

In most of the colonies, a very small minority of European colonists enjoyed a privileged status over the majority native population, who were held in a structurally inferior position. Coercive military power was used to establish and maintain administrative control, but the common objective was the capitalist development of productive resources, growing markets, and the expansion of trade, not the extraction of tribute as in ancient empires.

For example, in 1750 fewer than 1000 shareholders received nearly 90 percent of the profits from the British East India Company, and the 49 largest shareholders received one-fourth of the total annual profits (Dickson 1967:287). Much like the Mughal Empire, but headquartered in London, the East India Company was a vast empire with a chief official and 14 corporate directors commanding

63,000 employees, 160,000 troops, and 40 million native workers (Colquhoun 1815).

During the early period of British colonialism, the commercial elite, backed by the military power of the British navy, expanded their personal fortunes by plundering Great Tradition civilizations and the tribal world. Conquest provided revenue to the Crown as well as to private investors. In fact English piracy on Spanish shipments of gold and silver stolen from the Inca and Aztecs provided the highest return on investment. However, when captured territories had to be administered and policed, and roads and other infrastructure had to be built and maintained, the costs of colonialism quickly became a net loss for all but the very largest private investors (Clark 1936). The privileged economic elite promptly "socialized" the costs of colonialism by shifting them to the conquered peoples and through taxes to the British citizenry at large. The balance sheet shows that during the peak of imperial expansion from 1860 to 1912, the primary wealth benefits flowed to a tiny segment of the British elite composed of some 200,000 top shareholders: the bankers, military officers, government officials, Members of Parliament, and largest property owners. Thus, the real beneficiaries were the top 0.6 super-elite percent of 33 million British citizens (Davis and Huttenback 1986).

Investors extended their commercial enterprises far beyond the boundaries of the British Empire just as under the current postcolonial globalization process in the late twentieth century. The wealth of British capitalists grew so large that they could dominate markets and take advantage of investment opportunities everywhere in what had become an informal global empire centered on London. For example, by 1900 one man, Charles Morrison, a London financier and top landowner, personally controlled 10 percent of British investments in Argentina, which soon grew to £480 million (Cain and Hopkins 1993:290). At his death in 1909 Morrison left an estate valued at £10.9 million, and was one of 30 British multimillionaires at the time (Rubinstein 1981:41–44).

THE NEW FREE-MARKET GLOBAL ORDER

Colonialism was a costly system of economic growth subsidized by governments and taxpayers. It has now been totally superseded by a decentralized global market organized through an international system of financial institutions and regulatory bodies. Commercialization's triumph over the politicization process produced a world dominated by wealthy investors and the transnational corporations that they own and direct.

The institutional foundation of the new economic world order was the United Nations system, the World Bank (International Bank for Reconstruction and Development, IBRD), and the International Monetary Fund (IMF). This social structure did not just happen. It was not the only possible form of world order, and it was not inevitable. It was created by a handful of progressivist elite planners in 1944–1945, near the end of World War II. A total of perhaps a hundred advisors worked out the details, with help from the Council on Foreign Relations (CFR), a private American policy planning group, funded in part by the Rockefeller and Carnegie foundations (Domhoff 1990:113–144). These planners were not unself-interested. They were also advisors and officials at the highest level of the Roosevelt administration, and they were owners and managers of the largest American corporations, including the largest investment banks such as J. P. Morgan and Company (Shoup and Minter 1980). The new global institutional structures these planners designed facilitated the ascendency of the **financialization** process, but they were guided by a populist, humanitarian ideology. Following British economist John Maynard Keynes and American "New Deal" economists, they believed that the World Bank and the IMF would stabilize currency

---

financialization A cultural process involving the flow of finance capital, money, and securities, rather than the actual production and distribution of goods and services.

flows, make loans to governments for development purposes, and manage the global economy to promote commerce, prevent depressions, create employment, and distribute income to people to meet basic needs.

In practice, the new world order favored the financial elite and helped insure their global access to investment opportunities, while promoting American centered economic growth. It was no accident that the president of the World Bank must always be an American and that the American dollar is the standard international currency. In 1998 there were 182 member nations in the IMF, but just 9 nations, headed by the United States, controlled more than half of the voting power.

The flow of finance capital is now more important in commerce than the flow of actual goods and services (Phillips 1994). By the early 1990s as much as 90 percent of the world's commercial transactions involved stocks, bonds, and commodity futures (Barnet and Cavanagh 1994). The importance of financial capital is also reflected in the fact that by the year 2000, as noted above, 75 percent of American wealth was financial. The global market economy is free in that it is subject to less and less control by any national government or international political institutions. Centrally planned national economies, such as the former Soviet Union, have all but disappeared. International trade agreements, such as the GATT (General Agreement on Tariffs and Trade) and NAFTA (North American Free Trade Agreement), have greatly reduced national barriers to commerce such that commodities and finance capital now flow easily across borders. By 2003 the world's 6.3 billion people were being combined in a single commercial network, which is ultimately dependent on computerized financial transactions taking place in a few organized markets in the richest countries.

The rapid proliferation of consumer credit, such as through credit cards, also reflects the increasing importance of the financialization process. This process rapidly shifts wealth to financial elites, who already control large sums of finance capital, be-

cause, by taking advantage of the power of scale, they can realize handsome returns from very large financial exchanges with small profit margins.

In a sense, the prime beneficiaries of the global flow of finance capital are the approximately 6 million high-net-worth individuals (HNWI), primarily European and American multimillionaires with investable assets of more than a million dollars (Gemini Consulting 2003). In 2002, these private financial elites collectively controlled $27.2 trillion. Their wealth represented approximately 85 percent of global income. HNWI wealth was also growing at 7 percent a year, in effect producing income of nearly $2 trillion. This means that 0.1 percent of global people were receiving 6 percent of global income. Their investment decisions were shaping the world and profoundly influencing the lives of billions of people.

The prominence of financial wealth in the global economy means that as individuals the poor have become virtually irrelevant, even though in the aggregate they constitute an important market for certain low-cost consumer goods. At the bottom of the global hierarchy, the World Bank (2003) estimated that in 2002 there were 2.5 to 3 billion people in the world living on less than $2 a day. This suggests that nearly half of the world's people received less than 7 percent of global income and owned a much smaller proportion of the world's wealth. This means that most of the world's people have little ability to influence the decisions that shape their daily lives. The transnational corporations that dominate the economic sphere of the global system have become enormously powerful. For example, by 2002, Wal-Mart was the world's largest corporation with revenues of $245 billion. It operated 4,688 stores throughout the U.S. and in 9 other countries, employing more than a million people (Wal-Mart 2003). Only eighteen countries had higher gross national incomes than Wal-Mart's revenues. The largest individual owners of Wal-Mart were five members of the founder's family, who each held personal fortunes of $16.5 billion, each ranking as the world's seventh largest fortune, worth in the aggregate more than $82 billion.

TABLE 11.3   GLOBAL DISTRIBUTION OF BILLIONAIRES AND BILLIONAIRE FORTUNES, 2002

	Number of Billionaires	Percent of Billionaires	Aggregate $ Billions	Percent of Wealth
United States	222	47	$702	50
Other G-8	132	28	$376	27
European	39	8	$117	8
Asia-Pacific	39	8	$90	6
Latin America	22	5	$48	3
Middle East	20	4	$64	5
Africa	2	0	$4	0

DATA SOURCE: *Forbes Magazine,* March 17, 2003.

The level of social inequality produced by the global economy is difficult to comprehend. As economic growth accelerated during the 1990s the number of global billionaires soared from 101 in 1993 (Rogers 1993) to 476 in 2002 (Kroll and Goldman 2003). Total global billionaire wealth increased from $451 billion to more than $1.4 trillion. This was equivalent to 4.4 percent of global income in 2001. Measured as income produced by a predictable seven percent return on their $1.4 trillion in capital, these 476 individuals could expect to earn an aggregate of more than $98 billion in income a year. Only 36 countries had higher gross national incomes in 2001. Billionaire income of $98 billion would be sufficient to raise 134 million people (about the population of Bangladesh in 2001) above the World Bank's designation of extreme poverty of $730 per person per year ($2 per day per person). It would even elevate more than 5 million American four-person families above the official U.S. poverty level of $18,556 per year.

Nearly half of global billionaires were Americans, and together with the other G-8 nations (the "Group of Eight" with the world's largest economies: Canada, France, Germany, Italy, Japan, UK, the U.S., and Russia), they accounted for 75 percent of global billionaires (Table 11.3). There were only 2 billionaires in Africa.

There is a clear trend throughout human history for the few hundred super-elite individuals at the top of every society to increase their wealth

in step with growth in social income. Figure 11.11 demonstrates this trend by plotting average super-elite wealth by the size of social income for ten different societies, assuming that average minimum household subsistence in the imperial and early commercial worlds equals $1500. The difference in scale of super-elite income and absolute size of social income for different societies is so great that these data must be shown on a log scale. Significantly, in the societies represented, super-elite wealth and size of economy are strongly correlated and can be graphed as a straight line. These findings are further evidence for elite direction in cultural growth and confirm the folk wisdom that the rich get richer. The Asháninka are shown as the smallest society with the smallest super-elite wealth, even though in tribal societies the wealth difference between super-elite and "poor" households is insignificant in comparison to the inequalities of the imperial and commercial worlds. Asháninka household wealth is counted as $8500, rather than $1500, to reflect their social equality and greater access to natural resources.

The new global elite use their wealth to maintain a dominant influence in the world, or **cultural hegemony,** which maintains consumerism as a primary cultural ideal for the nonelite majority.

cultural hegemony Dominant influence by elites over the cultural symbols and beliefs that influence human behavior.

FIGURE 11.11 Super-elite wealth by social income in ten societies, 100 to 2002 AD.

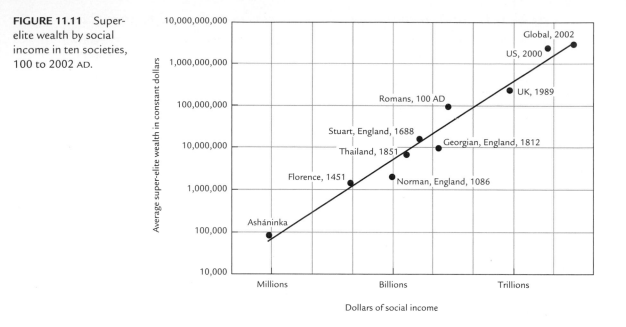

Commercial advertisers shape people's beliefs and the smallest details of their behavior through the mass media. For example, Coca-Cola—arguably the world's most successful brand—markets its soft drinks to 20 percent of the world's people. In 1992–1993, it had sales of more than $13 billion. Coca-Cola spent $392 million in the United States to persuade people to drink an average of 37 gallons of Coke products per capita per year, producing sales of $4.3 billion (Huey 1993). It is not surprising that in 1998, Warren Buffett, a principal Coca-Cola shareholder and corporate director, was perhaps the third-richest individual in the world, with a personal net worth estimated at $33 billion.

When the postcolonial era of national economic growth slowed in the 1980s, political economists promoted "New Growth Theory" favoring an even more *globally integrated* economy based on small and weak governments, minimal regulation of commerce, and removal of all trade barriers (Beach and Davis 1998; Johnson, Holmes, and Kirkpatrick 1998:4). This new commercially organized world economic order is directed by a loose network of economic planners who occupy key positions in newly created international economic institutions, such as the International Monetary Fund, the World Bank, and the World Trade Organization, and on the boards of the world's largest corporations. The promotion of economic growth is the single objective of this new global-scale power elite, but the planners are often divided over key policy approaches and conflicting interests.

SUMMARY

Capitalism is a commercial system of production and exchange that treats land, labor, technology, money, raw materials, and goods and services as commodities to be bought and sold for a profit. This cultural system is totally unique and has transformed the world. The wealthy elite who most benefit from the capitalist market economy have used industrial production based on fossil fuel energy sources, colonialism, and unequal exchange to integrate the diverse societies and cultures of the world into a single global economic system. An ideology of continuous economic expansion and high rates of consumption are central features of this system that are derived from more fundamental European beliefs in natural scarcity, insatiable wants, and a dualism between mind and body, humans and nature.

During the early stages of commercialization in medieval England, the number of poor actually increased. Capitalism required a financial revolution that made money the dominant means of organizing social power. The most successful mercantile capitalists used kinship and marriage to organize their far-flung business enterprises and transmit their growing commercial estates from generation to generation. Early economic theorists such as Adam Smith assumed that capitalist development directed by self-seeking entrepreneurs would ultimately benefit everyone. However, ethnographic data collected in nineteenth-century London showed that unrestrained economic growth produced enormous poverty and serious public health problems.

The global process of sugar production and consumption illustrated the early expansion of the global system. Commercially driven colonial empires, exemplified by the British empire at its peak, controlled much of the world during the first half of the nineteenth century. Since the breakdown of the colonial system after World War II, many supranational political and economic institutions, such as the United Nations and the World Bank, have assumed formal leadership of the global system. But the policies of these institutions are influenced by powerful nations and by giant multinational corporations that benefit from the global structure of inequality. A new cultural process, financialization, controlled by the wealthiest individuals and financial institutions, is emerging as the dominant force in the world.

The next chapter will examine the United States as an example of one of the most dominant national cultures in the present global system. Chapter 13 will explore the problem of poverty in the countries that are "peripheral" to the wealthy industrial core.

STUDY QUESTIONS

1. Define the following concepts: embedded economy, kin-ordered production, culture of consumption, mode of production, capitalist production, tributary production.
2. Distinguish between a market and nonmarket economy.
3. Define a capitalist political economy, and explain how it differs from the economic systems of ancient states.
4. Describe the structure of the global commercial economy as a world system.
5. What are the principal ideological features of the capitalist world system? Draw illustrations from Adam Smith and modern economists.
6. Discuss the specific changes in cultural organization that accompanied the Industrial Revolution in England. Refer to the role of technology, population, capital accumulation, inequality, and the enclosure movement.
7. What is the evidence for the argument that more people were impoverished than enriched by the cultural transformations that swept England between 1086 and 1890?
8. How were European economic conditions from 1086 to 1890 reflected in household organization and in kinship and marriage patterns?
9. What features of European cosmology and ideology supported capitalism?
10. Explain how dietary change (sugar and tea) in England was related to the Industrial Revolution and the expanding world system.
11. Describe the political and economic structure of modern colonialism in contrast to the empires of the past. Make specific comparisons between the Inca empire in the Andean world and the British empire in the modern world.

SUGGESTED READING

BODLEY, JOHN H. 2003. *The Power of Scale: A Global History Approach*. Armonk, New York: M. E. Sharpe.

CROSBY, ALFRED W. 1986. *Biological Imperialism: The Biological Expansion of Europe, 900–1900.* Cambridge, Eng.: Cambridge University Press. Discussion by a historian of the biological consequences of European colonialism on ecosystems and people throughout the world.

FERGUSON, NIALL. 2003. *Empire: How Britain Made the Modern World.* London: Allen Lane, Penguin.

SMITH, ADAM. 1776. *An Inquiry into the Nature and Causes of the Wealth of Nations,* vol. 1. London: Strahan and Cadell. The classic formulation of the key features of the early capitalist economy.

WALLERSTEIN, IMMANUEL. 1974. *The Modern World-System: Capitalist Agriculture and the Origins of the European World-Economy in the Sixteenth Century.* New York: Academic Press. The pioneer statement of world system theory.

WOLF, ERIC R. 1982. *Europe and the People Without History.* Berkeley: University of California Press. An anthropological treatment of European expansion since 1400, focusing on the political economy and showing how the capitalist system incorporated tributary and kin-based systems.

The concentration of vast wealth in a small number of American corporations has enormous consequences for not only the United States but for other countries too.

12

Capitalism in the United States

Learning Objectives

After studying this chapter you should be able to do the following.

1. Describe the distinctive features of U.S. cosmology or ideology in comparison with tribal and imperial cosmologies.

2. Distinguish between progressivist and neoconservative political ideologies in the U.S. and explain the shift from one to the other.

3. Evaluate the extent to which the realities of U.S. society reflect the ideals of the culture.

4. Make specific comparisons between Chinese and U.S. culture, referring to family life, economic practices, and core values.

5. Identify the distinctive, scale-related features of large business corporations and describe the role of elite decision-makers in making them dominant features of U.S. culture.

6. Describe the social structure of early U.S. textile factories, explaining the distribution of costs and benefits to households.

7. Describe the social structure and physical infrastructure of U.S. factory-farming food production systems in comparison with tribal and Great Tradition systems. Analyze the human costs and benefits of these systems.

8. Evaluate the importance of material conditions, cultural symbolism, and intentional human decision-making in shaping cultural patterns of consumption in the United States.

9. Evaluate the process of growth in the U.S. as related to the distribution of social power and human costs and benefits. Evaluate the evidence for elite-direction.

Thanks to the enormous success of both its ideological and material culture, the United States is often a model for the rest of the world and is certainly an appropriate anthropological subject. For many, the United States represents the ideals of freedom, democracy, equality, and material abundance. Its size and economic power give it enormous influence; this means that even such seemingly trivial matters as the American food preference for beef can have a profound impact on peoples in distant parts of the globe. Furthermore, its economic success makes the United States a critical source of stress in the global ecosystem. In the year 2000, Americans made up less than 5 percent of the world's population but consumed nearly 25 percent of the world's commercial energy.

Attempting to understand a country as large and complex as the United States is a formidable task, one that has engaged anthropologists and other social scientists for a long time. It requires anthropologists to ask basic questions about their own culture and its place in the world. This chapter focuses on aspects of American culture that offer the strongest contrasts with tribal cultures and the tribute-based civilizations discussed in Chapters 7–10. In the first section, we examine the unique cosmological and ideological features of American culture, highlighting Americans' beliefs about their political system and the proper relationship between business, government, and households. A contrast will be drawn between the American emphasis on individualism and the Chinese emphasis on kinship and family, based on the perspective of a Chinese-American anthropologist. This section also examines the historical context behind America's most sacred texts—the Declaration of Independence and the Constitution. Next, we focus specifically on the commercialization process by examining the organizational and technological changes behind the evolution of business enterprise and the rise of the giant corporation in nineteenth-century America. Ethnohistorical case studies of a Pennsylvania textile mill village, twentieth-century factory farming, and the cattle industry will illustrate the impact of commercialization on various aspects of American culture. Finally, we draw on a variety of American ethnographic materials to evaluate the human risks and rewards of the growth process itself.

AMERICAN CULTURAL IDEALS VERSUS REALITY

An American Profile

The United States is the world's fourth largest nation by land area, after Russia, Canada, and China. By 2002, when the United States had grown to approximately 288 million people, America ranked as the third largest national population in the world, after China and India. America is large enough to support great cultural diversity and is truly a complex culture. By the year 2000 the U.S. was a highly urbanized country. Approximately 80 percent of the population, 224 million people, were living in 256 metropolitan areas of 100,000 people or more. Forty-nine metropolitan areas contained a million people or more.

Approximately 75 percent of Americans self-identified their official "race" as "White" on the 2000 national census. More people (13 percent) identified as "Hispanic" than as "Black" or "African-American" (12 percent); however, because of their diversity, Hispanics could officially self-identify as any race. Nearly 4 percent of Americans identified as Asian, and about 2 percent called themselves "multi-racial," but only 1 percent identified as Native American, Alaska Natives, or Pacific Islanders (U.S. Census Bureau, Statistical Abstract of the United States 2002, Table 22). From 1991 to 2000 more than 9 million immigrants from some 62 countries became legal residents of the United States. More than 2 million came from Mexico (U.S. Census Bureau, Statistical Abstract of the United States 2002, Table 7).

In the year 2000, some 92 percent of the U.S. adult population (age 18 and over) claimed a religious preference, but only 69 percent were members of an organized religious community, and only 44 percent regularly attended religious services (U.S. Census Bureau, Statistical Abstract of the United States 2002, Table 64). This illustrates one difference between the formal culture and practice, or what people actually do. Approximately 83 percent of the adult population were Christian by preference, either Protestant (56 percent) or Catholic (27 percent). Approximately 2 percent were Jewish. Figures for 2003 show 6 million Jews, 5–6 million Muslims, some 2–3 million Buddhists, and more than a million Hindus in the United States (World Almanac 2004: 609–610).

As an object of anthropological investigation, the United States is unique among all the cultures examined so far in the great wealth of information available. Federal, state, and local governments have continuously generated vast volumes of statistical material covering all aspects of American life. Newspapers, films, and books abound and constitute a cultural record of unprecedented detail. The challenge for cultural anthropologists is to sift and sort through the existing data to reach useful conclusions about this complex culture. The analysis that follows draws on statistical data from national, county, and city levels in order to offer a more precise and ethnographically realistic picture for cross-cultural comparison.

Utopian Capitalism: An American Cosmology

Looking beyond the obvious cultural diversity of America, it is possible to identify a common cosmology that characterizes what most Americans believe about their culture. Americans may be political liberals or conservatives, Catholic or Protestant or Jewish. But a consistent cosmology crosscuts these differences and reveals a dominant worldview that is remarkably different from the worldviews found in both tribal cultures and the ancient agrarian civilizations we examined in earlier chapters. The most striking contrast is that in American culture, the economy is supreme, and all things are considered to be commodities to be regulated by the free market. There are three sectors to this economy: (1) business enterprises (the primary employers of labor and capital and the producers of products); (2) government (which taxes, spends, issues, and borrows money); and (3) individual households (which supply labor, own money, invest, and consume products).

The emphasis that Americans place on economic growth, and their belief that the world is defined by material scarcity, reflects the broader European cosmology discussed in Chapter 11. But this worldview is combined with the contradictory belief that production and consumption must forever expand. This conceptualization of the world is cross-culturally unusual, and it leaves isolated households remarkably vulnerable to autonomous economic forces that are assumed to be beyond the control of individuals. Most Americans believe in the supernatural, but specific religious beliefs are overshadowed by the overarching European belief that the economy is a physical thing that must grow to ensure everyone's well-being. Business corporations have an important place in the American cosmology, but, except for the very wealthiest families, there are no corporate kinship groups, and the isolated nuclear family replaces the extended family that is so prominent in noncommercial cultures. In comparison with Australian aboriginal and Amazonian cultures, the position of nature in the American cosmology is remarkable. Americans view nature as a part of *the environment,* which is separate from and often in conflict with humanity and *the economy.*

The autonomous market is believed to produce the culture as a whole, and as the driving force behind the economy, it has the same hallowed status. Like the economy, the market is conceived of as an entity quite apart from any physical marketplace, and a free market is assumed to work to benefit humans and society at large as Adam Smith imagined. Although many Americans realize that particular markets may be dominated by giant corporations or controlled by government regulations, the market is equated with *consumer demand* and is thus thought to represent what people want as expressed by what they choose to buy. Americans assume that markets are natural, and they make them the mysterious arbiters of societal well-being that call into being such diverse products as wholesome food, cars, cigarettes, and land mines.

Americans believe that their cultural universe is both unique and superior, because it is thought to maximize personal liberty and economic freedom. This is America's great strength. In this system of utopian capitalism, prosperity will be assured as long as individuals are free to buy and sell and to create and produce goods for the "free market." The self-serving actions of free people will produce continuous economic growth and material progress, which will ultimately benefit everyone. The only threats to this system are government interference with the free market, restrictions of individual liberty and private property rights, and reductions in individual incentive for economic activity through rewarding undeserving people with unearned material benefits. This grand view of the structure of American society and the functioning of the "free enterprise" system was clearly described by Dwight Eisenhower, who served as president from 1952 to 1960, during a period of especially rapid economic growth:

> The economy of the American people has served this nation faithfully and well. . . . It has afforded not only material comfort, but the resources to provide a challenging life of the mind and of the spirit. . . . Our economy has grown strong because our people have made jobs for each other and have not relied on the government to try to do it for them. Our economy is the result of millions of decisions we all make every day about producing, earning, saving, investing and spending. Both our individual prosperity, and our nation's prosperity, rest directly on the decisions all of us are making. (Wall Street 20th Century 1960:7)

In line with this emphasis on liberty and freedom is the belief that there is no hereditary aristocracy in America and that social class is unimportant, because everyone can rise to any economic level by their own intelligence, hard work, and creative energy. Public education makes prosperity available to everyone who truly wants to succeed. In this respect, wealth is an indirect measure of an individual's personal worth, and poverty indicates personal failure or irresponsibility. American society and culture are thought to reflect the interests of a broad middle class, whose members direct the economy and democratically elect the government. The economy itself is believed to be created and directed by the independent action of individual decision makers who make rational economic choices, freely choosing to buy or not buy commercial products that appear on the market. The ultimate measure of well-being in American culture is the rate of economic growth—this is the single concern that unites political conservatives, liberals, and radicals. Americans believe that only growth will create employment opportunities and make it possible for everyone to raise their standard of living.

Americans conceptually divide their society into two broad sectors: (1) the public sector, composed of the government, and (2) the private sector, composed of individuals and business corporations. The government is expected to provide military defense, public education, and highways, and to enforce contracts and protect private property; the government also promotes economic growth by following optimum monetary, tax, and spending policies. Business corporations provide jobs, products, and profits that benefit everyone, and they are owned by everyone (in the form of stock market shares) in a "people's capitalism." Individuals are employees and consumers. The entire system functions properly as long as government does not become too large and does not interfere with the freedom of business, and as long as individuals take full responsibility for their lives. Americans generally believe themselves to be free of racial, ethnic, or religious prejudices, assuming that distinctions between people of all nationalities will tend to disappear in the American "melting pot."

Throughout much of the twentieth century the prevailing American political ideology was "progressive." Elites who followed progressive ideology designed the United Nations and related institutions as discussed in Chapter 11. Domestically, progressivists believed that government should build public infrastructure, promote public education and social welfare programs to benefit society at large. They also thought that government should intervene in the economy to keep employment high, keep wages and prices in balance, and promote economic growth. Progressivists sought a just alliance between workers and capitalists, and favored the formation of labor unions to counterbalance the power of large corporations. This was called a "demand-side" economic policy, because it sought higher wages for workers, and redistributed tax revenues downward to households so that people could buy industrial products. The progressivist approach is well represented in the works of economists John Maynard Keynes (1936), and John Kenneth Galbraith (1952, 1958, 1967). It produced a rise in the proportion of national income received by the American middle class that peaked in 1960, and a related decline in the proportion received by the top twenty percent of households.

A change away from progressivist ideology began when America's economic elite became alarmed by a "crisis of capitalism" that occurred in the late 1960s and throughout the 1970s. This was a series of social and economic crises that included the Vietnam War, the youth counterculture, the peace movement, labor unrest, and social movements for civil rights, consumer rights, and environmental protection. All of this coincided with government scandals such as the Pentagon Papers in 1971 and Watergate in 1972–73, the American withdrawal from Vietnam in 1973, a slowing of economic growth, increased inflation, stagnant stock prices, and a decline in corporate profits. All of these problems were related to a sudden massive increase in oil prices by the Organization of Petroleum Exporting Countries (OPEC), the international oil cartel. The American elite responded by shifting toward a more conservative political ideology. Policy now emphasized "supply-side economics," or increasing production rather than consumer-purchasing power, and federal revenues shifted toward cor-

porations and large private investors, even as government regulation of commerce was reduced. This meant the ascendency of "New Growth" economic theory referred to in Chapter 11 and is often identified with the writings of economists Friedrich A. Hayek (1944) and Milton Friedman (1962). In the 1990s this approach has been called political neoconservatism and neoliberal, "free market" economics, and has been used to promote economic globalization. Corporate directors began moving manufacturing production to cheaper, more manageable labor overseas, and they invested heavily in computerization. All of these changes shifted wealth and income away from the lower and middle classes to the highest ranks of society (Philips 1990, 2002).

Cosmologies are cultural constructions that may not accurately reflect the practical realities in particular societies. The existence of factional disagreements in America over the proper balance of power between business and government suggests that the harmony implied in America's basic cosmology may not always exist. American beliefs about wealth and power are ambiguous, because wealth is highly desired but the wealthy are both envied and distrusted. America is believed to be a democracy in which everyone has an equal vote, but wealth inequality obviously gives some people more economic power than others, and this can become political power. The degree to which American cosmology corresponds with historical and ethnographic reality will be explored in the following sections.

America from a Chinese Perspective

Chinese anthropologist Francis Hsu grew up in China and has lived for many years in the United States and analyzed its culture. Hsu is a psychological anthropologist, interested in socialization, values, and personality. His deep familiarity with both Chinese and American culture allows him to make very insightful comparisons between the two cultures and provides an effective balance to the materialist bias of many American anthropologists.

Hsu (1972, 1981) argues that many of the key differences in economic life and class structure between Chinese and American culture can be attributed to what he considers to be the American core value of individual self-reliance versus the Chinese pattern of family dependence and filial piety. The emphasis that Americans place on self-reliance is represented by the ideal of the rugged individualist and a corresponding fear of dependence. For example, American children are socialized to value privacy, independence, and self-expression, and American parents are not supposed to interfere in the domestic lives of their adult children.

The Chinese emphasis on kinship and continuity of patrilineage highlights the virtues of dependency. Chinese children are socialized within families that include at least three generations and in-laws. They are cared for by a variety of elders. There is little individual privacy within a Chinese household, but individuals are always surrounded by many people who can be called on for physical and emotional support. There is little cultural incentive for an individual to pursue perpetual economic profit. An individual's primary responsibility is to parents and extended family, not self. Indeed, it is a source of pride for an aging Chinese parent to be taken care of by a child. By contrast, in the United States, one is expected to make it alone, and accepting economic aid from one's children might even be considered embarrassing.

Realistically, humans do depend on other people for many of their needs, and according to Hsu, culturally denying such dependence can generate psychological problems. Hsu maintains that the American ideal of self-reliance is likely to create emotional insecurity, which helps explain other seemingly contradictory American characteristics, such as racial and religious intolerance coexisting with an expressed belief in equality. Hsu suggests that personal insecurity drives Americans to accumulate material wealth to compensate and to demonstrate their self-worth. This not only makes Americans enormously competitive and intolerant of others but also serves the imperatives of a growth-centered capitalist economy. In contrast, the Chinese plow their earnings into family ceremonies, such as funerals, birthdays, and ancestor shrines, confident that they will be taken care of by their descendants.

The realities of American life pose some problems for Hsu's theory of self-reliance as a core value. The poorest classes in the United States likely survive by sharing with kin. Furthermore, the existence of economically based kinship groups among the American elite suggests that extended family dependency relations can be compatible with capitalist accumulation.

The role that Hsu ascribes to the American value of self-reliance fits well with the view that commercialization and profit making are the dominant cultural processes in commercial-scale cultures. Chinese civilization was created by a politicization process that does not require perpetual economic expansion. In support of this interpretation, Hsu observes that the small wealthy class in preindustrial China was composed of government bureaucrats, not merchants, and modern China has been very slow to industrialize. He also notes that most large Chinese cities are political capitals, whereas most large U.S. cities are commercial centers. American acquisitiveness generated economic growth and a relatively large middle class. This is not to argue that American values in themselves shaped the rest of American culture, but it suggests that values and personality are functionally connected to other economic and social variables.

A Mythic Framework: Founders and Sacred Texts

America's cosmology is supported by a mythic history and by the functional equivalent of sacred texts, in the form of the Declaration of Independence, the Constitution, and the written commentary in the Federalist Papers, all produced by the "Founding Fathers." The fifty-six men who signed the Declaration of Independence appealed directly to natural law with their lofty affirmation:

> We hold these Truths to be self-evident, that all Men are created equal, that they are endowed by their Creator with certain unalienable Rights, that among these are Life, Liberty, and the Pursuit of Happiness.

The Constitution, the legal framework for the federal government of the United States, was drafted in 1787 in the name of "We, the People." The purpose of the new government was to "establish Justice, insure domestic Tranquility, provide for the common defence, promote the general Welfare, and secure the Blessings of Liberty to ourselves and our Posterity."

Many popular beliefs about America's founding are contradicted by the historical record (McDonald 1958, 1979, 1985). The sentiments of the patriots of 1776 could have produced a loose federation of small-scale agrarian nations with high levels of local autonomy and individual freedom. There was no popular consensus that economic growth through the development of manufacturing and finance capital was a desirable goal or that a strong federal government was needed to protect business enterprise. On the contrary, many, including Thomas Jefferson, third U.S. president and author of the Declaration of Independence, and James Madison, fourth president and often called the Father of the Constitution, feared that unregulated commercial growth and subsequent wealth inequality would undermine democracy.

Those favoring a strong federal government did so for several reasons. Alexander Hamilton, first secretary of the treasury, wanted a strong banking and tariff system to promote industrialization, and a powerful navy to protect international commerce. The Federalist argument that a strong federal government was needed to protect business and promote growth was the opposite of "New Growth" neoliberal theory that identifies "big government" with growth-dampening regulations that would inhibit the "free market." However, protectionism made sense for those in the newly independent country who wanted to promote U.S. industrialization.

The Founding Fathers were idealistic statesmen, but the Constitution was not approved by popular vote. Historians have concluded that perhaps only 160,000 people, about 5 percent of the population, selected the delegates who attended the constitutional conventions in the various states, which in turn ratified the Constitution.

Only free adult males could vote, and some states required them to be property holders or to have certain levels of wealth. Historian Charles Beard (1913) maintained that the Constitution was an economic document, drafted and promoted by a small, consolidated group interested in protecting their personal, national-, and even international-level economic interests. The fifty-five men who drafted the Constitution were large landholders, merchants, and professionals, not poor farmers (see the box entitled "Robert Morris: Prince of Merchants, Patriot Financier"). More than half held government securities, nineteen were slave owners, and ten held bank shares. Although their personal economic interests often conflicted, they were all relatively wealthy men with significant economic power, and the document they produced did favor economic growth.

The Founding Fathers made a clear distinction between worthy, property-holding citizens and the propertyless. Propertyless people were considered to be too dependent to be informed citizens, and thus were assumed to be unfit to hold office or to vote. The Founders feared that popular democracy might lead to social disorder if an "overbearing majority" gained power and sought wealth redistribution. As a result, the Senate was designed as a "natural aristocracy" to balance the potential excesses of the more democratic House of Representatives. In the view of some historians, the social ideology of the federalists who assumed power in 1787 was not radically different from the elitist beliefs of the older European landed and wealthy aristocracy. Only the inherited titles were absent in America. However, the Constitution is an evolving, dynamic charter, and it produced an intricately balanced political system that can represent the democratic wishes of all the people.

The U.S. Constitution is a radical document. It expanded on the ideological transformations produced by the English Revolution of 1688 overturning belief in the "Divine Right of Kings" to rule, which had supported absolute monarchs throughout the imperial world for millennia. The idea that governments were established by "the people" to meet their needs was radical, but even more radical were the American ideals of human

Robert Morris: Prince of Merchants, Patriot Financier

A brief ethnographic sketch of the personal business interests of Robert Morris (1734–1806), considered the most prominent and powerful merchant and financier of the time, illustrates the extent of individual commercial power in preindustrial America and demonstrates how closely commercial power was linked with political power. This case study strongly suggests that commercial elites created America's political structure. Robert Morris was a politically active Philadelphia merchant, signer of the Declaration of Independence, and member of the Continental Congress, who handled the financial aspects of the Revolutionary War and the Continental Congress, helped draft the Constitution, and served on the Pennsylvania legislature and in the U.S. Senate. He was variously described by his contemporaries as a prince of merchants, patriot financier, and great man. He is still revered as a Founding Father, and his personal power certainly helped determine the course of cultural development in America.

Morris's economic interests were remarkably diverse and included manufacturing, shipping, and banking and finance; speculation in commodities, currency, land, and government securities; and trade with England, France, the West Indies, and India (Beard 1913, McDonald 1958, Ver Steeg 1954). Morris personally financed strategic troop movements during the Revolution, organized and was the largest shareholder in the original Bank of North America in Philadelphia, and organized and financed the first American trade expeditions to China. The key to his profit-making was *arbitrage,* buying low in one market and selling high in another market. He also secured handsome commissions from brokering large government

freedom as defined in the Bill of Rights adopted in 1791 to guarantee individual freedom of religion, speech, and press, and various other civil rights. The idea that individuals were entitled to equality of opportunity was also a radical break with the fundamentals of the imperial world.

The Founding Fathers on the Business of Politics

America is too large and too unequal to be a pure democracy. Instead, it is a representative democracy with officeholders elected by political subdivisions. American politics is largely a struggle between diverse commercial interest groups competing against one another to obtain favorable government policies. The competition is played out through national-level political parties. The Founding Fathers explicitly understood many of the economic conflicts inherent in a large-scale, commercially organized culture. The Constitution set the ground rules for an ongoing political struggle but could not resolve the underlying social conflicts because it ignored the reality of social class.

Madison enumerated "a landed interest, a manufacturing interest, a mercantile interest, a moneyed interest, and many lesser interests," but not a *household* interest, as necessary features of civilized nations. Madison foresaw that it would necessarily be the business of government to protect property and legislate a balance between these unavoidably conflicting commercial interests through the operation of factions and party politics. Setting the tone for the next two centuries, Hamilton defined the primary objective of politics and government as the promotion of commerce and effectively rejected the possibility

transactions, such as when he helped the French provision their American military expeditionary forces during the Revolution. He was an important member of nine major business partnerships and maintained numerous short-term partnerships, including business connections with at least five other delegates to the 1787 Constitutional Convention. For a time he owned millions of acres of undeveloped western land that was still controlled by Native Americans, and he brokered land purchases for European investors. He attempted to gain a monopoly over the tobacco trade with Europe, and he quickly bought up speculative property in Washington, D.C., as soon as the site was selected for the new national capital.

Politically, Morris was closely aligned with Alexander Hamilton and other prominent federalists who favored a strong federal government. He was a firm believer in free trade, maintaining that commerce should be "free as air to place it in the most advantageous state to mankind." Like Adam Smith, Morris praised the invisible hand, and he could imagine no conflict between his public and private life. Speaking of American entrepreneurs in general, he said: "Their own interest and the publick good goes hand in hand and they need no other prompter or tutor" (Ver Steeg 1954:38). However, he felt that only entrepreneurs themselves could be arbiters of the public good, and only they could define the proper balance of power between public and private. Morris's commercial vision certainly shaped America at a crucial moment in its history, but reckless speculation drove him into personal bankruptcy, and he was sent to debtors' prison in 1798, where he remained for three and a half years.

that there could be any significant class divisions in American society that would not be solved by economic growth. Anticipating the emergence of export-dependent agriculture, he argued that there was no conflict between mercantile and agrarian interests, because increased trade would benefit both (Federalist Papers No. 12). He rejected political representation by social class as "visionary." He believed that artisans and laborers would prefer to give their votes to merchants as their "natural representatives," patrons, and friends, who would have more "influence and weight" in deliberative assemblies.

Madison knew that elected legislators would not be totally impartial, but he felt that pluralism, the great diversity of interests, would prevent the abuse of political power. Hamilton thought that the poorest tenants and wealthiest landlords were "perfectly united" on the issue of keeping taxes low, and thus there was no class conflict between them. He assumed that the poorest and wealthiest would have an equal chance of being elected, because voters would simply elect whomever they were most confident with. However, Hamilton correctly expected government to be composed of landholders, merchants, and lawyers (Federalist Papers No. 35).

A simply binary political party system developed during the nineteenth century out of the original contrast between Jefferson's and Hamilton's visions for America. Jefferson's ideal of an agrarian nation became identified with slavery, western expansion, property rights, farmers, and labor, and evolved in stages into the modern Democratic party. Hamilton's Federalists promoted wage labor over slavery and favored industrialization, a national banking system, and large-scale capitalism; by 1854, they had evolved

TABLE 12.1   STAGES IN THE CONSTRUCTION OF CORPORATE AMERICA, 1790–PRESENT

Date	Development	Characteristics
1790–1850	Traditional business firms	Generalized mercantile partnerships Single-unit enterprises
1850–1900	Transportation, communication, and fuel revolutions	Multiunit enterprises Executive hierarchies Railroad empires
1850–1890	The Production and Distribution Revolution	High-volume throughput Vertically integrated production Emergence of wholesalers and mass market retailers
1880–1917	Modern industrial corporations	Vertical integration of mass production and mass marketing Multidivision, multinational enterprises Oligopolies, and Monopolies
1960–present	Conglomerates	Corporate mergers in unrelated industries

SOURCE: Based on Chandler (1977).

into the modern Republican party. This means that historically the Democratic party was politically conservative, and the Republican party was liberal. The meanings have now reversed, just as the meaning of "big government" has changed from its original pro-business identification, to its current anti-business image.

The Construction of Corporate America, 1790–1920

Twentieth-first-century America is dominated by those who own, direct, and manage a few hundred giant commercial corporations. Relative to ordinary humans, giant business corporations have the qualities of deities with superhuman form, immortality, and omnipotence. They are cultural constructions that have virtually taken the role of divine kings, but with computers adding omniscience to their powers. This may seem perfectly natural and inevitable, but nevertheless, corporate power of this scope and magnitude was a human creation and is not inevitable, and it is not the only way to organize commercial life. Corporate America was created by a handful of elites who purposefully used their political and economic power to design the legal and in-

stitutional structures to allow them increase the scale of business organizations and amass greater amounts of wealth (Table 12.1). They simultaneously constructed a national society and national scale markets. This corporatization process disempowered millions of small farmers and merchants living in small towns and villages, and totally changed their daily lives even though they resisted vigorously.

In 1790, perhaps fewer than 2000 people (approximately the top 0.5 percent of households) were wealthy enough to dominate the fledgling commercial economy and significantly influence political decisions and major cultural developments. America's leaders chose maximum growth, by combining Jefferson's vision of agrarian expansion with Hamilton's commercial industrialization approach. This was the best way for the wealthiest to expand their wealth, but it also opened new opportunities for European immigrants who were denied all hope of improving their living standards by hereditary aristocracies in their homelands.

After 1787, America's new political economy especially favored increased commercial activity. Over the next century, the nation's territory was tripled by a policy of military conquest that reduced the population of Native Americans by 95 percent. The U.S. Navy protected American shipping. The rural poor and impoverished European immigrants offered a steady labor force. Under these conditions, it suddenly became enormously rewarding for elites to develop new methods of production and new technology to speed the flow of goods. It would be deceptively easy to attribute corporatization to the effects of new technology. However, the steamships, railroads, and factory production systems that sustained large scale business corporations were as much social organizational changes as technological changes (Noble 1977). They were called into being and effectively owned and controlled by a few people. An equally plausible but different form of ownership and control would have produced a very different human outcome. Corporations, as designed by wealthy investors, were given the unique form of "socialized property" (Roy 1997, Zeitland 1989). The vast scale of corporations and the minute division of ownership among thousands and even millions of small owners allowed the corporate elite to concentrate power and socialize the costs. The few beneficial owners of a corporation, those owning five percent or more of the shares, can dominate the board of directors, control the company, and receive a disproportionate share of the profits. The more numerous small owners and society at large share the risks but do not hold enough power individually to enjoy significant benefits. Large owners can further socialize costs by using their political power to gain public subsidies for their businesses, even as they are insulated from catastrophic failures that can wipe out lower level managers, employees, and small shareholders.

The corporatization process unfolded quickly from 1810 to 1850 under the direction of a handful of merchants, investors, and intellectuals, based primarily in New England and the northeast, who created a national American commercial culture (Hall 1982). They designed and directed a small number of elite colleges that trained the leaders, who in turn created and ran the public schools and colleges, trusts and endowments, charities, banks, insurance companies, and factories that transformed America from a rural agrarian to a national commercial society organized by giant corporations.

How few were involved in this process is illustrated by 12 investors, the "Boston Associates," who initiated the factory system of textile production in America in 1813 (Dalzell 1987). By 1845, just 77 interconnected associates controlled $12 million in capital, and held 9 companies, with factories, dormitories, towns, waterworks, real estate investments, banks, and railroads. One associate had interests in 12 companies, a railroad, 2 banks, and an insurance company. Another prominent entrepreneur, John Jacob Astor (1763–1848) became America's first millionaire business tycoon by using his political influence to build a personal empire in the western fur trade, New York real estate development, and trade with China. By 1845 there were 715 super-elite individuals holding $100,000 or more in property in Boston, Brooklyn, New York, and Philadelphia. They used their wealth and influence to make themselves the primary human agents of culture change in America (Pessen 1973).

As it developed, corporatization depended on permissive federal and state legislation, and was supported by court decisions friendly to big business. For example, in 1819 U.S. Supreme Court Justice John Marshall ruled that business corporations could make contracts, own property, extend charters indefinitely, and bring suit in federal court. This made corporate business a new form of private property. Many pro-big-business-jurists and chief justices were trained by Chief Justice Joseph Story and associates at Harvard Law School from 1829 to 1845, which was supported from 1805 to 1846 by just 29 wealthy donors (Hall 1982, Newmyer 1987). By the 1880s large corporations were winning court challenges to state laws that restricted access to local markets to protect small businesses (McCurdy 1978). This allowed retail chain stores and door-to-door salesmen for national manufacturers to overpower local producers and merchants. Giant meat processors could then ship meat throughout the country, overruling local and state health laws. This created a national scale market for beef. In 1886 the Supreme Court made corporations "legal individuals" with rights of "due process" and "equal protection" under the fourteenth amendment, giving corporations rights to own other corporations. Recent court decisions even gave corporations rights of "free speech," even though their legal omnipotence gives them vastly greater powers and a much louder voice than ordinary citizens.

Railroads were the key to the scale increases in commerce. Demand from national and international investors for railroad securities contributed to the rise of powerful New York investment banks and brokerage houses. As railroads became complex systems, operational problems were solved when their top managers created a hierarchy of middle managers and lower-level supervisors. This required all the features of a modern business corporation including organizational charts, formal titles, job descriptions, lines of authority, regular reports, performance evaluations, and new accounting procedures. By the 1850s, the largest railroads were already being consolidated into the first giant holding companies—corporations that owned other corporations—by a few superwealthy stock speculators seeking to limit competition. American railroads soon became the largest business enterprises in the world. For example, in the 1890s, the Pennsylvania Railroad employed 110,000 workers, nearly three times the size of the United States military, and it took in more than a third of the revenue of the federal government (Chandler 1977).

Mass production of consumer goods is relatively easy, as long as energy and raw materials can be secured. The problem for commercial elites was how to promote mass distribution and consumption of their products. They created the first advertising agencies in the 1850s, and by the 1880s advertising was being used to market mass-produced consumer goods such as cigarettes and breakfast foods. Brands, patents, and trademarks soon became crucial new forms of property, used to control production and distribution in the national market, and to create customer loyalty for particular corporations. Early in the twentieth century new advertising campaigns were designed to persuade people of the moral legitimacy of giant corporations. For example, in the 1920s Bruce Barton's campaign on behalf of General Motors portrayed the company as one big family and the country as its neighborhood. In effect, advertisers attempted to create the corporate soul, just as the courts created the corporate body (Marchand 1998).

By the 1880s, giant, vertically integrated, multifunctional, multiunit, and often multinational business enterprises, controlled by a managerial class of corporate executives, dominated the American economy. These corporate giants created **oligopolies,** which allowed commercial bureaucrats to coordinate production and distribution decisions, effectively replacing the invisible hand of the market (Chandler 1977). The objective was to increase the volume, speed, and efficiency of commercial transactions, in order to reduce costs and generate a higher return on investments or to reduce competition by controlling markets. Large-scale business enterprises succeeded because they brought many formerly competing enterprises within a single organizational structure, thereby internalizing their diverse production, buying, and selling decisions within a single management hierarchy. Administrative coordination was the key. These institutional changes increased productivity and profits, because top managers could allocate resources more efficiently than could the managers of smaller firms competing in a decentralized marketplace with imperfect supply-and-demand information. The greatest transformation of corporate America occurred between 1898 and 1905 when the volume of the stock market expanded from tens of millions to billions of dollars (Roy 1997).

Rockdale: An American Industrial Village, 1825–1865

Anthropologist Anthony F. C. Wallace (1978) produced a remarkable historical ethnography of

FIGURE 12.1 Synthetic reconstruction of a typical Rockdale mill hamlet about 1850.

the small textile-producing community of Rockdale in southeastern Pennsylvania during the four decades from 1825 to 1865 (Figure 12.1). He spent 8 years poring over public records, newspapers, biographies, letters, and memorabilia to construct a richly detailed picture of the people of Rockdale. His study illuminates the difficult human problems that the new machine technology and the factory system produced as it developed under early American industrial capitalism.

In the 1820s, capitalist manufacturers intent on establishing new textile mills began buying up small, abandoned flour, paper, and lumber mills in the Rockdale district, southwest of Philadelphia. Their enterprises benefited from the federal government's policy of placing high tariffs on imported goods, rather than taxes, to encourage American manufacturing and to raise revenue. By 1850, there were 2000 people living in 351 households, in seven small hamlets along Chester Creek. Each hamlet was centered on a water-powered cotton mill, which provided the primary employment. Three local families, referred to by Wallace as "Lords of the Valley," owned most of the land and mills in Rockdale and determined the overall pattern of life.

Altogether, some 12 families of manufacturers, merchants, and gentlemen farmers sat at the top of the social hierarchy, forming a tightly integrated economic class. They lived in comfortable, well appointed, hilltop stone mansions. The men agreed on their probusiness politics; traveled regularly to Boston, New York, Washington, and nearby Philadelphia; and vacationed with their families at beach resorts. The wives and daughters of Rockdale's elite formed a close-knit sisterhood that included elites in neighboring communities. These women were well educated, well read, intellectually active, and musically and artistically accomplished. They had the leisure time to correspond and visit each other frequently, and write diaries and poetry. Beneath this elite group was a "middle class" assortment of 150 professionals, teachers, ministers, and artisans; and beneath them were 162 mill worker families, who lived very modestly. Workers lived in inexpensive tenements at the bottom of the hill near

oligopoly Concentrated economic power when a few sellers can control a market with many buyers by controlling the price and availability of goods.

the mill (Figure 12.1). The low residential position of workers also reflected their low social, intellectual, and emotional standing as a depressed class in the minds of upper-class people. For example, Sophie Du Pont, a member of the nearby Du Pont industrialist family and member of Rockdale high society, expressed amazement in her diary that working-class women could be emotionally distressed by sick children. People in that "class of life" were not expected to be particularly sensitive.

The economic distance between top and bottom in the hierarchy was enormous. The minimum capital cost of a mill and its machinery was approximately $12,000–35,000, which was far beyond the means of all but the wealthy. A typical mill worker family could earn about $250 a year and might bring in another $175 from boarders, for a total of $425. Basic household subsistence expenditures for food, fuel, and rent were $300, leaving $125 for clothing and all other expenses. This meant that with a stringent savings program, within a few years a healthy family might accumulate the $200 needed to move west and buy a small farm. Most of the mill workers hoped their jobs would be temporary. Many of them were recent immigrants from England and Ireland, where workers were clearly not as well off.

Relations between owners and workers were generally satisfactory; however, there remained an intrinsic conflict of interest, which eventually led to an open clash. The top four mill owners determined everyone's quality of life, because they could hire and fire workers at will, set wages and hours, buy new machines that displaced workers, and determine health and safety conditions. Profits were always more important than the security and well-being of worker households. Owners hired workers as a specified number of "hands" supplied by household units. Many children, including some younger than 10, routinely worked in the factories, although they were probably better off than children in comparable British mills. The Rockdale owners considered mistreatment to

be poor personnel management, as mill owner John Crozier testified in 1837: "When factories were first established in this vicinity, severe whipping was often practiced, but it was found not to be the best mode of management, and has been, in a great degree, abandoned" (Wallace 1978:180).

The 14-hour workday ran by the bell from 5 AM to 7 PM, with breaks for breakfast and dinner. The 6-day work week thus ran 72 hours. The mills were hot and poorly ventilated, and the air was thick with cotton fiber dust that gave workers chronic coughs. The work was so exhausting that young children sometimes fell asleep on the job. It was publicly acknowledged that factory conditions were mentally, morally, and physically unhealthy for children and less than ideal for adults. However, rather than calling for fundamental changes in the way factories were operated, religious reformers wanted the workers to improve themselves by attending Sunday School and becoming more responsible parents. The owners knew that working children did not have time for regular schooling, and many workers were illiterate. In principle, the Rockdale mill owners supported legislation that would shorten working hours and prohibit hiring workers younger than 12. But they refused to institute such social reforms, arguing that their mills would be economically uncompetitive unless all states had such laws. They blamed widows and lazy fathers and the absence of public assistance for child labor, not low wages. They recommended night school for working children. However, there were many female-headed households with small children in Rockdale, and many families were too poor to put their children in school. Obviously, the mills did not create a healthy social environment, but Crozier defended the economic necessity of child labor with impeccable functionalist logic: "The work of children cannot be shortened, without also abridging that of adults, as the labor of one is connected with that of the other, being part of a system, which, if broken in upon, destroys a connecting link in the chain of operations" (Wallace 1978:328).

For their part, Rockdale textile workers organized a labor union in 1836 and walked off their jobs in 1836 and again in 1842, demanding shorter hours and better pay. When the organizers were fired, strikers retaliated by destroying property. Later, some were fined and jailed. The commercial elite quickly aligned themselves with the religious establishment to denounce labor unions as anti-Christian, un-American, and immoral. Social reform became a Christian enterprise, but it did not threaten the established capitalist order.

The Rise of Factory Farming

The industrialization of farming and the general commercialization of the food system, which was well underway in Europe and America by the mid-twentieth century, must rank as a cultural transformation as significant as the domestication of plants and animals during the Neolithic. This great change is a continuation of the broad trend toward subsistence intensification that has accompanied each increase in the scale of human culture—more food is produced at greater energy cost and ecosystem degradation. This characterization may seem counterintuitive, but the true costs of industrialization have been masked by the cultural accounting system that only emphasizes human labor and monetary cost. In an industrial culture such as the United States, farms are operated like factories. Often the emphasis is on a single crop that is mass-produced at the lowest possible monetary cost for the maximum cash return. Economic imperatives compel the farmer to use labor-saving machinery to reduce costs and to employ chemical pesticides and fertilizers to increase production.

When viewed from a cultural ecological perspective, this **factory farming** raises troubling questions for the long-term viability of industrial civilization. As ecologist Howard Odum (1971) observed, the factory farm replaces self-maintaining biological processes, which are fueled by renewable solar energy, with urban-based cultural processes that require vast **energy subsidies** in the form of nonrenewable fossil fuels. Factory farming simplifies natural ecosystems, making them less stable while extracting a larger energy share for human consumption. An obvious problem with this system is that it also rapidly depletes fossil fuels and soils and thus cannot be sustained indefinitely.

Because it requires relatively few farm laborers and produces very high per-acre yields, factory farming appears deceptively productive. In 1970, when viewed at the national level, each kilocalorie of American farm labor returned 210 kilocalories (kcal) of food—four times the yield of intensive Chinese rice farming as discussed in Chapter 8. However, when the full energy costs of production were calculated—including fuel, electricity, fertilizer, and farm machinery—2 kilocalories of energy were expended to produce 1 kilocalorie of food energy (Steinhart and Steinhart 1974).

Such **deficit production** is only possible when subsidized by vast inputs of solar energy stored in nonrenewable fossil fuels. Furthermore, when food production costs are calculated to include the costs of industrial processing and marketing, which necessarily precede domestic consumption in a highly urbanized society, then a minimum of 8–12 kilocalories were expended in the production of 1 kilocalorie of food (Table 12.2). Even this figure underestimates the actual energy costs of the American food production system because it does not include all transport costs, especially the use of private automobiles in trips to the grocery store, or the costs of advertising commercialized

---

factory farming Commercial agriculture based on fossil fuel energy subsidies, mechanization, pesticides, chemical fertilizers, and large-scale monocropping.

energy subsidy The use of fossil fuels to increase food production above the rate that could be sustained through use of renewable energy sources.

deficit production The situation in which more calories are expended in food production than are produced for human food.

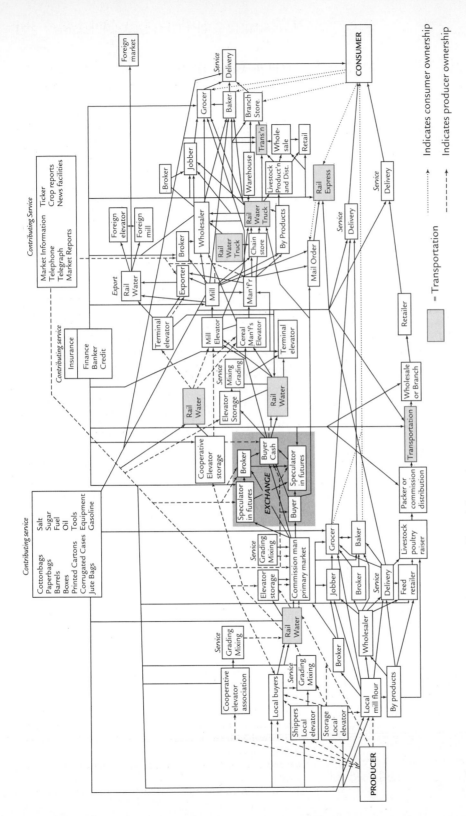

FIGURE 12.2 Chart showing the manufacturing of bread from wheat.

TABLE 12.2   ENERGY USE IN THE U.S. FOOD SYSTEM (IN 10^{12} KCAL), 1940 AND 1970

	1940	1970
Farm production*	124.5	526.1
Food processing†	285.8	841.9
Distribution‡	275.2	804.0
Totals	685.5	2172.0

SOURCE: Steinhart and Steinhart (1974).
*Farm production includes fuel, electricity, fertilizer, and irrigation and the costs of producing agricultural steel, farm machinery, and tractors.
†Processing includes production, machinery, packaging, transport fuel, and trucks and trailers.
‡Distribution includes commercial and domestic refrigeration and cooking.

food products and disposing of the trash by-products. A more realistic total would probably approach 20 kilocalories expended for each 1 consumed.

U.S. farm production was not fully industrialized until fossil fuel–powered farm machinery and agricultural chemicals became widely used after 1940. The social corollary of these technological changes was a decline in the rural population. The number of individual farms actually declined, but those that remained became much larger than before.

In America's large-scale subsistence system the food chain from farmer to consumer quickly became so complex that it drove up the price of food. Even by the 1920s there were so many steps between producer and consumer that the farmer received only 28 cents of the consumer's dollar spent on bread (Borsodi 1929:55). In 1949 a congressional committee documented the complexity of the wheat to bread network (Figure 12.2). They found that increased scale and complexity was accompanied by a greater concentration of economic power, as large food manufacturers and retailers bought up their suppliers and competitors, and fought to expand their market and increase the "value" of food (United States, House Committee on the Judiciary 1949). By the 1990s the farmer's average share of the food dollar had dropped to about 20 cents.

Wheat for Topsoil: Erosion and Plenty in Whitman County

The impact of farm industrialization at the local level can be illustrated using Census Bureau statistics for Whitman County in eastern Washington. Whitman County is the heart of the Palouse region, an area of steep, dunelike hills composed of deep loess soils, which were deposited by the wind 100,000 years ago (Figure 12.3). Climate and soil conditions in the Palouse are ideally suited for dry farming and help make Whitman County one of the world's leading wheat-producing regions. **Monocrop farming** of wheat was well underway in the Palouse by the 1880s.

According to Census Bureau figures, 27,000 people lived in rural Whitman County in 1910. Approximately 75 percent of the cash value of farm production was in grain. There were some 3000 farms, averaging 383 acres (155 hectares). The primary farm production inputs were human labor and horses. Because much of the feed for the 38,000 horses and mules was grown locally, the county enjoyed a high degree of energy self-sufficiency.

By 1987, the switch to industrialization in Palouse farming was strikingly apparent in Census Bureau data that showed a drastic reduction in human labor inputs, the virtual disappearance of horses, and an enormous increase in fossil fuels and chemical fertilizers (Figure 12.4). Yields of wheat per acre suddenly doubled and tripled. Between 1910 and 1940, approximately 30 bushels were produced per acre, but by 1987, yields averaged 69 bushels and sometimes reached 100. Such increases resulted from the use of newly developed "miracle grains," selectively bred to take maximum advantage of agricultural chemicals and machinery. This energy-intensive production system became known as the **Green Revolution**

---

monocrop farming   A system of growing one plant species, sometimes only a single variety, often in very large continuous stands.

Green Revolution   Dramatic increases in agricultural production from use of hybrid grains that produce high yields in return for high inputs of chemical fertilizers and pesticides.

FIGURE 12.3 Active soil erosion on a cultivated wheat field in Whitman County, Washington. Note the soil slumping on the steep hillside in the background.

The most ominous change was the steady loss of soil due to erosion caused by deep cultivation of steep slopes with heavy machinery. The U.S. Department of Agriculture (USDA) began an annual program to monitor the problem in 1939. In 1978, the USDA issued a report documenting the total loss of topsoil from 10 percent of the land and estimating that annual soil losses averaged 14 tons (13 metric tons) of soil per acre. This means that each metric ton of wheat produced costs 13.5 metric tons of topsoil. This kind of factory farming is truly mining the soil and cannot continue indefinitely.

Why would any culture institutionalize such a short-sighted technological system? This is a cultural problem that can best be understood by considering the dominant cultural role played by the economic elite in the United States. The logic of competitive commercial production aimed primarily at generating a cash profit forces U.S. producers to steadily accelerate output in order to gain economies of scale. Accelerated output is facilitated by technological innovation and by the concentration of economic control by a wealthy few. The concentration of economic power leads, in turn, to social inequality and many other long-term costs.

The American Cattle Complex: Good to Sell

One can easily make the case that a Cattle Complex exists in America just as in East Africa. But the contrasts between the two cattle systems highlight the role of economic elites in shaping commercial-scale industrial cultures. Cattle are significant in American culture not only because they are "good to eat" but more importantly, as Marvin Harris (1985) emphasizes, because cattle are "good to sell."

The elites who dominate the American cattle industry have used the most intensive production techniques to maximize the scale of their operation for the highest possible economic returns. Remarkably few people are the beneficial owners of

and was widely exported to the developing world in the 1970s and 1980s.

The social and environmental consequences of the technological changes in Palouse wheat farming were equally striking. As the demand for labor declined, by 1987 the total rural population had shrunk to less than half of what it had been in 1910. More significantly, the number of farms declined even more steeply, while total farm acreage remained approximately the same. This meant that individual farms tripled in size. Land became concentrated in fewer and fewer hands, such that 15 percent of the farms came to control 46 percent of the land.

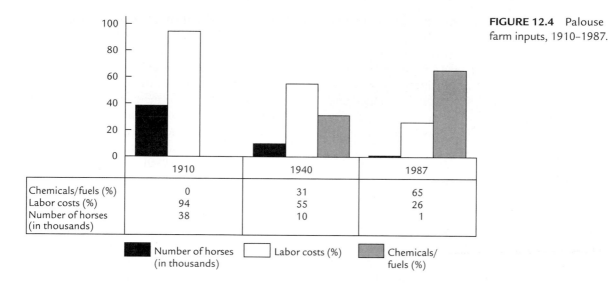

FIGURE 12.4 Palouse farm inputs, 1910–1987.

	1910	1940	1987
Chemicals/fuels (%)	0	31	65
Labor costs (%)	94	55	26
Number of horses (in thousands)	38	10	1

Number of horses (in thousands)   Labor costs (%)   Chemicals/ fuels (%)

the nation's beef. For example, the 1997 Census of Agriculture shows that the top 10 percent of farms and ranches owned half of the beef cattle in the United States, with the 212 largest farms having 2,500 cattle or more averaging herds of nearly 8,000 (USDA 1997, Table 28). Herd size followed the power law distribution, suggesting that the 10 largest herds may have averaged as many as 200,000 head of cattle. A single ranch of this gigantic size would provide some 10,000 American ranch households with median-sized herds of 20 animals, or would support some 30,000 East African cattle herder households. One of the largest ranches in the country, the King Ranch in Texas, covers 825,000 acres, more than 1000 square miles, but with an intensive feeding program, even a relatively small acreage ranch could support an enormous herd. For example, the Harris Ranch in California's San Joaquin Valley boasts an 800-acre feedlot with an annual capacity of 250,000 animals. This is vastly more animals than flowed annually through Emperor Ur-Nammu's livestock distribution center in ancient Nippur. The advantage of scale is reflected in market share, with the largest corporately owned cattle ranches receiving the largest share of the cattle market. The top 2 percent, 20,000 ranches, accounted for

50 percent of the $113 billion in cattle sales in 1997 (USDA 1997, Table 45).

Beef processing was also highly concentrated. Just three giant corporations, Tyson, Exel, and ConAgra accounted for 62 percent of the cattle slaughtered and processed commercially in the United States (Tyson Foods 2001:2). In 2002, one company, Tyson Foods, claimed to be the number one supplier of fresh, ground, and processed beef to U.S. retail grocers and food services and to Japan. Tyson also dominated poultry and pork processing, and with $23 billion in sales accounted for some 20 percent of the meat processing market (Statistical Abstract, 2001, Table 974, Tyson 2002). In 2001 Tyson's 300 plants and 120,000 employees were processing an average of 196,881 head of beef, 42.5 million chickens, and 338,288 pigs every week. This would be nearly 6 million pounds of beef per year and would supply 90 million Americans with their annual per capita consumption of 65 pounds of beef. Tyson also claimed to be the number one supplier of chicken to China and Russia, and frozen chicken to military commissaries. The principal beneficial owners of the company are members of the Tyson family and their close business partners. An enterprise of this scale is certainly profitable. Board chairman and CEO John Tyson received an annual salary and bonuses of more than $4.5 million. This degree of control, by so few, over all aspects of such a major element of subsistence is a remarkable cultural arrangement that certainly has *no* parallel in any domestic-scale cultures or ancient civilizations.

The scale of production shapes how cattle are handled, categorized, graded, slaughtered, and butchered and how the meat is named, packed, and distributed. In the tribal cultures of East Africa, cows are highly personalized, and slaughtering is a public and ritual act. The meat is distributed according to kinship relationships and is consumed immediately. In the United States, market cattle and meat are depersonalized commodities, the production of which is left entirely to specialists; few people have more than a vague idea of how their meat gets to them.

The production process is designed to move the animal to full slaughter weight as quickly as possible—usually within 24 months, although milk-fed calves may be slaughtered as veal at under 3 months. Calves may receive appetite stimulants and ear-implanted hormones to speed their growth. They are weaned at 6–9 months, either to be returned to the range as "stockers" to grow further or to be vaccinated and sold to feedlots as "feeders" to be "finished" for slaughter. At the feedlot, cattle receive more vaccinations and growth-hormone implants and are fattened on a weight-gain diet of grain, molasses, beef fat and by-products, and plant protein supplements, laced with antibiotics, vitamins, and growth steroids (Thomas 1986).

The entire production process is regulated by federal and state laws. Live cattle are sorted by federal inspectors into classes by sex condition—steer, bullock, bull, cow, and heifer—and into grades—prime, choice, select, standard, commercial, utility, cutter, and canner. Regulations specify every detail of the slaughtering process, even prescribing the rate (in head per hour) at which inspectors can examine specific parts of animals. Such detailed regulation and classification are necessary to ensure quality standards when ani-

mals move rapidly through a complex chain of buyers and sellers, each seeking to maximize monetary return.

Economies of scale are a major factor in slaughtering. Larger plants, using highly specialized technology, were able to increase the hourly kill-and-butcher rate from 100 head per hour during the 1970s to 300–350 head per hour in the 1980s, thereby reducing the unit price of processing by 25 percent (Pietraszek 1990). Faster butcher rates required a multitude of mechanized tools such as dehorners, dehiders, carcass splitters, brisket opener saws, bone saws, and primal cut saws. Further meat-processing operations use mechanical trimmers, dicers, massagers, tumblers, grinders, collagen films, patty machines, and vacuum stuffers. Meat cutting is a highly intensive, technical occupation in which the demand for increased efficiency produces a high rate of injuries in the workers.

Virtually every part of the animal finds some use. A beef carcass is split and quartered and then quickly reduced to six to ten primal and sub-primal cuts for wholesale. Numerous other edible by-products include gelatin, marshmallows, and canned meat. Inedible by-products include leather, buttons, and soap from beef tallow, as well as pet foods and animal feeds. A wide range of pharmaceuticals such as insulin, estrogen, and thyroid extract are also derived from cattle.

Large-scale factory meat production also produces low-wage jobs, impoverished communities, and environmental damage (Olsson 2002, Schlosser 2001, Stull and Broadway 2003). The scale and complexity of this form of subsistence and the speed of production also increase the risk of contamination. For example, in 2002 ConAgra voluntarily recalled some 19 million pounds of ground beef produced by its giant slaughterhouse in Greeley, Colorado, because of contamination by harmful E. coli bacteria (Schlosser 2002). Because it operated in a cultural system that socializes costs and maximizes economic returns, ConAgra officials were not required to publicly disclose all of the retail outlets that received their meat. Pressure from corporate lobbyists and generous political donations have encouraged lax enforcement of health regulations and self-inspection by producers, even as government regulatory agencies are underfunded and often staffed by former industry employees (Drew, Becker, & Blakeslee 2003).

The Cultural Construction of Consumption

Anthropologist Marvin Harris (1985) argues that cultural preferences for specific meats are largely determined by utilitarian, ecological, and economic factors. He attributes the American preference for beef to the forced removal of bison and Native Americans from the Great Plains in the 1870s and their replacement by cattle. The ranchers were, in turn, displaced by grain farmers, and cattle had to be grazed on the arid lands and in the logged-over forests further west. The real boom for beef, according to Harris, came after World War II when large numbers of American women began to work outside the home and fast-food dining on hamburgers suddenly opened a vast new market for beef. The key to the success of hamburger, which legally must be all beef, is that it can contain added beef fat, up to 30 percent. The added fat helps bind the meat when it is cooked. Thus, hamburger can be ground from relatively tough, range-fed steers, combined with the abundant fat trimmed from feedlot-fattened beef, which otherwise supply tender, marbled, and very expensive cuts of meat.

Utilitarian interpretations of cultural practices are helpful, but they imply that cultural development unfolds naturally and inevitably, suggesting that change will be adaptive and progressive. This leaves out both the cultural meanings in people's heads, as well as the elite decision-makers who expend massive resources on advertising to create these meanings. Rejecting economic **utilitarianism**, Marshall Sahlins reminds us that what people consume, as well as our concepts of economic scarcity, and by extension *poverty,* are all cultural constructions. In his famous statement on foragers as "the original affluent society," Sahlins observed that tribal foragers easily satisfy their wants by desiring little, whereas for Americans,

> scarcity is the peculiar obsession of a business economy, the calculable condition of all who participate in it. The market makes freely available a dazzling array of products, all these "good things" within a man's reach—but never his grasp, for one never has enough to buy everything. To exist in a market economy is to live out a double tragedy, beginning in inadequacy and ending in deprivation. All economic activity starts from a position of shortage . . . one's resources are insufficient to the possible uses and satisfactions. (1968:86)

Scarcity or poverty is thus not strictly a technological problem, and it is not inherent in nature; it is a cultural creation that is most elaborated by commercial-scale, industrial cultures. According to anthropologist Jules Henry (1963), the dependence of American culture on the deliberate creation of needs for goods and services constitutes a "psychic revolution" with far-reaching impacts on human thought and behavior.

Sahlins (1976b) offered a cultural symbolic analysis of American food practices suggesting that in American culture, because of its long cultural association with virility and strength, beef, and especially steak, has a central place in the diet. Pork takes second place, as a less preferred meat, while eating dogs or horses is virtually taboo.

Sahlins observed that in American culture, cattle and pigs form a structured set in opposition to horses and dogs (Figure 12.5). Cattle and pigs are treated as unnamed objects and are eaten, whereas dogs and horses are named subjects and are not eaten. Dogs and horses are seen as more "human"—both are talked to and petted, and dogs may live in the house and be buried upon death. Eating dogs would be like eating kin and implies cannibalism. Horses are more like servants, and eating them is only slightly less taboo. Pork is less preferred than beef, in part because

---

utilitarianism The use of economic profit, direct material advantage, or physical welfare, such as food and shelter, as an explanation for cultural practices.

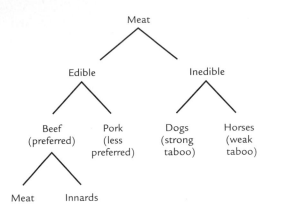

FIGURE 12.5 The cultural structure of meat edibility in the United States. (SOURCE: Based on Sahlins 1976b.)

pigs scavenge human food and are thus closer to people than cattle, such that eating pigs would be slightly cannibalistic.

A further cultural code of edibility is imposed on beef itself. Meat is culturally distinguished as the most edible part of the animal, in opposition to "innards" such as heart, tongue, and liver, which, like pork, imply cannibalism. Cuts of beef are subdivided into dozens of named categories and products, each priced according to its culturally defined desirability, such that eating a given cut reinforces one's social rank. Sahlins (1976b) stressed that pricing and desirability are not obviously related to supply and nutritional quality, because liver is highly nutritious and relatively scarce yet is much cheaper than steak, which is more abundant per animal.

The use of cultural products to encode social differences among categories of people resembles the use of animal species as totems to distinguish cultural groups in tribal cultures. However, this analysis focuses on "cultural intention," suggesting that the cultural system operates independently of human intention. In reality, what Americans eat, and what they believe they should eat can be intentionally changed. American food practices did change dramatically between 1940 and 2000 in response to decision-making, advertising, marketing, and political lobbying by the corporate directors of the food industry. Corporate concentration in the "fast food" industry

also shaped American eating patterns (Ritzer 2000). In 1940 Americans were primarily pork eaters, by 1960 they were beef eaters, but by 2000 Americans had become chicken eaters, eating more poultry than beef by weight (Statistical Abstract, 2002, Table 195). Between 1940 and 2000 Americans actually increased their daily consumption of protein, fats, carbohydrates, and total calories by an average of 16 percent. Apparent annual per capita consumption of refined sugar and corn syrup increased nearly 40 percent from 107 to 148 pounds. Soft drink consumption soared from 35 to 49 gallons between 1980 and 2000. These dietary changes are clearly related to official figures showing more than half of the population overweight and over 20 percent obese (Statistical Abstract, 2002, Table 190).

Changes of this magnitude in the practices of millions of people do not result from a nondirected, symbolically encoded cultural intention. American food practices are clearly influenced by the elite-directed drive to increase the scale of food production, marketing, and consumption. Much of this marketing is directed specifically at children and young people, who influence a significant share of household expenditures. In 2002 the directors of five candy and soft drink companies and four fast food giants spent a total of $6.5 billion on advertising, persuading people to eat more calories, more sugar and fat, and more transfatty acids known to elevate harmful cholesterol levels. This advertising spending is aimed at the top, "use sparingly," end of the official Food Guide Pyramid issued by the United States Department of Agriculture (USDA) in 2000 as a guide to daily food choices (Figure 12.6). The food pyramid was a compromise between food industry lobbyists who wanted to encourage consumption of all food commodities and independent nutritionists who wanted people to eat less of certain foods for their health (Nestle 2002). The pyramid phrase "use sparingly" is certainly not the same as "eat less." Other food pyramids are possible. For example, Figure 12.7 illustrates a healthy diet plan developed by Harvard nutritionist Walter Willet (2001) incorporating objective scientific research.

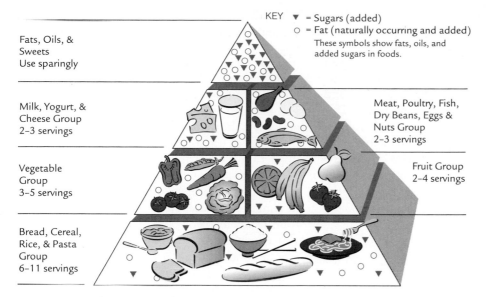

FIGURE 12.6   The USDA Food Guide Pyramid, 2000.

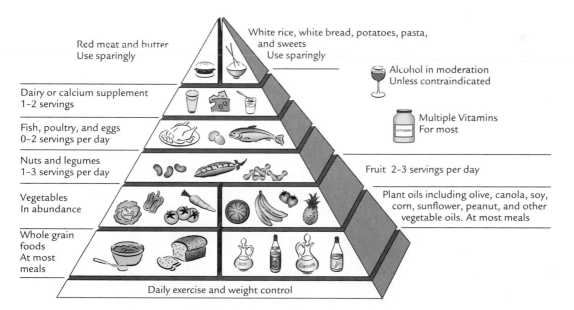

FIGURE 12.7   The Harvard healthy diet food pyramid (Willet 2001).

GROWTH, SCALE, AND POWER IN AMERICA

Growth is such a dominant element in American culture that it is important to closely examine its relationship to increases in culture scale and changes in the distribution of social power. This section uses broad ethnohistorical data for the country as a whole since 1776, as well as more detailed ethnography from New York City and the Palouse region of eastern Washington, to examine the social realities of 200 years of growth in the world's most successful commercial culture.

Growth in America: Wealth and Opportunity, 1776–1997

After his 9-month visit in 1831–1832, French political scientist Alexis de Tocqueville (1835–1840) described America as an egalitarian democracy, with a large middle class and few very rich or very poor. In his view, abundant resources, technological innovation, and hard work created equal economic opportunity in America. More recent observers point to the increasing numbers of wealthy as evidence of the benefits of American economic freedom, supporting the hope that economic growth makes it possible for everyone to become wealthy (Gilder 1981). However, three independent lines of evidence—probate estate records, census data, and tax assessments—suggest that for much of American history, social and economic reality seldom matched the widespread belief that growth made America a land of equal opportunity.

To estimate the distribution of wealth and income in the thirteen colonies immediately prior to the American Revolution of 1776, historian Alice Hanson Jones (1977, 1980) used detailed probate inventories of movable property and real estate in personal estates for 1773–1775, supplemented with tax lists, newspaper accounts, records of deeds and land grants, and church and town records of baptisms, marriages, and burials. Her findings suggest that the distribution of monetary income in 1776 was as top-heavy as in 1994,

when the top 5 percent of households received 20 percent of national household income, the middle 20 percent received 15 percent, and the bottom 20 percent received only 4 percent.

Remarkably, Lee Soltow's (1989) analysis of the distribution of property ownership recorded in the United States Census for 1798, 1850, 1860, and 1870 shows that political independence and a century of economic growth had no significant impact on the distribution of wealth in America. Soltow found extensive inequality in America throughout the nineteenth century. Perhaps half of American households owned no land. Soltow found such a strong correlation between wealth concentration and support for the Constitution that he concluded that it would not have been ratified by a popular vote because the poor saw no advantages in a strong federal government.

Other historians have used tax assessment data to examine the distribution of wealth in New York City during the nineteenth century when especially rapid urban growth occurred (Jaher 1972, 1982; Pessen 1971, 1973). Pessen documented very rapid wealth concentration during the first half of the century. In 1845, the top 1 percent held half of all wealth in property, and the top 4 percent owned an incredible 81 percent, including shares in New York's emerging corporate businesses (primarily banks and insurance companies). During this time, New York City's wealth grew faster than its population. Per capita wealth actually quadrupled, but the rich got much richer.

Careful analysis of the family connections of the economic elite showed conclusively that nineteenth-century New York was not a city of equal opportunity, because one needed inherited social status and wealth to prosper. Jaher found that the nineteenth-century New York economic elite proved to be closely integrated by kinship and marriage connections and were even forming marriage alliances with the European aristocracy. In 1898, 42 percent of New York's 1368 millionaires were related by blood or marriage (Jaher 1982:255). Ninety-five percent of New York's wealthiest individuals were born into already wealthy families; only 2 percent started out poor. The wealthy proved to be very secure, with most holding their wealth intact during their lifetimes and successfully passing it on to the next generation, even through severe economic downturns.

Even though wealth was heavily concentrated at the very top of the social hierarchy in nineteenth-century America, there was still significant upward mobility in comparison with the virtually frozen hierarchy in Europe. Low-income American households were able to move up the economic ladder, but much of their increase was a function of aging within the domestic cycle and very gradual accumulation of small savings. Soltow (1975:53) estimated that in 1870, 43 percent of adult males were poor, because they held total estates worth less than $100. Perhaps 52 percent of Americans were middle class, in the sense that they held at least $100 in property. Fewer than 10 percent were wealthy.

According to contemporary observers, in the 1850s accumulated wealth of $60,000, which would have generated an annual income of $3,000, was sufficient to provide the good life: "a comfortable house—servants, a good table—wine—a horse—books—'country quarters,'—a plentiful wardrobe—the ability to exercise hospitality" (cited in Pessen 1971:997). Only the top 0.5 percent of the urban population were in this category. If mid-nineteenth-century wealth accumulations of a mere $60,000 made one quite comfortable, it is understandable that $150,000 was considered to be a very substantial fortune, yet Soltow (1975:112) estimated that there were already 41 American millionaires in 1860, 545 in 1870, and, as we have seen, 1368 in New York City alone by 1898.

By 1890, small farms were being rapidly replaced by giant farms, and small businesses by giant corporations. With the closing of the frontier and the rise of manufacturing, about half the population had become urban, and most people needed income-producing jobs to survive. There were perhaps 25 million new poor who were unable to produce enough income to comfortably meet basic needs. During the twentieth century, further growth produced even more poverty.

Economic Elites and Urban Poverty, New York City, 1863–1914

All of the social stresses generated by rapid growth occurred in New York City during the nineteenth century, making this city an ideal place to examine scale and power issues. A remarkable geography of power had emerged in New York City by 1845, with city government, party politics, corporate finance, and massive private wealth situated side by side (see the box entitled "Machine Politics in New York City, 1845–1873"). On the lower end of Manhattan Island stood City Hall, immediately flanked on the East River side by Tammany Hall and on the Hudson River side by the residence of John Jacob Astor, then richest man in the country. The New York Stock Exchange was located half a mile to the south in the Wall Street financial district. By 1890, New York had become, after London, the largest and the wealthiest city in the world. Home of the Statue of Liberty, it was the primary port of entry for immigrants. It handled more than half of all U.S. international trade and provided headquarters for America's largest corporations. With 2.5 million people, New York was the nation's largest urban center, with the greatest ethnic and religious diversity. Perhaps most importantly from our perspective, it also had the most powerful economic elites and the worst urban slums in the country.

In 1890, New York's economic elites probably consisted of fewer than 2500 very wealthy individuals, representing no more than 0.5 percent of the city's households. The elite were a diverse lot, representing Anglo-American Protestants, German Christians, and German Jews. Many elites were members of aristocratic merchant and landholding families, while others were newly rich bankers, corporate entrepreneurs, and professionals. Members of these distinct elite groups sometimes had conflicting political and economic interests and belonged to different social, professional, and commercial associations. But they

Machine Politics in New York City, 1845–1873

By the mid-nineteenth century New York City had grown so large ordinary people could have little significant political influence as individuals. An organized political bureaucracy was required to select candidates and rally electoral support for them. The party system stood between individuals and the government and is often described as *machine politics*. For example, in New York City in 1845, the 68,000 potential voters out of the city's 400,000 people were effectively controlled by a Democratic party apparatus run by 2400 people. The party bureaucracy was organized on three levels, with a 51-man General Committee at the top and seventeen ward committees, each responsible for two to eight election districts of 500 voters (Gronowicz 1998). There were also dozens of party-affiliated associations that fostered an active social life for people at all levels of New York society.

The political machine in New York was called Tammany Hall, after the building where the General Committee met, which was owned by the Tammany Society, a politically oriented social club originally formed to assist immigrants. The Tammany machines selected candidates and brought out the votes for some ninety-one elected or appointed offices, from state governor and U.S. senators and representatives to police commissioner and street inspector. From 1868 to 1873, the political machine was completely controlled by William "Boss" Tweed, who previously had held a series of public offices in the U.S. Congress, the New York State Senate, and the City of New York. He gained control of the city treasury and used false accounting to systematically steal millions of dollars.

Boss Tweed and Tammany Hall became synonymous with bribery, corruption, and political patronage. But the Democratic party in New York cross-cut all social classes and reached out to small artisans and laborers, especially Irish Catholic immigrants. Because of its support for slavery, however, the party became outrageously racist toward the city's African Americans. Party politics in New York certainly helped working people adjust to the uncertainties of urban life, but it also helped the city's most powerful commercial interests expand their financial empires.

also were integrated by kinship and marriage ties, and all benefited from the tremendous economic growth that was occurring, especially in railroads, banking, oil, and manufacturing.

The wealthiest of the city's 200 or so most prominent citizens was John D. Rockefeller (1839–1937), who was personally worth perhaps $200 million in the 1890s. J. P. Morgan (1837–1913) probably ranked second, with an estate valued at $77.6 million in 1913. It is important to distinguish the personal wealth of

these superwealthy from their actual social, political, and economic power, which was represented by the total assets of the corporations they controlled and the foundations they endowed.

Rockefeller and Morgan were at the top of a web of interlocking financial imperia centered in New York. In 1904 investment analyst John Moody approvingly described the Rockefeller-Morgan "family tree" as an interconnected alliance of trusts that dominated the financial, commercial, and industrial interests of the coun-

FIGURE 12.8 The interlocking Rockefeller–Morgan commercial imperia of industrial trusts and financial institutions in 1904. (Moody 1904).

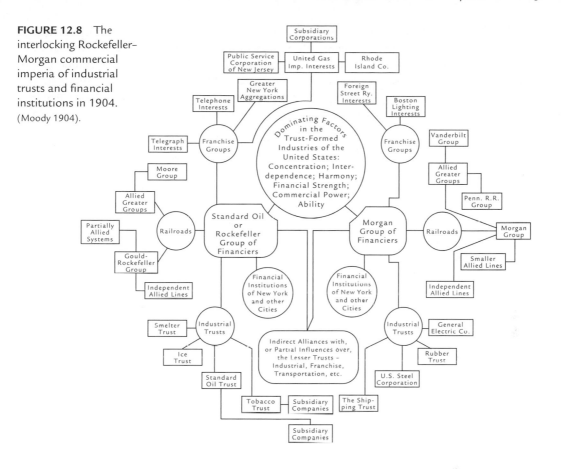

try (Figure 12.8). Trusts were the early form of holding companies. They were giant companies that owned other companies. Moody thought such concentrated power was good, inevitable, and a "law of nature." He argued, "[N]o amount of blind public opposition or restrictive legislation can prevent this constant change from small scale to large scale" (Moody 1904:44). Even more emphatically, he declared, "The modern trust is the natural outcome or evolution of society conditions and ethical standards which are recognized and established among men to-day as being necessary elements in the development of civilization" (Moody 1904:44).

Hearings held in Washington, D.C., in 1912–1913, by the House Subcommittee on Banking and Currency, the Pujo Committee, provided a rare glimpse of the financial power of J. P. Morgan.

Summaries of this material by Supreme Court Justice Louis Brandeis (1914) showed that as an investment banker operating through J. P. Morgan & Co., Morgan stood at the top of a complex web of commercial relationships. Through the directors of companies in which he held controlling interests, Morgan exerted direct and indirect influence over 34 large banks and trust companies, 10 insurance companies, 32 transportation systems, 12 public utilities, and 135 other corporations, with combined assets of $45 billion. His power was such that he virtually dominated all sectors of the national economy.

Morgan had effectively gained control over other people's money, such that he could assemble vast transfers of capital between "his" corporations and extract hefty commissions in the process. Decisions that he and his associates made influenced employment conditions and the well-being of millions of low-paid working people throughout the country. Morgan's economic focus was national and international. He had little interest in or influence over New York's domestic issues, although he was president of a prominent New York social club. As a principal owner of Manhattan's elevated railway line, Morgan unsuccessfully resisted the city's plans to build a publicly financed subway system. New York's elites were so divided on public policy that it was difficult for even one of the most powerful economic elites to impose his will everywhere.

Immigration caused the population of metropolitan New York to more than double between 1850 and 1880, and again between 1880 and 1910, providing a rental bonanza for slum landlords. There was enormous pressure on housing, and the large landowners responded by replacing single-family houses built on narrow lots with tenements housing three or more families, which would yield higher rents but at a much reduced quality of life for the residents. The costs and benefits in this development process were clear. The New York housing market was a free-market paradise, with no pesky building codes requiring fire escapes and the like to interfere with developers' natural desire to maximize profits. The result was shoddy, even dangerous construction and unhealthy, overpriced housing for most of the city's people, who were overwhelmingly poor. Social reformers condemned crowded living conditions as conducive to immorality among the poor. It took a series of cholera outbreaks, centered in the tenements, to enable reform-minded physicians to persuade the city to establish a Metropolitan Board of Health in 1866. The government was forced to grudgingly acknowledge that inferior housing was a public health problem.

Journalist photographer Jacob Riis (1904) vividly portrayed conditions in New York's crowded tenements in *How the Other Half Lives*. Riis succeeded in arousing public indignation that spurred the government to action. Investigators for the New York State Tenement House Commission found in 1900 that 2.3 million people,

approximately 70 percent of the population of metropolitan New York, lived in crowded, unsanitary tenements (DeForest and Veiller 1903). The average floor space in these small apartments approximated 4.7 square meters per person. This figure almost precisely matched the 4.6 square meters (10 by 10 feet) of floor space that Charles Booth (1892–1903) had used to identify the residences of the London poor. Remarkably, this was about half the floor space enjoyed by a typical Asháninka household. Furthermore, it was much less than the 6–10 square meters of floor space per person that seems to represent a crosscultural constant for all precommercial cultures (Brown 1987, Naroll 1962).

In Ward 10, the Jewish quarter, a forty-five-block area on Manhattan's Lower East Side, 76,000 people were living in three- to seven-story tenements, with as many as 200 people to a house (Figure 12.9). Buildings were dark and poorly ventilated, and many had only a single outside water tap and pit toilet for all families. Sometimes hallway water-closet toilets were situated on each floor to be shared by two to four families. There were no baths or showers. Not surprisingly, over one 5-year period, there were thirty-two cases of tuberculosis and thirteen cases of diphtheria in one sample block jammed with 2781 people, and 660 families requested public assistance.

These wretched living conditions made turn-of-the-century New York a center of labor unrest and union and socialist activism that eventually resulted in small increases in wages and acceptance of the 8-hour workday. Building codes were also gradually modified. The elites were often divided on what policies the city should pursue, which made it possible for working-class people to influence events with their votes. Some elites favored a form of municipal socialism in which tax dollars and private investment would improve the commercial prospects of the city by developing better public transit systems, public education, public health and housing, municipal government, and cultural institutions (Hammack 1982:56). The largest economic elites were reluctant to support reforms because they were

FIGURE 12.9 Model of a representative block in Ward 10, in Manhattan's Lower East Side, 1900.

suspicious of government involvement in the "free market," did not want their taxes to increase, and had much broader economic interests than in the city itself. Others blamed the city's problems on socialists, anarchists, immorality, and ethnic and religious diversity.

Social Power, Personal Imperia, and Family in the U.S., 1980–2003

In the last decades of the twentieth century, social power became even more concentrated in America as neoliberal economic policies made it easier for investors to seek the highest returns on financial capital. America has become a global economic and military superpower, but unlike societies in the ancient imperial world, it is not a totalitarian system. No single person, not the President, not the richest person, and not the CEO of the largest corporation commands the entire system. America is also not run by a small, secret, conspiratorial group. Rather, America is a heterarchy, with economic, political, ideological, and military power divided into multiple hierarchies controlled by various, often shifting elites.

In 2003 political power in the United States was commanded nationally by 630 top officials in the Federal Government, including the President, cabinet secretaries, Supreme Court Justices, Senators and Representatives, and the directors of government agencies. Although the country is a formal democracy, only 51 percent of eligible

voters voted in the 2000 presidential election. Federal expenditures were $2 trillion, and Federal financial wealth and property were worth some $7 trillion. The President also commanded the vastly powerful American military, with a $408 billion budget and 2.6 million active and reserve military personnel, many posted all over the world. The American military budget exceeded the expenditures of the next 29 countries ranked by troop strength, suggesting that some Americans seek global military supremacy (Mann 2003, Myers 2003). The United States had more than 1100 long-range ballistic missiles, including intercontinental (ICBMs) and submarine launched (SLBMs), and 315 strategic bombers, capable of delivering some 3500 nuclear warheads virtually anywhere in the world. These nuclear weapons of mass destruction were backed by massive, technologically superior conventional forces, giving America's military leaders the ability to project overwhelming military power or threats of violent force worldwide at will.

The American economy in 2002 was approximately $10 trillion in gross domestic product (GDP), the market value of all the goods and services produced in the United States. This was roughly one third of global GDP. The degree to which economic power was concentrated in the hands of the directors and beneficial owners of commercial business corporations is indicated by the $7.4 trillion in revenues flowing through the 500 largest publically traded corporations in

2001, which was more than 40 percent of all corporate revenues. Fortune 500 companies owned $19 trillion in assets. The 400 wealthiest American individuals in 2000 were collectively worth $946 billion. Those who commanded great personal wealth or the collective assets of giant corporations were able to shape the culture by their decisions to invest in certain activities, or to produce certain products.

Ideological power is the ability to influence what people know and believe. In America this power resides with the directors of media corporations, the religious institutions, government agencies, educational institutions, foundations, and various nonprofit organizations, as well as, perhaps most importantly, with those who directed $243 billion in national advertising in 2000. National advertising expenditures were more than half of the amount spent on all public education from kindergarten through high school. Forty percent of national advertising was expended by the top 100 advertisers, and nearly half was for television ads. The commercial broadcast media draws virtually all of its revenue from advertising. This means that radio and television are primarily marketing tools. The emphasis on television advertising is understandable, with Americans over 18 on the average watching 35 hours per week. The American media was concentrated in fewer than 20 corporations controlling most of the television, radio, publishing, music, and film in the country (McChesney 2000). This meant that a very small number of people determined what Americans watched, read, and heard, and the primary message was that consumption of certain brands brings happiness. Advertising manipulates individual self-interest and is less concerned with the interests of society, because society is not a market. The other role of the mass media is "manufacturing consent," or persuading people to believe that the existing culture is the best possible way of life and that those in charge are making the right decisions (Herman and Chomsky 2002).

When any power elite uses the media primarily to sell products, it becomes an unreliable source of information about the real world. Reliance on television is especially problematic because it is more likely to offer highly selective, emotional images and contrived events rather than objective, in-depth information, that can be intellectually interpreted (Mander 1978, Boorstin 1985).

America is too large and complex for one person to rule, but individual elites can move between power hierarchies, commanding personal imperia that crosscut different power domains. They can use their personal connections to enormous advantage. This is not different from the personal networks of power that exist in all societies. However, because America is such a large-scale system, with so much concentrated power, the potential for unintended negative consequences of misguided decision-making is very high. Conflicts of interest and corruption are also part of the system. Furthermore, elites do not always follow the rules (Simon 1999). The problem is that mistakes by well-intended super-elites commanding a super-power can affect the entire world.

Giant commercial corporations now dominate American life. Corporations are given the same rights as individuals, but unlike individuals and sole-proprietorship businesses, corporations can live forever and grow ever more powerful. Corporations also are not limited to particular places, and they can project their commercial power throughout the world. Furthermore, corporate structure and limited liability makes it difficult to hold corporations responsible for the total costs of their activities, even when they are criminal.

The scale of giant corporations can be illustrated by Philip Morris, the fourteenth-largest industrial corporation in the world in 1991 and seventh-largest in the United States. Philip Morris sold a staggering $50 billion worth of products in 1993, an amount far exceeding the national budgets of many countries. As a huge conglomerate, Philip Morris contained some 222 operating companies, subsidiaries, units, and divisions in the United States, and forty-two countries. From top to bottom, there were at least four major organizational levels, such that the corporation, with its 210,000 employees worldwide, was structurally as complex as a political state. Philip Morris produced hundreds of food items. The company has had an enormous impact on American life through its employment practices, its choice of plant locations, and the health effects of the products it markets.

By 2002 Philip Morris's directors had restructured the company into a giant conglomerate composed of Philip Morris USA, Philip Morris International, Kraft Foods, and Philip Morris Capital Corporation, all under the new parent company name of Altria. The company had expanded its global reach, and shed 44,000 employees since 1993, but its revenue had risen to $80 billion.

Thomas R. Dye (1983) and a team of graduate students at Florida State University painstakingly compiled and sorted biographical data on elites and concluded that 5778 individuals controlled America's giant corporations, the federal government, the news media, and the primary cultural institutions in the early 1980s. Some of these people were elected officials, but many are completely unknown outside the networks of power. Similarly, a very small number of owners and managers exercise real power over American business. My investigation of Securities and Exchange Commission filings in 1994 revealed that a mere ten people helped direct thirty-seven American companies whose combined assets of $2 trillion represented nearly 10 percent of all corporate assets in the country. One individual directed five companies with $549 billion in total assets, or 2.5 percent the national total. In 1995, a mere 600 people directed America's fifty largest companies, accounting for 16 percent of the country's business revenues and exceeding the combined revenues of all noncorporate businesses and nonprofit organizations. This change in the scale of business enterprise transforms commercial life in small American communities, making participation in markets difficult for many small-business owners. Concentrated wealth of this magnitude gives enormous freedom to a privileged few to produce and direct the economic processes that shape our future.

The Carlyle Group, a private equity corporation based in Washington, D.C., is a good example of how super-elite personal imperia work in America and globally. In 2003 Carlyle's directors

managed $17.5 billion in investments, primarily in private business and real estate throughout the world. Its principal investors were a few hundred high net worth individuals (HNWIs), with $5 million or more to invest, including members of America's 400 wealthiest. Carlyle has been characterized as an "iron triangle," because it conducts business by exploiting connections between powerful individuals who have held high ranking positions in the American military, the Federal Government, and private corporations, including important defense contractors (Briody 2003). Along with CEOs from major corporations, among Carlyle's senior officers and advisors in 2003 were former U.S. Secretaries of State and Defense, a former Director of the Federal Office of Management and Budget, and former Chairmen of the U.S. Federal Communications Commission and the Securities and Exchange Commission. Since its founding in 1987, the Carlyle group has included among its members and advisors former President George W. Bush, former UK Prime Minister John Major, and present U.S. Secretary of State Colin Powell. Carlyle associates play multiple roles as investors, corporate officers, and often as former or future government officials. This is much like the "fiscal-military state" under early European capitalism, and creates wealth by capitalizing on personal connections and insider knowledge that crosscuts power domains.

Anthropologist Marvin Harris (1981) attributed increased crime and family breakdowns to the rise of oligopoly in American business and the related shift from industrial production to services and information. These economic processes accelerated in the United States during the 1980s and 1990s, as changes in tax laws, deregulation of financial institutions, and the removal of global trade barriers prompted giant corporations to increase their financial power through leveraged buyouts and downsizing. This vast transformation, which has been called **deindustrialization**

deindustrialization The replacement of factory employment with service sector employment in formerly industrial countries as production jobs are moved to low-wage countries.

(Bluestone and Harrison 1982), parallels the social disruptions caused by the Industrial Revolution. Millions of American workers are losing their manufacturing jobs and are being forced to take low-paying, in-person service jobs. At the same time, as the economy grows, financial markets soar, and the privileged few—wealthy investors and corporate executives—prosper. Upper-middle-class professionals may use "assortive mating"—marrying another well-paid professional—to double their income and join the financial elites (Lasch 1995). Meanwhile, downsized production workers and service workers can gamble on the lottery.

Giant corporations, because of their size, can eliminate competition and control markets to such an extent that locally owned businesses may have difficulty surviving. Large corporations also derive a significant proportion of their profits from buying and selling smaller corporations, rather than directly from production, and this reduces their long-term commitment to consumers, employees, or the local communities where their factories are located.

The increasing financial power of giant corporations is associated with a loss of power and control in local communities. Anthropologist James Toth (1992), who conducted ethnographic research on a small Pennsylvania town, found that the deindustrialization process reduced economic decision making by local businesspeople. Small businesses, local manufacturing plants, and independent contractors were being replaced by subsidiary electronics firms, shopping malls, banks, and realty agencies controlled by conglomerates headquartered in other cities, other states, and even other countries. This process drained financial capital from the local community.

Anthropologist Katherine Newman (1988, 1993) estimates that 10.6 million Americans lost their jobs to corporate downsizing between 1981 and 1992. To assess the impact of this process, she gathered life histories and conducted intensive interviews with hundreds of Americans, including members of sixty families in a suburban New Jersey community. Newman found that many middle-class people who were experienc-

ing declining living standards felt that the American Dream of continuous economic progress was passing them by. They accepted this as evidence of personal failure, rather than attributing it to larger economic forces. Anthropologist June Nash (1989, 1994) found the same passive acceptance of economic misfortune among the 5000 workers in Massachusetts who were laid off when General Electric moved their plant to Canada in 1986. Displaced workers may find lower-paying jobs, but they are often forced to sell their homes, and their households experience the stress of downward mobility.

The vast changes in American business have directly impacted family life. Few married women worked outside of the home in the 1890s, but since 1965 the declining value of wages has forced many women to seek employment in an effort to maintain a constant standard of living. Economic stresses are reflected in higher divorce rates and an increase in single-parent households. Furthermore, careful, large-scale statistical studies have demonstrated a direct relationship between income level and stability and mortality (Gregorio et al. 1997). Differences in social class mean that in contemporary America, just as in nineteenth-century London and New York, well-paid professionals and managers live longer than laborers. Government reports have consistently shown that poor children are unlikely to see doctors or be vaccinated, and poor adults are more likely to be in poor health, to lack health insurance, and to die from chronic diseases (National Center for Health Statistics 1998). Medical researcher Richard G. Wilkinson (1996, 1997) argues that a high level of social inequality raises mortality at lower social levels, because inequality reduces social cohesion and increases stress. This connection between social cohesion, stress, and health is strongly supported by a 30-year longitudinal study of health in Roseto, Pennsylvania, an Italian American village of 1500 people, from approximately 1960 to 1990 (Wolf and Bruhn 1993). The Roseto villagers were the descendants of immigrants who came to Pennsylvania in the 1880s. Researchers found that, as long as their family and clan structure remained strong, the villagers were almost

TABLE 12.3   AMERICAN HOUSEHOLDS BY ECONOMIC POWER, CLASS, AND IMPERIA, 1998

Classes	Economic Type	Income Range	Net Worth	Households	Portfolio	Imperia
Capitalist 8%	Directors	$1 million+	$ millions– $ billions	0.4 million	$ millions– $ trillions	Super-Elite 0.5%
	Owners	$100,000– $999,999	$100,000– $ millions	5.6 million	$ millions	Elite 8%
Producer- Consumer 92%	High Consumers skilled wage & salary, small entrepreneurs	$10,000– $99,999	median $60,000	55.8 million	none	Maintenance 79%
	Low Consumers unskilled wage- earners	<$10,000	median $3,600	8.9 million		Poor 13%

completely free from heart attacks. The incidence of heart attacks increased sharply when they began to lose social cohesion in the mid-1960s, even though other risk factors did not significantly change.

Americans are reluctant to talk about social class, but researchers such as Ferdinand Lundberg (1937, 1968), C. Wright Mills (1956), and G. William Domhoff (1967, 1983) have concluded that a very small upper class, perhaps the top 0.5 percent of the country, enjoys a disproportionate share of the benefits of the American economy and have a disproportionate influence over events. Indeed, in 1998, the $727 billion in combined wealth held by the 400 richest Americans was more than sixty times the wealth held by all the colonists in 1774, on the eve of the American Revolution (Jones 1980: Table 3.1). Many of the wealthiest Americans know one another and may interact socially, but they no longer form a cohesive, self-conscious social class. They share a common interest in perpetuating economic growth but may disagree on details of political policy.

In my own analysis of the well-being of American households in 1998 (Bodley 2003:46–53), I found that the top 8 percent, about 6 million households, were elites and super-elites with incomes of $100,000 or more, and net worths ranging into the millions and billions of dollars (Table 12.3). They were America's capitalists.

They owned approximately half of the personal wealth in the country, especially income generating property and financial assets, from which they received unearned income, and the luxury of saving and investing. Other households were producer-consumers. They were dependent on wages and salaries from their employers for their livelihoods, but had little power to influence their conditions of employment. The median net worth of the middle 79 percent of the population who were maintenance level was only $60,000. Most children could not inherit a significant estate. Upward mobility was difficult for producer-consumers, because, as in early modern England, even middle-income households were forced to spend most of their income on maintenance. An Asháninka visiting America in 1998 would have been amazed by the level of social inequality. He would also have been surprised to discover that more than 10 percent of American adults lived alone in single-person households; 18 percent of family households had no husband present.

The distribution of social power in America clearly seems to be the result of elite-directed growth processes. This interpretation is supported by ethnographic research on the well-being of households in eastern Washington state showing an association between growth in the size of urban places and increasing concentration of property ownership and poverty (see the box entitled "Property, Growth, and Power in the Palouse, 1997").

Property, Growth, and Power in the Palouse, 1997

I examined the well-being of households in different-sized communities in the Palouse region of eastern Washington State to test whether wealth-producing growth, and the resulting increases in population and economic value, produced more poor households (Bodley 1999). I also wondered if there would be local-level evidence that growth was directed by the people who most benefited from increases in community scale.

Rather than relying on census data on income, intrusive survey questionnaires, or official definitions of poverty, I used publicly available property assessments to measure the well-being of Palouse households. I inferred that households owning property assessed at less than $10,000 would be too poor to easily meet their basic needs. Households owning $10,000 or more but less than $75,000 in property could maintain themselves comfortably but would have difficulty saving. Households with $75,000 or more in property would be able to save, invest, and steadily increase their economic level.

By carefully sorting through computerized data from the county assessors, I found that individuals owned nearly $10 billion worth of urban property in the Palouse. This was sufficient to put every household comfortably above the maintenance level, but instead the top 20 percent of owner-residents actually owned nearly 70 percent of all individually owned property. Many of the wealthiest property owners did not even live in the Palouse. Incredibly, the top three owners held more property than all 10,200 people who lived in the twenty smallest towns.

Most significantly, community scale proved to be the best predictor of household well-being. More households were better off in small urban places with fewer than 2500 people. The average value of property ownership increased with community scale, but the wealthiest households gained disproportionately, and there was an enormous increase in the absolute number of poor households in larger towns. There were proportionately more maintenance-level households and more home ownership in the smallest villages. There were few poor villagers, and they were better off than the poor in larger places. The communities that grew the least showed the least wealth concentration and large property owners appeared to have less influence on municipal government. Property elites who generated wealth from the higher property values that accompanied urban growth needed progrowth municipal policies to expand city boundaries and change zoning restrictions. Not surprisingly, the communities that had grown the most proved to be places where big property owners were the most represented in the municipal government.

These findings suggest that in this case, wealth-promoting government policies were designed by the wealthy to serve the needs of the wealthy. Growth appeared to work against the interests of a significant number of households because elevated property values priced low-income households out of the housing market.

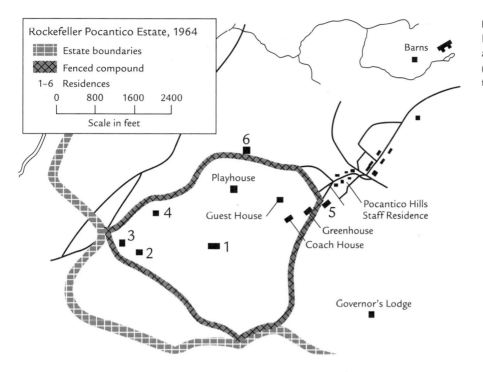

FIGURE 12.10 The Rockefeller family estate at Pocantico, 1964. (SOURCE: Estate diagram from Pyle 1964.)

The Rockefeller Dynasty

The remarkable Rockefeller family (Figures 12.10, 12.11) illustrates the extent to which wealth can be amassed in a commercial culture, be transmitted across four generations, and be used to exert enormous cultural, political, and commercial influence in the United States and in the world. The patriarch of the family, John D. Rockefeller (1839–1937), founded the Standard Oil Company in 1870 and gained monopolistic control over the American petroleum industry. The government dissolved the Standard Oil trust in 1911, but John D. Sr. had already become fabulously wealthy. In 1913, he established the Rockefeller Foundation with an endowment of $100 million "to promote the well-being of mankind throughout the world." Through the foundation and other charitable organizations, the family promoted worldwide public health, Christian missions, technical research, and public education (including anthropology) on an unprecedented scale. By the 1930s, John D. Sr. had controlling interests over a vast financial em-

pire consisting of stockholdings and directorships in some 287 companies, with assets estimated at over $20 billion at that time (Colby and Dennett 1995, Collier and Horowitz 1976, Rochester 1936:56).

The Rockefeller family's personal estate has been wisely stewarded by the family and has grown significantly over the years. In 1998, *Fortune* magazine estimated the family's combined wealth at $8 billion (Gorham, Kafka, and Neelakantan 1998). The Rockefeller Foundation was the nation's tenth-largest foundation with assets of $2.7 billion, and the Rockefeller Brothers Fund was worth $409 million (*The Foundation Directory,* 1998:xi). The family's interests were long centered in Chase Manhattan Bank, the International Basic Economy Corporation, and the Rockefeller Center in New York. But their interests were dispersed in a complex web of national and international financial holdings and properties that included mines in Chile and oil and supermarkets throughout Latin America. John D. Sr. and John D. Jr. maintained residences in

FIGURE 12.11 The Rockefeller family genealogy and household groups in 1964. Numbers correspond to houses shown in Figure 12.10. Households 5–9 were located within, or adjacent to the Pocantico Estate, but outside the fenced compound.

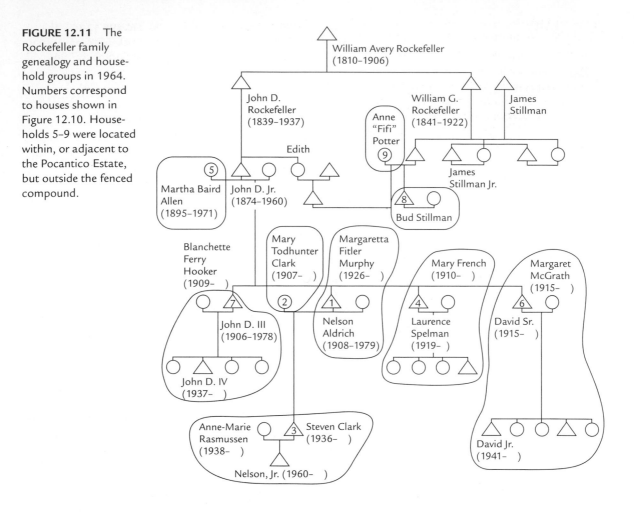

Manhattan, New Jersey, Maine, and Florida, and Nelson owned huge ranches in Venezuela and Brazil. But most members of the family lived on the 3600-acre Pocantico estate, 25 miles north of downtown Manhattan (Figures 12.10 and 12.11). This vast estate was carefully consolidated in various family trust funds, many of them managed through a family corporation, Rockefeller Family and Associates, headquartered in Rockefeller Center. Rockefeller family members were influential in building the World Trade Center and donated the property for the United Nations building. The Rockefellers also have been leaders in nature conservation and the arts, and their public policy interests have been fostered through support for conferences and organizations such as the Council on Foreign Relations.

The Rockefellers generally did not hold political offices, although Nelson served as governor of New York from 1958 to 1970, and as vice president of the United States from 1974 to 1977. Nelson's brother Winthrop served as governor of Arkansas from 1967 to 1971 and as lieutenant governor in 1998. John D. IV was a U.S. senator and governor of West Virginia. Many close associates of the family, including Henry Kissinger, Walt Rostow, and Dean Rusk, served in high-level appointments in the federal government.

SUMMARY

America is unquestionably the dominant economic and political-military power in the global system and is viewed by its own citizens as an ideal cultural model for the entire world. However, certain aspects of the culture raise important questions about its effectiveness in providing for the health and well-being, social cohesion, and stability for all of its citizens. The American cultural ideal of invidualism contrasts sharply with the Chinese emphasis on kinship, which is more representative of tribal cultures. Individualism can make life less secure for Americans.

Economic growth is a crucial feature of America's cosmology. Economic growth can make it more difficult for any culture to maintain a balance with natural resources and ecosystems. Ethnohistoric examples from the nation's founding through the nineteenth century reveal the contradictions between the concentrated social power produced by growth in economic and social scale and the American emphasis on democracy, economic freedom, and equal opportunity. The key cultural transformation, which provided the real foundation of American culture, was in the evolution of business into ever-large-scale organizational forms that were capable of taking full commercial advantage of industrial technology.

The ethnographic example of the industrial village of Rockdale, Pennsylvania, from 1825 to 1865 illustrates the social inequality that sustained America's commercial development. The ethnographic examples of factory farming and cattle raising show how the commercialization and industrialization of food production and consumption transformed the organization of American life. Inequality in the distribution of economic power is perhaps the greatest threat to social cohesion and cultural continuity in America. Inequality in the United States involves differential access to status and prestige, productive resources, income, and economic and political power generally. The existence of this kind of inequality is an objective contradiction in a country that enjoys formal democracy and a high degree of personal freedom. American culture demonstrates that the human problem of social inequality, which seems to be an intrinsic feature of states, is not necessarily solved by capitalist market economies and continuous economic expansion. It is important to understand the cultural significance of inequality in America and the way in which production and consumption is carried out, because at a global level the wealthiest industrial nations occupy the top of an international hierarchy of nations in which most of humanity is desperately impoverished.

STUDY QUESTIONS

1. Discuss the cultural ecological features of factory farming in comparison with less intensive subsistence systems. Refer to monocrop, Green Revolution, energy input–output ratios, energy subsidy, social consequences, stability, and ecosystem degradation.

2. How is economic and social power distributed in the United States?

3. In what sense is it legitimate to speak of a Cattle Complex in the United States? Make specific comparisons between the role of cattle in the United States and their role in an East African cattle culture. Briefly describe the pathway that American cattle follow as commodities from production to consumption.

4. Using the American beef industry as an example, show how market forces influence specific production and processing practices and promote inequality and social conflict.

5. Discuss how the realities of American society reflect American cosmology.

6. Use the Rockdale case study to illustrate the human impact of industrial development and wage labor.

7. What economic interests did the Founding Fathers represent? Were these interests reflected in the American Constitution?

8. To what extent is it reasonable to speak of social class in America? What are the correlates of social class?

9. Use New York City in 1890 to illustrate the urban problems of particular forms of growth.
10. To what extent is American growth from 1790 to the present related to the distribution of social power?
11. What cultural ecological factors contributed to the importance of beef in the United States, and how do these factors compare with the influence of symbolic and ideological factors over dietary practices?
12. Describe how scarcity and consumption are culturally constructed in America.

SUGGESTED READING

DeVita, Philip R., and James D. Armstrong. 1993. *Distant Mirrors: America as a Foreign Culture*. Belmont, Calif.: Wadsworth. Interpretations of American culture and descriptions of their experiences as outsiders by fourteen foreign scholars, primarily anthropologists.

Domhoff, G. William. 1998. *Who Rules America?: Power and Politics in the Year 2000*. Mountain View, Calif.: Mayfield. An updated version of Domhoff's 1967 book about elite domination of the American political economy.

Hsu, Francis L. K. 1981. *Americans and Chinese: Passage to Difference*. Honolulu: The University Press of Hawaii. A comparative analysis of American and Chinese culture by a Chinese psychological anthropologist.

Phillips, Kevin. 2002. *Wealth and Democracy: A Political History of the American Rich*. New York: Broadway Books. This is a detailed historical overview and critical analysis of wealth concentration in America since 1776, by a leading authority on political and economic issues.

Spradley, James P., and Michael A. Rynkiewich. 1975. *The Nacirema: Readings on American Culture*. Boston: Little, Brown. A collection of ethnographically based studies of diverse aspects of American culture.

Economic globalization has forced millions
of people into urban slums and squatter
settlements.

13

The Impoverished World

Learning Objectives

After studying this chapter you should be able to do the
following.

1. Describe the ethnographic realities of daily life in the
   impoverished world based on examples from Brazil and
   Bangladesh, identifying the political and economic factors
   that create these conditions.

2. Describe the human consequences of the Green Revolution in Bangladesh.

3. Describe the different approaches that the United Na-
   tions and its specialized agencies, such as the World
   Bank, have taken toward global poverty since 1945.
   Assess their effectiveness.

4. Describe the ideological assumptions of utopian capitalism and test its predictions of progress against the
   evidence.

5. Explain why many anthropologists do not consider
   overpopulation to be the primary cause of poverty.

6. Describe the American government's official approach
   to international development since 1945 in comparison
   with UN agencies, and development anthropologists.

7. Describe and assess the effectiveness of radical alternative development strategies that directly empower
   the poor.

417

During the decades following World War II, the disparity in material welfare between the wealthy industrial nations and the rest of the world steadily widened, as did the gap between rich and poor within individual countries. Even as decolonization and technological progress proceeded, increasing millions of people throughout the world came to live in absolute poverty. By 1980, an estimated 730 million people (excluding China) were living on diets considered inadequate by international standards and had extremely limited access to material resources. By the late 1980s, dramatic increases in poverty were occurring throughout the world. Real living standards plunged while public spending for social services declined as many countries found themselves deeply in debt to First World lenders. When the new millennium began, 1.2 billion people were thought to be living in extreme poverty. That was roughly the entire population of the world in 1850. Nearly a billion urban people did not have access to basic sanitation. Viewed objectively, this would not seem to be an adaptive form of cultural evolution and lends more credibility to the theory that economic globalization is elite-directed.

Development, as it has been practiced throughout most of the twentieth century, has systematically undermined the self-maintenance abilities of rural communities, leaving them highly vulnerable to outside exploitation. Nearly half of the global population was urbanized, but the lives of most were totally dependent on sources of employment and material resources that they did not control. The primary ideological justification for elite-directed economic growth was that it would ultimately improve everyone's lives, but the outcome of decades of development suggests that a fundamental reassessment of the entire issue is required.

This chapter begins with a close look at the human realities of impoverishment using case material from Brazil and Bangladesh, where communities have been impoverished by technologically based development programs that leave grossly unequal power structures in place. Next, we examine the international development establishment since 1945, focusing on the United Nations and related agencies and the United States. We examine the complex structure of development at the global level, considering the flow of resources, costs, and benefits, and show why development often works against the interests of local communities. Next, we discuss diverse anthropological perspectives on development, peasantries, and poverty. Finally, we present a famous anthropological experiment in community development in the Andes to show that even when local power structures are altered, development that undermines the unique strengths of local communities may still leave rural peoples impoverished.

DAILY REALITY IN THE IMPOVERISHED WORLD

National-level statistics show that for job-dependent people, low wages and underemployment produce malnutrition, high infant mortality, and wretched living conditions on a vast scale. However, the impersonal statistics diminish the human reality. A close look at real people, households, and communities gives a more complete view of the impoverishment produced by elite-directed growth in the commercial world. The harsh reality is that when the quest for economic growth and wealth accumulation dominates the humanization process, children may be deprived of food, their most urgent human need. By contrast, tribal cultures placed human needs first and guaranteed food security to everyone.

Infant Mortality in Brazil

During the 1980s, anthropologist Nancy Scheper-Hughes (1992) conducted extensive research on women living in a northeast Brazilian squatter town, which she called Bom Jesus. The growth of giant sugar plantations in this region since the 1950s had pushed subsistence farmers off their lands, forcing them to survive on inadequate wages. During the 1980s, men who worked in the sugarcane fields were paid the legal minimum of $10 a week, while women received $5. At the same time, a family of four required $40 a week to meet their minimum food needs, because even the most basic foods, such as beans, could no longer be grown locally. As a result, sugar workers and their families had to adapt to a situation of chronic malnutrition. Babies were dying, just as Adam Smith (1776) had predicted, but unfortunately wages were not improving because Brazil's poor had little political or economic power.

The impoverished sugarcane workers were surviving on an average of 1500 calories a day, virtually concentration camp rations. Regional statistics showed that 80 percent of the population, some 30 million people, constituted an impoverished underclass. Surprisingly, Scheper-Hughes (1992) found that people were actually able to survive under these conditions, even though two-thirds of their children were clinically undernourished and one-fourth were nutritionally dwarfed by their starvation diets. Women experienced high rates of miscarriage, and many of their babies were born underweight. Most disturbing was Scheper-Hughes' discovery that in 1987, infants in the community of Bom Jesus were dying at the rate of 211 per 1000. By 1998 this figure was exceeded only by national-level infant mortality rates in 5 African countries—Malawi, Mali, Mozambique, Niger, and Sierra Leone—with figures ranging from 213 to 283. This compared with a low of 5 in Japan, Sweden, and Switzerland. The reality of this human cost of social inequality is partially buried in the regional statistic showing an aggregate infant mortality rate for northeast Brazil of 116 per 1000. This is still a very high rate, but even this figure is obscured by Brazil's national-level statistic of just 57 infant deaths per 1000 in 1993. The same obfuscation occurs with statistics that use per capita GNP (gross national product) as the primary measure of economic growth and prosperity. Indeed, Brazil has experienced an economic miracle. In 1971, its total GNP was just $421 per capita; by 1993, it had reached $2930 per capita. In 2003 the World Bank ranked Brazil as an upper-middle income

nation with a per capita GNP of $3070, even though, based on 1997 figures, the Bank estimated that 8 million Brazilians were living in "extreme poverty," with the equivalent of less than $1 a day per capita, and 28 million were "poor," with less than $2 a day per capita. The Bom Jesus household of 4 was living on 54 cents per capita per day.

Low wages put Brazilian working families in a terrible dilemma. Anthropologists Daniel Gross and Barbara Underwood (1971) investigated sisal plantation workers in the same region. They found that sisal workers, like sugarcane workers, were forced to buy the cheapest high-calorie food and systematically starve their children to give their working men enough food energy to keep them in the fields.

Protein-calorie deficiency diseases, such as kwashiorkor and marasmus, cause a wasting away of body tissues and have dramatic effects on children (Trowell 1954). Malnutrition is also known to damage the developing brain during early infancy (Montagu 1972), and it can inhibit a child's intellectual ability by making the child less active. Fortunately, new research suggests that some of these effects are reversible if malnourished children can be given adequate nutrition early enough (Brown and Pollitt 1996).

Real detective work is required to measure the actual human cost of poverty. Scheper-Hughes visited the local cemetery and obtained the handwritten birth and death records from the registry books in Bom Jesus to learn how many babies were dying. She also collected full reproductive histories from 100 women and found that an average older (post-menopausal) woman had seen 4.7 of her children die. During the worst conditions, the infant mortality rate in Bom Jesus soared to 493 per 1000 in 1 year.

The women of Bom Jesus certainly understood the general nature of their impoverishment. As one woman declared, "Our children die because we are poor and hungry" (Scheper-Hughes 1992:313). However, similar to laid-off factory workers in the United States, the poor of Bom Jesus blamed themselves. They treated their own poor health as a problem of "nerves," which could be treated with tranquilizers and vitamins purchased at the pharmacy. Scheper-Hughes is emphatic about the real causes of sickness and death in Bom Jesus:

> I do not want to quibble over words, but what I have been seeing on the Alto de Cruzeiro [the slum in Bom Jesus] for two and a half decades is more than "malnutrition," and it is politically as well as economically caused, although in the absence of overt political strife or war. Adults, it is true, might be described as "chronically undernourished," in a weakened and debilitated state, prone to infections and opportunistic diseases. But it is overt hunger and starvation that one sees in babies and small children, the victims of a "famine" that is endemic, relentless, and political-economic in origin. (1992:146)

The global financialization process itself has intensified the human costs of impoverishment. The Brazilian government borrowed heavily to finance economic growth and cut expenditures on public health in 1985 to help make its loan payments.

Medical anthropologist Paul Farmer is both a physician and an anthropologist and has worked among the poorest peoples in Haiti since 1983. He found conditions in Haiti as extreme as in the Brazilian northeast. National figures showed 65 percent of the Haitian people as officially poor in 1987. Haitians worked on coffee plantations for 7 to 15 cents per day and faced an epidemic of tuberculosis and AIDS, as well as hunger, rape, and political torture (Farmer 1994, 2001, 2003). Historically, Haitian poverty was preceded by the extermination of the Amerindians by Spanish invaders in the sixteenth century, followed by the importation of African slaves by the English and French in the eighteenth-century trade triangle, and finally by repeated episodes of political violence and rule by tyrannical dictators in the twentieth century.

Farmer describes the everyday condition of the Haitian poor as **structural violence**. This means that poverty involves more than economic deprivation, and it calls attention to the inequities of social power that cause this kind of pre-

ventable human suffering. Structural violence means that relatively more powerful individuals are socially and culturally able to violate the most fundamental of human social, economic, civil and political rights of less powerful individuals and communities, resulting in human suffering, loss of human dignity, torture, rape, disease, malnutrition, vulnerability, and death. Structural violence includes both the infrastructural dimensions of inadequate income and insufficient resources, as well as the tyrannical use of state political and military power to oppress poor people, the inhumane use of concentrated economic power by economic elites, and superstructural forms of oppression based on race, gender, and ethnicity. Structural violence is produced by dangerous concentrations of social power, which throughout human history have been the predictable outcome of elite-directed growth.

The scale of structural violence in the twentieth century was unprecedented. Political rulers caused the deaths of perhaps as many as 200 million people through direct violence in wars, genocidal massacres, and internal repression, disproportionately targeting the poor and powerless. This was more than the entire population of the world a mere 1500 years ago (Rummel 1997). The Nazis killed some 21 million civilians between 1933 and 1945, and the Soviets some 62 million between 1917 and 1987 (Rummel 1997:4, 70). This level of violence was made possible by the availability of fossil fuels and new armaments produced by giant commercial corporations.

Land and Food in Impoverished Bangladesh

The following pair of quotes encapsulate the way impoverishment was experienced by many south Asian villages and identify the commercial processes involved:

> Between 1933 and 1960 the village became poorer, and was polarized into two groups of households, one owning insufficient land to support an average household, and another owning a sufficient or excessive amount of it. (Van Schendel 1981:82)

Thus, international systems of production and finance are changing the ways that the rich and poor [of Bangladesh] eat and lead their lives.
(Lindenbaum 1987:436)

Bangladesh, formerly East Pakistan (1947–1971), is a primarily Muslim nation centered on the Ganges–Brahmaputra delta region known as East Bengal, in the northeast corner of the Indian subcontinent at the head of the Bay of Bengal. In 1990, the World Bank listed Bangladesh as one of the world's poorest nations, fifth from the bottom with a per-capita GNP of $170 (World Bank 1988–1995).

Given such precarious economic conditions, it is not surprising that several hundred thousand people died in famines in Bangladesh in 1974. In 1996 one-third of the Bangladeshi population was officially below the national poverty line, but by international standards 35 million people were living in extreme poverty on less than $1 per capita per day, and 95 million were poor at less than $2 per capita per day—this is more than the entire population of the neolithic tribal world. Fifty-six percent of children under five were malnourished. Nearly half of adult men, and 70 percent of women were illiterate and thus disadvantaged in a commercial world. Nevertheless, the economy was growing at 5 percent a year, and by 2001 Bangladesh had more than doubled its per capita GDP to $360. Bangladesh remained in the low-income global rank of nations even though it had received enormous amounts of development aid from international lenders and assistance from nongovernmental organizations (NGOs), including $13.8 billion in Official Development Aid (ODA) from 1982 to 1988, and 4.6 million tons of food aid from the United States from 1985 to 1988. The Bangladesh experience suggests that economic growth and development assistance may not reduce poverty when the structure of social inequality remains unchanged.

As part of the UN-sponsored Millennium Development Goals, the government of Bangladesh published a Poverty Reduction Strategy Program (PRSP) in 2003 calling for "eradicating hunger, chronic food insecurity, and extreme destitu-

tion . . ." The government wanted to cut in half the absolute number of poor, achieve universal primary education for boys and girls, eliminate gender disparity in education, gain large reductions in infant mortality, child malnutrition, and maternal mortality, make reproductive health services available to everyone, reduce or eliminate social violence, and prevent environmental degradation (Bangladesh 2003:7–8). These were admirable goals, but the "Pro-Poor" growth measures advocated by planners included more intensive rice production, biotechnology, more information technology, increased **foreign direct investment** (FDI), and "reforming" state-owned enterprises, including utilities, by privatization. These elite-directed measures were in line with the New Growth, neoliberal economic policies prevailing among globalization planners in the United States. Such measures would further increase scale, and seem unlikely to transform the underlying cultural structures of inequality.

To better understand poverty in Bangladesh it will be helpful to review its historical development. Under the Muslim rulers of the Mughal Empire (sixteenth to eighteenth centuries), East Bengal supported a prosperous cotton industry. The peasantry collectively controlled the land and remained economically self-sufficient, although they had to pay taxes to the zamindars, the title of local elites who were the appointed agents of the Muslim state. Shortly after the British completed their conquest of the region in 1765, they legally recognized the zamindar tax collectors as the rural landowners. Turning the zamindars into landlords, as well as tax collectors, amplified village-level inequalities. However, by giving the zamindars more power, it also made it easier

---

structural violence Human suffering that is the direct result of social and cultural structures that enable more powerful individuals to violate the basic human rights of less powerful individuals.

foreign direct investment When businesses headquartered in a given country buy productive assets in another country and retain control over them.

for the new British rulers to maintain political stability and ensured a steady flow of taxes and profits for the shareholders of the British East India Company. The British also suppressed the indigenous cotton industry and converted the peasantry into agricultural laborers for the production of jute as an export crop to supply British-owned mills in Calcutta and England.

Thus, preexisting social structures created by state authority laid the foundation for the profound impoverishment of Bangladesh in the twentieth century. Despite various changes in the central government and apparent reforms in land laws, rural elites have tenaciously maintained their grip over the best agricultural land in Bangladesh. Their favored social standing, which ultimately was supported by the state, permitted them to benefit at the expense of their less-favored fellow villagers when agricultural development programs became important during the 1970s. Thus, Bangladesh demonstrates that the incorporation of a regional state into the global system can increase internal inequality and reduce the quality of life for much of the population (Figure 13.1).

The impoverishment process in Bangladesh is well documented at the village level in some two dozen modern ethnographic studies (for example, see Hartmann and Boyce 1983, Jansen 1986, Van Schendel 1981). A representative case is Goborgari, a single village described by the Dutch researcher Willem Van Schendel (1981).

Goborgari is a Bengali-speaking, mixed Hindu and Muslim village situated on a level alluvial plain north of the Ganges and west of the Brahmaputra River in northern Bangladesh. Goborgari was primarily settled by immigrants during the nineteenth and early twentieth centuries. A government survey showed that in 1933 Goborgari was a small village of nineteen relatively egalitarian and self-sufficient farming households. There were no landless households and few large landholders, and the average acreage per household stood at approximately 4.3 acres (1.7 hectares), which was adequate for basic needs. The situation had changed dramatically by 1977. The

FIGURE 13.1   Bangladeshi village. Bangladesh was the fifth-poorest nation in the world in 1990 according to the World Bank. Millions of impoverished people, such as these villagers, live in the flood-prone Ganges–Brahmaputra delta.

population had increased from 30 people to 392. Total acreage increased, and cultivation was greatly intensified with irrigation and with double, even triple, cropping, but most people were impoverished (Table 13.1).

It might appear that natural population increase was the primary cause of impoverishment in Goborgari, but a closer look shows that this was not the case. Much of the growth of Goborgari since 1933 was because landless villagers moved in from other areas. More importantly, even with a tenfold population increase, subsis-

TABLE 13.1   CHANGE IN A DEVELOPING BANGLADESHI VILLAGE, GOBORGARI, 1933 AND 1977

	1933	1977
Population	30	392
Households	19	75
Average household size	1.5	5.2
Average acres/household	4.3	1.5
Households landless (%)	0	32
Land owned by richest 10% of households (%)	10	46
Households not self-sufficient in rice	n.d.	60%

SOURCE: Van Schendel (1981). n.d. = no data

tence resources still would have been marginally adequate if land were equitably distributed. If Goborgari had been organized as an egalitarian society, land resources and the risks of food production would have been shared equally. The primary crop in Goborgari by 1977 was the newly introduced Green Revolution **high-yield variety** (HYV) of rice, which increased production by a third. The problem with the new HYV rice, which was promoted by government extension agents, was that it required access to land and high levels of water and chemicals. Despite these technological improvements, the village was still relatively impoverished in comparison with earlier conditions. Average household acreage dropped to 1.5 acres (0.6 hectare), which was insufficient to meet basic household needs. Thirty-two percent of households were suddenly landless, and the richest 10 percent of households owned 46 percent of the land. A full 63 percent of households were below the 2-acre line, which was the minimal acreage needed to produce what villagers considered to be a "moderately contented living" derived from full-time farming. It is likely that all households in 1933 were self-sufficient in rice, although there is no available figure. It is known that inequality was minimal, and no households were landless.

The land situation was more complex than the facts of legal ownership suggest because land quality and productivity varied and land frag-

mentation made cultivation difficult. An average household might own 1.5 acres (0.6 hectare) in six and one-half separate pieces. A significant amount of land was also either mortgaged or sharecropped under an arrangement in which the sharecropper could keep half of the production. Holding a mortgage or rights to sharecrop a given piece of land gave a degree of control over "unowned" land and made it considerably more difficult to assess the actual degree of poverty and inequality in the village. Virtually as critical as control over land was ownership of a plow and team of draft animals, yet only 33 percent of households owned a full team. A farmer who did not own a team could not sharecrop, and hiring a team to plow one's own land meant reduced yields and increased expenses. To a limited extent, sharecropping gave the poorest villagers a chance to make up their deficiencies; nevertheless, 60 percent of all households were not self-sufficient in rice. They could not produce enough rice to meet their minimal nutritional requirements and were even farther from producing a marketable surplus to help meet their physical needs for moderately contented living by local standards.

high-yield variety High-yield plant varieties developed by selective breeding as part of the Green Revolution.

TABLE 13.2   HOUSEHOLD ECONOMIC CATEGORIES IN GOBORGARI, 1977

Category*	Households		Population	
	(no.)	(%)	(no.)	(%)
A: Substandard	15	20	74	19
B: Low	32	43	147	38
C: Moderate	16	21	90	23
D: Comfortable	12	16	81	20

SOURCE: Van Schendel (1981).
*Etic categories distinguished by Van Schendel: (A) Substandard: virtually landless, tattered clothing, hungry; income insufficient for year. (B) Low: plow less than 2 acres, basic annual food and clothing. (C) Moderate: more than 2 acres, 1–3 month's surplus. (D) Comfortable: metal-roofed house, tube well, expensive clothes, bicycle, wristwatches, as status symbols; surplus of 3 months or more. Native economic categories within Goborgari: (1) Chhotolok: laborers, cannot produce rice. (2) Moidhom: sharecroppers, must also buy rice. (3) Dewani: eat rice they produce; wealthy landowners in other villages. (4) Mashari: wealthy, owners of 10–25 acres. (5) Adhoni: very wealthy, owners of more than 25 acres.

Because agricultural self-sufficiency was out of reach of two-thirds of the villagers, they were forced to supplement their incomes with seasonal part-time labor, with petty—and sometimes illegal—business operations, and with whatever irregular and poorly paid service employment they could find. Under these conditions, most villagers faced continual economic emergencies and scarcity, and serious poverty and inequality appeared to be steadily increasing. These conditions closely resembled the circumstances that faced English peasants during the enclosure movement and compelled millions of Bangladeshi to migrate to the cities in search of wage employment.

When he attempted to estimate the actual economic status of Goborgari households, Van Schendel found that cash values were inadequate to cover all of the significant economic exchanges that took place in the village and the varying requirements of individual households. Instead, Van Schendel used a 4-point scale based on the villagers' own estimates of monthly household maintenance requirements and standard of living. Villagers implicitly recognized at least four standards of living within the village, which Van Schendel labeled A (substandard), B (low), C (moderate), and D (comfortable) (Table 13.2), according to a household's ability to produce sufficient rice for its total annual needs. The poorest 20 percent of households (category A) often went hungry and could not afford respectable clothing. The top 16 percent of households (category D) enjoyed an annual surplus that would allow them to maintain their modest comforts and simple luxuries for more than 3 months beyond a given agricultural year. Households in the 2 middle categories existed on a very narrow margin.

The economic position of the village as a whole could be affected by war, famine, and fluctuations in the price of cash crops. Upward or downward mobility of individual households was determined by a variety of specific factors. Where the margin of economic viability is narrow, illness, a single poor crop, an expensive wedding or funeral, a robbery, or litigation can push a household into extreme poverty.

The local rural elite were wealthy landowners who could live relatively comfortably, even though in comparison with the national-level urban elite they did not appear wealthy. The rural elite were heavily dependent on the labor of sharecroppers who worked their land, and they made significant profit from lending money to the chronically indebted peasantry at exorbitant rates. The rural elite thus had a vested interest in maintaining the long-established peasant landholding system, which was defined by a large, high-density agrarian population, living under very marginal conditions. The system's basic features—especially landless laborers, sharecroppers, mortgages, and high rates of indebtedness—severely inhibit upward mobility.

Bangladesh and the Green Revolution

As discussed in Chapter 12, the Green Revolution refers to the use of institutionalized agricultural research, large-scale capital resources, and energy-intensive technology to increase per-acre food productivity in the developing world. This approach to agricultural development began in 1943 when the Rockefeller Foundation funded a special project in cooperation with the Mexican government to improve the yield of grain crops by selective breeding. By the early 1960s, the program had successfully produced a dwarf hybrid wheat capable of tripling yields. In 1966, the Mexican research center became an international agricultural research institute known as CIMMYT (International Center for the Improvement of Wheat and Maize). By 1977, after an intensively funded international campaign, Mexican dwarf HYV (high-yield-variety) wheat was being grown on half of the wheatland throughout the developing world and was replacing many indigenously produced varieties and other crops (CGIAR 1980). CIMMYT became a model for a dozen other similar centers, which spread throughout the developing world under the sponsorship of CGIAR (Consultative Group on International Agricultural Research).

The HYV grains are often presented as the primary factors behind the large per-acre yields of the Green Revolution; however, these production increases were won at a cost. The local crops that the new plants replaced were produced by many generations of local people to fit local environmental conditions and the requirements of small-scale, self-sufficient production techniques. The new plants have been called high-response varieties to emphasize that they depend on expensive inputs (Palmer 1972). The "miracle grains" are extremely demanding plants. They only produce high yields under optimum conditions. They require a specific amount of water and large quantities of chemical fertilizer. They are also vulnerable to disease and pests because they are a genetic monocrop; thus, successful production also requires generous applications of chemical pesticides. They are often dwarf forms because a short stock is needed to support the heavy head of grain, but this leaves the plants more vulnerable to flooding and means that they cannot be grown in many otherwise favorable areas. The special requirements of the new varieties mean that only the largest farmers with the best land and the best connections with the government can take advantage of the new technology and can afford the risk of occasional crop failure (Lappe, Collins, and Fowler 1979).

Joining the Green Revolution means that small farmers are linked to a complex global political economy in which the seeds they plant, the tools they use, and the most critical factors affecting their security, such as land, marketing, wages, and credits, are all removed from effective village control. Ultimately, the fate of "developing" rural villagers is determined by the heads of governments, banks, corporations, foundations, and other international development agencies, all operating through many interconnected bureaucracies. Under the Green Revolution, village-level agricultural production is connected to global-level institutions, by way of national-level institutions, through a series of unequal exchanges, or inputs and outputs, in which power is concentrated at the top at each level and costs and benefits are unevenly distributed.

Figure 13.2 illustrates the three levels—global, national, and village—at which the Green Revolution is organized and lists some of the exchanges between levels. Although the public purpose of this kind of agricultural development is "to help poor peasants feed themselves," at the global level it can be seen that important political and economic benefits accrue to the elites of the

FIGURE 13.2 Input–output structure of the Green Revolution.

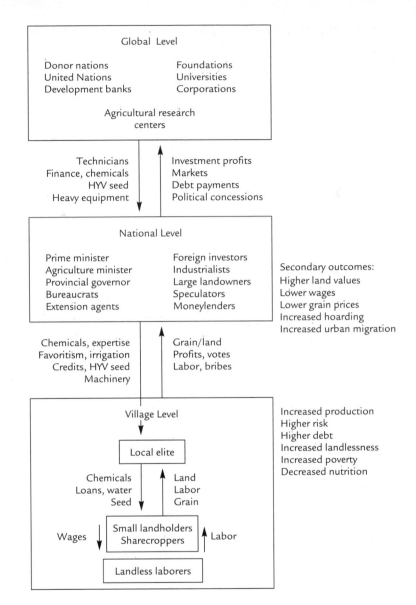

donor nations. Many elites at the national level also derive important benefits in the form of food surpluses, land, profits, cheap labor, bribes, and votes. National elites, including government officials at all levels in the bureaucracy and the wealthy in private enterprises (who are often also in government), control the technological and financial inputs, as well as the natural resources of land and water, that make the HYVs produce. In exchange, the developing countries have accepted an increasing burden of debt to international donors and often find that they must submit to specific conditions in order to keep up their payments. Thus, a form of international debt peonage has become part of the development process. Ironically, at the village level, the local elite repeat the unequal exchanges of higher levels, such that the majority of the rural population becomes impoverished, not nourished and empowered, by the Green Revolution.

Impoverishment was one of the unintended secondary outcomes that accompanied increased production as the Green Revolution reached the village level (Figure 13.2). This occurred as part of an interconnected process in which the new technology was linked to increased debt and landlessness and reduced nutrition in the villages. Nutrition declined because the monocrop HYVs replaced other food crops, while declining incomes made it more difficult for no-longer self-sufficient villagers to buy food. At the national level, land values increased along with grain hoarding by speculators, while grain prices fell. Many rural people forfeited their small landholdings when they were unable to pay off their debts. Increased mechanization reduced the demand for farm labor, and wages fell, driving many people to seek low-paying jobs in the cities. Elites at every level benefited from all of this while the total level of poverty increased (Lappe, Collins, and Fowler 1979). Arguably, this growth process produced unintended structural violence.

Green Revolution impoverishment is well illustrated in Bangladesh. The local elite used their political connections to gain control of the tube wells required for irrigating the HYV crops. They also "cultivated" the government extension agents with bribes to make sure that the seeds, expertise, chemicals, and machinery came to them first. The elite dominated village agricultural cooperatives and effectively controlled whatever technological inputs reached the lower-class small landholders and sharecroppers. Skillful manipulation of their political and economic advantages helped the local elite to systematically appropriate the land of less fortunate fellow villagers, while extracting their labor and grain. The landless laborers at the bottom of the village hierarchy had only their labor to exchange for inadequate wages.

Wheat steadily displaced rice and other crops as a primary food staple in Bangladesh because HYV wheat proved more suitable in Bangladesh than HYV rice. This crop change, however, has also had unexpected cultural consequences (Lindenbaum 1987). The traditional Bangladeshi diet consists of rice, lentils, fish, and vegetables. As inexpensive HYV wheat became widely available, it became the dominant food. The poor, who can afford little else, were forced to abandon their preferred foods and eat wheat three meals a day even though this meant a decline in the caloric and nutritional quality of their diet. Culturally, rice remained the most important food and was considered the essential element of a meal, whereas wheat was treated as a foreign snack food and was understandably associated with disease by villagers.

Some development experts have argued that the expansion of wheat production in Bangladesh benefits women because many women, who were formerly employed as rice hullers but were displaced by machines, may now find employment harvesting and threshing wheat. However, this work is taken only by the poorest women because it violates *purdah* restrictions, is very heavy and difficult work, and must take place during the hottest time of year.

THE FAILED PROMISE OF GROWTH, 1950–2000

During the last half of the twentieth century, the previous era of colonialism was replaced by a new era of international development. New international agencies, many of them formed in the aftermath of World War II, together with governments, philanthropic foundations, and private agencies, jointly engaged in a massive effort to improve public health and increase economic productivity. The assumption was that such development would raise living standards and reduce poverty throughout the world, but the reality was that the number of poor actually increased. Development failed to achieve its stated goals because poverty was treated primarily as a

TABLE 13.3 UN DEVELOPMENT ISSUES AND STRATEGIES, 1950–2015

Decade	Issues	Strategies
1950–1959	Disease Poverty Ignorance	Public health programs Public education Technology transfer Promotion of economic growth
1960–1969	Population Urban growth Income inequality	Integrated economic and social growth UN Development Decade
1970–1979	Social equity Global disparity Human environment	Second UN Development Decade Unified economic-social-political approach
1980–1989	Foreign debt Energy cost Economic downturn	Third Development Decade Human development Popular participation Grassroots development Appropriate technology International development cooperation
1990–1999	Poverty	Labor-intensive development Human-capital improvement
2000–2015	Millennium Development Goals	Eradicate extreme hunger and poverty Achieve universal primary education Promote gender equality and empower women Reduce child mortality Improve maternal health Combat HIV/AIDS, malaria, and other diseases Ensure environmental sustainability Develop a global partnership for development

SOURCES: United Nations (1952, 1963, 1975), UNDP (2003), and World Bank (1988, 1989, 1990, 1991).

technical problem, rather than a cultural problem of scale and power.

The United Nations and Development Decades

The United Nations (UN) is the most prominent international organization concerned with global development issues. The UN Charter, which was formally adopted in 1945 by fifty-one nations, specifies that the promotion of "social progress and better standards of living" and "economic and social advancement of all peoples" are among the principal aims of the United Nations. Over the years since its founding, the United Nations has focused on a changing series of development issues and has proposed a variety of development strategies (Table 13.3). To formulate and implement its development effort, the UN has also constructed an elaborate institutional framework of specialized agencies, councils, commissions, funds, and programs, each chartered by formal resolutions.

By the end of World War II, it was obvious to world leaders that much of the world was seriously impoverished. Vast numbers of people in many countries were living under conditions that were intolerable from a humanitarian perspective. Furthermore, because impoverished peoples made poor producers and consumers in the global

TABLE 13.4   SOCIAL CONDITIONS IN NORTH AMERICA, ASIA, AFRICA, AND
LATIN AMERICA, 1947–1949

	North America	Asia	Africa	Latin America
Birth rate/1000	25	42.5	42.5	40
Death rate/1000	10	30	27.5	17
Natural increase	15	12.5	15	23
Infant mortality/1000 births*	31.8	88	177	119.9
Life expectancy at birth†	68.7	27	33	39

SOURCE: United Nations (1952).
*National averages in the Asian countries Ceylon, Federation of Malaya, and Singapore; in the African country Sierra Leone; and in the Latin American countries Chile, Mexico, and Venezuela.
†National averages in the North American country United States (whites), in the Asian country India (1921–1931), in the African country Mauritius, and in the Latin American country Peru (Lima, 1933–1935).

economy and were potential sources of political instability, it was in their "enlightened self-interest" for wealthy industrialized countries to attempt to alleviate world poverty. War-caused impoverishment could be solved by reconstruction, but most authorities assumed that global poverty was caused by a vicious cycle of disease, ignorance, and poverty and would be eliminated by the transfer of industrial technology and education from rich to poor countries. In 1948, the United Nations began the international campaign to improve the human condition by issuing the Universal Declaration of Human Rights, which stated, "Everyone has the right to a standard of living adequate for the health and well-being of himself and of his family, including food, clothing, housing and medical care" (United Nations 1952:22). This was a truly revolutionary document, comparable to the American Declaration of Independence and the U.S. Bill of Rights in its support of human freedom.

As its first major development initiative, in 1949 the United Nations began its Expanded Program of Technical Assistance for Economic Development of Under-Developed Countries. In 1950, the United Nations placed fifty technical experts in sixteen countries and expended $20 million on projects, while a UN affiliate, the International Bank for Reconstruction and Development (IBRD), or the World Bank, loaned $279 million to governments for large-scale develop-

ment projects. This action showed that global poverty was considered to be a problem that would respond to increased technical proficiency and economic expansion.

Because, according to the UN Charter, the Economic and Social Council (ECOSOC) was expected to "help solve international problems in the economic, social, humanitarian and cultural fields," the General Assembly in 1949 asked it to prepare a general report on the world social situation. The council report, issued in 1952, found that conditions were shockingly "inadequate" for more than half of the world's people, with dramatically higher fertility, crude mortality, and infant mortality rates and much lower life expectancy rates for populations in Asia, Africa, and Latin America, in comparison with North America. For example, infant mortality in some African countries was more than five times the North American rate, and life expectancy throughout much of the world was half that of North Americans (Table 13.4).

The council report offered no absolute definition of *underdevelopment* or *poverty*. But it did provide figures showing that two-thirds of the world's population had only 17 doctors per 100,000 people and earned only $41 per person per year, whereas the "developed" 20 percent of the world earned $461 per person and had 106 doctors per 100,000 people. Such inequality had obvious implications for public health.

During the 1950s, UN experts treated the economic and social aspects of development as separate issues, and they focused on improving specific target indicators at national levels, especially in the area of public health. Initial efforts focused on relatively easily combated mass diseases such as malaria, yaws, hookworm, tuberculosis, and gastrointestinal diseases, which accounted for much of the elevated mortality in the world and which responded readily to the insecticide DDT and to penicillin. Nutritional diseases, such as beriberi (vitamin B deficiency) and kwashiorkor (protein deficiency), were considered to be more intractable because they were caused by "ignorance and poverty" rather than microbes. For many development planners, disease was the most basic problem. As the council report explained,

> A community burdened with ill-health is an impoverished community. There is a vicious circle: disease—underproduction—poverty—poor health services—more disease, which is manifest in those underdeveloped countries where the majority of a people are afflicted with gross diseases which rob them of vitality and initiative and which create social lethargy. . . . The control of disease . . . is a precondition of economic and social development. The advance of any community depends on the extent to which it reduces the burden of ill health which squanders human resources, wastes food in nourishing bacteria and parasites, produces social lethargy, and prevents people and countries from developing their full capacities. (United Nations 1952:22, 36)

This emphasis on technical progress steadily accelerated in the 1950s. By 1960, after a decade of major development effort and steady improvement in highly visible areas of public health and formal education, several ominous global trends had become inescapably obvious. In its 1963 Report on the World Situation, the UN Economic and Social Council observed that global population increased by 19 percent during the 1950s. Such a dramatic increase was partly due to a rapid decline in death rates. At a global level, the crude death rate dropped from an estimated 26

per 1000 in 1937 to 18 by 1960, while fertility rates remained approximately constant. A demographic change of this magnitude was absolutely unprecedented in human history and gave rise to the term *population explosion*. In specific countries, the figures were truly remarkable. For example, in Ceylon (Sri Lanka), overall mortality dropped from 25 to 10.1 per 1000 people, and infant mortality from 183 to 69 per 1000 live births. The global impact of these changes was much higher than most demographers had at first expected and led to a doubling in world population between 1950 and 1990.

Ironically, the world population increase experienced by 1960, in the absence of changes in wealth distribution, meant that the absolute number of impoverished people actually increased, even though the proportion of impoverished may have declined as a percentage of total population in certain countries. Significantly, the UN report also observed that the gap between developed and less developed countries had widened in regard to consumption of material goods and per-capita national income, while inequality within individual developing countries increased. The UN report was emphatic on this point:

> In many less developed countries, growth in national income appears to have been shared disproportionately by the minority already well-to-do, while in richer countries certain disadvantaged minorities have continued to lag behind the majorities in growth of income. (1963:2)

Even before the official report detailing the failures of previous development efforts was released, UN planners called for "integrated development" and initiated a 10-year plan designating the 1960s as the UN Development Decade. The Development Decade Resolution, adopted unanimously by the UN General Assembly in 1961, specified that each developing country should achieve a target annual growth rate of 5 percent in national income by 1969.

During the 1970s, a "unified" or "holistic approach" was recommended by development planners to solve the inequality problems recognized a decade earlier. A Second UN Development Decade was proclaimed in 1971, calling on poor countries to increase their annual growth rates of gross national product (GNP) per person by 3.5 percent, their annual agricultural output by 4 percent, and their manufacturing output by 8 percent. Even if these growth rates had been realized, the gap between rich and poor nations would only have been reduced if the rich nations had remained at a constant level, but that did not happen.

Midway through the Second Development Decade, the original goal of a better standard of living for all peoples was still far out of reach. A new UN report found that development had not achieved "any significant narrowing of disparities in income or levels of living" (United Nations 1975:1), either within individual countries or between different countries at the global level. National development was helping to create wealthy national elites even as the absolute number of severely impoverished people continued to grow. Frustrated UN planners were forced to conclude that "policies geared to national or macro-growth objectives do not of themselves give rise to a more equitable distribution of income" (United Nations 1975:13).

During the 1970s, people became more aware that the existence of the global market economy made conditions in the developing world different from conditions existing in Europe during the Industrial Revolution. This implied that technological changes by themselves would not achieve development. In 1974, the United Nations even recommended the creation of a "New International Economic Order" based on more equitable trade relations between nations. During the 1980s, however, the rise in energy costs, the burden of development debts, and the related problems of inflation and economic recession dampened hopes for a new economic order.

Although the implications of expanding impoverishment were still not fully understood, new development issues continued to emerge. By the mid-1970s, the obvious failure of many projects at the local level made it desirable to refer to the need for "popular participation" in development. This meant some degree of decentralization and involvement of local "target populations" in planning. A further issue emerging at this time was the environment, because many large-scale development projects were degrading the "human environment," simplifying ecosystems, lowering the quality of soil and water, and generating pollution.

As the Third UN Development Decade came to an end in 1990, the World Bank estimated that more than 1 billion people were living in absolute poverty, with annual incomes of less than $370 per person (Figure 13.3) (World Bank 1990).

The wealth disparity between nations after five decades of concerted development effort is dramatically illustrated by the World Bank's international rank order of nations by annual per-capita GNP based on 2001 data (World Bank 2002, Table 1.1). The wealthiest nation, Switzerland, showed a per-capita GNI (gross national income, the equivalent of gross national product) of $38,330, which was 479 times greater than that of the poorest nation, Congo, of $80.

The World Bank's ranking of nations shows that only 28 nations, with 16 percent of the world's population, were high-income nations with per-capita GNIs of $9206 or more, whereas 55 nations were considered low income with per-capita GNIs of $745 or less. Low income correlated with poor scores on many indicators of social well-being. For example, the average infant mortality rate in low-income countries was 107 per 1000 live births in 1998, nearly 18 times the rate of high income countries. The 55 poorest nations included some 2.5 billion people, over 40 percent of the world's population.

Nations may also be ranked by the size of their economies. This matters because the rulers of the most powerful nations command all dimensions of social power, and can shape the world to a degree that is almost unimaginable. Figure 13.4 shows that nations are ranked by economic power according to the power law. Growth in the scale of the global economy from $2 trillion to over $30 trillion between 1965 and 2001 did not change the relative power ranking of nations, although

FIGURE 13.3   El Salvadoran peasant family. At the end of the Third UN Development Decade in 1990, there were more than 1 billion people living in absolute poverty. In 1988 the World Bank considered El Salvador to be a lower-middle-economy country based on GNP per capita.

power became enormously concentrated at the top. In 1965 the 5 most powerful nations controlled 60 percent of global GDP. In 1991 the top 4 nations controlled 58 percent. If the international distribution of economic power remained the same, and global economic growth continued at an annual rate of 5 percent a year, it would reach $335 trillion by the year 2050, and the top-ranked nation would have an economy of more than $100 trillion. The richest individuals would be trillionaires, with the ability to endow foundations, influence politics, and shape events in the world far greater than ordinary billionaires. With continued growth by 2075 the global economy would reach more than a quadrillion dollars ($1.E+15) and the top nation's economy would exceed $360 trillion.

Figure 13.5 shows that for 142 nations with populations of 1 million or more, population size is positively correlated with size of economy ($R^2 = 0.42$), with larger nations tending to have larger economies. High *per-capita* GNI in combination with a large economy can produce more concentrated wealth and makes nations more powerful in the global commercial world. In Figure 13.5, per-capita GNI is reflected in the World Bank rankings of high income ($9206 or more), upper-middle income ($2976 to $9205), lower-middle ($746 to $2975), and low income ($745 or less). At a given population size, larger economies have higher per capita income. A large economy gives a nation's rulers a large voice in global trade policy and finance. It also makes a large, powerful military possible. The political leaders

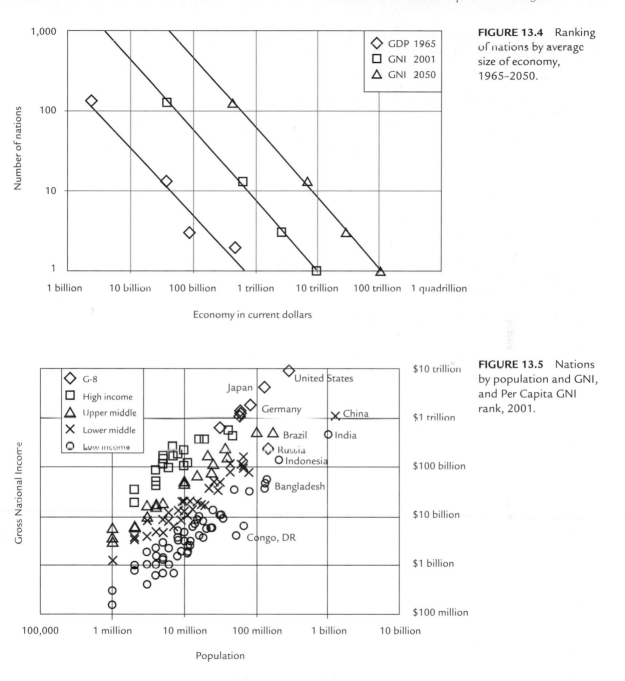

FIGURE 13.4 Ranking of nations by average size of economy, 1965–2050.

FIGURE 13.5 Nations by population and GNI, and Per Capita GNI rank, 2001.

of the United States, the most powerful nation, are able to influence the United Nations and its specialized agencies, especially the World Bank and the IMF, by holding formal offices, voting, and funding. The rulers of the most powerful nations convene periodically as the Group of Eight (G-8; see Chapter 11) to coordinate economic policies. Global elites, including former political leaders, the very wealthy, and the heads of giant corporations also meet formally for planning purposes as members of the Trilateral Commission, and the World Economic Forum. Economic and political elites in the G-8 nations at the top of the hierarchy of nations are the primary architects of the formal social structure of the global system. Unfortunately, in spite of prevailing utopian ideologies that promote economic growth, *elite-directed* growth has not significantly improved conditions in the impoverished world.

The level of economic inequality observed between nations could not exist in the tribal world because there was no significant wealth accumulation. Extreme inequality is produced in the commercial world by unequal exchange sustained by unequal political power. In effect, global wealth is a political distribution. The global political economy is designed to redistribute wealth and income from lower- to upper-ranked nations.

Utopian Futurists and the Growth of Global Poverty, 1965–2000

The culture of economic development had its roots in the recommendations of various economic specialists and planners who produced influential books during this period predicting a utopian future in a fully commercialized world. But these utopian visions were flawed by a narrow view of human cultural history and by a focus on national-level measures of economic activity. To better understand what went wrong, it will be helpful to examine the thinking behind international development efforts and to compare the reality of global poverty with the predictions.

In 1967, Hudson Institute futurists Herman Kahn and Anthony Wiener published their predictions for a "surprise free" world in the year 2000, assuming a continuation of what they called the *multifold trend* of technological progress and economic growth. Their multifold trend is the commercialization process. They traced it back to the eleventh and twelfth centuries—precisely where we began in Chapter 11 with our examination of

the rise of money and markets in medieval Europe. Kahn and Wiener were convinced that unrestricted economic growth was benefitting the world. They optimistically expected that for at least the next 30 years, every nation would follow what they imagined to be the *natural* progression of development stages from takeoff, through maturity, to the high mass consumption outlined so elegantly in M.I.T. economist Walt Rostow's influential 1960 book *The Stages of Economic Growth*. Rostow conceived of economic *takeoff* as a watershed event in which the "forces making for economic progress . . . [would] come to dominate the society" and overcome the "old blocks and resistances to steady growth" (1960:7). As advisor to presidents Kennedy and Johnson, Rostow's utopian vision of unlimited growth supported the thinking and interests of America's top intellectual, political, and economic leaders. In reality, of course, many of these people were themselves the "forces making for economic progress" that ultimately directed the global flow of finance capital.

In line with Rostow's view, the Hudson Institute futurists expected world population to double and the global economy to increase more than fivefold by the year 2000. They predicted that 25 percent of the world's population would bask in the luxury of "post-industrial" societies by the end of the century, while the rest of the world steadily grew to maturity and mass consumption. Kahn and Wiener expected growth to dramatically improve economic conditions in the less developed nations, although the absolute gap between rich and poor would increase.

The Hudson Institute futurists were correct in their prediction that the global economy would increase fivefold by the year 2000 and global population would double, but they were wrong about how the human benefits of this growth would be distributed. By the year 2000 poverty was much more prevalent and wealth far more concentrated than expected. Where did they and other elite planners go wrong? A serious shortcoming of utopian projections was their focus on **gross national product (GNP)** or **gross domestic** product (GDP). These macroeconomic statistics, and their income equivalents are far removed from real people. They measure only values priced by the market. They typically leave out "services" performed in the household or exchanges between kin that do not involve money. They also do not include negative "externalities" that impoverish people, such as activities that deplete natural resources or damage communities, because these things are outside of the market. Even when presented as per capita, to account for differences in population between nations, until 1990 these measures did not consider the actual distribution of income to people by rank within different countries or differences between income ranks at the global level. Aggregate measures made it possible to be optimistic about the benefits of economic growth, because they obscured the reality that a larger economy, measured as more products or more total income, often benefits only a few people.

The real issue is how income relates to human well-being. Beginning with its 1990 *World Development Report,* the World Bank for the first time began to measure in detail the extent of global poverty. As shown previously, World Bank researchers established an appallingly low poverty line of $275 per person per year in 1985 PPP dollars (purchasing power parity, an adjustment for price differences between countries). This was a minimum income baseline for extreme poverty, and $370 was designated as an upper poverty line. PPP dollars tend to inflate the value of local commodities, and the World Bank's poverty lines were "arbitrary," but even so the $370 PPP poverty line produced the "staggering" and "shameful" figure of more than one billion impoverished people for 1985 (World Bank 1990:1).

My own estimate of global household well-being (Bodley 2000:376–388) used a generalized version of the World Bank's estimates of the percentile distribution of income in different countries available as of 1995 (World Bank 1995, Table 30) applied to global population and income in 1965 and 1997. I used $2500 as the

global poverty line to more realistically reflect the living standard prevailing in the high-income nations that most benefit from global economic growth. It seems reasonable to uniformly apply a single, high, but still modest, threshold for economic prosperity, given that the economic elite treat capital and labor as part of a single pool within a single world economy. Poverty creates human suffering, and human suffering is not culturally relative. I used $12,500 as the line between maintenance-level people and the global elite, assuming that at this level people would be able to accumulate wealth by saving and investing. My figures expand the concept of poverty by attempting to include all those who must borrow to meet basic needs and are unable to own land or their own homes, together with the World Bank's "absolute poor," within a single "poor" category. Using these consistent categories, and adjusting for inflation, it is possible to ask whether economic globalization since 1965 produced more wealth than poverty in the world.

My calculations for 1997 show more than 4 billion (70 percent) poor people, 1.23 billion (25 percent) maintenance-level people, and 300 million (5 percent) growth-level people (Figure 13.6 and Table 13.5). The figures also show a decline in the proportion who were poor by this new standard, but their actual numbers increased much more dramatically than the World Bank's categories suggest. By 1997, there were 260 million new individuals with growth-level incomes worldwide, but this increase was more than overshadowed by a new cohort of 1.25 billion poor. The wealthiest 5 percent of the world's population enjoyed 40 percent of global income. The 25 percent of maintenance-level people in the global "middle class" also had more than their share

---

gross national product (GNP) The total output of a country's goods and services, by monetary value; includes profits from foreign activities.

gross domestic product (GDP) The total output of goods and services produced within a country, by monetary value.

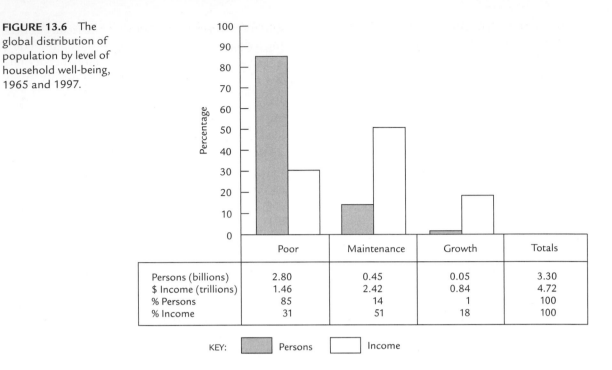

FIGURE 13.6 The global distribution of population by level of household well-being, 1965 and 1997.

	Poor	Maintenance	Growth	Totals
Persons (billions)	2.80	0.45	0.05	3.30
$ Income (trillions)	1.46	2.42	0.84	4.72
% Persons	85	14	1	100
% Income	31	51	18	100

KEY: Persons   Income

with 40 percent of the wealth, whereas the 70 percent of the world who were poor were left with less than 20 percent of global income. Clearly, if we accept this global standard of economic well-being, growth since 1965 impoverished more people than it enriched.

It has only been possible to look at income distribution across the globe with some accuracy since the late 1990s, when very detailed household level surveys became available for most of the world. These surveys counted the income that people in different countries actually received. Branko Milanovic (2002) made some surprising discoveries from the first careful examination of such surveys from 216 countries, covering some 84 percent of the world's people, and 93 percent of GDP in 1988 and 1993. Milanovic found that income was much more skewed toward the top than previous official estimates had suggested. In 1993 the bottom 20 percent of the global population received about 2 percent of total income, whereas the top 20 percent received 73 percent,

and the global middle 20 percent received only 6 percent (Figure 13.7).

In the tribal world, where relative equality prevailed, there would be no ranking by income— each 20 percent of households would received 20 percent of income. It was remarkable that in the commercial world over the 5 years between 1988 and 1993, those in the bottom 80 percent of global society actually lost income share, whereas the top 20 percent gained nearly 5 percentage points. Income was being redistributed upward to those least in need. My analysis of the distribution of global income and wealth by household shows a similar distribution (Table 13.6).

The adoption of the Millennium Development Goals (MDG) (Table 13.3) by delegates from 189 countries at the UN Millennium Summit in 2000 was a recognition that, in spite of the prevailing optimism about economic growth, poverty was not being reduced. The UNDP (United Nations Development Program) Human Development Report for 2003 (UNDP 2003:39) called

TABLE 13.5   THE GLOBAL DISTRIBUTION OF POPULATION AND INCOME, BY LEVEL OF HOUSEHOLD WELL-BEING, 1965 AND 1997.

1965	Poor	Maintenance	Elite	Totals
Persons	2,800,000,000	450,000,000	50,000,000	3,300,000,000
$ Income/capita	521	5378	16,800	1430
Percent persons	85	14	1	100
Percent income	31	51	18	100
1997	Poor	Maintenance	Elite	Totals
Persons	4,060,000,000	1,460,000,000	310,000,000	5,830,000,000
$ Income/capita	919	5637	24,903	3376
Percent persons	70	25	5	100
Percent income	19	42	39	100

SOURCES: *Information Please Almanac Atlas and Yearbook 1967,* United Nations 1968a, 1968b: Table 7B, *World Almanac and Book of Facts 1998,* World Bank 1995.

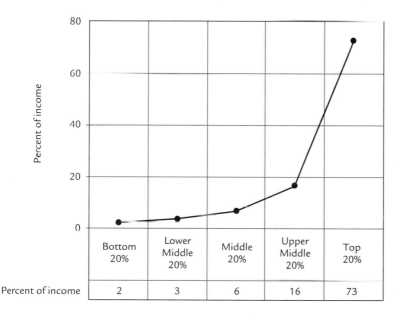

Percent of income	2	3	6	16	73

FIGURE 13.7   Percent distribution of global per capita income by quintile, 1993 (Milanovic 2002).

the distribution of global income inequality at the beginning of the millennium "grotesque," citing Milanovic's (2002) findings. This critical view contrasts with that of the optimists who saw improvement between 1987 and 1998 when the *percentage* of "extremely poor," as defined by the Bank, dropped from 28.5 percent to 26.2 per-

cent. At the same time the absolute number of extremely poor increased from 880 million to 895 million (World Bank 2001:23, Table 1.1). However, the World Bank's understanding of poverty in 2001 was much more comprehensive than in the past. In its World Development Report on "attacking poverty" (World Bank 2001),

TABLE 13.6   DISTRIBUTION OF GLOBAL INCOME AND NET WORTH BY HOUSEHOLD RANK, 1999

Class	Households	Average Net Worth	Average Income	Imperia
Billionaire	538	$3,213,011,152	$321,301,115	Super-Elite 0.6% of Households 9% of Income
Ultra HNWI	56,462	$116,386,242	$11,638,624	
HNWI	7,143,000	$2,617,948	$261,795	
Elite	52,800,000	$100,000	$170,415	Elite 4.4% of Households 30% of Income
Middle Class	300,000,000	$50,000	$41,992	Maintenance 25% of Households 42% of Income
Poor	840,000,000	$3000	$6784	Poor 70% of Households 19% of Income

Totals: 6 billion people, 1.2 billion households, $29.9 trillion World Bank global income, 1999.

SOURCES: Super-Elite Income (Gemini 2001), Elite, Maintenance, Poor Distributions (Bodley 2000:378, Bodley 2003, Table 8.1), Global Income (World Bank 2001).

for the first time the Bank made a systematic effort to let the poor themselves define their experience of poverty. They interviewed more than 60,000 poor people in 60 countries for a "Voices of the Poor" study. The World Bank declared that fighting poverty is its mission, and its new definition of poverty is well represented in the following:

> To be poor is to be hungry, to lack shelter and clothing, to be sick and not cared for, to be illiterate and not schooled. . . . Poor people are particularly vulnerable to adverse events outside their control. They are often treated badly by the institutions of state and society and excluded from voice and power in those institutions" (World Bank 2001:15).

In spite of their new insights on poverty the World Bank still optimistically maintained that growth in scale, seen as market globalization and technological advance, could be mobilized to serve the interests of the poor. The report correctly observed that the poor need more economic opportunity, more political empowerment, and an effective safety net to increase their security in the event of crises. However, the World Bank also stressed that it was important to have the right

institutional and social foundations in place to manage the "vulnerability" of the poor and encourage their "participation to ensure inclusive growth." The emphasis was on "stimulating overall growth," and the report asserted that "traditional elements of strategies to foster growth—macroeconomic stability and market-friendly reforms—are essential for reducing poverty." (World Bank 2001:vi). The World Bank was now describing poverty in terms that resembled Paul Farmer's concept of structural violence, but in practice did not endorse radical redistribution of social power.

The Roots of Poverty: Overpopulation or Development?

The critical problem in the commercial world is that economic elites use political power to advance their interests, and the scale of business corporations and governments is such that only a few people have staggering amounts of power at their command while the majority are disempowered. The impoverished world is not only about people being poor in income and wealth, it is about people being disempowered in the broadest sense. Being disempowered means not having the ability to influence government or gain access to the social, cultural, or natural capital needed for survival, basic maintenance, and successful household reproduction.

Since the 1960s, when the population explosion began to be recognized as a global problem, overpopulation has often been identified as the primary cause of impoverishment in the developing world. It has been easy to attribute hunger and malnutrition to "too many people" and "too little food," as biologist Paul Ehrlich did in his influential book, *The Population Bomb* (1968). However, a close examination of the evidence shows that impoverishment is not that simple. People die in famines because food is scarce, but food is scarce because people lack *entitlement* to food—that is, either they are unable to produce food directly, they are landless, or they are unable to purchase food (Sen 1981). Thousands died in famines in Bangladesh in 1943 and 1974 because they did not have the social power to give them access to food.

Defense strategist Thomas Homer-Dixon (1991) makes a population pressure argument similar to Ehrlich's, warning that population growth is linked to environmental stress and "environmentally induced economic decline" that causes poverty, social upheaval, and conflict. He states this explicitly:

> As developing societies produce less wealth because of environmental problems, their citizens will probably become increasingly discontented by the widening gap between their actual level of economic achievement and the level they feel they deserve. (1991:109)

Homer-Dixon warns that the desperate poor might then attempt to impose "distributive justice," which would only lead to authoritative, abusive regimes. What Homer-Dixon fails to consider is that the growth of global capitalism and the global financialization process itself produce environmental stress and shift the costs to poor countries, regions, and communities.

Anthropologists who have examined the population stress argument in specific regions have consistently found that the distribution of landownership, and related political factors, was the crucial cause of both poverty and environmental deterioration—not population density. For example, William Durham (1979) conducted an indepth ethnohistorical and ethnographic analysis of the dynamics of population and land scarcity in Honduras and El Salvador for 1892–1974. He found that the expansion of commercial agriculture by large landholders on the most productive lands forced the peasantry into marginal lands. Increasingly, anthropologists treat these issues as problems of *political ecology*, rather than population pressure (Durham 1995).

Susan George (1992) observed that between 1982 and 1990, rich countries in the Northern Hemisphere transferred $927 billion in economic assistance, charity, loans, and private investment capital to poor debtor nations in the Southern Hemisphere to finance poor countries' economic growth. The investor nations received $1.345 trillion in return, for a modest profit of $418 billion. The developing nations used the money for massive projects such as dams, highways, power plants, manufacturing facilities, and vast agricultural programs. Much of this money came directly back to the rich nations that supplied some of the heavy equipment and material. These projects often contributed directly to environmental stress, and because they favored the interests of the wealthy, they also contributed to the further impoverishment of millions. Many poor people were pushed off their small landholdings by wealthy developers and were forced onto marginal lands on steep slopes, and forested regions, where further environmental damage is taking place.

The impoverishing dynamics of this financially driven process were intensified, beginning in the 1980s, by the **structural adjustments** that were imposed by the World Bank and the International Monetary Fund (IMF) to help poor debtor nations repay their international loans.

---

structural adjustments Austerity measures designed to increase foreign exchange through increased exports.

FIGURE 13.8 The structure of international technical assistance.

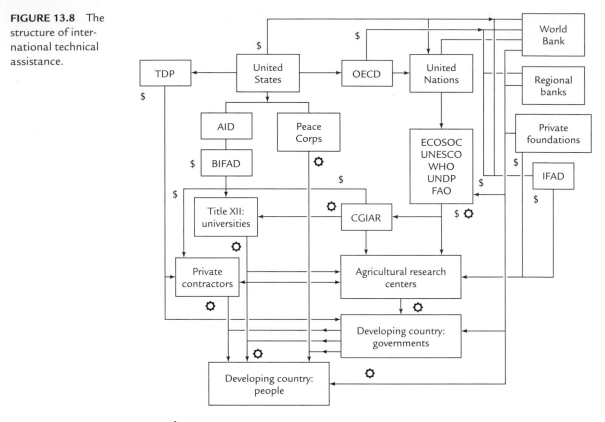

KEY: ✿ Technical assistance $ Financial assistance

Structural adjustments involve currency devaluations, reduced social support programs, and increased pressure to produce for export, which further stress the poor and the environment.

The United States, AID, and the Development Industry

The formal structures through which technical assistance and development finance reach the developing world consist of many complex bureaucracies linked in a ponderous network. Priorities are set by relatively few key organizations at the top that make decisions that affect the smallest details of life for millions of people living in remote villages throughout the impoverished world. Development decisions pass through so many hands before actually being implemented that the entire enterprise is extremely costly and often proves counterproductive. Understanding how this can happen requires some knowledge of aid categories, specific organizations, their functions, and interconnections.

The United Nations and related agencies offer what is called **multilateral development assistance** because it is financed by many nations and thus must offer assistance without political considerations or special trade preconditions. All development assistance given by individual countries is called **official development assistance (ODA)**. It must either be a gift or grant or be loaned at less than commercial rates. The largest aid category was bilateral assistance, or ODA supplied directly from one country to another. **Bilateral development assistance** can, and often does, have political and trade conditions attached and thus can serve the interests of the donor. A donor country might give only to "friendly" countries and then require them to spend their aid money on goods and services provided by the donor.

Figure 13.8 presents a simplified view of the network through which technical assistance is channeled from the United States and the Organization for Economic Cooperation and Development (OECD) countries to developing nations as bilateral aid and through the major multilateral aid organizations. This figure emphasizes agricultural technology. The acronyms appearing in Figure 13.8 are identified in the box entitled "International Assistance Agencies."

Global poverty has been consistently treated as a technological problem, partly because professional elites who are far removed from the daily realities of poverty formulate and finance development policies. Development is much more than a humanitarian concern; it has become a thoroughly institutionalized and highly complex industry with important political and economic functions for the wealthy donors that may be unrelated to the needs of the poor.

The assistance policies of the United States deserve a closer look because they play such a major role in the development process. U.S. development policies and programs were formally initiated by Point Four in President Truman's 1949 inaugural address, in which he declared, "We must embark on a bold new program for making the benefits of our scientific advance and industrial progress available for the improvement and growth of underdeveloped areas."

This was at the beginning of the Cold War, and the objective of Point Four development assistance was to use U.S. technology to advance U.S. interests in the world as part of Truman's policy of Soviet "containment." This less explicit objective was the cultural imperative to maintain a global system that would insure the availabil-

ity of resources to support America's economic growth into the distant future. The U.S. development effort received a major boost in 1961 under President Kennedy when the Agency for International Development (AID), the Peace Corps, and the Alliance for Progress were all launched (Figure 13.9). In the same year, Kennedy urged the UN General Assembly to create the UN Development Decade program. Between 1962 and 1969, a staggering $33.5 billion worth of food commodities and economic assistance flowed directly to developing countries and through development banks and the Peace Corps (U.S. Department of Commerce 1990).

Significant changes were brought about in U.S. policies by the 1975 Freedom from Hunger Title XII amendments to the Foreign Assistance Act of 1961, further reinforcing the narrow view that world hunger was primarily a technological problem. The Title XII amendments directed AID to recruit U.S. universities to apply "science to solving food and nutrition problems of the developing countries" (U.S. Code 1982, Title 22, Section 2220a). The assumption of this legislation was that because agricultural research, especially by the land-grant universities, had successfully increased farm productivity in the United States, this was the best way to deal with hunger in the impoverished world. The potential costs in energy, resources, and social inequality of implementing American-style factory farming in the developing world were disregarded.

U.S. development policy shifted again in the 1980s under the Reagan administration. Although continuous economic growth and technological

---

multilateral development assistance Aid that is donated by several countries and channeled through a single international agency such that it can be free of political favoritism.

official development assistance (ODA) Aid given by a government for development purposes, including both direct gifts and low-rate loans.

bilateral development assistance Aid that is given directly from one country to another and that may be given under conditions that favor the donor.

International Assistance Agencies

AID   Agency for International Development: Founded in 1961 to administer the U.S. government's foreign economic assistance program.

BIFAD   Board for International Food and Agricultural Development: Founded in 1977 to promote U.S. land-grant university involvement in AID agricultural development activities under the provisions of the Title XII amendment to the Foreign Assistance Act.

CGIAR   Consultative Group on International Agricultural Research: Formed in 1971 to coordinate and sponsor international agricultural research centers in various countries; a major promoter of the Green Revolution.

ECOSOC   Economic and Social Council: An official body of the UN organization with primary responsibility for coordinating development activities in the United Nations and related agencies.

FAO   Food and Agricultural Organization of the United Nations: The UN special agency formed in 1945 to promote food production; directs the Freedom from Hunger campaign.

IFAD   International Fund for Agricultural Development: Founded in 1976 to assist the poorest countries make technological improvements in food production.

OECD   Organization for European Economic Cooperation and Development: Formed in 1961 and composed primarily of wealthy industrial nations, its member countries provide official development assistance (ODA) to developing countries, either individually (bilateral assistance) or on a multilateral basis.*

TDP   Trade and Development Program: Created in 1980 to help U.S. technicians conduct feasibility studies for development projects in middle-income developing countries that might not otherwise qualify for technical assistance; serves to promote the export of U.S. technology.

UNDP   UN Development Programme: Established in 1966 to coordinate all development activities of the United Nations and related agencies.

UNESCO   UN Educational, Scientific and Cultural Organization: A UN special agency, established in 1946, that promotes international welfare.

WHO   World Health Organization: A UN special agency, established in 1948, that promotes public health in developing countries.

---

*Multilateral development agencies provide support that has been pooled from many sources. OECD members in 1990 were Australia, Austria, Belgium, Canada, Denmark, Finland, France, West Germany, Greece, Iceland, Ireland, Italy, Japan, Luxembourg, Netherlands, New Zealand, Norway, Portugal, Spain, Sweden, Switzerland, Turkey, United Kingdom, United States, and Yugoslavia.

FIGURE 13.9 Peace Corps volunteers inspecting a rural water system in the Bolivian Andes. The Peace Corps, initiated by President Kennedy in 1961, has played an important role in America's development aid program.

advance remained the primary development objectives, "free market forces" and the "private sector" were now considered "the principal engines of sustainable development" (United States AID 1985:iv). AID's new development objectives were, in some cases perhaps realistically, less than the goals set by the United Nations for the Third Development Decade. For example, the United Nations wanted infant mortality rates to be 50 per 1000 live births or below by the year 2000, but AID set below 75 as the target. Privatization called for the increased commercialization of agricultural systems while emphasizing biotechnol-

ogy. Seed and fertilizer companies were to become "extension agents," and many poor farmers were encouraged to produce export crops instead of locally consumed subsistence crops. The problem with applying this approach to the impoverished world is that market forces select for large-scale enterprises and inequality. In the United States, as shown in Chapter 12, this process makes small farms "uneconomical" and forces much of the rural population into the cities. Furthermore, many poor peasants simply lack the financial resources to take the expensive risks that producing for the international export market requires. Critics also charge that some aid programs may be an obstacle to democratic development because they support unpopular governments and thereby delay necessary land reform while devaluing the products of local farmers (Lappe, Collins, and Kinley 1981; Lappe, Schurman, and Danaher 1987).

Given the close links between America's national interests as defined by its ruling elite and America's official approach to international development issues and global poverty, it is relevant to consider the "National Security Strategy" issued by President George W. Bush in September of 2003. The basic premise of the Strategy is that since the end of the Cold War there is only one "sustainable model for national success: freedom, democracy, and free enterprise." The assumption is that "Free trade and free markets have proven their ability to lift whole societies out of poverty." The Strategy calls for foreign policies that will "ignite a new era of global economic growth through free markets and free trade" (U.S. White House 2003:17). These priorities also appear in the jointly issued "Strategic Plan" of the U.S. State Department and the Agency for International Development for 2004–2009, which stresses the dominance of private direct investment and public-private partnerships (U.S. State Department of State and U.S. AID 2003). This development strategy conspicuously aims at "reducing" poverty rather than eradicating it, and the method is by raising productivity, not by seeking to redistribute power to the poor. Global free trade is more about the interests of international investors than about meeting the needs of the poor.

ALTERNATIVE DEVELOPMENT STRATEGIES

The dominant development strategy pursued by the most powerful international agencies calls for high-energy industrial technology and rapid growth in the total output of goods and services as measured by GNP per capita. It is recognized that, just as in the early centers of capitalist development in Europe and North America, poverty and inequality may actually increase as economic growth occurs, but many assume that everyone will eventually benefit as long as growth remains strong. Many agencies acknowledge that the world's poorest groups may need some special assistance and perhaps even low-cost, environmentally sensitive "appropriate technology," but still emphasize the importance of perpetual economic growth.

The only major alternative to the perpetual growth approach to development is wealth redistribution emphasizing social justice. In effect, this is a development process that would return priority to the humanization goals championed by tribal cultures. Ideally, the satisfaction of basic human needs with maximum social equality would be the objective of this kind of development. This alternative is inherently difficult because it offers no immediate benefits to the wealthy and powerful; however, it has been tried in a few cases with some success, as the following examples show.

Wealth Redistribution as Development in India

The state of Kerala in southwest India represents an unusual attempt at development directed by the poor to meet their needs. This was a social transformation process organized by poor farmers, workers, and tenants, who engaged in decades of political struggle to transform a cultural system that was dominated by inequities of caste

and grossly concentrated wealth and power. This struggle for social justice, as analyzed by Richard Franke and Barbara Chasin (1989), has important implications for development theory. When Franke and Chasin assessed Kerala's economy in 1989, it had not grown significantly, as measured by per-capita GNP, and unemployment remained high. But the people's basic needs were being more effectively satisfied than in many countries where more economic growth had occurred.

According to Franke and Chasin (1989), protests against caste injustices opened the way for a broad range of social reforms. The Kerala variant of the Hindu caste system required some of the most extreme and degrading forms of ritual separation in India. Lower-caste people were kept in perpetual servitude to higher-caste people while being denied access to marketplaces, temples, schools, and public roads. In a series of peaceful mass protests against these indignities during the 1920s and 1930s, low-caste people and their political supporters in the Indian Communist party used open violations of the taboos to win political reforms that eventually eased caste restrictions. "Eat-ins" were held in which higher-caste political organizers ate with untouchables in their homes, thus publicly violating the Hindu concepts of purity and pollution that sustained caste differences. Anticaste movements eventually combined with labor movements and peasant unions, and together they succeeded in forcing the government to adopt wide-ranging political reforms that restructured society, redistributing wealth and power. These reform movements were conducted without resorting to armed violence, even though protesters were often murdered and imprisoned.

Before land reform was implemented in 1969, Kerala's agricultural land, the basic source of wealth and subsistence in the state, was controlled primarily by an upper class of Brahman landlords, who constituted about 2 percent of the population. The Brahmans owned both the irrigated rice fields and the plots where poor farmers built their house compounds and maintained small food-producing gardens. The landlords leased their land to a class of superior tenants, who often subleased to inferior tenants, who, if possible, hired untouchables to do the actual farmwork. Poor farmers were often perpetually in debt yet were forced to pay 50–94 percent of their gross harvest to landlords or face eviction. The land reform process turned former tenants into landowners while compensating the former landlords. Limits were also set on the size of landholdings.

Specific food distribution programs, some underway since early in the twentieth century, have included school lunch programs, free daily meal programs for infants and their mothers, and a system of ration shops selling basic foodstuffs to the poorest households at controlled prices. These programs appear to have had a significant effect. Regional food surveys in Kerala in the 1980s suggested that people were getting approximately 2300 kilocalories per day. This was above the national average of 2126 kilocalories and much more than the 1500 kilocalories that the impoverished sugarcane workers in northeast Brazil were receiving, as discussed earlier. Childhood growth studies show that Kerala's young children are doing slightly better than the average for India, even though per-capita income is actually lower in Kerala.

Political reformers in Kerala regarded adequate housing, clean water, sanitation, and vaccinations as public health issues and campaigned for government programs to make these basic needs available to everyone. These goals have not been fully achieved, but the government has been successful in making health services, including doctors, primary health care centers, and hospitals, more available in Kerala than in other parts of India. The clearest measure of the overall success of this wealth redistribution effort can be seen in Kerala's figures for adult literacy (78 percent), life expectancy (68 years), and infant mortality (27 per 1000 live births), which were significantly better than the Indian 1986 average of 43 percent, 57 years, and 86 per 1000, respectively. Kerala's infant mortality rate of 27 was a spectacular achievement in comparison with the

rate of 211 that Scheper-Hughes (1992) found in Bom Jesus in the Brazilian northeast in 1987. Improvements in infant mortality, life expectancy, and education, together with government pension programs, have reduced the incentive to raise large families, particularly for poor farmers. When these social gains were combined with government-supported family-planning programs and general improvements in the status of women, birth rates declined significantly in comparison with the rest of India.

Conventional development programs emphasize economic opportunities for men and often adversely affect the economic contribution of women in the household. This is certainly the case in India and is a factor in the recent increase in bride burnings, as discussed in Chapter 9. Thus, it is significant that the health status of women in Kerala is better than elsewhere in India. This improvement in the status of women is due in part to effective social support programs and has occurred despite high rates of female unemployment.

Kerala is a historically unique case, but it suggests that informed underclass groups can organize themselves and use democratic political processes to overcome the disadvantages imposed by the inequities of wealth and power. This kind of redistribution occurred in the absence of economic growth. In this post–Cold War world, it is also important to recognize that in many impoverished countries, leftist or socialist political organizations may be able to contribute positively to development, where externally financed and directed programs may have failed to meet the needs of the most impoverished classes.

Development Anthropology and Peasants

Cultural anthropologists enthusiastically supported post–World War II international development efforts by turning their attention to rural peasantries and the urban poor. Many researchers shifted their focus from the functional equilibrium of tribal cultures to the realities of poverty, the process of cultural change, and the "obstacles" to modernization or development progress. This research shift corresponded to changes within anthropology itself. Since 1950, many anthropologists have found full-time employment in development. In 1968, roughly three-quarters of the new PhDs in American anthropology still took academic positions. But by 1982, when there were few new academic positions, only 28 percent found teaching positions, and many of the others took positions as development anthropologists (Weaver 1985). For example, in 1980, there were fifty anthropologists doing development work as full-time employees of AID. This was probably greater than the total number that ever worked as colonial anthropologists for the British empire. In the 1980s, many more American anthropologists conducted temporary contract work through universities or private firms (Hoben 1982). One such firm, the Institute for Development Anthropology, held contracts with AID and the FAO for over $5.8 million in 1987 and had conducted projects in forty-eight countries. "Development" is clearly what many contemporary anthropologists do, often within an academic framework.

The anthropological approach to development and poverty has gone through significant changes since the 1950s. Initially, some prominent anthropologists uncritically accepted the established view that poverty was caused by ignorance and disease—in effect blaming the poor, or their culture, for poverty while ignoring the inequalities of economic and political power that sustained poverty. However, since the 1970s many applied anthropologists have sought to empower the poor. For example, in 2004 the Institute for Development Anthropology described its mission as "to promote environmentally sustainable development through poverty elimination, equitable economic growth, respect for human rights, gender equity, and cultural pluralism." In keeping with those objects it designed projects "to enhance the rights of low-income populations to land, natural resources, food, shelter, health, education, income, employment and participation

in democratic and transparent polities" (www.developmentanthropology.org).

Many anthropologists have long been aware of the complex ethical issues they face when working for development agencies (Manners 1956). Applied or development anthropologists now subscribe to formal codes of ethical conduct, but many difficult judgments must still be made. Development contractors necessarily have a dual, sometimes irreconcilable, responsibility to their employers and to the people who will be affected by development projects. They must consider the political agenda of funding agencies and the differential costs and benefits at all levels. Predicting all consequences of development changes is not possible, and even the most well-intended programs can still increase poverty and inequality.

Because target populations, the assumed beneficiaries of development programs, often have little power, it is vital that their views be taken into account. When local communities control their own resources and are able to support relatively self-maintaining communities, they often resist development programs designed to integrate them into the global system. Some early development writers attributed resistance to ethnocentrism on the part of the target people, suggesting that they mistakenly believed their own culture to be superior (Arensberg and Niehoff 1964). Other social engineers even recommended that change agents try to make people feel inadequate so they would desire change (Goodenough 1963). Development anthropologists, however, have increasingly recognized that resistance to change is often justified.

As development efforts were first beginning, some anthropologists correctly identified critical features of peasant culture that acted as apparent obstacles to the kind of development progress envisioned by government planners. However, these researchers also emphasized the rationality and practicality of peasant culture. For example, Robert Redfield (1947) used his "folk society" concept as an ideal type, to draw a contrast between the **peasantry** and members of urban societies. Redfield's folk society was defined by cultural features that also characterize tribal societies, such as small population, homogeneity, high social solidarity, simple division of labor, and economic self-sufficiency. In Redfield's view, peasants were members of former tribal societies that had been incorporated by states. State intervention, however, caused significant cultural changes in the folk society, including inequality, loss of autonomy, and impoverishment.

Focusing on political economy, Eric Wolf (1955, 1957) defined peasants as subsistence agriculturalists who control their own land but do not produce primarily for the market to make a profit. Wolf suggested that a common characteristic of peasants in Latin America and Island Southeast Asia is their organization as **closed corporate communities** in defense against conquest and exploitation by outsiders backed by state authority. Closed corporate communities either own land communally or regularly redistribute ownership of individual plots to ensure equal access for all members. To protect their lands, peasants also try to exclude outsiders and discourage members from becoming too involved with the larger national society. Peasant communities are corporations in that they seek to be self-perpetuating and self-sufficient. They promote internal security by means of **wealth-leveling devices** such as expensive rituals and feasting that tend to reduce economic inequality, while inhibiting economic growth and capital accumulation by consuming potential surplus within the community (Figure 13.10).

When cultural features of the closed corporate community are practiced by peasants, they are a defense against state exploitation. These same features may also be found in tribal societies, where they inhibit the concentration of internal political and economic power that led to the state in the first place. Given this self-defense emphasis, peasants often prefer to grow their own locally adapted crops for their proven hardiness, and they emphasize domestic food crops

FIGURE 13.10 Women are making corn tortillas during a fiesta in San Pedro Chenalhó, Chiapas, Mexico. Corn, a symbol of fertility and regeneration, is the primary food eaten and circulated in fiestas. Many domestic-scale subsistence agriculturalists engage in rituals and feasting that promote cohesiveness.

peasantry Village farmers who provide most of their own subsistence but who must pay taxes and are politically and often, to some extent, economically dependent on the central state government.

closed corporate community Communally organized peasants who exclude outsiders and limit the acquisition of wealth and power by their own members.

wealth-leveling device Any cultural means, such as ritual feasting, used to redistribute wealth within a community and thereby reduce inequality.

over market crops. They are also likely to reject exotic and expensive agricultural technologies to avoid debt and loss of independence. Peasants maximize subsistence security, and they value social support networks and strategic reserves over risk taking. Such cultural objectives may be conservative, but they are not ignorant or irrational.

George Foster (1965, 1969) identified the "image of limited good" as the key cognitive orientation in peasant societies. **Limited good** refers to the assumption that "all desired things in life . . . exist in finite and unexpandable quantities" (Foster 1969:83). This view was a direct expression of a stable, egalitarian, predominantly nonmarket economy and meant that a wealthy peasant was gaining his wealth at the expense of his less fortunate neighbors. The contrasting principle of **unlimited good** assumes that "with each passing generation people on average will have more of the good things of life." Unlimited good is part of the ideology of utopian capitalism and is not what most people in the world are experiencing in practice. Unfortunately, many development elites allowed their belief in unlimited good to mistakenly conclude that peasants were poor because they believed in equality, not because they were oppressed and exploited. (See the box entitled "The Culture of Poverty" for a closer look at this controversy.)

Andean Development: The Vicos Experiment

The Cornell Peru Project conducted at the hacienda of Vicos in the Peruvian Andes from 1952 to 1963 is one of the best-known development anthropology projects (Dobyns, Doughty, and Lasswell 1971). This was a unique, long-term development effort, planned and directed by anthropologists as a **participant intervention** experiment in cultural change designed to empower the peasantry. Using research funds provided by the Carnegie Corporation of New York, the project codirectors, American anthropologist Allan Holmberg, then of Cornell Uni-

versity, and Peruvian anthropologist Mario Vazquez, rented the colonial-style hacienda of Vicos where some 2000 peasants lived as virtual serfs on a 60-square-mile (mi^2) (155-square-kilometer [km^2]) estate. The anthropologists then used their position as managers of the hacienda to gradually turn political power back to the peasants and help them regain control over their ancestral land. This was a novel approach to development and was widely considered a success; however, as an externally imposed solution, the project did not enhance the potential of small-scale indigenous Andean communities.

The **hacienda** system in the Peruvian Andes in 1952 was a continuation of colonial social structures created by the Spaniards following their conquest of the Inca empire in the sixteenth century. The original Spanish conquerors created great landed estates for themselves out of the best lands. These estates, or *encomiendas*, like European manors, included rights to extract labor and produce from the natives who were already residents on the land. After Peru became independent from Spain, the descendants of the conquerors retained their dominant position in Andean society, and many of the *encomienda* estates remained in place as vast haciendas and plantations.

The Andean haciendas were agricultural estates with a dominant landowner and a dependent labor force that produced primarily for subsistence and local markets (Miller 1967, Mintz and Wolf 1957). In the twentieth century, haciendas were often administered by absentee owners who intentionally kept the resident natives impoverished so that many would be forced to provide cheap labor. The hacienda was divided sharply into two classes that were each further stratified. Power was concentrated at the top with the *hacendado*, the Spanish owner, and his hired administrators. The *hacendado*, or *patron*, used his landholding to enhance his personal wealth and status and was supported in his power by regional and national political authorities and church officials.

Hacienda laborers, or *peones* (Quechua-speaking indigenous peoples), were granted small subsistence holdings, often on marginal lands, and were allowed to graze their livestock on the estate. As rent, the *peones* were obligated to work three days a week for the hacienda, for which they received a token wage. They were also required to provide the hacienda free service and the labor of their animals on demand. The *peones* were treated as ignorant children by the *patron* and his managers. As serfs, they were expected to show exaggerated, hat-in-hand respect for those in charge. Uncooperative *peones* were subject to imprisonment and fines, although formerly they might have been beaten. Hacienda officials created support by dispensing small favors and sometimes acted as godparents to specific native families. Ritual co-parenthood, the institution of *compradazgo,* established an informal alliance between families of different social ranks.

When the Vicos participant intervention experiment began, the anthropologist-*patrons* immediately began to move the *peones* into administrative positions in the hacienda, replacing the former managers. Next they abolished free service and began to pay decent wages to their new native employees. Profits from agricultural production were returned to the community in the form of agricultural improvements and schooling. A formal group of community leaders was organized to participate directly in the planning of the entire project, and weekly meetings were held with all workers to discuss problems. In 1957, the project leaders petitioned the government for a decree of expropriation that would allow the natives to obtain full ownership of the hacienda. This action aroused the ire of the local elite, who accused the project of being a Communist plot, but after five years of persistent effort and the intervention of the U.S. ambassador and supportive officials within the Peruvian government, the Vicos hacienda was sold to its former serfs in 1962. The Cornell Peru Project terminated the next year. Holmberg attributed the apparent success of his experiment to its approach to political power:

> The element of power proved to be the key that permitted the Cornell Peru Project to open the door

to change; the devolution of power to the people of Vicos proved to be the mechanism that made the new system viable. (1971:62)

The emphasis on changing the local power structure in Vicos was certainly innovative in development anthropology; in retrospect, however, it is difficult to precisely evaluate the long-term impact of the project. Surveys conducted up to 1964 showed measurable improvements in nutrition, education, and some indicators of material prosperity (Dobyns, Doughty, and Lasswell 1971). Nevertheless, the project and the economic opportunities it presented were designed to favor the "most progressive" community members, and it is possible that a new elite was created. More cash wealth was flowing into the community, and agricultural production had apparently increased, but it is unclear how the new wealth was being distributed or how long the community could remain competitive in the national economy.

The community did make some critical trade-offs in its "modernization." Responding to the program's directives, they formed an agricultural cooperative organized along capitalist lines as a profit-making agricultural corporation. This move carried significant risks because it weakened or replaced many pre-Inca subsistence practices, and this may explain why researchers found that by 1963, household heads showed a substantial increase in several clinical measures of anxiety (Alers 1971). To buy the land, the new Vicos corporation assumed a substantial long-term debt

---

limited good A belief often found in peasant communities that total wealth is limited and that anyone who acquires too much is taking away from others. This is a justification for wealth leveling.

unlimited good The belief in continuous economic growth often used to justify wealth inequality.

participant intervention A form of culture change in which those in control become members of the system they seek to change.

hacienda A Latin American agricultural estate with dependent laborers that produced for local rather than global markets and was designed to maintain the social status and lifestyle of the *hacendado* landowner.

The Culture of Poverty

Anthropologist Oscar Lewis studied Latin American urban poor in Mexico, Puerto Rico, and New York and described some seventy specific features of the *culture of poverty*. Lewis (1959, 1966a, 1966b) found the poor to be relatively unorganized, yet "disengaged" from and suspicious of the political and economic institutions of urban society, even though they lived within cities. The poor lived in crowded slums (Figure 13.A), were chronically unemployed and short of food and cash, and were forced to make small, expensive purchases and to borrow at exorbitant rates. Marriages were often not legalized and easily dissolved. Poor families were unstable, and often matricentered, and children quickly assumed adult roles. Lewis found that as individuals, the poor tended to be fatalistic, with feelings of inferiority and dependency. They were present-oriented, were unwilling to defer gratification, and had little sense of history or their place in society.

FIGURE 13.A The slums of Bombay, an extreme example of urban poverty conditions. Whatever cultural patterns the world's urban poor may share, they are a response to conditions imposed by dominant classes and institutions.

with the government for half of the total purchase price. Many Vicos families also assumed large individual debts with the Peruvian government's agricultural bank to pay for the expensive new agricultural inputs required for profitable market production.

Even the new production technology involved additional trade-offs, but the project planners treated the development process as "enlightenment," virtually disregarding the centuries of accumulated agricultural knowledge already present in Vicos and the genetic value of local crop vari-

Lewis argued that these behavior patterns formed a culture of poverty that served "adaptive functions" in response to economic deprivation. He thought that poverty traits defined a self-perpetuating subculture, which he attempted to describe in positive terms. The culture of poverty, however, proved controversial because many poverty traits were negative stereotypes about the poor, which attributed poverty to ignorance. Lewis himself often acknowledged the negative aspects of poverty traits and even referred to them as pathologies. He also attributed the culture of poverty to specific conditions in the political economy, especially a capitalist economy with high unemployment, inadequate government assistance, an absence of supportive descent groups, and a dominant class that prizes wealth and attributes economic achievement to personal effort. Lewis argued that the culture of poverty was not just a response to deprivation, because not all impoverished groups shared these traits. Furthermore, he considered poverty culture to be an inadequate solution to poverty conditions. Lewis also suggested that poverty culture was self-perpetuating through socialization and might actually prove more difficult to eradicate than poverty itself. Thus, with the culture of poverty concept, Lewis, no doubt inadvertently, lent support to those who would blame the poor for their poverty. It also made it easier for some to reject public policies that would work to provide better schooling, training programs, employment opportunities, access to health care, and general public services to poor households and neighborhoods.

Critics found serious deficiencies with the culture of poverty concept. Charles Valentine (1968, 1969, 1971) objected to Lewis's use of the culture concept because Lewis relied on autobiographical oral histories of a few individual poor families. It is difficult to determine what, if any, actual subculture they represented. These families displayed numerous idiosyncrasies incompatible with the culture of poverty model. The poor neighborhoods of which they were part were also more organized than might be expected; however, larger organizational patterns do not stand out when analysis remains at the family level. The individuals in the sample families were often more "engaged" with the world around them than the model of passivity and ignorance suggests. Valentine argued that regardless of the distinctive traits the poor may share, poverty does not constitute a self-perpetuating subculture, because poverty traits are a response to conditions imposed by dominant classes and institutions. Lewis certainly would have agreed with the last part of this interpretation.

---

eties. Stephen Brush and his associates (Brush, Carney, and Huaman 1981) have shown that high-yield hybrid potatoes produced by agricultural scientists have many disadvantages for Andean communities. The new potatoes are grown as a monocrop that requires exotic debt-producing inputs, and the crop must be sold on the national government-controlled market. By contrast, local communities control all the skills and other "inputs" required to produce and distribute native potatoes. Oxen and foot plows are locally produced and maintained. Unlike tractors, they require no imported fuel and are highly reliable. There are more than 2000 varieties of traditional potatoes, each developed for special qualities of taste, storability, and hardiness under specific local conditions. These potatoes, greatly preferred by Andean people, are readily bartered and sold in the local markets.

Anthropologist Paul Doughty (2002), who first visited Vicos in 1960, revisited in 1997 and provides an overview of the project's achievements and problems. He found that the trend toward material prosperity was continuing; however, in 1996, the people of Vicos formally disbanded their agricultural cooperative and replaced community land ownership with individual private ownership.

The Vicos project closely resembled Peru's later agrarian reform program of 1969, which also expropriated haciendas and promoted commercial agriculture. However, it is significant that although many Andean communities were eager to gain control over their lands under the new land reform program, they stubbornly and sometimes violently refused to form cooperatives and resisted agricultural "modernization." Diane Hopkins (1985) suggests that this refusal to cooperate with the government program was not because the peasants were ignorant and backward. They simply did not want the government to become their new *patron,* and they rationally preferred their own forms of agricultural production.

At the local level, the Andean system is based on barter of food products between communities, exchanges of labor based on *ayni* (simple reciprocity), and household ownership of widely dispersed plots. This form of land ownership is a distinctively tribal cultural pattern and assumes relative equality and self-sufficiency while it minimizes risk and makes effective use of local resources. In the Andean setting, small, intensively utilized plots, though disparaged by agricultural economists as **minifundia,** can be highly productive. The national agrarian reform plan calls for the peasants to be integrated into the national economy by means of agricultural cooperatives

in debt to the government and dependent on the market economy. The advantage for the government of such an arrangement is that it gives it greater control over the peasantry and provides inexpensive food to support urban industrialization. This kind of rural development might make some farmers wealthy, but it brings substantial risks and means that local control systems will be effectively lost.

SUMMARY

Since the 1950s, poverty has been conceptualized as a development or modernization problem. Development planners assumed that people were poor because they were underdeveloped, and they were underdeveloped because they were technologically backward and culturally conservative. Hoping to reduce poverty, the developed countries optimistically financed the transfer of agricultural technologies, dam and highway construction, and other large-scale developments designed to promote economic growth throughout the world. Unfortunately, these efforts have not significantly reduced poverty.

Initially, anthropologists enthusiastically endorsed this development model and worked in small communities to identify the cultural barriers to economic progress. It became apparent, however, that traditional cultures were not the primary cause of poverty. National and international efforts to raise GNP in many cases actually further impoverished local communities by promoting debt and dependency and intensified internal inequalities that reduced access to basic resources. Anthropological data also show that many cultural traits, which development planners may consider to be causes of poverty, are rational coping mechanisms to conditions of extreme deprivation. Similarly, overpopulation cannot be a sole cause

---

minifundia Tiny landholdings of the Latin American peasantry.

of poverty. Although population growth has certainly intensified poverty, the relationship is complex. Poverty and the development process itself have both fostered population growth.

The scale and power approach suggests that poverty will not be solved by increasing the scale of production or making everyone dependent on global market exchanges. The evidence presented in previous chapters showed that poverty was essentially absent in autonomous tribal cultures but was first created by the inequality inherent in the social ranking of political-scale cultures. Poverty was further intensified by the process of colonialism and the global system of stratification that emerged with commercialization. To be effective, development efforts designed to reduce poverty must deal with the inequalities of wealth and power that exist at all levels of the global system.

STUDY QUESTIONS

1. How did UN experts conceptualize the problem of global poverty in 1950? What specific indicators of underdevelopment did they refer to? What was the vicious cycle? What solutions did they call for?

2. In what sense can it be said that poverty has increased since 1950? Refer to poverty indicators, absolute numbers of impoverished people, and GNP rankings between nations.

3. Describe the official charter and the institutional basis for the UN's approach to development, referring to the following: UN Charter, Universal Declaration of Human Rights, technical assistance, integrated development, Development Decades, Economic and Social Council, World Bank, FAO, UN Development Programme.

4. Define the following development-related concepts: official development assistance, multilateral assistance, bilateral assistance, and gross national product.

5. Describe how the issues and strategies of the UN's approach to development have changed in the decades since 1950.

6. Define underdevelopment and poverty, discussing the conceptual and cultural problems that limit the usefulness of your definitions.

7. In what sense can development itself be considered an industry?

8. Describe the major categories of U.S. foreign assistance and the institutional pathways that it follows to reach impoverished villagers in the developing world. Refer to multilateral aid, bilateral aid, military aid, development aid, food aid, and the economic support fund. What evidence is there that factors other than humanitarian concerns influence foreign aid?

9. Explain how the following concepts reflect changing priorities in official U.S. approaches to development: Point Four, Freedom from Hunger, privatization, free market, biotechnology.

10. How does U.S. food aid benefit U.S. interests?

11. Discuss how colonialism, social structure, population growth, and technological advance were related to poverty in Bangladesh at both national and village levels.

12. Describe village social structure in Bangladesh emphasizing access to land, labor, technology, food, and cash income in relation to standard of living.

13. What is meant by structural violence and what does it add to the understanding of poverty?

14. Discuss cultural obstacles to development programs, referring to folk society, closed corporate community, and limited good.

15. What was the culture of poverty, according to Lewis? Why was this concept so controversial, and how was it related to public policy issues? What conceptual and methodological problems have been identified?

16. Define the following terms and concepts related to Latin American and Andean peasantries: *encomienda, hacendado, patron, peones, compradazgo,* hacienda, plantation, *minifundia, ayni.*

17. Describe the social structure of the Vicos hacienda when the Cornell Peru Project began in 1952. Explain how the participant intervention experiment was conducted and discuss the results.

18. Why did some Andean communities refuse to participate fully in Peru's agrarian reform program? Identify specific points of conflict, referring to production technologies, cooperatives, *ayni,* risk, debt, market economy, subsistence economy, barter exchange, and land ownership.

SUGGESTED READING

HARTMANN, BETSY, AND JAMES K. BOYCE. 1983. *A Quiet Violence: View from a Bangladesh Village*. San Francisco: Institute for Food and Development Policy. A detailed case study of development in Bangladesh, which expands on the coverage provided in this chapter.

LAPPE, FRANCES MOORE, JOSEPH COLLINS, AND DAVID KINLEY. 1981. *Aid as Obstacle: Twenty Questions About Our Foreign Aid and the Hungry*. San Francisco: Institute for Food and Development Policy.

UNDP (UNITED NATIONS DEVELOPMENT PROGRAM). 2003. *Human Development Report. Millennium Development Goals: A compact among nations to end human poverty*. New York: Oxford University Press. Update on the UNDP's efforts to eradicate poverty.

WORLD BANK. 2001. *World Development Report 2000/2001: Attacking Poverty*. Oxford: Oxford University Press. Special edition of the World Bank's Annual Development Report, focusing on global poverty.

Quichua children in the Ecuadorean Amazon
inspect an oil pipeline traversing their territory.

14

Indigenous Peoples

Learning Objectives

After studying this chapter you should be able to do the
following.

1. Explain the political significance of the term "indigenous
   peoples" and discuss the problem of labeling such
   peoples.
2. Evaluate realist and idealist policy approaches to
   indigenous peoples by analyzing their human impact.
3. Describe the process of colonial expansion into tribal
   territories and its negative consequences using specific
   examples from East Africa, Australia, and Amazonia.
4. Describe and evaluate the diverse approaches that
   anthropologists have used in the attempt to understand
   and influence public policy on indigenous people's
   confrontation with the commercial world.
5. Describe and evaluate the diverse approaches that
   international organizations have adopted in regard to
   indigenous people's confrontation with the commercial
   world.
6. Explain what cultural autonomy means for indigenous
   people and why it would be desirable.

Indigenous peoples are members of formerly independent tribal societies who are engaged in a contemporary struggle for autonomy and survival in a world dominated by national governments and commercial elites. Previous chapters detailed the cultural background of these peoples as they existed under independent conditions (Chapters 2–5). In this chapter, we examine the conceptual, philosophical, and political issues involved in defining the place of indigenous peoples within the global system. First, we discuss the complexities of devising a non-ethnocentric concept of indigenous peoples. Next, we review the genocide and ethnocide that they suffered along the frontiers of national expansion. Finally, we examine the great humanitarian policy debate carried on by anthropologists, missionaries, and government officials since the 1830s over how states should relate to tribal peoples and their cultures.

To maintain maximum cultural context, we discuss these complex issues using extended case studies drawn from Australia (see Chapter 2) and Amazonia (see Chapter 3). The background of the International Labour Organization's controversial Conventions 107 and 169 and the promising new United Nations Universal Declaration on Rights of Indigenous Peoples are examined in detail because these are the most important modern international conventions on indigenous peoples.

INDIGENOUS PEOPLES AND THE GLOBAL CULTURE

The Politics of Labels: Defining Indigenous Peoples

The labels that one employs in any discussion of "indigenous peoples" are a critical matter because use of any specific label implies a particular understanding of what indigenous people are like and how they should be treated. Choice of labels may also be an expression of political domination or superiority. For example, use of such labels as "Stone Age tribe" implies that an indigenous group is an anachronism, perhaps lost or at least in the wrong time and place. A "Stone Age tribe" may also be seen as especially weak, childlike, helpless, and naive. In the interests of cross-cultural understanding, anthropologists generally prefer to use the self-selected terms that specific cultural groups apply to themselves.

As threatened tribal peoples became politically involved in self-defense movements early in the 1970s, many native leaders gradually adopted the term **indigenous** as a self-designation to use in pressing their claims in international forums such as the United Nations. Within the political arena, *indigenous* refers to the original inhabitants of a region and is posed in opposition to the colonists, usurpers, and intruders who came later in search of new resources to exploit. As a political category, indigenous people includes members of peasant groups and ethnic communities who have been absorbed by states but who still strongly identify with their cultural heritage and claim special rights to territory and resources on that basis.

In reference to most areas of the world, indigenous is an appropriate label for international discourse. However, if priority of residence in a territory is considered the most critical aspect of the concept of indigenous peoples, then the term *indigenous* must be applied cautiously in specific areas because indigenous peoples have sometimes displaced or absorbed other, more indigenous inhabitants. Archaeological evidence would be needed to sort out the details of settlement priority in some areas of Africa and South America. In general, however, the priority of indigenous groups relative to modern invaders connected with modern states and global culture is obvious.

Indigenous does not distinguish between people living in tribal cultures or in political-scale chiefdoms or who were incorporated as peasants into states and empires. However, it is adherence to such tribal traits as community-level resource management, high levels of local self-sufficiency, and relative social equality that makes indigenous peoples so distinctive. It is also these traits that generate conflict with larger-scale cultures that seek to extinguish local control systems and create dependency in order to extract resources. Indigenous peoples are likely to resist any external pressures for change that undermine their autonomy, yet their small size and lack of political organization make them especially vulnerable to outside intervention and give them special claims before the international community. The term *indigenous* is often preferable to similar terms such as *native,* which in some settings carries negative connotations because of its use by colonial powers. In other areas, *native* may be a self-designation used interchangeably with *indigenous.* Indigenous, now a self-appellation, has no negative connotations for the people who use it. This usage calls attention to both cultural uniqueness and the political oppression, or at least the disadvantage, that indigenous peoples must often endure from the larger-scale cultures surrounding them.

Colonizing peoples also used generic labels such as *Indian* or *aborigine* in much the same way as the term *native,* to refer to original inhabitants. Indigenous peoples may themselves also use these terms, but in this case, a negative connotation is not implied.

Historically, anthropologists have used the terms *savage, primitive, uncivilized,* and *preliterate* to call attention to cultural differences. These terms have sometimes enjoyed a certain scientific respectability, but they have not successfully avoided the popular negative connotation of backwardness. Some writers used *primitive* in the sense of primary or original and emphasized positive cultural features (Bodley 1975, 1976, Diamond 1968), but the term has now been abandoned.

Tribal is sometimes used synonymously with *indigenous* and is an acceptable self-designation in many areas of the world. In this chapter, *tribal* will refer to indigenous groups that maintain significant degrees of independence. However, the term is usually avoided in Africa because in modern political circles, *tribal* may be used pejora-

tively to imply backwardness and ethnic division. Many anthropologists also reject the term on technical grounds, because tribes, as political divisions, were created by colonial administrators. Furthermore, as was shown in earlier chapters, tribal cultures were not organized into discrete polities under centralized leadership. *Tribe* is also used to refer to a stage in cultural evolution, and missionaries often use the term to mean "ethnic group."

The problem of terminology also applies to labels given to specific cultural groups. Ethnic group names that find their way into the anthropological and popular literature may be pejorative labels applied by neighbors who despise the group in question. For example, the term *Eskimo* is an outsider term applied to people who call themselves "Inuit." Other names, like tribes, may be artificial creations of colonial governments.

Indigenous people self-identify as members of small-scale cultures and consider themselves to be the original inhabitants of the territories they occupy. In 2001, there were an estimated 200 million indigenous peoples scattered throughout the world, often in remote areas containing valuable natural resources (Figure 14.1). They are aware of the advantages of their cultural heritage in comparison with life in the larger-scale systems surrounding them.

Because indigenous people claim a territorial base and a history of independence, they resemble politically organized states and sometimes call themselves "nations." Geographer Bernard Nietschmann (1988) adopted the term **nations** in place of *tribes* to refer to indigenous people, pointing out that nations have a common territory, language, and culture, in contrast to modern states that are often composed of diverse

---

indigenous Peoples who are the original inhabitants of a territory and who seek to maintain political control over their resources and their cultural heritage.

nation A people with a common language, culture, and territory and who claim a common identity.

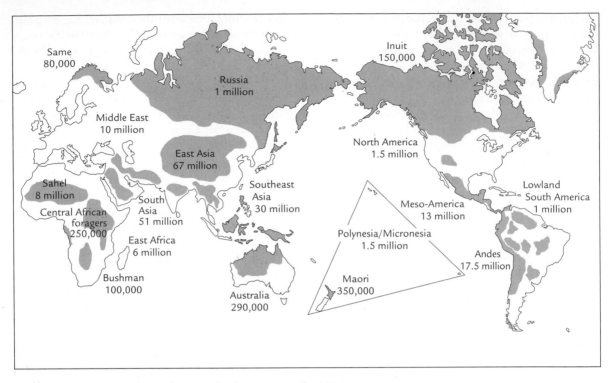

FIGURE 14.1   Estimated populations of indigenous people, 2001. (SOURCE: IWGIA 2001.)

ethnic groups. Many newly independent states were created out of former colonies with little regard for the integrity of the indigenous peoples, which they incorporated and turned into internal colonies as their territories were thrown open for development.

Policy Alternatives: Realists Versus Idealists

Over the past 500 years, the fate of indigenous peoples has been determined by government policy. Indigenous peoples have flourished when they have remained autonomous, beyond the reach of state power, but they have had great difficulty maintaining their cultural integrity and physical well-being when state power has been used against them. The extreme power differential between tribal societies and politically organized, commercial societies gives state government elites

an obvious advantage whenever direct confrontations have occurred. When indigenous peoples have prevailed, it is because of the moral force of their arguments at times when governments have been sensitive to human rights concerns. However, as the discussion in the following sections demonstrates, humanistic policies have not always been sufficient to protect the integrity of tribal societies.

The enormous human suffering caused by the commercially driven expansion of European civilization generated humanitarian concern almost immediately, but this concern was tempered by an acceptance of the reality of state power. One of the earliest and most outspoken advocates of humane treatment of indigenous people was Bartolome de Las Casas, a Catholic priest who accompanied the Spanish conquistadores to the New World in 1502. He participated in the conquest, attempting to convert the "Indians" to

Christianity, but became convinced by experience that the Spanish system of colonialism was unjust. He freed the indigenous serfs on his *encomienda* and began a lifelong campaign against the exploitation and mistreatment of the Indians. Las Casas composed a series of works condemning the worst abuses of colonialism, especially the *encomienda* system. In public debates with leading Spanish intellectuals, he championed the basic humanity of indigenous peoples, successfully challenging the concept that non-Christian Indians were subhumans who could be mistreated with impunity. Las Casas gained royal support in Madrid for his views, but the reforms he proposed were never effectively implemented in the New World (Dussel 1975).

Even if the policies that Las Casas proposed had been implemented, it is unlikely that the integrity of tribal cultures would have been secured because his policies did not question the legitimacy of the conquest itself. A fundamental philosophical difference between **realist** and **idealist** approaches separates even the most humanistic state policies toward indigenous peoples. Realist policies, such as those advocated by Las Casas, seek to moderate the negative consequences of conquest but do not challenge the authority of the state to use its power to reduce the political and economic autonomy of nonstate, tribal cultures. Thus, from the Spanish conquest to the present, realist humanitarian policies would permit the intrusion of state power and commercial interests into indigenous territories for the extraction of indigenous labor and resources; for mining, lumbering, and ranching; and for the construction of dams, highways, and other projects.

State policies based on the opposing idealist philosophy set limits on state power and recognize the local political authority and territorial sovereignty of tribal societies. Such an approach has been the de facto practice beyond the frontiers of state power and during the earliest phases of conquest, but historically, states have dominated tribal societies in the long run. In recent decades, indigenous peoples have been able to negotiate greater autonomy, and there are indications at the international level that idealist policies are gaining support. This is the **self-determination** demanded by contemporary indigenous political leaders. Such devolution of power is a promising alternative, even for local communities that have been incorporated by Great Tradition civilizations for a long time and by capitalist nations within the global culture. Self-determination may be the best way for communities to meet the basic human needs of small-scale societies.

COLONIALISM AND TRIBAL CULTURES

Since the beginning of European colonial expansion, authorities on international law maintained that indigenous peoples held legitimate group rights to political sovereignty and territory that could be taken from them only by treaty or military conquest. Tribal groups were considered to be autonomous sovereign nations. Of course, tribal nations were often militarily weaker than the colonial powers that invaded their territories and were often easily defeated in war, but the important, internationally acknowledged legal point was that a formal written document had to define the relationship between the invading power and the tribal nation. Such a document would specify the details of land ownership and the degree of independence that the indigenous group might enjoy. This left room for the abuses of ethnocide, genocide, and ecocide that accompanied colonialism and sparked the great debate over humanitarian policy. At the same time, failure to sign treaties, as was the case in Australia, deferred the question of specific rights and provided a basis

---

realist A policy position that maintains that indigenous peoples must surrender their political and economic autonomy and be integrated into dominant state societies.

idealist A policy position that advocates cultural autonomy for indigenous peoples as a basic human right.

self-determination The right of any people to freely determine its own cultural, political, and economic future.

for modern negotiations. Former agreements may also be renegotiated in reference to the higher international standards of conduct toward indigenous peoples that have steadily evolved along with the emergence of the global system.

Ethnocide, Genocide, and Ecocide

During the first, preindustrial phase of capitalist expansion, which was underway by 1450, several European powers, such as Spain, Portugal, England, and France, gained political domination over large areas in North and South America, the Caribbean, and the islands of the eastern Atlantic. This was the beginning of a colonial process of conquest and incorporation that continued into the twentieth century.

Historian Alfred Crosby (1986) notes that the Guanches, the original inhabitants of the Canary Islands in the Atlantic 200 miles (322 kilometers [km]) off the northwest coast of Africa, were perhaps the first tribal societies to be conquered by the advancing Europeans. The Guanches, who numbered some 80,000, appear to have been egalitarian village farmers with no metal tools. They resisted successive waves of French, Portuguese, and Spanish invaders from 1402 until the Spaniards gained full control of the islands in 1496.

The Guanches who survived the conquest were dispossessed, exiled, and enslaved. Their culture was destroyed, and by 1540, the Guanche had virtually disappeared as a people. The Spaniards stripped the forests and sold the timber and other resources of the Canaries. They replaced the native flora and fauna with European species and established sugarcane plantations based on slave labor. Deforestation initiated flooding and erosion and then caused the local climate to become arid. All of the negative impacts of colonial expansion—**ethnocide, genocide,** and **ecocide**—were underway in the Canaries when Christopher Columbus passed through in 1492 on his first crossing of the Atlantic.

In 1800, at the beginning of the Industrial Revolution, preindustrial states still existed in China, Japan, and Africa, and traditional kingdoms and chiefdoms in India, the Middle East, and the Pacific still retained considerable autonomy. The great Western colonial powers had made claims over 55 percent of the world's land area but exercised effective control over only 33 percent of the world (Clark 1936). Approximately half the world was still controlled by relatively autonomous and largely self-sufficient tribal cultures, containing perhaps 200 million people, roughly 20 percent of the global population (Figure 14.2). Over the next 150 years, virtually all tribal territory was conquered by colonizing industrial states, and perhaps 50 million tribal peoples died. This process created the modern world system, but at an enormous cost in the ethnocide, genocide, and ecocide suffered by the peoples and territories forcibly incorporated by the new system.

Incorporation, in this context, means that natural resources and or human labor begin to flow into the world system from formerly "external" areas. From the viewpoint of the peoples and cultures being incorporated, incorporation sets in motion a process of demographic disruption and destroys political and economic autonomy. Demographic disruption first appears as drastic depopulation when people are enslaved and killed by invaders and when they die from newly introduced diseases to which they have little immunity. Mortality is increased when culturally established support networks are interrupted and food systems disturbed. Epidemic diseases that make everyone sick at once can be devastating in a tribal society.

Much of the increased mortality occurred as a direct result of violence perpetrated against tribal peoples during their conquest by outsiders. In rare cases, governments followed a policy of deliberate genocide in an effort to totally exterminate a tribal population, and many government officials organized military campaigns against tribal groups. The largest tribal loss of life probably resulted from the actions of individual colonists who sought to profit from tribal territories before governments established formal political control. On the **uncontrolled frontier,** colonial

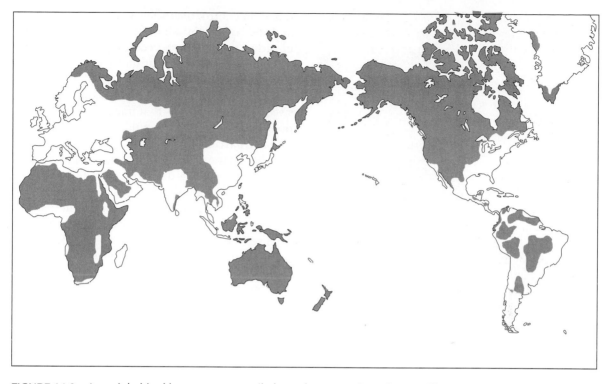

FIGURE 14.2   Areas inhabited by autonomous tribal peoples, approximately 200 million people (20 percent of the global population), 1800.

governments, as a matter of policy, allowed their citizens to systematically kill and exploit tribal peoples (Bodley 1999) (Figure 14.3). Where tribal peoples were not needed as a source of labor, they were classified as "nonhuman" savages and were killed with impunity to remove them from the land.

Increased mortality is a special threat to the survival of tribal cultures that rely on fertility-limiting cultural practices to maintain their small, low-density, low-growth populations. Many of these groups simply disappeared when the frontier overtook them, and only their territories remained to be incorporated.

The loss of political autonomy by tribal peoples occurs when state governments gain enough power over a tribal territory to prevent tribal groups from acting in their own defense to expel outsiders. This can occur following military con-

quest, or it can be accomplished by formal treaty signing or some less formal process by which government control is extended over a formerly autonomous tribal area. In most cases, the relative difference in power between tribal cultures and states is so extreme that the state can impose control over a tribal territory virtually at will, although it can be a costly and time-consuming process.

State political control usually is symbolized by the appointment of political authorities and

ethnocide The forced destruction of a cultural system.
genocide The extermination of a human population.
ecocide The degradation of an ecosystem.
uncontrolled frontier A tribal territory that is invaded by colonists from a state-organized society but where the government chooses not to regulate the actions of the colonists.

FIGURE 14.3 Contemporary engraving of an attack against Australian aborigines. The uncontrolled frontier phase of capitalist expansion often involved direct physical violence against indigenous peoples.

maintain control over their subsistence resources in order to remain self-sufficient. Drastic depopulation can reduce the economic viability of a tribal group, but competition with colonists over resources, especially when the tribal land base is reduced by government decree, is often the decisive factor. Any factors that undermined the traditional subsistence base would push tribal peoples toward participation in the market economy, whether as wage laborers or **cash croppers.**

There was also a desire to secure some of the manufactured goods, such as metal tools and factory clothing, produced by the world system's industrial centers. However, the "pull" forces in themselves were insufficient to compel tribal peoples into large-scale participation in the market economy without a strong "push." Whenever their subsistence economy remained strong, tribal peoples were often poorly motivated target workers, and colonial administrators resorted to legal measures such as special taxes and planting laws to force reluctant tribal groups into the market economy. Once initiated, involvement in the market economy can become self-reinforcing because wage labor leaves little time for subsistence activities and cash cropping can degrade the local ecosystem and reduce its potential for subsistence production.

The cost of industrial expansion was minimized or ignored by the economists and politicians who championed growth with "differential benefits" for the colonized and the colonizers, but anthropologists who conducted fieldwork on the colonial frontiers observed the devastation firsthand and often attempted to minimize it.

The Humanitarian Response

Throughout their expanding colonial empire, the British used military force against resisting indigenous peoples, but they consistently drew up formal treaties to legalize the transfer of political authority and tribal lands to Europeans. British policy in Australia was a striking exception because the presence of the aborigines as mobile foragers was never legally acknowledged and no

the introduction of a police force. State functions such as taxation, military recruitment, and census taking usually follow, along with the imposition of a legal system, courts, and jails. Administrative issues to be dealt with by colonial officials concerned specifying the differential rights of the native population and the colonizing population to land and other natural resources. Special regulations defined the conditions under which natives would be employed and how native culture could be expressed.

The loss of economic autonomy is fostered by political conquest because tribal groups must

treaties were signed. The abuses of British colonialism, which flourished under such legalism, inspired a dedicated group of British humanitarians led by Thomas Fowell Buxton, who formed the Anti-Slavery Society in 1823 and successfully campaigned for a ban on slavery throughout the empire by 1833.

In 1835, Buxton, like Las Casas, turned his attention to the larger humanitarian issue of the negative impact of colonialism on tribal peoples. Buxton, as a member of Parliament, persuaded the House of Commons to appoint a Select Committee to formulate official policies to protect the rights of tribal peoples and to ensure their just treatment. The committee conducted an extensive survey of the impact of European civilization on tribal groups throughout the empire and issued a massive report concluding that European colonialism was "a source of many calamities to uncivilized nations" (an excerpt appears in Bodley 1988:63–69). The report elaborated:

Too often, their territory has been usurped; their property seized; their numbers diminished; their character debased; the spread of civilization impeded. European vices and diseases introduced among them (House of Commons 1837:5)

The committee recommended specific corrective measures that it hoped would bring justice to tribal peoples without hindering the growth of British colonies. The most important measure acknowledged the inherent conflict between invading settlers and indigenous peoples and recommended that colonial governors in consultation with the queen and Parliament, and not local legislatures, should safeguard the rights of indigenous peoples. The committee also called for curbs on alcohol, strict controls on contract labor to prevent debt slavery, and a prohibition on the acquisition of tribal lands by settlers, arguing that there was enough empty land to satisfy the needs of settlers. Legal dispossession of tribal peoples could still take place, but it required an act of Parliament; in such cases, dispossessed natives were to be protected and educated by missionaries who would be supported by the revenues

the crown received from the sale of tribal lands. Thus, under the most liberally envisioned form of British justice at the time, the rights of natives were narrowly defined and remained secondary to the economic needs of the colonizers. This policy approach could be characterized as realist because it advocated no major changes in the existing political relationship between a dominant state power and a subordinate indigenous people. However, even these enlightened policies were seldom effectively enforced.

After the Select Committee issued its report, the committee's work was continued by the Aborigines Protection Society (APS), an advocacy group formed by committee members under the direction of Thomas Hodgkin in 1836 to "promote the advancement of Uncivilized Tribes." The APS was a model humanitarian organization that played a decisive role throughout the nineteenth century in keeping government attention focused on the painful human cost of colonialism for tribal peoples and lobbying for protective policies. Through its network of branch societies and corresponding members, the APS was able to closely monitor the condition of native peoples throughout the empire and directly petition government officials to take humanitarian action.

Proimperialist humanitarian concern for the welfare of indigenous peoples did not envision the persistence of independent tribal cultures and tended to discourage any cultural diversity. The APS remained a firm supporter of British imperialism, but even this limited application of the principle of human rights to indigenous people was an important development in the ideological system of the emerging global system.

Early international conventions containing humanitarian provisions designed to protect indigenous peoples were sometimes outrageously ethnocentric. For example, when the major imperialist powers met in Berlin in 1884–1885 to facilitate the colonial partitioning of Africa, they

cash cropping The raising of crops for market sale rather than domestic consumption.

FIGURE 14.4   Sir William E. Maxwell (seated on right), governor of the British Gold Coast colony, and a contingent of native police, 1895. The photo represents the political and military power used by Europeans to carry out the "civilizing crusade" formalized by the Berlin Africa Conference of 1884–1885.

described their action as a "civilizing crusade" and pledged to support all efforts "to educate the natives and to teach them to understand and appreciate the benefits of civilization" (General Act of the 1884–1885 Berlin Africa Conference). European elites took control to protect their political and economic interests, justifying their action as an effort to end the illegal slave trade (Figure 14.4). By 1892, the Brussels Act effectively mandated ethnocide as part of the "uplift," or civilization, process by declaring that the colonizing powers should civilize tribal peoples and "bring about the extinction of barbarous customs."

In 1907, the APS tried to persuade the international Hague Peace Conference to ban wars of extermination and punitive military raids against relatively defenseless tribal groups. This would have been a logical extension of the rules of war covered in the various Geneva Conventions, which began in 1864 with the establishment of the International Red Cross. Unfortunately, the APS proposal was not placed on the agenda because the British prime minister objected.

Toward the end of World War I, the APS had another opportunity to promote the rights of indigenous peoples during international discussions on the fate of Germany's former colonies.

These territories were scattered throughout Africa and the Pacific and contained some 30 million indigenous people, many still living independently. The APS recognized that, ideally, this would be the time to grant full political sovereignty to existing tribal nations and grant self-determination to detribalized groups. However, the APS rejected tribal independence because it would have threatened the colonial system, even though it was obvious that "protection and uplift" policies had not prevented massive depopulation of tribal areas. These policy debates, which ultimately determined the fate of countless tribal groups, were permeated with paternalistic, racist, and demeaning language. Tribal peoples were variously referred to as backward races, subject races, and child races. Under the mandate system, established by the League of Nations Covenant in 1919 to administer former German colonies, tribal peoples were called "peoples not yet able to stand by themselves under the strenuous conditions of the modern world." They were to be administered according to the principle that "the well-being and development of such peoples form a sacred trust of civilization" (League Covenant, Article 22).

Applied Anthropology and Tribal Peoples

As the British colonial system matured and increasing numbers of tribal peoples were brought under formal administrative control, the value of anthropological knowledge became obvious to colonial authorities, and many anthropologists went to work for the empire. In many respects, anthropology, as an academic discipline and as a profession, was a product of colonial expansion. It was no accident that major anthropological associations were formed in Great Britain, the United States, and France during the nineteenth century and that their publications, such as the *American Anthropologist* and the *Journal of the Royal Anthropological Institute of Great Britain and Ireland*, were filled with ethnographic notes gleaned from native peoples on

the colonial frontiers by administrators, missionaries, military men, and ethnologists.

The practical utility of anthropological knowledge for imperialist countries was recognized quickly. For example, Colonel A. H. Lane-Fox Pitt-Rivers, in his opening address to the anthropology section of the British Association for the Advancement of Science in 1871, declared,

> Nor is it unimportant to remember that Anthropology has its practical and humanitarian aspect, and that, as our race is more often brought in contact with savages than any other, a knowledge of their habits and modes of thought may be of the utmost value to us in utilizing their labour, as well as in checking those inhuman practices from which they have but too often suffered at our hands. (1872:170–171)

From the 1870s through the 1930s, as the colonial empires reached their height, two themes were frequently discussed at the meetings of anthropological associations: (1) how to salvage the ethnographic data that were being destroyed by colonial expansion and (2) how to increase the practical value of anthropology for the empire. Lane-Fox Pitt-Rivers (1882) coined the term *applied anthropology* and declared, "no subject is more capable of being turned to useful account than the scientific study of mankind" (1882:507). By the turn of the century, British anthropologists had become enthusiastic imperialists. In 1901, C. H. Read, president of the Anthropological Institute, specifically emphasized the utility of anthropology for "private enterprise" such as the great trading and colonization companies, observing,

> We should . . . be in a position to give the officers of such companies valuable information for the conduct of their affairs with natives, and thus be of distinct value to commercial enterprise. (1901:15)

Anthropologists of the Anthropological Institute and the Folklore Society addressed a formal memorandum to the Colonial Secretary in London, proposing the creation of a special commission, including anthropologists, to study native culture in areas of South Africa where colonial development was creating serious tensions between colonists and native peoples. The memorandum blamed native unrest on misunderstanding of native culture and argued that besides its obvious scientific value, anthropological knowledge would facilitate colonial administration because

1. It will enable the Government to ascertain what customs may be recognized, and what customs must be forbidden or modified, and how to effect this object with the least disturbance to tribal conditions and native prejudices.

2. It will save time and ensure certainty in the administration of justice, and obviate many difficulties in other departments of government.

3. It will afford the Government authoritative materials for legislation adjusting the arrangements for native labour in the mines, and generally dealing with the relations between the natives and European settlers. (Anthropological Institute 1903:70–74)

After many more petitions and endorsements by various scientific committees, colonial administrations finally began to hire government anthropologists and recommended anthropological training for administrators. In a short period of time in the 1920s and 1930s, applied anthropology became institutionalized in the British empire. In 1921, A. R. Radcliffe-Brown was appointed to an anthropology professorship in South Africa where he became a popular lecturer on the "native problem." Radcliffe-Brown stressed that understanding the "laws" of cultural development would give administrators "control over the social forces." More specifically, in 1923 he argued that knowing

the functions of native institutions . . . can afford great help to the missionary or the public servant who is engaged in dealing with the practical problems of the adjustment of the native civilization to the new conditions that have resulted from our occupation of the country. (Radcliffe-Brown 1958:32)

Applied anthropologists did not expect to be too directly involved in policymaking, for that was to be left to administrators. Applied anthropologists avoided value judgments about colonialism while hoping that anthropological knowledge would be used to minimize the damage that imperialist expansion was causing to native peoples. Aside from standard functionalist analysis, the major object of research for applied anthropologists was **acculturation,** or culture change (Redfield, Linton, and Herskovits 1936); both of these were ethically neutral concepts that masked the harsh political realities of imperialism.

Acculturation studies inventoried highly visible changes such as the adoption by tribal peoples of European clothing, crops, implements, language, and Christianity and the corresponding abandonment of traditional cultural features. The loss of political and economic autonomy was not usually examined as acculturation. In reality, firsthand contact meant conquest and dispossession of native peoples by colonial soldiers and settlers. Acculturation was forced culture change and was primarily an unequal process in which tribal peoples were subordinated and exploited. However, applied anthropologists in the service of the empire could hardly be expected to draw attention to the negative side of imperialism.

The real native problem that perplexed colonial administrators was how to keep the natives from resorting to armed resistance while settlers were depriving them of their lands and how to turn them into docile taxpayers and willing and effective laborers on their former lands. Culture change was supposed to be slow to avoid detribalization, which would make control more difficult and could lead to depopulation and labor shortages.

The primary recommendation from applied anthropologists was for administrators to use **indirect rule** to maintain political control. This meant using local native chiefs to serve as government agents and intermediaries and creating them when they did not already exist. **Direct rule** by European officers was culturally insensitive and prohibitively expensive.

Bronislaw Malinowski, a prominent British functionalist, was emphatic on the advantages of indirect, or dependent, rule:

In fact, if we define dependent rule as the control of Natives through the medium of their own organization, it is clear that only dependent rule can succeed. For the government of any race consists rather in implanting in them ideas of right, of law and order, and making them obey such ideas. (1929:23)

The Native Problem in Kenya

Kenya colony in East Africa illustrates the political domination and economic exploitation that occurred as European powers forced much of Africa into the capitalist global system in the late nineteenth and early twentieth centuries. As discussed in Chapter 4, Nilotic-speaking cattle peoples and Bantu farmers effectively adapted their tribal cultures to the distinctive ecosystems of East Africa some 2000 years ago. Around AD 800, the expanding Islamic empire reached the East African coast and established small centers that became important conduits for the slave and ivory trade. There was no Arab settlement in the interior, and the indigenous peoples retained their economic and political autonomy despite the disruption of the slave trade. The Maasai dominated the best pasturelands, centered in the Rift Valley, and raided their neighbors for cattle.

By the 1870s, European explorers ventured into the East African interior in increasing numbers. In 1886, Germany declared a protectorate over part of what is now Tanzania, taking advantage of a series of treaties arranged between African "chiefs" and German colonists. In the same year, Britain and Germany agreed to divide the entire East African region between themselves. Officially, the justification for British intrusion was to help end the slave trade and improve the condition of the Africans, in line with the rules established by the Berlin Africa Conference of 1884–1885 (Figure 14.5).

In 1896, the British government created the East Africa Protectorate and established fortified outposts and used punitive expeditions, frequently pitting Maasai allies against their Bantu neighbors, to impose a *Pax Britannica*. The administrative arrangements that followed gave the European

THE RHODES COLOSSUS
STRIDING FROM CAPE TOWN TO CAIRO.

FIGURE 14.5 Cecil Rhodes, prime minister of Britain's Cape Colony in southern Africa, astride the African continent. This 1892 political cartoon symbolizes the arrogance of European colonialism.

minority complete political power over more than 2 million disenfranchised Africans who were expected to serve as units of labor and pay their taxes while learning the "benefits of civilization." The process of using political and economic force to create a dependent underclass of laborers resembles the enclosure movement that

---

acculturation The concept used by colonial applied anthropologists to describe the changes in tribal culture that accompanied European conquest but that minimized the role of coercion and the loss of tribal autonomy.

indirect rule The situation in which European colonial administrators appointed local natives to serve as mediating officials, or chiefs, to help them control local communities.

direct rule The use of European colonial administrators to control a native community at the local level.

prepared the way for industrial capitalism in England (see Chapter 11).

The consolidation of political and economic control over the protectorate was a complex process that the British administration carried out in stages as specific legislation was drafted. The cool and fertile highlands were declared uninhabited and opened for European settlement, even though they were the center of Maasai territory. In 1920, the protectorate became the Crown Colony of Kenya. In 1924, areas of European settlement were given a separate administrative system, while "native" provinces and districts were placed under a chief native commissioner, senior provincial commissioners, and district commissioners—all Europeans. Village "chiefs" were appointed by the administration and treated like government employees with very limited authority. A simple system of native courts was given limited authority to maintain order at the local level. From the start, the political structure was designed to favor European interests at the expense of Africans. The colony's legislative council was dominated by twenty officially appointed European administrators. The interests of indigenous Africans were represented by two European appointees among twenty unofficial council members.

In 1911, there were only 3175 Europeans in the East Africa protectorate, which also contained an indigenous African population that was estimated at 2.5–4 million. The number of Europeans increased fourfold, to 12,529 by 1926, but even after the European population reached 30,524 in 1948, it still constituted barely 0.05 percent of the total population (Buell 1928, Hailey 1950).

Europeans were drawn to the protectorate by promises of low taxes and abundant resources, cheap land, and cheap African labor, all waiting to be exploited. Lumber, grain, livestock, rubber, copra, and gold were soon flowing to world markets, along with the hides, horns, and ivory of big game animals that were being slaughtered in great numbers by European hunters. By 1908, the

value of exported East African natural resources exceeded 400,000 pounds sterling annually (Great Britain Board of Trade 1909) (Figure 14.6). Nearly one-fourth of these resources were destined for the United Kingdom, and two-thirds went to the world's major industrial powers: the United Kingdom, the United States, France, and Germany (Great Britain Board of Trade 1909) (Figure 14.7).

The British administration gained control over African land simply by enacting the necessary legislation. The only concern was that the appearance of justice and legality be maintained so that humanitarians in London would not protest in Parliament. The Crown Lands Ordinance of 1902 merely specified that the government could not sell land that the Africans were actually occupying, but it provided that "unoccupied" lands could be "leased" to colonists in lots of 1000 acres (405 hectares) for 99 years. The Crown Lands Ordinance of 1915 left no doubt about who would control the land by declaring that all African lands were "crown lands" and could be alienated by the government. This policy permitted a tiny European elite to systematically acquire the best agricultural lands while dispossessing the indigenous owners.

More than 40,000 Maasai were forced to give up more than half of their territory under the terms of a treaty in 1904, by which they agreed to move into northern and southern reserves, abandoning the central Rift Valley to a handful of European settlers. The Maasai reserves were supposed to last "so long as the Maasai as a race shall exist" (Buell 1928:312). However, in 1911, the northern reserve turned out to be good farmland, and by 1913, the protesting Maasai were consolidated on the much poorer southern reserve.

Harvard political scientist Raymond Buell examined the Maasai case and concluded that the government's action was legally unjustified, but he suggested that the Maasai themselves were partly responsible for the loss of their land because their culture was unsuitable. In exaggerated and ethnocentric terms that showed a complete

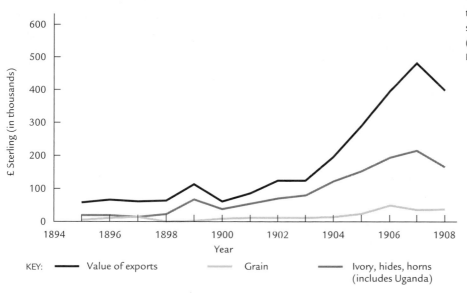

KEY: ——— Value of exports   ——— Grain   ——— Ivory, hides, horns (includes Uganda)

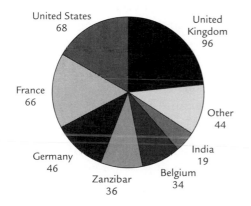

FIGURE 14.7   Destination and value, in pounds sterling (in thousands), of exports from the East Africa protectorate, 1908. (SOURCE: Great Britain Board of Trade 1909.)

misunderstanding of Maasai culture, Buell described them as

> aimless and wandering pastoralists, owning economically worthless but continually increasing cattle. Their military organization was a constant

menace to other natives, while their warrior villages were a corrupting influence inside of the tribe. (1928:315–316)

Between 1907 and 1912, a series of native reserves were proposed on "crown land" for African use in order to officially open land for European settlement. However, colonists objected that such reserves might be self-sustaining, and Africans would not need to work for Europeans in order to support themselves. Government commissions recommended that reserves be drawn up to suit the needs of only the immediate African population with the expectation that population growth would soon force people to seek wage labor. In 1919, Governor Northey justified such a policy with an appeal to the ideology of capitalist economics:

> No one wants to take away any land that natives occupy or are using productively, but we can say, in these days of productivity and development, and world-wide shortage of food and raw materials, that Crown lands not made productive, may, by law, be made so as required. (Buell 1928:319)

This emphasis on productive use was somewhat misplaced, in view of the fact that in 1922, Europeans were cultivating only 6 percent of the land that they had appropriated. The inequities in the land system were obvious. Some 9000 Europeans were occupying 3.8 million acres (1.5 million hectares), with 422 acres (171 hectares) of prime land per capita. By 1926, twenty-three native reserves were actually established, and 2.5 million Africans were crowded into 29.9 million acres (12.1 million hectares), leaving them with only 12 often very poor acres (5 hectares) per capita.

Africans who wished to develop their land along European lines faced significant difficulties. They could not legally purchase land outside the reserves or individually own land within the reserves. The colonists encouraged dispossessed Africans to remain on their former lands as squatters, because African squatters were legally required to work 6 months per year for the landowners.

Hut and poll taxes were designed to provide revenue to help fund the administration and to force the Africans to find wage labor on European farms. The total African contribution to the state's revenue in direct taxes was twenty-five times the European contribution between 1900 and 1925 (Ross 1927). Africans also paid indirect taxes in the form of 10 percent custom duties that were added to the price of cloth, beads, and other trade goods. Because the total value of cash-crop farming on the native reserves covered barely two-thirds of the African tax, Africans were compelled to seek outside employment. Professional labor recruiters toured the reserves and paid local chiefs for rounding up workers. These efforts met with success because the number of employed Africans rose from 12,000 in 1912 to over 185,000 in 1927—approximately 14 African laborers for every man, woman, and child in the European population.

The attitude of Europeans toward African labor is illustrated by the British Masters and Servants Ordinances of 1906, which made it a crime punishable by a fine of a month's wages and up to a month in prison for a "servant" to be late to work, to be absent without permission, or to insult or disobey an employer. Six months' imprisonment was the punishment for quitting. In 1915, all African males over 16 were required to register with the government, be fingerprinted, and carry identity papers. This procedure helped, but desertion remained enough of a problem because of low wages and poor working conditions that in 1925 the government approved a proposal to establish special detention camps for labor offenders.

British colonial policies were unusually harsh in Kenya because European settlement was a primary objective, unlike in British colonies in West Africa, where the climate was considered unsuitable for European settlement. Indirect rule was also more easily practiced in West Africa, where traditional kingdoms were more common. In Kenya, indigenous peoples found it difficult to follow traditional cultural patterns in the absence of political and economic autonomy, and they were legally excluded from effective participation in the capitalist economy introduced by their British conquerors. The obvious inequities of the situation ultimately led to the Mau Mau armed rebellion of 1952–1959 and political reforms culminating in Kenya's independence from colonial rule in 1963.

THE AUSTRALIAN ABORIGINAL POLICY DEBATE

The experience of Australian aborigines further demonstrates how the political fate of tribal groups often is determined by government policies, which, in turn, are shaped by the demands of varied special-interest groups exercising political power. In Australia, as in East Africa, anthropologists have often played a role in shaping and supporting government policies toward indigenous peoples.

Genocidal Protection and Uplift

The European invasion of Australia began in 1788 with the founding of Port Jackson, now

Sydney, as a penal colony. Because the aborigines were not settled farming peoples and had no chiefs, colonial administrators declared Australia to be an "empty wasteland" and dispensed with treaty signing. The aborigines were granted no legal existence and no official claim to their land. As elsewhere, genocide and ethnocide followed the Australian frontiers of European settlement. Except where aborigines were useful as labor, they were systematically eliminated by poison, disease, and shooting as if they were wild animals. Tasmania's aboriginal population was reduced from 5000 to 111 within 30 years. In western Victoria, 4000 aborigines were reduced to 213 within 40 years, and 10 years later no one remained who could reliably describe the culture (Corris 1968). Witnesses before the Select Committee in the 1830s reported "many deeds of murder and violence" committed by settlers on the Australian frontier. This situation persisted well into the twentieth century. According to A. G. Price, in the Northern Territory in 1901, "It was notorious, that the blackfellows were shot down like crows and that no notice was taken" (1950:107–108).

Appeals by the Aborigines Protection Society (APS) led to the establishment of aboriginal reserves and protectors of natives in Australia by 1850. These actions did not prevent the wholesale extinction of aborigines in many areas of Australia, but they did demonstrate that such injustice was officially disapproved. Aboriginal reserves at this time were not considered to be aboriginal lands where aborigines could live independently; instead, they served a dual protection and "uplift" role. Reserves were to contain mission schools and farms where aborigines would learn civilized skills.

The fact, which no one disputed, was that aborigines were facing extinction as a result of frontier violence and dispossession. By contrast, from 1788 to 1880, the European population increased to 3 million. And by 1920, there were 5 million Europeans and barely 60,000 aborigines, a mere 20 percent of the widely accepted estimate of 300,000 for the pre-European population. All authorities anticipated a continuing decline in the aboriginal population, and many predicted their total extinction. Everyone agreed that the European invasion was responsible, but the government still followed the inadequate "protection and uplift" approach devised by the House of Commons Select Committee and the Aborigines Protection Society in the 1830s.

By 1880, the sparsely settled Northern Territory, which contained 17 percent of Australia's land area, had become the last great frontier. There were fewer than 700 Europeans throughout the territory's 500,000 square miles (mi^2) (1.3 million square kilometers [km^2]) stretching from the desert center of Australia to the tropical north coast. This vast, seemingly inhospitable region was the ancestral homeland of unknown thousands of aborigines still living independently. European Australians saw the territory as a great pastoral frontier, and there was still no national policy permitting the aborigines to defend themselves, their resources, and their culture against the final invasion that was just beginning.

The government encouraged immigration into the territory to promote economic development, fully aware that the aborigines would be victimized. To minimize the damage, humanitarians like Sydney's Archdeacon Lefroy (1912) recommended federal control of all aborigines by a permanent Native Commission and urged the formation of reserves on which aborigines could be preserved and "uplifted" by becoming cattle ranchers. A committee of the Australasian Association for the Advancement of Science, which included pioneer Central Australian ethnographers Baldwin Spencer and Francis Gillen, drafted a resolution to the government that incorporated Lefroy's proposals. The committee emphasized that aborigines were "a valuable labor asset" in the pastoral economy as a justification for a preservation policy. There was no attempt to protect aboriginal culture, except in museums, or to defend aboriginal political autonomy; instead, the emphasis was on "the well-being and preservation of the native race," presumably as units of labor

(ANZAAS 1914). However, even these modest ameliorative proposals were ineffective.

By 1920, there were some 4000 Europeans and 600,000 cattle in the Northern Territory, steadily advancing against an aboriginal population estimated at 17,000 who faced a grim future. A mere 30,000 square miles (77,770 km^2), barely 6 percent of the territory, had been designated for aboriginal reserves, even though the aborigines were still the majority population, outnumbering Europeans more than four to one. The reserves contained cattle stations and missions where the aborigines were to be "civilized," just as the Aborigines Protection Society envisioned in the nineteenth century.

Reserves, Assimilation, and Land Rights

As the situation for aborigines in the Northern Territory became increasingly desperate, anthropologist Frederic Wood Jones (1928) issued a stinging condemnation of the established policy of limited protectionism and uplift. In an emotional presidential address to the anthropology section of the Australasian Association for the Advancement of Science in 1926, Wood Jones declared that "civilizing" the aborigine, whether on missions or cattle stations, meant extermination. Using missionary reports, he showed that the aborigines in the best condition were those most remote from civilization. Missionized aborigines were unhealthy and ill-housed and continued to die. Arguing that the missions were a form of humanitarian euthanasia that had failed in every sense, Wood Jones concluded, "I fail to see any sort of justification for a belief that salvation for the Australian native can ever lie in this direction" (1928:504).

Wood Jones was just as critical of the government effort to provide welfare to the aborigines on the fringes of civilization. He suggested that it was a form of conscience money that served to hide the fact that aboriginals were being dispossessed. He also challenged the belief that the aborigine could be converted to a "coolie" population to provide cheap labor for the pastoral stations. He pointed out that although individuals might become successful station hands, they did not reproduce to replace themselves. There seemed to be no substitute for the traditional independent life.

He further argued that the existing reserves were "fictions and frauds" because they existed only on paper and were revoked whenever outside economic interests demanded entry: "There are no real reserves in Australia where the aborigine is free to live, what everyone is agreed on calling, a life uncontaminated by the white man" (1928:513).

A "real reserve" in Wood Jones' terms would be one that allowed the continuation of tribal "culture and traditions." Melbourne anthropologist Donald Thomson (1938) proposed making Arnhem Land, in the far north of the Northern Territory, just such a reserve after he conducted a government-commissioned field investigation there in 1935–1937. Some 1500 aborigines were still living independently in Arnhem Land, and when five Japanese fishermen and a policeman were killed on the reserve, the government hoped Thomson could help settle the matter peacefully. Thomson was trained in functionalist applied anthropology by Radcliffe-Brown at Sydney, but he was also a close associate of Wood Jones. Thomson's sympathies were clearly with the aborigines. He concluded that the killings were self-defense, and he recommended that Arnhem Land be made an absolutely inviolable reserve, with missionaries and ranchers excluded, in order to allow the aborigines freedom to maintain their nomadic settlement pattern, culture, and social structure. This was perhaps the first time that an idealist policy approach was seriously proposed for Australia.

This approach was soundly rejected by Sydney anthropologist A. P. Elkin, who represented the vested interests of the government and missionary organizations. Elkin was an influential and outspoken advocate of "justice" for aborigines. But he also wanted to secure a place for both anthropology and missions in the business of smoothing what he considered to be the inevitable **assimilation** of aborigines from their independent tribal life into a settled existence within civilized Australian society. Trained by Radcliffe-Brown and Malinowski in functionalist applied anthropology, Elkin became a leading expert on aboriginal culture. However, he also accepted Radcliffe-Brown's ominous dictum that "the Australian Aborigines, even if not doomed to extinction as a race, seem at any rate doomed to have their cultures destroyed" (1934:3).

As an anthropologist, Elkin clearly understood the centrality of totemism in aboriginal culture. But he considered it an obsolete and ignorant belief that was to be replaced by "a religious and philosophical outlook which will enable them [the aborigines] to see that their own spiritual life and the future of natural species is not bound up with the integrity of particular spots on the earth's surface" (1934:7). Oblivious to his own ethnocentrism and convinced that the culture was doomed, Elkin went on to suggest, "Wise teaching on religion and in the rudiments of science should do much to enable the natives to pass through the difficult transition period for which we are responsible" (1934:7).

The irony of this is that the aborigines were right on this very critical issue. Totemism was not a matter of tribal ignorance over which the aborigines needed to be educated. The spiritual life of aborigines and the future of their natural resources are inextricably linked to the ultimate integrity of their sacred sites, but it was nearly 40 years before government policy grudgingly came to acknowledge this point with the Northern Territory Land Rights Act of 1971. Accepting the validity of the totemic system would have meant also acknowledging the legitimacy of the aboriginal claim to full control over their land, resources, and political and economic independence.

Rather than advocating aboriginal rights, Elkin called for a "positive policy" for aborigines, based on close collaboration between church and state to promote "education as well as law, order, harmony, and pacification." Elkin was a religious man, ordained in 1915 as an Anglican priest, and was in charge of a parish until 1937. Combining his religious role with his training as an applied

anthropologist, he advised missionaries to "build on the religious life of the natives, modifying it where necessary, and seeking its fulfillment along Christian lines" (Elkin 1933:6).

Elkin opposed any aboriginal claim to the land that would stand in the way of outside development interests. In his view, keeping whites off the reserves "of course, cannot be done once gold or valuable land be found in them." Elkin's policy approach was probably related to his position in the Sydney anthropology department, which he began to chair in 1934. The department developed an applied program under Radcliffe-Brown's earlier direction and with Rockefeller Foundation grants. The Sydney program was designed to support the government's colonial development policies, and Elkin emphatically disassociated his department from any support for aboriginal autonomy:

> It should be stated quite clearly and definitely that anthropologists connected with the Department in the University of Sydney have no desire to preserve any of the aboriginal tribes of Australia or of the islands in their pristine condition as "museum specimens" for the purpose of investigation; this charge is too often made against anthropologists . . . for change is coming, and anthropologists, like all good members of a "higher" and trustee race, are concerned with the task of raising primitive races in the cultural scale. (1934:3)

Twenty years later, Elkin's assimilation approach was still the government's solution to the "aboriginal problem." In 1952, Paul Hasluck, minister for territories, publicly attacked "a few" unnamed anthropologists whose "mystical" belief in "changeless primitive culture" had led them to advocate strict inviolability of aboriginal reserves. Hasluck declared contemptuously, "My view is that no society can live in such an isolated dreamland as that" (Hasluck 1953:156).

---

assimilation Ethnocide without genocide; the loss of distinctive cultural traits as a population surrenders its autonomy and is absorbed into a dominant society and culture.

Of course, the real issue was not the existence of culture change, but the political independence of tribal peoples and whether outsiders should be allowed to dictate the kind of changes that occur on tribal land. Hasluck inadvertently admitted that the government had no intention of respecting the boundaries of tribal reservations when he rhetorically asked, "Do we expect that they can remain static even if protected by imaginary lines, drawn around reserves, when a new and active society and culture are brought into their country?" (1953:157).

Hasluck knew that the reserves were a sham, that the government would not permit tribal autonomy, yet he shamelessly argued that good social science culture change theory had led him to such a conclusion. The ethnocentric policy that Hasluck promoted was uncompromising assimilationist, which he described in the following terms:

> A policy of assimilation means, to my mind, that we expect that, in the course of time, all persons of aboriginal blood or mixed-blood in Australia will live in the same manner as white Australians do, that they will have full citizenship, and that they will, of their own desire, participate in all the activities of the Australian community. (1953:163)

The government continued this rigid policy of rejecting aboriginal self-determination and land rights into the 1970s when politically active aboriginal organizations began to publicly demand legal ownership of traditional lands. The protest began in 1971 when the government rejected aboriginal claims of ownership to the Arnhem Land Reserve. The aboriginal landowners wanted to protect their sacred sites by preventing a multinational mining company from strip mining bauxite inside the reserve. By 1973, the protest began to take on international dimensions, and the government appointed an Aboriginal Land Rights Commission to find a solution. The result was the Aboriginal Land Rights (Northern Territory) Act of 1976, which provided a legal mechanism for aboriginal communities to gain title to their traditional lands. This was a major victory for aborigines, although the act provided only limited protection from outside development and

was later weakened by amendments. The real significance of the act was that it meant that the government was finally acknowledging the legitimacy of aboriginal culture and the right of aborigines to maintain themselves as independent communities.

DECOLONIZATION AND HUMAN RIGHTS

The decolonization era, which began with the founding of the United Nations in 1945, was also the beginning of a gradual shift away from the paternalistic and ethnocentric bias of even the most humanitarian of colonial policies toward indigenous peoples. The United Nations and affiliated organizations such as the International Labour Organisation (ILO) provided an international framework within which the concept of human rights was steadily expanded to include indigenous peoples as cultural groups and to legitimize their struggle for self-determination. The extension of fundamental human rights to indigenous peoples has been a slow and difficult process requiring decisive participation by indigenous peoples themselves.

The United Nations and Indigenous Peoples

The UN Charter provided an opening for indigenous rights, but it still contained ethnocentric thinking. Article 1 of the charter proclaimed support for "the principle of equal rights and self-determination of peoples," but it did not define *peoples*. The only provisions in the charter specifically applicable to indigenous peoples were in Chapters XI–XIII describing the international trusteeship system. The "Declaration Regarding Non-Self-Governing Territories" in Article 73 ethnocentrically speaks of "territories whose peoples have not yet attained a full measure of self-government." This language was obviously ethnocentric when applied to Pacific Islanders with functioning chiefdoms, but it was equally patronizing to call small-scale cultures "nonself-governing" when they clearly managed their own internal affairs without formal government. Many "nonself-governing territories" were already under the League of Nations mandate system, and the framers of the UN Charter borrowed from the League of Nations Covenant when they referred to a "sacred trust" to promote "the well-being of the inhabitants of these territories." There are demeaning references to "stages of advancement" and "constructive measures of development," which were direct carryovers from the "protection and uplift" civilizing policies of the colonial era.

From the perspective of indigenous peoples, the early institutionalization of international development under the UN system represented a direct continuation of the old colonialism under new leadership. Fortunately, additional international covenants helped expand the concept of human rights, providing a framework on which indigenous political leaders could build. For example, Article 22 of the 1948 UN Declaration of Human Rights states that everyone is entitled to the realization of the "cultural rights indispensable for his dignity and the free development of his personality." This was amplified by the International Covenant of Human Rights, adopted by the UN General Assembly in 1966:

> In those states in which ethnic, religious or linguistic minorities exist, persons belonging to such minorities shall not be denied the right, in community with the other members of their group, to enjoy their own culture, to profess and practice their own religion or to use their own language.

This is a significant statement because it refers specifically to the human rights of cultural groups as group rights, whereas most earlier international declarations have referred to individual human rights.

ILO Convention 107

The first attempt to write an international convention devoted entirely to the relationship between indigenous peoples and governments was undertaken by the ILO in 1946 in cooperation with the United Nations, UNESCO, FAO, and WHO. Anthropologists were directly involved in this historic 11-year effort, which culminated in 1957 when the General Conference of the ILO adopted "Convention (No. 107) concerning the protection and integration of indigenous and other tribal and semi-tribal populations in independent countries" (United Nations 1959).

ILO Convention 107, a curiously ambiguous document that attempted to raise a new standard for the rights of indigenous peoples, fell short of its goal because it failed to incorporate the viewpoint of indigenous peoples themselves. Convention 107 made a strong statement in support of the human rights of tribal individuals while endorsing government programs that directly undermined tribal cultures. The key contradiction is found in Article 7:

> These populations shall be allowed to retain their own customs and institutions where these are not incompatible with the national legal system or the objectives of integration programmes.

This convention merits careful study because the issues that it defined are still being debated. This section details the background to the writing of Convention 107 to show how ethnocentric misunderstanding of indigenous peoples can undermine even the most well-intended humanitarian efforts.

The ILO was created at the end of World War I as a League of Nations affiliate concerned with international labor conditions and standard of living. It became a UN affiliate, and by 1980, its membership included 144 countries. The ILO's original interest in indigenous peoples was restricted to labor problems in colonial territories. In 1946, the ILO expanded its concerns to include general issues of economic development and indigenous peoples, and it established a Committee of Experts on Indigenous Labor.

The general approach to "the problem of Indigenous populations" expressed at the committee's first meeting in 1951 indicated that indigenous peoples would be treated ethnocentrically as impoverished and underdeveloped people in need of development. This narrow interpretation closely followed the UN Economic and Social Council view of global poverty and underdevelopment, which launched the United Nations' development campaign at precisely the same moment (see Chapter 13). According to the ILO experts, indigenous people were disadvantaged because they were backward and ignorant. Their legal "rights" were being denied because they were not able to participate fully in development progress. The solution was formal education, economic development, new forms of political organization, and special legislation.

The ILO experts identified **integration** of indigenous peoples into the national society as the best policy objective. Integration would help tribal peoples "progress" and raise their "cultural level" so that they could overcome their social and economic "inferiority," but integration left little room for the existence of independent tribal societies. The committee noted that tribal culture might already seem "attractive" and that change might disturb prior ecological balances, but they concluded that "the scientist must accept the fact that social change is inevitable as a result of the general economic and social development of the community" (ILR 1951:64).

At the same time, the committee expressed confidence that applied social science could overcome any problems. However, recognizing the potential for damage, efforts were to be made to set "standards that would prevent the indigenous groups from being overwhelmed" by change. Governments were to create special vocational training programs to provide

> the aboriginals with proper opportunity to develop fully their occupational abilities, so as to improve their conditions of life, to obtain the greatest benefit to the national economy and to assist in their assimilation into the cultural life of the nation. (ILR 1951:65)

It was argued that vocational training could be used to improve the existing subsistence economy of a tribal group in order to raise their liv-ing standard, but it could also be used to modify the culture more directly (Figure 14.8). The report specifically recommended that in some cases, "an attempt should be made to change the direction of the traditional activities of the group" (ILR 1951:65). It was suggested that special extension agents could deliver "oral advice" to tribal peoples on such matters as agricultural methods, handicrafts, and "good habits of living" (ILR 1951:66).

A second ILO Committee of Experts was convened in 1954 to discuss how to protect and integrate forest-dwelling indigenous groups such as Amazonians. This fifteen-member committee was also flawed by ethnocentric preconceptions, even though it was chaired by New Zealand anthropologist Ernest Beaglehole and included two other prominent anthropologists, Horace Miner, an American, and Darcy Ribeiro, a Brazilian. The committee's agenda was limited to helping forest dwelling "populations" adapt to forced development change. The committee acknowledged that the expansion of "technologically advanced societies" into formerly isolated tribal refuges was disturbing ecological balances and cultural patterns, breaking up tribal communities, marginalizing tribal individuals, and leaving them easy prey to economic exploitation. However, instead of condemning the invasion of tribal lands, the experts blamed the victims by declaring that tribal groups were "marginalized" because "they have failed to identify themselves with the values of technologically advanced societies" (ILR 1954:422).

By accepting the state's right to invade tribal areas in the interest of economic development, the Committee of Experts was placed in an ambiguous and contradictory position, and this contradiction was incorporated into ILO Convention 107. The experts endorsed a tribal right to self-fulfillment, to retention of traditional lands, and to free movement across national boundaries. However, the committee refused to condemn the greatest threat to these noble objectives—the state's right to "integrate" tribal peoples on its own terms.

FIGURE 14.8 An Asháninka shaman processing sheets of raw rubber for sale at a mission station in the Peruvian Amazon. This vocational activity operated within an extremely exploitative system of labor that was not effectively addressed by the ILO.

The Committee of Experts described all tribal groups as occupying various stages on their way toward "inevitable" integration with national society. Totally independent tribes represented the first stage of integration. When the integration process was inadequately directed, Stage 2 was characterized by violence, disease, disorder, ecological disruption, and other direct assaults on tribal culture. Stage 3 involved collapse of the tribal system and social disintegration, followed by marginalization of former tribal individuals in Stage 4. The experts argued optimistically that these negative outcomes could be avoided by more carefully planned integration programs, backed

by special protective legislation. They envisioned a limited "cultural autonomy" for tribal peoples, who would be integrated into a pluralistic national society, where economic development would mutually benefit all groups. Successfully integrated tribal groups would "identify themselves with the values of technologically advanced societies." This positive outcome mirrored the "benefits of civilization" approach advocated by the nineteenth-century humanitarians and was equally prone to failure.

Like the anthropologists who identified the obstacles to economic progress in peasant cultures, the ILO experts recognized that successfully adapted indigenous groups might resist imposed integration. The committee found that "isolated" tribal peoples were healthy and self-sufficient, yet this was called "an undesirable state of segregation" (ILR 1954:424) because it perpetuated tribal culture, thereby blocking successful integration. Committee chair Ernest Beaglehole (1954) was explicit on the value of applied anthropology in implementing culture change programs:

> The anthropologist, through his detailed knowledge of indigenous life, can note the areas of resistance, blockage and susceptibility to change, so that local patterns will be circumvented or utilised in order to reduce friction and resistance. (1954:432)

Because force was not supposed to be employed in helping tribal groups realize their "inexorable destiny," the central problem for planners was "how to produce a shift from the satisfactions that indigenous forest dwellers find in their own societies to the satisfactions normally found in modern society" (Beaglehole 1954:424).

The experts proposed a four-point program for a combined "protection-integration" action plan:

integration The absorption of a formerly autonomous people into a dominant state society, with the possible retention of ethnic identity.

1. The safeguarding, preservation and development of the indigenous forest-dwelling population's economic base

2. The raising of its standard of living

3. The development of medical and health action with the object of maintaining at least the same health conditions as existed before contact with the invading society

4. The development of fundamental education (Beaglehole 1954:425)

This program may have sounded promising, but it supported external conquest and invasion and was founded on outrageously ethnocentric assumptions. In a series of resolutions, the committee declared that tribal peoples were socially and economically "impoverished," their subsistence was "inadequate," and they were unhygienic. They needed outside technical experts to teach the "best agricultural, stock-rearing, forestry and handicraft techniques." They needed to be taught how to work efficiently, maintain subsistence reserves, and prevent waste and resource depletion and "irrational" deforestation. They needed to be instructed how to ensure the equitable distribution of water resources. And they needed to grow more crop varieties and increase their economic independence.

Ironically, undisturbed tribal peoples were doing just fine in all of these areas before outside intrusion; "integration" created the very conditions of impoverishment that it intended to prevent. This negative view of tribal culture likely resulted, in part, because the first session of the Committee of Experts was primarily concerned with the most depressed and exploited Andean peasantry and tended to generalize their unhappy condition to *all* tribal peoples while attributing its cause to the indigenous culture rather than the national political and economic structures that encouraged oppression.

The committee's final resolutions were contradictory because, although they advocated respect for tribal culture "as a legitimate way of life," they also accepted the self-fulfilling prophecy that tribal peoples were "doomed to change." Committee members were divided over whether change should be rapid or slow, but they agreed that development would be imposed. As Horace Miner explained, "The realist recognizes the inevitability of increasing encroachment of civilization on the remaining outposts of preliterate culture" (1955:441).

The drafting of ILO Convention 107 presented anthropologists with a golden opportunity to create a blueprint for the independence of tribal cultures, but the momentum of global economic development was too strong. Convention 107 failed to support indigenous rights because it made the economic goals of commercial-scale state cultures the primary objective. In 2004 ILO 107 was still in force in 18 countries including countries with large tribal populations such as Bangladesh, India, Iraq, and Pakistan.

Indigenous Organizations and ILO Convention 169

In the 1960s and 1970s, indigenous peoples throughout the world began to form political organizations to press their demands for full control over their traditional lands and communities. Indigenous organizations emerged at local, national, and international levels. In Amazonia, the Shuar of Ecuador were among the first to organize when they formed a federation in 1964 to unite communities that were fragmented by land invasions. Similar groups exist in other Amazon countries, including Peru. At the international level, the World Council of Indigenous Peoples (WCIP) was formed in 1975, with delegates drawn from indigenous organizations from throughout the world. The WCIP was one of the first indigenous organizations to have NGO (nongovernmental organization) status with the United Nations. This allowed it to play a consultative role in deliberations before the Economic and Social Council and UN affiliates such as the ILO. The primary objective of the WCIP was "to ensure political, economic, and social justice to indigenous peoples."

At the Fourth Assembly of the WCIP, which was held in Panama in 1984, some 300 indigenous people from twenty-three countries drew up a Declaration of Principles of Indigenous Rights. This declaration clearly lists the international standards that should define their position relative to state governments and international institutions. Three of the most critical principles are the following:

> Principle 1. All indigenous peoples have the right of self-determination. By virtue of this right they may freely determine their political status and freely pursue their economic, social, religious and cultural development.
>
> Principle 9. Indigenous peoples shall have exclusive rights to their traditional lands and its resources; where the lands and resources of the indigenous peoples have been taken away without their free and informed consent such lands and resources shall be returned.
>
> Principle 12. No action or course of conduct may be undertaken which, directly or indirectly, may result in the destruction of land, air, water, sea ice, wildlife, habitat or natural resources without the free and informed consent of the indigenous peoples affected.

Indigenous organizations are supported by various religious, environmentalist, and human rights groups in many countries. International organizations such as Cultural Survival, IWGIA (the International Work Group for Indigenous Affairs), and Survival International, which are directed by anthropologists, have played important support roles for indigenous organizations by raising funds and by helping them establish national and international contacts where their views can be expressed.

A new possibility for raising the international standard on the rights of indigenous peoples arose in 1985 when the ILO decided to revise its 1957 Convention 107 on the protection and integration of indigenous peoples. Even though Convention 107 was ratified by only twenty-six states, it remained the principal international convention on indigenous rights. The ILO hoped to remove the integrationist tone of the old convention, while keeping the basic document intact. Indigenous groups and their supporters wanted a revised convention to be a strong statement in support of indigenous rights to self-determination and urged removal of the old convention's ethnocentric emphasis on integration and development and its ambiguity concerning indigenous land rights.

A new Committee of Experts took up the question in Geneva at formal meetings in 1986, 1988, and 1989. This time, indigenous people were permitted at least token representation, but the final wording and approval of the revision rested with the hundred or so experts who represented employers, governments, and workers, and not with indigenous people. The WCIP, the IWGIA, and Survival International were allowed to speak as NGOs, but they could exercise only indirect influence. The proceedings were also attended by official and unofficial indigenous observers representing various native groups from North and South America, India, and Australia, but they remained on the sidelines (Gray 1987).

As discussion proceeded, two familiar arguments emerged, and the specific terms used and precise definitions became critical matters. Experts representing the ILO, employers, and some governments urged realism and proposed that indigenous peoples be granted the right to participation and consultation in the process of integration and development. Indigenous people assumed that participation and consultation still meant integration, and they insisted on self-determination, with indigenous consent and control over government policies that might affect them. They wanted the power to veto undesirable development programs and refused to be seen as passive participants in programs already designed by others. The realists also wanted to retain the original language of Convention 107 that referred to "populations," thereby avoiding references to specific cultural characteristics that defined *peoples* as groups. Recognizing that cultural uniqueness was the most fundamental issue, indigenous people insisted that the term *people* should replace *population* in a new convention.

The indigenous representatives objected to the old convention's derogatory references to "stages" of development and integration. They also wanted to greatly expand references to "land" to refer to "territories of the earth" to emphasize their claims to land, water, ice, and air. Indigenous people considered themselves to be "custodians" of inalienable resources, not *owners* in the market economy sense. When the final deliberations appeared to be supporting the old integrationist approach, the Australian aboriginal delegation withdrew in protest. Delivering an impassioned speech, aboriginal representative Geoff Clarke declared,

> We define our rights in terms of self-determination. We are not looking to dismember your States and you know it. But we do insist on the right to control our territories, our resources, the organisation of our societies, our own decision-making institutions, and the maintenance of our own cultures and ways of life. . . . Do you think that we are unaware of the actual meaning of words like consultation, participation and collaboration? Would you be satisfied with "consultation" as a guarantee for your rights? Unless governments are obligated to obtain our consent, we remain vulnerable to legislative and executive whims that inevitably will result in further dispossession and social disintegration of our peoples. The victims are always the first to know how the system operates. (IWGIA Yearbook 1988, 1989:184–185)

A final revision was approved by the ILO in 1989 as Convention 169. It did eliminate most of the ethnocentric language, but the contradictory emphasis on integration remained. The term *people* was introduced but was avowed to have no legal significance. Over the objections of indigenous leaders, governments retained responsibility for development and policymaking, with indigenous peoples relegated to "participation" and "cooperation." There were references to respect for indigenous culture and recognition of land rights, but the qualifications and escape clauses were so numerous that in many respects, less real protection was provided than in the original covenant. Not surprisingly, the new convention has been widely rejected by indigenous peoples (Gray 1990). As of 2004 17 countries

had ratified ILO 169, including Brazil, Colombia, Ecuador, Peru, and Venezuela, where important Amazonian indigenous groups live.

The Universal Declaration on Rights of Indigenous Peoples

Indigenous political organizations have presented their viewpoints on indigenous rights before a variety of UN human rights forums, beginning in 1977 when more than fifty indigenous leaders were invited to attend the International Conference on Discrimination Against Indigenous Populations in the Americas, organized in Geneva by the special UN Committee on Human Rights. Similar conferences followed, and in 1982 a special Working Group on Indigenous Peoples (WGIP) was established by the UN Sub-Commission on the Prevention of Discrimination and Protection of Minorities, of the UN ECOSOC Commission on Human Rights. The WGIP was directed to draft a Universal Declaration of Indigenous Rights for final adoption by the UN General Assembly in 1992. In this case, there was direct involvement of many indigenous groups in the proceedings and in the drafting of the declaration. In contrast to the ILO Convention, the real concerns of indigenous peoples with guaranteeing self-determination and preventing genocide, ethnocide, and ecocide were specifically addressed.

The UN Human Rights Commission finally approved a draft of the Universal Declaration in 1994, with the expectation that it would be adopted by the UN General Assembly during the International Decade of the World's Indigenous Peoples 1995–2004. The draft resolution included 42 articles, and was extremely comprehensive (UN, Commission on Human Rights 1994). It endorsed such crucial rights as the right for indigenous people to be free of genocide and forced removal of children from the families (Article 6), and free of ethnocide and cultural genocide, including forced removals and dispossession from "their lands, territories or resources," or forced assimilation or integration (Articles 7 and 10). The draft declaration also included the right to the repatriation of human remains, such as skeletons in museum collections, and the return of cultural properties, such as ceremonial objects. Another crucial right was the right to control cultural and intellectual property, including genetic resources (Article 29). This is especially important in a commercial world where giant agricultural and pharmaceutical companies patent genetic material and restrict their availability to generate revenue. Indigenous peoples own their cultivated plant varieties, but do not typically turn ownership into a commercial advantage (Cleveland and Murray 1997).

These rights represent a significant departure from the ethnocentric uplift and limited protectionism of the colonial era. They also represent a clear repudiation of the forced-integration policies that were called "inevitable" by the realists during the modern era of economic development. These new indigenous rights, if they are fully recognized by the international community, will provide a firm basis for the coexistence of indigenous peoples within the global system. However, as the draft declaration declares in Article 29, "These rights constitute the minimum standards for the survival and the well-being of the indigenous peoples of the world."

The following case study from Amazonia shows how indigenous groups are continuing to be dispossessed by national development and integration programs that ignore these most basic of human rights.

NATIONAL INTEGRATION IN AMAZONIA

Because ILO Convention 107 was written with the welfare of indigenous Amazonians specifically in mind and because most Amazonian countries signed the convention, it is especially relevant to examine the effects of national integration programs that have been carried out in Amazonia and to consider policy alternatives.

Historically, the European invasion of Amazonia nearly annihilated the indigenous populations. In 1500, when Amazonia was first claimed by Europeans, there may have been as many as 6.8 million native residents (Denevan 1976), but by 1970, the population had declined by nearly 90 percent to less than 1 million. ILO committee member Darcy Ribeiro (1957) reported that in Brazil, more than one-third of the indigenous groups known in 1900 were extinct by 1957, the year Convention 107 was adopted. In 1968, the Brazilian government revealed that officials of its Indian Protection Service had conspired with wealthy landowners to remove indigenous people from their lands using machine guns, dynamite, poison, and disease. Thousands must have died in an extermination process that rivaled the worst abuses of the early colonial period. Native dispossession and deaths were accelerated when construction of the transamazon highway system began in 1970, followed by large-scale colonization, agricultural development, mining, and hydroelectric projects (Davis 1977).

Indigenous peoples in the Ecuadorean and Peruvian Amazon were unable to prevent multinational oil corporations from prospecting and development within their territories. This has caused such destructive pollution to the fragile rain forest ecosystem (Figure 14.9), that Ecuadorean indigenous groups brought suit against Chevron Texaco in 2003 claiming up to $1 billion in damages.

The Asháninka Versus Global Development

The Asháninka (Campa) of eastern Peru, who were introduced in Chapters 1 and 3, provide a useful case study of the integration process in Amazonia. In the 1960s, some 21,000 Asháninka were still the principal occupants of their vast homeland in the forested eastern foothills of the Andes in central Peru. They were highly self-sufficient and only minimally involved with the market economy. Their first contacts with Europeans occurred in the 1500s, and over the next two centuries, Franciscan missionaries gradually established outposts throughout the region and imposed their own culture change program. However, the Asháninka resented Franciscan disapproval of polygyny and other restrictions on their freedom. They destroyed the missions in 1742 and enjoyed complete independence for more than 100 years, demonstrating that the integration process was reversible, not inevitable.

The situation began to change in the 1870s when the Republic of Peru turned to Amazonia as a frontier of national expansion. Asháninka territory was critical to government planning because it controlled the river pathways to the Amazon, but explorers and missionaries entering the area were frequently met with a rain of Asháninka arrows. Military force and gift giving eventually overcame most Asháninka resistance and cleared the way for colonists. A regional economic boom began after the Pichis Trail was successfully opened in 1891 as a mule road through the Asháninka homeland to a navigable point on the Pichis River, and a huge tract of Asháninka land was deeded to an English company for a coffee plantation. This development activity caused many Asháninka to experience all the negative aspects of the uncontrolled frontier and led to further hostilities. In 1913–1914, frustrated Asháninka warriors armed themselves with guns and attacked missions and outposts in the Pichis Valley, killing 150 settlers before they, in turn, were defeated by troops.

After these events, the government took little interest in the region until the 1960s. Scattered groups of fully independent Asháninka dominated the remote areas, while the more accessible riverine zones were only lightly settled by outsiders who established missions, small cattle ranches, and farms, following successive economic waves of rubber and lumber extraction. The Asháninka still maintained a viable culture after more than 400 years of colonial intrusion. But their future was increasingly threatened by a shift in government policy that began in 1960 with the Plan Peruvia, which selected some 45,000

FIGURE 14.9   Oil workers dumping contaminated wastewater into an open pit in the Ecuadorean Amazon.

square miles (116,550 km^2) in Amazonia, including most of the Asháninka area, for long-term economic development. A special unit (ONERN) was established, with U.S. AID funds, to evaluate the natural resources in the zone and to formulate a detailed development proposal. Military engineer units, supported by U.S. military assistance programs, began constructing a network of "penetration" highways that would provide the primary infrastructure for the project.

In 1965, Peruvian president Fernando Belaunde-Terry (1965) announced a definitive economic "conquest" of Amazonia. Ignoring the native population, he characterized the region as underpopulated and underexploited and promised that developing Amazonia would solve the overpopulation, poverty, food shortages, and land scarcity of the Andean and coastal zones. Indeed,

Peru's population had tripled since 1900 and exceeded 10 million by 1965. However, the real issue was inequality, not population growth, because the Inca empire had supported an even larger population without invading Amazonia. The government's development program was simply an accelerated eastward extension of the national market economy, which had already generated Andean poverty and was now impoverishing the Native Amazonians. The new, multimillion-dollar program was eventually cofinanced by U.S. AID, the UN Development Programme, the World Bank, and the Inter-American Development Bank, contributing to a vast increase in Peru's external public debt, from $856 million in 1970 to $12.4 billion in 1988. This debt arrangement helped make Peru a poor client state and made the fate of the Amazonians and the forest ecosystem ultimately dependent on management decisions made at the global level.

My own investigations in the region between 1965 and 1969 (Bodley 1970, 1972b) showed that when Belaunde-Terry's project began, some 2500 Asháninka still remained fully self-sufficient, whereas many others were drawn into exploitive **debt bondage** with patrons who offered cheap merchandise in exchange for labor (Figure 14.10). Many Asháninka had already joined Protestant mission communities and were establishing a marginal and precarious niche in the expanding regional market economy. These new mission communities did not control an adequate land base and were quickly depleting local subsistence resources, increasing their dependence on purchased goods. This placed the Asháninka at an enormous disadvantage in economic competition with the wealthier and more sophisticated colonists who were invading their lands.

The Asháninka were largely ignored by development planners. For example, air-photo planning maps had "empty wasteland" printed over plainly visible Asháninka garden plots. In the Tambo-Pajonal planning unit, a 5500-square-mile (14,245-km²) roadless area occupied by 4000 Asháninka, plans called for 560 miles (901 km)

of roads and the introduction of 145,000 settlers (ONERN 1968). There were legal provisions for granting limited land titles to the Asháninka in accord with the general principles of Convention 107 but no provision for those who preferred not to be integrated into the national economy.

Because these events coincided with the widely publicized Brazilian massacres, many anthropologists began making public statements on indigenous rights at this time. The 39th Americanist Congress, assembled in Lima, Peru, in 1970, issued "recommendations" condemning ethnocide and calling threatened Amazonian communities "oppressed peoples" in need of "national liberation." In 1971, Stefano Varese, a Peruvian anthropologist who had also worked with the Asháninka, joined with Ribeiro and nine other anthropologists to draft the Declaration of Barbados (Bodley 1990). They stated that native lands were being treated as **internal colonies,** and they called on governments, the missions, anthropologists, and especially the indigenous peoples themselves to work for liberation. Varese (1972), optimistic that Peru's new approach to agrarian reform would reduce the exploitation and dependency of forest peoples, proposed that special government teams encourage native groups to mobilize politically in their own defense.

The Cultural Autonomy Alternative

In 1972, I proposed that the government demarcate the entire interfluvial upland zone as inviolable "Asháninka Land" (Figure 14.11). Development by outsiders would have been permanently prohibited in this vast 29,000-square-mile (75,110-km²) territory, which encompassed most of the traditional Asháninka homeland (Bodley 1972b). This

debt bondage An exploitive economic relationship that is managed to keep individuals in virtually perpetual indebtedness.
internal colony A territory within a state containing an indigenous population that is denied the right of self-determination.

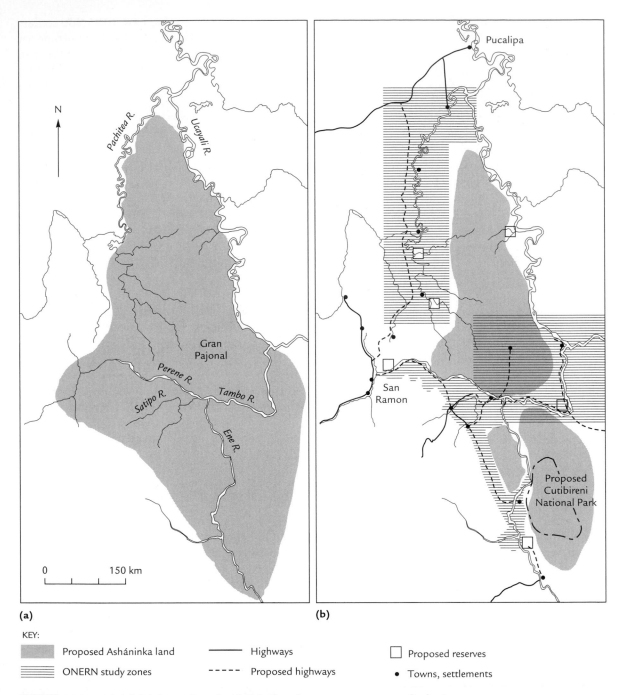

KEY:

- ▨ Proposed Asháninka land
- ▤ ONERN study zones
- —— Highways
- - - - - Proposed highways
- ☐ Proposed reserves
- • Towns, settlements

FIGURE 14.11 (*a*) Asháninka territory in 1850 before the most recent wave of colonization and development by outsiders; (*b*) the Asháninka land cultural alternative proposed in 1972, shown in relation to new colonization and economic development zones.

FIGURE 14.10
A newly recruited Asháninka labor crew being interviewed by the author in 1969.

was realistic given the ONERN studies showing that most of this area was unsuitable for commercial agriculture, contained no important mineral resources, and was best maintained as a protected watershed. In lowland areas where integration was already underway, I recommended that very large reserves be established on the best agricultural soils to give market-oriented Asháninka a competitive advantage. Later I called this approach the **cultural autonomy** alternative because it would allow tribal cultures the opportunity to maintain their independence; it specified three key points:

1. National governments and international organizations must recognize and support tribal rights to their traditional land, cultural autonomy, and full local sovereignty.

2. The responsibility for initiating outside contacts must rest with the tribal people themselves: outside influences may not have free access to tribal areas.

3. Industrial states must not compete with tribal societies for their resources. (Bodley 1975:169)

Granting this degree of autonomy to the Asháninka in 1972 would have forced drastic modifications in the government's programs, but the institutional momentum for large-scale development was so strong that my proposal was ignored. However, some aspects of cultural autonomy were coincidentally incorporated in the Manu Park, a 5800-square-mile (15,022-km²) environmental sanctuary established in the southern Peruvian Amazon in 1973. Independent tribal groups already living within the park, such as the Matsigenka, were allowed to remain undisturbed as long as they did not exploit park resources for commercial purposes (d'Ans 1972, 1981). More than 20 years later, cultural autonomy was implicitly included in the 1994 draft Universal Declaration of Indigenous Rights under Article 31:

cultural autonomy Self-determination by a cultural group.

Indigenous peoples, as a specific form of exercising their right to self-determination, have the right to autonomy, or self-government in matters relating to their internal and local affairs, including culture, religion, education, information, media, health, housing, employment, social welfare, economic activities, land and resources management, environment and entry by non-members, as well as ways and means for financing these autonomous functions.

The cultural autonomy alternative was initially rejected by some anthropologists who argued that it was based on an idealized concept of traditional cultures and would prevent the necessary political mobilization and economic development of indigenous peoples (Aaby 1977, Varese 1972). Of course, cultural autonomy must ultimately be supported by governments, but it can be implemented by indigenous peoples themselves. It is a strategy for allowing indigenous groups to chart their own course, not a strategy that nonindigenous experts can use to impose their own concept of development on target groups. What matters is whether indigenous peoples are allowed to control their own resources and cultural destiny. The anticultural autonomy arguments repeated the earlier Australian debate over aboriginal policy. Some missionaries firmly opposed native autonomy in Amazonia, arguing that it was "unrealistic" and "romantic" and would artificially deny indigenous people the benefits of Christianity (Wise, Loos, and Davis 1977). Like Elkin, they maintained that missionary intervention would help the natives overcome maladaptive culture traits such as infanticide and shamanism and that Christianity would provide "spiritual help in facing the difficult life of the 20th century" (1977:521).

In 1974, anthropologist Richard Chase Smith (1977) proposed a development plan that would have allowed significant autonomy for the Yanesha (Amuesha), western neighbors of the Asháninka, while protecting the vulnerable rain forest environment. Smith recommended creation of a 1200-square-mile (3108-km²) zone, divided into three

blocks to include contiguous communal reserves, deeded to specific Yanesha communities to protect natural resources for their exclusive use; tribal territory for all Yanesha as a cultural group; and a national park as an environmental preserve.

Smith's plan was initially approved by the Peruvian Ministry of Agriculture but was tabled by 1980 when the government actually began to implement its own project to bring 150,000 agricultural colonists into the Pichis–Palcazu Valleys and create a city of 20,000 people. No territory was deeded to the 12,000 resident Asháninka and Yanesha for them to control as cultural groups, and less than half the fifty-one scattered indigenous communities were given discrete village titles. This left the original inhabitants either landless or with fragmented blocks of land that were inadequate for traditional subsistence activities or long-term commercial agriculture (Swenson and Narby 1986). Protests by a coalition of native organizations, religious and human rights groups, and anthropologists (*Amazonia Indigena* 1981) brought only token reforms represented by village land titles, community development advisors, and agricultural credits that fostered debt.

The World Bank, which provided $46 million for the Pichis Valley Project and cosponsored many similar projects that deprived indigenous groups of their resources and autonomy, responded to critics by issuing a position paper arguing that with "interim safeguards" it was possible to promote large development projects and still defend tribal people (Goodland 1982). The bank's report advocated support for "cultural autonomy . . . until the tribe adapts sufficiently." Thus, they seemed to reject genuine cultural autonomy as a permanent policy.

Anthropologists Sally Swenson and Jeremy Narby, who investigated conditions in the Pichis Valley in the mid-1980s, observed that development policies at international, national, and regional levels need to be changed if indigenous groups like the Asháninka are to benefit from development. They urged that indigenous political organizations be allowed to participate directly in planning affecting them, and declared,

> A more appropriate approach would discourage colonization and place priority on the participation in development by current inhabitants; recognize native rights to, and title land sufficient for, subsistence and commercial production; and recognize the rationality of current native land use, incorporating native knowledge of the rainforest environment into development. (Swenson and Narby 1986:24)

This course was taken in the Upper Ucayali region of Asháninka territory beginning in 1987, when the Indigenous Organisation of the Atalaya Region (OIRA) was founded. The group soon brought together more than a hundred Asháninka communities, joining a larger regional indigenous organization, the Inter-Ethnic Association for the Development of the Peruvian Rainforest (AIDESEP), formed in 1980. These organizations were part of the worldwide political mobilization of indigenous peoples, and they provided an effective basis for the Asháninka to implement their own cultural autonomy alternative. In 1988, with the help of AIDESEP, the Atalaya Asháninka denounced the debt-bondage exploitation practiced by the colonizing *patrons* before a special multi-agency government commission. Next, with the help of IWGIA and funds from the Danish government development agency (DANIDA), they succeeded in implementing the community land title provisions of the 1978 Peruvian Law of Native Communities. They demarcated their own territories to reflect their subsistence requirements, creating contiguous territories to block out *patrons* (Gray n.d., Hvalkof and Gray 1990). By 1993, 113 Asháninka communities in the region had secure land titles. Many of the colonists had withdrawn after being compensated for their holdings. The Asháninka were proudly reasserting their culture. An Asháninka man, dressed in *cushma* and face paint, told IWGIA's Andrew Gray how he felt about their new autonomy:

> We have no problems with colonists. There are no patrons or "colonos." Just Asháninka. We wanted titles for our lands and to work in the fields, harvest yuca [manioc], sow rice, pineapple. That is why we need land. In the future I want to live quietly. We in our community want to live in peace, drinking our masato [manioc beer]. We hunt animals throughout our land. We have a school now too. We think that our organization OIRA helps us and we are very pleased. (Gray n.d.:24)

In 1995 the Asháninka community of Marankiari Bajo on the Perené River incorporated itself as CIAMB, Comunidad Indígena Asháninka Marankiari Bajo (Indigenous Asháninka Community). The community counted 1027 inhabitants and 246 families in 1997 and began maintaining a web site in 1999 (www.rcp.net.pe/ashaninka/). The organization proudly proclaimed itself to be an "autonomous and independent communal organization."

SUMMARY

Since the policy debate began over how states should deal with tribal peoples, only two basic positions have been argued. A fundamental philosophical conflict exists between the realists, who advocate policies to help indigenous people adjust to the "inevitable" changes brought by colonialism or postcolonial national integration and economic development, and the idealists, who oppose the state-sponsored invasion of indigenous territories by colonists or externally imposed development projects. This philosophical split has obvious political implications for indigenous peoples. If the realists set national and international policies, indigenous peoples are likely to disappear as distinct cultural groups, whereas the idealist position will foster indigenous self-determination that will make cultural survival possible.

The initial involvement of anthropology in the colonial enterprise was in the context of British colonialism. The specific process of colonial development in East Africa paralleled the conquest, exploitation, and marginalization of Native Americans in the New World, under both colonial powers and independent countries such as the United States.

Virtually all tribal cultures that anthropologists have described ethnographically have been adversely affected by the commercial world. Our discussion of these cultures in Chapters 2–5 largely ignored this possibility by treating tribal cultures as if they existed only within tribal worlds. However, more complex cultures clearly have varied impacts on smaller-scale cultures. In Chapters 6–10, we pointed out that ancient kingdoms and empires often absorbed tribal societies or forced them to organize into states in their own defense. In the modern era, industrial civilization has exerted an enormous economic and political influence in drawing tribal cultures into the emerging global system.

Throughout the nineteenth and the first half of the twentieth century, the realist policy approach of adjustment and integration clearly dominated. However, since World War II, a more evolved international concept of human rights, fostered by the UN system, has for the first time created conditions under which indigenous peoples themselves could develop their own formal political organizations and promote their own idealist perspective. This has given them the opportunity to directly shape international standards for the interaction between small-scale cultures and the larger state- and global-level forces surrounding them.

STUDY QUESTIONS

1. Distinguish between the realist and the idealist positions on policy toward indigenous peoples. Refer to specific examples, organizations, individuals, policies, or international conventions.
2. Define *indigenous people*. Differentiate between *indigenous people* and *indigenous population*. What are the limitations of the term *indigenous*? In what sense is *indigenous people* a political concept?
3. Why are the terms *tribal* and *primitive* sometimes avoided by anthropologists?
4. What features of small-scale cultures can be identified with indigenous peoples?
5. In what sense can indigenous peoples be referred to as *nations*?
6. Describe the philosophical position and the policy recommendations of the Select Committee and the Aborigines Protection Society. How were they actually applied?
7. In what way did colonial policy toward Australian aborigines depart from standard British practice? How do you account for this?
8. Describe the different policies advocated by Wood Jones, Thomson, and Elkin in Australia. How did they defend their views?
9. In what way could the League of Nations mandate system, the UN Charter, and ILO Convention 107 be said to endorse ethnocentric policies that might be used to undermine the human rights of indigenous peoples?
10. What UN declarations or covenants provide a basis for the human rights of indigenous peoples?
11. Distinguish between the human rights of individuals and those of groups.
12. What were the assumptions of the anthropologists involved in drafting ILO Convention 107? How were they expressed in the convention?
13. Describe how Peru's economic development policies affected the Asháninka and their neighbors. What alternative policies were proposed?
14. What is meant by "internal colonialism"? Use examples from Australia and Peru.
15. Using the East Africa Protectorate and Kenya as an example, explain how political and economic power was used by colonial administrations to create structural inequalities and unequal accumulation.
16. What are the most important human rights that indigenous peoples themselves define as the minimum conditions for their survival?

SUGGESTED READING

BODLEY, JOHN H. 1988. *Tribal Peoples and Development Issues: A Global Overview.* Mountain View, Calif.: Mayfield. An edited collection of materials including case studies, policy positions, assessments, and recommendations on indigenous peoples and development issues throughout the world from the nineteenth century to 1988.

BODLEY, JOHN H. 1999. *Victims of Progress,* 4th ed. Mountain View, Calif.: Mayfield. Examines the official policies and underlying motives that have shaped the interaction between indigenous peoples and members of commercial-scale culture, since the early nineteenth century; includes many case studies drawn from throughout the world.

DAVIS, SHELTON H. 1977. *Victims of the Miracle: Development and the Indians of Brazil.* Cambridge, Eng.: Cambridge University Press. A critical analysis of the Brazilian government's development policies in the Amazon region and their impact on the native peoples.

15

The Future in the Global Greenhouse

Tropical deforestation contributes to economic growth, global warming, and loss of biodiversity.

Learning Objectives

After studying this chapter you should be able to do the following.

1. Compare the adaptive success of tribal and commercial cultures, referring to impact on nature and long-term sustainability.

2. Describe and evaluate the evidence that the availability of natural resources will limit growth of the commercial culture.

3. Explain the Greenhouse Effect, and describe its human causes and consequences.

4. Evaluate the Malthusian argument that population growth will naturally outstrip food supply, reviewing arguments for and against the theory.

5. Evaluate the argument that technological advances will remove limits to growth.

6. Review the global crises that humanity has faced up to the present, describing the human agents, decisions, and outcomes.

7. Critically evaluate power and scale solutions to the sustainability crisis, comparing them with other approaches.

As Bronislaw Malinowski (1944) pointed out long ago, culture is a mixed blessing because, in providing for basic human needs, it creates new, culturally derived needs and new problems for people to solve. Culture is both problem and solution, and the problems increase as culture scale increases. For example, farming as a means of subsistence intensification helped feed more people in a smaller area, but it also made it more difficult to maintain population stability and social equality. The problems generated by tribes and chiefdoms often were highly localized and occurred so imperceptibly that cultural adjustments were readily found and the tendency was toward equilibrium. The emergence of commercial culture, however, has completely changed the problem of human adaptation. The rate of culture change has become so rapid, and its scale so vast, that it is becoming increasingly difficult to respond effectively to new problems.

Today the world is threatened simultaneously by social and political conflict, impoverishment, resource depletion, and environmental deterioration on a level few would have anticipated at the beginning of the twentieth century. These problems exist at the global, national, and local level and are so serious that the future of humanity and the biosphere itself is at risk for the first time in human existence. It would not be too dramatic to say that a global crisis exists. Major cultural adjustments will be required during this century to prevent a collapse of global society and culture and a widespread breakdown of the humanization process.

The commercialization process that created the global culture has totally transformed and homogenized the planet in an astonishingly short time. Many of the most pervasive items of daily life, such as computers, televisions, jet aircraft, nuclear power, and mass-produced organic compounds, have come into worldwide use only since 1950. The scale and quality of fossil fuel–based industrial production and the unprecedented increases in global population and consumption over the past 200 years are depleting resources and altering the biosphere in ways that threaten

FIGURE 15.1   Large-scale deforestation damages watersheds and contributes to global warming.

the future viability of the global culture itself (Figure 15.1).

Previous cultural processes—whether the humanization that generated language and tribal culture, settled village life, and farming and herding, or the politicization process that created social stratification, cities, and states—did not have such a sudden destabilizing effect. Tribal cultures manipulated natural ecosystems to satisfy basic nutritional needs, but the changes that they induced occurred over millennia, and the tendency was toward equilibrium of population and resource consumption. Politically organized societies promoted population growth and intensive food production to support political structures and social inequality. The environmental alterations produced by traditional states and empires were often drastic, but they occurred over centuries and were regional, not global, in their effects. The rise and fall of particular empires were common and relatively insignificant events in the broad sweep of culture, but the breakdown of the commercial world would be devastating.

Commercial culture, driven by its consumption-based market economy, dominates the world with its perpetually expanding quest for new resources and markets. This cultural domination is itself a problem because it leads to cultural homogeneity, which can reduce human adaptive potential. A multicultural world is not only a more diverse and interesting place but also a way to develop and test alternative cultural solutions to common problems. Since 1950, vast resources have been dedicated to national defense, international development, and environmental protection, but many of these problems have only become more severe. Much of this problem-solving effort has been directed by specialists who offered purely technical solutions for what they assumed were isolated technical problems. The example of global poverty, examined in Chapter 13, suggests that the problems of commercial culture are actually cultural, not technical, problems. They are related to the most fundamental aspects of commercial culture and are thus best approached by a generalist anthropological perspective that takes cultural scale and diversity into account.

In this chapter, we assess the long-term outlook for the world's peoples and cultures by focusing on three major issues: (1) the potential for serious resource shortfalls, (2) environmental deterioration such as through global warming and deforestation, and (3) ways in which a sustainable world might be designed.

LIMITS TO GROWTH IN A FINITE WORLD

The Success of the Commercial Culture

One of the most widely held ideological features of commercial culture is the deceptive belief that evolutionary progress has given people greater control over nature while increasing human security and adaptability. For example, anthropologist Yehudi Cohen (1974) treated hunting-gathering, cultivation, and industrialism as technological stages on the road toward "freedom from environmental limitations." Cohen argued that progress meant a more secure food supply, suggesting with a seemingly trivial example that the ability to produce and market frozen strawberries represented "perhaps one of man's greatest achievements."

When viewed from a culture scale, rather than a strictly technological perspective, frozen berries illuminate some of the critical problems of commercial culture because commercialized berries primarily exist to make a profit for the stockholders of large food corporations, not to increase human food security. Nonrenewable fossil fuels are expended in berry production, refrigerated transport, and storage. Even more significantly, when Cohen wrote, many of America's supermarket strawberries were being produced by giant U.S. agribusinesses using Mexican land and labor in an exploitative international system that perpetuated poverty and inequality while damaging the environment (Feder 1978, Lappe, Collins, and Fowler 1979). Arguing that this is culturally "adaptive," either locally or globally, would be difficult.

The adaptive success of commercial culture is sometimes defined by its "natural" ability to expand in population and territory at the expense of less "advanced" cultures. This has even been offered as an indirect explanation for the genocidal destruction of indigenous peoples. For example, in 1915, Paul Popenoe assured the members of the 19th International Congress of Americanists that Native Americans were a "weak stock" that was being "killed off by natural selection." In 1960, anthropologist David Kaplan formulated a law of cultural dominance to explain the spread of industrial civilization: "That cultural system which more effectively exploits the energy resources of a given environment will tend to spread in that environment at the expense of less effective systems" (1960:75).

This "law" was offered as an ethically neutral scientific generalization, but it implied that ethnocide was inevitable and did not adequately define "effectiveness" of energy exploitation. Significantly, Kaplan acknowledged that in certain especially marginal environments, such as deserts and the arctic, tribal cultures could indeed be considered adaptive successes, even in an environment that might temporarily be invaded by outsiders. In the same volume where Kaplan wrote, Marshall Sahlins and Elman Service agreed and commented in reference to peoples like the mobile foraging Inuit (Eskimo):

> Nor are those cultures that we might consider higher in general evolutionary standing necessarily more perfectly adapted to their environments than lower. Many great civilizations have fallen in the last 2,000 years, even in the midst of material plenty, while the Eskimos tenaciously maintained themselves in an incomparably more difficult habitat. The race is not to the swift, nor the battle to the strong. (1960:26–27)

Writing somewhat later, anthropologists Richard Lee and Irven DeVore, who in 1966 organized the first major international conference on foraging peoples, expressed concern over the "unstable ecological conditions" created by industrial civilization and were even more emphatic about the adaptive achievements of mobile foragers, declaring that they were "the most successful and persistent adaptation man has ever achieved" (Lee and DeVore 1968).

Reproductive success may be a very poor measure of human adaptive success because beyond a certain point the growth of any population must cease. There were ten times as many people in the world in 1990 as in 1650, but the world in 1990 was measurably less secure. Humans are consumers ultimately dependent on the energy produced by green plants through photosynthesis, which is powered by a fixed quantity of solar energy. Biologist Isaac Asimov (1971) estimated that the planet could support a maximum of 20 trillion tons of consumer biomass. Any expansion in the human population must inevitably displace other species. The commercial culture with its 2003 population of 6.3 billion people makes far different demands on the biosphere than the 0.5 billion people in the world in 1650 at the beginning of the commercial revolution. In 1986, it was estimated that humans were already appropriating some 40 percent of the food energy produced by green plants (Brown and Postel 1987, Vitousek et al. 1986). The pinnacle of cultural evolutionary achievement, if narrowly defined by short-term human reproductive success, would be reached when all natural "competitors" were eliminated and every gram of living material was available for human consumption. Asimov projected that in theory, this could occur by 2436.

The sudden planetary dominance of the commercial culture has initiated a dramatic decline in biodiversity that may equal in magnitude the mass extinctions of the geological past, including the disappearance of the dinosaurs at the end of the Cretaceous and the loss of marine animals at the end of the Permian (Wilson 1989, Wilson and Peter 1988). Foraging peoples may have contributed to the more recent extinctions of some of the megafauna, such as the woolly mammoth, at the end of the Ice Age (see Chapter 2), but natural changes in climate and vegetation likely were primarily responsible for those losses (Webster 1981, Grayson and Meltzer 2002).

Habitat destruction, or ecocide, caused by the expansion of commercial ranching, farming, and logging has been destroying species at a catastrophic rate. Much of the loss of nature has occurred since 1700 (Turner II et al. 1990). Careful reconstructions of global changes in land use suggest that, between 1700 and 1990, 14 percent of desert lands, nearly a third of the world's forest lands, nearly 50 percent of grasslands, and 75 percent of the shrubland have been converted to cropland and pasture (Goldewijk 2001). This drastic transformation of the earth from nature to culture was accompanied by tremendous loss in the absolute number of wild plants and animals. To put this in human terms, it can be estimated that in the paleolithic world populated by 8 million people there were approximately 14,000 breeding wild birds per person. In 2000 there were fewer than 15 birds per person (Gaston, Blackburn, and Goldewijk 2003).

Tropical rain forests, which were sustainably used by tribal peoples and are critical for maintaining global biodiversity and climate control, have not been protected by the commercial culture. Analysis of satellite imagery showed that worldwide 8 million hectares (20 million acres) of tropical forest were being cleared or visibly degraded between 1990 and 1997 (Achard et al. 2002). Globally, this is a loss of undisturbed forest of 1.7 percent a year, although some areas of the Brazilian Amazon were being cleared at the rate of 4.4 percent a year. Because tropical forests are so rich in species, deforestation accelerates the loss of biodiversity (Wilson 2002). Tropical deforestation also reduces the capacity of the earth to store carbon and thus contributes to global warming. Reforestation by second-growth trees and tree plantations represents such a small amount of biomass that it does not make up for the loss of mature forest.

The International Union for the Conservation of Nature's 2003 Red List of Threatened Species listed one-third of the world's 11,126 known mammals and birds as threatened with extinction, or nearing extinction. Two hundred and ten species, including more than half of all primates, were already totally extinct, or extinct in the wild (www.iucn.org). Environmental changes associated with global warming are apparently a greater threat to biodiversity than direct habitat destruction. A careful review of possible species losses suggests that between 18 and 37 percent of species in a sample of ecosystems covering 20 percent of the earth's land area would be "committed to extinction" by 2050 as a result of climate change caused by global warming (Thomas et al. 2004).

The present rate of species extinction may be as much as 10,000 times greater per year than occurred naturally (Wilson 2002). Much of the world's present wealth of species was produced over the past 200 million years. Extinction is an irreversible process. Loss of biological diversity is maladaptive for humans because it makes the biosphere less able to support human life. It also involves an economic loss because it is often more costly to replace natural goods and services with their cultural counterparts. Species are now disappearing before they are even scientifically described and their possible uses identified. Un-

fortunately, the extensive biological knowledge accumulated by tribal cultures for many otherwise "unknown" species is also disappearing as genocide and ethnocide continue.

Risks and Rewards in a Commercial Culture

When commerce becomes the most critical cultural influence on human welfare, households must deal with a new set of risks and opportunities for rewards. These risks and rewards are also inequitably distributed within society and are experienced differently by people at different income and wealth levels, at different life cycle stages, and even by gender. The primary risks faced by households in tribal cultures are seasonal cycles and unpredictable variations in natural phenomena, such as weather, that threaten everyone's subsistence. By contrast, commerce can amplify or dampen natural cycles and random variations and can shift the risks and rewards to different social groups. Commerce has dynamics of its own that are not always related to natural cycles, as economist Paul Samuelson summarized in his introductory text:

> Business conditions never stand still. Prosperity is followed by a panic or a crash. National income, employment, and production fall. Prices and profits decline, and men are thrown out of work. Eventually the bottom is reached, and revival begins. The recovery may be slow or fast. It may be incomplete, or it may be so strong as to lead to a new boom. The new prosperity may represent a long, sustained plateau of brisk demand, plentiful jobs, buoyant prices, and increasing living standards. Or it may represent a quick, inflationary flaring up of prices and speculation, to be followed by another disastrous slump. (1964:250–251)

These fluctuations in volume of production, consumption, and commercial activity are characteristic of money economies, and they can affect particular industries or entire market economies at regional, national, and even global levels. They are sometimes called the *business cycle,* but this implies a degree of predictability that may not be justified, because commerce has become so large and complex so quickly that historical experience may be an unreliable guide to the future. What is certain is that large fluctuations in commerce can have extreme human impacts. American economists have long recognized 20-year cyclical patterns in building construction and capital investment. Longer cycles, or great waves, of commercial activity lasting 50 years or more have also been described (Goldstein 1988). Employment, money supply, income, interest rates, investment, and saving rates vary according to cycle phase. Expansion and contraction in industrial investment, rather than agricultural cycles, have now become the dominant commercial risk in much of the world. Business cycles and associated market fluctuations also are a major source of economic opportunities that wealthy investors can manipulate to produce even larger fortunes. Investors who buy low and sell high can create enormous profits from very small percentage gains on large-scale transactions. This speculative arbitrage can itself create chaotic swings in the market and is a very different process from long-term investment in the production of goods and services that benefits society at large. All of this economic volatility would be more manageable in smaller-scale, culturally regulated markets in which many small enterprises operated. The large scale at which business enterprise is organized, rather than commerce itself, is perhaps the most important threat to sustainability. Many observers argue that giant corporations are now more powerful than governments and have become *the* dominant forces shaping the global culture (Estes 1996, Grossman and Adams 1996, Korten 1996, Mander 1996).

Commercial Culture and Resource Depletion

Because commercial culture is most distinguished by its elevated rates of resource consumption, the question of resource balance is critical for any assessment of the future of commercial culture. In theory, culture growth, like the growth of any organism, must be limited by the essential material that is in shortest supply, as predicted in

1840 by German chemist Justus von Liebig's law of the minimum. Identifying any single, irreplaceable natural resource required by the commercial culture, however, would be difficult, although petroleum would be a likely candidate. Resource depletion by itself is an inadequate predictor of cultural viability because resources are culturally defined and major economic and social instabilities are produced by more comprehensive changes in ecosystems or climate, as will be examined later.

From the very beginning of the industrial era, a number of scholars, including economist Adam Smith (1776), demographer Thomas Malthus ([1798] 1895), and pioneer conservationist George Marsh (1864), warned that the earth would not support endless economic progress. In 1873, scientists from the American Association for the Advancement of Science even petitioned the U.S. Congress to legislate conservation measures. However, the colonial expropriation of the resources controlled by tribal cultures and great tradition civilizations postponed the inevitable shortages and fostered an ideology of unlimited growth.

The global issue of resource depletion was not even seriously addressed at the international level until 1949 when the United Nations convened 700 scientists from fifty nations to assess the resource demands of global economic development. At that time, H. L. Keenleyside, Canadian deputy minister of mines and resources, reported that between 1900 and 1949, more world mineral resources had been consumed than at any time in the past. He thought that the mineral situation was not yet critical but warned that

> it is clear that the combination of an increasing population and rising standards of living will place a strain on our metal resources which will almost certainly in the end prove beyond the capacity of man and nature to supply. . . . [Unless] there is a fundamental change in the economic fabric of human society we will ultimately be faced with the exhaustion of many of our mineral resources. (1950:38)

Since the 1940s, American planners and resource scientists have kept a careful eye on the supply of strategically significant resources. This was prudent, given America's disproportionate consumption levels, as was demonstrated as early as 1952 in a study commissioned by President Truman, which amplified the Keenleyside report. Truman's commission estimated that between 1914 and 1950, Americans by themselves had consumed more of the world's fuels and minerals than the combined total of *all* previous consumption.

Given the inequities built into the global system, resource shortages likely will not be shared equally by peoples in different regions. Most U.S. assessments of resource limitations have been remarkably optimistic. For example, a major study to predict "America's Needs and Resources" up to 1960, commissioned by the Twentieth Century Fund in 1947, acknowledged that domestic mineral resources would eventually be exhausted but assumed that free access to foreign resources would support an "expanding American economy" for many decades (Dewhurst 1947). Another study in 1963 concluded that, given continued imports and substitution of synthetics for natural materials, no critical shortages would prevent Americans from tripling their consumption of natural resources by the year 2000 (Landsberg 1964). However, a 1975 report, "Mineral Resources and the Environment," issued by the National Academy of Sciences, was much more pessimistic and called on the government to establish a national policy of resource conservation, recycling, and reduced energy consumption. The report ominously declared, "Man faces the prospect of a series of shocks of varying severity as shortages occur in one material after another, with the first real shortages perhaps only a matter of a few years away" (National Research Council 1975:26).

Curiously, the commercial economy is designed to thrive on resource depletion while theoretically denying its existence. According to an influential text, *The Economics of Natural Resource Availability,* by resource economists Harold Barnett and Chandler Morse (1963), there can be no limits on economic growth because market forces and technological advance will inevitably create new resources. Barnett and Morse

argued that industrial progress makes nature "subservient to man." They emphatically declared, "The notion of an absolute limit to natural resource availability is untenable when the definition of resources changes drastically and unpredictably over time" (Barnett and Morse 1963:7).

Such an economic ideology, when uninhibited by political controls, or an objective view of the physical world, allows resources to be systematically depleted. Historically, different types of trees, whales, and fossil fuels have been exploited as long as prices and production costs made it profitable. Orthodox market theory suggests that a given resource will be replaced by a cheaper substitute the moment that it becomes too scarce or expensive to harvest. This makes economic sense, but it can lead to extinction.

Theoretically, solar-based cultures can last perhaps 5 billion years, when the sun is predicted to burn out, but a fossil fuel–dependent commercial-scale culture is mining a limited energy source that is rapidly being depleted. There are no absolute figures on the total supply of fossil fuels, but a study commissioned by President Jimmy Carter in 1977 to guide government planning up to the year 2000 estimated that at 1976 production rates, oil would be depleted within 77 years, natural gas in 170 years, and coal in 212 years (Barney 1980, vol. 2). Any such estimates are purely hypothetical and are based on assumptions about population levels, consumption rates, production technologies, use efficiencies, prices, and politics; nevertheless, the magnitude of the supply problem is inescapable and has been acknowledged by geologists for many years. Petroleum expert M. King Hubert (1969) estimated that even with the most optimistic estimates, oil production would peak about the year 2000 and would essentially stop by the end of the twenty-first century. In Figure 15.2 Hubert gives two estimates of the total amount of world oil in existence that could ever be extracted, either 1.35 trillion barrels (1350 billion) or 2.1 trillion (2100 billion). Taking the larger, more optimistic figure, he calculates that 80 percent of total world production of oil would occur within a mere 64 years.

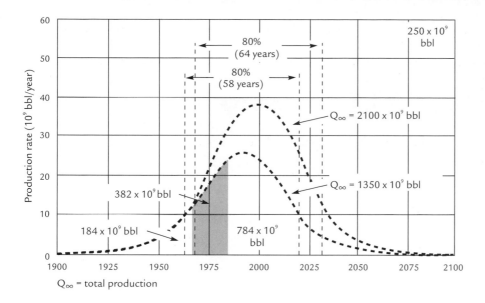

FIGURE 15.2

A chart of the complete cycles of world crude-oil production. Petroleum is perhaps commercial culture's most vital nonrenewable resource, yet its total availability is strictly limited. (SOURCE: Hubert 1969:196.)

Hubert's estimate that global petroleum production would peak at 25 billion barrels a year in 1995 was almost exactly the 25.5 billion barrels estimated for 1995 by the U.S. Department of Energy (2003b Table G2). At that rate of consumption, the world's proven oil reserves of 1 trillion barrels would last 37 years, up to the year 2038, but of course new oil will still be discovered. As a nonrenewable resource, it seems certain that oil will eventually be used up, and this reality is well understood by the leaders of the industry, such as Mike Bowlin, then CEO of ARCO, who commented in 1999, "We've embarked on the beginning of the Last Days of the Age of Oil" (Brown 2000:12).

Because the United States is the world's largest consumer of energy, American elites are key actors in the global commercial system. In 2004, U.S. official forecasters projected that total annual energy consumption would continue to grow, increasing more than 40 percent from 97 quadrillion Btu's in 2000 to 136.5 quadrillion Btu's by the year 2025 (U.S. Department of Energy 2004). This is critically important not only because of America's dependence on fossil fuels in the form of oil, coal, and natural gas (Figure 15.3), which are nonrenewable and contribute

to global warming, but because much of this is imported oil. This means that five Middle East Islamic countries, Iraq, Iran, Kuwait, Saudi Arabia, and the United Arab Emirates, which together control two-thirds of global oil reserves, are enormously important to the continued maintenance and growth of America's energy-intensive cultural system. These cultural realities also give enormous social power to a few individuals and a handful of elite families that rule these countries. Oil revenues accumulate in oil producing nations and ironically have been used to finance terrorist attacks against American interests.

Limits to Growth and the Global Environment

The Club of Rome study, *The Limits to Growth* (Meadows et al. 1972), published in 1972, was the first comprehensive predictive model of the global system to incorporate the interaction of cultural and biological components and to look relatively far into the future. The Club of Rome is unusual among futurist groups because it is an informal international organization formed in 1968 under the sponsorship of an Italian industrialist to study the global system and the "predicament

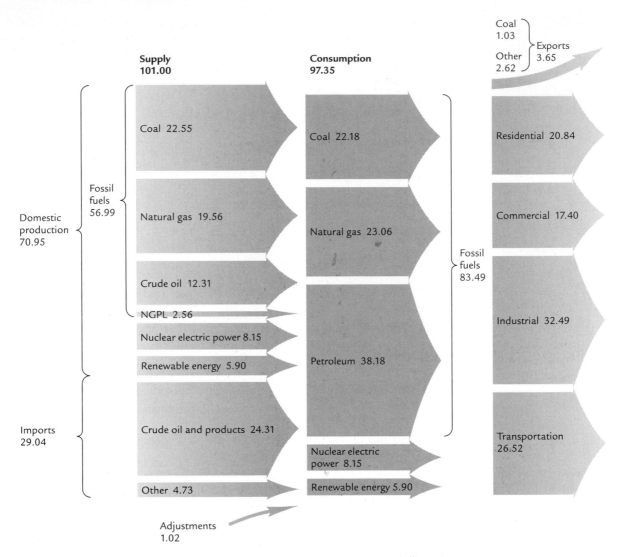

FIGURE 15.3   American energy flow overview, 2002 (numbers given in quadrillion Btus).

of mankind." The *Limits to Growth* study was produced by a seventeen-member international team of experts who worked with a sophisticated "world model" computer program developed by Jay Forrester of the Massachusetts Institute of Technology. The model took a systems approach and considered the positive and negative feedbacks between population, agriculture, industry, natural resources, and pollution. The objective

was to see how long the global system could function if the exponential growth trends already observed in the world economy and population from 1900 to 1970 were to continue indefinitely.

The Club of Rome study consistently predicted a system collapse before 2100 because of the seemingly inescapable limits to growth (Figure 15.4). Even when the researchers doubled world resources and assumed that pollution could be

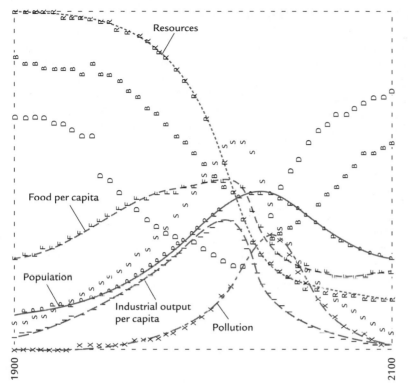

FIGURE 15.4
Graph of potential system collapse. According to this famous computer projection from the 1972 *Limits to Growth* study, if historical trends in population and economic growth continued with no change, the global commercial culture would collapse well before 2100. (SOURCE: Meadows et al. 1972:124.)

Key: B = Crude birth rate (births per 1000 people per year)
    D = Crude death rate (deaths per 1000 people per year)
    S = Service per person (dollar equivalent per person per year invested in education, healthcare, and household maintenance)

controlled and population stabilized, the global system still collapsed. In the "standard run" of the world model, industrial production peaks sometime after the year 2000, due to dwindling resources. Population continues to increase until death rates rise due to pollution, declining food output, and reduced medical services. The only way to prevent system collapse was to stabilize both population and economic growth.

Technological optimists charged that the *Limits to Growth* study was either too simple or too complex, and there were accusations that it was simply a demonstration of the preconceived "doomsday" assumptions of the model's designers (Cole 1973). Twenty years later, the original authors of *Limits to Growth* published a new

study reaffirming their earlier findings (Meadows, Meadows, and Randers (1992). They stressed that their concern was sustainability, not fixing a doomsday date, and argued that resource consumption and pollution had already exceeded sustainable rates in many countries.

The 1977 Carter Commission *Global 2000* study referred to earlier was an independent and more conservative reexamination of the near future for the global system, carried out with a larger budget and the cooperation of thirteen U.S. government agencies. The *Global 2000* researchers assumed fewer negative feedbacks and limited their projections to the year 2000, but they still found that population would continue to increase and that there could be serious water shortages, deforestation, desertification (expansion of arid lands), deterioration of agricultural lands, and massive extinctions, together with more poverty and political tension. The commissioners concluded,

> The most knowledgeable professional analysts in the executive branch of the U.S. Government have reported to the President that, if public policies around the world continue unchanged through the end of the century, a number of serious world problems will become worse, not better . . . the world in 2000 will be more crowded, more polluted, less stable ecologically, and more vulnerable to disruption. . . . Serious stresses involving population, resources, and environment are clearly visible ahead . . . the world's people will be poorer. (Barney 1977, vol. 1:xvi, 1)

BIOSPHERE ALTERATION

Human-induced changes in global climate, which most experts conclude are now underway, are an ominous indication that critical natural thresholds have already been crossed. During the 1980s, a sequence of environmental events occurred that made it difficult for even the most optimistic planners to deny the possibility that the commercial culture would need to make major adjustments to ensure its long-term survival. In 1982, German scientists announced that acid rain caused by industrial pollution was destroying European forests. In 1985, British scientists reported a thinning in the ozone layer over Antarctica, which was attributed to release of chlorofluorocarbons (CFCs) used in refrigerants and as propellants in spray cans. In 1986, world population passed the 5-billion mark; the Soviet nuclear reactor at Chernobyl exploded, spewing radiation worldwide; and an article in the British science journal *Nature* reported measurable evidence that global warming was taking place due to elevated levels of carbon dioxide (CO_2), the greenhouse effect (Jones, Wigley, and Wright 1986). Negative feedbacks of the sort predicted by the *Limits to Growth* model are taking place.

The Rising Tide: Global Environmental Change

Global warming is probably the single most dramatic and far-reaching environmental impact of industrial development. The natural cycles of the past 2 million years would suggest that the world is more than halfway through an interglacial period and should be cooling, but instead the world has actually warmed over the past 100 years. The greenhouse effect, which has been recognized as a theoretical possibility since the nineteenth century, assumes that increased atmospheric CO_2 gas from the burning of fossil fuels would heat the earth like the glass of a greenhouse by trapping solar heat near the earth's surface. Evidence that human activities were impacting global climate was presented at the first UN-sponsored World Climate Conference in 1979, but it was nearly a decade before a full institutional response began. However, further proof of the greenhouse effect continued to emerge. Precise measurements showed an increase of nearly 8 percent in atmospheric CO_2 between 1958 and 1984 (Landsberg 1989), and CO_2 gas bubbles trapped in Antarctic ice showed relative stability over the previous 10,000 years (Graedel and Crutzen 1989).

Carbon is stored in natural "sinks," or reservoirs, either as organic matter, especially in forest biomass, or in coal and oil, or in the ocean. In the natural carbon cycle, CO_2 is taken up by plants during photosynthesis. It is also stored chemically in the ocean. Carbon is released back into the atmosphere as CO_2 by respiration, decomposition, and other chemical and biological processes. Large-scale human burning of fossil fuels and forests imbalances the cycle by withdrawing carbon from storage faster than it can be reabsorbed by the forests and oceans (Figure 15.5).

In the 1980s, CO_2 was considered to be responsible for more than half of the predicted global warming, while other less common but more active greenhouse gases such as methane, CFCs, and nitrous oxide contributed the remainder. Although methane is produced naturally as

FIGURE 15.5 The amount of emissions in the atmosphere rose by 8 percent between 1958 and 1984. Emissions such as from this coal-burning power plant contributed to this increase.

swamp gas and by termites, significant quantities are also produced by fermentation in rice paddies and in the digestive tracts of domestic cattle (Ciccrone 1989). CFCs are a commercial product that chemists synthesized in the 1920s. Their ability to destroy the ozone that screens the earth from ultraviolet radiation has been suspected since 1974 (Rowland 1989).

It is impossible to predict with absolute confidence how much warming will occur; however, the Intergovernmental Panel on Climate Change (IPCC), established in 1988 by the World Meteorological Organization and the UN Environment Program, has produced the most comprehensive overview of the problem available. The IPCC issued its first report in 1991, the second in 1996,

and published a four-volume Third Assessment Report in 2001. IPCC researchers organized their effort in three working groups to examine respectively the scientific aspects of climate change, its impacts, and possible responses. The Third Assessment Report was based on thirteen years of work by hundreds of scientists and contributions from dozens of research institutes from throughout the world. It was backed up by numerous special reports and technical papers.

The IPCC's (2001a, 2001b) findings show unmistakable evidence of global warming caused by human activities. Burning of fossil fuels and land development have caused atmospheric concentrations of CO_2, the principal greenhouse gas, to increase by 31 percent from 280 ppm (parts per million) in 1750 to 368 ppm in the year 2000. Global CO_2 remained relatively constant over the thousand years before 1750, when global commercial development began to expand dramatically. Average global surface temperature increased by 0.6°C (1°F) during the twentieth century. In the Northern Hemisphere this was greater than in any century during the last thousand years, and the 1990s were the warmest decade of the millennium. It appears that climate change is already causing social and economic damage from floods, droughts, and other severe weather events. Glaciers are retreating, arctic ice is thinning, permafrost is melting, winter snow cover is declining, northern rivers and lakes are thawing two weeks earlier than a century ago, growing seasons are increasing, and plant and animal distributions, flowering, and breeding seasons are changing. Global mean sea level increased at 1 to 2 mm annually during the twentieth century, for a total of some 6 inches. Sea level rise is caused by expansion of the ocean as it warms as well as by water added from melting glaciers and ice fields.

Food Production and the Malthusian Dilemma

Many researchers and policy planners have examined food production as a key variable limiting global population, but this is not a simple matter. Theoretically, treating global limits as a subsistence carrying-capacity issue should be possible, but carrying capacity can only be defined for a specific cultural system and technology in a given environment. This is difficult to do even for tribal cultures, where food is produced directly to satisfy human needs, because neither environment nor technology are constants, as the long history of subsistence intensification demonstrates. In the global system, food production is only indirectly concerned with human nutritional requirements; it is primarily directed by political and economic objectives. Indeed, when food and the means to produce it are controlled by governments, multinational corporations, and market economies, the connection between food production and carrying capacity must be approached with caution. Hungry people and empty granaries in a given country do not necessarily mean that environmentally defined production limits have been exceeded. Similarly, steadily increasing grain output at the global level may not mean that technology has defeated nature. Diminishing returns and environmental deterioration are real and can be described at both local and global levels.

In 1798, English economist and demographer Thomas Malthus (1766–1834) correctly observed that human population has the biological capacity to grow faster than food production, but he did not realize that tribal cultures can maintain a relative balance between food and population without suffering chronic hunger. Ignoring the culturally determined demographic imbalances and inequities that were generating hunger in the newly emerging global system, Malthus mistakenly concluded that misery worked "naturally" as the primary check on population growth. He supported his findings with historical data demonstrating that famine and hunger elevated mortality in states and empires. But he did not realize that he was also observing the action of cultural variables acting together with natural limits.

The Malthusian argument conveniently provided nineteenth-century policymakers with a justification for keeping public welfare low because it implied that only a certain level of human suffering would prevent overpopulation. This aspect of Malthusian theory has since been widely discredited, especially by demographic transition theorists. During the early post–World War II decades of economic development, some technological optimists argued that Malthus was also wrong about the ultimate limits of food production. However, granted that poverty and misery are cultural, not natural, checks on population, Malthus was indeed correct about the general relationship between food and population, even if it is difficult to define. Because of diminishing returns and the limits of water, soil, and energy, there are practical limits to subsistence intensification in any given region and at a global level. However, determining what the actual limits are is complicated by the intervention of governments, markets, and the fossil fuel subsidy in the food production process.

Any estimates of a maximum sustainable global population must consider not only physical limits but also cultural variables such as political and economic organization, as well as technology. In 1905, when world population stood at 1.5 billion, Harvard geologist Nathaniel Shaler (1841–1906) warned that world food production could not support a threefold increase to 4.5 billion people. That was probably a realistic estimate for the early twentieth-century world in which agricultural production was not fossil fuel–based and remained largely self-sustaining. This was still the situation at midcentury, when world population reached 2.5 billion, and only marginal or highly erodible lands remained undeveloped (Brown and Postel 1987). Given that poverty-inducing colonial inequities were perpetuated in the decolonized world, massive Malthusian crises were probably delayed by the introduction of the expensive technological inputs that began with the post–World War II campaign for economic development. During the technological optimism of the 1950s, there were projections that world population might reach 30 billion by 2075, but geochemist Harrison Brown (1956) calculated

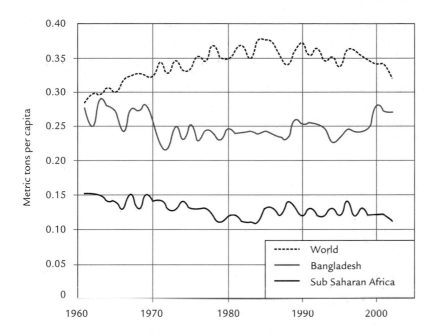

FIGURE 15.6
Per-capita cereal pro-
duction, 1961–2002.
(SOURCE: Food and Agri-
culture Organization of the
United Nations, FAOSTAT,
online database,
www.fao.org)

that such a population would literally eat up the world, even if it could feed directly on rock and seawater. Joel E. Cohen (1995) provides an exhaustive overview of global population and human carrying-capacity issues, together with an inventory of estimates of maximum population from Leeuwenhoek's 1679 figure of 13.4 billion to a 1994 Dutch Government figure of 11 to 44 billion.

The availability of food is of course a critical limiting factor for human population, with grain directly providing about half of human nutrition and feeding much of the world's livestock. At a global level, cereal grain production per capita generally increased since 1960 (Figure 15.6), seemingly disproving Malthus on the general relationship between food and population. However, the per-capita cereal production trends for Bangladesh and sub-Saharan Africa have been downhill, and global cereal production relative to population may have peaked in about 1985. Nevertheless, the real food problem lies in the way the global food system is organized, and the way wealth and income are distributed in the commercial world. The Bangladesh case study in Chapter 13 showed how energy and capital in-

tensive production systems amplified poverty, making it more difficult for people to feed themselves, or buy food. The history of global poverty shows that hunger is primarily a social and cultural, not a technical, production problem. There is no economic incentive for giant agribusinesses to allow the poor access to productive resources and livable wages. However, it is highly profitable for agribusinesses to expend precious energy and capital on the production of corn and soybeans to be converted into corn syrup and expensive protein for the world's wealthiest to consume.

In the commercial world food production and distribution is dominated by the elites who own and direct a relatively few giant corporations, whose primary goal is generating maximum profit for shareholders. For example, Monsanto, with nearly $5 billion in revenues in 2003, dominated the biotechnology seed market, with its licensed genetic traits planted in 150 million acres. Monsanto's Roundup™ was the world's top herbicide, and Monsanto's branded corn and soybean seeds were number one or two in the North American, Latin American, and Asian markets. By the last quarter of the twentieth century, just five privately held corporations already controlled the marketing and transport of most of the world's grain (Morgan 1979, Sewell 1992). In 2003, one food processing corporation, Archer Daniels Midland (ADM), operated the world's largest storage and transportation network for grain and oil seed, and claimed to be the world's largest processor of corn and cocoa and one of the largest processors of wheat and oilseeds (ADM 2003). ADM's publicity declared, "Our production and distribution networks make it possible for us to contribute to satisfying the nutritional needs of billions of people" (www.admworld.com). Their revenues of $30 billion in 2003 exceeded the individual GDPs of 92 of the world's 153 nations. Another company, Arbor Acres, subsidiary of Aviagen, claimed to be the largest broiler chicken breeding company in the world, controlling 44 percent of the global market in 85 countries.

The problem with an elite-directed global food system is that it is not designed to serve human needs. Because food is a commodity and elites use it for both political and economic advantage, commercial food often does a poor job of reducing hunger and malnutrition. Concentrated economic power in food production and distribution means that most people do not have access to the land, labor, and tools needed to produce food directly, and low incomes make it difficult for poor people to buy nutritionally adequate food. Furthermore, food produced and extensively marketed by giant corporations often does not promote an optimal diet. The UN Food and Agriculture Organization (2003:4) estimated that there were 798 million chronically hungry or undernourished people in the world in the year 2000. That is more than the entire population of the world in 1750. As many as 2 billion people were malnourished (UN, WHO/FAO 2002:5). There may have been a total of 3 billion malnourished, or half the world, if over-consumption is included along with nutritional deficiency (Gardner and Halweil 2000). Multinational corporations benefit from the "nutritional transformation" (see Chapter 5) shift to high-fat, energy-dense commercial foods that contributes to a wide range of

costly noncommunicable diseases such as diabetes and obesity. The shareholders of Monsanto and ADM benefit along with Coca-Cola and Pepsi from the sale of high-calorie soft drinks containing high quantities of corn syrup sweeteners, but few nutrients.

The elite objective of economic globalization favors the largest, most powerful agribusinesses and food corporations and works against food self-sufficiency at local and national levels, even though smaller-scale food systems and markets are more likely to be more sustainable, more equitable, and more responsive to nutritional needs. Given the economic and social inequalities that have been caused by colonialism and globalization, many areas of Asia, the Middle East, and Latin America may be approaching or exceeding the limits of sustainable food production under present conditions (Keyfitz 1989). Short-term production shortfalls can be compensated for by tapping stored grain or by diverting grain from cattle feed directly to human consumption. However, any redistribution of this sort would be mediated by the global grain market and the political economy, and in 1989, only the United States, Canada, western Europe, Australia, and New Zealand were net grain exporters. Any long-term declines in the world food balance will compel the commercial culture to institute profound adjustments.

Numerous lines of evidence suggest that food production is already badly overextended in many countries, under prevailing cultural conditions. Food scientist Georg Borgstrom (1965) pointed out that developed countries were supplementing their agricultural production by drawing extensively on marine fisheries and market-based international trade. Borgstrom used the concept of ghost acres to refer to land that a given country would need to put into production to produce an amount of animal protein equal to its net food imports and fishery production. Ghost acres allow a country to subsidize what might otherwise be unsustainable economic growth by shifting production costs to the oceans or the farmlands of other countries. Obvious examples are Middle East desert countries that trade oil for food, but richly endowed agricultural countries such as the United States also take advantage of favorable trade conditions to import large amounts of food from poorer countries. In the 1960s, Borgstrom estimated that Japan's ghost acres were six times greater than its agricultural acreage. Since then, innovations in the fishing industry—such as the use by Japan, Taiwan, and South Korea of miles-long monofilament drift nets that sweep all the fish from vast areas of ocean—have extended ghost acreage to clearly unsustainable levels.

The concept of ghost acres also applies to Peruvian fish meal that is exported to the United States for use as chicken food, to native-grown oilseed cakes fed to European cattle, and to beef that is raised in former Amazonian rain forests and shipped to the United States. These seemingly irrational economic exchanges occur because they generate profit in a market system that does not count all production costs.

The danger of reliance on ghost acres is that global finance—including investment capital, tax subsidies, special loans, and grants—has produced a capital-intensive factory-fishing system, which is displacing small-scale, subsistence-level fisheries and harvesting fish faster than they can be replenished. Ecologist Carl Safina (1995) has shown that between 1970 and 1990, the world's factory-fishing fleet actually doubled, and the world's major fisheries reached their production peaks between 1973 and 1989 and are now declining, in some dramatic cases by more than 50 percent. Some of the richest fisheries, such as the famous Grand Banks off Newfoundland, have been closed, yet the market price of fish has been buffered by shifts to other fisheries and the artificial subsidies to the industry.

Diminishing returns to inputs in fisheries and agriculture seem to be an inescapable law of nature (see Chapter 10). The rapid early increase in food production after 1950 can be largely attributed to a 22 percent increase in world cropland, as previously undeveloped marginal lands were plowed and irrigated. These lands had been un-

developed because they would not support intensive use or because the cost of their development was previously considered too high. Further production increases required large amounts of fossil fuel energy and chemical fertilizer. Between 1950 and 1986, irrigated land increased nearly threefold, world fertilizer use increased ninefold, and energy use in agriculture increased nearly sevenfold. Much of this increase in agricultural effort was a result of the intervention of the global institutions of development examined in Chapter 13.

As diminishing returns theory would predict, increased yields have required steadily larger inputs of energy and fertilizer. In 1950, a ton of grain required 0.44 barrel of oil to produce, but in 1986, the same ton cost 1.14 barrels. Declining yields in relation to fertilizer inputs, despite the widespread use of high-yield-variety hybrids, suggest that many crops may be reaching the limits of photosynthetic efficiency, beyond which no further gains can be achieved regardless of the input (Brown 1989).

Such intensive production systems cannot be sustained for long because energy and fertilizer will inevitably become more costly. Elevated production is also mining highly erodible soils and withdrawing irrigation waters from underground aquifers at greater than replacement rates (Brown 1987, Brown and Postel 1987). Many marginal areas that were pushed too quickly into production have since been abandoned due to desertification, waterlogging, salination, and erosion.

Technological Optimism and Scale Subsidies

Taking a more optimistic approach, some experts suggest that world food production might still support up to 10 billion people, given full application of environmentally "appropriate" technology. Economist Pierre Crosson and soils and climate specialist Norman Rosenberg, both of Resources for the Future, are skeptical of "apocalyptic scenarios," suggesting that damage to marginal soils may be overestimated. They point to the Green Revolution grain-yield achievements of the 1965–1985 period and a continued slowing of the annual growth rate of world population as cause for optimism. Advocating more high-tech progress, they called for "a steady stream of new agricultural technologies that can only come from the CGIAR system (see Chapter 13) and national research institutions in both the developed and the developing countries" (Crosson and Rosenberg 1989:132).

Many agricultural scientists hope that accelerated application of biotechnology will lead to new nitrogen-fixing plant varieties that will require less fertilizer or to plants that will tolerate salt and drought. Furthermore, lasers and mechanical improvements might increase irrigation efficiency, and new cropping techniques might reduce pesticide requirements.

Lester Brown (1989) warns that biotechnology is unlikely to yield further dramatic production increases, and many genetic "improvements" may be accompanied by trade-offs that will actually lower yields. Robert Chandler, founding director of the International Rice Research Institute, CGIAR's oldest research center, is also cautious about the long-term potential for continued yield expansion. Chandler was a leading architect of the Green Revolution in Asia, but predicted in 1989 that Indian rice production might keep pace with population for only another 20 years. Finding it "extremely unlikely" that Asian rice yields would ever be increased to more than double their then current levels, Chandler cautioned,

> It must be realized that the greatest gains in varietal improvement have already been made. There are limits not only to the amount of arable land and to fresh water supplies for irrigation but to the genetic improvement of plants. . . . We should remember that we cannot increase average world precipitation or the quantity of solar radiation, the two most important factors limiting crop production. (1990:174)

Chandler's predictions are supported by the fact that total Asian rice production doubled between 1962 and 1983, but increased by only 25 percent over the next 20 years.

TABLE 15.1   SCALE SUBSIDIES: NEGATIVE OUTCOMES OF SUBSIDIZED LARGE-SCALE AGRICULTURAL INTENSIFICATION

Land Clearing	deforestation
	soil erosion
	loss of biodiversity
	greenhouse gases
	desertification
Shortened Fallow	soil erosion
Irrigation	salinization
	water depletion
Chemical Fertilizer	water contamination
Mechanization	loss of small producers
Pesticides	water contamination
	resistant organisms
	health hazards
	loss of biodiversity
Monocrops	loss of biodiversity
	reduced crop rotation
	soil erosion
Giant Agribusiness	greenhouse gases
	soil erosion
	overproduction
	social inequity
	loss of small producers

SOURCE: Myers and Kent 2001:39–62.

The high-tech, energy- and capital-intensive food production system is sustained by what can be called scale subsidies. A scale subsidy is social support in the form of taxes, higher prices, or negative costs for activities that in this case promote larger-scale food systems. In effect, global society as a whole pays the negative costs for the unsustainable form of agricultural intensification chosen by the leaders of giant agribusinesses (Table 15.1). Scale subsidies can be called "perverse subsidies" to the extent they are "adverse to society's overall and long-term interests" (Myers and Kent 2001:4). This is a different evaluation from their potential to generate profits for investors, and calls attention to the difference between short-term benefits to the few and long-term costs to the many. The annual costs of agricultural perverse subsidies to global society in 2000 were conservatively estimated at $510 billion (Myers and Kent 2001). Total perverse subsidies in agriculture, energy systems, roads, water, fisheries, and forestry approach $2 trillion. These estimates include, for example, a calculation that agricultural pesticide use in the United States in the 1990s produced social and environmental costs of $8.3 billion in public health impacts, groundwater contamination, loss of wild birds and domestic animals, pesticide resistance, and loss of natural enemies. Producers benefitted from this subsidy because they spent only $6.5 billion for the pesticides, passed those costs on to consumers in the form of higher prices, and gained $26 billion in crops saved (Pimentel and Greiner 1997).

TOWARD A SUSTAINABLE WORLD

Most global planners agree that significant cultural changes will be required if the global system is to remain intact through the end of the twenty-first century. In 1987, the report of the Brundtland Commission on environmental deterioration officially advocated sustainable development as a solution to global poverty and environmental deterioration (WCED 1987). The commission defined sustainable development as "development that meets the needs of the present without compromising the ability of future generations to meet their own needs" (WCED 1987:43). Sustainability is now a widely endorsed planning goal, as shown by frequent use of the expression "sustainable agriculture" and the oxymoron "sustainable economic growth." Institutionalized planning, however, still sets relatively short-term goals, often focused on single technologically defined issues such as global warming or food production. More fundamental problems, such as the need for a redistribution of political and economic power to create a more balanced and equitable world, are not being adequately addressed.

If progress is now equated with sustainability, the obvious failure of utopian capitalism to produce a demonstrably sustainable cultural system after 500 years of continuous growth suggests that increased scale and the more concentrated social power that growth produces may themselves be the primary obstacles to progress. Phrasing the sustainability problem in these terms opens the door to very exciting possibilities, because growth, scale, and power are cultural constructions that can be changed. People can gain control over the cultural processes that produce instability. This final section discusses how social and economic scale relate to the distribution of power, examines the problems inherent in commercialization, and considers what cultural changes can produce sustainable development.

Responding to Global Warming

In order to explore possible responses to global warming, IPCC Working Group III used six scenarios to simulate the effects that different cultural development pathways might have on future increases in global CO_2 levels up to the year 2100. The scenarios were grouped into four "families" by differences in the degree of economic development and globalization. A1 scenarios assume rapid economic growth with high consumption and a cultural convergence of world regions. The A2 scenario assumes lower economic growth with considerable regional differences. B1 assumes globalization with an emphasis on service and information, social equity, environmental protection, and resource efficiency, rather than energy-intensive material consumption. B2 resembles B1, but calls for local and regional development rather than global convergence. The A1 scenario most closely resembles the pathway global elites have followed since 1950, and is subdivided into three variations by energy system. A1FI continues with American-like fossil fuel intensive development. A1T assumes increasing reliance on nonfossil fuel energy sources, and A1B assumes a balanced energy system.

Following the A1FI, fossil-fuel intensive, development-as-usual future would produce the worst possible future with CO_2 levels at well over 900 ppm, global temperature nearly 5°C

(7°F) warmer than in 2000, and sea levels perhaps 0.5 meters (20 inches) higher. According to IPCC impact assessments detailed in Working Group II's report on "Impacts, Adaptation, and Vulnerability" (IPCC 2001a), A1FI outcomes would produce (1) risks to unique and threatened ecosystems; (2) large increases in extreme weather events; (3) negative impacts for most regions of the world; (4) overall negative impacts to markets and people; and (5) high risks of "future large scale discontinuities" (IPCC 2001a:11). The list of negative impacts is long and includes increased disease, loss of crops, water shortages, impoverishment, and, of course, flooding of coastal areas. Atolls and low Pacific islands would quickly become uninhabitable. Flooding and storm surges could force tens of million, and perhaps hundreds of million of people, out of densely settled river deltas, such as Bangladesh, and important rice producing areas would be lost (Nicholls, Hoozemans, and Marchand 1999). This is an altogether scary picture.

Not surprisingly, the "best" scenarios, A1T, B1, and B2 achieve the lowest CO_2 levels by 2100, but unfortunately, without other major policy interventions to drastically reduce CO_2 emissions, by 2100 global CO_2 levels would exceed 500 ppm, average global temperatures could be 2.5°C (4.5°F) higher (Figure 15.7), and sea levels could rise 0.3 meters (nearly a foot) above 2000 levels (Figure 15.8).

The United Nations Framework Convention on Climate Change (UNFCCC), adopted by the UN in 1992, calls on nations to "protect the climate system for the benefit of present and future generations of humankind, on the basis of equity and in accordance with their common but differentiated responsibilities and respective capabilities" (UNFCCC 2003). The objective is to stabilize greenhouse gases to prevent dangerous, human-induced climate changes. A crucial feature of the convention is its sorting of nations into three groups: (1) Annex I—industrialized nations, including the OECD (Organization for Economic Cooperation and Development) and Eastern European nations that were formerly part of or aligned with the Soviet Union; (2) Annex II—the wealthiest nations, the OECD; and (3) Non-Annex I—all poorer, less-industrialized nations (UNFCCC 2003). The membership of former Soviet block nations in both Annex I and II was an acknowledgment that these countries faced special problems in the transition from Soviet-style socialism to capitalism. According to the Framework Convention, Annex I nations were expected to reduce their CO_2 levels to 1990 levels by the year 2000. Even though 1990 levels would still be much too high, this would be a very positive step because in 2002 these countries consumed 83 percent of global GDP yet were only 23 percent of global population. There is, of course, a strong connection between high GDP in a country and high CO_2 emissions wherever fossil fuel-intensive development predominates.

Annex II nations were expected to provide financial and technical assistance to help poorer nations reduce their carbon emissions and deal with the effects of global warming. This seems reasonable, given that these rich nations represent less than 20 percent of global population with more than 80 percent of global GDP. The elites of these nations, and especially the American elite, are most responsible for producing the greenhouse gases that are causing global warming. The Framework Convention makes special provisions for very poor, "least-developed countries" (LDCs), because they are expected to suffer some of the most severe effects of global warming, yet will be least able to protect themselves or to mitigate the damage.

The Kyoto Protocol, adopted by the participants in the Framework Agreement in 1997, introduces specific measures to reduce global warming. It calls for the nations most responsible for greenhouse gas to reduce their emissions to five percent below their 1990 levels by 2008–2012. It creates an entirely new accounting system to keep track of each nation's progress toward meeting its overall reduction goals. The system gives credits for carbon stored in "sinks" and allows Annex I countries to conduct joint implementation projects moving and trading measured emission

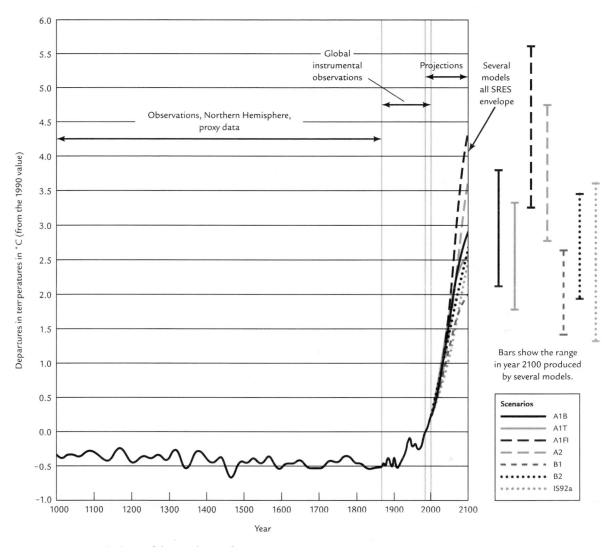

FIGURE 15.7 Variations of the Earth's surface temperature: years 1000 to 2100. SRES refers to the scenarios described in detail in the Special Report on Emissions Scenarios, a background report for the IPCC's Third Assessment Report.

reduction units (ERUs), removal units (RMUs), and certified emission reductions (CERs). Equally important are measures to remove government subsidies that support environmentally harmful industries.

The Kyoto Protocol would not eliminate global warming, but it is an important step and represents the first international effort to confront the most serious threats to sustainable development in the commercial world. However, the initial failure of the United States to ratify the Kyoto Protocol has greatly diminished its effectiveness. This is especially significant because the United States was responsible for 36 percent of CO_2 emissions by Annex I nations in 1990. The official American position can be attributed to a

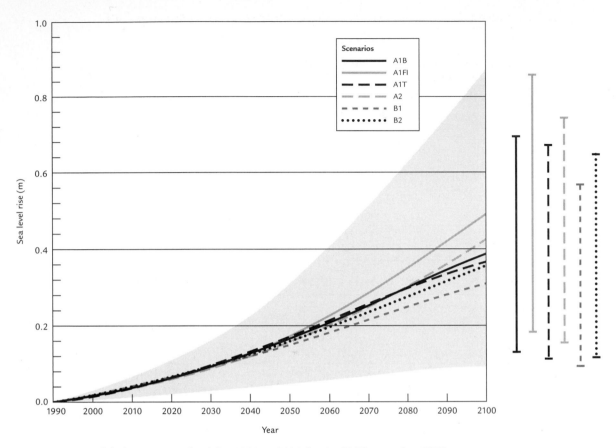

FIGURE 15.8   Global average sea level rise 1990 to 2100 for the SRES scenarios. SRES refers to the scenarios described in detail in the Special Report on Emissions Scenarios, a background report for the IPCC's Third Assessment Report.

handful of very powerful oil industry elites, their investors, and political supporters, whose short-term interests would presumably be threatened by any reduction in oil consumption (Leggett 2001).

Global Crises and Cultural Response, 12,000 BP–AD 2050

The global crisis that humanity faces at the beginning of the twenty-first century is not entirely unprecedented. As detailed in previous chapters, humans have already transformed their cultures in response to four major global crises (Table 15.2). This demonstrates that we have an enormous

capacity to adapt to new situations, and shows that no particular cultural development is inevitable or beyond human control. Other cultural worlds are possible. Ten thousand years ago at the end of the last Ice Age, people faced a warming world and rising sea levels. They adapted in at least three different ways. Some, such as Australian aborigines, kept their existing cultural system intact while gradually downscaling the size of their total population and of their territories. This option maintained the tribal world of mobile foragers. Others, such as Amazonian peoples and African cattle herders, opted to live in smaller territories and denser societies by adopt-

TABLE 15.2   GLOBAL CRISES AND CULTURAL RESPONSES, 12,000 BC–AD 2050

Agents	Decision	Outcome
I. Paleolithic Crisis: Post-Glacial Global Warming and Sea Level Rise, 12,000–5,000 BP		
Tribal Foragers	Downscale Society & Territory	Cultural Continuity of Mobile Forager World
Tribal Foragers	Intensify Subsistence Technology, Sedentarization	Creation of Neolithic Villager World
Aggrandizers, Political Elites	Concentrate Political Power, Urbanize, Conquer	Creation of Imperial World
II. Crisis of Feudalism: Scale Limits of Imperial World, AD 1300–1790		
European Elites	Depose Divine Monarchy, Concentrate Economic Power, Promote: Colonialism, Capitalism, Democratic Regimes	Creation of Commercial World
III. Crisis of Capitalism: Cyclical Economic Depressions and Wars, 1929–1950		
Euro-American Elites	Distribute Income Down, Promote: Decolonization, Energy- & Capital-Intensive Growth, Global Institutions, Human Rights	Creation of Progressive Global Order
IV. Crisis of Capitalism: Economic Downturn, Social Protest, 1970–1980		
Global Elites	Distribute Wealth & Income Up, Promote: Multinational Corporations, Energy- & Capital-Intensive Development	Creation of Global Economy
V. Sustainability Crisis: Environmental Degradation, Poverty, Social Protest, 1990–2050		
Global Citizens	Promote: Human Economic and Social Rights, Freedom, Social Equity, and Sustainability. Redistribute Social Power, Downscale Societies	Creation of Sustainable Global Society

ing more intensive food production systems and domestic technologies. This choice created the tribal world of Neolithic villagers. These tribal transformations were directed by everyone, and must have happened so gradually that everyone benefitted. A third option, which became possible under certain conditions, was to allow a few aggrandizing individuals to concentrate social power to permit survival for the majority, but at reduced levels of physical well-being and free-

dom. This decision ultimately created the imperial world of Pacific Island chiefdoms, the Ur-Namur Empire in ancient Mesopotamia, the Andean empires, and the Great Tradition civilizations in China and South Asia, but also produced many negative side effects for people and nature.

The chiefdoms, kingdoms, and empires of the imperial world went through repeated cycles of growth, collapse, and extinction, but these events did not become a global crisis until these cultures reached an effective growth ceiling during a period of deteriorating global climate. The European elite responded to the crisis of feudalism by concentrating economic power and ultimately creating the commercial world as a global capitalist system. Global capitalism allowed a few individuals and institutions to concentrate enormous levels of power, but by 1929 confronted its first crisis—a worldwide economic collapse, followed by massive social unrest, and a destructive global war. The Euro-American elites responded by constructing a progressive global social order based on the ideals of human rights and social justice and capital- and fossil fuel-intensive economic growth. Unfortunately, in practice economic growth often overrode the ideals of human rights and justice.

By 1970 a second crisis of capitalism was underway as it became apparent to many people that the system was not working to benefit them as they expected and might not be sustainable. This time global elites responded by concentrating more power and promoting even more intensive growth to create a larger, more integrated, global economy. By 1990 with global warming beginning, global poverty unsolved, and social unrest and conflict increasing, including global terrorism and massive habitat destruction and extinctions, it was clear that the global system was not sustainable as constructed.

Another major cultural transformation is required. The global warming crisis alone will force people to adjust over a very long period. Even if CO_2 emissions are stabilized and reduced by 2050, temperatures may take centuries to stabilize, and sea levels are expected to rise for millennia.

Power and Scale Solutions

Recognizing the dynamics of growth, scale, and power as the source of the present sustainability crisis points the way to solutions. Elite-directed growth has created a succession of crises for humanity over the past five thousand years. Societies and economies cannot grow forever and survive in a finite world. Clearly, elite solutions have failed, because they have been self-interested and too narrowly focused to maintain viable societies. Likewise, concentrated social power has proven maladaptive, because it has given too few too much ability to transform the world.

Our first priority in achieving a sustainable global culture will be to gain universal acceptance for the principle that all of humanity, all citizens of the world, need to be decision-makers and agents of cultural transformation. This will require full implementation of existing human rights conventions covering economic and social rights, as well as basic civil rights. Next, international institutions need to be reconstituted to fully protect human freedom, redistribute social power, and work for social justice in the global system. Effective international tribunals will be needed to hold individual and corporate tyrants responsible for human rights violations.

Redistributing social power to all citizens of the world will be a major undertaking. It will mean universalizing truly democratic political institutions at local, regional, national, and global levels. This would be facilitated in some cases by redistricting to downscale political units in order to give citizens more effective control over elected officials and more influence in larger representative forums. The principles of democratic political order are already widely accepted but poorly practiced. Military power can be downscaled by effective implementation of existing international arms conventions, especially those dealing with Weapons of Mass Destruction. Great nations may also subdivide into several smaller nations, thereby reducing the threat of massive military power.

Redistributing ideological power will require full implementation of existing human rights applied to religious belief and practice. It will also require universal recognition of freedom of the press, speech, and assembly as incorporated in the American Bill of Rights and the European Union Charter of Fundamental Rights, and full application to all media. This may require limits on concentrated commercial ownership and control of the media, as well as limitations on commercial advertising.

TABLE 15.3   SOCIAL SCALE AND THE *SUMMUM BONUM*

Individual Objectives	Organization, Institutions	Optimum Population Scale	Post-Optimum Socialized Objectives
HUMANIZATION reproduction, maintenance	HOUSEHOLD	5–25 household	social health
SOCIABILITY companionship	VILLAGE clubs, taverns	500 village, community	social welfare
PROSPERITY leisure & wealth	TOWN factories, markets	5000 town, region	economic growth GNP
SECURITY security, peace, justice, defense	CITY courts, city hall, armories	10,000–20,000 city, nation, absolute extended maximum 15 million	military power empire
EXPRESSIVE CULTURE	METROPOLIS, STATE theaters, churches, museums, galleries universities	100,000–200,000 metropolis, nation, technological maximum 15 million	national glory

SOURCE: Kohr (1977).

Redistributing economic power will require a broader concept of wealth to include conventional financial and tangible forms of wealth, as well as natural capital, social and cultural capital, and human capital. Encouraging unlimited accumulation of private financial capital will not be the primary objective of the political economy in a sustainable world order. Different property regimes may be needed to preserve capital and meet human needs. Natural capital would not be available for short-term private benefits, because it would provide $33 trillion in global services for such vital ecosystem services as climate regulation, water regulation, soil formation, and the production of edible biomass and organic materials by ecosystems (Costanza et al. 1997). The GDP measure of income will need to be adjusted to account for perverse subsidies, and democratic public institutions will need to devise means to distribute income to meet the requirements of social justice and sustainability.

The objective of these cultural transformations would not only be to construct a sustainable global system but to create a world in which social units and institutions would be the best size to optimize human well-being, making it possible for people to enjoy "the good life" or the *summum bonum*, as defined by their particular culture. The *summum bonum* concept recognizes the individual need to maintain and reproduce a successful household, to socialize, to be prosperous and secure, and to enjoy expressive culture (Table 15.3). It is likely that all of these individual needs could be met within optimum-sized societies having local communities of 500, towns of 5000, regional urban centers of 50,000, and a metropolis of a few hundred thousand—all within a national society of up to 15 million (Kohr 1977). As societies grow larger, individual needs are "socialized," becoming objectives of the whole society, such as economic growth or national glory. These are "post-optimum" objectives; socialization concentrates power and promotes further growth and quickly becomes a very costly and inefficient way to meet human needs. Many energy-intensive technologies can be considered "scale commodities," because their primary function is to sustain post-optimum scale systems.

Small, optimum-sized societies and economies already exist. There are 29 nations, such as Luxembourg and Iceland with populations of 10 million or less, including 15 nations with high per-capita incomes. Switzerland, with the highest per-capita income in the world, has only 7 million people organized as a small confederation. There are 22 independent Swiss cantons and communes, and the largest city has only 343,000 people. Switzerland has existed since 1291. There are also many proposals for new global structures such as the Earth Charter and the Common Agreement on Investment and Society, which proposes a World Economic Parliament.

Toward a Multiscale Cultural World

We can create sustainable cultures. But this will require the construction of a world system composed of many independent regional cultures, each working to establish a humane balance between the cultural processes that sustain households and those that sustain communities, polities, and commercial activities. Domestically organized indigenous cultures could thrive in such a multiscale world while national polities also remained secure. The Basques of northern Spain have already shown that sustainable cultural systems can be designed that effectively integrate industrial technologies and commercialization within an existing nation-state (see the box entitled "The Mondragón Cooperatives").

Designing sustainable cultures will require a *localization* process to diffuse social power by limiting growth and reducing the scale of both government and business enterprise. Localization built on existing local and regional governments would make democratic decision making by all adults a reality. It would also make it easier for workers to act as business owner-managers and for business profits to benefit local communities. Diffusing social power would allow local communities to regulate growth and scale by giving priority to the maintenance and reproduction of healthy households. The optimum balance between political and economic power could then

be democratically established by each cultural community.

To make these changes, people in each region of the world need to be free to manage culture scale and social power in ways that are most sustainable in their particular cultural and natural settings. Truly sustainable development should demand nothing less, but this is precisely the opposite of the wealth-concentrating growth program being promoted by the experts at the World Trade Organization, the World Bank, and the International Monetary Fund, who make global commercial competitiveness the top priority. Unfortunately, dollars are not democratic. The poor do not have equal opportunity in this kind of world, and localities are pitted against each other. The next great cultural development must put the interests of all people first by letting local communities and households set growth and development priorities. A useful guiding principle can be found in the concept of *Pareto optimality,* which is the ideal point at which development stops, that being when no one can get richer without making someone else poorer. Sustainable development policies could be most readily implemented by culturally homogeneous local communities, as is often the case with indigenous peoples. Large urban centers may also often have culturally distinct neighborhoods, but in many cases, locality, rather than culture, would necessarily be the basis of political mobilization. People in diverse communities and political constituencies may find a common ground in efforts to implement the humanitarian objectives enshrined in existing human rights charters, such as the UN's Universal Declaration of Human Rights.

Our long-run self-interest demands that we diffuse social power and reduce the scale of culture to manageable human proportions. We can begin this essential evolutionary correction by moving now to construct public policies that will strengthen the political and economic powers of households, local and regional communities, and noncommercial institutional structures, including voluntary associations. We need to abandon the goal of perpetual economic growth as an end in

The Mondragón Cooperatives

A successful, highly democratic, and economically just cultural system has been operating quietly in northern Spain since the 1950s (Morrison 1991, Whyte and Whyte 1988). Stubbornly independent Basques have created an integrated regional society of some 250,000 people, based on a system of numerous small-scale, worker-owned cooperatives centered on the town of Mondragón. Each Mondragón cooperative is limited in size to no more than 500 members, who each have an equal vote in management decisions. There are no giant, remotely owned corporations. The scale limit is crucial, because the Basques have learned that it is almost impossible for larger production units to remain truly democratic. Likewise, the pay scale normally increases by no more than a factor of six from top to bottom, which both rewards hard work and sets a ceiling on executive pay. Everyone shares in annual profits, and a proportion goes to support local community projects and the Basque cultural heritage.

Mondragón cooperatives manufacture world-class computerized robots and a wide range of exported industrial goods and consumer durables. They also run their own consumer co-ops and cooperative banking, social insurance, education, and child care services that respond directly to the needs of local people. The Mondragón mission statement makes employment, community, equity, education, and environment the primary objectives, and Basque cultural autonomy is a key to their achievement. The Basques are a unique people, who claim to be descendants of the Ice Age peoples who produced the great paintings on the cave walls at Lascaux and Altamira 30,000 years ago. In fact, their language and genetic roots do connect them with the most ancient Europeans. The Basques have learned that general welfare and domestic tranquility can best be achieved when everyone is allowed to manage the human, cultural, and natural resources that produce wealth.

This example shows how localization processes are actually being implemented in a particular region. The Basques are attempting to maintain high degrees of local cultural autonomy based on economic self-reliance. They are using industrial technology and capitalist economics within an integrated network of worker-owned, small-scale corporate business enterprises that strive to be highly democratic and egalitarian while supporting households and local communities. Cooperative enterprises may also help dampen the negative human impact of long-wave capitalist economic cycles in particular regions (Booth 1987).

itself and focus instead on the design of our cultural systems in order to truly democratize social power. We need to focus on allocation rather than production. The incentives for destabilizing wealth concentration can be reduced by progressive tax laws that promote philanthropy. Corporate welfare can be channeled to small businesses. Corporations that misuse their power or engage in criminal conduct can be dechartered. The Tobin Tax on international currency transactions can be implemented. Tax laws that reward mergers and speculative finance can be eliminated. Perhaps most importantly, we must deny anonymity to anyone with massive power. The public must have full information about power networks and the ways power is used.

The commercial culture's two unresolved interconnected problems—impoverishing concentrations of social power and the impossibility of perpetual growth in a finite world—are both exaggerated by increases in scale. A more humane culture would use market forces to reward equitable and sustainable allocations of material prosperity. Democratic processes could bring both scale and power under control. Local and regional markets designed to draw on locally owned and managed resources could enhance every community's potential for self-reliance—much like tribal indigenous cultures that based their success on maintaining a permanent stake in particular places. Local residents would shift their finance capital out of remote mutual funds and foreign corporations into local enterprises in which investors have a direct, permanent stake. The efficiencies that local, small-scale enterprises gain by reducing the need for transportation costs, advertising, large CEO salaries, and ever-larger shareholder profits might offset the scale advantages that remote giant enterprises now enjoy. As energy costs rise and as the human costs of global business become more apparent, small-scale alternatives will become more attractive, and people will choose to bring their capital home. Many communities are already experimenting with local currencies and reviving regional produce markets. An energizing positive feedback will begin as citizens become increasingly disillusioned with remote and unresponsive political systems and turn to their own local and regional governments for solutions. Economic crises in the global system will only speed this inevitable cultural development process.

SUMMARY

The most fundamental issue facing humanity is this: How can a global commercial culture based on perpetual growth and inequality survive in a finite world? Truly successful cultural adaptation demands a long-term balance between available resources and consumption. In theory, there are measurable limits beyond which cultures cannot expand without degrading their resources and threatening their own existence. Industrial systems that rely primarily on fossil fuels will necessarily be a short-lived phenomenon lasting a few centuries at best. By contrast, cultural systems designed for lower levels of consumption can maintain a balance with renewable sources of solar energy and thus could exist for millions of years.

The ominous possibility exists that critical carrying-capacity limits may already have been exceeded, given the present structure of the commercial culture. Whether or not human-induced global warming is already underway, people now clearly have the capability to disrupt the life-support systems of the planet in a way that would have been inconceivable a mere 200 years ago. Food production systems are being strained in many areas of the world; unless distribution systems and consumption patterns can be modified, it is unlikely that even the most optimistic technological solutions will prevent Malthusian crises.

There are alternative solutions to create a more secure human future. Our comparative analysis of cultural systems from an anthropological culture-scale perspective suggests that an equitable and secure world needs to combine the best features of domestic-, political-, and commercial-scale cultural patterns. Social justice and preservation of the biosphere will require effective management by highly autonomous local communities, democratic regional governments, and fully representative global institutions.

STUDY QUESTIONS

1. In what sense can cultural development be called a mixed blessing that both solves problems and creates new ones? Use specific examples from each level of culture scale.
2. What are the problems with using increasing cultural control over nature and human reproductive success as measures of greater human

adaptability? Refer to consumer biomass, bio-diversity, and resource depletion.

3. What is the basis for the optimism of resource economists and futurist planners who argue that there are no limits to the availability of resources?

4. Compare the Club of Rome *Limits to Growth* study and the *Global 2000* report, referring to basic assumptions, methods, and conclusions.

5. Discuss the dynamics of global warming, referring to the greenhouse effect, greenhouse gases, fossil fuels, carbon cycle, carbon sinks, sea-level rise, and thermal expansion. What degree of warming and sea-level rise is predicted over the next century?

6. Why is there uncertainty about the rate and pace of global climate and sea-level changes? Why do some challenge the consensus view?

7. What are the likely consequences of global warming?

8. Why is it difficult to apply a carrying-capacity model to the global system? What variables need to be considered in setting a global maximum for human population? What different estimates have been proposed?

9. Critique the Malthusian model of food production and population growth. Refer to natural and cultural checks on population, diminishing returns, and absolute limits on food production.

10. What evidence is there that global food production systems may already be overextended? What factors set absolute limits on food production?

11. Distinguish between predominantly technological approaches to world problems and those that are more broadly cultural. Provide specific examples.

12. What is the argument in favor of the devolution of political and economic power as a solution to world problems?

SUGGESTED READING

BROWN, LESTER R.(ED.). 1984–. *State of the World* (annual). New York and London: Norton. Annual surveys of global conditions and prospects covering such issues as food, health, and economics.

COHEN, JOEL E. 1995. *How Many People Can the Earth Support?* New York and London: W. W. Norton. Thorough examination of global population and carrying-capacity issues.

DURNING, ALAN THEIN. 1992. *How Much Is Enough? The Consumer Society and the Future of the Earth*. The Worldwatch Environmental Alert Series. New York and London: Norton. Argues that people in the richest countries must reduce their consumption of resources.

IPCC. 2001. *Climate Change 2001: Synthesis Report*. A Contribution of Working Groups I, II, and III to the Third Assessment Report of the Intergovernmental Panel on Climate Change [Watson, R.T. and the Core Writing Team (eds)]. Cambridge, United Kingdom and New York, NY: Cambridge University Press. The IPCC is the principal international scientific body concerned with global warming.

KOHR, LEOPOLD. 1977. *The Overdeveloped Nations: The Diseconomies of Scale*. New York: Schocken Books. An economist shows how size creates global problems.

MEADOWS, DONELLA H., DENNIS L. MEADOWS, JORGEN RANDERS, AND WILLIAM W. BEHRENS, III. 1972. *The Limits to Growth*. New York: Universe. The first widely publicized computer simulation of the global system, designed to diagnose problems and seek solutions.

MYERS, NORMAN AND JENNIFER KENT. 2001. *Perverse Subsidies: How Tax Dollars Can Undercut the Environment and the Economy*. Washington, D.C.: Island Press. A thorough discussion of how subsidies impact the global system, with examples from many countries.

Glossary

acculturation   The concept used by colonial applied anthropologists to describe the changes in tribal culture that accompanied European conquest but that minimized the role of coercion and the loss of tribal autonomy.

acephalous   A political system without central authority or permanent leaders.

achieved status   Social position based on a person's demonstrated personal abilities apart from social status ascribed at birth.

adaptation   The long-term cultural process of maintaining a balance between population levels and natural resources within a given environment.

affine   A relative by marriage.

age-class system   A system in which individuals of similar age are placed in a named group and moved as a unit through the culturally defined stages of life. Specific rituals mark each change in age status.

age grade   A culturally defined stage of an age-class system such as childhood, adolescence, parenthood, and old age.

agnatic   Kin who are related through male links.

agricultural intensification   Changes in farming technology, such as shortened fallow periods, use of fertilizers, new crops, or irrigation, in order to produce more food per year in a given area, often at greater energy cost.

agromanagerial despotism   Wittfogel's explanation for the rise of the Mesopotamian state, arguing that the first rulers controlled irrigation and agriculture.

ancestor worship   A religious system based on reverence for specific ancestors and sometimes involving shrines, rituals, and sacrifice.

animism   A belief in spirits that occupy plants, animals, and people. Spirits are supernatural and normally invisible but may transform into different forms. Animism is considered by cultural evolutionists to be the simplest and earliest form of religion.

animistic thinking   The soul concept used by tribal individuals as an intellectual explanation of life, death, and dream experiences, part of Tylor's theory of animism as the origin of religion.

aristocracy   A political system in which a small, privileged elite rule.

ascribed status   The social status that one is born into; includes gender, birth order, lineage, clan affiliation, and connection with elite ancestors.

assimilation   Ethnocide without genocide; the loss of distinctive cultural traits as a population surrenders its autonomy and is absorbed into a dominant society and culture.

band   A group of twenty-five to fifty people who camp and forage together.

bigman   A self-made leader in a tribal culture. His position is temporary, depending on personal ability and consent of his followers.

bilateral development assistance   Aid that is given directly from one country to another and that may be given under conditions that favor the donor.

bride-service   The cultural expectation that a newly married husband will perform certain tasks for his in-laws.

bride-wealth   Goods, often livestock, that are transferred from the family of the groom to the family of the bride in order to legitimize the marriage and the children of the couple.

bureaucracy   A centralized command and control structure with officials arranged in an administrative hierarchy.

capital   Marx's term for land and tools as the means of production; also refers generally to accumulated wealth used for productive purposes.

capital accumulation   Expansion of wealth and the means of production that can be devoted to further production.

capitalist production   A mode of production in which a few people control the means of production and purchase the labor of those who could not otherwise support themselves.

carrying capacity   The number of people who could, in theory, be supported indefinitely in a given environment with a given technology and culture.

cash cropping   The raising of crops for market sale rather than for domestic consumption.

caste   An endogamous, ranked, occupationally defined group, known as *jati* in India, and based on differences in ritual purity and impurity.

central place   A settlement that serves as the focus of a regional communication network.

circumscription   Carneiro's explanation for the development of political centralization—that villagers may be forced to surrender their autonomy if they are unable to move away from authorities because of geographic barriers or neighboring societies.

city-states   Political-scale cultures based on relatively self-sufficient city-states, drawing their primary support from their immediate surroundings.

clan   A named group claiming descent from a common but often remote ancestor and sharing a joint estate.

closed corporate community   Communally organized peasants who exclude outsiders and limit the acquisition of wealth and power by their own members.

cognates   Related words found in more than one language and that were derived from a common proto-language.

cognatic line   A descent line that is traced to a common ancestor and that need not rely on exclusively male or female links.

collective representations   Ideas, or thoughts, and emotions common to a society as a whole, especially in reference to the supernatural.

commercialization   The production and maintenance of private profit-making business enterprise.

commercial-scale culture   A cultural system organized by impersonal market exchanges, commercial enterprises, contracts, and money, and potentially encompassing the entire world.

commodities   Basic goods that are produced for their exchange value in a market economy to generate profit to be accumulated as capital.

complementary opposition   A situation in which people assume a group identity in political opposition to another group at the same level.

consanguine   A relative by culturally recognized descent from a common ancestor; sometimes called a "blood" relative.

core   The wealthy industrial countries at the center of the world system where the recipients of unequal exchange reside.

cosmogony   An ideological system that seeks to explain the origin of everything: people, nature, and the universe.

cosmology   An ideological system that explains the order and meaning of the universe and people's places within it.

cross-cousin   The son or daughter of one's mother's brother or father's sister, and often considered to be in a marriageable category.

cultural autonomy   Self-determination by a cultural group.

cultural hegemony   Preponderant influence, or authority, by an elite in the production and reproduction of a society's moral order and associated cultural beliefs, symbols, and practices.

cultural relativism   Understanding other cultures by their own categories, which are assumed to be valid and worthy of respect.

culture   Socially transmitted, often symbolic, information that shapes human behavior and that regulates human society so that people can successfully maintain themselves and reproduce. Culture has mental, behavioral, and material aspects; it is patterned and provides a model for proper behavior.

culture scale   Order-of-magnitude differences among cultures on various socioeconomic dimensions, based on different modes of organizing social power.

debt bondage   An exploitive economic relationship that is managed to keep individuals in virtually perpetual indebtedness.

deferred exchange   A form of trade in which gift giving is reciprocated with a return gift at a later time, thus providing an excuse for maintaining contacts and establishing alliances between potentially hostile groups.

deficit production   The situation in which more calories are expended in food production than are produced for human food.

deindustrialization   The replacement of factory employment with service sector employment in formerly industrial countries as production jobs are moved to low-wage countries.

demand sharing   Requesting food or other things from kin who are obligated to give.

descent group   A social group based on genealogical connections to a common ancestor.

diminishing returns   The situation in which output values will decline as effort is increased in any production system.

direct rule   The use of European colonial administrators to control a native community at the local level.

disembodied economy   The concept of an economy as something that can be understood apart from the rest of society and culture, especially with a capitalist mode of production.

domestic mode of production   Material production organized at the household level, with distribution between households based on reciprocal sharing.

domestic-scale culture   A cultural system characterized by small, kinship-based societies, often with only 500 people, in which households organize production and distribution.

ecocide   The degradation of an ecosystem.

embedded economy   An economy that can only be observed and understood within the context of the social, political, and religious systems of the culture.

emic   Cultural meanings derived from inside a given culture and presumed to be unique to that culture.

endogamy   Marriage within a specified group.

energy subsidy   The use of fossil fuels to increase food production above the rate that could be sustained through use of renewable energy sources.

estate   Property held in common by a descent group, perhaps including territory, sacred sites, and ceremonies.

ethnic group   A dependent, culturally distinct population that forms part of a larger state or empire and that was formally autonomous.

ethnocentrism   Evaluating other cultures from the perspective of one's own presumably superior culture.

ethnocide   The forced destruction of a cultural system.

ethnographic method   Reliance on direct participant observation, key informants, and informal interviews as a data-collecting technique.

ethnographic present   An arbitrary time period when the process of culture change is ignored in order to describe a given culture as if it were a stable system.

etic   Cultural meanings as translated for cross-cultural comparison.

exchange value   The value of goods when used as commodities.

exogamy   Marriage outside a culturally defined group.

exploitation   Unjust use of someone to differentially benefit another, especially when one social class is deprived of basic necessities while the elites live in luxury.

extended family   A joint household based on a parent family and one or more families of its married children.

factory farming   Commercial agriculture based on fossil-fuel energy subsidies, mechanization, pesticides, chemical fertilizers, and large-scale monocropping.

feudalism   A political system in which village farmers occupy lands owned by local lords to whom they owe loyalty, rent, and service.

feuding   Chronic intergroup conflict that exists between communities in the absence of centralized political authority. It may involve a cycle of revenge raids and killing that is difficult to break.

filial piety   *Hsiao*, the ritual obligation of children to respect their ancestors, and especially the duty of sons to care for shrines of their partrilineal ancestors.

filiation   A parent–child relationship link used as a basis for descent-group membership.

financialization   A cultural process involving the flow of finance capital, money, and securities, rather than the actual production and distribution of goods and services.

folk-urban continuum   Robert Redfield's concept of a gradual distinction between the Little Tradition culture of rural commoners and the Great Tradition culture of the urban elites in a political-scale culture.

foreign direct investment   When businesses headquartered in a given country buy productive assets in another country and retain control over them.

forest fallow system   A system of cultivation in which soil nutrients are restored by allowing the forest to regrow.

fraternal polyandry   When a woman marries two or more men who are brothers.

fuel revolution   The large-scale adoption of fossil fuels such as coal and oil.

functionalism   The assumption that particular cultural traits may have a role in maintaining the culture.

genealogical method   Tracing the marriage and family relationships among people as a basis for identifying cultural patterns in a community.

generalized reciprocity   The distribution of goods and services by direct sharing. It is assumed that in the long run giving and receiving balances out, but no accounts are maintained.

genitor   The biological father of a child.

genocide   The extermination of a human population.

gerontocracy   An age hierarchy that is controlled or dominated by the oldest age groups.

glottochronology   A method of estimating the relative date at which related languages separated from a common ancestral language, by calculating the percentage of cognates shared between the related languages.

Great Tradition   The culture of the elite in a state-organized society with a written tradition that is not fully shared by nonliterate, village-level commoners.

Green Revolution   Dramatic increases in agricultural production from use of hybrid grains that produce high yields in return for high inputs of chemical fertilizers and pesticides.

gross domestic product   (GDP)   The total output of goods and services produced within a country, by monetary value.

gross national product   (GNP)   The total output of a country's goods and services, by monetary value; includes profits from foreign activities.

hacienda   A Latin American agricultural estate with dependent laborers that produced for local rather than global markets and was designed to maintain the social status and lifestyle of the *hacendado* landowner.

headman   A political leader who coordinates group activities and is a village spokesman but who serves only with the consent of the community and has no coercive power.

high-yield variety   High-yield plant varieties developed by selective breeding as part of the Green Revolution.

hominid   A member of the human family, distinct from the great apes.

household   A social unit that shares domestic activities such as food production, cooking, eating, and sleeping, often under one roof, and is usually based on the nuclear or extended family.

humanization   The production and maintenance of human beings, human societies, and human cultures, based on social power organized at the household, or domestic, level.

hypergamy   Marriage to someone of higher rank. For example, Hindu women may marry men of a higher subcaste.

hypogamy   Marriage to someone of lower rank.

idealist   A policy position that advocates cultural autonomy for indigenous peoples as a basic human right.

immiseration   Malthusian impoverishment, a declining standard of living attributed to continuous population growth on a limited-resource base.

imperia   Imperium (singular) An individual's personal power network, including everyone that one might command, or call on for assistance, as well as the institutional structures that one might direct.

impurity   Low ritual status attributed to association or contact with polluting biological events or products.

inclusive fitness   A sociobiological concept referring to the degree to which individuals are successful in passing on a high proportion of their genes to succeeding generations.

indigenous   Peoples who are the original inhabitants of a territory and who seek to maintain political control over their resources and their cultural heritage.

indirect rule   The situation in which European colonial administrators appointed local natives to serve as mediating officials, or chiefs, to help them control local communities.

integration   The absorption of a formerly autonomous people into a dominant state society, with the possible retention of ethnic identity.

internal colony   A territory within a state containing an indigenous population that is denied the right of self-determination.

invisible hand   The capitalist belief that market forces, operating through supply and demand, will lead to continuous economic growth and benefit everyone.

key informant   A member of the host culture who helps the anthropologist learn about the culture.

kindred   Ego based, overlapping network that includes all of an individual's relatives.

kin-ordered production   A mode of production organized at the domestic or kinship level and producing primarily for domestic use rather than exchange.

kinship terminology   An ego-centered system of terms that specifies genealogical relationships of consanguinity and affinity in reference to a given individual.

law of cultural differentiation   A statement of the cultural relativity of cognitive ability or basic intelligence. It assumes that no single culture-bound test can adequately test cognitive ability because different cultures produce different cognitive abilities in individuals.

law of participation   The assumption that a thing can participate in or be part of two or more things at once; identified by Lévy-Bruhl as the principle underlying his concept of prelogical thought.

law of sympathy   Frazer's explanation for the logic underlying magic, sorcery, and shamanism. He thought that tribal peoples believed that anything ever connected with a person, such as hair or blood, could be manipulated to influence that person.

levirate   A cultural pattern in which a woman marries a brother of her deceased husband.

liminal phase   An ambiguous phase of ritual transition in which one is on the threshold between two states.

limited good   A belief often found in peasant communities that total wealth is limited and that anyone who acquires too much is taking away from others. This is a justification for wealth leveling.

Little Tradition   Ritual beliefs and practices followed by nonliterate commoners, especially rural villagers who are part of a larger state-level society.

liturgical government   The use of ritually prescribed interpersonal relations and religious, moral authority as a primary means of social control in a state-level society.

male supremacy complex   A functionally interrelated series of presumably male-centered traits, including patrilocality, polygyny, inequitable sexual division of labor, male domination of headmanship and shamanism, and ritual subordination of women.

mana   An impersonal supernatural force thought to reside in particular people and objects. In the Pacific islands, *mana* is the basis of chiefly power.

marginal returns   The increase in the total output produced by the additional input; in subsistence production, the additional amount above what was produced the previous year, resulting from the increased effort.

matrilocality   Residence near the wife's kin, normally near her parents.

minifundia   Tiny landholdings of the Latin American peasantry.

moiety   One part of a two-part social division.

monocrop farming   A system of growing one plant species, sometimes only a single variety, often in very large continuous stands.

monumental architecture   Large-scale permanent structures, such as temples, palaces, or tombs, that require large labor forces and central planning.

multilateral development assistance   Aid that is donated by several countries and channeled through a single international agency such that it can be free of political favoritism.

multilinear evolution   Steward's theory that, given similar conditions, cultures can develop independently along similar lines. For example, he argued that irrigation agriculture led to state organization several times.

myth   A narrative that recounts the activities of supernatural beings. Often acted out in ritual, myths encapsulate a culture's cosmology and cosmogony and provide justification for culturally prescribed behavior.

mythical thought   Lévi-Strauss' term for the thinking underlying myth and magic; logically similar to scientific thought but based on the science of the concrete and used to serve aesthetic purposes and to solve existential problems.

nation   A people with a common language, culture, and territory and who claim a common identity.

natural symbols   Inherent qualities of specific plants and animals used as signs or metaphors for issues that concern people.

noumenal   Noumena (plural). Mental constructs, concepts, things that people know through the mind, rather than phenomena observed, or perceived through the senses.

nuclear family   The primary family unit of mother, father, and dependent children.

official development assistance   (ODA)   Aid given by a government for development purposes, including both direct gifts and low-rate loans.

oligopoly   Concentrated economic power when a few sellers can control a market with many buyers by controlling the price and availability of goods.

participant intervention   A form of culture change in which those in control become members of the system they seek to change.

participant observation   Field method in which the observer shares in community activities.

pater   The culturally legitimate, or sociological, father of a child.

patrilineage   A lineage based on descent traced through a line of men to a common male ancestor and sharing a joint estate.

patrilineal descent   Descent traced through a line of men to a male ancestor.

patrilocal band   A theoretical form of band organization based on exogamy and patrilocal residence.

patrilocality   A cultural preference for a newly married couple to live near the husband's parents or patrilineal relatives.

patron   A Spanish term for someone who extends credits or goods to a client who is kept in a debt relationship.

peasantry   Village farmers who provide most of their own subsistence but who must pay taxes and are politically and often, to some extent, economically dependent on the central state government.

periphery   Capital-poor areas that supply raw materials and labor to the core; this area was integrated into the early capitalist world system through conquest and coercion.

phoneme   The minimal unit of sound that carries meaning and is recognized as distinctive by the speakers of a given language.

political economy   A cultural pattern in which centralized political authority intervenes in the production and distribution of goods and services.

political-scale culture   A cultural system characterized by centrally organized societies with thousands or millions of members and energy-intensive production directed by political rulers.

politicization   The production and maintenance of political power.

polyandry   When a woman marries two or more men.

polygyny   A form of marriage in which a man may have more than one wife.

polytheism   A religious system based on belief in many gods or deities.

prelogical thinking   Lévy-Bruhl's characterization of the collective representations of tribal peoples, which he thought reflected concrete thought and a mystic reality unique to domestic-scale cultures.

primogeniture   Preferential treatment to a couple's first-born offspring or oldest surviving child; may be a basis for establishing social rank.

purity   Ritually superior status; a category in logical opposition to impurity.

rank   Social position in a status hierarchy.

realist   A policy position that maintains that indigenous peoples must surrender their political and economic autonomy and be integrated into dominant state societies.

redistribution   A form of exchange in which goods, such as foodstuffs, are concentrated and then distributed under the control of a central political authority.

reverse dominance hierarchy   System whereby the members of a village or community intentionally limit the power of leaders, keeping them subservient to the group will.

rite of passage   A ritual marking culturally significant changes in an individual's life cycle, such as birth, puberty, marriage, old age, and death.

Sapir-Whorf hypothesis   Suggests that one's view of the world is shaped by language, such that the speakers of different languages may live in different perceptual worlds.

scale subsidy   Social support in the form of taxes or tribute for activities that promote growth in scale, or that maintain a larger scale society when benefits are inequitably distributed.

scapulimancy   Divination by interpreting the pattern of cracks formed in heated animals' scapula or turtle shells.

science of the concrete   Thought based on perceptions and signs, images, and events, as opposed to formal science based on concepts.

section system   A social division into four (sections) or eight (subsections) intermarrying, named groups, which summarize social relationships. Members of each group must marry only members of one other specific group.

segmentary lineage system   A system in which complementary opposition and genealogical principles of unilineal descent are used by residential groups as a basis for political mobilization in the absence of centralized political leadership.

selective female infanticide   According to cultural materialist theory, a cultural pattern in which infant girls are selectively killed or neglected in favor of boys, who will become hunters and warriors.

self-determination   The right of any people to freely determine its own cultural, political, and economic future.

shaman   A part-time religious specialist with special skills for dealing with the spirit world; may help his community by healing, by divination, and by directing supernatural powers against enemies.

shamanic state of consciousness (SSC)   An interpretation of the shamanic trance phenomenon that distinguishes it from the altered state of consciousness of schizophrenics. A shaman may enter and leave the SSC at will, remains aware of his surroundings, and uses the SSC for socially beneficial purposes.

slash and burn   A farming technique in which forest is cleared and burned to enrich the soil for planting; a forest fallow system depending on forest regrowth.

social class   A group of people in a stratified society, such as elites and commoners, who share a similar level of access to resources, power, and privilege.

social Darwinism   A political philosophy that treats other societies as biologically and culturally inferior, and therefore "unfit" for survival.

social power   An individual's ability to get what he or she wants, even when others might object.

social product   The value of the aggregate annual production of a society, measured either as production or consumption.

social status   A position that an individual occupies within a social system; defined by age, gender, kinship relationships, or other cultural criteria and involving specific behavioral expectations.

social stratification   A ranking of social statuses such that the individuals of a society belong to different groups having differential access to resources, power, and privileges.

society   An interacting, intermarrying population sharing a common culture.

sororal polygyny   When a man marries two or more women who are sisters.

sororate   A man marries his deceased wife's sister.

specialist   An individual who provides goods and services to elites in hierarchically organized societies. Such a specialist does not produce his or her own food but is supported from the surplus that is politically extracted by central authorities.

staple economy   The state-controlled production, storage, and distribution of subsistence staples, such as potatoes and maize in the Inca case, to support nonfood-producing specialist groups and to provide emergency aid.

structural adjustments   Austerity measures designed to increase foreign exchange through increased exports.

structural violence   Human suffering that is the direct result of social and cultural structures that enable more powerful individuals to violate the basic human rights of less powerful individuals.

structure   The social, economic, and political organization of a culture, which is shaped by the technological base, or infrastructure, according to Harris' cultural materialist theory.

subsistence economy   Production and distribution carried on at the local community level, primarily for local consumption.

subsistence intensification   Technological innovations that produce more food from the same land area but often require increased effort.

superstructure   The mental, ideological, or belief systems, as expressed in the religion, myth, and rituals of a culture. According to Harris' cultural materialist theory, superstructure is shaped by the structure.

surplus   Subsistence production that exceeds the needs of the producer households and that is extracted by political leaders to support nonfood-producing specialists.

symbol   Anything with a culturally defined meaning.

tabu   Actions that are forbidden under the sanction of supernatural punishment. *Tabus* may be imposed by chiefs and are supported by chiefly *mana*.

theocracy   State government based on religious authority or divine guidance. The Chinese emperor was the highest civil and religious leader.

totem   In Australia, specific animals, plants, natural phenomena, or other objects that originate in the Dreaming and are the spiritual progenitors of aboriginal descent groups. Elsewhere refers to any cultural association between specific natural objects and human social groups.

transhumance   Seasonal movement of livestock herds to maintain optimum grazing conditions; often involves altitudinal shifts.

tribe   A politically autonomous, economically self-sufficient, territorially-based society, that can reproduce a distinct culture and language, and form an in-marrying (endogamous) society.

tributary production   A mode of production in which products are extracted as surplus from a self-supporting peasantry and used to support the state.

uncontrolled frontier   A tribal territory that is invaded by colonists from a state-organized society but where the government chooses not to regulate the actions of the colonists.

unequal exchange   Market-based exchanges in which one party is consistently able to accumulate a disproportionate share of the profit or wealth.

unilineal descent group   Membership based on descent traced through a line of ancestors of one sex to a common ancestor.

unlimited good   The belief in continuous economic growth often used to justify wealth inequality.

use value   The value of goods produced for domestic consumption, usually within a kin-ordered mode of production.

utilitarianism   The use of economic profit, direct material advantage, or physical welfare, such as food and shelter, as an explanation for cultural practices.

village-states   Politically centralized societies based on an urban administrative and ceremonial center drawing their support from self-sufficient peasant villagers scattered over a vast region.

wealth economy   The state-controlled production, storage, and distribution of wealth objects that support the status hierarchy.

wealth-leveling device   Any cultural means, such as ritual feasting, used to redistribute wealth within a community and thereby reduce inequality.

world system   An international hierarchy of diverse societies and cultures integrated into a single economic system based on unequal exchange that allows wealth to accumulate in the core.

Bibliography

AABY, PETER. 1977. "What Are We Fighting For? 'Progress' or 'Cultural Autonomy'?" In *Cultural Imperialism and Cultural Identity,* edited by Carola Sanbacka, pp. 61–76. Transactions of the Finnish Anthropological Society, No. 2. Helsinki: Finnish Anthropological Society.

ACHARD, FRÉDÉRIC, HUGH D. EVAO, HANS-JÜRGEN STIBIG, PHILIPPE MAYAUX, JAVIER GALLEGO, TIMOTHY RICHARDS, JEAN-PAUL MALINGREAU. 2002. "Determination of Deforestation Rates of the World's Humid Tropical Forests." *Science* 297(5583):999–1002.

ADAMS, RICHARD N. 1988. *The Eighth Day: Social Evolution as the Self-Organization of Energy.* Austin: University of Texas Press.

ADAMS, ROBERT McC. 1981. *Heartland of Cities: Surveys of Ancient Settlement and Land Use on the Central Floodplain of the Euphrates.* Chicago and London: University of Chicago Press.

ADAMS, ROBERT McC. 1982. "Property Rights and Functional Tenure in Mesopotamian Rural Communities." In *Societies and Languages of the Ancient Near East: Studies in Honour of I. M. Diakonoff,* pp. 1–14. Warminster, Eng.: Aris & Phillips.

ADM (ARCHER DANIELS MIDLAND). 2003. ADM 2003 Annual Report: Positioning our Global Franchise.

AHMED, LEILA. 1982. "Western Ethnocentrism and Perceptions of the Harem." *Feminist Studies* 8(3):521–534.

ALBERT, BRUCE. 1985. "Temps du Sang, Temps des Cendres. Représentations de la Maladie, Système Rituel et Espace Politique chez les Yanomami du Sud-est (Amazonie Bresilienne)." Ph.D. dissertation, Université de Paris X (Nanterre).

ALERS, J. OSCAR. 1971. "Well Being." In *Peasants, Power, and Applied Social Change: Vicos as a Model,* edited by Henry Dobyns, Paul Doughty, and Harold Lasswell, pp. 115–136. Beverly Hills, Calif., and London: Sage.

ALEXANDER, RICHARD D. 1987. *The Biology of Moral Systems.* New York: Aldine De Gruyter.

ALKIRE, WILLIAM H. 1965. *Lamotrek Atoll and Inter-Island Socioeconomic Ties.* Studies in Anthropology, no. 5. Urbana: University of Illinois Press.

ALLCHIN, BRIDGET, AND F. RAYMOND ALLCHIN. 1982. *The Rise of Civilization in India and Pakistan.* Cambridge, Eng.: Cambridge University Press.

ALLCHIN, F. RAYMOND. 1982. "The Legacy of the Indus Civilization." In *Harappan Civilization: A Contemporary Perspective,* edited by Gregory Possehl, pp. 325–333. New Delhi: Oxford and IBH.

ALLEN, HARRY. 2002. *The Hunter Gatherer Mode of Thought and Change in Aboriginal Northern Australia.* Presented at the Ninth International Conference on Hunting and Gathering Societies, Heriot-Watt University, Edinburgh, Scotland.

ALTMAN, J. C. 1987. *Hunter-Gatherers Today: an Aboriginal economy in north Australia.* Canberra: Australian Institute of Aboriginal Studies.

ALVA, WALTER. 1990. "New Tomb of Royal Splendor." *National Geographic* 117(6):2–15.

ALVA, WALTER AND CHRISTOPHER B. DONNAN. 1993. *Royal Tombs of Sipán.* Los Angeles: Fowler Museum of Cultural History, University of California.

AMAZONIA INDIGENA. 1981. "Pronunciamiento Sobre el Projecto Especial Pichis-Palcazu." *Amazonia Indigena* 1(3):3–5

AMBROSE, STANLEY H. 1984. "The Introduction of Pastoral Adaptations to the Highlands of East Africa." In *From Hunters to Farmers: The Causes and Consequences of Food Production in Africa,* edited by J. Desmond Clark and Steven Brandt, pp. 212–239. Berkeley: University of California Press.

AMERICAN ANTHROPOLOGICAL ASSOCIATION. 2002. *El Dorado Task Force Papers. Final Report,* May 18. 2 Volumes.

AMERICAN PSYCHIATRIC ASSOCIATION (APA). 1980. *Diagnostic and Statistical Manual of Mental Disorders,* 3rd ed. Washington, D.C.: American Psychiatric Association.

AMERICAN PSYCHIATRIC ASSOCIATION (APA). 2000. *Diagnostic and Statistical Manual.* Text Revision (DSM-IV-TR™).

AMMERMAN, ALBERT J., AND L. L. CAVALLI-SFORZA. 1984. *The Neolithic Transition and the Genetics of Populations in Europe.* Princeton, N.J.: Princeton University Press.

ANDERSON, RICHARD L. 1990. *Calliope's Sisters: A Comparative Study of Philosophies of Art.* New York: Prentice-Hall.

ANTHROPOLOGICAL INSTITUTE OF GREAT BRITAIN AND IRELAND. 1903. "A Plea for the Scientific Study of the Native Laws and Customs of South Africa: A Memorial Addressed by the Anthropological Institute and the Folklore Society to H.M. Secretary of State for the Colonies; and Subsequent Correspondence." *Man* 3(37):70–74.

ANZAAS (Australia and New Zealand Association for the Advancement of Science). 1914. "Welfare of Aborigines Committee." Report of the Fourteenth Meeting of the Australasian Association for the Advancement of Science, 450–452.

ARENS, W. 1979. *The Man Eating Myth: Anthropology and Anthropophagy.* New York: Oxford University Press.

ARENSBERG, CONRAD M., AND ARTHUR H. NIEHOFF. 1964. *Introducing Social Change: A Manual for Americans Overseas.* Chicago: Aldine.

ARNOLD, JEANNE E. 1993. "Labor and the Rise of Complex Hunter-Gatherers." *Journal of Anthropological Archaeology* 12(1):75–119.

ASCHER, MARCIA, AND ROBERT A. ASCHER. 1981. *Code of the Quipu: Study in Media, Mathematics, and Culture.* Ann Arbor: University of Michigan Press.

ASHTON, T. S. 1969. *The Industrial Revolution 1760–1830.* London: Oxford University Press.

ASIMOV, ISAAC. 1971. "The End." *Penthouse* (January).

BAILEY, ROBERT C., G. HEAD, M. JENIKE, B. OWEN, R. RECHTMAN, AND E. ZECHENTER. 1989. "Hunting and Gathering in Tropical Rain Forest: Is It Possible?" *American Anthropologist* 91(1):59–82.

BANGLADESH. MINISTRY OF FINANCE. 2003. *Bangladesh: A National Strategy for Economic Growth, Poverty Reduction and Social Development.*

BARNARD, ALAN. 2002. "The Foraging Mode of Thought." In *Self- and Other-Images of Hunter-Gatherers,* edited by Henry Stewart, Alan Barnard, and Keiichi Omura, pp. 1–24. Senri Ethnological Studies No. 60. Osaka: National Museum of Ethnology.

BARNET, RICHARD J., AND JOHN CAVANAGH. 1994. *Global Dreams: Imperial Corporations and the New World Order.* New York: Simon & Schuster.

BARNETT, HAROLD, AND CHANDLER MORSE. 1963. *Scarcity and Growth: The Economics of Natural Resource Availability.* Baltimore: Johns Hopkins University Press.

BARNEY, GERALD O. (ED.). 1977–1980. *The Global 2000 Report to the President of the United States,* 3 vols. New York: Pergamon Press.

BATEMAN, JOHN. 1883. *The Great Landowners of Great Britain and Ireland,* 4th ed. London: Harrison.

BAUER, BRIAN S. 1996. "Legitimization of the State in Inca Myth and Ritual." *American Anthropologist* 98(2):327–337.

BEACH, WILLIAM W., AND GARETH DAVIS. 1998. "The Institutional Setting of Economic Growth." In *1998 Index of Economic Freedom,* edited by Bryan T. Johnson, Kim R. Holmes, and Melanie Kirkpatrick, pp. 1–10. Washington, D.C., and New York: The Heritage Foundation and Dow Jones & Co.

BEAGLEHOLE, ERNEST. 1954. "Cultural Factors in Economic and Social Change." *International Labour Review* 69(5): 415–432.

BEARD, CHARLES A. 1913. *An Economic Interpretation of the Constitution of the United States.* New York: Macmillan.

BECKWITH, MARTHA WARREN. 1951. *The Kumulipo: A Hawaiian Creation Chant.* Chicago: University of Chicago Press.

BEHRENS, CLIFFORD A. 1986. "Shipibo Food Categorization and Preference: Relationships Between Indigenous and Western Dietary Concepts." *American Anthropologist* 88(3):647–658.

BEIDELMAN, T. O. 1966. "The Ox and Nuer Sacrifice: Some Freudian Hypotheses About Nuer Symbolism." *Man* 1(4): 453–467.

BEIDELMAN, T. O. (ED.). 1971. "Nuer Priest and Prophets: Charisma, Authority, and Power Among the Nuer." In *The Translation of Culture: Essays to E. E. Evans-Pritchard,* pp. 375–415. London: Tavistock.

BELAUNDE-TERRY, FERNANDO. 1965. *Peru's Own Conquest.* Lima: American Studies Press.

BELL, DIANE. 1983. *Daughters of the Dreaming.* Sydney: McPhee Gribble/Allen & Unwin.

BELL, DIANE. 1987. "Aboriginal Women and the Religious Experience." In *Traditional Aboriginal Society: A Reader,* edited by W. H. Edwards, pp. 237–256. South Melbourne: Macmillan.

BELLWOOD, PETER S. 1985. *Prehistory of the Indo-Malaysian Archipelago.* New York and Sydney: Academic.

BENEDICT, RUTH. 1934. *Patterns of Culture.* Boston: Houghton Mifflin.

BERGMAN, ROLAND W. 1974. "Shipibo Subsistence in the Upper Amazon Rainforest." Ph.D. dissertation, Department of Geography, University of Wisconsin–Madison. Ann Arbor, Mich.: University Microfilms.

BERLIN, BRENT. 1972. "Speculations on the Growth of Ethnobotanical Nomenclature." *Language in Society* 1:51–86.

BERLIN, BRENT, AND ELOIS ANN BERLIN. 1983. "Adaptation and Ethnozoological Classification: Theoretical Implications of Animal Resources and Diet of the Aguaruna and Huambisa." In *Adaptive Responses of Native Amazonians,* edited by Raymond Hames and William Vickers, pp. 301–325. New York: Academic Press.

BERLIN, BRENT, DENNIS E. BREEDLOVE, AND PETER H. RAVEN. 1973. "General Principles of Classification and Nomenclature in Folk Biology." *American Anthropologist* 75(1):214–242.

BERLIN, BRENT, AND PAUL KAY. 1969. *Basic Color Terms: Their Universality and Evolution.* Berkeley and Los Angeles: University of California Press.

BERN, JOHN. 1979. "Ideology and Domination: Toward a Reconstruction of Australian Aboriginal Social Formation." *Oceania* 50(2):118–132.

BERNARDI, BERNARDO. 1985. *Age Class Systems: Social Institutions and Polities Based on Age.* Cambridge, Eng.: Cambridge University Press.

BERREMAN, GERALD. 1960. "Caste in India and the United States." *American Journal of Sociology* 66:120–127.

BERREMAN, GERALD D. 1979. *Caste and Other Inequities: Essays on Inequality.* Meerut, Uttar Pradesh, India: Ved Prakash Vatuk, Folklore Institute.

BERRY, J. W., AND S. H. IRVINE. 1986. "Brocolage: Savages Do It Daily." In *Practical Intelligence: Nature and Origins of Competence in the Everyday World,* edited by Robert Sternberg and Richard Wagner, pp. 271–306. Cambridge, Eng.: Cambridge University Press.

BETZIG, LAURA L. 1986. *Despotism and Differential Reproduction: A Darwinian View of History.* New York: Aldine.

BETZIG, LAURA L. 1993. "Sex, Succession, and Stratification in the First Six Civilizations: How Powerful Men Reproduced, Passed Power on to Their Sons, and Used Power to Defend Their Wealth, Women, and Children." In *Social Stratification and Socioeconomic Inequality,* edited by Lee Ellis, pp. 37–74. Westport, Conn.: Praeger.

BICKERTON, DEREK. 1990. *Language and Species.* Chicago and London: University of Chicago Press.

BIRD-DAVID, NURIT. 1992. "Beyond 'The Original Affluent Society': A Culturalist Reformulation." *Current Anthropology* 33(1):25–47.

BIRDSELL, JOSEPH B. 1957. "Some Population Problems Involving Pleistocene Man." *Cold Spring Harbor Symposium on Quantitative Biology* 22:47–70.

BIRDSELL, JOSEPH B. 1973. "A Basic Demographic Unit." *Current Anthropology* 14(4):337–350.

BLOCHMANN, H. (Translator). 1939. The *Aini Akbari by Abu Fazl'Allami.* Second Edition. Calcutta: Royal Asiatic Society of Bengal.

BLUESTONE, BARRY, AND BENNETT HARRISON. 1982. *The Deindustrialization of America.* New York: Basic Books.

BOAS, FRANZ. 1911. *The Mind of Primitive Man.* New York: Macmillan.

BOAS, FRANZ. 1945. *Race and Democratic Society.* New York: J. J. Agustin.

BOCQUET-APPEL, JEAN-PIERRE, AND CLAUDE MASSET. 1981. "Farewell to Paleodemography." *Journal of Human Evolution* 11:321–333.

BODLEY, JOHN H. 1970. "Campa Socio-Economic Adaptation." Ph.D. dissertation, University of Oregon. Ann Arbor, Mich.: University Microfilms.

BODLEY, JOHN H. 1972a. "A Transformative Movement Among the Campa of Eastern Peru." *Anthropos* 67:220–228.

BODLEY, JOHN H. 1972b. *Tribal Survival in the Amazon: The Campa Case.* IWGIA (International Work Group for Indigenous Affairs) Document, no. 5. Copenhagen: IWGIA.

BODLEY, JOHN H. 1973. "Deferred Exchange Among the Campa Indians." *Anthropos* 68:589–596.

BODLEY, JOHN H. 1975. *Victims of Progress.* Menlo Park, Calif.: Cummings.

BODLEY, JOHN H. 1976. *Anthropology and Contemporary Human Problems.* Menlo Park, Calif.: Cummings.

BODLEY, JOHN H. 1981a. "Deferred Exchange Among the Campa: A Reconsideration." In *Networks of the Past: Regional Interaction in Archaeology,* edited by Peter Francis, F. J. Kense, and P. G. Duke, pp. 49–59. Calgary: University of Calgary Archaeological Association.

BODLEY, JOHN H. 1981b. "Incquality: An Energetic Approach." In *Social Inequality: Comparative and Developmental Approaches,* edited by Gerald Berreman, pp. 183–197. New York: Academic Press.

BODLEY, JOHN H. 1988. *Tribal Peoples and Development Issues: A Global Overview.* Mountain View, Calif.: Mayfield.

BODLEY, JOHN H. 1990. *Victims of Progress,* 3rd ed. Mountain View, Calif.: Mayfield.

BODLEY, JOHN H. 1992. "Anthropologist at Work: Inequality & Exploitation in the Peruvian Amazon." In *Discovering Anthropology,* by Daniel R. Gross, p. 483. Mountain View, Calif.: Mayfield Publishing.

BODLEY, JOHN H. 1993. "Human Rights, Development and the Environment in the Peruvian Amazon: The Asháninka Case." In *Who Pays the Price? Examining the Sociocultural Context of Environmental Crisis.* A Society for Applied Anthropology Report on Human Rights and the Environment Submitted to the United Nations Commission on Human Rights Sub-Commission for the Prevention of Discrimination and Protection of Minorities, edited by Barbara R. Johnston, pp. 158–162. Oklahoma City: Society for Applied Anthropology.

BODLEY, JOHN H. 1996. *Anthropology and Contemporary Human Problems,* 3rd ed. Mountain View, Calif.: Mayfield.

BODLEY, JOHN H. 1999. *Victims of Progress,* 4th ed. Mountain View, Calif.: Mayfield.

BODLEY, JOHN H. 1999. "Socio-Economic Growth, Culture Scale, and Household Well-Being: A Test of the Power-Elite Hypothesis." *Current Anthropology* 40(5):595–620.

BODLEY, JOHN H. 2001. "Growth, Scale, and Power in Washington State." *Human Organization* 60(4):367–379.

BODLEY, JOHN H. 2003. *The Power of Scale: A Global History Approach.* Armonk, New York: M.E. Sharpe.

BODLEY, JOHN H., AND FOLEY BENSON. 1979. *Cultural Ecology of Amazonian Palms.* Reports of Investigations, no. 56. Laboratory of Anthropology, Washington State University.

BODMER, W., AND LUIGI CAVALLI-SFORZA. 1970. "Intelligence and Race." *Scientific American* 223:19–29.

BOEHM, CHRISTOPHER. 1993. "Egalitarian Behavior and Reverse Dominance Hierarchy." *Current Anthropology* 34(3): 227–254.

BOORSTIN, DANIEL J. 1985. *The Image: A Guide to Pseudo-Events in America.* New York: Atheneum.

BOOTH, CHARLES. 1892–1903. *Life and Labour of the People in London.* London and New York: Macmillan.

BOOTH, DOUGLAS E. 1987. *Regional Long Waves, Uneven Growth, and the Cooperative Alternative.* New York: Praeger.

BORGSTROM, GEORG. 1965. *The Hungry Planet,* 2nd ed. New York: Macmillan.

BORSODI, RALPH. 1929. *The Distribution Age: A Study of the Economy of Modern Distribution.* New York: D. Appleton.

BOSERUP, ESTER. 1965. *The Conditions of Economic Growth.* Chicago: Aldine.

BOSERUP, ESTER. 1970. *Women's Role in Economic Development.* London: Allen & Unwin.

BOSTER, J. 1983. "A Comparison of the Diversity of Jivaroan Gardens with That of the Tropical Forest." *Human Ecology* 11(1):47–68.

BOURLIERE, FRANÇOIS, AND M. HADLEY. 1983. "Present-Day Savannas: An Overview." In *Ecosystems of the World 13: Tropical Savannas,* edited by François Bourliere, pp. 1–17. New York: Elsevier.

BOWDLER, S. 1977. "The Coastal Colonisation of Australia." In *Sunda and Sahul: Prehistoric Studies in Southeast Asia, Melanesia and Australia,* edited by J. Allen, J. Golson, and R. Jones, pp. 205–246. London: Academic Press.

BOYD, ROBERT, AND PETER J. RICHERSON. 1985. *Culture and the Evolutionary Process.* Chicago and London: University of Chicago Press.

BOYER, PASCAL. 2000. "Functional Origins of Religious Concepts: Ontological and Strategic Selection in Evolved Minds." *Journal of the Royal Anthropological Institute* 6:195–214.

BRAIDWOOD, ROBERT J. 1964. *Prehistoric Men,* Sixth Edition. Chicago: Chicago Natural History Museum.

BRAIDWOOD, ROBERT J., AND BRUCE HOWE. 1960. *Prehistoric Investigations in Iraqi Kurdistan.* Studies in Ancient Oriental Civilization, no. 31. Chicago: University of Chicago Press.

BRAND, MICHAEL AND GLENN D. LOWRY. 1987. *Fatehpur-Sikri.* Bombay: Marg Publications.

BRANDEIS, LOUIS D. 1914. *Other People's Money and How the Bankers Use It.* New York: Frederick A. Stokes.

BREWER, JOHN. 1989. *The Sinews of Power: War, Money and the English State, 1688–1783*. New York: Alfred A. Knopf.

BRIODY, DAN. 2003. *The Iron Triangle: Inside the Secret World of the Carlyle Group*. Hoboken, New Jersey: John Wiley.

BROWN, BARTON MCCAUL. 1987. "Population Estimation from Floor Area: A Restudy of 'Naroll's Constant.'" *Behavior Science Research* 21(1–4):1–49.

BROWN, CECIL H. 1977. "Folk Botanical Life-Forms: Their Universality and Growth." *American Anthropologist* 79(2):317–342.

BROWN, CECIL H. 1979a. "Folk Zoological Life-Forms: Their Universality and Growth." *American Anthropologist* 81(4): 791–817.

BROWN, CECIL H. 1979b. "Growth and Development of Folk Botanical Life Forms in the Mayan Language Family." *American Anthropologist* 6(2):366–385.

BROWN, DONALD E. 1991. *Human Universals*. Philadelphia: Temple University Press.

BROWN, HARRISON. 1956. "Technological Denudation." In *Man's Role in Changing the Face of the Earth*, edited by William Thomas, Jr., pp. 1023–1032. Chicago: University of Chicago Press.

BROWN, J. LARRY, AND ERNESTO POLLITT. 1996. "Malnutrition, Poverty and Intellectual Development." *Scientific American* 274(2):38–43.

BROWN, LESTER R. 1987. "Sustaining World Agriculture." In *State of the World 1987*, edited by Lester Brown et al., pp. 122–138. New York and London: Norton.

BROWN, LESTER R. 1989. "Reexamining the World Food Prospect." In *State of the World 1987*, edited by Lester Brown et al., pp. 41–58. New York and London: Norton.

BROWN, LESTER R. 1994. "Facing Food Insecurity." In *State of the World 1994: A Worldwatch Institute Report on Progress Toward a Sustainable Society*, edited by Lester Brown et al., pp. 177–197. New York: Norton.

BROWN, LESTER R. 2000. "Challenges of the New Century." In *State of the World 2000: A Worldwatch Institute Report on Progress Toward a Sustainable Society*, edited by Lester R. Brown, Christopher Flavin, Hilary French, and Linda Starke, pp. 1–21. New York and London: Norton.

BROWN, LESTER R., AND SANDRA POSTEL. 1987. "Thresholds of Change." In *State of the World 1987*, edited by Lester Brown et al., pp. 3–19. New York and London: Norton.

BROWN, MICHAEL F. 1984. "The Role of Words in Aguaruna Hunting Magic." *American Ethnologist* 11(3):545–558.

BRUSH, STEPHEN B. 1976. "Man's Use of an Andean Ecosystem." *Human Ecology* 4(2):147–166.

BRUSH, STEPHEN B., HEATH J. CARNEY, AND ZOSIMO HUAMAN. 1981. "Dynamics of Andean Potato Agriculture." *Economic Botany* 35(1):70–88.

BUELL, RAYMOND L. 1928. *The Native Problem in Africa*, vol. 1. New York: Macmillan.

BUHLER, G. 1886. "The Laws of Manu." In *The Sacred Books of the East*, edited by F. M. Muller. Oxford, Eng.: Clarendon Press.

BUNSEN, C. C. J. 1854. *Outlines of the Philosophy of Universal History Applied to Language and Religion*, 2 vols. London: Longman.

BURBANK, VICTORIA KATHERINE. 1994. *Fighting Women: Anger and Aggression in Aboriginal Australia*. Berkeley: University of California Press.

BURGER, RICHARD L., AND NIKOLAAS J. VAN DER MERWE. 1990. "Maize and the Origins of Highland Chavin Civilization: An Isotopic Perspective." *American Anthropologist* 92(1):85–95.

BURNELL, ARTHUR COKE, AND EDWARD W. HOPKINS (EDS.). 1884. *The Ordinances of Manu*. London: Trubner.

BURTON, JOHN W. 1980. "Women and Men in Marriage: Some Atuot Texts (Southern Sudan)." *Anthropos* 75:710–720.

BURTON, JOHN W. 1981. "Ethnicity on the Hoof: On the Economics of Nuer Identity." *Ethnology* 20(2):157–162.

CAIN, P. J. AND A. G. HOPKINS. 1993. *British Imperialism: Innovation and Expansion 1688–1914*. London and New York: London.

CANNON, WALTER B. 1942. "'Voodoo' Death." *American Anthropologist* 44(2):169–181.

CARNEIRO, ROBERT L. 1960. "Slash-and-Burn Agriculture: A Closer Look at Its Implications for Settlement Patterns." In *Men and Cultures: Selected Papers of the International Congress of Anthropological and Ethnological Sciences*, edited by A. Wallace, pp. 229–234. Philadelphia: University of Pennsylvania Press.

CARNEIRO, ROBERT L. 1978a. "The Knowledge and Use of Rain Forest Trees by the Kuikuru Indians of Central Brazil." In *The Nature and Status of Ethnobotany*. Anthropological Papers, no. 67, edited by R. Ford, pp. 210–216. Ann Arbor: Museum of Anthropology, University of Michigan.

CARNEIRO, ROBERT L. 1978b. "Political Expansion as an Expression of the Principle of Competitive Exclusion." In *Origins of the State: The Anthropology of Political Evolution*, edited by R. Cohen and E. R. Service, pp. 205–223. Philadelphia: Institute for the Study of Human Issues.

CARNEIRO, ROBERT L. 1981. "The Chiefdom: Precursor of the State." In *The Transition to Statehood in the New World*, edited by Grant Jones and Robert Kautz, pp. 37–79. Cambridge, Eng.: Cambridge University Press.

CARNEIRO, ROBERT L. 1983. "The Cultivation of Manioc Among the Kuikuru of the Upper Xingu." In *Adaptive Responses of Native Amazonians*, edited by Raymond Hames and William Vickers, pp. 65–111. New York: Academic Press.

CARNEIRO, ROBERT L., AND STEPHEN F. TOBIAS. 1963. "The Application of Scale Analysis to the Study of Cultural Evolution." *Transaction of the New York Academy of Sciences* (ser. 2) 26:196–207.

CARRUTHERS, BRUCE G. 1996. *City of Capital: Politics and Markets in the English Financial Revolution*. Princeton, N.J.: Princeton University Press.

CAVALLI-SFORZA, LUIGI LUCA, AND FRANCESCO CAVALLI-SFORZA. 1995. *The Great Human Diasporas: The History of Diversity and Evolution*. Reading, Mass.: Addison-Wesley.

CAVALLI-SFORZA, LUIGI LUCA, AND M. FELDMAN. 1981. *Cultural Transmission and Evolution*. Princeton, N.J.: Princeton University Press.

CAVALLI-SFORZA, LUIGI LUCA, PAOLO MENOZZI, AND ALBERTO PIAZZA. 1994. *The History and Geography of Human Genes*. Princeton, N.J.: Princeton University Press.

CAWTE, JOHN. 1974. *Medicine Is the Law: Studies in Psychiatric Anthropology of Australian Tribal Societies*. Honolulu: University Press of Hawaii.

CAWTE, JOHN E. 1976. "Malgri: A Culture-Bound Syndrome." *Culture-Bound Syndromes, Ethnopsychiatry, and Alternate Therapies*. Vol. 4 of *Mental Health Research in Asia and the*

Pacific, edited by William Lebra, pp. 22–31. Honolulu: University Press of Hawaii.

CGIAR (CONSULTATIVE GROUP ON INTERNATIONAL AGRICULTURAL RESEARCH). 1980. *Consultative Group on International Development.* Washington, D.C.: CGIAR.

CHADWICK, SIR EDWIN. 1842. *Report . . . on an Inquiry Into the Sanitary Conditions of the Labouring Population of Great Britain.* London: W. Clowes and Sons.

CHAGNON, NAPOLEON A. 1968a. *Yanomamo: The Fierce People.* New York: Holt, Rinehart & Winston.

CHAGNON, NAPOLEON A. 1968b. "Yanomamo Social Organization and Warfare." In *War: The Anthropology of Armed Conflict and Aggression,* edited by Morton Fried, Marvin Harris, and Robert Murphy, pp. 109–159. Garden City, N.Y.: Doubleday.

CHAGNON, NAPOLEON A. 1979. "Is Reproductive Success Equal in Egalitarian Societies?" In *Evolutionary Biology and Human Social Behavior: An Anthropological Perspective,* edited by Napoleon Chagnon and William Irons, pp. 374–401. North Scituate, Mass.: Duxbury Press.

CHAGNON, NAPOLEON A. 1983. *Yanomamo: The Fierce People,* 3rd ed. New York: Holt, Rinehart & Winston.

CHAGNON, NAPOLEON A. 1988. "Life Histories, Blood Revenge, and Warfare in a Tribal Population." *Science* 239(4843): 985–992.

CHAGNON, NAPOLEON. 1992. *The Yanomamo,* 4th ed. New York: Holt, Rinehart & Winston.

CHAI, CH'U, AND WINBERG CHAI. 1967. "Introduction." In *Li Chi: Book of Rites,* vol. 1, translated by James Legge, pp. xxiii–lxxxiv. New Hyde Park, N.Y.: University Books.

CHANDLER, ALFRED D., JR. 1977. *The Visible Hand: The Managerial Revolution in American Business.* Cambridge, Mass., and London: The Belknap Press of Harvard University Press.

CHANDLER, ROBERT F., JR. 1990. "Thoughts on the Global Issues of Food, Population, and the Environment." In *Sharing Innovation: Global Perspectives on Food, Agriculture, and Rural Development,* edited by Neil Kotler, pp. 169–185. Washington, D.C., and London: Smithsonian Institution Press.

CHANDLER, TERTIUS. 1987. *Four Thousand Years of Urban Growth.* Lewiston, N.Y.: St. David's University Press.

CHANG, KWANG-CHIH. 1980. *Shang Civilization.* New Haven, Conn., and London: Yale University Press.

CHANG, KWANG-CHIH. 1983. *Art, Myth, and Ritual: The Path to Political Authority in Ancient China.* Cambridge, Mass.: Harvard University Press.

CHANG, KWANG-CHIH. 1986. *Archaeology of Ancient China,* 4th ed. New Haven, Conn.: Yale University Press.

CHANG, T. T. 1983. "The Origin and Early Culture of the Cereal Grains and Food Legumes." In *The Origins of Chinese Civilization,* edited by D. N. Keightley, pp. 65–94. Berkeley: University of California Press.

CHAO, KANG 1986. *Man and Land in Chinese History: An Economic Analysis.* Stanford, Calif.: Stanford University Press.

CIBA FOUNDATION. 1977. *Health and Disease in Tribal Societies.* CIBA Foundation Symposium 49, pp. 49–67. Amsterdam: Elsevier/Excerpta Medica/North-Holland.

CICERONE, RALPH J. 1989. "Methane in the Atmosphere." In *Global Climate Change: Human and Natural Influences,* edited by S. Fred Singer, pp. 91–112. New York: Paragon House.

CLAESSEN, HENRY J. M., AND PETER SKALNIK (EDS.). 1978. "The Early State: Theories and Hypotheses." In *The Early State,* pp. 3–29. The Hague, Paris, and New York: Mouton.

CLARK, GROVER. 1936. *The Balance Sheets of Imperialism: Facts and Figures on Colonies.* New York: Columbia University Press.

CLARK, J. DESMOND. 1984. "Prehistoric Cultural Continuity and Economic Change in the Central Sudan in the Early Holocene." In *From Hunters to Farmers: The Causes and Consequences of Food Production in Africa,* edited by J. Desmond Clark and Steven Brandt, pp. 113–126. Berkeley: University of California Press.

CLASTRES, PIERRE. 1977. *Society Against the State: The Leader as Servant and the Humane Uses of Power Among the Indians of the Americas.* New York: Urizen Books.

CLEAVE, T. L. 1974. *The Saccharine Disease.* Bristol, Eng.: John Wright.

CLEVELAND, DAVID A. AND STEPHEN C. MURRAY. 1997. "The World's Crop Genetic Resources and the Rights of Indigenous Farmers." *Current Anthropology* 38(4):477–515.

CODRINGTON, R. H. 1981. *The Melanesians.* Oxford, Eng.: Clarendon Press.

COHEN, JOEL E. 1995. *How Many People Can the Earth Support?* New York and London: Norton.

COHEN, LEONARD A. 1987. "Diet and Cancer." *Scientific American* 257(5):42–48.

COHEN, MARK NATHAN. 1989. *Health and the Rise of Civilization.* New Haven, Conn., and London: Yale University Press.

COHEN, YEHUDI (ED.). 1974. *Man in Adaptation,* 2nd ed. Chicago: Aldine.

COHN, BERNARD. 1996. *Colonialism and Its Forms of Knowledge.* Princeton: Princeton University Press.

COLBY, GERARD, AND CHARLOTTE DENNETT. 1995. *Thy Will Be Done: The Conquest of the Amazon: Nelson Rockefeller in the Age of Oil.* New York: HarperCollins, HarperPerennial.

COLCHESTER, MARCUS. 1984. "Rethinking Stone Age Economics: Some Speculations Concerning the Pre-Columbian Yanomama Economy." *Human Ecology* 12(3):291–314.

COLE, H. S. D. (ED.). 1973. *Models of Doom.* New York: Universe.

COLLIER, JANE FISHBURNE. 1988. *Marriage and Inequality in Classless Societies.* Stanford, Calif.: Stanford University Press.

COLLIER, PETER, AND DAVID HOROWITZ. 1976. *The Rockefellers: An American Dynasty.* New York: Holt, Rinehart & Winston.

COLQUHOUN, PATRICK. 1815. *A Treatise on the Wealth, Power, and Resources of the British Empire.* London: Joseph Mawman.

CONRAD, GEOFFREY W. 1981. "Cultural Materialism, Split Inheritance, and the Expansion of Ancient Peruvian Empires." *American Antiquity* 46:3–26.

CONRAD, GEOFFREY W., AND ARTHUR A. DEMAREST. 1984. *Religion and Empire: The Dynamics of Aztec and Inca Expansionism.* Cambridge, Eng.: Cambridge University Press.

COOK, EARL. 1971. "The Flow of Energy in an Industrial Society." *Scientific American* 224(3):134–144.

COOK, NOBLE DAVID. 1991. *Demographic Collapse: Indian Peru, 1520–1620.* Cambridge: Cambridge University Press.

CORRIS, PETER. 1968. *Aborigines and Europeans in Western Victoria.* Occasional Papers in Aboriginal Studies, no. 12, Ethnohistory Series, no. 1. Canberra: Australian Institute of Aboriginal Studies.

COSTANZA, ROBERT, ET AL. 1997. "The Value of the World's Ecosystem Services and Natural Capital." *Nature* 387(6630): 253–259.

COUGHENOUR, M. B., J. E. ELLIS, D. M. SWIFT, D. L. COPPOCK, K. GALVIN, J. T. McCABE, AND T. C. HART. 1985. "Energy Extraction and Use in a Nomadic Pastoral Ecosystem." *Science* 230(4726):619–625.

COWLISHAW, GILLIAN. 1978. "Infanticide in Aboriginal Australia." *Oceania* 48(4):262–283.

CROSBY, ALFRED W. 1986. *Biological Imperialism: The Biological Expansion of Europe, 900–1900.* Cambridge, Eng.: Cambridge University Press.

CROSSON, PIERRE R., AND NORMAN J. ROSENBERG. 1989. "Strategies for Agriculture." *Scientific American* 261(3):128–135.

CRUMLEY, CAROLE L. 2001. "Communication, Holism, and the Evolution of Sociopolitical Complexity." In *From Leaders to Rulers,* edited by Jonathan Haas, pp. 19–33. New York: Kluwer Academic.

CUMBERLAND, KENNETH BRAILEY. 1956. *Southwest Pacific: A Geography of Australia, New Zealand and Their Pacific Neighborhoods.* London: Methuen.

DAHL, GUDREN, AND ANDERS HJORT. 1976. *Having Herds: Pastoral Herd Growth and Household Economy.* Stockholm Studies in Social Anthropology, no. 2. Stockholm: Department of Social Anthropology, University of Stockholm.

DALES, GEORGE F. 1964. "The Mythical Massacre at Mohenjo-Daro." *Expedition* 6(3):36–43.

DALES, GEORGE F. 1965. "Civilization and Floods in the Indus Valley." *Expedition* 7(4):10–19.

DALES, GEORGE F. 1966. "The Decline of the Harappans." *Scientific American* 214(5):92–100.

DALES, GEORGE F. 1982. "Mohenjodaro Miscellany: Some Unpublished, Forgotten, or Misinterpreted Features." In *Harappan Civilization: A Contemporary Perspective,* edited by Gregory Possehl, pp. 97–106. New Delhi: Oxford and IBH.

DALES, G. F., AND R. L. RAIKES. 1968. "The Mohenjo–Daro Floods: A Rejoinder." *American Anthropologist* 70(5):957–961.

D'ALTROY, TERENCE N. 2002. *The Incas.* Oxford: Blackwell.

D'ALTROY, TERENCE N., AND TIMOTHY K. EARLE. 1985. "Staple Finance, Wealth Finance, and Storage in the Inka Political Economy." *Current Anthropology* 26(2):187–206.

DALZELL, JR. ROBERT F. 1987. *Enterprising Elite: The Boston Associates and the World They Made.* Cambridge, Mass. and London: Harvard University Press.

D'ANS, ANDRÉ-MARCEL. 1972. "Les Tribus Indigènes du Parc National du Manu." *Proceedings of the 39th International Americanists Congress* 4:95–100.

D'ANS, ANDRÉ-MARCEL. 1981. "Encounter in Peru." In *Is God an American? An Anthropological Perspective on the Missionary Work of the Summer Institute of Linguistics,* edited by Søren Hvalkof and Peter Aaby, pp. 145–162. Copenhagen and London: IWGIA and Survival International.

DAVIS, LANCE E. AND ROBERT A. HUTTENBACK. 1986. *Mammon and the Pursuit of Empire: the Political Economy of British Imperialism, 1860–1912.* Cambridge: Cambridge University Press.

DAVIS, SHELTON H. 1976. "The Yanomamo: Ethnographic Images and Anthropological Responsibilities." In *The Geological Imperative: Anthropology and Development in the Amazon Basin of South America,* edited by Shelton Davis and Robert

Mathews, pp. 7–23. Cambridge, Mass.: Anthropology Resource Center.

DAVIS, SHELTON H. 1977. *Victims of the Miracle: Development and the Indians of Brazil.* Cambridge, Eng.: Cambridge University Press.

DAWKINS, R. 1989. *The Selfish Gene.* New York: Oxford University Press.

DAY, KENT C. 1982. "Ciudedelas: Their Form and Function." In *Chan Chan: Andean Desert City,* edited by Michael Moseley and Kent C. Dean, pp. 55–66. Albuquerque: University of New Mexico Press.

DeFOREST, ROBERT W., AND LAWRENCE VEILLER (EDS.). 1903. *The Tenement House Problem: Including the Report of the New York State Tenement House Commission of 1900.* 2 vols. New York: Macmillan.

DENEVAN, WILLIAM. 1976. *The Native Population of the Americas in 1492.* Madison: University of Wisconsin Press.

DENNETT, GLENN, AND JOHN CONNELL. 1988. "Acculturation and Health in the Highlands of Papua New Guinea." *Current Anthropology* 29(2):273–299.

DEWHURST, J. FREDERIC (ED.). 1947. *America's Needs and Resources: A Twentieth Century Fund Survey Which Includes Estimates for 1950 and 1969.* New York: Twentieth Century Fund.

DIAKONOFF, I. M. 1987. "Slave-Labour vs. Non-Slave Labour: The Problem of Definition." In *Labor in the Ancient Near East,* edited by Marvin A. Powell, pp. 1–3. American Oriental Series, Vol. 68. New Haven, Conn.: American Oriental Society.

DIAMOND, STANLEY. 1968. "The Search for the Primitive." In *The Concept of the Primitive,* edited by Ashley Montagu, pp. 99–147. New York: Free Press.

DICKENS, CHARLES. (1852–1853) 1953. *Bleak House.* Garden City, N.Y.: The Literary Guild of America.

DICKSON, F. P. 1981. *Australian Stone Hatchets: A Study in Design and Dynamics.* Sydney: Academic Press.

DICKSON, P. G. M. 1967. *The Financial Revolution in England: A Study in the Development of Public Credit 1688–1756.* London: Macmillan.

DIRKS, NICHOLAS B. 1989. "The Original Caste: Power, History and Hierarchy in South Asia." *Contributions to Indian Sociology* 23(1):59–77.

DIRKS, NICHOLAS B. 2001. *Castes of Mind: Colonialism and the Making of Modern India.* Princeton and Oxford: Princeton University Press.

DIVALE, WILLIAM, AND MARVIN HARRIS. 1976. "Population, Warfare and the Male Supremacist Complex." *American Anthropologist* 78(3):521–538.

DOBYNS, HENRY E., AND PAUL L. DOUGHTY. 1976. *Peru: A Cultural History.* New York: Oxford University Press.

DOBYNS, HENRY F., PAUL L. DOUGHTY, AND HAROLD D. LASSWELL (EDS.). 1971. *Peasants, Power, and Applied Social Change: Vicos as a Model.* Beverly Hills, Calif., and London: Sage.

DOLE, GERTRUDE. 1964. "Shamanism and Political Control Among the Kuikuru." In *Beiträge zur Völkerkunde Südamerikas Festgabe für Herbert Baldus zum 65. Geburtstag,* edited by Hans Becher, pp. 53–62. *Völkerkundliche Abhandlungen,* Vol. 1, Des Niedersächsischen Landesmuseum.

DOLE, GERTRUDE. 1978. "The Use of Manioc Among the Kuikuru: Some Implications." In *The Nature and Status of Ethnobotany.* Anthropological Papers, no. 67, edited by

R. Ford, pp. 217–247. Ann Arbor: Museum of Anthropology, University of Michigan.

DOMHOFF, G. WILLIAM. 1967. *Who Rules America?* Englewood Cliffs, N.J.: Prentice-Hall.

DOMHOFF, G. WILLIAM. 1983. *Who Rules America Now? A View for the '80s.* Englewood Cliffs, N.J.: Prentice-Hall.

DOMHOFF, G. WILLIAM. 1990. *The Power Elite and the State.* New York: Aldine de Gruyter.

DOUGHTY, PAUL L. 2002. "Ending Serfdom in Peru: The Struggle for Land and Freedom in Vicos." In *Contemporary Cultures and Societies of Latin America,* edited by Dwight B. Heath. Prospect Heights, Ill.: Waveland Press.

DOUGLAS, MARY. 1966. *Purity and Danger: An Analysis of Concepts of Pollution and Taboo.* New York: Praeger.

DOW, JAMES. 1986. "Universal Aspects of Symbolic Healing: A Theoretical Synthesis." *American Anthropologist* 88(1):56–69.

DREW, CHRISTOPHER, ELIZABETH BECKER, AND SANDRA BLAKESLEE. 2003. "Despite Mad-Cow Warnings, Industry Resisted Safeguards." *New York Times,* Dec. 28.

DREWNOSKI, ADAM AND BARRY M. POPKIN. 1997. "The Nutrition Transition: New Trends in the Global Diet." *Nutrition Review* 55(2):31–43.

DULL, JACK L. 1990. "The Evolution of Government in China." In *Heritage of China: Contemporary Perspectives on Chinese Civilization,* edited by Paul Ropp, pp. 55–85. Berkeley: University of California Press.

DUMONT, LOUIS. 1970. *Homo Hierarchicus: An Essay on the Caste System.* Chicago: University of Chicago Press.

DUPUY, T. N. 1979. *Numbers, Predictions and War: Using History to Evaluate Combat Factors and Predict the Outcome of Battles.* New York: Bobbs-Merrill.

DURHAM, WILLIAM H. 1979. *Scarcity and Survival in Central America: Ecological Origins of the Soccer War.* Stanford, Calif.: Stanford University Press.

DURHAM, WILLIAM H. 1991. *Coevolution: Genes, Culture, and Human Diversity.* Stanford, Calif.: Stanford University Press.

DURHAM, WILLIAM H. 1995. "Political Ecology and Environmental Destruction in Latin America." In *The Social Causes of Environmental Destruction in Latin America,* edited by Michael Painter and William H. Durham, pp. 249–264. Ann Arbor: University of Michigan Press.

DUSSEL, ENRIQUE. 1975. "Bartolome de Las Casas." *Encyclopaedia Britannica* 10:684–686.

DYE, THOMAS R. 1983. *Who's Running America? The Reagan Years.* Englewood Cliffs, N.J.: Prentice–Hall.

DYSON-HUDSON, RADA, AND NEVILLE DYSON-HUDSON. 1969. "Subsistence Herding in Uganda." *Scientific American* 220(2):76–89.

EARLE, PETER. 1989. *The Making of the English Middle Class: Business, Society and Family Life in London 1660–1730.* Berkeley and Los Angeles: University of California Press.

EARLE, TIMOTHY. 1978. *Economic and Social Organization of a Complex Chiefdom: The Halelea District, Kaua'i, Hawaii.* Anthropological Papers, no. 63. Ann Arbor: Museum of Anthropology, University of Michigan.

EARLE, TIMOTHY. 1987. "Specialization and the Production of Wealth: Hawaiian Chiefdoms and the Inka Empire." In *Specialization, Exchange, and Complex Societies,* edited by Elizabeth Brumfiel and Timothy Earle, pp. 64–75. Cambridge, Eng.: Cambridge University Press.

EARLE, TIMOTHY K. 2001. "Institutionalization of Chiefdoms: Why Landscapes Are Built." In *From Leaders to Rulers,* edited by Jonathan Haas, p. 105–124. New York: Kluwer Academic/Plenum.

EARLS, JOHN, AND IRENE SILVERBLATT. 1978. "La Realidad Fisica y Social en la Cosmologia Andina." *Proceedings of the International Congress of Americanists* 42(4):299–325.

EASTMAN, LLOYD E. 1988. *Family, Fields, and Ancestors: Constancy and Change in China's Social and Economic History, 1550–1949.* New York: Oxford University Press.

EASTWELL, HARRY D. 1982. "Voodoo Death and the Mechanisms for Dispatch of the Dying in East Arnhem, Australia." *American Anthropologist* 84(1):5–18.

EBREY, PATRICIA. 1990. "Women, Marriage, and the Family in Chinese History." In *Heritage of China: Contemporary Perspectives on Chinese Civilization,* edited by Paul Ropp, pp. 197–223. Berkeley: University of California Press.

ECK, DIANA L. 1985. *Darsan: Seeing the Divine Image in India.* Chambersburg, Pa.: Anima Books.

EDGERTON, LYNNE T. 1991. *The Rising Tide: Global Warming and World Sea Levels.* Washington, D.C., and Covelo, Calif.: Island Press.

EDGERTON, ROBERT B. 1992. *Sick Societies: Challenging the Myth of Primitive Harmony.* New York: Free Press.

EHRENBERG, RICHARD. 1928. *Capital and Finance in the Age of the Renaissance: A Study of the Fuggers and Their Connections.* New York: Harcourt, Brace.

EHRLICH, PAUL. 1968. *The Population Bomb.* New York: Ballantine Books.

EISENBURG, J., AND R. THORINGTON, JR. 1973. "A Preliminary Analysis of a Neotropical Mammal Fauna." *Biotropica* 5(3):150–161.

EKELUND, ROBERT B., JR., AND ROBERT F. HEBERT. 1983. *A History of Economic Theory and Method,* 2nd ed. New York: McGraw-Hill.

ELKIN, A. P. 1933. "Wanted: A Positive Policy." *Sydney Morning Herald,* Oct. 13, p. 6.

ELKIN, A. P. 1934. "Anthropology and the Future of the Australian Aborigines." *Oceania* 5(1):1–18.

ENARD, WOLFGANG, ET AL. 2002. "Molecular evolution of FOXP2, a gene involved in speech and language." Author's *Nature* advance online publication, 14 August 2002 (doi:10.1038/nature01025).

ENGELS, DONALD W. 1978. *Alexander the Great and the Logistics of the Macedonian Army.* Berkeley: University of California Press.

ENGELS, FRIEDRICH. 1973. *The Condition of the Working Class in England.* Moscow: Progress.

ERDOSY, GEORGE. 1988. *Urbanization in Early Historic India.* BAR International Series 430. Oxford, Eng.: Oxford University Press.

ESTES, RALPH. 1996. *Tyranny of the Bottom Line: Why Corporations Make Good People Do Bad Things.* San Francisco: Berrett-Kohler.

EVANS-PRITCHARD, E. E. 1940. *The Nuer: A Description of the Modes of Livelihood and Political Institutions of a Nilotic People.* New York and Oxford, Eng.: Oxford University Press.

EVANS-PRITCHARD, E. E. 1951. *Kinship and Marriage Among the Nuer.* Oxford, Eng.: Oxford University Press.

EVANS-PRITCHARD, E. E. 1953. "The Nuer Conception of Spirit in Its Relation to the Social Order." *American Anthropologist* 55(2, pt. 1):201–214.

FAIRSERVIS, WALTER A., JR. 1967. "The Origin, Character, and Decline of an Early Civilization." *American Museum Novitates* 2302:1–48.

FARMER, PAUL. 1994. *The Uses of Haiti.* Monroe, Maine: Common Courage Press.

FARMER, PAUL. 2001. *Infections and Inequalities: The Modern Plagues.* Berkeley: University of California Press.

FARMER, PAUL. 2003. *Pathologies of Power: Health, Human Rights, and the New War on the Poor.* Berkeley: University of California Press.

FEDER, ERNEST. 1978. *Strawberry Imperialism: An Enquiry into the Mechanisms of Dependency in Mexican Agriculture.* The Hague: Institute of Social Studies.

FEDERALIST PAPERS (Alexander Hamilton, James Madison, John Jay, papers No. 1–85, originally published 1787–1788, numerous editions have been republished).

FEHER, JOSEPH. 1969. *Hawaii: A Pictorial History.* Bernice P. Bishop Museum Special Publication, no. 58. Honolulu: Bishop Museum Press.

FEI, HSIAO-TUNG, AND CHIH-I CHANG. 1945. *Earthbound China: A Study of Rural Economy in Yunnan.* Chicago: University of Chicago Press.

FERGUSON, R. BRIAN. 1995. *Yanomami Warfare: A Political History.* Santa Fe: School of American Research Press.

FERGUSON, R. BRIAN, AND NEIL L. WHITEHEAD (EDS.). 1992. *War in the Tribal Zone: Expanding States and Indigenous Warfare.* Santa Fe: School of American Research Press.

FEUERWERKER, ALBERT. 1990. "Chinese Economic History in Comparative Perspective." In *Heritage of China: Contemporary Perspectives on Chinese Civilization,* edited by Paul Ropp, pp. 224–241. Berkeley: University of California Press.

FIELD, C. R. 1985. "The Importance to Rendille Subsistence Pastoralists of Sheep and Goats in Northern Kenya." In *Small Ruminants in African Agriculture,* edited by R. T. Wilson and D. Bourzat, pp. 188–197. Addis Ababa, Ethiopia: International Livestock Centre for Africa.

FIRTH, RAYMOND. [1936] 1957. *We the Tikopia: A Sociological Study of Kinship in Primitive Polynesia,* 2nd ed. New York: Barnes & Noble.

FIRTH, RAYMOND. [1940] 1967. "The Work of the Gods." In *Tikopia,* 2nd ed. London: Athlone Press.

FIRTH, RAYMOND. [1965] 1975. *Primitive Polynesian Economy.* New York: Norton.

FISCHER, DAVID HACKETT. 1996. *The Great Wave: Price Revolutions and the Rhythm of History.* New York: Oxford University Press.

FITTKAU, E., AND H. KLINGE. 1973. "On Biomass and Trophic Structure of the Central Amazonian Rain Forest Ecosystem." *Biotropica* 5(1):2–14.

FLANNERY, KENT V. 1965. "The Ecology of Early Food Production in Mesopotamia." *Science* 147(3663):1247–1256.

FLANNERY, KENT V. 1972a. "The Cultural Evolution of Civilizations." *Annual Review of Ecology and Systematics* 3:399–426.

FLANNERY, KENT V. 1972b. "The Origins of the Village as a Settlement Type in Mesoamerica and the Near East: A Comparative Study." In *Man, Settlement and Urbanism,* edited by P. J. Ucko, R. Tringham, and G. W. Dimbleby, pp. 25–53. London: Duckworth.

FLETCHER, ROLAND. 1995. *The Limits of Settlement Growth: A Theoretical Outline.* Cambridge: Cambridge University Press.

FLOOD, JOSEPHINE. 1980. *The Moth Eaters.* Atlantic Highlands, N.J.: Humanities Press.

FLOOD, JOSEPHINE. 1983. *Archaeology of the Dreamtime.* Honolulu: University of Hawaii Press.

FLOWERS, NANCY M. 1983. "Seasonal Factors in Subsistence, Nutrition, and Child Growth in a Central Brazilian Indian Community." In *Adaptive Responses of Native Amazonians,* edited by Raymond Hames and William Vickers, pp. 357–390. New York: Academic Press.

FLYNN, JOHN T. 1941. *Men of Wealth: The Story of Twelve Significant Fortunes from the Renaissance to the Present Day.* New York: Simon & Schuster.

FOSTER, GEORGE M. 1965. "Peasant Society and the Image of Limited Good." *American Anthropologist* 67(2):293–315.

FOSTER, GEORGE M. 1969. *Applied Anthropology.* Boston: Little, Brown.

FOUNDATION DIRECTORY. 1998. Vol. 20. New York: Columbia University Press.

FOUTS, ROGER S. 1994. "Transmission of a Human Gestural Language in a Chimpanzee Mother–Infant Relationship." In *The Ethological Roots of Culture,* edited by R. A. Gardner et al., pp. 257–270. Dordrecht, Boston, and London: Kluwer Academic.

FRANK, ANDRÉ GUNDER. 1967. *Capitalism and Underdevelopment in Latin America.* New York: Monthly Review Press.

FRANKE, RICHARD W., AND BARBARA H. CHASIN. 1989. *Kerala: Radical Reform as Development in an Indian State.* Food First Development Report No. 6. San Francisco: The Institute for Food and Development Policy.

FRATKIN, ELLIOT. 1989. "Household Variation and Gender Inequality in Ariaal Pastoral Production: Results of a Stratified Time-Allocation Survey." *American Anthropologist* 91(2):430–440.

FRATKIN, ELLIOT. 1998. *Ariaal Pastoralists of Kenya: Surviving Drought and Development in Africa's Aris Lands.* Boston and London: Allyn and Bacon.

FRATKIN, ELLIOT AND ERIC ABELLA ROTH. 1990. "Drought and Economic Differentiation Among Ariaal Pastoralists of Kenya." *Human Ecology* 18(4):385–402.

FRAZER, JAMES G. 1990 [1890] 1900. *The Golden Bough,* 3 vols. London: Macmillan.

FRAZER, SIR JAMES. 1910. *Totemism and Exogamy,* 4 vols. London: Macmillan.

FREED, STANLEY A., AND RUTH S. FREED. 1981. "Sacred Cows and Water Buffalo in India: The Uses of Ethnography." *Current Anthropology* 22(5):483–490.

FREEDMAN, MAURICE. 1966. *Chinese Lineage and Society: Fukien and Kwangtung.* London School of Economics, Monographs on Social Anthropology, no. 33. London: Athlone Press.

FREEDMAN, MAURICE. 1979. *The Study of Chinese Society.* Stanford, Calif.: Stanford University Press.

FRIED, MORTON H. 1983. "Tribe to State or State to Tribe in Ancient China." In *The Origins of Chinese Civilization,* edited by D. N. Keightley, pp. 467–493. Berkeley: University of California Press.

FRIEDMAN, MILTON. 1962. *Capitalism and Freedom,* with the assistance of Rose D. Friedman. Chicago: University of Chicago Press.

GALATY, JOHN G. 1982. "Being 'Maasai'; Being 'People-of-Cattle': Ethnic Shifters in East Africa." *American Ethnologist* 9(1):1–20.

GALBRAITH, JOHN KENNETH. 1952. *American Capitalism: The Concept of Countervailing Power.* Boston, Houghton.

GALBRAITH, JOHN KENNETH. 1958. *The Affluent Society.* Boston: Houghton Mifflin.

GALBRAITH, JOHN KENNETH. 1967. *The New Industrial State.* Boston: Houghton Mifflin.

GALE, FAY (ED.). 1983. *We Are Bosses Our-Selves: The Status and Role of Aboriginal Women Today.* Canberra: Australian Institute of Aboriginal Studies.

GARDNER, GARY AND BRIAN HALWEIL. 2000. "Nourishing the Underfed and Overfed." In *State of the World 2000: A Worldwatch Institute Report on Progress Toward a Sustainable Society,* edited by Lester R. Brown, Christopher Flavin, Hilary French, and Linda Starke, pp. 59–78. New York and London: Norton.

GARDNER, R. ALLEN, AND BEATRIX T. GARDNER. 1994a. "Development of Phrases in the Utterances of Children and Cross-Fostered Chimpanzees." In *The Ethological Roots of Culture,* edited by R. A. Gardner et al., pp. 223–255. Dordrecht, Boston, and London: Kluwer Academic Press.

GARDNER, R. ALLEN, AND BEATRIX T. GARDNER. 1994b. "Ethological Roots of Language." In *The Ethological Roots of Culture,* edited by R. A. Gardner et al., pp. 199–222. Dordrecht, Boston, and London: Kluwer Academic Press.

GASTON, KEVIN J., TIM M. BLACKBURN, AND KEES KLEIN GOLDEWIJK. 2003. "Habitat conversion and global avian biodiversity loss." *Proceedings of the Royal Society of London Series B,* 270(1521):1293–1300.

GATES, BILL, WITH NATHAN MYHRVOLD AND PETER REARSON. 1996. *The Road Ahead,* 2nd ed. New York and London: Penguin Books.

GEERTZ, CLIFFORD. 1963. *Agricultural Involution: The Process of Ecological Change in Indonesia.* Berkeley: University of California Press.

GEIST, VALERIUS. 1994. "Culture and Its Biological Origins: A View from Ethnology, Epigenesis and Design." In *The Ethological Roots of Culture,* edited by R. A. Gardner et al., pp. 441–459. Dordrecht, Boston, and London: Kluwer Academic Press.

GELB, I. J. 1965. "The Ancient Mesopotamian Ration System." *Journal of Near Eastern Studies* 24(3):230–243.

GEMINI CONSULTING. 1998. *World Wealth Report 1998.* New York: Gemini Consulting.

GENNEP, ARNOLD L. VAN. 1909. *Les Rites de Passage.* Paris: E. Nourry.

GEORGE, SUSAN. 1992. *The Debt Boomerang: How Third World Debt Harms Us All.* Boulder, Colo.: Westview Press.

GIBSON, MCGUIRE. 1976. "By Stage and Cycle to Sumer." In *The Legacy of Sumer.* Vol. 4 of *Bibliotheca Mesopotamia,* edited by Denise Schmandt-Besserat, pp. 51–58. Malibu, Calif.: Undena Publications.

GILDER, GEORGE. 1981. *Wealth and Poverty.* New York: Basic Books.

GIVEN-WILSON, C. 1991. "Wealth and Credit, Public and Private: The Earls of Arundel 1306–1397." *The English Historical Review* 418:1–26.

GLADWIN, THOMAS. 1970. *East Is a Big Bird.* Cambridge, Mass.: Harvard University Press.

GLICKMAN, MAURICE. 1972. "The Nuer and the Dinka: A Further Note." *Man* 7(4):586–594.

GLUCKMAN, MAX. 1956. *Custom and Conflict in Africa.* New York: Barnes & Noble.

GODELIER, MAURICE. 1975. "Modes of Production, Kinship, and Demographic Structures." In *Marxist Analyses and Social Anthropology,* edited by Maurice Bloch, pp. 3–27. New York: Wiley.

GOLDEWIJK, KEES KLEIN. 2001. "Estimating Global Land Use Change over the Past 300 Years: The HYDE Database." *Global Biogeochemical Cycles* 15(2):417–433.

GOLDMAN, IRVING. 1970. *Ancient Polynesian Society.* Chicago and London: University of Chicago Press.

GOLDSCHMIDT, WALTER. 1969. *Kambuya's Cattle.* Berkeley: University of California Press.

GOLDSMITH, RAYMOND. 1987. *Premodern Financial Systems: A Historical Comparative Study.* Cambridge: Cambridge University Press.

GOLDSTEIN, JOSHUA S. 1988. *Long Waves: Prosperity and War in the Modern Age.* New Haven, Conn., and London: Yale University Press.

GOOD, ANTHONY. 2000. "Congealing Divinity: Time, Worship and Kinship in South Indian Hinduism." *Journal of the Royal Anthropological Institute* 6:273–292.

GOOD, KENNETH. 1991. *Into the Heart: One Man's Pursuit of Love and Knowledge Among the Yanomama.* New York: Simon & Schuster.

GOODALL, J. 1986. *The Chimpanzees of Gombe.* Cambridge, Mass.: Belknap Press.

GOODENOUGH, WARD HUNT. 1963. *Cooperation in Change: An Anthropological Approach to Community Development.* New York: Wiley.

GOODENOUGH, WARD H. 1965. "Yankee Kinship Terminology: A Problem in Componential Analysis." Part 2. *American Anthropologist* 67(5):259–287.

GOODLAND, ROBERT. 1982. *Tribal Peoples and Economic Development: Human Ecological Considerations.* Washington, D.C.: International Bank for Reconstruction and Development/World Bank.

GOODY, JACK. 1976. *Production and Reproduction: A Comparative Study of the Domestic Domain.* Cambridge, Eng.: Cambridge University Press.

GOODY, JACK. 1977. *The Domestication of the Savage Mind.* Cambridge: Cambridge University Press.

GORHAM, KAFKA, AND NEELAKANTAN. 1998. "The Forbes 400: The Richest People in America." *Forbes* 162(8):165–428.

GOSH, A. 1982. "Deurbanization of the Harappan Civilization." In *Harappan Civilization: A Contemporary Perspective,* edited by George Possehl, pp. 321–324. New Delhi: Oxford and IBH.

GOULD, RICHARD A. 1969. "Subsistence Behavior Among the Western Desert Aborigines of Australia." *Oceania* 39(4):253–273.

GOULD, RICHARD A. 1970. *Spears and Spear-Throwers of the Western Desert Aborigines of Australia.* American Museum Novitates, no. 2403. New York: American Museum of Natural History.

GOULD, RICHARD A. 1980. *Living Archaeology.* Cambridge, Eng.: Cambridge University Press.

GOULD, RICHARD A. 1981. "Comparative Ecology of Food-Sharing in Australia and Northwest California." In *Omnivorous Primates: Gathering and Hunting in Human Evolution,* edited by Robert Harding and Geza Teleki, pp. 422–454. New York: Columbia University Press.

GOULD, STEPHEN JAY. 1981. *The Mismeasure of Man*. New York: Norton.

GOULDING, MICHAEL. 1980. *The Fishes and the Forest: Explorations in Amazonian Natural History*. Berkeley: University of California Press.

GRAEDEL, THOMAS E., AND PAUL. J. CRUTZEN. 1989. "The Changing Atmosphere." *Scientific American* 261(3):58–68.

GRAINGER, A. 1980. "The State of the World's Forests." *Ecologist* 10(1):6–54.

GRAY, ANDREW. n.d. *Freedom and Territory: Slavery in the Peruvian Amazon*. Unpublished manuscript.

GRAY, ANDREW. 1987. "IWGIA Report on the ILO Meeting of Experts to Discuss the Revision of Convention 107 Geneva, 1–10 September, 1986." In *IWGIA Yearbook 1986: Indigenous Peoples and Human Rights*, pp. 73–92. Copenhagen: IWGIA.

GRAY, ANDREW. 1990. "The ILO Meeting at the UN, Geneva, June 1989: Report on International Labour Organisation Revision of Convention 107." In *IWGIA Yearbook 1989*, pp. 173–191. Copenhagen: IWGIA.

GRAYSON, DONALD K. AND DAVID J. MELTZER. 2002. "Clovis Hunting and Large Mammal Extinction: A Critical Review of the Evidence." *Journal of World Prehistory* 16:1–68.

GREAT BRITAIN BOARD OF TRADE. 1909. *Statistical Abstracts for the Several British Colonies, Possessions, and Protectorates in Each Year from 1894 to 1908*, no. 46. London: His Majesty's Stationery Office.

GREGORIO, DAVID I., STEPHEN J. WALSH, AND DEBORAH PATURZO. 1997. "The Effects of Occupation-Based Social Position on Mortality in a Large American Cohort." *American Journal of Public Health* 87(9):1472–1475.

GRONOWICZ, ANTHONY. 1998. *Race and Class Politics in New York City Before the Civil War*. Boston: Northeastern University Press.

GROSS, DANIEL R. 1975. "Protein Capture and Cultural Development in the Amazon Basin." *American Anthropologist* 77(3):526–549.

GROSS, DANIEL R., AND BARBARA A. UNDERWOOD. 1971. "Technological Change and Caloric Costs: Sisal Agriculture." *American Anthropologist* 73(2):725–740.

GROSSMAN, RICHARD L., AND FRANK T. ADAMS. 1996. "Exercising Power over Corporations Through State Charters." In *The Case Against the Global Economy and for a Turn Toward the Local*, edited by Jerry Mander and Edward Goldsmith, pp. 374–389. San Francisco: Sierra Club Books.

GUDSCHINSKY, SARAH C. 1956. "The ABC's of Lexicostatistics (Glottochronology)." *Word* 12:175–210.

GULLIVER, P. H. 1955. *The Family Herds: A Study of Two Pastoral Tribes in East Africa, the Jie and Turkana*. London: Routledge & Kegan Paul.

HADINGHAM, EVAN. 1987. *Lines to the Mountain Gods: Nazca and the Mysteries of Peru*. New York: Random House.

HAGESTEIJN, RENÉE. 1989. *Circles of Kings: Political Dynamics in Early Continental Southeast Asia*. Verhandelingen van het Koninklijk Institut Voor Taal-, Land- en Volkenkunde No. 138. Dordrecht, Holland: Foris Publications.

HAILEY, WILLIAM MALCOLM. 1950. *Native Administration in the British African Territories. Part One, East Africa: Uganda, Kenya, Tanganyika*. Colonial Office. London: His Majesty's Stationery Office.

HALL, PETER DOBKIN. 1982. *The Organization of American Culture, 1700–1900: Private Institutions, Elites, and the Origins of American Nationality*. New York: New York University Press.

HALLPIKE, C. R. 1979. *The Foundations of Primitive Thought*. Oxford, Eng.: Clarendon Press.

HALLPIKE, C. R. 1986. *The Principles of Social Evolution*. Oxford, Eng.: Clarendon Press.

HAMES, RAYMOND. 1987. "Game Conservation or Efficient Hunting?" In *The Question of the Commons: The Cultural Ecology of Communal Resources*, edited by Bonnie McCoy and James Acheson, pp. 92–107. Tucson: University of Arizona Press.

HAMILTON, ANNETTE. 1979. "A Comment on Arthur Hippler's Paper 'Culture and Personality Perspective of the Yolngu of Northeastern Arnhem Land: Part 1.'" *Mankind* 12(2):164–169.

HAMMACK, DAVID C. 1982. *Power and Society: Greater New York at the Turn of the Century*. New York: Russell Sage Foundation.

HANCOCK, DAVID. 1995. *Citizens of the World: London Merchants and the Integration of the British Atlantic Community, 1735–1785*. Cambridge: Cambridge University Press.

HANDY, E. S. C., AND E. G. HANDY. 1972. *The Native Planters in Old Hawaii: Their Life, Lore, and Environments*. Bernice P. Bishop Museum bull. 233. Honolulu: Bishop Museum Press.

HANKS, LUCIEN M. 1972. *Rice and Men: Agricultural Ecology in Southeast Asia*. Chicago: Aldine.

HANKS, LUCIEN M. 1975. "The Thai Social Order as Entourage and Circle." In *Change and Persistence in Thai Society*, edited by G. William Skinner and A. Thomas Kirsch, pp. 197–218. Ithaca and London: Cornell University Press.

HARDIN, C. L. AND L. MAFFI (EDS.). 1997. *Color Categories in Thought and Language*. Cambridge: Cambridge University Press.

HARDIN, GARRETT. 1968. "The Tragedy of the Commons." *Science* 162(3859):1243–1248.

HARNER, M. J. 1980. *The Way of the Shaman*. New York: Harper & Row.

HARRIS, MARVIN. 1965. "The Myth of the Sacred Cow." In *Man, Culture, and Animals*, edited by A. P. Vayda and A. Leeds, pp. 217–228. Washington, D.C.: American Association for the Advancement of Science.

HARRIS, MARVIN. 1966. "The Cultural Ecology of India's Sacred Cattle." *Current Anthropology* 7(1):51–59.

HARRIS, MARVIN. 1971a. "A Comment on Heston: An Approach to the Sacred Cow of India." *Current Anthropology* 12(2):199–201.

HARRIS, MARVIN. 1971b. *Culture, Man, and Nature: An Introduction to General Anthropology*. New York: Crowell.

HARRIS, MARVIN. 1974. *Cows, Pigs, Wars, and Witches: The Riddles of Culture*. New York: Random House.

HARRIS, MARVIN. 1980. *Cultural Materialism: The Struggle for a Science of Culture*. New York: Random House/Vintage Books.

HARRIS, MARVIN. 1981. *America Now: The Anthropology of a Changing Culture*. New York: Simon & Schuster.

HARRIS, MARVIN. 1984. "A Cultural Materialist Theory of Band and Village Warfare: The Yanomamo Test." In *Warfare, Culture, and Environment*, edited by R. Brian Ferguson, pp. 111–140. New York: Academic Press.

HARRIS, MARVIN. 1985. *Good to Eat: Riddles of Food and Culture.* New York: Simon & Schuster.

HARRIS, MARVIN. 1988. *Culture, People, Nature: An Introduction to General Anthropology,* 5th ed. New York: Harper & Row.

HARTMANN, BETSY, AND JAMES K. BOYCE. 1983. *A Quiet Violence: View from a Bangladesh Village.* San Francisco: Institute for Food and Development Policy.

HASLUCK, PAUL M. 1953. "The Future of the Australian Aborigine." Twenty-ninth Meeting of the Australian and New Zealand Association for the Advancement of Science, Sydney. *Australian and New Zealand Association for the Advancement of Science* 29:155–165.

HASSAN, FEKRI A. 1981. *Demographic Archaeology.* New York: Academic Press.

HASTORF, CHRISTINE A. 1993. *Agriculture and the Onset of Political Inequality Before the Inka.* Cambridge, Eng.: Cambridge University Press.

HAWKES, JAMES F., AND KRISTEN O'CONNELL. 1981. "Affluent Hunters? Some Comments in Light of the Alyawarra Case." *American Anthropologist* 83(3):622–626.

HAYDEN, BRIAN. 1977. "Stone Tool Functions in the Western Desert." In *Stone Tools as Cultural Markers: Change, Evolution and Complexity,* edited by R. V. S. Wright, pp. 178–188. Prehistory and Material Culture Series, no. 12. Canberra: Australian Institute of Aboriginal Studies.

HAYDEN, BRIAN. 1995. "Pathways to Power: Principles for Creating Socioeconomic Inequalities." In *Foundations of Social Inequality,* edited by T. Douglas Price and Gary M. Feinman, pp. 15–86. New York and London: Plenum Press.

HEADLAND, THOMAS N., KENNETH L. PIKE, AND MARVIN HARRIS. 1990. *Emics and Etics: The Insider/Outsider Debate.* Newbury Park, Calif.: Sage.

HECKER, HOWARD M. 1982. "Domestication Revisited: Its Implications for Faunal Analysis." *Journal of Field Archaeology* 9:217–236.

HEILBRONER, ROBERT, AND LESTER C. THUROW. 1987. *Economics Explained.* Englewood Cliffs, N.J.: Prentice-Hall.

HEMMING, JOHN. 1978. *Red Gold: The Conquest of the Brazilian Indians.* Cambridge, Mass.: Harvard University Press.

HENRY, JULES. 1963. *Culture Against Man.* New York: Random House.

HERMAN, EDWARD S. AND NOAM CHOMSKY. 2002. *Manufacturing Consent: The Political Economy of the Mass Media.* New York: Pantheon.

HERRNSTEIN, RICHARD J. 1971. "IQ." *Atlantic Monthly* (September):43–64.

HERRNSTEIN, RICHARD J., AND CHARLES MURRAY. 1994. *The Bell Curve: Intelligence and Class Structure in American Life.* New York: Free Press.

HERSKOVITS, MELVILLE J. 1926. "The Cattle Complex in East Africa." *American Anthropologist* 28(1):230–272, 28(2): 361–388, 28(3):494–528, 28(4):633–664.

HESTON, ALAN. 1971. "An Approach to the Sacred Cow of India." *Current Anthropology* 12(2):191–197.

HEYERDAHL, THOR. 1952. *American Indians in the Pacific: The Theory Behind the Kon-Tiki Expedition.* London: Allen & Unwin.

HIATT, L. R. 1984a. *Aboriginal Landowners: Contemporary Issues in the Determination of Traditional Aboriginal Land Ownership.* Oceania Monograph, no. 27. Sydney: University of Sydney.

HIATT, L. R. 1984b. "Your Mother-in-Law Is Poison." *Man* 19(2):183–198.

HIATT, L. R. 1987. "Aboriginal Political Life." In *Traditional Aboriginal Society,* edited by W. H. Edwards, pp. 174–188. South Melbourne: Macmillan.

HIATT, L. R. 2002. *Edward Westermarck and the Origin of Moral Ideas.* Presented at the Ninth International Conference on Hunting and Gathering Societies, Heriot-Watt University, Edinburgh, Scotland.

HILL, KIM, AND A. MAGDALENA HURTADO. 1996. *Ache Life History: The Ecology and Demography of a Foraging People.* New York: Aldine.

HIPPLER, ARTHUR. 1977. "Cultural Evolution: Some Hypotheses Concerning the Significance of Cognitive and Affective Interpenetration During Latency." *Journal of Psychohistory* 4(4):419–460.

HIPPLER, ARTHUR. 1978. "Culture and Personality Perspective of the Yolngu of Northeastern Arnhem Land: Part 1. Early Socialization." *Journal of Psychological Anthropology* 1(2): 221–244.

HIPPLER, ARTHUR. 1981. "The Yolngu and Cultural Relativism: A Response to Reser." *American Anthropologist* 83(2):393–397.

HOBEN, ALLAN. 1982. "Anthropologists and Development." *Annual Review of Anthropology* 11:349–375.

HOEBEL, E. ADAMSON. 1968. *The Law of Primitive Man.* New York: Atheneum.

HOLMES, REBECCA. 1995. "Small is Adaptive: Nutritional Anthropometry of Native Amazonians." In *Indigenous Peoples and the Future of Amazonia,* edited by Leslie E. Sponsel, pp. 121–148. Tucson and London: The University of Arizona Press.

HOLTZMAN, JON. 2002. "Politics and Gastropolitics: Gender and the Power of Food in Two African Pastoralist Societies." *JRAI* 8(2):259–278.

HOMER-DIXON, THOMAS F. 1991. "On the Threshold: Environmental Changes as Causes of Acute Conflict." *International Security* 16(2):76–116.

HOMEWOOD, K. M., AND W. A. RODGERS. 1984. "Pastoralism and Conservation." *Human Ecology* 12(4):431–441.

HOMMON, ROBERT J. 1986. "Social Evolution in Ancient Hawai'i." In *Island Societies: Archaeological Approaches to Evolution and Transformation,* edited by Patrick V. Kirch, pp. 55–68. Cambridge: Cambridge University Press.

HOPKINS, DIANE E. 1985. "The Peruvian Agrarian Reform: Dissent from Below." *Human Organization* 44(1):18–32.

HORNBORG, ALF. 2001. *The Power of the Machine: Global Inequalities of Economy, Technology, and Environment.* Walnut Creek, CA: Alta Mira Press.

HORNBORG, ALF. 2002. *Beyond Universalism and Relativism.* Presented at the Ninth International Conference on Hunting and Gathering Societies, Heriot-Watt University, Edinburgh, Scotland.

HOUSE OF COMMONS. 1837. *Report from the Select Committee on Aborigines (British Settlements).* Imperial Blue Book, no. 7, 425. British Parliamentary Papers.

HOWARD, ALAN. 1967. "Polynesian Origins and Migrations: A Review of Two Centuries of Speculation and Theory." In *Polynesian Culture History: Essays in Honor of Kenneth P. Emory,* edited by Genevieve Highland, Roland Force, Alan Howard,

Marion Kelly, and Yosihiko Sinoto, pp. 45–101. Bernice P. Bishop Museum Special Publication, no. 56. Honolulu: Bishop Museum Press.

Hsu, Francis L. K. 1963. *Clan, Caste, and Club.* Princeton, N.J.: Van Nostrand.

Hsu, Francis L. K. (Ed.). 1972. "American Core Value and National Character." In *Psychological Anthropology,* pp.240–262. Cambridge, Mass.: Schenkman.

Hsu, Francis L. K. 1981. *Americans and Chinese: Passage to Difference.* Honolulu: University Press of Hawaii.

Hubert, M. King. 1969. "Energy Resources." In *Resources and Man,* edited by National Academy of Sciences, pp. 157–242. San Francisco: Freeman.

Huey, John. 1993. "The World's Best Brand." *Fortune,* May 31, pp. 44–54.

Hummel, Ralph P. 1987. *The Bureaucratic Experience.* New York: St. Martin's Press.

Hunn, Eugene. 1985. "The Utilitarian Factor in Folk Biological Classification." In *Directions in Cognitive Anthropology,* edited by Janet Dougherty, pp. 117–140. Urbana and Chicago: University of Illinois Press.

Hutton, J. H. 1963. *Caste in India: Its Nature, Function, and Origins,* 4th ed. London: Oxford University Press.

Hvalkof, S., and Andrew Gray. 1990. "Inscription and Titling of Native Communities in the Ucayali Department." In *Supervision Report on Land Titling Project, Peruvian Amazon.* Report to IWGIA, Copenhagen.

Hyslop, John. 1984. *The Inka Road System.* New York: Academic Press.

Ii, John Papa. 1983. *Fragments of Hawaiian History.* Bernice P. Bishop Museum Special Publication, no. 70. Honolulu: Bishop Museum Press.

ILR (International Labour Review). 1951. "Reports and Enquiries: First Session of ILO Committee of Experts on Indigenous Labour." *International Labour Review* 64(1): 61–84.

ILR (International Labour Review). 1954. "Reports and Enquiries: The Second Session of the ILO Committee of Experts on Indigenous Labour." *International Labour Review* 70(5):418–441.

Ilyatjari, Nganyintja. 1983. "Women and Land Rights: The Pitjantjatjara Land Claims." In *We Are Bosses Our-Selves: The Status and Role of Aboriginal Women Today,* edited by Fay Gale, pp. 55–61. Canberra: Australian Institute of Aboriginal Studies.

Information Please Almanac Atlas and Yearbook 1967. 1966. New York: Simon & Schuster.

IPCC (Intergovernmental Panel on Climate Change). 1991. *Climate Change: The IPCC Response Strategies.* Washington, D.C., and Covelo, Calif.: Island Press.

IPCC. 2001a. *Climate Change 2001: Impacts, Adaptation, and Vulnerability.* Contribution of Working Group II to the Third Assessment Report of the Intergovernmental Panel on Climate Change, edited by James J. McCarthy, James J. Osvaldo F. Canziani, Neil A. Leary, David J. Dokken, Kasey S. White. Cambridge, United Kingdom and New York, N.Y.: Cambridge University Press.

IPCC, 2001b. *Climate Change 2001: Synthesis Report.* Contribution of Working Groups I, II, and III to the Third Assessment Report of the Intergovernmental Panel on Climate Change, edited by R. T. Watson, and the Core Writing Team.

Cambridge, United Kingdom and New York, N.Y.: Cambridge University Press.

Irvine, S. H., and J. W. Berry. 1988. "The Abilities of Mankind: A Revaluation." In *Human Abilities in Cultural Context,* edited by S. H. Irvine and J. W. Berry, pp. 3–59. Cambridge, Eng.: Cambridge University Press.

Isbell, William H. 1978. "Environmental Perturbations and the Origin of the Andean State." In *Social Anthropology: Beyond Subsistence and Dating,* edited by Charles Redman, Mary Jane Berman, Edward Curtin, William Langhorne, Jr., Nina Versaggi, and Jeffery Wanser, pp. 303–313. New York: Academic Press.

IWGIA (International Workgroup for Indigenous Affairs). 1989. *IWGIA Yearbook 1988: Indigenous Peoples and Human Rights.* Copenhagen: IWGIA.

IWGIA (International Workgroup for Indigenous Affairs). 2001. The Indigenous World 2000/2001. Copenhagen: IWGIA.

Jacobsen, Thorkild. 1976. *The Treasures of Darkness: A History of Mesopotamian Religion.* New Haven, Conn., and London: Yale University Press.

Jacobsen, Thorkild, and Robert McC. Adams. 1958. "Salt and Silt in Ancient Mesopotamian Agriculture." *Science* 128 (3334):1251–1258.

Jacobson, Doranne. 1982. "Purdah and the Hindu Family in Central India." In *Separate Worlds: Studies of Purdah in South Asia,* edited by Hanna Papanek and Gail Minault, pp. 81–109. Delhi: Chanakya Publications.

Jacobson, Jodi L. 1989. "Abandoning Homelands." In *State of the World 1987,* edited by Lester Brown et al., pp. 59–76. New York and London: Norton.

Jaher, Frederic Cople. 1972. "Nineteenth-Century Elites in Boston and New York." *Journal of Social History* 6(1):32–77.

Jaher, Frederic Cople. 1982. *The Urban Establishment: Upper Strata in Boston, New York, Charleston, Chicago, and Los Angeles.* Urbana: University of Illinois Press.

Jansen, Eirik G. 1986. *Rural Bangladesh: Competition for Scarce Resources.* Oslo: Universitetsforlaget, Norwegian University Press.

Janssen, Marco A., Timothy A. Kohler, and Marten Scheffer. 2003. "Sunk-Cost Effects and Vulnerability to Collapse in Ancient Societies." *Current Anthropology* 44(5): 722–728.

Jensen, Arthur. 1969. "How Much Can We Boost I.Q. and Scholastic Achievement?" *Harvard Educational Review* 29:1–123.

Johannes, Robert E. 1981. *Words of the Lagoon: Fishing and Marine Lore in the Palau District of Micronesia.* Berkeley: University of California Press.

Johns. C. H. W. 1926. *The Oldest Code of Laws in the World: The Code of Laws Promulgated by Hammurabi, King of Babylon b.c. 2285–2242.* Edinburgh: T. & T. Clark.

Johnson, Allen. 1975. "Time Allocation in a Machiguenga Community." *Ethnology* 14(3):301–310.

Johnson, Allen. 1983. "Machiguenga Gardens." In *Adaptive Responses of Native Amazonians,* edited by Raymond Hames and William Vickers, pp. 29–63. New York: Academic Press.

Johnson, Allen. 1985. "In Search of the Affluent Society." In *Anthropology: Contemporary Perspectives,* edited by David Hunter and Phillip Whitten, pp. 201–206. Boston: Little, Brown. (Reprinted from *Human Nature,* September 1978.)

JOHNSON, ALLEN. 2003. *Families of the Forest: The Matsigenka Indians of the Peruvian Amazon*. Berkeley: University of California Press.

JOHNSON, ALLEN, AND CLIFFORD A. BEHRENS. 1982. "Nutritional Criteria in Machiguenga Food Production Decisions: A Linear-Programming Analysis." *Human Ecology* 10(2):167–189.

JOHNSON, BRYAN T., KIM R. HOLMES, AND MELANIE KIRKPATRICK (EDS.). 1998. *Index of Economic Freedom*. Washington, D.C., and New York: The Heritage Foundation and Dow Jones.

JOHNSON, GREGORY ALAN. 1973. *Local Exchange and Early State Development in Southwestern Iran*. Anthropological Papers, no. 51. Ann Arbor: Museum of Anthropology, University of Michigan.

JONES, ALICE HANSON. 1977. *American Colonial Wealth: Documents and Methods*. 3 Vols. New York: Arno Press.

JONES, ALICE HANSON. 1980. *Wealth of a Nation to Be: The American Colonies on the Eve of the Revolution*. New York: Columbia University Press.

JONES, P. D., T. M. L. WIGLEY, AND P. B. WRIGHT. 1986. "Global Temperature Variations Between 1861 and 1984." *Nature* 322(6078):430–434.

JONES, RHYS, AND BETTY MEEHAN. 1978. "Anbarra Concept of Colour." In *Australian Aboriginal Concepts*, edited by L. R. Hiatt, pp. 20–39. Canberra: Australian Institute of Aboriginal Studies.

JULIEN, CATHERINE J. 1982. "Inka Decimal Administration in the Lake Titicaca Region." In *The Inca and Aztec States 1400–1800*, edited by George Collier, Renato Rosaldo, and John Wirth, pp. 119–151. New York: Academic Press.

KAHN, HERMAN, AND ANTHONY J. WIENER. 1967. *The Year 2000: A Framework for Speculation on the Next Thirty-Three Years*. New York: Macmillan.

KAMIN, LEON J. 1995. "Behind the Curve." *Scientific American* 272(2):99–103.

KAPLAN, DAVID. 1960. "The Law of Cultural Dominance." In *Evolution and Culture*, edited by Marshall Sahlins and Elman Service, pp. 69–92. Ann Arbor: University of Michigan Press.

KATZ, SOLOMON H., AND MARY M. VOIGT. 1986. "Bread and Beer: The Early Use of Cereals in the Human Diet." *Expedition* 28(2):23–34.

KAY, PAUL, AND WILLETT KEMPTON. 1984. "What Is the Sapir-Whorf Hypothesis?" *American Anthropologist* 86(1):65–79.

KEATINGE, RICHARD W. 1981. "The Nature and Role of Religious Diffusion in the Early Stages of State Formation: An Example from Peruvian Prehistory." In *The Transition to Statehood in the New World*, edited by Grant Jones and Robert Kautz, pp. 172–187. Cambridge, Eng.: Cambridge University Press.

KEATS, DAPHNE M., AND JOHN A. KEATS. 1988. "Human Assessment in Australia." In *Human Abilities in Cultural Context*, edited by S. H. Irvine and J. W. Berry, pp. 283–298. Cambridge, Eng.: Cambridge University Press.

KEELEY, LAWRENCE H. 1996. *War Before Civilization*. New York and Oxford: Oxford University Press.

KEEN, IAN. 2000. "A Bundle of Sticks: The Debate Over Yolngu Clans." *Journal of the Royal Anthropological Institute* 6(3):419–436.

KEENLEYSIDE, H. L. 1950. "Critical Mineral Shortages." In *Proceedings of the United Nations Scientific Conference on the Conservation and Utilization of Resources*, pp. 38–46, August–September 1949, Lake Success, N.Y.: United Nations.

KEIGHTLEY, DAVID N. 1990. "Early Civilization in China: Reflections on How It Became Chinese." In *Heritage of China: Contemporary Perspectives on Chinese Civilization*, edited by Paul Ropp, pp. 15–54. Berkeley: University of California Press.

KELLOGG, WILLIAM W. 1989. "Carbon Dioxide and Climate Changes: Implications for Mankind's Future." In *Global Climate Change: Human and Natural Influences*, edited by S. Fred Singer, pp. 37–65. New York: Paragon House.

KELLY, RAYMOND C. 1985. *The Nuer Conquest: The Structure and Development of an Expansionist System*. Ann Arbor: University of Michigan Press.

KEMP, BARRY J. 1989. *Ancient Egypt: Anatomy of a Civilization*. London and New York: Routledge.

KENCHINGTON, RICHARD. 1985. "Coral-Reef Ecosystems: A Sustainable Resource." *Nature & Resources* 21(2):18–27.

KENNEDY, KENNETH A. R. 1982. "Skulls, Aryans and Flowing Drains: The Interface of Archaeology and Skeletal Biology in the Study of the Harappan Civilization." In *Harappan Civilization: A Contemporary Perspective*, edited by Gregory Possehl, pp. 289–295. New Delhi: Oxford and IBH.

KESWANI, PRISCILLA SCHUSTER. 1996. "Hierarchies, Heterarchies, and Urbanization Processes: The View from Bronze Age Cyprus." *Journal of Mediterranean Archaeology* 9:211–250.

KEYFITZ, NATHAN. 1989. "The Growing Human Population." *Scientific American* 261(3):119–126.

KEYNES, JOHN MAYNARD. 1936. *The General Theory of Employment, Interest and Money*. London: Macmillan.

KHARE, R. S. 1976a. *Culture and Reality: Essays on the Hindu System of Managing Foods*. Simla: Indian Institute of Advanced Study.

KHARE, R. S. 1976b. *The Hindu Hearth and Home*. New Delhi: Vikas Publishing.

KING, F. H. 1911. *Farmers of Forty Centuries or Permanent Agriculture in China, Korea and Japan*. Madison, Wis.: Mrs. F. H. King.

KING, GREGORY. 1936. *Two Tracts*, edited by Jacob H. Hollander (original edition 1696). Baltimore: The Johns Hopkins Press.

KIRCH, PATRICK VINTON. 1984. *The Evolution of the Polynesian Chiefdoms*. Cambridge: Cambridge University Press.

KIRCH, PATRICK VINTON. 1985. *Feathered Gods and Fishhooks: An Introduction to Hawaiian Archaeology and Prehistory*. Honolulu: University of Hawaii Press.

KIRCH, PATRICK VINTON. 2000. *On the Road of the Winds: An Archaeological History of the Pacific Islands Before European Contact*. Berkeley: University of California Press.

KIRCH, PATRICK V. 2001. "Polynesian Feasting in Ethnohistoric, Ethnographic, and Archaeological Contexts: A Comparison of Three Societies." In *Feasts: Archaeological and Ethnographic Perspectives on Food, Politics, and Power*, edited by Michael Dietler and Brian Hayden, pp. 168–184. Washington and London: Smithsonian Institution Press.

KIRCH, PATRICK VINTON, AND DOUGLAS E. YEN. 1982. *Tikopia: The Prehistory and Ecology of a Polynesian Outlier*. Bernice P. Bishop Museum, bull. 238. Honolulu: Bishop Museum Press.

KIRSCH, A. THOMAS. 1973. *Feasting and Social Oscillation: Religion and Society in Upland Southeast Asia*. Data Paper: Number 92, Southeast Asia Program, Department of Asian Studies, Cornell University, Ithaca, New York.

KLENGEL, HORST. 1987. "Non-Slave Labor in the Old Babylonian Period: The Basic Outlines." In *Labor in the Ancient Near East,* edited by Marvin A. Powell, pp. 159–166. American Oriental Series, Vol. 68. New Haven, Conn.: American Oriental Society.

KLICH, L. Z. 1988. "Aboriginal Cognition and Psychological Nescience." In *Human Abilities in Cultural Context,* edited by S. H. Irvine and J. W. Berry, pp. 427–452. Cambridge, Eng.: Cambridge University Press.

KNUDSON, KENNETH E. 1970. "Resource Fluctuation, Productivity, and Social Organization on Micronesian Coral Islands." Ph.D. dissertation, University of Oregon.

KOHR, LEOPOLD. 1977. *The Overdeveloped Nations: The Diseconomies of Scale.* New York: Schocken Books.

KOHR, LEOPOLD. 1978. *The Breakdown of Nations.* New York: Dutton.

KOMLOS, JOHN. 1998. "Shrinking in a Growing Economy? The Mystery of Physical Stature during the Industrial Revolution." *The Journal of Economic History* 58(3):779–802.

KONDRATIEFF, NIKOLAIR. 1984. *The Long Wave Cycle.* New York: Richardson & Snyder.

KORTEN, DAVID C. 1996. *When Corporations Rule the World.* West Hartford, Conn.: Kumarian Press; and San Francisco: Berrett-Koehler.

KOSSE, KRISZTINA. 1990. "Group Size and Societal Complexity: Thresholds in the Long-Term Memory." *Journal of Anthropological Archaeology* 9(3):275–303.

KRAMER, SAMUEL NOAH. *The Sumerians: Their History, Culture, and Character.* Chicago: University of Chicago Press.

KRANTZ, GROVER S. 1978. *Interproximal Attrition and Modern Dental Crowding.* Occasional Papers in Method and Theory in California Archaeology, no. 2, pp. 35–41. Society for California Archaeology.

KRANTZ, GROVER S. 1980. *Climatic Races and Descent Groups.* North Quincy, Mass.: Christopher.

KROEBER, A. L. 1948. *Anthropology.* New York: Harcourt, Brace & World.

KROLL, LUISA AND LEA GOLDMAN. 2003. "Billionaires: Survival of the Richest." *Forbes Magazine,* March 17, 2003.

KUPER, ADAM. 1982. "Lineage Theory: A Critical Retrospect." *Annual Review of Anthropology* 11:71–95.

LA LONE, DARRELL E. 1982. "The Inca as a Nonmarket Economy: Supply on Command Versus Supply and Demand." In *Contexts for Prehistoric Exchange,* edited by Jonathon Ericson and Timothy K. Earle, pp. 291–316. New York: Academic Press.

LAMBRICK, H. T. 1967. "The Indus Flood-Plain and the 'Indus' Civilization." *Geographical Journal* 133(4):483–495.

LANDSBERG, HANS H. 1964. *Natural Resources in America's Future: Patterns of Requirements and Availabilities 1960–2000.* Baltimore: Johns Hopkins University Press.

LANDSBERG, HELMUT E. 1989. "Where Do We Stand with the CO_2 Greenhouse Effect Problem?" In *Global Climate Change: Human and Natural Influences,* edited by S. Fred Singer, pp. 87–89. New York: Paragon House.

LANE-FOX PITT-RIVERS, A. H. 1882. "Anniversary Address to the Anthropological Institute of Great Britain and Ireland." *Journal of the Royal Anthropological Institute* 11(4):488–509.

LANNING, EDWARD P. 1967. *Peru Before the Incas.* Englewood Cliffs, N.J.: Prentice-Hall.

LAPPE, FRANCES MOORE, JOSEPH COLLINS, AND CARRY FOWLER. 1979. *Food First: Beyond the Myth of Scarcity.* New York: Ballantine Books.

LAPPE, FRANCES MOORE, JOSEPH COLLINS, AND DAVID KINLEY. 1981. *Aid as Obstacle: Twenty Questions About Our Foreign Aid and the Hungry.* San Francisco: Institute for Food and Development Policy.

LAPPE, FRANCES MOORE, RACHEL SCHURMAN, AND KEVIN DANAHER. 1987. *Betraying the National Interest.* New York: Grove Press.

LARICK, ROY. 1986. "Age Grading and Ethnicity in the Style of Loikop (Samburu) Spears." *World Archaeology* 18(2):269–283.

LARRICK, JAMES W., JAMES A. YOST, JON KAPLAN, GARLAND KING, AND JOHN MAYHALL. 1979. "Patterns of Health and Disease Among the Waorani Indians of Eastern Ecuador." *Medical Anthropology* 3(2):147–189.

LASCH, CHRISTOPHER. 1995. *The Revolt of the Elites and the Betrayal of Democracy.* New York: Norton.

LATHRAP, DONALD W. 1970. *The Upper Amazon.* New York: Praeger.

LATHRAP, DONALD W. 1977. "Our Father the Cayman, Our Mother the Gourd: Spinden Revisited, or a Unitary Model for the Emergence of Agriculture in the New World." In *Origins of Agriculture,* edited by C. A. Reed, pp. 713–751. The Hague: Mouton.

LEACH, EDMUND. 1964. *Political Systems of Highland Burma: A Study of Kachin Social Structure.* London School of Economics Monographs on Social Anthropology No. 44. London: The Athlone Press, University of London.

LEE, RICHARD B. 1981. "Is There a Foraging Mode of Production?" *Canadian Journal of Anthropology* 2(1):13–19.

LEE, RICHARD, AND IRVEN DEVORE (EDS.). 1968. "Problems in the Study of Hunters and Gatherers." In *Man the Hunter,* pp. 3–12. Chicago: Aldine.

LEFROY, ARCHDEACON. 1912. *The Future of Australian Aborigines.* Report of the Thirteenth Meeting of the Australasian Association for the Advancement of Science, Sydney, pp. 453–454.

LEGGE, JAMES. 1967. *Li Chi: Book of Rites,* 2 vols. New Hyde Park, N.Y.: University Books.

LEGGETT, JEREMY. 2001. *The Carbon War: Global Warming and the End of the Oil Era.* New York: Routledge.

LEONOWENS, ANNA HARRIETTE. 1870. *The English Governess at the Siamese Court: Being Recollections of Six Years in the Royal Palace at Bangkok.* Boston: Fields, Osgood.

LEONOWENS, ANNA HARRIETTE. 1953. *Siamese Harem Life.* New York: Dutton.

LEVINE, TERRY Y. 1992. "Inka State Storage in Three Highland Regions: A Comparative Study." In *Inka Storage Systems,* edited by Terry Y. Levine, pp. 107–148. Norman and London: University of Oklahoma Press.

LEVISON, M., R. G. WARD, AND J. W. WEBB. 1973. *The Settlement of Polynesia: A Computer Simulation.* Minneapolis: University of Minnesota Press.

LÉVI-STRAUSS, CLAUDE. 1944. "The Social and Psychological Aspects of Chieftainship in a Primitive Tribe: The Nambikuara of Northwestern Matto Grosso." *Transactions of the New York Academy of Sciences* 7:16–32.

LÉVI-STRAUSS, CLAUDE. [1949] 1969. *The Elementary Structures of Kinship.* Boston: Beacon Press.

LÉVI-STRAUSS, CLAUDE. 1963. *Totemism.* Boston: Beacon Press.

LÉVI-STRAUSS, CLAUDE. 1966. *The Savage Mind.* Chicago: University of Chicago Press.

LÉVI-STRAUSS, CLAUDE. 1969. *The Raw and the Cooked: Introduction to a Science of Mythology 1.* New York: Harper & Row.

LÉVI-STRAUSS, CLAUDE. 1973. *From Honey to Ashes: Introduction to a Science of Mythology 2.* New York: Harper & Row.

LÉVI-STRAUSS, CLAUDE. 1978. *The Origin of Table Manners: Introduction to a Science of Mythology 3.* New York: Harper & Row.

LEVY, REUBEN. 1962. *The Social Structure of Islam.* London: Cambridge University Press.

LÉVY-BRUHL, LUCIEN. [1922] 1923. *Primitive Mentality.* New York: Macmillan.

LÉVY-BRUHL, LUCIEN. 1926. *How Natives Think [Les Fonctions Mentales dans les Sociétés Inférieures].* New York: Knopf.

LEWIS, BERNARD. 1960. *The Arabs in History.* New York: Harper Torchbooks.

LEWIS, D. 1976. "Observations on Route-Finding and Spatial Orientation Among the Aboriginal Peoples of the Western Desert Region of Central Australia." *Oceania* 46(4):249–282.

LEWIS, OSCAR. 1959. *Five Families: Mexican Case Studies in the Culture of Poverty.* New York: Basic Books.

LEWIS, OSCAR. 1966a. "The Culture of Poverty." *Scientific American* 215(4):19–25.

LEWIS, OSCAR. 1966b. *La Vida: A Puerto Rican Family in the Culture of Poverty—San Juan and New York.* New York: Random House.

LINDENBAUM, SHIRLEY. 1987. "Loaves and Fishes in Bangladesh." In *Food and Evolution: Toward a Theory of Human Food Habits,* edited by Marvin Harris and Eric Ross, pp. 427–443. Philadelphia: Temple University Press.

LINDERT, PETER H. AND JEFFREY G. WILLIAMSON. 1982. "Revising England's Social Tables 1688–1812." *Explorations in Economic History* 19:385–408.

LINDERT, PETER H. AND JEFFREY G. WILLIAMSON. 1983. "Reinterpreting Britain's Social Tables, 1688–1913." *Explorations in Economic History* 20:94–109.

LINNEKIN, JOCELYN. 1985. *Children of the Land: Exchange and Status in a Hawaiian Community.* New Brunswick, New Jersey: Rutgers University Press.

LINNEKIN, JOCELYN. 1990. *Sacred Queens and Women of Consequence; Rank, Gender, and Colonialism in the Hawaiian Islands.* Ann Arbor: University of Michigan Press.

LIPPMAN, WALTER. 1929. *A Preface to Morals.* New York: Macmillan.

LITTLE, MICHAEL A., AND GEORGE E. B. MORREN, JR. 1976. *Ecology, Energetics, and Human Variability.* Dubuque, Iowa: Brown.

LIZOT, JACQUES. 1977. "Population, Resources and Warfare Among the Yanomami." *Man* 12(3/4):497–517.

LIZOT, JACQUES. 1985. *Tales of the Yanomami: Daily Life in the Venezuelan Forest.* Cambridge, Eng.: Cambridge University Press.

LOBEL, PHIL S. 1978. "Gilbertese and Ellice Islander Names for Fishes and Other Organisms." *Micronesica* 14(2):177–197.

LOUNSBURY, FLOYD G. 1964. "A Formal Account of the Crow- and Omaha-Type Kinship Terminologies." In *Explorations in Cultural Anthropology,* edited by Ward Goodenough, pp. 351–393. New York: McGraw-Hill.

LOURANDOS, HARRY. 1985. "Intensification and Australian Prehistory." In *Prehistoric Hunter-Gatherers: The Emergence of Cultural Complexity,* edited by Douglas Price and James A. Brown, pp. 385–423. New York: Academic Press.

LOURANDOS, HARRY. 1987. "Pleistocene Australia: Peopling a Continent." In *The Pleistocene Old World: Regional Perspectives,* edited by Olga Soffer, pp. 147–165. New York: Plenum.

LOZOFF, BETSY, AND GARY M. BRITTENHAM. 1977. "Field Methods for the Assessment of Health and Disease in Pre-Agricultural Societies." In *Health and Disease in Tribal Societies,* pp. 49–67. CIBA Foundation Symposium, no. 49. Amsterdam: Elsevier/Excerpta Medica/North-Holland.

LUTEN, DANIEL B. 1974. "United States Requirements." In *Energy, the Environment, and Human Health,* edited by A. Finkel, pp. 17–33. Acton, Mass.: Publishing Sciences Group.

LYONS, WILLIAM H. 1995. "Sleepy in Sarnath: Forager Time Storage and Food Resources of Semiarid Regions." Paper presented at the 49th Annual Northwest Anthropological Conference, Moscow, Idaho.

MAGER, NATHAN H. 1987. *The Kondratieff Waves.* New York: Praeger.

MAISELS, CHARLES KEITH. 1990. *The Emergence of Civilization: From Hunting and Gathering to Agriculture, Cities, and the State in the Near East.* London and New York: Routledge.

MALINOWSKI, BRONISLAW. 1929. "Practical Anthropology." *Africa* 2(1):22–38.

MALINOWSKI, BRONISLAW. 1944. *A Scientific Theory of Culture.* Chapel Hill: University of North Carolina Press.

MALO, DAVID. 1951. *Hawaiian Antiquities,* 2nd ed. Bernice P. Bishop Museum Special Publication, no. 2. Honolulu: Bernice P. Bishop Museum.

MALTHUS, THOMAS R. [1798, 1807] 1895. *An Essay on the Principle of Population.* New York: Macmillan.

MANDER, JERRY. 1978. *Four Arguments for the Elimination of Television.* New York: Quill.

MANDER, JERRY. 1996. "The Rules of Corporate Behavior." In *The Case Against the Global Economy and for a Turn Toward the Local,* edited by Jerry Mander and Edward Goldsmith, pp. 309–322. San Francisco: Sierra Club Books.

MANN, MICHAEL. 1986. *The Sources of Social Power,* Vol. 1, *A History of Power from the Beginning to AD 1760.* Cambridge, Eng.: Cambridge University Press.

MANNERS, ROBERT A. 1956. "Functionalism, Realpolitik, and Anthropology in Under-Developed Areas." *America Indigena* 16(1):7–33.

MANNHEIM, BRUCE. 1991. *The Language of the Inka Since the European Invasion.* Austin: University of Texas Press.

MARANO, LOUIS A. 1973. "A Macrohistoric Trend Toward World Government." *Behavior Science Notes, HRAF Quarterly Bulletin* 8(1):35–39.

MARCHAND, ROLAND. 1998. *Creating the Corporate Soul: The Rise of Public Relations and Corporate Imagery in American Big Business.* Berkeley: University of California Press.

MARKS, JONATHAN. 1995. "Egalitarianism and Human Biodiversity." *Anthropology Newsletter* 36(9):20.

MARSH, GEORGE PERKINS. 1864. *Man and Nature: Physical Geography as Modified by Human Action.* New York: Scribner.

MARTIN, P. S. 1967. "Prehistoric Overkill." In *Pleistocene Extinctions,* edited by P. S. Martin and H. E. Wright, Jr., pp. 75–120. New Haven, Conn.: Yale University Press.

MARX, KARL, AND FRIEDRICH ENGELS. 1967. *The Communist Manifesto*. London: Penguin Books.

MAYER, ADRIAN C. 1970. *Caste and Kinship in Central India: A Village and Its Region*. Berkeley and Los Angeles: University of California Press.

MAYHEW, BRUCE H., AND PAUL T. SCHOLLAERT. 1980a. "Social Morphology of Pareto's Economic Elite." *Social Forces* 59(1):25–43.

MAYHEW, BRUCE H., AND PAUL T. SCHOLLAERT. 1980b. "The Concentration of Wealth: A Sociological Model." *Sociological Focus* 13(1):1–35.

MAYHEW, HENRY. 1861–62. *London Labour and the London Poor*, 4 vols. London: Griffin, Bohn. (Reprinted 1968. New York: Dover.)

MCARTHUR, MARGARET. 1960. "Food Consumption and Dietary Levels of Groups of Aborigines Living on Naturally Occurring Foods." In *Records of the American-Australian Scientific Expedition to Arnhem Land*. Vol. 2 of *Anthropology and Nutrition*, edited by Charles Mountford, pp. 90–135. Melbourne: Melbourne University Press.

MCCABE, J. TERRENCE. 1990. "Turkana Pastoralism: A Case Against the Tragedy of the Commons." *Human Ecology* 18:81–103.

MCCABE, J. TERRENCE. 2003. "Sustainability and Livelihood Diversification Among the Maasai of Northern Tanzania." *Human Organization* 62(2):100–111.

MCCARTHY, F. D., AND MARGARET MCARTHUR. 1960. "The Food Quest and Time Factor in Aboriginal Economic Life." *Records of the American-Australian Scientific Expedition to Arnhem Land*. Vol. 2 of *Anthropology and Nutrition*, edited by Charles Mountford, pp. 145–194. Melbourne: Melbourne University Press.

MCCAY, BONNIE J., AND JAMES M. ACHESON (EDS.). 1987. *The Question of the Commons: The Culture and Ecology of Communal Resources*. Tucson: University of Arizona Press.

MCCHESNEY, ROBERT W. 2000. *Rich Media, Poor Democracy: Communication Politics in Dubious Times*. New York: The New Press.

MCCLOSKEY, DONALD N. 1976. "English Open Fields as Behavior Towards Risk." *Research in Economic History* 1: 124–170.

MCCORRISTON, JOY. 1997. "The Fiber Revolution: Textile Extensification, Alienation, and Social Stratification in Ancient Mesopotamia." *Current Anthropology* 38(4):517–549.

MCCOY, JOHN. 1970. "Chinese Kin Terms of Reference and Address." In *Family and Kinship in Chinese Society*, edited by Maurice Freedman, pp. 209–226. Stanford, Calif.: Stanford University Press.

MCCURDY, CHARLES W. 1978. "American Law and the Marketing Structure of the Large Corporation, 1875–1890." *The Journal of Economic History* 38(3):631–649.

MCDONALD, DAVID. 1977. "Food Taboos: A Primitive Environmental Protection Agency (South America)." *Anthropos* 72: 734–748.

MCDONALD, FORREST. 1958. *We the People: The Economic Origins of the Constitution*. Chicago: University of Chicago Press.

MCDONALD, FORREST. 1979. *E. Pluribus Unum: The Formation of the American Republic*, 2nd ed. Indianapolis, Ind.: Liberty Press.

MCDONALD, FORREST. 1985. *Novus Ordo Seclorum: The Intellectual Origins of the Constitution*. Lawrence: University Press of Kansas.

MCEVEDY, COLIN, AND RICHARD JONES. 1978. *Atlas of World Population History*. Middlesex, England and New York: Penguin Books.

MCGREW, W. C. 1992. *Chimpanzee Material Culture*. Cambridge, Eng.: Cambridge University Press.

MCNEILL, WILLIAM H. 1982. *The Pursuit of Power: Technology, Armed Force, and Society since A.D. 100*. Chicago: The University of Chicago Press.

MCNEIL, WILLIAM H. 1987. *A History of the Human Community: Prehistory to the Present*. Englewood Cliffs, N.J.: Prentice-Hall.

MEAD, MARGARET. 1942. *And Keep Your Powder Dry: An Anthropologist Looks at America*. New York: Morrow.

MEAD, MARGARET. 1961. *New Lives for Old*. New York: New American Library.

MEADOWS, DONELLA H., DENNIS L. MEADOWS, AND JORGEN RANDERS. 1992. *Beyond the Limits: Confronting Global Collapse, Envisioning a Sustainable Future*. Post Mills, Vt.: Chelsea Green.

MEADOWS, DONELLA H., DENNIS L. MEADOWS, JORGEN RANDERS, AND WILLIAM W. BEHRENS III. 1972. *The Limits to Growth*. New York: Universe.

MEEHAN, BETTY. 1982. "Ten Fish for One Man: Some Anbarra Attitudes Towards Food and Health." In *Body, Land and Spirit: Health and Healing in Aboriginal Society*, edited by Janice Reid, pp. 96–120. St. Lucia: University of Queensland Press.

MEGGERS, BETTY J. 1954. "Environmental Limitation on the Development of Culture." *American Anthropologist* 56(5, pt. 1):801–824.

MEGGERS, BETTY J. 1971. *Amazonia: Man and Culture in a Counterfeit Paradise*. Arlington Heights, Ill.: AHM.

MEILLASSOUX, CLAUDE. 1981. *Maidens, Meal and Money: Capitalism and the Domestic Community*. Cambridge, Eng.: Cambridge University Press.

MELLAART, J. 1967. *Çatal Hüyük: A Neolithic Town in Anatolia*. London: Thames & Hudson.

MERRILEES, D. 1968. "Man the Destroyer: Late Quaternary Changes in the Australian Marsupial Fauna." *Journal of the Royal Society of Western Australia* 51:1–24.

MESAROVIC, MIHAJLO, AND EDUARD PESTEL. 1974. *Mankind at the Turning Point: The Second Report of the Club of Rome*. New York: New American Library.

MICHAEL, FRANZ. 1964. "State and Society in Nineteenth-Century China." In *Modern China*, edited by Albert Feuerwerker, pp. 57–69. Englewood Cliffs, N.J.: Prentice-Hall.

MIGLIAZZA, ERNEST C. 1982. "Linguistic Prehistory and the Refuge Model in Amazonia." In *Biological Diversification in the Tropics*, edited by Ghillean Prance, pp. 497–519. New York: Columbia University Press.

MILANOVIC, BRANKO. 2002. "True World Income Distribution, 1988 and 1993: First Calculations Based on Household Surveys Alone." *The Economic Journal* 112(476):51–92.

MILLER, DANIEL. 1985. "Ideology and the Harappan Civilization." *Journal of Anthropological Archaeology* 4:34–71.

MILLER, EDWARD, AND JOHN HATCHER. 1995. *Medieval England: Towns, Commerce and Crafts 1086–1348*. London and New York: Longman.

MILLER, SOLOMON. 1967. "Hacienda to Plantation in Northern Peru: The Processes of Proletarianization of a Tenant Farmer Society." In *Contemporary Change in Traditional Societies*.

Vol. 3, *Mexican and Peruvian Communities,* edited by Julian Steward, pp. 133–225. Urbana: University of Illinois Press.

MILLS, C. WRIGHT. 1956. *The Power Elite.* New York: Oxford University Press.

MINER, HORACE M. 1955. "Planning for the Acculturation of Isolated Tribes." *Proceedings of the 31st International Congress of Americanists* 1:441–446.

MINTZ, SIDNEY W. 1985. *Sweetness and Power: The Place of Sugar in Modern History.* New York: Viking Press/Penguin Books.

MINTZ, SIDNEY W., AND ERIC R. WOLF. 1957. "Haciendas and Plantations in Middle America and the Antilles." *Social and Economic Studies* 6:380–412.

MONTAGU, ASHLEY. 1972. "Sociogenic Brain Damage." *American Anthropologist* 74(5):1045–1061.

MOODY, JOHN. 1904. *The Truth About the Trusts: A Description and Analysis of the American Trust Movement.* New York: Moody Publishing.

MOORE, ANDREW M. T. 1983. "The First Farmers in the Levant." In *The Hilly Flanks and Beyond: Essays on the Prehistory of Southwestern Asia,* pp. 91–111. Studies in Ancient Oriental Civilization, no. 36. Chicago: Oriental Institute, University of Chicago.

MOORE, A. M. T., G. C. HILLMAN, AND A. J. LEGGE. 2000. *Village on the Euphrates: From Foraging to Farming at Abu Hureyra.* New York: Oxford University Press.

MORGAN, DAN. 1979. *Merchants of Grain.* New York: Viking Press.

MORGAN, LEWIS HENRY. 1851. *League of the Ho-de-no-saunee, or Iroquois.* Rochester, N.Y.: Sage.

MORGAN, LEWIS HENRY. 1877. *Ancient Society.* New York: Holt.

MORRIS, CRAIG, AND DONALD E. THOMPSON. 1985. *Huanaco Pampa: An Inca City and Its Hinterland.* London: Thames & Hudson.

MORRISON, ROY. 1991. *We Build the Road as We Travel.* Philadelphia: New Society Publishers.

MOSELEY, MICHAEL EDWARD. 1975. *The Maritime Foundations of Andean Civilization.* Menlo Park, Calif.: Cummings.

MOSELEY, MICHAEL E., AND K. C. DAY (EDS.). 1980. *Chan Chan: The Desert City and Its Hinterland.* Albuquerque: University of New Mexico Press.

MOSELEY, MICHAEL E., AND CAROL J. MACKEY. 1973. "Chan Chan, Peru's Ancient City of Kings." *National Geographic* 143(3):318–345.

MOUNTFORD, CHARLES P. 1965. *Ayers Rock: Its People, Their Beliefs, and Their Art.* Honolulu: East-West Center Press.

MUNN, NANCY D. 1969. "The Effectiveness of Symbols in Murngin Rite and Ritual." In *Forms of Symbolic Action: Proceedings of the 1969 Annual Spring Meeting of the American Ethnological Society,* edited by Robert Spencer, pp. 178–207. Seattle and London: American Ethnological Society.

MUNN, NANCY D. 1973. *Walbiri Iconography: Graphic Representation and Cultural Symbolism in a Central Australian Society.* Ithaca, N.Y., and London: Cornell University Press.

MURAL, MARY, FLORENCE PEN, AND CAREY D. MILLER. 1958. *Some Tropical South Pacific Island Foods: Description, History, Use, Composition, and Nutritive Value.* Hawaii Agricultural Experiment Station, bull. 110. Honolulu: University of Hawaii Press.

MURDOCK, GEORGE P. 1949. *Social Structure.* New York: Macmillan.

MURDOCK, GEORGE P. 1981. *Atlas of World Cultures.* Pittsburgh: University of Pittsburgh Press.

MURPHY, ROBERT F. 1957. "Intergroup Hostility and Social Cohesion." *American Anthropologist* 58:414–434.

MURPHY, ROBERT F. 1960. *Headhunter's Heritage.* Berkeley: University of California Press.

MURPHY, YOLANDA, AND ROBERT F. MURPHY. 1974. *Women of the Forest.* New York and London: Columbia University Press.

MURRA, JOHN V. 1960. "Rite and Crop in the Inca State." In *Culture in History: Essays in Honor of Paul Radin,* edited by Stanley Diamond, pp. 393–407. New York: Columbia University Press.

MURRA, J. V. 1972. "'El Control Vertical' de un Maximo de Pisos Ecologicos en la Economia de las Sociedades Andinas." In *Vista de la Provincia de Leon de Huanuco (1562),* Vol. 2, edited by Inigo Ortiz de Zuniga, pp. 429–476. Huanuco, Peru: Universidad Hermillo Valdizan.

MYERS, FRED R. 1980. "The Cultural Basis of Politics in Pintupi Life." *Mankind* 12(3):197–214.

MYERS, NORMAN AND JENNIFER KENT. 2001. *Perverse Subsidies: How Tax Dollars Can Undercut the Environment and the Economy.* Washington, D.C.: Island Press.

MYERS, RICHARD B. 2003. "Shift to a Global Perspective." *Naval War College Review* 56(4):9–17.

NAROLL, RAOUL. 1962. "Floor Area and Settlement Population." *American Antiquity* 27(4):587–589.

NAROLL, RAOUL. 1967. "Imperial Cycles and World Order." *Peace Research Society (International) Papers* 7:83–101.

NASH, JUNE. 1989. *From Tank Town to High Tech: The Clash of Community and Industrial Cycles.* Albany: State University of New York Press.

NASH, JUNE. 1994. "Global Integration and Subsistence Insecurity." *American Anthropologist* 96(1):7–30.

NATIONAL CENTER FOR HEALTH STATISTICS. 1998. *Health, United States, 1998.* Washington, D.C.: U.S. Government Printing Office.

NATIONAL PROVISIONER. 1990a. *National Provisioner* 202(2).

NATIONAL PROVISIONER. 1990b. *National Provisioner* 202(9).

NATIONAL RESEARCH COUNCIL, COMMITTEE ON MINERAL RESOURCES AND THE ENVIRONMENT. 1975. *Mineral Resources and the Environment.* Washington, D.C.: National Academy of Sciences.

NEEL, JAMES V. 1970. "Lessons from a 'Primitive' People." *Science* 170(3960):815–822.

NESTLE, MARION. 2002. *Food Politics: How the Food Industry Influences Nutrition and Health.* Berkeley: University of California Press.

NEWCOMER, PETER J. 1972. "The Nuer Are Dinka: An Essay on Origins and Environmental Determinism." *Man* 7(1):5–11.

NEWMAN, KATHERINE S. 1988. *Falling from Grace: The Experience of Downward Mobility in the American Middle Class.* New York: Free Press.

NEWMAN, KATHERINE S. 1993. *Declining Fortunes: The Withering of the American Dream.* New York: Basic Books.

NEWMYER, R. KENT. 1987. "Harvard Law School, New England Legal Culture, and the Antebellum Origins of American Jurisprudence." *The Journal of American History* 74(3): 814–835.

NICHOLLS, ROBERT J., FRANK M. J. HOOZEMANS, AND MAR-
CEL MARCHAND. 1999. "Increasing flood risk and wetland
losses due to global sea-level rise: regional and global analyses." *Global Environmental Change* 9 (supplement 1), pages
S69–S87.

NIETSCHMANN, BERNARD. 1988. "Third World Colonial Expansion: Indonesia, Disguised Invasion of Indigenous Nations." *Tribal Peoples and Development Issues: A Global
Overview*, edited by John H. Bodley, pp. 191–207. Mountain
View, Calif.: Mayfield.

NILES, SUSAN A. 1999. *The Shape of Inca History: Narrative and
Architecture in an Andean Empire.* Iowa City: University of
Iowa Press.

NISSEN, HANS J. 1986. "The Archaic Texts from Uruk." *World
Archaeology* 17(3):317–334.

NOBLE, DAVID F. 1977. *America by Design: Science, Technology, and the Rise of Corporate Capitalism.* New York: Alfred
A. Knopf.

NOBLE, DAVID F. 1993. *Progress Without People: In Defense of
Luddism.* Chicago: Keer.

NOLL, RICHARD. 1984. "The Context of Schizophrenia and
Shamanism." *American Ethnologist* 11(1):191–192.

OATES, JOAN. 1993. "Trade and Power in the Fifth and Fourth
Millennia BC: New Evidence from Northern Mesopotamia."
World Archaeology 24(3):403–422.

OCHOLLA-AYAYO, A. B. C. 1979. "Marriage and Cattle Exchange Among the Nilotic Luo." *Paideuma* 25:173–193.

O'CONNELL, JAMES F., AND KRISTEN HAWKES. 1981. "Alya-
wara Plant Use and Optimal Foraging Theory." In *Hunter-
Gatherer Foraging Strategies,* edited by B. Winterhalder and
E. A. Smith, pp. 99–125. Chicago: University of Chicago Press.

ODUM, HOWARD T. 1971. *Environment, Power, and Society.*
New York: Wiley Inter-Science.

OLIVER, DOUGLAS L. 1989. *Oceania: The Native Cultures of
Australia and the Pacific Islands,* 2 vols. Honolulu: University
of Hawaii Press.

OLSSON, KAREN. 2002. "The Shame of Meatpacking." *The Nation* 275(8):11–16.

ONERN (OFICINA NACIONAL DE EVALUACIÓN DE RECURSOS
NATURALES). 1968. *Inventario, Evaluación e Integración de
los Recursos Naturales de la Zona del Rio Tambo-Gran Pajonal.* Lima: ONERN.

ORLOVE, BENJAMIN S. 1987. "Stability and Change in Highland
Andean Dietary Patterns." In *Food and Evolution: Toward a
Theory of Human Food Habits,* edited by Marvin Harris and
Eric Ross, pp. 481–515. Philadelphia: Temple University Press.

ORTNER, S. 1996. *Making Gender: the Politics and Erotics of
Culture.* Boston: Beacon Press.

ORWIN, C. S., AND C. S. ORWIN. 1967. *The Open Fields.* Oxford, Eng.: Clarendon Press.

PALMER, INGRID. 1972. *Science and Agricultural Production.*
Geneva: UN Research Institute for Social Development.

PAPANEK, HANNA. 1982. "Purdah: Separate Worlds and Sym-
bolic Shelter." In *Separate Worlds: Studies of Purdah in South
Asia,* edited by Hanna Papanek and Gail Minault, pp. 3–53.
Delhi: Chanakya.

PARKINSON, C. NORTHCOTE. 1957. *Parkinson's Law and Other
Studies in Administration.* Boston: Houghton Mifflin.

PARRY, JONATHAN P. 1979. *Caste and Kinship in Kangra.* London: Routledge & Kegan Paul.

PAULSON, ALLISON C. 1974. "The Thorny Oyster and the Voice
of God: Spondylus and Strombus in Andean Prehistory."
American Antiquity 39(4):597–607.

PERKINS, DWIGHT H. 1969. *Agricultural Development in China
1368–1968.* Chicago: Aldine.

PERRY, W. J. 1923. *The Children of the Sun.* London: Methuen.

PESSEN, EDWARD. 1971. "The Egalitarian Myth and the American Social Reality: Wealth, Mobility, and Equality in the 'Era
of the Common Man.'" *The American Historical Review*
76(4):989–1034.

PESSEN, EDWARD. 1973. *Riches, Class, and Power Before the
Civil War.* Lexington, Mass.: Heath.

PETERS, LARRY G., AND DOUGLASS PRICE-WILLIAMS. 1980.
"Towards an Experiential Analysis of Shamanism." *American
Ethnologist* 7(3):397–418.

PETERSON, NICOLAS. 1986. *Australian Territorial Organization.*
Oceania Monograph, no. 30. Sydney: University of Sydney.

PETERSON, N. 1997. *Demand Sharing: Sociobiology and the
Pressure for Generosity among Foragers.* In *Scholar and Scep-
tic: Australian Aboriginal Studies in Honour of L. R. Hiatt,*
edited by F. Merlan, J. Morton and A. Rumsey, pp. 171–190.
Aboriginal Studies Press, Canberra.

PHILLIPS, KEVIN. 1990. *The Politics of Rich and Poor: Wealth
and the American Electorate in the Reagan Aftermath.* New
York: Random House.

PHILLIPS, KEVIN. 1994. *Arrogant Capital: Washington, Wall
Street, and the Frustration of American Politics.* Boston: Little, Brown.

PHILLIPS, KEVIN. 2002. *Wealth and Democracy: A Political History of the American Rich.* New York: Broadway Books.

PHILLIPSON, DAVID W. 1985. *African Archaeology.* Cambridge,
Eng.: Cambridge University Press.

PIETRASZEK, GREG. 1990. "Cattlemen Face Future Competition
with Confidence." *National Provisioner* 202(12):5–8.

PIKE, KENNETH L. 1954. *Language in Relation to a Unified Theory of the Structure of Human Behavior,* vol. 1. The Hague:
Mouton.

PILLSBURY, JOANNE. 1996. "The Thorny Oyster and the Origins
of Empire: Implications of Recently Uncovered Spondylus Imagery from Chan Chan, Peru." *Latin American Antiquity*
7(4):313–340.

PIMENTEL, DAVID, AND ANTHONY GREINER. 1997. "Environmental and Socio-Economic Costs of Pesticide Use." In *Techniques for Reducing Pesticide Use: Economic and Environmental
Benefits,* edited by David Pimentel, pp. 51–78. Chichester, England: John Wiley & Sons.

PLOG, STEPHEN. 1995. "Equality and Hierarchy: Holistic Ap-
proaches to Understanding Social Dynamics in the Pueblo
Southwest." In *Foundations of Social Inequality,* edited by
T. Douglas Price and Gary M. Feinman, pp. 189–206. New
York and London: Plenum Press.

POLANYI, KARL. 1977. *The Livelihood of Man.* New York: Academic Press.

POPKIN, BARRY M. 1998. "The Nutrition Transition and its
Health Implications in Lower-Income Countries." *Public
Health Nutrition* 1(1):5–21.

PORTEUS, S. D. 1917. "Mental Tests with Delinquents and Australian Aboriginal Children." *Psychological Review* 24(1):
32–42. (Reprinted in *The Psychology of Aboriginal Australians,* edited by G. E. Kearney, P. R. de Lacey, and G. R.
Davidson, pp. 29–37. Sydney: Wiley, 1973.)

PORTEUS, S. D. 1931. *The Psychology of a Primitive People.* London: E. Arnold.

POSPISIL, LEOPOLD. 1972. *The Ethnology of Law.* Addison-Wesley Module in Anthropology, no. 12. Reading, Mass.: Addison-Wesley.

POSSEHL, GREGORY L. 1967. "The Mohenjo-Daro Floods: A Reply." *American Anthropologist* 69(1):32–40.

POSSEHL, GREGORY L. 1977. "The End of a State and Continuity of a Tradition: A Discussion of the Late Harappa." In *Realm and Region in Traditional India,* edited by Richard Fox, pp. 234–254. Program in Comparative Studies on Southern Asia, Duke University. Monograph and Occasional Papers Series, Monograph no. 14. Durham, N.C.

POUMISAK, JIT (pseudonym SOMSAMAI SRISUDRAVARNA). 1987. "The Real Face of Thai Saktina Today." In *Thai Radical Discourse: The Real Face of Thai Feudalism Today,* editor and translator Craig J. Reynolds, pp. 43–148. Studies on Southeast Asia, Cornell University, Ithaca, New York.

PRICE, A. G. 1950. *White Settlers and Native Peoples.* London: Cambridge University Press.

PRICE, WESTON ANDREW. 1945. *Nutrition and Physical Degeneration: A Comparison of Primitive and Modern Diets and Their Effects.* Redlands, Calif.: Weston Price.

PUKUI, MARY KAWENA AND SAMUEL H. ELBERT. 1986. *Hawaiian Dictionary.* Honolulu: University of Hawaii Press.

PYLE, TOM. 1964. *Pocantico: Fifty Years on the Rockefeller Domain.* New York: Duell, Sloan & Pearce.

QUILTER, JEFFREY, AND TERRY STOCKER. 1983. "Subsistence Economies and the Origins of Andean Complex Societies." *American Anthropologist* 85(3):545–562.

RABB, THEODORE K. 1967. *Enterprise and Empire: Merchant and Gentry Investment in the Expansion of England, 1575–1630.* Cambridge, Mass.: Harvard University Press.

RABIBHADANA, AKIN. 1969. *The Organization of Thai Society in the Early Bangkok Period, 1782–1873.* Data Paper: Number 74, South East Asia Program, Department of Asian Studies. Cornell University, Ithaca, New York.

RADCLIFFE-BROWN, A. R. 1913. "Three Tribes of Western Australia." *Journal of the Royal Anthropological Institute* 43: 143–195.

RADCLIFFE-BROWN, A. R. 1918. "Notes on the Social Organization of Australian Tribes." *Journal of the Royal Anthropological Institute* 48:222–253.

RADCLIFFE-BROWN, A. R. 1929. "The Sociological Theory of Totemism." Proceedings of the Fourth Pacific Science Congress. (Reprinted in *Structure and Function in Primitive Society,* edited by A. R. Radcliffe-Brown, pp. 117–132. New York: Free Press, 1965.)

RADCLIFFE-BROWN, A. R. 1941. "The Study of Kinship Systems." *Journal of the Royal Anthropological Institute.* (Reprinted in *Structure and Function in Primitive Society,* edited by A. R. Radcliffe-Brown, pp. 49–89. New York: Free Press, 1965.)

RADCLIFFE-BROWN, A. R. 1958. Presidential Address to Section E. South African Association for the Advancement of Science, July 1928. (In *Method in Social Anthropology: Selected Essays by A. R. Radcliffe-Brown,* edited by M. N. Srinivas. Chicago: University of Chicago Press.)

RADIN, PAUL. 1971. *The World of Primitive Man.* New York: Dutton.

RAIKES, ROBERT L. 1964. "The End of the Ancient Cities of the Indus." *American Anthropologist* 66(2):284–299.

RAIKES, ROBERT L. 1965. "The Mohenjo-Daro Floods." *Antiquity* 38(155):196–203.

RAMOS, ALCIDA R. 1987. "Reflecting on the Yanomami: Ethnograpic Images and the Pursuit of the Exotic." *Cultural Anthropology* 2(3):284–304.

RANDALL, ROBERT A., AND EUGENE S. HUNN. 1984. "Do Life-Forms Evolve or Do Uses for Life? Some Doubts About Brown's Universals Hypotheses." *American Ethnologist* 1(2): 329–349.

RAO, S. R. 1982. "New Light on the Post-Urban (Late Harappan) Phase of the Indus Civilization in India." In *Harappan Civilization: A Contemporary Perspective,* edited by Gregory Possehl, pp. 353–359. New Delhi: Oxford and IBH.

RAPPAPORT, ROY A. 1977a. "Maladaptation in Social Systems." In *The Evolution of Social Systems,* edited by J. Friedman and M. J. Rowlands, pp. 49–71. London: Duckworth.

RAPPAPORT, ROY A. 1977b. "Normative Models of Adaptive Processes: A Response to Anne Whyte." In *The Evolution of Social Systems,* edited by J. Friedman and M. J. Rowlands pp. 79–87. London: Duckworth.

RAWSKI, EVELYN S. 1987. "Popular Culture in China." In *Tradition and Creativity: Essays on East Asian Civilization,* edited by Ching-I Tu, pp. 41–65. New Brunswick, N.J., and Oxford, Eng.: Transaction Books.

READ, C. H.. 1901. "Presidential Address." *Journal of the Royal Anthropological Institute* 31:14–15.

READ, DWIGHT W. 2002. "A multitrajectory, competition model of emergent complexity in human social organization." *Proceedings of the National Academy of Sciences* Vol. 99, Supplement 3, 7251–7256.

REDFIELD, ROBERT. 1941. *The Folk Culture of Yucatan.* Chicago: University of Chicago Press.

REDFIELD, ROBERT. 1947. "The Folk Society." *American Journal of Sociology* 52(4):295–298.

REDFIELD, ROBERT, RALPH LINTON, AND MELVILLE J. HERSKOVITS. 1936. "Memorandum for the Study of Acculturation." *American Anthropologist* 38(1):149–152.

REDMAN, CHARLES L. 1978a. "Mesopotamian Urban Ecology: The Systemic Context of the Emergence of Urbanism." In *Social Archaeology: Beyond Subsistence and Dating,* edited by Charles Redman, Mary Jane Berman, Edward Curtin, William Langhorne, Jr., Nina Versaggi, and Jeffery Wanser, pp. 329–347. New York: Academic Press.

REDMAN, CHARLES L. 1978b. *The Rise of Civilization: From Early Farmers to Urban Society in the Ancient Near East.* San Francisco: Freeman.

REEVES, ROSSER. 1961. *Reality in Advertising.* New York: Knopf.

REICH, ROBERT B. 1992. *The Work of Nations.* New York: Vintage Books/Random House.

REICHEL-DOLMATOFF, GERARDO. 1971. *Amazonian Cosmos: The Sexual and Religious Symbolism of the Tukano Indians.* Chicago: University of Chicago Press.

REICHEL-DOLMATOFF, GERARDO. 1976. "Cosmology as Ecological Analysis: A View from the Rain Forest." *Man* 11(3): 307–318.

RENFREW, COLIN. 1989. "The Origins of Indo-European Languages." *Scientific American* 261(4):106–114.

RESER, JOSEPH. 1981. "Australian Aboriginal Man's Inhumanity to Man: A Case of Cultural Distortion." *American Anthropologist* 83(2):387–393.

RIBEIRO, DARCY. 1957. *Culturas e Linguas Indigenas do Brasil.* Separata de Educação e Ciencias Soçais, no. 6. Rio de Janeiro: Centro Brasileiro de Pesquisas Educaçionais.

RICHARDS, PAUL W. 1973. "The Tropical Rain Forest." *Scientific American* 229(6):58–67.

RIFKIN, JEREMY. 1992. *Beyond Beef: The Rise and Fall of the Cattle Culture.* New York: Plume, Penguin.

RIIS, JACOB A. 1904. *How the Other Half Lives: Studies Among the Tenements of New York.* New York: Scribner.

RITZER, GEORGE. 2000. *The McDonaldization of Society.* Thousand Oaks, Calif.: Pine Forge Press.

RIVIERE, PETER. 1969. *Marriage Among the Trio: A Principle of Social Organization.* Oxford, Eng.: Clarendon Press.

ROBERTS, CLAYTON AND DAVID ROBERTS. 1980. *A History of England: Prehistory to 1714.* Volume 1. Englewood Cliffs, N.J.: Prentice-Hall.

ROBERTS, RICHARD G., RHYS JONES, AND M. A. SMITH. 1990. "Thermoluminescence Dating of a 50,000-Year-Old Human Occupation Site in Northern Australia." *Nature* 345:153–156.

ROCHESTER, ANN. 1936. *Rulers of America: A Study of Finance Capital.* New York: International.

RODSETH, LARS, RICHARD W. WRANGHAM, ALISA M. HARRIGAN, BARBARA B. SMUTS. 1991. "The Human Community as a Primate Society." *Current Anthropology* 32(3):221–254.

ROE, PETER G. 1982. *The Cosmic Zygote: Cosmology in the Amazon Basin.* New Brunswick, N.J.: Rutgers University Press.

ROGERS, ALISON. 1993. "Billionaires: The World's 101 Richest People." *Fortune,* June 28, pp. 36–66.

ROSS, JANE BENNETT. 1984. "Effects of Contact on Revenge Hostilities Among the Achuara Jivaro." In *Warfare, Culture, and Environment,* edited by R. Brian Ferguson, pp. 83–109. New York: Academic Press.

ROSS, W. McGREGOR. 1927. *Kenya from Within: A Short Political History.* London: Allen & Unwin.

ROSTOW, W. W. 1960. *The Process of Economic Growth.* New York: Norton.

ROWE, JOHN H. 1982. "Inca Policies and Institutions Relating to the Cultural Unification of the Empire." In *The Inca and Aztec States 1400–1800,* edited by George Collier, Renato Rosaldo, and John Wirth, pp. 93–118. New York: Academic Press.

ROWLAND, F. SHERWOOD. 1989. "Chlorofluorocarbons, Stratospheric Ozone, and the Antarctic 'Ozone Hole.'" In *Global Climate Change: Human and Natural Influences,* edited by S. Fred Singer, pp. 113–155. New York: Paragon House.

ROY, MANISHA. 1975. *Bengali Women.* Chicago and London: University of Chicago Press.

ROY, WILLIAM G. 1997. *Socializing Capital: The Rise of the Large Industrial Corporation in America.* Princeton, N.J.: Princeton University Press.

RUBINSTEIN, DON. 1978. "Native Place-Names and Geographic Systems of Fais, Caroline Islands." *Micronesica* 14(1):69–82.

RUBINSTEIN, W. D. 1981. *Men of Property: The Very Wealthy in Britain Since the Industrial Revolution.* New Brunswick, N.J.: Rutgers University Press.

RUHLEN, MERRITT. 1987. *A Guide to the World's Languages,* Vol. 1, *Classification.* Stanford, Calif.: Stanford University Press.

RUMMEL, R. J. 1997. *Death by Government.* New Brunswick, N.J.: Transaction.

RUTTAN, LORE M., AND MONIQUE BORGERHOFF MULDER. 1999. "Are East African Pastoralists Truly Conservationists?" *Current Anthropology* 40(5):621–652.

SAFINA, CARL. 1995. "The World's Imperiled Fish." *Scientific American* 273(4):46–53.

SAHLINS, MARSHALL. 1958. *Social Stratification in Polynesia.* Seattle: University of Washington Press.

SAHLINS, MARSHALL. 1961. "The Segmentary Lineage: An Organization of Predatory Expansion." *American Anthropologist* 63(2, pt. 1):322–345.

SAHLINS, MARSHALL. 1963. "Poor Man, Rich Man, Big-Man, Chief: Political Types in Melanesia and Polynesia." *Comparative Studies in Society and History* 5:285–303.

SAHLINS, MARSHALL. 1965. "On the Ideology and Composition of Descent Groups." *Man* 65 (July/August):104–107.

SAHLINS, MARSHALL. 1968. "Notes on the Original Affluent Society." In *Man the Hunter,* edited by Richard Lee and Irven DeVore, pp. 85–89. Chicago: Aldine.

SAHLINS, MARSHALL. 1972. *Stone Age Economics.* Chicago: Aldine.

SAHLINS, MARSHALL. 1976a. "Colors and Cultures." *Semiotica* 16:1–22.

SAHLINS, MARSHALL. 1976b. *Culture and Practical Reason.* Chicago and London: University of Chicago Press.

SAHLINS, MARSHALL. 1976c. *The Use and Abuse of Biology: An Anthropological Critique of Sociobiology.* Ann Arbor: University of Michigan Press.

SAHLINS, MARSHALL. 1985a. *Islands of History.* Chicago: University of Chicago Press.

SAHLINS, MARSHALL. 1985b. "Hierarchy and Humanity in Polynesia." In *Transformations of Polynesian Culture,* edited by A. Hooper and J. Huntsman. Auckland: The Polynesian Society.

SAHLINS, MARSHALL. 1996. "The Sadness of Sweetness: The Native Anthropology of Western Cosmology." *Current Anthropology* 37(3):395–428.

SAHLINS, MARSHALL, AND ELMAN SERVICE (EDS.). 1960. *Evolution and Culture.* Ann Arbor: University of Michigan Press.

SAMUELSON, PAUL A. 1964. *Economics: Introductory Analysis.* New York: McGraw-Hill.

SAUNDERS, BARBARA. 2000. "Revisiting Basic Color Terms." *Journal of the Royal Anthropological Institute* 6:81–99.

SCHATTENBURG, PATRICIA. 1976. "Food and Cultivar Preservation in Micronesian Voyaging." Miscellaneous Work Papers. *University of Hawaii Pacific Islands Program* 1:25–51.

SCHEPER-HUGHES, NANCY. 1992. *Death Without Weeping: The Violence of Everyday Life in Brazil.* Berkeley: University of California Press.

SCHLOSSER, ERIC. 2001. *Fast Food Nation: The Dark Side of the All-American Meal.* Boston: Houghton Mifflin.

SCHLOSSER, ERIC. 2002. "Bad Meat: The Scandal of Our Food Safety System." *The Nation* 275(8):6–7.

SCHMANDT-BESSERAT, DENISE. 1982. "The Emergence of Recording." *American Anthropologist* 84(4):871–878.

SCHNEIDER, HAROLD K. 1979. *Livestock and Equality in East Africa: The Economic Basis for Social Structure.* Bloomington and London: Indiana University Press.

SCHNEIDER, STEPHEN H. 1989. "The Changing Climate." *Scientific American* 261(3):70–79.

SCHWARTZBERG, JOSEPH E. 1977. "The Evolution of Regional Power Configurations in the Indian Subcontinent." In *Realm and Region in Traditional India,* edited by Richard Fox, pp. 197–233. Monograph and Occasional Papers Series, Monograph no. 14. Durham, N.C.: Program in Comparative Studies on Southern Asia, Duke University.

SEEBOHM, FREDERIC. 1905. *The English Village Community Examined in Its Relations to the Manorial and Tribal Systems and to the Common or Open Field System of Husbandry: An Essay in Economic History.* London: Longmans, Green.

SEN, AMARTYA. 1981. *Poverty and Famines: An Essay on Entitlement and Deprivation.* Oxford, Eng.: Clarendon Press.

SERVICE, ELMAN R. 1960. "The Law of Evolutionary Potential." In *Evolution and Culture,* edited by Marshall Sahlins and Elman Service, pp. 93–122. Ann Arbor: University of Michigan Press.

SERVICE, ELMAN. 1962. *Primitive Social Organization.* New York: Random House.

SERVICE, ELMAN R. 1975. *Origins of the State and Civilization: The Process of Cultural Evolution.* New York: Norton.

SEWELL, TOM. 1992. *The World Grain Trade.* New York: Woodhead-Faulkner.

SHALER, NATHANIEL S. 1905. *Man and the Earth.* New York: Duffield.

SHAMASASTRY, R. (TRANS.). 1960. *Kautilya's Arthasastra.* Mysore, India: Mysore.

SHAPIRO, WARREN. 1981. *Miwuyt Marriage: The Cultural Anthropology of Affinity in Northeast Arnhem Land.* Philadelphia: Institute for the Study of Human Issues.

SHOUP, LAURENCE H. AND WILLIAM MINTER. 1980. "Shaping a New World Order: The Council on Foreign Relations' Blueprint for World Hegemony." In *Trilateralism: The Trilateral Commission and Elite Planning for World Management,* edited by Holly Sklar, pp. 135–156. Boston: South End Press.

SHWEDER, RICHARD A. 1982. "On Savages and Other Children." *American Anthropologist* 84(2):354–366.

SILVERBLATT, IRENE. 1987. *Moon, Sun, and Witches: Gender Ideologies and Class in Inca and Colonial Peru.* Princeton, New Jersey: Princeton University Press.

SILVERMAN, JULIAN. 1967. "Shamans and Acute Schizophrenia." *American Anthropologist* 69(1):21–31.

SIMON, DAVID R. 1999. *Elite Deviance.* Sixth Edition. Boston: Allyn and Bacon.

SIMOONS, FREDERICK J. 1979. "Questions in the Sacred Cow Controversy." *Current Anthropology* 20(3):467–476.

SINDIGA, ISAAC. 1987. "Fertility Control and Population Growth Among the Maasai." *Human Ecology* 15(1):53–66.

SISKIND, JANET. 1973. *To Hunt in the Morning.* London: Oxford University Press.

SKINNER, G. WILLIAM. 1964. "Marketing and Social Structure in Rural China (Part 1)." *Journal of Asian Studies* 24(1):3–43.

SKLAIR, LESLIE. 1991. *Sociology of the Global System.* Baltimore: Johns Hopkins University Press.

SLURINK, POUWELL. 1994. "Causes of Our Complete Dependence on Culture." In *The Ethological Roots of Culture,* edited by R. A. Gardner et al., pp. 461–474. Dordrecht, Boston, and London: Kluwer Academic Press.

SMITH, ADAM. 1776. *An Inquiry into the Nature and Causes of the Wealth of Nations,* Vol. 1. London: Strahan & Cadell.

SMITH, ANDREW B. 1984. "Origins of the Neolithic in the Sahara." In *From Hunters to Farmers: The Causes and Consequences of Food Production in Africa,* edited by J. Desmond Clark and Steven Brandt, pp. 84–92. Berkeley: University of California Press.

SMITH, E. A. 1988. "Risk and uncertainty in the 'original affluent society': Evolutionary Ecology of Resource-Sharing and Land Tenure." In *Hunters and Gatherers, vol. 1, History, Evolution, and Social Change,* edited by T. Ingold, D. Riches, and J. Woodburn, pp. 222–251. Berg, Oxford.

SMITH, G. ELLIOT. 1928. *In the Beginning: The Origin of Civilization.* New York: Morrow.

SMITH, RICHARD CHASE. 1977. *The Amuesha-Yanachaga Project, Peru: Ecology and Ethnicity in the Central Jungle of Peru.* Survival International Document 3. London: Survival International.

SMITH, WILBERFORCE. 1894. "The Teeth of Ten Sioux Indians." *Journal of the Royal Anthropological Institute* 24:109–116.

SNOOKS, GRAEME DONALD. 1993. *Economics Without Time: A Science Blind to the Forces of Historical Change.* London: Macmillan Press.

SOLTOW, LEE. 1975. *Men and Wealth in the United States 1850–1870.* New Haven, Conn., and London: Yale University Press.

SOLTOW, LEE. 1989. *Distribution of Wealth and Income in the United States in 1798.* Pittsburgh: University of Pittsburgh Press.

SOUTHALL, AIDAN. 1976. "Nuer and Dinka Are People: Ecology, Ethnicity and Logical Possibility." *Man* 11:463–491.

SPENCER, CHARLES S. 1990. "On the Tempo and Mode of State Formation: Neoevolutionism Reconsidered." *Journal of Anthropological Archaeology* 9(1):1–30.

SPENCER, HERBERT. 1967. *The Evolution of Society: Selections from Herbert Spencer's Principles of Sociology,* edited by Robert Carneiro. Chicago: University of Chicago Press.

SPENCER, PAUL. 1965. *The Samburu: A Study of Gerontocracy in a Nomadic Tribe.* Berkeley: University of California Press.

SPENCER, PAUL. 1988. *The Maasai of Matapato: A Study of Rituals of Rebellion.* Bloomington and Indianapolis: Indiana University Press.

SPOKESMAN REVIEW. 1991. "Biggest Beef Packer Put on Auction Block." *Spokesman Review,* February 29.

SPONSEL, LESLIE E. 1998. "Yanomami: An Arena of Conflict and Aggression in the Amazon." *Aggressive Behavior* 24(2):97–122.

SRINIVAS, M. N. 1959. "The Dominant Caste in Rampura." *American Anthropologist* 61(1):1–16.

STANNARD, DAVID E. 1989. *Before the Horror: The Population of Hawai'i on the Eve of Western Contact.* Honolulu: Social Science Research Institute, University of Hawaii.

STATISTICAL ABSTRACT OF THE UNITED STATES. *See* United States, Department of Commerce, Bureau of the Census.

STEADMAN, DAVID W. 1995. "Prehistoric Extinctions of Pacific Island Birds: Biodiversity Meets Zooarchaeology." *Science* (Feb. 24) 267:1123–1131.

STEIN, GIL. 1986. "Herding Strategies at Neolithic Gritille: The Use of Animal Bone Remains to Reconstruct Ancient Economic Systems." *Expedition* 28(2):35–42.

STEIN, GIL. 1994. "Economy, Ritual, and Power in 'Ubaid Mesopotamia." In *Chiefdoms and Early States in the Near East: The Organizational Dynamics of Complexity,* edited by Gil Stein and Mitchell S. Rothman, pp. 35–46. Monographs in World Archaeology No. 18. Madison, Wisc.: Prehistoric Press.

STEINHART, JOHN S., AND CAROL E. STEINHART. 1974. "Energy Use in the U.S. Food System." *Science* 184 (4134):307–316.

STEINKELLER, PIORTR. 1991. "The Administrative and Economic Organization of the Ur III State: The Core and the Periphery." In *The Organization of Power: Aspects of Bureaucracy in the Ancient Near East,* edited by McGuire Gibson and Robert D. Biggs, pp. 15–33. Studies in Ancient Oriental Civilization, No. 46. The Oriental Institute of the University of Chicago.

STEWARD, JULIAN H. 1936. "The Economic and Social Basis of Primitive Bands." In *Essays in Anthropology in Honor of Alfred Louis Kroeber,* pp. 331–350. Berkeley: University California Press.

STEWARD, JULIAN H. 1955. *Theory of Culture Change.* Urbana: University of Illinois Press.

STOKEN, DICK. 1993. *The Great Cycle: Predicting and Profiting from Crowd Behavior, the Kondratieff Wave, and Long-Term Cycles.* Chicago: Probus.

STONE, ELIZABETH C. 1987. *Nippur Neighborhoods.* Studies in Ancient Oriental Civilization No. 44. Oriental Institute of the University of Chicago. Chicago, Illinois.

STONE, LINDA. 1997. *Kinship and Gender: An Introduction.* Boulder, Colo.: Westview Press.

STONE, LINDA, AND CAROLINE JAMES. 1995. "Dowry, Bride-Burning, and Female Power in India." *Women's Studies International Forum* 18(2):125–134.

STOVER, LEON N., AND TAKEKO KAWAI STOVER. 1976. *China: An Anthropological Perspective.* Pacific Palisades, Calif.: Goodyear.

STULL, DONALD D. AND MICHAEL J. BROADWAY. 2003. *Slaughterhouse Blues: The Meat and Poultry Industry in North America.* Belmont, Calif.: Wadsworth/Thomson Learning.

SWANSON, G. E. 1960. *The Birth of the Gods.* Ann Arbor: University of Michigan Press.

SWENSON, SALLY, AND JEREMY NARBY. 1986. "The Pichis–Palcazu Special Project in Peru—a Consortium of International Lenders." *Cultural Survival Quarterly* 10(1):19–24.

TAAGEPERA, REIN. 1978a. "Size and Duration of Empires: Systematics of Size." *Social Science Research* 7:108–127.

TAAGEPERA, REIN. 1978b. "Size and Duration of Empires: Growth-Decline Curves, 3000 to 600 B.C.." *Social Science Research* 7:180–196.

TAAGEPERA, REIN. 1997. "Expansion and Contraction Patterns of Large Polities: Context for Russia." *International Studies Quarterly* 41:475–504.

TAINTER, JOSEPH A. 1988. *The Collapse of Complex Societies.* Cambridge, Eng.: Cambridge University Press.

TAMBIAH, STANLEY JEYARAJA. 1985. *Culture, Thought, and Social Action: An Anthropological Perspective.* Cambridge, Mass., and London: Harvard University Press.

THOMAS, CHRIS D. ET AL. 2004. "Extinction Risk From Climate Change." *Nature* 427(6970):145–148.

THOMAS, NICHOLAS. 1989. "The Force of Ethnology." *Current Anthropology* 30(1):27–41.

THOMAS, VERL M. 1986. *Beef Cattle Production: An Integrated Approach.* Philadelphia: Lea & Febiger.

THOMSON, DONALD F. 1938. *Recommendations of Policy in Native Affairs in the Northern Territory of Australia,* no. 56.-F.2945. Canberra: Parliament of the Commonwealth of Australia.

THUROW, LESTER C. 1996. *The Future of Capitalism: How Today's Economic Forces Shape Tomorrow's World.* New York: Morrow.

TIERNEY, PATRICK. 2000. *Darkness in El Dorado: How Scientists and Journalists Devastated the Amazon.* New York: Norton.

TINDALE, NORMAN B. 1974. *Aboriginal Tribes of Australia: Their Terrain, Environmental Controls, Distribution, Limits, and Proper Names.* Berkeley: University of California Press.

TINDALE, NORMAN B. 1981. "Desert Aborigines and the Southern Coastal Peoples: Some Comparisons." In *Ecological Biogeography of Australia,* vol. 3, pt. 6, edited by Allen Keast, pp. 1853–1884. *Monographiae Biologicae,* vol. 41. The Hague: Dr. W. Junk.

TOCQUEVILLE, ALEXIS DE. 1835–40. *Democracy in America* (original *De la démocratie*), various editions.

TODD, IAN A. 1976. *Çatal Hüyük in Perspective.* Menlo Park, Calif.: Cummings.

TOMASELLO, MICHAEL. 1994. "The Question of Chimpanzee Culture." In *Chimpanzee Culture,* edited by Richard W. Wrangham, Frans B. M. de Waal, and W. C. McGrew, pp. 301–317. Cambridge, Mass.: Harvard University Press.

TOTH, JAMES. 1992. "Doubts About Growth: The Town of Carlisle in Transition." *Urban Anthropology* 21(1):2–44.

TOWNSEND, ROBERT M. 1993. *The Medieval Village Economy: Study of the Pareto Mapping in General Equilibrium Models.* Princeton, N.J.: Princeton University Press.

TROWELL, HUGH C. 1954. "Kwashiorkor." *Scientific American* 191(6):46–50.

TURNER II, B. L., WILLIAM C. CLARK, ROBERT W. KATES, JOHN F. RICHARDS, JESSICA T. MATHEWS, WILLIAM B. MEYER (EDS.). 1990. *The Earth as Transformed by Human Action: Global and Regional Changes in the Biosphere over the Past 300 Years.* Cambridge: Cambridge University Press.

TURNER II, CHRISTY G. 1989. "Teeth and Prehistory in Asia." *Scientific American* 260(2):88–96.

TYLOR, EDWARD B. 1871. *Primitive Culture.* London: Murray.

TYLOR, EDWARD B. 1875. "Anthropology." *Encyclopaedia Britannica,* Vol. 1.

TYSON FOODS. 2001. *Investor Fact Book.* Springdale, Arkansas.

TYSON FOODS. 2002. *Tyson Annual Report 2002.* Springdale, Arkansas.

UNITED NATIONS. 1959. *International Labour Organisation Convention (No. 107) Concerning the Protection and Integration of Indigenous and Other Tribal and Semi-Tribal Populations in Independent Countries.* United Nations Treaty Series, no. 4738. New York: United Nations.

UNITED NATIONS. 1968a. *Statistical Yearbook 1967.* New York: United Nations.

UNITED NATIONS. 1968b. *Yearbook of National Accounts Statistics 1967.* New York: United Nations.

UNITED NATIONS, COMMISSION ON HUMAN RIGHTS. 1994. *Report of the Sub-Commission on Prevention of Discrimination and Protection of Minorities On Its Forty-Sixth Session.* Geneva, 1–26 August, 1994. E/CN.4/1995/2, E/CN.4/Sub.2/1994/56.

UNITED NATIONS, DEPARTMENT OF ECONOMIC AND SOCIAL AFFAIRS. 1963. *Report on the World Social Situation.* New York: United Nations.

UNITED NATIONS, DEPARTMENT OF ECONOMIC AND SOCIAL AFFAIRS. 1975. *1974 Report on the World Social Situation.* New York: United Nations.

UNITED NATIONS, DEPARTMENT OF SOCIAL AFFAIRS. 1952. *Preliminary Report on the World Situation: With Special Ref-*

erence to Standards of Living, E/CN.5/267/rev.1. New York: United Nations.

UNITED NATIONS, FOOD AND AGRICULTURE ORGANIZATION. 2003. *The State of Food Insecurity in the World 2003: Monitoring Progress Towards the World Food Summit and Millennium Development Goals.* Rome: UN FAO.

UNITED NATIONS, WHO/FAO. UNITED NATIONS, WORLD HEALTH ORGANIZATION/FOOD AND AGRICULTURE ORGANIZATION. 2003. *Joint WHO/FAO Expert Consultation on Diet, Nutrition and the Prevention of Chronic Diseases.* WHO Technical Report Series 916. Geneva.

UNDP (UNITED NATIONS DEVELOPMENT PROGRAM). 2003. *Human Development Report. Millennium Development Goals: A compact among nations to end human poverty.* New York: Oxford University Press.

UNFCCC (UNITED NATIONS FRAMEWORK CONVENTION ON CLIMATE CHANGE). 2003. *Caring for Climate: A Guide to the Climate Change Convention and the Kyoto Protocol.* Bonn, Germany: Climate Change Secretariat.

UNITED STATES, AID (AGENCY FOR INTERNATIONAL DEVELOPMENT). 1985. *Blueprint for Development: The Strategic Plan of the Agency for International Development.* Washington, D.C.: Government Printing Office.

UNITED STATES CONGRESS. 1974. *Nomination of Nelson A. Rockefeller to be Vice President of the United States. Hearings Before the Committee on the Judiciary, House of Representatives, Ninety-Third Congress.* Serial No. 45.

UNITED STATES DEPARTMENT OF COMMERCE, BUREAU OF THE CENSUS. 1990. *Statistical Abstract of the United States: 1990,* 110th ed. Washington, D.C.: Government Printing Office.

UNITED STATES DEPARTMENT OF ENERGY. 2003a. *Annual Energy Review 2002.* Energy Information Administration. (www.eia.doe.gov).

UNITED STATES DEPARTMENT OF ENERGY. 2003b. *International Energy Annual 2001.* Energy Information Administration. (www.eia.doe.gov).

UNITED STATES DEPARTMENT OF ENERGY. 2004. *Annual Energy Outlook 2004: With Projections to 2025.* Energy Information Administration. (www.eia.doe.gov).

UNITED STATES DEPARTMENT OF STATE AND USAID. 2003. *Security, Democracy, Prosperity: Strategic Plan Fiscal Years 2004-2009: Aligning Diplomacy and Development Assistance.* Department of State/USAID Publication 11084.

UNITED STATES HOUSE COMMITTEE ON THE JUDICIARY. 1949. *Study of Monopoly Power. Hearings Before the Subcommittee on Study of Monopoly Power of the Committee on the Judiciary, House of Representatives, Eighty-First Congress.* First Session. Serial No. 14, Pt. 1. Washington, DC: U.S. Government Printing Office.

UNITED STATES, WHITE HOUSE. 2003. *The National Security Strategy of the United States of America.* (Sept. 17, 2003).

URTON, GARY. 1981. *At the Crossroads of the Earth and Sky: An Andean Cosmology.* Austin: University of Texas Press.

VALENTINE, CHARLES A. 1968. *Culture and Poverty: Critique and Counter-Proposals.* Chicago and London: University of Chicago Press.

VALENTINE, CHARLES A. 1971. "The 'Culture of Poverty': Its Scientific Significance and Its Implications for Action." In *The Culture of Poverty: A Critique,* edited by Eleanor Burke Leacock, pp. 193-225. New York: Simon & Schuster.

VALENTINE, CHARLES A., ET AL., 1969. "Culture and Poverty: Critique and Counterproposals." *Current Anthropology* 10(2/3):181-201.

VAN SCHENDEL, WILLEM. 1981. *Peasant Mobility: The Odds of Life in Rural Bangladesh.* Assen: Van Gorcum.

VARESE, STEFANO. 1972. "Inter-Ethnic Relations in the Selva of Peru." In *The Situation of the Indian in South America,* edited by W. Dostal, pp. 115-139. Geneva: World Council of Churches.

VATUK, SYLVIA. 1982. "Purdah Revisited: A Comparison of Hindu and Muslim Interpretations of the Cultural Meaning of Purdah in South Asia." In *Separate Worlds: Studies of Purdah in South Asia,* edited by Hanna Papanek and Gail Minault, pp. 54-78. Delhi: Chanakya.

VERDON, MICHEL. 1982. "Where Have All Their Lineages Gone? Cattle and Descent Among the Nuer." *American Anthropologist* 84(3):566-579.

VER STEEG, CLARENCE L. 1954. *Robert Morris Revolutionary Financier.* Philadelphia: University of Philadelphia Press.

VITOUSEK, PETER M., PAUL R. EHRLICH, ANNE H. EHRLICH, AND PAMELA A. MATSON. 1986. "Human Appropriation of the Products of Photosynthesis." *BioScience* 36(6):368-373.

VOIGT, MARY. 1987. "Relative and Absolute Chronologies for Iran Between 6500 and 3500 BC." In *Chronologies in the Near East,* edited by O. Aurenche, J. Evin, and F. Hours, pp. 615-646. BAR International Series 379(ii). Oxford, Eng.: BAR.

WAETZOLDT, HARTMUT. 1987. "Compensation of Craft Workers and Officials in the Ur III Period." In *Labor in the Ancient Near East,* edited by Marvin A. Powell, pp. 117-141. American Oriental Series, Vol. 68. New Haven, Conn.: American Oriental Society.

WAKE, CHARLES STANILAND. 1872. "The Mental Conditions of Primitive Man as Exemplified by the Australian Aborigine." *Journal of the Royal Anthropological Institute* 1:78-84.

WALES, H. G. QUARITCH. 1934. *Ancient Siamese Government and Administration.* London: Bernard Quaritch.

DE WALL, FRANS. 1982. *Chimpanzee Politics: Power and Sex Among Apes.* London: Jonathan Cape.

WALLACE, ANTHONY F. C. 1978. *Rockdale: The Growth of an American Village in the Early Industrial Revolution.* New York: Knopf.

WALLERSTEIN, IMMANUEL. 1974. *The Modern World-System: Capitalist Agriculture and the Origins of the European World-Economy in the Sixteenth Century.* New York: Academic Press.

WALLERSTEIN, IMMANUEL. 1990. "Culture as the Ideological Battleground of the Modern World-System." *Theory, Culture & Society* 7:31-55.

WALL STREET 20TH CENTURY. 1960. *A Republication of the Yale Daily News' Wall Street 1955.* New Haven, Conn.: Yale Daily News.

WAL-MART. 2003. *Annual Report, 2003.* Bentonville, Arkansas.

WALSH, J., AND R. GANNON. 1967. *Time Is Short and the Water Rises.* Camden, N.J.: Nelson.

WARNER, W. L. 1958. *A Black Civilization.* New York: Harper.

WCED (WORLD COMMISSION ON ENVIRONMENT AND DEVELOPMENT). 1987. *Our Common Future.* Oxford, Eng.: Oxford University Press.

WEAVER, THOMAS. 1985. "Anthropology as a Policy Science: Part II, Development and Training." *Human Organization* 44(3):197-205.

WEBER, MAX. [1904–1905] 1930. *The Protestant Ethic and the Spirit of Capitalism.* New York: Scribner.

WEBER, MAX. 1968. *Economy and Society: An Outline of Interpretive Sociology,* edited by Guenther Roth and Claus Wittich. Three volumes. New York: Bedminster Press.

WEBSTER, DAVID. 1981. "Late Pleistocene Extinction and Human Predation; A Critical Overview." In *Omnivorous Primates: Gathering and Hunting in Human Evolution,* edited by Robert Harding and Geza Teleki, pp. 556–595. New York: Columbia University Press.

WEI-MING, TU. 1990. "The Confucian Tradition in Chinese History." In *Heritage of China: Contemporary Perspectives on Chinese Civilization,* edited by Paul Ropp, pp. 112–137. Berkeley: University of California Press.

WEISS, GERALD. 1975. *Campa Cosmology: The World of a Forest Tribe in South America.* Anthropological Papers, no. 52(5). New York: American Museum of Natural History.

WENDORF, FRED, AND ROMUALD SCHILD. 1984. "The Emergence of Food Production in the Egyptian Sahara." In *From Hunters to Farmers: The Causes and Consequences of Food Production in Africa,* edited by J. Desmond Clark and Steven Brandt, pp. 93–101. Berkeley: University of California Press.

WERNER, DENNIS. 1983. "Why Do the Mekranoti Trek?" In *Adaptive Responses of Native Amazonians,* edited by Raymond Hames and William Vickers, pp. 225–238. New York: Academic Press.

WESTERMARK, EDWARD. 1922. *The History of Human Marriage,* 5th ed. New York: Allerton Book Co.

WESTERN, DAVID, AND VIRGINIA FINCH. 1986. "Cattle and Pastoralism: Survival and Production in Arid Lands." *Human Ecology* 14(1):77–94.

WHEATLEY, PAUL. 1971. *The Pivot of the Four Quarters: A Preliminary Enquiry into the Origins and Character of the Ancient Chinese City.* Chicago: Aldine.

WHEELER, JANE C. 1984. "On the Origin and Early Development of Camelid Pastoralism in the Andes." In *Animals and Archaeology,* vol. 3, edited by Juliet Clatton-Brock and Caroline Grigson, pp. 395–410. BAR International Series, no 202. Oxford, Eng.: BAR.

WHITE, J. PETER, AND JAMES F. O'CONNELL. 1982. *Prehistory of Australia, New Guinea and Sahul.* New York: Academic Press.

WHITE, LESLIE A. 1949. *The Science of Culture.* New York: Grove Press.

WHYTE, WILLIAM FOOTE, AND KATHLEEN KING WHYTE. 1988. *Making Mondragón: The Growth and Dynamics of the Worker Cooperative Complex.* Ithaca, NY: ILR Press.

WILKINSON, RICHARD G. 1996. *Unhealthy Societies: The Afflictions of Inequality.* London and New York: Routledge.

WILKINSON, RICHARD G. 1997. "Comment: Income, Inequality, and Social Cohesion." *American Journal of Public Health* 87(9):1504–1506.

WILLETT, WALTER C. 2001. *Eat, Drink, and Be Healthy.* New York: Simon & Schuster.

WILLIAMS, NANCY M. 1986. *The Yolngu and Their Land: A System of Land Tenure and the Fight for Its Recognition.* Stanford, Calif.: Stanford University Press.

WILSON, ALLAN C., AND REBECCA L. CANN. 1992. "The Recent African Genesis of Humans: Genetic Studies Reveal That an African Woman of 200,000 Years Ago Was Our Common Ancestor." *Scientific American* 266(April):68–73.

WILSON, EDWARD O. 1989. "Threats to Biodiversity." *Scientific American* 261(3):108–116.

WILSON, EDWARD O. 2002. *The Future of Life.* New York: Alfred A. Knopf.

WILSON, EDWARD O., AND FRANCES M. PETER (EDS.). 1988. *Biodiversity.* Washington, D.C.: National Academy Press.

WILSON, PETER J. 1988. *The Domestication of the Human Species.* New Haven, Conn., and London: Yale University Press.

WINTER, IRENE J. 1991. "Legitimation of Authority Through Image and Legend: Seals Belonging to Officials in the Administrative Bureaucracy of the Ur III State." In *The Organization of Power: Aspects of Bureaucracy in the Ancient Near East,* edited by McGuire Gibson and Robert D. Biggs, pp. 59–100. Studies in Ancient Oriental Civilization, No. 46. The Oriental Institute of the University of Chicago.

WINTERHALDER, BRUCE. 1993. "Work, Resources and Population in Foraging Societies." *Man* 28(2):321–340.

WISE, MARY RUTH, EUGENE E. LOOS, AND PATRICIA DAVIS. 1977. "Filosofiá y Métodos del Instituto Linguistico de Verano." *Proceedings of the 42nd International Americanists Congress* 2:499–525.

WITTFOGEL, KARL A. 1957. *Oriental Despotism: A Study of Total Power.* New Haven, Conn.: Yale University Press.

WOLF, ARTHUR P. 1968. "Adopt a Daughter-in-Law, Marry a Sister: A Chinese Solution to the Problem of the Incest Taboo." *American Anthropologist* 70(5):864–874.

WOLF, ARTHUR P. (ED.). 1974. "Gods, Ghosts, and Ancestors." *Religion and Ritual in Chinese Society,* pp. 131–182. Stanford, Calif.: Stanford University Press.

WOLF, ARTHUR P. 1995. *Sexual Attraction and Childhood Association: A Chinese Brief for Edward Westermarck.* Stanford, Calif.: Stanford University Press.

WOLF, ERIC R. 1955. "Types of Latin American Peasantry." *American Anthropologist* 57(3, pt.1):452–471.

WOLF, ERIC R. 1957. "Closed Corporate Peasant Communities in Mesoamerica and Central Java." *Southwestern Journal of Anthropology* 13(1):1–18.

WOLF, ERIC R. 1969. *Peasant Wars of the Twentieth Century.* New York: Harper & Row.

WOLF, ERIC R. 1982. *Europe and the People Without History.* Berkeley: University of California Press.

WOLF, MARGERY. 1968. *The House of Lim: A Study of a Chinese Farm Family.* New York: Appleton-Century-Crofts.

WOLF, STEWARD, AND JOHN G. BRUHN. 1993. *The Power of Clan: The Influence of Human Relationships on Heart Disease.* New Brunswick, N.J., and London: Transaction Books.

WOODBURN, JAMES. 1982. "Egalitarian Societies." *Man* 17(3):431–451.

WOOD JONES, FREDERIC. 1928. "The Claims of the Australian Aborigine." *Report of the Eighteenth Australasian Association for the Advancement of Science* 18:497–519.

WOODRUFF, WILLIAM. 1966. *The Impact of Western Man.* London: Macmillan.

WOOLLEY, SIR LEONARD. 1982. *Ur "of the Chaldees."* London: Herbert Press.

WOOLLEY, SIR LEONARD AND P. R. S. MOOREY. 1982. *Ur 'Of the Chaldees.'* Ithaca, New York: Cornell University Press.

WORLD ALMANAC AND BOOK OF FACTS. 1998. Mahwah, N.J.: World Almanac Books.

WORLD ALMANAC AND BOOK OF FACTS. 2004. New York: World Almanac Books.

WORLD BANK. 1988–1995. *World Development Report*. New York: Oxford University Press.

WORLD BANK. 2001. *World Development Report 2000/2001: Attacking Poverty*. Oxford: Oxford University Press.

WORLD BANK. 2002. *World Development Report 2003: Sustainable Development in a Dynamic World*. Oxford: Oxford University Press.

WRIGHT, ARTHUR F. 1977. "The Cosmology of the Chinese City." In *The City in Late Imperial China*, edited by G. William Skinner, pp. 33–73. Stanford, Calif.: Stanford University Press.

WRIGHT, ERIK OLIN. 1997. *Class Counts: Comparative Studies in Class Analysis*. Cambridge: Cambridge University Press.

WRIGHT, HENRY T. 1969. *The Administration of Rural Production in an Early Mesopotamian Town*. Anthropological Papers, no. 38. Ann Arbor: Museum of Anthropology, University of Michigan.

WRIGHT, JOHN W. 1990. *The Universal Almanac*. Kansas City, Mo.: Andrews & McMeel.

WYATT, DAVID K. 1968. "Family Politics in Nineteenth Century Thailand." *Journal of Southeast Asian History* 9(2):208–228.

YALMAN, NUR. 1963. "On the Purity of Women in the Castes of Ceylon and Malabar." *Journal of the Royal Anthropological Institute* 93:25–58.

YDE, JENS. 1965. *Material Culture of the Waiwai*. Nationalmuseets Skrifter. Ethnografisk Roekke 10. Copenhagen: National Museum.

YENGOYAN, ARAM A. 1981. "Infanticide and Birth Order: An Empirical Analysis of Preferential Female Infanticide Among Australian Aboriginal Populations." In *The Perception of Evolution: Essays Honoring Joseph B. Birdsell*, edited by Larry Mai, Eugenia Shanklin, and Robert Sussman, pp. 255–273. Anthropology UCLA, vol. 7, nos. 1 and 2. Los Angeles: Department of Anthropology, University of California.

YOFFEE, NORMAN. 1988a. "The Collapse of Ancient Mesopotamian States and Civilization." In *The Collapse of Ancient States and Civilizations*, edited by Norman Yoffee and George Cowgill, pp. 44–68. Tucson: University of Arizona Press.

YOFFEE, NORMAN. 1988b. "Orienting Collapse." In *The Collapse of Ancient States and Civilizations*, edited by Norman Yoffee and George Cowgill, pp. 1–19. Tucson: University of Arizona Press.

ZEITLAND, MAURICE. 1989. *The Large Corporation and Contemporary Classes*. New Brunswick, N.J.: Rutgers University Press.

ZETTLER, RICHARD L. 1991. "Administration of the Temple of Inanna at Nippur Under the Third Dynasty of Ur: Archaeological and Documentary Evidence." In *The Organization of Power: Aspects of Bureaucracy in the Ancient Near East*, edited by McGuire Gibson and Robert D. Briggs, pp. 101–114. Studies in Ancient Oriental Civilization, No. 46. The Oriental Institute of the University of Chicago.

ZIPF, GEORGE KINGSLEY. 1949. *Human Behavior and the Principle of Least Effort*. Cambridge, Mass.: Addison Wesley Press.

ZUIDEMA, R. TOM. 1990. *Inca Civilization in Cuzco*. Austin: University of Texas Press.

Credits

Index

Note: Page numbers in italics *indicate illustrations, tables and figures.*